Practical Law Office Management

Fourth Edition

Options.

We understand that affordable options are important. Visit us at cengage.com to take advantage of our new textbook rental program, which can be bundled with our MindTap products!

Over 300 products in every area of the law: MindTap, textbooks, online courses, reference books, companion websites, and more – Cengage Learning helps you succeed in the classroom and on the job.

Support.

We offer unparalleled course support and customer service: robust instructor and student supplements to ensure the best learning experience, custom publishing to meet your unique needs, and other benefits such as Cengage Learning's Student Achievement Award. And our sales representatives are always ready to provide you with dependable service.

Feedback.

As always, we want to hear from you! Your feedback is our best resource for improving the quality of our products. Contact your sales representative or write us at the address below if you have any comments about our materials or if you have a product proposal.

Accounting and Financials for the Law Office • Administrative Law • Alternative Dispute Resolution • Bankruptcy Business Organizations/Corporations • Careers and Employment • Civil Litigation and Procedure • CP Exam Preparation • Computer Applications in the Law Office • Constitutional Law • Contract Law • Criminal Law and Procedure • Document Preparation • Elder Law • Employment Law • Environmental Law • Ethics • Evidence Law • Family Law • Health Care Law • Immigration Law • Intellectual Property • Internships • Interviewing and Investigation • Introduction to Law • Introduction to Paralegalism • Juvenile Law • Law Office Management • Law Office Procedures • Legal Research, Writing, and Analysis • Legal Terminology • Legal Transcription • Media and Entertainment Law • Medical Malpractice Law • Product Liability • Real Estate Law • Reference Materials • Social Security • Torts and Personal Injury Law • Wills, Trusts, and Estate Administration • Workers' Compensation Law

---

Cengage

5 Maxwell Drive
Clifton Park, New York 12065-2919

For additional information, find us online at: **cengage.com**

Practical Law Office Management

Fourth Edition

Cynthia Traina Donnes, M.A.

Cengage

Australia • Brazil • Canada • Mexico • Singapore • United Kingdom • United States

Cengage

Practical Law Office Management,
Fourth Edition
Cynthia Traina Donnes

SVP, GM Skills & Global Product Management: Dawn Gerrain

Product Director: Matthew Seeley

Product Manager: Katie McGuire

Senior Director, Development: Marah Bellegarde

Senior Product Development Manager: Larry Main

Senior Content Developer: Melissa Riveglia

Senior Product Assistant: Diane Chrysler

Vice President, Marketing Services: Jennifer Ann Baker

Marketing Manager: Scott Chrysler

Senior Production Director: Wendy Troeger

Production Director: Andrew Crouth

Senior Content Project Manager: Betty L. Dickson

Managing Art Director: Jack Pendleton

Software Development Manager: Joe Pliss

Cover Image: ©GaudiLab/Shutterstock.com

WCN: 01-100-101

Library of Congress Control Number: 2015949200

ISBN: 978-1-305-57792-3

Cengage
200 Pier 4 Boulevard
Boston, MA 02210
USA

Printed in the United States of America
Print Number: 06 Print Year: 2022

To my supportive family, friends, and colleagues

Brief Contents

Contents

3 Ethics and Malpractice 117

6 Client Trust Funds and Law Office Accounting 313

7 Calendaring, Docket Control, and Case Management 387

Preface

Another class, another boring textbook. Right? Wrong! Law office management is a dynamic subject and a great class. It will make you a better paralegal. You will learn about real-life problems encountered on the job and how to deal with them successfully. You will understand the importance of performing quality work for clients. You will learn methods for improving your communication skills and your ability to work with clients successfully. You will be shown how to track and bill your time correctly, and how to use your time effectively. You will find explanations throughout the book on how to avoid ethical problems that may come up. Law office management is anything but boring.

The goal of *Practical Law Office Management* is to educate paralegal students regarding law office management procedures and systems. Law firms, as well as paralegals themselves, must have good management skills to survive in today's competitive marketplace. This text is written for the student who wants to understand effective law practice management techniques and systems whether or not he or she will go on to become a law office administrator.

This text is not intended to be an "armchair" text on the theories and principles of management, nor is it a text on how to set up a law office. Rather, this text presents a practical discussion of law office management with realistic applications.

The information presented is national in scope and assumes no prior knowledge of management or the legal field. Sociology, theories, and jargon are kept to an absolute minimum. To present a flavor of how a real law office operates, step-by-step explanations, "how-to" tips, practical charts, recent trends in law office management and software, and many practical ideas on law office management from the paralegal's perspective are provided. Information is presented in a manner that encourages students to think independently and to learn by participating.

This book, among other things, will explain what management generally expects of paralegals, and will present good law office systems and practical information about law office management.

Paralegals must learn to manage themselves in addition to performing their normal duties. This book will help the student manage him- or herself in addition to teaching basic law office systems, such as timekeeping and billing, docket control, financial management, file and library management, technology, and more. If the student takes the time to learn the management systems in this book, he or she will perform tasks more efficiently, with greater accuracy, and with less work. Sound too good to be true? That is what good management is all about.

A book on law office management has inherent limitations because there are many different management styles, techniques, and philosophies, depending on the size and type of firm (e.g., small-, medium-, and large-sized firms, corporate legal departments), location of the firm (urban, rural, east, west), and so forth. In addition, law office management is such a diverse area that most people cannot agree on all the topics that should be covered. In light of these inherent problems, a vast and varied amount of information from many different angles is presented.

Ethics

The importance of ethics is stressed throughout the text. Assuring a high ethical standard in the law office is a major function of law office management. It is very important to your career that you be educated regarding ethical issues and adopt a high ethical standard as a way of life. Every chapter in the text has an in-depth section on ethics. In "Chapter 3—Ethics and Malpractice," the codes of ethics for both the National Association of Legal Assistants (NALA) and the National Federation of Paralegal Associations (NFPA) are included. Ethical-related cases also appear at the end of most chapters. The cases discuss major ethical points covered in the chapter from real life, actual settings. As much as possible, the cases involve paralegals and/or legal assistants.

Organization of Text

The text is organized into nine chapters. Chapter 1 is an introduction to the legal environment, including a discussion about members of the legal team found in most law offices, information about the different sizes and types of law practices as well as law firm governance. Chapter 2 is a broad introduction to law office management and covers 11 major areas regarding the topic, giving students a broad "30,000-foot view" of law office management and an excellent framework for the rest of the book. However, from Chapter 2 onward, the chapters stand on their own and do not depend on the preceding chapter(s). Thus, instructors can assign the chapters in whatever order they believe is appropriate.

Changes to the Fourth Edition

The fourth edition of *Practical Law Office Management* offers major enhancements over the third edition. The text has been completely updated to reflect current management practices and technological advances. Some of the more significant changes include the following:

- The text has been updated with one of the top recommended software programs utilized by law offices, and provides more kinds and types of practice, hands-on exercises than any other law office management text. The text includes updated lessons for ethics/conflict of interest checks, docket control and client management, time and billing as well as trust accounting and Excel exercises. The text continues to have On the Web Exercises (for every chapter), Projects (for every chapter), thought-provoking Practical Applications (for every chapter), excellent Web Site Links (for every chapter), great ethical cases included at the end of most chapters (many of which are new), Suggested Reading (for every chapter), and "Test Your Knowledge" (for every chapter). The text really tries to be *practical* and *hands-on* to offer the student many learning opportunities.

- The Boutique Plan of the software product Clio is utilized with the text. Clio is a cloud-based program that provides case management/docket control, financial management, time and billing, and trust accounting, among other things. A common issue between packaging demonstration software with a text is that the author and publisher of the text cannot control the software product or manufacturer. Software manufacturers sometimes put limitations on the demonstration version, or make other changes that are detrimental to our adopters. We are delighted that Clio has provided a resource link for a fully functional version of the program for 12 months. We believe that this will greatly enhance our ability to provide a solid software product with top-of-the-line software support.
- Updated ethical cases have been added to the text. Whenever possible, the cases involve actual paralegals and/or legal assistants in the facts of the cases. Most of the cases involve truly interesting fact patterns and present excellent learning opportunities for students.
- Hands-on exercises for Microsoft Excel continue to be provided with Chapter 5, Legal Timekeeping and Billing; and with Chapter 6, Client Trust Funds and Law Office Accounting. All of the exercises are law-office-management based and give the student experience with building practical spreadsheets regarding these important topics. The exercises are fun and full of learning opportunities.
- Most of the charts and graphs in the text have been updated and are current.
- The text continues to have a strong ethical foundation that is covered in every chapter and with many of the exercises. All of the ethics citations have been updated to include any revisions with states' rules of professional conduct that follow the current *Model Rules of Professional Conduct* from the American Bar Association.
- Coverage of technological advances has been added to every chapter.

Special Features

- Strong, practical coverage of ethics throughout the text
- Ethical cases regarding law office management topics in most chapters
- Citations to states' rules of professional conduct including recent updates based on the *Model Rules.*
- Hands-on exercises and Clio office and case management software for five chapters.
- Introductions that "set the stage" for most chapters
- Up-to-date charts, figures, and graphs to illustrate concepts
- Key terms/concepts defined in the margin
- List of Web sites by topic for each chapter
- List of suggested reading for each chapter
- Expanded discussion questions, practical applications, and exercises at the end of each chapter
- Chapter objectives listed for each chapter
- Suggestions on how to succeed as a paralegal and avoid problems
- "On the Web Exercises" for each chapter
- Projects for each chapter
- Microsoft Excel tutorials for two chapters

Software Tutorials and Hands-On Exercises

The text accommodates legal programs that have access to computers by including software tutorials at the end of many of the chapters. However, these are simply an added feature and computer use is completely optional. This text can be used fully by legal programs that choose not to use computers.

The software tutorials included in the text are completely interactive and allow the student hands-on experience with the software programs. In addition, all of the tutorials are specifically related to law offices and legal applications so that the student learns not only how to operate the software but also how to use it in a law office. An educational version of Clio is provided free of charge for students who purchase the text. Clio runs on any operating system. The demo expires 365 days after it is first installed. Clio is a full-featured legal software program that includes functionality in:

- Legal timekeeping and billing
- Trust accounting
- Docket control
- Conflict of interest
- Client relationship management

Step-by-step hands-on exercises are included in the text for each of these areas, along with exercises for Microsoft Excel regarding client trust funds/budgeting, timekeeping, and billing.

Supplemental Teaching and Learning Materials

Premium Web Site

The Premium Web site includes resources for instructors and students. The card in the text includes an access code for this book's Premium Web site. Go to login.cengagebrain.com to access the Clio demo and updates to the text.

Instructor Companion Site

The online Instructor Companion Site provides the following resources:

Instructor's Manual and Test Bank

- The Instructor's Manual and Test Bank have been greatly expanded to incorporate changes in the text and to provide comprehensive teaching support. The Instructor's Manual contains instructional tips, suggested class activities, chapter outlines, and answers to the text questions. A comprehensive test bank with a variety of question types and answer key is also provided.

PowerPoint Presentations

Customizable Microsoft PowerPoint® Presentations focus on key points for each chapter. (Microsoft PowerPoint® is a registered trademark of the Microsoft Corporation.)

Cengage Learning Testing Powered by Cognero is a flexible, online system that allows you to:

- author, edit, and manage test bank content from multiple Cengage Learning solutions
- create multiple test versions in an instant
- deliver tests from your LMS, your classroom, or wherever you want

Start right away!
Cengage Learning Testing Powered by Cognero works on any operating system or browser.

- No special installs or downloads needed
- Create tests from school, home, the coffee shop—anywhere with Internet access

What will you find?

- *Simplicity at every step.* A desktop-inspired interface features drop-down menus and familiar intuitive tools that take you through content creation and management with ease.
- *Full-featured test generator.* Create ideal assessments with your choice of 15 question types (including true/false, multiple choice, opinion scale/Likert, and essay). Multilanguage support, an equation editor, and unlimited metadata help ensure your tests are complete and compliant.
- *Cross-compatible capability.* Import and export content into other systems.

To access additional course materials, please go to login.cengage.com, then use your SSO (single sign-on) login to access the materials.

To the Student

Law office management is exciting and ever changing. It is my hope that you will find this book useful as a reference tool in your professional career and that you will use some ideas of this book to climb the ladder of success. Remember that just because you graduate from a paralegal program, you do not get to start at the top. Everyone has to start at the bottom and work his or her way up. Do not be surprised or disappointed if you start at an entry-level job. The experience you will gain is priceless, and through hard work and determination, you will move up more quickly than you think, being the better for it because you will have earned it. Also remember to help your coworkers. You will not be able to succeed without their help. Treat them like you would like to be treated, put the interests of your law office ahead of your own, and you will go far.

If you have an interesting idea, have solved some problem in law office management, or just have a story to tell and you would not mind me using it as an example in a subsequent edition of this book, please do not hesitate to contact me. I am always interested in learning from you. I wish you the best of luck in your endeavors. Cynthia Traina Donnes, New Orleans, LA.

Acknowledgments

A special part of writing a book is acknowledging those invaluable people that worked on this project. Many thanks for all of your help and support.

Reviewers Thanks to the reviewers of this fourth edition for their time and suggestions to improve the text.

Sally Bisson
College of Saint Mary
Omaha, NE

Anthony DiSomma
Heald College
Stockton, CA

Kenneth O'Neil Salyer
Education Consultant
Louisville, KY

Cengage Learning

A special thanks goes to the wonderful people at Cengage Learning, including Katie McGuire, Product Manager, whose encouragement and positive outlook made this undertaking manageable. To Melissa Riveglia, Senior Content Developer, whose patience, help, and support were invaluable and without her this book would not have been possible. They are a wonderful team to work with. Many other people provided help by double-checking the accuracy of the hands-on exercises, including Jeffrey Schwartz at Cengage and Shelby Hejjas at Clio.

Colleagues and Friends

"Thanks" goes to my lifelong friends for their support and encouragement to pursue this textbook. As well, many colleagues have provided invaluable input and suggestions, especially members of the School of Continuing Studies at Tulane University. I am truly grateful to be affiliated with an organization that is open-minded and promotes creativity. Many thanks to Kathryn Beachy, Sallie Davis, and Robyn Ice for supporting me during this project.

Family

A special thanks goes to my husband, Bert, and our children, Dominic, Erin, Antonia, David, Louis, and Sara, along with their spouses and significant others for their love and support throughout this process. The long hours and hectic schedules during weddings and family losses required patience and understanding. I could not have done this without all of you.

Cynthia Traina Donnes
New Orleans, LA

Please note that the Internet resources are of a time-sensitive nature and URL addresses may often change or be deleted.

Note:
Demo access to Microsoft Office Applications (Excel) is not included with the text.

Technical Support
If you are having problems accessing the Clio program included with this text, contact Cengage Learning Technical Support at http://cengage.com/support. Please keep in mind this is third-party software and there is limited support Cengage can provide.

If you are experiencing issues while using the software, contact your instructor.
Please keep in mind that software is of a changing nature. Please visit the text's accompanying Premium Web site to access the Clio demo, updates to the demo, and updates to the corresponding hands-on exercises.

1

The Legal Team, Law Practices, and Law Firm Governance

Chapter Objectives

After you read this chapter, you should be able to:

- Discuss the titles and duties of each member of the legal team.
- Explain the trends in paralegal salaries.
- Discuss the different types of law practices.
- Identify alternative law office organizational structures.

The law firm was more than 40 years old and well established in the legal community. Recently, however, the firm had several senior partners retire and with their retirement, the loss of a major client. Additionally, the firm had just purchased a new building, relocated in a restored downtown area which had proven to be more accessible to clients. The building was completely renovated to include retail space on the bottom floor, residential space on the top two floors, a roof top conference facility, and three floors dedicated to law office space. Losing the resources of a major client created a substantial income deficit for the remaining partners now saddled with an enormous mortgage payment for the new building. The current partners decided they should move in a new direction to generate more business and ensure the firm's survival. They focused on the flood of new attorneys coming out of law school with very little job prospects, integrating a virtual law office layout with the current firm. It offered a space sharing concept designed with sophisticated software and technology along with a mentoring program to help the new attorneys get started, which in turn would provide new business for the firm.

The partners quickly realized they needed help to implement their plan and hired a management consulting firm. The remaining lawyers were not administrators, they spent most of their time in court or meeting with clients. After careful analysis of the firm's goals, the consultants suggested the firm develop a governance structure that was streamlined and decisive. They hired a legal administrator to handle contract lawyers with space sharing, remote use of office resources, and scheduling for attorney mentoring. They hired a marketing specialist with computer experience to develop a Web site and advertising strategies. The technology utilized would require information technology (IT) resources, so the firm decided to outsource the services, with an eye on creating an in-house IT department to maintain its network and computer systems. The firm was well on its way to catching up with practicing law in the age of technology.

Law offices are organizations that provide legal services to clients, but they are fundamentally a business. Like any business, their function is to make money, operate at a profit, and earn money for their owners. This chapter introduces you to the legal team members who provide services to clients and management to a law office; salary trends of paralegals; different types of law practices that operate in the legal field; and various organizational structures used by law firms.

The Legal Team

legal team

A group made up of attorneys, administrators, law clerks, librarians, paralegals/legal assistants, secretaries, clerks, and other third parties. Each provides a distinct range of services to clients and has a place on the legal team.

In a law office, many people make up the legal team. The **legal team** consists of attorneys, administrators, law clerks, librarians, paralegals, secretaries, clerks, and other third parties (see Exhibit 1-1). Each person provides a distinct range of services to clients, and each has his or her place on the legal team. The positions and job duties in any law office depend on the type and size of the office. A list of job titles and a general description of common duties and responsibilities are provided in this section. It should be noted that job titles are just that—they are "titles" only. Attorneys and law office administrators are far more impressed with a person's actual performance than with a job title.

Attorney

attorneys

Licensed professionals who counsel clients regarding their legal rights, represent clients in litigation, and negotiate agreements between clients and others.

Attorneys counsel clients regarding their legal rights, represent clients in litigation, and negotiate agreements between clients and others. Once licensed, they can legally represent clients in court, keeping in mind that every state, through its respective bar association, regulates the practice of law. A licensed attorney is responsible for providing competent representation and ensuring that all members of the legal team are aware of the ethical duties owed to the client. Depending on the size of the law office, attorneys may also have administrative duties. There are several kinds of attorneys.

partner or shareholder

An owner in a private law practice who shares in its profits and losses.

PARTNER/SHAREHOLDER A **partner** or **shareholder** is an attorney-owner in a private law practice who shares in its profits and losses. In the partnership form of business, an owner of the business is called a partner. In the corporate form of business, an owner is called a shareholder. Partners and shareholders serve primarily the same purpose; it is only the legal structure that is different. For simplicity, "partner" will be used to refer collectively to partners and shareholders, but "shareholder" could also have been used.

Partners attend partnership meetings and vote in the management decisions of the firm. Partners must also make monetary contributions to the firm if the need arises. Partners are sometimes called "equity partners," since they share in the profits or losses of the firm. To become a partner, an attorney must either be an attorney who founded the firm or be voted into the position by the existing partners. Typically, partners do not receive a "salary" but may receive a periodic draw, which is an advance against future profits.

managing partner

An attorney in a law firm chosen by the partnership to run the firm, make administrative decisions, and set policies.

In some firms, a **managing partner** is chosen by the partnership to run the firm, make administrative decisions, and set policies. The managing partner reports to the partnership on the progress of the firm. Managing partners are typically elected to serve for a set amount of time, such as one or two years. Depending on the size of the firm, a managing partner may spend part or all of his or her time on management duties. In smaller law offices, a managing partner will practice law in addition to running the firm, while in large firms, managing the practice is typically a full-time job.

associate attorney

Attorney who is a salaried employee of the law firm, does not have an ownership interest in the firm, does not share in the profits, and has no vote regarding management decisions.

ASSOCIATE ATTORNEYS An **associate attorney** does not have an ownership interest in the law firm and does not share in the profits. The associate is only an employee of the firm who receives a salary and has no vote regarding management decisions. Associates can be hired directly out of law school or come from other firms. Associates who are hired from other firms are known as lateral hires or lateral hire associates. Associates who are candidates for a future partnership are said to be on a partnership track. An associate is usually with the firm between

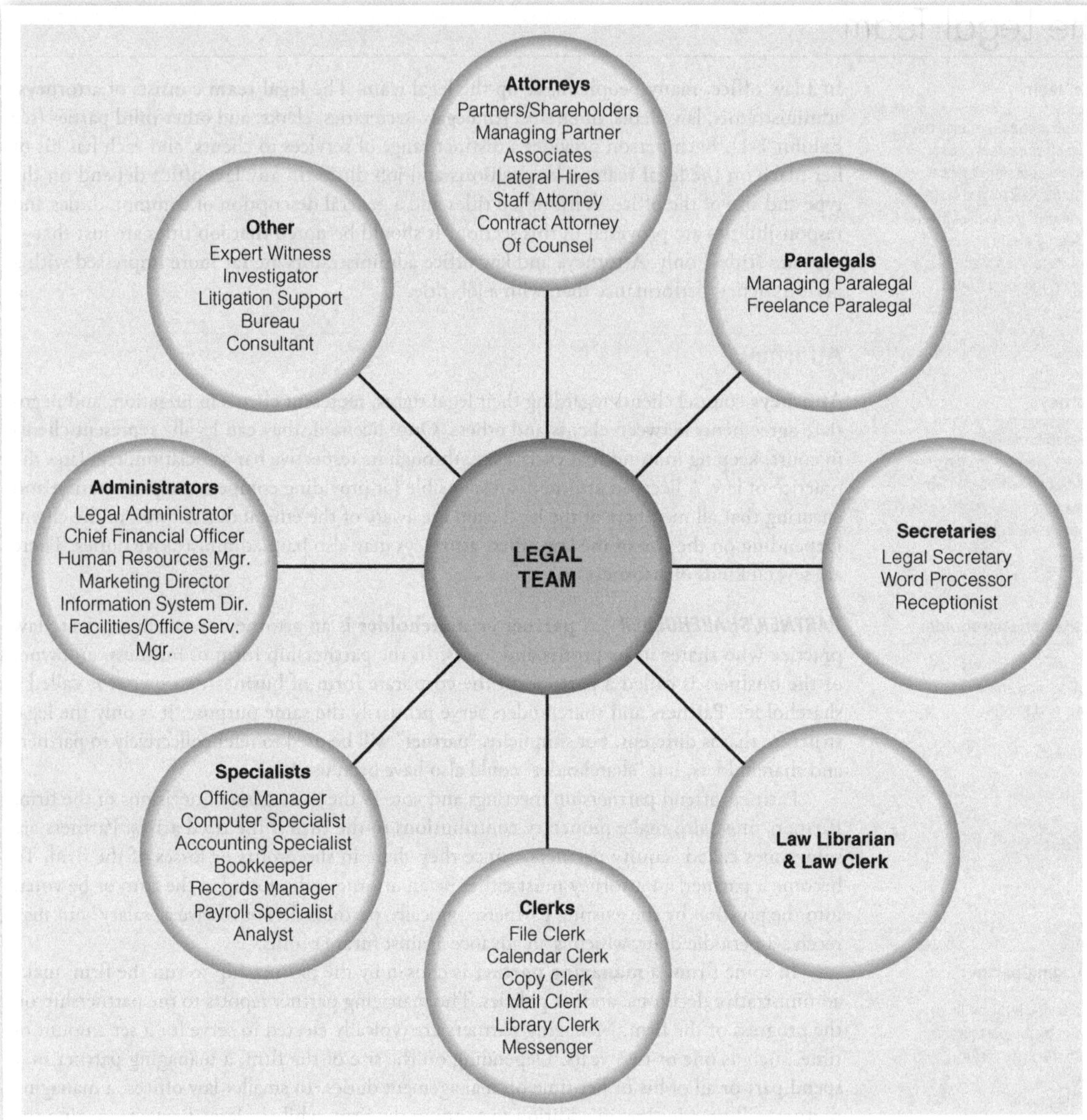

Exhibit 1-1 The Legal Team

non-equity partner

One who does not share in the profits or losses of the firm but may be included in some aspects of management and may be entitled to certain benefits.

5 and 10 years before he or she is a candidate for a partnership position, depending on the size of the firm. In large metropolitan firms, the time may be longer. An associate passed over for partnership may or may not leave the firm to practice elsewhere. Sometimes, to keep good associate attorneys who have nevertheless been passed over for partnership, the firm creates a position known as a non-equity partner. A **non-equity partner** does not share in the profits

or losses of the business but may be included in some aspects of the management of the firm and may be entitled to other benefits not given to associates. A **staff attorney** is another type of associate. A staff attorney is an attorney hired by a firm with the knowledge and understanding that he or she will never be considered for partnership. Finally, a **contract attorney** is an associate attorney who is temporarily hired by the law office for a specific job or period. When the job or period is finished, the relationship with the firm is over.

staff attorney

An attorney hired by a firm with the knowledge and understanding that he or she will never be considered for partnership.

contract attorney

An attorney temporarily hired by the law office for a specific job or period. When the job or period is finished, the relationship with the firm is over.

OF COUNSEL The **"of counsel"** position is a flexible concept but generally means that the attorney is affiliated with the firm in some way, such as a retired or semiretired partner. "Of counsel" attorneys lend their names to a firm for goodwill and prestige purposes, in order to attract additional clients and business to the firm. An "of counsel" attorney may be paid on a per-job basis or may be an employee of the firm. He or she does not usually share in the profits of the firm. The "of counsel" arrangement is also used when an attorney is considering joining a firm as a partner and wants to work on a trial basis first.

of counsel

An attorney affiliated with the firm in some way, such as a retired or semiretired partner.

Legal Administrators

Legal administrators are usually found in medium and large firms, although they are beginning to be used in small firms as well. They are responsible for some type of law office administrative system such as general management, finance and accounting, human resources, marketing, and computer technology. Legal administrators are typically non-attorneys who have degrees in business or related fields or who have been promoted through the ranks; most report directly to a committee or a partner.

legal administrators

Person responsible for some type of law office administrative system, such as general management, finance and accounting, human resources, marketing, or computer systems.

Legal administrators draft annual budgets, prepare and interpret management reports, supervise the fiscal operations of the business, hire and fire support staff, and are responsible for implementing effective systems. In actuality, managers are hired to relieve partners or managing committees of operational burdens. Experienced paralegals are sometimes promoted to become law office managers, which can be a positive career move. Depending on the size of the law firm, the legal administrator will have a varied range of job duties (see Exhibit 1-2). An excellent source of information regarding law office administration is the Association of Legal Administrators (ALA) [http://www.alanet.org].

Paralegals

Paralegals, sometimes referred to as legal assistants, are a unique group of people who assist attorneys in the delivery of legal services. Through formal education, training, and experience, paralegals have knowledge and expertise regarding the legal system to perform substantive legal work under the supervision of a lawyer, either employed or retained by lawyers and/or law firms, corporations, governmental agencies, or other entities. Some parts of the country as well as some legal organizations use the term *paralegal* and *legal assistant* interchangeably, still others consider the two terms clearly distinguishable. The American Bar Association (ABA) provides a definition, which uses both terms interchangeably, as does several other organizations and this text. Exhibit 1-3 shows three separate definitions for a paralegal or legal assistant consistent with the American Bar Association (ABA), National Federation of Paralegal Associations (NFPA), National Association of Legal Assistants (NALA), and American Association for Paralegal Education (AAfPE). However, in some parts of the country, as well as some legal organizations, there are various distinctions between the two terms.

paralegals

A unique group of people who assist attorneys in the delivery of legal services. They have knowledge and expertise regarding the legal system in order to provide substantive and procedural law that qualifies them to do work of a legal nature under the supervision of an attorney.

Exhibit 1-2 Legal Administrator Job Description

Source: Association of Legal Administrators.

Summary of Responsibilities

Handles the law office's overall business functions and operations including control and financial planning, handling personnel matters, and systems and facilities maintenance along with identifying necessary organizational changes. Legal administrator will report to a management committee, chairman of the board, or managing partner and participates in management meetings as well as sharing strategic planning, marketing, and practice management with the appropriate partners for cost-effective management throughout the organization.

The legal administrator, whether directly or indirectly through a management team, is responsible for all of the following:

Management of Facilities

Handles design and space planning, reprographics, record storage, telecommunications, mail, messenger, reception/switchboard services, and other facilities management duties.

Management of Systems

Handles computer system designs for the legal practice and litigation support, telecommunications, information services, records management, library management, document assembly, office automation, information storage and retrieval, system analysis, cost/benefit analysis, and operational audits.

Management of Finances

Handles everything from banking, cash flow control, general ledger accounting, billing and collections to payroll, pension plans, trust accounting, and tax reporting. Other financial management functions include profit and variance analysis, budgeting, planning, and forecasting.

Management of Human Resources

Handles the legal, paralegal, and support staff including job design, recruitment, employee selection, training and development, motivational resources, employee performance and evaluation, salary administration, employee relations including counseling, disciplinary actions, and discharge. Additional functions include benefits administration and workers' compensation along with maintaining personnel data systems and resource allocation.

Legal administrators are the members of the business's management team and will either manage and/or contribute considerably to the following:

Practice Management

Handles recruitment of lawyers along with training and development, supervising paralegals, overseeing work product, professional standards, substantive practice systems, and other practice management duties.

General Management

Handles business and organizational development, tactical and strategic firm planning, quality control, risk management, and other management duties.

Marketing

Handles legal services marketing to enhance the firm's visibility and image for preferred practice areas which includes client development and management, business opportunity forecasts, client development, and profit analysis.

A 2012 NALA survey found that 84% of participants were referred to as *paralegals* and only 11% were referred to as *legal assistants*, a significant change from the 2004 NALA survey where 30% were called *legal assistant* and 62% used *paralegal.*

The ABA has also recognized the contribution of paralegals and legal assistants to the legal profession by creating an associate membership category for them, which allows them

Exhibit 1-3 Definitions of a Legal Assistant/Paralegal

Sources: National Federation of Paralegal Associations (NFPA); National Association of Legal Assistants (NALA); National Association for Paralegal Education (AAfPE).

Organization	Definition of Legal Assistant or Paralegal
National Federation of Paralegal Associations (NFPA)	"A Paralegal/Legal Assistant is a person qualified through education, training or work experience to perform substantive legal work that requires knowledge of legal concepts and is customarily, but not exclusively, performed by a lawyer. This person may be retained or employed by a lawyer, law office, governmental agency or other entity or may be authorized by administrative, statutory or court authority to perform this work."
National Association of Legal Assistants (NALA)	Paralegals, also known as legal assistants, per the organization's July 2001 resolution is defined pursuant to the ABA's definition as "a person qualified by education, training or work experience who is employed or retained by a lawyer, law office, corporation, governmental agency, or other entity who performs specifically delegated substantive legal work for which a lawyer is responsible."
American Association for Paralegal Education (AAfPE)	"Paralegals perform substantive and procedural legal work as authorized by law, which work, in the absence of the paralegal, would be performed by an attorney. Paralegals have knowledge of the law gained through education, or education and work experience, which qualifies them to perform legal work. Paralegals adhere to recognized ethical standards and rules of professional responsibility."

to participate in relevant activities and join sections and divisions of the ABA. Many state and county bar associations also allow paralegals and legal assistants to participate as associate members in their organizations. Paralegals and legal assistants have two of their own national professional associations—NFPA and NALA—among others that they may join, which offer paralegals many resources and benefits. Exhibit 1-4 shows NALA's home page and Exhibit 1-5 shows NFPA's home page.

Although paralegals perform many tasks, they are strictly prohibited from giving legal advice to clients, from representing clients in court proceedings, from accepting client cases, and from setting a fee in a matter. This is covered in more detail in Chapter 3.

freelance or contract paralegals

Works as an independent contractor with supervision by and/or accountability to an attorney; is hired for a specific job or period.

Traditionally, a paralegal works under the direct supervision of an attorney and is accountable to that attorney. Some paralegals, however, work independently as **freelance** or **contract paralegals**; they are self-employed, marketing their services to the legal community on a per-job basis, enjoying the freedom to set their own hours and be their own bosses. Freelance paralegals often work off-site for a number of attorneys or legal organizations at the same time, while still working under the supervision of attorneys. They control time scheduling that is coordinated with the attorneys and the clients. The most important concern is that the work is done. The paralegal or legal assistant can determine the rate for their services, which is paid to them by the attorney. It's a win–win situation.

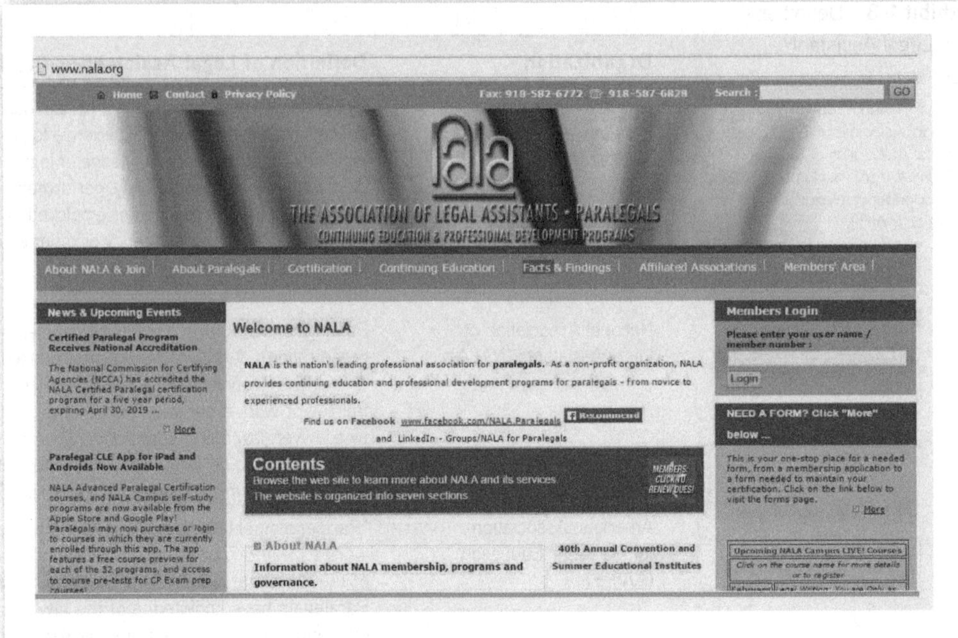

Exhibit 1-4 Home Page of the NALA Web Site

Source: National Association of Legal Assistants (NALA).

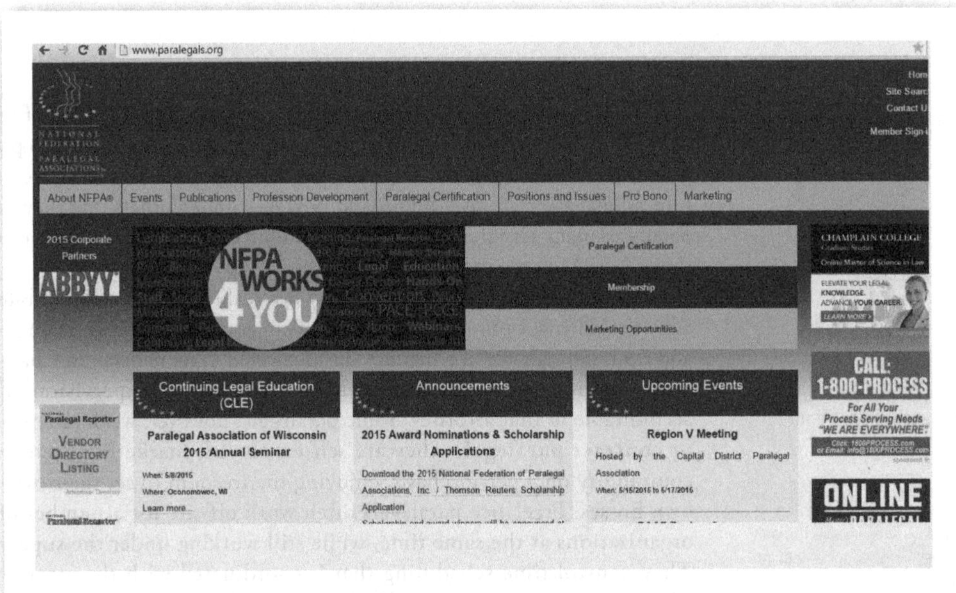

Exhibit 1-5 Home Page of the NFPA Web Site

Source: National Federation of Paralegal Associations (NFPA).

independent legal assistants

Services provided to clients in which the law is involved, but individuals providing the services are not accountable to a lawyer.

limited license legal technician

In states where legislation has provided, a person qualified by education, training, and work to engage in the limited practice of law in the approved practice area as per the state's rules.

paralegal managers

Oversees a paralegal program in a legal organization, including preparing work plans, hiring, training, and evaluating paralegals.

Independent legal assistants or **legal technicians** present some complicated issues with paralegals/legal assistants, in particular, ethical issues concerning unauthorized practice of law, discussed further in Chapter 3. Independent legal assistants provide services to clients, which involves the law, generally providing self-help services to the public. However, these individuals are not accountable to a lawyer. A **limited license legal technician**, in states where legislation has been passed, is a person qualified by education, training, and work to engage in the limited practice of law in the approved practice area as per the state's laws. In 2013, Washington passed legislation allowing non-attorneys, under carefully regulated circumstances, with specialized training and certification to practice law in a limited capacity. Washington State Rule 28—Limited Practice Rule for Limited License Legal Technicians. Other states such as California and Oregon have formed task forces to consider the adoption of Limited License Legal Technician. Still other states are considering similar options to address the needs for affordable and quality legal assistance without hiring an attorney, while still protecting the public interest.

Some larger legal organizations have **paralegal managers** who oversee the firm's paralegal program, and are responsible for administering all firm policies pertaining to paralegals. The firm's paralegals report either directly or indirectly to the paralegal manager. Paralegal managers develop work plans and standards, prepare staffing plans and bill rates, recruit and hire, provide training and development, monitor workloads, and conduct evaluations of the paralegals.

A recent survey by the National Association of Legal Assistants (NALA) found that more than 85% of the respondents had earned some kind of college education (see Exhibit 1-6). Both NFPA and NALA have voluntary certification exams, and some states offer certifications as well.

Paralegal Roles, Responsibilities, and Employment

People unfamiliar with the legal profession might assume that paralegals spend a great deal of time in court; this is a common misconception. A considerable amount of the paralegal's time is spent researching background information, plowing through reams of files, summarizing depositions, drafting pleadings or correspondence, and organizing information. It is not always exciting, but it is essential work with every case; often, the facts gathered, researched, and presented determine a case's outcome. Many of the paralegal's duties do not involve a courtroom, preparation of wills, real estate closing transactions, drafting discovery, or preparation of business corporation papers.

Response	Percent	Responses
High-school diploma	13%	176
Associate degree	31%	421
Bachelor's degree	47%	634
Master's degree	8%	112
Ph.D.	1%	13

Exhibit 1-6 General Education Degree Attained for Practicing Paralegals

Source: National Association of Legal Assistants, 2013 National Utilization and Compensation Survey Report, Table 1.4, General Education Degree Attained available at http://www.nala.org/Upload/file/PDF-Files/Certification/Report-for%20web%20site.pdf.

Defining a paralegal's job duties is not an easy task, given the wide variety and versatility of the profession. Exhibit 1-7 shows some of the more frequent duties paralegals perform. Notice that assisting at trial is the lowest on the chart. A majority of the paralegal/legal assistants responding to the survey in Exhibit 1-7 draft letters and case correspondence, work with and manage files and cases, calendar and keep track of case deadlines, work with computer systems, draft pleadings and formal court documents, work on miscellaneous office matters, and work with clients on a daily basis.

Most paralegals practice in a particular area of the law. Exhibit 1-8 shows the areas in which paralegals/legal assistants most frequently practice. Notice in Exhibit 1-8 that 37% of the participants surveyed indicated that they specialized in civil litigation. Litigation provides many employment opportunities for paralegals.

In addition to practicing in many different areas of the law, paralegals are employed in different kinds of legal organizations (see Exhibit 1-9). Approximately three-fourths of all the paralegals work in private law offices. Exhibit 1-9 also shows that about 62% of the paralegals/legal assistants surveyed worked in relatively small firms with 10 or fewer attorneys. The size of the law office has an effect on the job duties and salaries of paralegals. In small law offices, paralegals usually compose and draft their own documents on a computer and do their own

Exhibit 1-7

Paralegal Duties

Source: National Association of Legal Assistants, 2015 National Utilization and Compensation Survey Report, Table 2.16, Functions and Duties/ Frequencies.

Duty	Daily	Weekly	Monthly	Rarely	Total Responses*
Case management	72%	18%	6%	4%	1036
Draft correspondence	68%	21%	7%	4%	1274
Calendar deadlines	60%	21%	8%	11%	1129
Other	56%	10%	12%	22%	281
Automation systems/ computers	54%	20%	11%	15%	910
Draft pleadings	46%	29%	15%	10%	999
Assist with client contact	39%	27%	17%	17%	1109
Office matters	45%	19%	15%	21%	955
General, factual research	34%	33%	21%	12%	1198
Fact checking	39%	31%	15%	14%	997
Document analysis/ summary	36%	30%	19%	15%	1072
Court filings	33%	32%	15%	20%	984
Investigation	23%	31%	22%	23%	885
Personnel management	25%	14%	9%	52%	569
Client/witness interviews	10%	23%	26%	40%	831
Train employees	11%	13%	24%	53%	681
Cite checking	8%	17%	26%	49%	788
Prepare/attend closings	6%	9%	20%	66%	482
Law library maintenance	6%	4%	11%	78%	501
Deposition summaries	4%	10%	25%	61%	714
Prepare/attend depositions	3%	16%	36%	45%	644
Assist/attend mediations	0%	7%	32%	59%	549
Assist at trial	76%	20%	2%	2%	719

***Respondents were asked to skip the item if their work does not require the duty.**

Exhibit 1-8
Paralegal Specialty Areas of Practice
Source: National Association of Legal Assistants, 2015, National Utilization and Compensation Survey Report, Table 2.20, Specialty Areas of Practice by Number of Responses.

Specialty Areas	Percent of Respondents Selecting the Specialty	Number of Respondents
Civil litigation	37%	520
Family law	24%	179
Personal injury law	23%	277
Administrative/government/ public including compliance	22%	282
Insurance law	22%	233
Corporate law	18%	337
Social security	17%	88
Trusts and estates	16%	225
Criminal	16%	158
Real estate	15%	287
Intellectual property	15%	183
Contract	14%	337
Banking/finance	14%	168
Probate	13%	227
Commercial	12%	226
Health care	11%	118
Immigration	10%	78
Tax	9%	114
Workers compensation	8%	152
Oil and gas	8%	106
Bankruptcy	7%	178
Office management	6%	196
Construction	5%	135
Nonprofit	5%	92
Multistate litigation	4%	95
Collections	3%	190
Mergers/acquisitions	3%	124
Securities/antitrust	2%	84
Legislation/lobbying	1%	84

secretarial tasks. In larger firms, paralegals may supervise secretarial personnel or share secretary staff with other legal professionals. Exhibit 1-9 shows that about 45% of all paralegal/legal assistants are supervised by an attorney and about 43% are supervised by an administrator, manager, or the head of the department. Another interesting fact shown in Exhibit 1-9 is that as the number of attorneys in firms increase, the ratio of attorneys to paralegals goes down dramatically. In a sole practitioner's office, the ratio of attorneys to paralegal is 0.8:1, but in a firm with more than 100 attorneys, the ratio is 4.6:1.

Paralegal Compensation

Exhibit 1-10 contains a national survey of paralegal/legal assistant compensation. This survey found that the average compensation for all paralegal/legal assistants was $56,648 per year. The survey found that paralegal/legal assistants in tax intellectual property, securities/antitrust, and corporate law departments receive higher compensation on average

Exhibit 1-9
Paralegal Employment Statistics

Employer	Percent	Respondents
Private law firm	61%	660
Corporation	16%	178
Public sector/government	11%	124
Insurance company	3%	31
Self-employed	2%	20
Nonprofit organization	1%	23
Bank	1%	15
Court system	1%	9
Health/medical	1%	11

Source: National Association of Legal Assistants, 2015 National Utilization and Compensation Survey Report, Table 2.1, Type of Employer.

Number of Attorneys	Percent	Respondents
1 (sole practitioner)	12%	112
2–5	32%	294
6–10	18%	166
11–20	7%	124
21–50	13%	137
51–100	7%	62
More than 100	3%	31

Source: National Association of Legal Assistants, 2015 National Utilization and Compensation Survey Report, Table 2.10, Number of Attorneys in Firm.

Supervised by	Percent	Respondents
One or more attorneys	45%	478
Office administrator/manager	29%	305
Paralegal manager	7%	74
Department head	6%	66
No supervision (or other)	3%	34
General counsel	5%	56
Management committee	1%	11

Source: National Association of Legal Assistants, 2015 National Utilization and Compensation Survey Report, Table 2.8, Overall Supervision of Support Staff.

Number of Attorneys	Ratio of Attorneys to Legal Assistants
1	0.8
2–5	1.5
6–10	2.1
11–15	2.3
16–20	2.6
21–40	3.6
41–60	4.6
61–100	5.3
More than 100	4.6

Source: National Association of Legal Assistants, 2015 National Utilization and Compensation Survey Report, Table 2.11, Ratio of Attorneys to Legal Assistants.

Exhibit 1-10 Paralegal Compensation Survey

By Years of Legal Experience	Average Total Compensation	Respondents
1–5 years	$41,150	127
6–10 years	$52,061	155
11–15 years	$57,051	129
16–20 years	$61,622	185
21–25 years	$62,608	128
Over 25 years	$65,393	309
All years	$62,148	

Source: National Association of Legal Assistants, 2015 National Utilization and Compensation Survey Report, Table 4.7, Annual Salary and Compensation by Total Years of Legal Experience.

By Region	Average Total Compensation	Respondents
Region 7: Far West	$63,744	114
Region 1: New England/East	$63,396	40
Region 5: Southwest	$61,097	235
Region 6: Rocky Mountains	$60,621	49
Region 3: Plains States	$56,211	142
Region 4: Southeast	$56,123	381
Region 2: Great Lakes	$55,223	82

Source: National Association of Legal Assistants, 2015 National Utilization and Compensation Survey Report, Table 4.11, Annual Salary and Compensation by Region.

By Practice Area	Average Total Compensation (Greater than 40% of time in practice area)	Respondents
Antitrust/securities	$115,780	7
Tax law	$71,858	19
Corporate law	$70,225	112
Contract law	$67,715	112
Intellectual property law	$67,215	45
Employment/labor law	$60,780	65
Real estate law	$58,005	89
Insurance law	$56,436	91
Administrative/government/public	$56,154	111
Civil litigation	$55,856	337
Personal injury	$53,857	121
Bankruptcy	$50,454	29
Criminal	$48,314	38
Family law/domestic relations	$42,117	69
Antitrust/securities	$115,780	7

Source: National Association of Legal Assistants, 2015 National Utilization and Compensation Survey Report, Table 4.14, Total Compensation by Specialty Area Greater than 40% of Time.

(continued)

Exhibit 1-10 Paralegal Compensation Survey *(continued)*

Number of Attorneys	Average Total Compensation	Respondents
1	$55,916	123
2-5	$56,809	334
6-10	$59,209	183
11-15	$55,463	87
16-20	$61,765	54
21-25	$63,197	47
26-30	$57,462	39
31-40	$60,204	58
41-50	$56,811	36
51-75	$58,340	67
76-100	$70,447	21
More than 100	$64,777	34

Source: National Association of Legal Assistants, 2015 National Utilization and Compensation Survey Report, Table 4.13, Annual Salary and Compensation by Number of Attorneys.

Fair Labor Standards Act

Federal law that sets minimum wage and overtime pay requirements for employees.

exempt

The employee is not required to be paid overtime wages over 40 hours per week.

nonexempt

The employee is required to be paid overtime wages (time and a half) over 40 hours per week.

than do legal assistants in other areas of practice. The survey also found that: (1) paralegals with more experience earned higher pay than those with less experience, (2) paralegals working in the far west and New England/eastern areas earned higher compensation than those working in other areas of the United States, and (3) paralegals working in smaller firms tended to make less money than paralegals working in large law firms (see Exhibit 1-10).

EXEMPT V. NONEXEMPT The **Fair Labor Standards Act (FLSA)** is a federal law that sets minimum wage and overtime pay requirements for employees. It requires that overtime pay (one-and-one-half times their normal rate) be paid to employees who work in excess of 40 hours per week. Employees do not need to be paid overtime if they fall into one of the four "white-collar" exemptions: executive, administrative, professional, or outside sales. If an employee is **exempt**, he or she is not required to be paid overtime wages. If an employee is **nonexempt**, he or she is required to be paid overtime wages. According to a recent survey of paralegals/legal assistants, 52.2% of respondents indicated that they were classified as "exempt" by their employers and were not paid overtime wages.

Employment of paralegals and legal assistants is projected to grow 17% from 2012 to 2022, faster than the average for all occupations.

As law firms try to increase the efficiency of legal services and lower their expenses, they are expected to hire more paralegals and legal assistants. This occupation attracts many applicants, and competition for jobs will be strong. Experienced, formally trained paralegals with strong computer and database management skills should have the best job prospects. In addition, many firms will prefer paralegals with experience and specialization in high-demand practice areas. Bureau of Labor Statistics, U.S. Department of Labor, Occupational Outlook Handbook, 2014-15 Edition, Paralegals and Legal Assistants, *on the Internet at* http://www.bls.gov/ooh/legal/paralegals-and-legal-assistants.htm

The issue of whether paralegals should be exempt or nonexempt is hotly debated. The United States Department of Labor, which administers the FLSA, has long taken the position that paralegals are nonexempt and are thus entitled to overtime pay for hours worked in excess of 40 per week because their "duties do not involve the exercise of discretion and independent judgment required by the regulations" (see Wage & Hour Opinion Letters [available at http://www.dol.gov/esa/whd/opinion/opinion.htm] dated March 20, 1998; February 19, 1998; April 13, 1995; February 10, 1978). As recently as 2005 (see Wage & Hour Opinion Letter dated January 7, 2005, FLSA2005-9), the Department of Labor stated that a paralegal was not exempt from the FLSA even if the paralegal possessed a four-year degree, had a paralegal certificate, had taken continuing legal education classes, and had been practicing as a paralegal for 22 years. The Department relied on section 541.301(3)(7), which states that "[p]aralegals and legal assistants generally do not qualify as exempt learned professionals because an advanced specialized academic degree is not a standard prerequisite for entry into the field. Although many paralegals possess general four-year advanced degrees, most specialized paralegal programs are two-year associate degree programs from a community college or equivalent institution."

The advantage of this long-held position by the Department of Labor is that if a paralegal is deemed nonexempt, then he or she is entitled to overtime pay, which can be an attractive benefit. Unfortunately, the ruling arguably diminishes the profession by holding that it is not of a prestigious enough nature to warrant exempt status. The ruling from the Department of Labor was criticized by many that felt it failed to consider the advanced education and continuing legal education of paralegals and legal assistants, the profession's status as well as the substantive duties performed by paralegals and legal assistants for which independent judgment is routinely exercised. In 1994, a jury in the case of *Riech v. Page & Addison, P.C.* (Case No. 3-91-CV-2655-P in the United States District Court, Northern District of Texas, Dallas Division) found that the legal assistants at the Page & Addison law firm were exempt from overtime requirements. Nevertheless, the Department of Labor did not change its general position on the matter. Interestingly, many law firms still do not pay overtime compensation to paralegals/legal assistants, even after the rulings by the Department of Labor on the subject; according to Exhibit 1-11, only 52% of firms always pay overtime compensation for paralegals.

The Judicial System's Recognition of the Paralegal Profession

The United States Supreme Court case of *Missouri v. Jenkins*, 491 U.S. 274, 109 S.Ct. 2463, 105 L.Ed. 2d 229 (1989), established that the paralegal profession had come of age. In that case, the plaintiff was successful on several counts under a federal statute in a civil rights lawsuit

Do You Receive Overtime Compensation?	Percent	Respondents
Always paid	52%	497
Sometimes paid	7%	64
Never paid	22%	206
Compensatory time off	19%	180

Exhibit 1-11 Paralegal Overtime Compensation

Source: National Association of Legal Assistants, 2015 National Utilization and Compensation Survey Report, Table 2.4, Overtime Compensation.

that was attempting to recover attorney's fees from the defendant. The federal statutory language allowed the prevailing party to recover "reasonable attorney's fees" from the adverse party. The plaintiff argued for the right to recover the time that both attorneys and paralegal had spent working on the case. The defendant argued that paralegal time was not "attorney's fees." Alternatively, the defendant argued that if required to pay for paralegal time, the amount should be about $15 an hour, a representation of the overhead costs to the firm of a paralegal.

The Court found that paralegals carry out many useful tasks, and that "reasonable attorney's fees" refers to a reasonable fee for the work produced, whether by attorneys or paralegals, and could be compensable as long as the work was not of a clerical nature. The Court also found that under the federal statute, paralegal time should be compensable at the prevailing market rates. The Court noted that the prevailing rate at that time for paralegal in that part of the United States was about $40 an hour and held that the plaintiff was entitled to receive that amount for paralegal hours expended on the case. This important case defined a paralegal position not as a secretarial or clerical position but as a professional, fee-generating profession.

Former Chief Justice Warren Burger stated that the "expanded use of well-trained assistants, sometimes called 'paralegals,' has been an important development. The advent of the paralegal enables law offices to perform high quality legal services at a lower cost. Possibly we have only scratched the surface of this development."

While *Missouri v. Jenkins* was a landmark decision for paralegals, the case involved a federal court interpreting a specific federal statute, the Civil Rights Act. Because fee questions occur in many different situations, it is possible for a court under a different statute to reach a different conclusion. Since *Missouri v. Jenkins*, many federal and state courts have allowed for recovery of paralegal billable hours [see *Baldwin v. Burton*, 850 P.2d 1188, 1200-01 (Utah 1993), *Cooper v. Secretary of Dept. of Health and Human Services*, No. 90-608V, 1992 WL 63271 at 3 (Cl. Ct. March 11, 1992), *Consolo v. George*, 58 F.3d 791 (1st Cir. 1995), *Department of Transp., State of Fla. v. Robbins & Robbins, Inc.* 700 So. 2d 782, Fla. App. 5 Dist. (1997), *Guinn v. Dotson* (1994) 23 Cal. App. 4th 262, *In re Mullins*, 84 F.3d 459 (D.C. Cir. 1996), and *Taylor v. Chubb Group of Insurance Companies,* 874 P.2d 806 (Ok. 1994). *Role Models American, Inc. v. Brownlee*, 353 F.3d 962 (C.A.D.C., 2004)].

Paralegal Profitability for Law Offices

The use of paralegals is a financially profitable proposition and represents a win–win situation for both the law office and client. Law offices charge clients for paralegal time. Paralegal billing rates are substantially more than the salaries law offices pay them, so law offices make a profit by billing paralegal time. In addition, clients are typically very willing to pay for paralegal time because the billable rate is substantially less than what an attorney would charge to do the same work.

Office Manager

office managers

Manager who handles day-to-day operations of the law office, such as accounting, supervision of the clerical support staff, and assisting the managing partner.

Office managers are typically found in smaller firms. They handle day-to-day operations of the law office, including activities such as timekeeping and billing, supervision of the clerical support staff, assisting the managing partner in preparing a budget, and making recommendations with regard to changes in systems and purchases. Office managers typically do not have degrees in business. They are usually not given as much decision-making power as administrators and, unlike administrators, usually assist a managing partner in managing the law office. Nonetheless, good office managers are important for the survival of smaller firms. Experienced paralegals are sometimes promoted to office manager positions.

Law Clerk

law clerk

A law student working for a law firm on a part-time basis while he or she is finishing a law degree. Law clerk duties revolve almost exclusively around legal research and writing.

A **law clerk** is usually a student who works for a law firm on a part-time basis while he or she is finishing a law degree. Law clerk duties revolve almost exclusively around legal research and writing. Law clerks perform research, write briefs and motions, and prepare memorandums of law.

Law Librarian

law librarian

A librarian is responsible for maintaining a law library, conducting legal research, and managing library resources.

A **law librarian** conducts legal research using both computerized and manual methods; acquires and preserves library materials; is an expert in legal and nonlegal research methods/tools; advises attorneys and legal professionals on legal research methods; maintains, classifies, indexes, and stores library materials; manages the library/legal research budget, and may coordinate the use of electronic resources, such as Westlaw, LexisNexis, and other services.

Legal Secretaries

legal secretaries

Employees who provide assistance and support to other law office staff by preparing documents, composing correspondence, scheduling appointments, and performing other tasks.

Legal secretaries provide a variety of services to attorneys and paralegals. Typical duties include preparing documents, composing routine correspondence, proofreading, reading and routing mail, scheduling appointments, organizing material, filing, answering the phone and screening calls, faxing, copying, responding to e-mails, responding to clients, and other tasks. Exhibit 1-12 shows that about 52% of paralegals have limited or full access to secretarial support. Secretaries include legal secretaries, receptionists, and word processing secretaries. Competent legal secretaries have highly specialized skills and perform many services for law firms. Legal secretaries, like paralegals, have their own local, regional, state, and national associations. It is not uncommon for a person to start employment with a law office as a legal secretary and work his or her way up to paralegal, office manager, or another position.

Secretarial Assistance	Percent	Respondents
Have personal secretary	2%	19
Share secretary with one or more attorneys	24%	251
Share secretary with one or more paralegals	5%	48
Have limited access to a secretary (perform some of own secretarial duties)	17%	183
Have access to word processing staff or secretarial pool	4%	45
No secretarial service	48%	511

Exhibit 1-12 Secretarial Support Provided to Legal Assistants

Source: National Association of Legal Assistants, 2015 National Utilization and Compensation Survey Report, Table 2.2, Kinds of Secretarial Assistance Provided.

Receptionists are commonly found in all law offices, and their duties include answering the phone, greeting clients, opening the mail, and making photocopies. Word processing secretaries are commonly found in larger law offices. They type, format, and produce documents using word processing software.

It is not uncommon for friction to exist between paralegals and secretaries. Problems may occur in law offices where there are no clear descriptions of job duties, where paralegals are required to do some clerical or administrative work, and where secretaries perform higher level research or case management from time to time. This blurring of the lines sometimes causes confusion about who is supposed to do what; when this happens, pressure is added to the working relationship. Some secretaries also resent paralegals performing higher-level work than they themselves are allowed to perform. In addition, some secretaries refuse or resist performing clerical work for paralegals because they view paralegals as peers. In any case, paralegals and secretaries must work together as members of the same team. They must put the needs of the team first and always support their coworkers, because eventually they will need their help.

Clerks

clerks

Employees who provide support to other staff positions in a variety of miscellaneous functions.

Clerks provide support to other staff positions in a variety of functions. Law offices may have a wide variety of clerks, including mail clerks, copy clerks, file clerks, process servers, messengers, calendar clerks, and billing clerks. Much of their work involves data entry and physically handling files and documents.

Other Legal Team Members

expert witness

A person who has technical expertise in a specific field and agrees to give testimony for a client at trial.

A variety of other people and organizations make up the legal team. Other team members may include expert witnesses, investigators, litigation support bureaus, and consultants. An **expert witness** is a person who has technical or scientific expertise in a specific field and agrees to give testimony for a client at trial. Professional investigators are sometimes hired to gather facts and evidence regarding a case. Litigation support service bureaus may be used in cases that have hundreds or thousands of documents to organize and records to computerize for trial. Specialists may also be hired, such as computer specialists, accountants, bookkeepers, records managers, payroll specialists, and analysts. Some large firms employee analysts who are experts in their fields, such as biologists, chemists, and others. These analysts advise the firm and their clients on extremely complex cases. Law offices use business, marketing, and other types of consultants to give them advice on how to run their operation efficiently. Law offices may also use temporary or permanent staffing firms and may outsource jobs, projects, or services as needed, including copying, mail services, and records management.

Types of Law Practices

To a certain extent, how law office management operates depends on the type of law office. Therefore, it is necessary to review the different types of law practices and their functional effect on management. Usually, people think of the private law firm as the only type of law practice, but there are others, including corporate law, government, and legal service practices.

Corporate Law Practice

Some businesses, including large corporations, banks, retailers, manufacturers, transportation companies, publishers, insurance companies, and hospitals, have their own in-house legal departments. Attorneys employed by a corporate law department are often referred to as "in-house counsel." In a corporate legal department, attorneys and paralegals have just one client: the business itself. However, some corporate legal departments see each division or department in the corporation as an individual client for whom they must provide quality legal services.

Corporations with their own legal departments are generally large, with millions of dollars in assets. Unlike private law firms, a corporate legal department is not involved in many administrative functions, such as accounting, since the corporation itself provides these services. Corporate legal departments do not record billable hours, since all costs are covered by the corporation. However, corporate legal departments must still budget, track, and plan activities, and they are responsible for the overall efficiency of their department. Corporate law departments handle a variety of legal concerns in such areas as contracts, labor relations, employee benefits, federal tax laws, intellectual property, environmental law issues, Security Exchange Commission (SEC) filings, general litigation, real estate law, and workers' compensation claims, among others.

Most corporate legal departments are too small to handle all the legal needs of the corporation, so the law departments hire private law firms that specialize in the additional areas they need. This is sometimes referred to as having "outside counsel." The chief attorney for a corporate legal department is called the **general counsel**. The general counsel, in addition to having legal duties, may also be the corporate secretary. The general counsel typically reports to the chief executive officer and interacts closely with the board of directors of the corporation. Many corporate law departments have practice groups that specialize in certain areas, such as litigation, regulatory work, taxes, contracts and intellectual property work, and more.

general counsel

The chief for a corporate legal department.

Staffing in corporate legal departments includes secretaries, paralegals, law clerks, administrators, and attorneys (see Exhibit 1-13). Most corporate legal departments employ one or more paralegals. The job duties a paralegal performs in a corporate legal department are similar to those performed in other types of practices and may include preparing deposition summaries, performing legal research, and drafting documents. Like paralegals in private law firms, paralegals in corporate legal departments might also specialize in specific areas, such as litigation, real estate, or business law.

Government Practice

Government attorneys, like corporate attorneys, have just one client. In most local, state, and federal agencies, a legal department represents the interests of *each* particular agency. Government attorneys representing agencies or governmental bodies may be involved in contract law, bankruptcy law, tax law, employment law, property law, and environmental law, to name a few. Each state also has an attorney general's office; the attorney general operates as the state's chief law enforcement officer and attorney. In many instances, when a state or state agency is sued, the attorney general's office represents the state. In addition, many other types of government attorneys exist, including local district and city attorneys, state attorney generals, and U.S. attorneys.

Exhibit 1-13
Corporate Law Department Organizational Chart

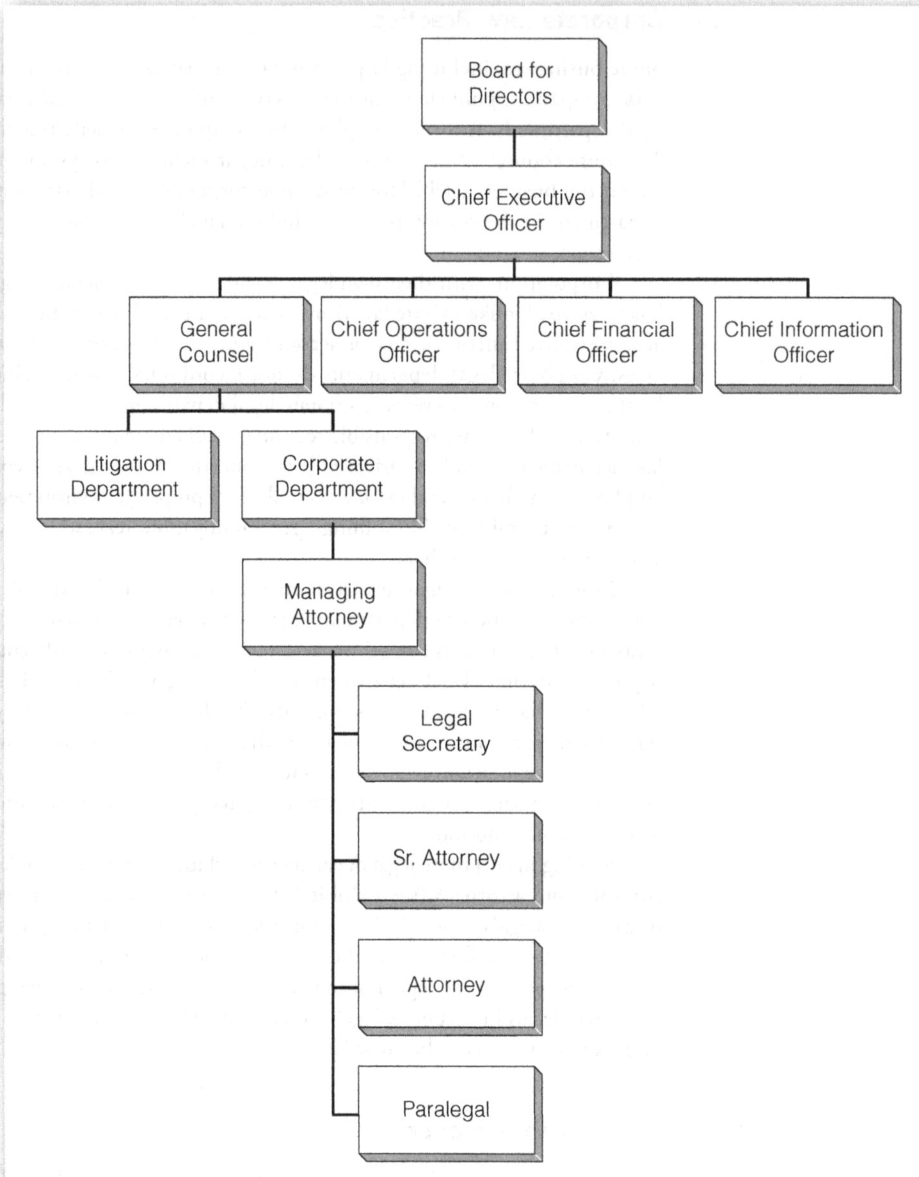

In many ways, practicing for the government is similar to practicing for a large corporation. Government attorneys, like corporate attorneys, do not record billable hours and are not responsible for as many management duties as are their counterparts in private law firms. Government practices differ from corporate legal department practices in that politics plays a role; government attorneys and paralegals are also paid according to their civil service classification. Staffing for government legal departments consists of secretaries, investigators, paralegals, law clerks, and attorneys. The job duties of paralegals in government practices vary depending on the area of practice, and these duties may be tested in various civil service exams that are a prerequisite to hiring.

Legal Services Offices

legal services office

A not-for-profit law office that receives grants from the government and private donations to pay for representation of disadvantaged persons who otherwise could not afford legal services.

A **legal services office**, sometimes called a legal clinic or legal aid office, is a not-for-profit law office that receives grants from the government and private donations to pay for representation of disadvantaged persons who otherwise could not afford legal services. In some cases, legal services offices or clinics are operated by law schools, bar associations, or other nonprofit entities as a public service to the community. Clients pay little or no fees for legal services. Legal services offices typically represent the disadvantaged in areas relating to child support, child custody, disability claims, bankruptcies, landlord-tenant disputes, and mental health problems. Staffing for legal services offices includes secretaries, paralegals, law clerks, and attorneys. In legal services practices, paralegals may be used fairly extensively and are usually given a wide variety of tasks because their use is cost effective. Legal services offices typically handle civil matters, while government public defenders' offices handle criminal matters for low-income clients.

Private Law Practices

The most common way that attorneys practice law is in a private law firm (see Exhibit 1-14). A private law practice is a firm that generates its own income by representing clients. Private law firms, like any business, are operated to make a profit for their owners. Private law firms represent a variety of clients and come in all shapes and sizes, from a sole practitioner to international megafirms.

The terminology is somewhat arbitrary, and may depend on the relative size of your community, but, for this text, a small firm is a law office that has fewer than 20 attorneys; a medium-size firm usually has from 20 to 75 attorneys; and a large firm can employ from 75 to hundreds of attorneys. There are also megafirms that employ between 500 and 1000 attorneys or more. Private practices, no matter the size, have their own unique styles, methods, clients, cultures, and ways of doing things. As of 2012, there were nearly 1.3 million attorneys in the United States, according to the American Bar Association's Market Research Department, Exhibit 1-14 shows the types and sizes of practices they join.

Sole Practitioner

A sole practitioner is an attorney who individually owns and manages the practice. Anyone who works for the attorney is considered an employee. Sole practitioners sometimes hire another attorney as an employee, who is not entitled to any share of the practice's profits. Although the sole practitioner has the advantage of freedom and independence, he or she is also ultimately responsible for all, or nearly all, of the legal work and management duties of the law office. It is important that overhead costs stay as small as possible, if the sole practitioner is to succeed. Overhead costs are the expenses incurred month after month and include such things as rent (thus the term "overhead"), utilities, the lease of equipment (such as copiers and computers), and support staff salaries. These are costs incurred whether the attorney is serving one client or 100. Sole practitioners typically have small offices with a very small law library.

Exhibit 1-14 Percent of Attorneys by Practice Type/Size

Practice Type	Percent
Private practice	75%
Government	8%
Corporate/private industry	8%
Retired/inactive	4%
Judiciary	3%
Education	1%
Legal aid/public defender	1%
Private association	1%

Source: *The Lawyer Statistical Report*, American Bar Foundation, 2004 Edition.

Private Practitioners

Practice Type	Percent
1	49%
2-5	14%
6–10	6%
11–20	6%
21–50	6%
51–100	4%
More than 100	16%

Sources: *The Lawyer Statistical Report*, American Bar Foundation, 1985, 1994, 2004, 2012 Editions.

Sole practitioners are typically generalists, meaning they handle a wide variety of cases, such as probate, family law, criminal law, and personal injury. The sole practitioner typically refers a case outside of his or her area of expertise to another attorney who is skilled in that matter. Sole practitioners need good management skills for their practice to survive. This may pose a problem, because management duties take the sole practitioner away from the actual practice of law, which is the activity that brings in the money. Exhibit 1-14 shows that nearly half of all attorneys in the United States are sole practitioners.

Staffing can include a secretary, paralegal, law clerk, and possibly an associate attorney; these positions may even be part time. Paralegals working in a sole practitioner's office enjoy a great deal of responsibility and diversity in their jobs. Duties include conducting legal research, drafting pleadings and discovery materials, word processing, and interviewing witnesses. Because sole practitioners are generalists, their paralegals work in many areas of the law. In a solo practice, the paralegal has the opportunity to learn firsthand about law office management and to perform management functions.

Law Firms

Law firms have two or more attorneys in practice together. There are 47,563 law firms in the United States (not counting sole practitioners), according to the American Bar Association. While there is not as much freedom as in sole practice, law firms do not incur as much risk. If a sole practitioner becomes ill, loses a large client, or faces other such catastrophes, the sole practitioner's income may be endangered. These problems may be alleviated in law firms, because more than one attorney is available. Law firms are usually categorized as small, medium, or large.

THE SMALL LAW FIRM The small firm usually has fewer than 20 attorneys. Notice in Exhibit 1-14 that nearly 76% of all attorneys in the United States practice as either a sole practitioner or in a small firm. Most small firms have a staff member—such as an office manager or an administrator—who helps with the day-to-day operations of the business. However, a partner or managing partner is usually responsible for major management decisions such as hiring, firing, distributing profits, and setting salaries. Small firms usually concentrate in a few areas of the law but may also have attorneys who are general practitioners.

A small law office that specializes in only one or two areas of the law is sometimes called a **boutique firm**. The boutique firm normally has several attorneys who practice in the same specialty. Paralegals who work for boutique firms also usually become specialists in that particular area of the law.

boutique firm

A small law office that specializes in only one or two areas of the law.

Disadvantages that hinder small firms include cash-flow problems, lack of time to recruit, hire, and train new staff, little time for management, and long hours. Staffing positions include clerks, secretaries, paralegals, office managers, law clerks, and attorneys. Small firms offer paralegals a relatively large variety of tasks to perform.

THE MEDIUM-SIZE FIRM The medium-size firm usually has from 20 to 75 attorneys. Typically, medium-size firms are organized into subject-area departments. Medium-size firms differ from small firms in that most medium-size firms have professional administrators who manage many aspects of the business. Administrators usually report to a managing partner or a committee that has overall management responsibilities. Medium-size firms typically have multiple offices, and it is not uncommon for them to have sophisticated computer systems. Staffing often consists of administrators, law librarians, receptionists, secretaries, paralegals, law clerks, and attorneys. Paralegals in medium-size firms have a more structured existence than in smaller firms; the diversity of duties and areas of practice are not as broad. However, the legal assistant may learn a particular area of law in greater depth. In addition, the internal structure and lines of communication are more intense and more important than in small firms, where colleagues tend to be more familiar with one another.

THE LARGE FIRM The large firm has between 75 and several hundred attorneys. A few large firms, sometimes called "megafirms," have 500–1000 or more attorneys. Most large firms have practice groups or departments. A large firm might have 15 or more different practice groups, including antitrust, bankruptcy, environmental, estate planning, intellectual property, international, labor/employment law, litigation, patents, trademarks, copyright, property, and tax. The internal structure of these firms is more similar to the structure of business corporations than to other types of law firms. Staffing in large firms typically includes various classes of paralegals, law clerks, and attorneys, in addition to the positions shown in Exhibit 1-15. Large firms often have large corporations as clients. Many have offices throughout the United States, and some have international offices. Large firms also tend to have resources such as large law libraries, a word processing department, and extensive, technologically advanced computer systems connecting all their offices for information exchange.

Disadvantages encountered by large firms include recruiting and retaining good employees in the vital areas of the practice, getting departments to communicate and work together, and controlling the bureaucracy itself. Large law firms usually employ a large number of

Exhibit 1-15 Large Law Firm Administrative Staff Positions

Accounts payable clerk	Legal secretary/administrative assistant
Accounts receivable clerk	Library specialist
Analyst	Litigation support specialist
Bookkeeper	Mail clerk
Chief financial officer	Messenger/driver
Controller	Paralegal manager
Computer specialist	Payroll specialist
Copy room clerk	Proofreader
Credit/collections manager	Purchasing manager
Data processing operator	Purchasing clerk
Director of marketing	Receptionist
Docket clerk	Records/file manager
Employee benefits manager	Recruiter
Equipment manager	Risk manager
Facilities manager	Trainer
File room clerk	Time and billing assistant
Human resource manager	Word processor
Legal administrator	Word processing supervisor
Law librarian	

paralegals and treat them formally and professionally, requiring them to attend department meetings, assist attorneys in depositions, and travel as needed. The physical space occupied by a large firm is more lavish than in small- and medium-size firms, usually occupying several floors in a large office building.

Plaintiff/Defense Firms

Private law practices may categorize themselves as either more or less plaintiff or defense oriented, no matter what the size of the law office. Plaintiff-oriented firms, as the name implies, represent clients who bring claims against others. Plaintiff-oriented firms tend to be smaller, not as well funded, and have fewer employees than defense-oriented firms. Cash flow in plaintiff firms may not be as stable as in defense-oriented firms because, in many cases, they take clients on a contingency fee basis; that is, the law office recovers fees for the case only if it wins.

Defense-oriented firms, on the other hand, have the luxury of billing defendants—who are typically businesses—according to the time spent on the case. This gives defense-oriented firms a more stable cash flow, enabling them to hire more personnel, purchase advanced equipment, and spend more on litigation services, such as hiring expert witnesses and taking as many depositions as needed. Nonetheless, effective management is needed in both plaintiff- and defense-oriented firms.

No matter the type of legal organization, good management, including sound financial management, cost-efficient hiring and training of personnel, efficient use of equipment, and overall leadership, is important.

Law Firm Mergers and Acquisitions

Law firm mergers are commonplace in the U.S. legal market. Law firms merge for different reasons. A law firm might merge as a growth strategy, in order to quickly expand their personnel and client base. A law firm might merge in order to create a presence in a new geographic area or to move into a new practice specialty. A law firm might merge in order to create a national or international practice. A law firm might also merge if it is financially weak or if key partners have left or are retiring, as a way to save what's left of the practice. Law firm mergers can be complicated for a number of reasons, including conflict of interest problems (if the firms are representing different parties in a legal action), law office culture differences, staffing issues, financial resources, client satisfaction, computer compatibility, political power struggles, and other issues. Nonetheless, they occur regularly among private law practices throughout the United States.

Geographic Service Areas

In years past, a law firm operated in a single location, and the office typically attracted clients within a limited geographic area around that location. That model no longer works in the current legal marketplace. The Internet, sophisticated computer networks that can tie offices together from across the country or around the world, and large, multi-office law firms have changed that paradigm. Many law firms have developed a geographic strategy regarding business expansion and how they define where and what their marketplace and client base will be. Geographic service strategies include: local, statewide, regional/multistate, national, international, and industry specific. When considering law practices, size is just one factor; it is also important to take geographic and business strategy into account, along with where they see themselves going in the short and long terms. Geographic and business strategies are also important in that they play a significant part in how firms are managed and operated, and these issues can cause a great deal of disagreement and problems between the owners of a firm who may not see eye to eye on these issues.

Law Practice Organization Structures

Law practices have different organization or management structures. Private law practices are managed by a powerful managing partner, by all partners, or by committees. Corporate and government law practices have either a centralized or decentralized management structure.

Legal Forms of Private Law Firms

Management structures of law firms are affected by the firm's legal status. A law firm can be formed as a sole proprietorship, partnership, corporation, or, in some states, a limited liability company. Before the management structure of law offices can be considered, the legal status of those law offices must be explained.

SOLE PROPRIETORSHIP In a sole proprietorship, the proprietor, in this case an attorney, runs the business, receives all profits, and is personally responsible for all losses and liabilities of the law office. However, a sole proprietorship is a distinct type of legal structure, and a sole practitioner does not have to use the sole proprietorship form; many sole practitioners are incorporated.

PARTNERSHIP The partnership's legal structure allows two or more attorneys to associate themselves together and to share in the profits or losses of the business. Many group practices use this structure. When a law office is established as a partnership, the founding attorneys are usually named as partners. As growth takes place, the partnership may hire additional associate attorneys.

All the partners are jointly and severally liable for the actions of the firm. This means if one partner commits malpractice and injures a client, each partner may be held individually or jointly responsible. Partners are also personally liable for the debts of the partnership. Partnerships typically use committees to make policy decisions, and partners meet regularly to discuss partnership business.

PROFESSIONAL CORPORATION The professional corporation allows a single shareholder or a group of shareholders from the same profession, such as attorneys, to join together to share in the outcomes of a business. When a law office is established as a professional corporation, the founding attorney or attorneys receive shares in the business. As in a partnership, associates are not owners and are only paid a salary. Shareholders can vote to offer additional shares of the business to associates and expand the ownership of the law firm. All attorneys are employees of the corporation and are paid a salary. Besides a salary, shareholders are also paid a dividend. The amount of the dividend depends on the profitability of the corporation and on the number of shares owned. Shareholders are not personally responsible for the debts of the professional corporation. The corporate form requires the election of officers and a board of directors.

LIMITED LIABILITY COMPANY The limited liability company (LLC) is a hybrid form of legal structure; it is a combination of the corporate and partnership forms. The LLC form of structure is valid in many states. The main advantage of an LLC is that it allows for limited personal liability of company debts for its owners (like a corporation), but is treated like a partnership for income tax purposes.

Private Law Firm Management Structures

The type of management or governing structure used to manage the business aspect of the firm is the choice of the firm itself, but the legal structure of the business may dictate some of that management structure. For example, a corporation—by law—must have a board of directors. Many law practices struggle with the problem of determining who runs the firm and who has the final say on firm decisions. Possible management structures include one powerful managing partner, rule by all partners/shareholders, and rule by management committee or board.

powerful managing partner

A management structure in which a single partner is responsible for managing the firm.

THE POWERFUL MANAGING PARTNER In a **powerful managing partner** management structure, a single partner manages the firm. The managing partner is responsible for day-to-day operations of the partnership, while partners vote on major firm decisions (see Exhibit 1-16). The managing partner may have a specific term of office. In some firms, the position is rotated among the practicing partners. In many firms, the managing partner spends anywhere from 60% to 100% of his or her time on management responsibilities. This form allows other partners to spend more time practicing law, but it places the managerial duties on one partner and reduces the managing partner's time to practice law. The powerful managing partner structure is autocratic: power rests with only one person. In some cases, the other partners may feel that they are without a voice in the management of the firm.

The strong managing partner structure works well in small- to medium-sized law practices where the managing partner is well-regarded and well-liked; makes sound business decisions so that the firm is profitable and stable; is an effective delegator, leader, and manager; and where the practice is not expanding rapidly. One benefit of this structure is that decisions

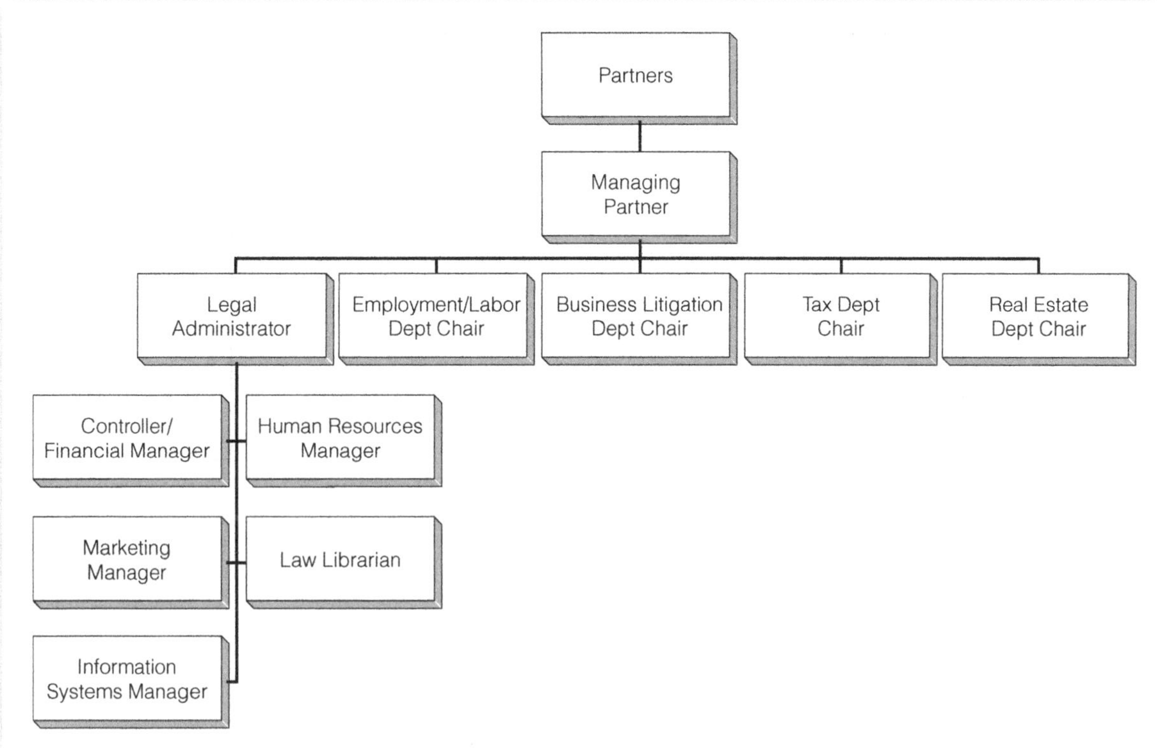

Exhibit 1-16 Powerful Managing Partner Structure

are made relatively quickly and decisively because the power principally lies with one person. The managing partner structure tends to break down, however, when the managing partner makes an unpopular decision, when there is not enough partner oversight to satisfy the other partners, when the firm is not profitable, or where there is substantial conflict or questions about the direction of the firm.

rule by all partners/shareholders

A management structure in which all partners/shareholders are included in decisions that affect the firm.

RULE BY ALL PARTNERS/SHAREHOLDERS **Rule by all partners/shareholders** is a management structure in which all partners/shareholders make decisions that affect the firm (see Exhibit 1-17). All the partners or shareholders meet whenever management policies or decisions need to be made. This is a democratic structure, since all the partners have a say in firm decisions and policies. Although this structure allows partners'/shareholders' involvement in all decisions of the firm, as the number of partners/shareholders increases, the effectiveness of the group may decrease; a larger group may foster indecision and a lack of direction.

rule by management committee/board

Management structure that uses a committee structure to make management decisions for the firm.

RULE BY MANAGEMENT COMMITTEE/BOARD The **rule by management committee/board** management structure uses a committee structure to make management decisions for the firm (see Exhibit 1-18). Committees are made up of 5–10 members depending on the size of the firm, and are typically composed of partners or shareholders. Common committees include the library committee, automation or technology committee, finance committee, and personnel committee. These committees usually report to a management or executive committee.

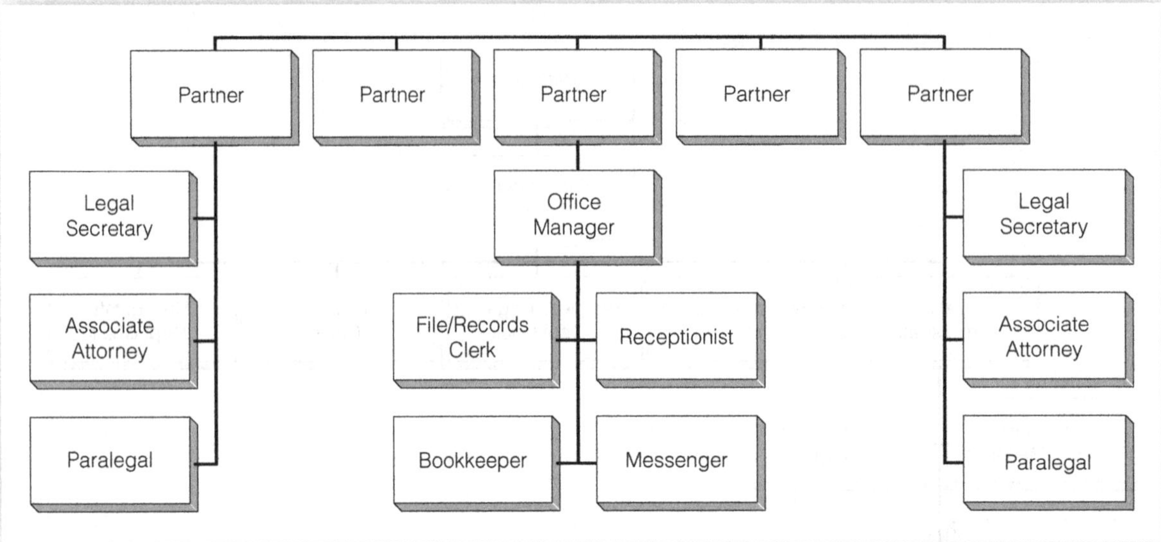

Exhibit 1-17 Rule by All Partners/Shareholders

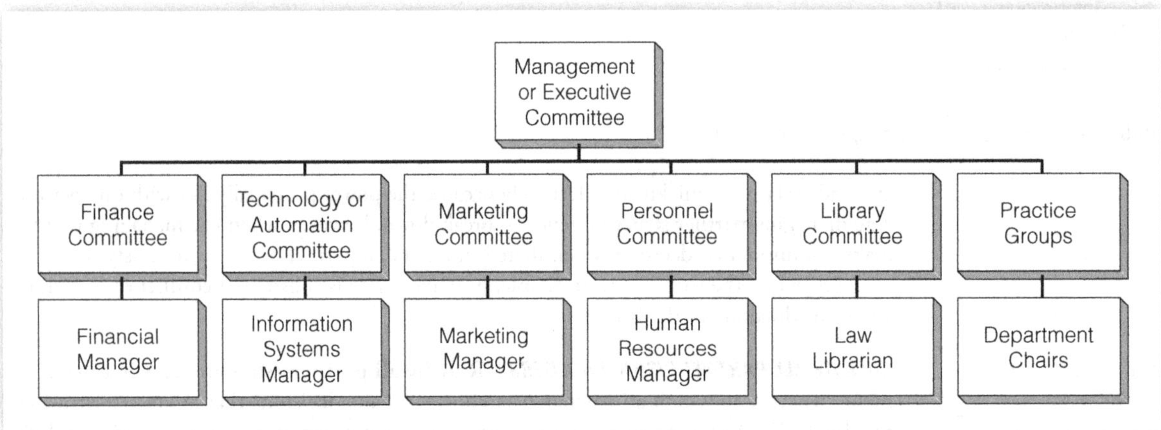

Exhibit 1-18 Rule by Management Committee Structure

If the committee gets too large, the actions of the committee slow down greatly and can hamper the effectiveness of the firm. Participation in a committee can be simply based on the interest of a partner or shareholder, a seniority system, or an election or a representation system, depending on how the firm wants to organize the committee selection process. A representation system, for example, is where a practice group (such as an employment and labor law practice group) elects or selects a chair, and that chair then represents the whole group on the executive or management committee. Committee systems are typically used in medium to large law firms.

Corporate, Government, and Legal Aid Organization Structures

Corporate and government law practices have different organizational and management structures than private law firms. Corporate law departments can be centralized or decentralized. In the past, many—but not all—were centralized, meaning they were usually located in the firm's corporate headquarters but provided legal services to the whole company. Many government practices take a decentralized approach; most state and federal agencies have their own legal departments that provide legal services only to that particular agency. Like most private law firms, corporate and government practices can have different divisions within the practice, such as litigation or labor law. Although many corporate departments are centralized and many government practices are decentralized, the choice depends on the type, size, and dynamics of the organization.

The management structure of corporate and government practices is dependent upon the corporation's or agency's own organizational structure as well. Many corporate and government departments have a general counsel responsible for the overall management of the department (see Exhibit 1-18). The power of the general counsel is similar to that of the powerful managing partner in private law firms. However, the power is diluted, since the general counsel must still act under the auspices of the overall corporate structure or of the legislative or other public body in the government practice.

Legal services practices, because they are usually nonprofit corporations, are overseen by a board of directors (see Exhibit 1-19). The board of directors might be made up of law professors, attorneys in private practice, judges, and other interested persons. The board usually hires an executive director who is responsible for the day-to-day operations of the practice. The executive director has attorneys, paralegals, clerical staff, and administrators who report to him or her.

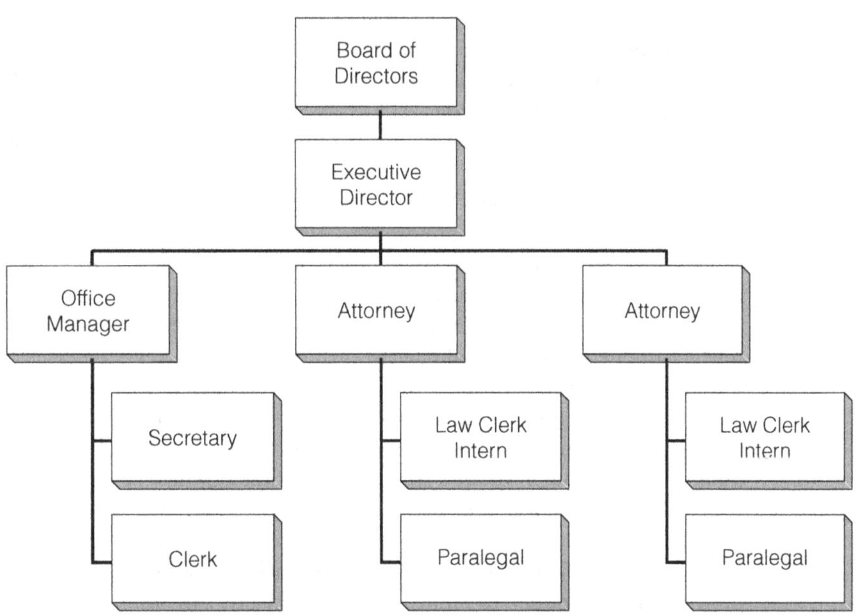

Exhibit 1-19 Legal Services/Aid Structure

Summary

Many people make up the legal team in a law office, including attorneys, administrators, paralegals/legal assistants, law librarians, legal secretaries, and clerks, among others. An attorney is a licensed professional who counsels clients regarding their legal rights. A partner or shareholder is an attorney-owner in a private law practice. A managing partner is an attorney who runs the firm in some law practices. An associate attorney is a paid employee of the law firm who does not, however, share in the profits of the business. An "of counsel" attorney is a lawyer who is affiliated with a law practice in some way, such as being semiretired, or who is paid by the firm on a per-job basis.

A legal administrator is responsible for a certain type of law office administrative system, such as general management, human resources, finance and accounting, marketing, or computer systems. Legal administrators typically have degrees in business or related fields.

Paralegals/legal assistants are a unique group of persons who assist attorneys in the delivery of legal services. They have knowledge and expertise regarding the legal system and substantive and procedural law that qualifies them to do work of a legal nature under the supervision of an attorney. The Department of Labor has consistently found that paralegals/legal assistants are nonexempt under the Fair Labor Standards Act and are thus entitled to overtime pay (one-and-one-half times their normal rate) for work in excess of 40 hours per week.

Law librarians conduct legal research, acquire and preserve library materials, advise attorneys and legal assistants on research strategies, classify and index materials, and maintain the law firm library.

Law practices include corporate law departments, government practices, legal service/aid practices, and private law firms. Corporate legal departments are found in large corporations and are usually headed up by a general counsel, the attorney responsible for the in-house legal services provided to the company.

Government law practices include attorneys who work in local, state, and federal agencies, as well as in state attorney general offices, and criminal prosecutors who work in all levels of government, among others.

Legal services/aid offices provide legal services to disadvantaged persons who otherwise could not afford it. Legal services/aid offices are nonprofit organizations and are funded by government and private donations.

Most attorneys practice in private law offices; approximately 48% of all attorneys are sole practitioners who own and manage their own law practices. Law firms come in all sizes, including small firms with fewer than 20 attorneys, medium-sized firms with 20–75 attorneys, and large firms with 75 to as many as 1000 attorneys. Many practices distinguish themselves either as plaintiff or defense firms, and law firm mergers are commonplace in the U.S. legal market. Through business strategy and technology, law firms can have different geographic service areas, including clients who are local, statewide, regional/multistate, national, international, or industry specific.

Law firms can take different legal forms, including a sole proprietorship, partnership, professional corporation, or limited liability company. Law firms can also use different governance structures, including a powerful managing partner structure, ruled by all partners/shareholders, or ruled by management committee.

Key Terms

associate attorney
attorneys
boutique firm
clerks
contract attorney
expert witness
Fair Labor Standards Act (FLSA)
exempt
nonexempt
freelance/contract paralegals
general counsel
independent paralegal
law clerk
law librarian
legal administrators
legal assistants
legal secretaries
legal services office
legal team
managing partner
non-equity partner
"of counsel"
office manager
paralegal manager
partner or shareholder
powerful managing partner
rule by all partners/shareholders
rule by management committee/board
staff attorney

Test Your Knowledge

Test your knowledge of the chapter by answering these questions.

1. What is the difference between a partner or shareholder and an associate attorney?
2. Partners are sometimes called __________________ partners because they share in the profits and losses of the firm.
3. What are the duties of a managing partner?
4. What is a lawyer called who is a salaried employee and does not have an ownership interest or share profits in the law firm?
5. An associate is usually with a firm between 5 and __________________ years before being a candidate for a partnership position.
6. A __________________ partner does not share in the profits or losses of the firm but may be included in some aspects of management of the firm and be entitled to certain benefits.
7. What is a temporary associate attorney who is hired for a specific job or period called?
8. An attorney affiliated with a firm in some way, such as being retired or semiretired from the firm, may have the designation "of __________________."
9. Legal administrators are usually found in __________________ and __________________ -sized law firms.
10. Name three areas of responsibility for a legal administrator.
11. True or false: a paralegal or legal assistant can become an associate member of the American Bar Association.
12. A unique group of persons who assist attorneys in the delivery of legal services are called __________________.
13. Paralegals who work as independent contractors but are still supervised and report to an attorney are called __________________.
14. True or false: drafting correspondence is the number one duty of most legal paralegals.
15. True or false: most paralegals attend depositions and trials.

16. True or false: the number one specialty area for paralegals is civil litigation.
17. According to the United States Department of Labor, are paralegals and legal assistants exempt or nonexempt under the Fair Labor Standards Act?
18. Why is the U.S. Supreme Court case of *Missouri v. Jenkins* important to the paralegal profession?
19. Office managers are usually found in __________ -sized law firms.
20. The four types of law practices are __________, __________, __________, and __________.
21. The head lawyer of a corporate law department is called a __________.
22. A not-for-profit law office that receives grants from the government and private donations to represent disadvantaged persons or people who cannot afford legal services is called a __________.
23. The majority of attorneys in the United States work in __________ practice.
24. A small law office that specializes in only one or two areas is sometimes called a __________ firm.
25. Private law practices have four options from which to choose their legal status. A sole proprietorship is one; what are the other three?
26. A management structure in a private law firm where one partner is responsible for managing the firm is called a __________.
27. The three types of management structures for private law firms are __________, __________, and __________.

Practical Applications

1. Compare and contrast *Missouri v. Jenkins,* 491 U.S. 274, 109 S.Ct. 2463, 105 L.Ed. 2d 229 (1989) and *Role Models American, Inc. v. Brownlee,* 353 F.3d 962 (C.A.D.C., 2004), which allowed recovery of paralegal fees, with *Joerger v. Gordon Food Service, Inc.*, 224 Mich. App. 167, 568 N.W.2d 365 (Mich.App., June 13, 1997), which did not allow recovery.

2. You are a new paralegal in an eight-attorney law firm. Your supervising attorney has instructed you to give clerical work to a legal secretary named Pat. Pat has been with the firm for many years and considers herself to have as much legal experience as any paralegal. She has made it perfectly clear that she will not peaceably make copies for you or help you in any way with any clerical work. Pat does not bill clients for her time, but you must. You are required to bill 1750 hours annually. You know that you are not allowed to record billable hours for time you spend doing clerical work. You are responding to a Request for Production of Documents in a case in litigation, and you estimate that it will take five hours to copy the documents. How would you handle the matter?

3. You are in your last semester of school, about to graduate with a paralegal degree, and you plan to begin looking for a job. Government practice would give you job security; a corporate law department would be interesting and provide opportunities for advancement; a legal aid office would give you the feeling that you were helping others; a private law office would be exciting and fast-paced; and being a freelance paralegal would let you be your own boss. What type of job would you select, and why?

4. Interview two legal professionals in your area. Find out about their jobs and the firms that they practice in, such as how many attorneys each firm has, what practice areas they specialize in, what types of jobs/positions are included in their "legal team," whether or not they use paralegal in their practice (and if so, what tasks the paralegal perform), what is the legal structure of the firm (e.g., partnership, professional corporation, etc.), how the firm is managed, and what type of clients the firms serve or target. Prepare a report regarding your findings.

On the Web Exercises

1. Paralegal Compensation In this exercise, you will research average or median compensation for paralegals or legal assistants at different experience levels. You can even see market salary for a given city and state on a few sites. Complete the table below for paralegals in your city and state (if the site will allow it) based on the different levels of experience. Collect data from three different sources (this may or may not be possible). If you cannot get data specific for your city, either use regional information, if available, or national data. Likewise, if you cannot get the exact experience levels that the table reflects, simply record what you can find. Use the "notes" section of the table to cite any irregularities or anything you need to clarify. The object of this exercise is to get rough estimates of salary levels.

Start your research at http://www.salary.com. Note: information on that site is free as long as you do not customize the data (which is not necessary for this exercise). If possible, try to get data that includes base pay and bonus pay (this is sometimes called "total compensation"). Print a copy of the results, showing the total compensation (if possible) for each search. Complete the table below or enter the table into a word processor. Include the name of the source of the data and the year the survey is dated, if a date is given. Turn in your table, your printed search results, and a short analysis of what you found. What did you find? Were you surprised by any of the results? How did the results from the different sources compare? Following are possible sources to research.

Possible Paralegal Salary Web Sites

Web Site	Description
http://www.salary.com	Contains salary data by city and state for hundreds of jobs.
http://www.nala.org/Upload/file/PDF-Files/News-Articles/15SEC4.pdf	National Association of Legal Assistants—National Utilization and Compensation Survey Report (see compensation section). If the link does not work, try going to http://www.nala.org and then to "General Information," "The Paralegal Profession," "Current Survey Info." Alternatively, at the "Search This Site" command, try typing in "National Utilization and Compensation Survey" and then click on "Survey Report."
http://www.paralegals.org	This is the site for the National Federation of Paralegal Associations. They regularly publish national compensation data for paralegals. Try going to the home page, click on "Site Search," and then type "compensation" to locate their compensation and benefits report.
http://www.google.com, http://www.yahoo.com, or other general search engines	Try searching for "paralegal compensation" or related terms. You may pull up other sites or newspaper articles with relevant data.

Paralegal or Legal Assistant Total Compensation (Average or Median Salary)

City: ______________________ State: ______________________

Years of Experience	Source 1 Name of Source:_______ Date of Data:	Source 2 Name of Source:_______ Date of Data:	Source 3 Name of Source:_______ Date of Data:
Paralegal 0–2 years	$ ____________________	$ ____________________	$ ____________________
Paralegal 2–5 years	$ ____________________	$ ____________________	$ ____________________
Paralegal 5–8 years	$ ____________________	$ ____________________	$ ____________________
Paralegal 8+ years	$ ____________________	$ ____________________	$ ____________________
Notes:			

2. Law Firm Web Sites In this exercise, you will find three law firm Web sites on the Internet, review them, and research information about the firms. Start your research by going to http://lawyers.findlaw.com or to www.findlaw.com and clicking on the "Find Lawyers" button. Click on "Law Firms" and then select any city or state you would like. You do not need to select a specialty. Then, click "Search." Alternatively, you can use any general search engine, such as http://www.google.com or http://www.yahoo.com, to search for law firms. Try to find three law firms, such as a solo practitioner, a small- to medium-size firm (2–75 lawyers), and a large law firm (75 or more attorneys). View the "Profile" on Findlaw, go to the firm's Web site, and complete the table below or enter the table into a word processor. If you have difficulty finding large law firms, try using a general search engine to search for "large law firm."

Question	Law Firm 1	Law Firm 2	Law Firm 3
Web address			
Law firm name			
What is the total approximate number of attorneys in the entire firm?			
What is the total number of offices the firm has?			
What is the geographic service area for the firm (local, state, regional, national, or international)?			
What is the number of practice areas the firm has?			
List a few of the main practice areas in which the firm specializes.			
What is the firm's legal structure (if listed) (e.g., sole proprietorship, partnership, professional corporation [PC], or limited liability company [LLC])?			
What kind of attorneys does the firm have ("of counsel," partner, associate, etc.)?			
In addition to marketing information, does the site contain resources, articles, or other information clients or members of the public might find helpful?			

3. Legal Service/Aid Offices In this exercise, you will find a legal services/aid office near you. Start by going to http://www.lsc.gov and clicking on the map of the United States. Click on your state and find the closest legal services offices. Go to the office's Web site, if there is a link to it. Alternatively, you can use a general search engine to search for "(state name) legal services aid office." Refer to the office's Web site to learn about their mission, the total number of attorneys, what kind of matters the office handles, the funding level of the office, and other general information. Type a one-page summary of what you found.

Projects

1. Compare and Contrast Paralegal Definitions Conduct an in-depth analysis and write a report on what a paralegal or legal assistant does, according to the (1) American Bar Association, (2) National Legal Assistant Association, (3) National Federation of Paralegal Associations, and (4) American Association for Paralegal Education. Compare the definitions. What are the similarities and differences? Consider the nature of the group and the interests they represent. Does this influence how they define what a paralegal does? Go behind the definitions and look at the functions and tasks that paralegals actually perform, according to each group. What kind of activities do they say that paralegals should perform? Are there any caveats or limitations on the duties? Which organization's definition do you like the best, and why?

2. Paralegal and **Legal Assistants—Exempt or Nonexempt under the Fair Labor Standards Act** Research and write an in-depth report regarding the question of whether paralegals/legal assistants are exempt or nonexempt under the Fair Labor Standards Act (FLSA). Your report should, at a minimum, include answers to the following questions.

- What is the FLSA?
- What is the difference between an exempt and a nonexempt employee?
- What are the so-called white collar exemptions to the FLSA?
- What is the position of the United States Department of Labor regarding the exemption status of legal assistants under the law, and why?
- What positions do the national paralegal/legal assistant associations take on the matter?
- What is your opinion regarding this matter?

There is a tremendous amount of information on the Fair Labor Standards Act. Starting points for research on this subject include: the National Association of Legal Assistants [http://www.nala.org], the National Federal of Paralegal Associations [http://www.paralegals.org], the United States Department of Labor FLSA compliance page [http://www.dol.gov/dol/compliance/comp-flsa.htm], and the United States Department of Labor FLSA Opinion Letters [http://www.dol.gov/whd/opinion/opinion.htm] (see January 7, 2005, FLSA2005-9). If you have access to Westlaw, LexisNexis, or case law, you may also find these resources helpful in researching this issue.

Case Review

In the Matter of a Member of the State Bar of Arizona, JEFFREY PHILLIPS, Attorney No. 13362, 244 P.3d 549 (2010)

244 P.3d 549 (2010)
(Cite as: 244 P.3d 549)

Supreme Court of Arizona

In the Matter of a Member of the State Bar of Arizona,
JEFFREY PHILLIPS, Attorney No. 13362
No. SB-10-0036-D

December 16, 2010, Decided

PELANDER, Justice

P1 We granted review in this attorney disciplinary case to determine whether the Hearing Officer erroneously used a vicarious liability standard in finding that Petitioner Jeffrey Phillips violated Arizona Rules of Professional Conduct ("ERs") 5.1(a) and 5.3(a), and whether the recommended suspension of six months and one day was appropriate. Although we accept the Hearing Officer's determination that Phillips violated ERs 5.1(a) and 5.3(a), we reduce the suspension to six months.

I. Facts and Procedural Background

P2 Phillips is the founder and managing attorney of Phillips & Associates ("P&A"), a large law firm based in Phoenix. A self-styled "consumer law firm," P&A handles a high volume of cases, having represented approximately 33,000 clients between 2004 and 2006. At the time of the disciplinary proceedings, P&A employed 250 people, including thirty-eight lawyers. The firm's practice was limited to criminal defense, bankruptcy, and personal injury.

P3 Phillips no longer represents clients, but instead supervises and manages the firm. His duties include setting firm policy on billing, accounting, and intake procedures. Although Phillips has general control over the firm, during the relevant period he had delegated primary responsibility for the criminal division to Robert Arentz, and for the bankruptcy division to Robert Teague.

P4 In 2002, Phillips was the subject of disciplinary proceedings resulting in his conditionally admitting to violations of ERs 5.1, 5.3, and 7.1, and agreeing to a censure and two-years' probation. The judgment and order entered in 2002 included detailed probationary terms relating to the management of P&A. Those terms required specific changes to P&A's intake procedures, accounting procedures, and ethics training. Among other things, the 2002 order required the following:

> Prior to entering into a written attorney/client agreement for the firm, an Arizona licensed attorney must speak with the client and approve the legal fees to be charged and retention of the Firm [sic] by the client.
>
> ...
>
> Bonuses paid to intake personnel cannot be based exclusively on either the number of clients who retain the firm or on the amount of fees received from those clients. The criteria for determining bonuses must be provided to the intake personnel in writing.
>
> ...
>
> All attorneys and other billable staff members who work on criminal cases shall keep contemporaneous time records to enable the firm to conduct a "backward glance" at the conclusion of a case in order to determine whether a refund is due.
>
> ...
>
> The firm shall provide a written accounting of time spent and fees incurred within 15 days of a request by a client. When a client terminates the firm's representation in a criminal case and the firm has been permitted to withdraw by the court, the firm shall, within fifteen (15) days following receipt of the Order permitting withdrawal, provide to the client a written accounting of the time spent, fees incurred, and when appropriate, a refund of unearned fees.

Phillips successfully completed his probation in 2004.

P5 Between August 2006 and May 2008, the Bar issued a series of probable cause orders against Phillips and Arentz. The Bar filed a formal complaint against them in October 2007 and, after several amendments, ultimately charged twenty-two counts, alleging violations of ERs 1.1, 1.2, 1.3, 1.4, 5.1, 5.3, 7.1, and 8.4.

P6 A hearing was held over eleven days in 2008. The Hearing Officer heard testimony from many witnesses, including former P&A clients, current and former P&A attorneys, and experts for both Phillips and the Bar.

P7 In detailed findings of fact, conclusions of law, and recommendations, the Hearing Officer found that Phillips had violated ERs 5.1(a), 5.3(a) and 7.1, and Arentz had violated ERs 5.1(a) and (b), 5.3(a) and (b), and 1.5(a). Phillips had a total of twelve. The Hearing Officer found that all the clients involved in the matters giving rise to the allegations were unsophisticated. He recommended that Arentz be suspended for sixty days, and that Phillips be suspended for six months and one day. The Hearing Officer also recommended that Phillips and Arentz be placed on two years' probation upon reinstatement.

P8 The Hearing Officer's findings regarding Phillips's ethical violations can be generally categorized as follows:

A. Caseloads of Bankruptcy Attorneys

P9 The Hearing Officer found that Phillips violated ER 5.1(a) as alleged in Counts 3 and 4, which related to the caseloads of P&A's bankruptcy attorneys, each of whom carried as many as 500 cases at a time. A former P&A attorney testified that, upon joining the firm, she was immediately responsible for 540 cases. Counts 3 and 4 involved circumstances in which clients' needs were not met because of the high volume of cases assigned to bankruptcy attorneys. In both counts, the Hearing Officer also found that, because of the number of attorneys handling a given case, inadequate attention was paid to the problems presented in the case and the client was confused and not adequately informed.

P10 Count 3 specifically involved a breakdown in communication between the attorney and the client, missed hearings by the attorney, and a failure to keep the client reasonably informed. Count 4 involved P&A's practice of having one attorney handle all of the firm's "341 meetings," which are short, informal meetings that debtors are required to attend after filing a bankruptcy petition under Chapter 7 or Chapter 13 of the federal Bankruptcy Code. The P&A attorney handled forty files per day and at times would have six to seven 341 meeting within thirty minutes. Count 4 included a client's complaint that a P&A attorney had missed a 341 meeting and failed to act with reasonable diligence. The Hearing Officer concluded that Phillips violated ER 5.1(a) in both counts for establishing and maintaining a business model in which such ethical violations were likely to occur.

B. Intake and Retention Procedures

P11 Another category of violations related to P&A's intake and retention procedures. Prospective clients who visit the firm's offices do not immediately meet with an attorney. Instead, they are provided a blank fee agreement and a general questionnaire. After completing the questionnaire, the prospective client meets with a P&A legal administrator, a nonlawyer tasked with retaining clients. Legal administrators are paid a base salary and monthly bonuses, based, in part, on the number of cases that the legal administrator retains. After obtaining general information from the client, the legal administrator meets with a lawyer who sets the fee. After the fee agreement is prepared, the client speaks with a lawyer to make sure the client understands the fee agreement, who the lawyer will be, and the scope of P&A's representation. The Hearing Officer found that this process, known as "closing," was often not completed by an attorney knowledgeable in the relevant practice area.

P12 On Counts 9, 12, and 17, the Hearing Officer found P&A's retention policies, as implemented, impeded potential clients from obtaining the information needed to make informed decisions about retention. With respect to Counts 9 and 12, the Hearing Officer found that a P&A legal administrator gave a client's family member unreasonable expectations about the representation, suggesting that the firm would be able to reduce the client's sentence in criminal proceedings.

P13 In Count 9, the client's father was told that the firm should be able to reduce his son's sentence. An attorney signed a fee agreement describing the scope of the services as "mitigation of sentencing." The client, however, had already entered into a plea agreement with a stipulated sentence, and no one at P&A advised the client or his father of the unlikelihood of mitigating the sentence. Despite the client's expectations, the client's sentence was not reduced.

P14 In Count 12, a client's mother signed a fee agreement after being told by a legal representative that the firm should be able to help reduce her son's sentence. As the firm was aware, however, the client had already stipulated to a particular sentence. The client's mother met with a bankruptcy attorney, who did not know what a stipulated plea agreement was. A criminal attorney did not meet with her until the day of sentencing, when she was informed that her son would receive the sentence stipulated in the plea agreement.

P15 The Hearing Officer found that Phillips and Arentz violated ERs 5.1(a) and 5.3(a) in both counts because the firm's retention practices did not require a knowledgeable attorney to speak with the potential client before entering into a fee agreement, and the firm used nonlawyers in its retention process. Similarly, in Count 17, a client with a suspended driver's license met only with a bankruptcy attorney and a legal administrator before hiring P&A to represent him. The client wanted to have his license reinstated but also had an unadjudicated DUI charge. The scope of services set forth in the fee agreement did not match the client's expectations. The firm did not follow the client's decisions regarding the scope of the representation, and the firm waited weeks before telling the client his driver's license could not be reinstated until the DUI charge was resolved. The firm also failed to inform the client prior to retention that the firm could not accomplish his goals. The Hearing Officer found that both Phillips and Arentz violated ER 5.1(a).

C. Conduct by Legal Administrators

P16 The Hearing Officer also found violations of ER 5.3 arising from P&A's providing legal administrators with bonuses based, in part, on the number of clients retained. Count 8 involved a legal administrator who used "high pressure tactics" to attempt to dissuade a client from terminating P&A's representation. Count 19 involved a client who retained the firm for defense of a DUI charge and, as the firm was aware, was also in the process of becoming a United States citizen. When the client asked to terminate P&A's representation after meeting with a legal administrator and a bankruptcy attorney, the client was subjected to intimidation and false statements from a P&A employee. At one point, the employee warned the client that he was "looking to lose his citizenship," and the employee insinuated that if the client stopped payment on the retainer check, the firm could have the police investigate his immigration status. After making several unsuccessful attempts to obtain documents he had furnished to P&A, the client was only able to recover the papers after hiring new counsel.

P17 Although the P&A employees' tactics violated P&A's policies, the Hearing Officer concluded that Phillips and Arentz violated ER 5.3(a) in both counts because legal administrators' bonuses were tied, in part, to client retention. These incentives provided "the motive for the misconduct." The words in the firm's policy manual prohibiting such conduct were insufficient to insulate managers and supervisors from ethical responsibility when the actual ongoing practices were to the contrary.

D. Refund Policy

P18 In Count 11, the Hearing Officer found that P&A employees failed to act promptly on a client's termination request. The firm took more than five months to refund money to the client despite repeated requests for a refund. The Hearing Officer found that both Arentz and Phillips violated ERs 5.1(a) and 5.3(a) for failing to have practices in place to prevent difficulty in obtaining a refund. [1]

FN1. The Hearing Officer also found (in Count 20) that Phillips negligently violated ER 7.1 by writing and using a materially misleading television advertisement in 2007 regarding P&A's DUI defense services and a new DUI law. But the Hearing Officer found that violation did not "warrant significant discipline" because it was neither knowing nor actually injurious; rather, his recommended sanction was based solely on Phillips's knowing violations of ERs 5.1(a) and 5.3(a).

E. Disciplinary Commission Decision

P19 On review, pursuant to Rule 58, Arizona Rules of the Supreme Court, the Disciplinary Commission considered the parties' objections to the Hearing Officer's decision and held oral argument. In December 2009, by a vote of 6-2, the Commission adopted the Hearing Officer's findings of fact, conclusions of law, and recommendations. The two dissenting Commission members found no basis for disturbing the Hearing Officer's factual findings but concluded that "the recommended discipline is too severe" and that lesser sanctions were appropriate - suspensions of thirty days for Arentz and ninety days for Phillips.

P20 Phillips and Arentz jointly petitioned for review. This Court granted review on only two discrete issues Phillips raised: whether the Hearing Officer erroneously applied a vicarious liability standard in finding ethical violations by Phillips, and whether the recommended sanction for him is appropriate. We denied review of any issues raised by Arentz, thereby leaving undisturbed his sixty-day suspension. The Bar did not file a cross-petition for review to challenge the recommended sanction for Arentz. We therefore limit our discussion to the two issues regarding Phillips on which review was granted.

II. Managerial and Supervisory Liability

P21 Phillips first argues that the Hearing Officer used an improper standard of vicarious liability in finding violations of ERs 5.1(a) and 5.3(a) because his analysis was based solely on the ethical breaches of other firm employees. We disagree.

P22 HN1Go to this Headnote in the case. Ethical Rule 5.1(a) provides that a partner or an attorney with comparable managerial authority "shall make reasonable efforts to ensure that the firm has in effect measures giving reasonable assurance that all lawyers in the firm conform to the Rules of Professional Conduct." Similarly, ER 5.3(a) provides that a partner or a lawyer with comparable managerial authority must make "reasonable efforts to ensure that the firm has in effect measures giving reasonable assurances that" nonlawyers employed by the firm or associated with the lawyer comply with the professional obligations of the lawyer.

P23 These duties require not only supervision, but also that the supervising attorney establish "internal policies and procedures" providing reasonable assurances that lawyers and nonlawyers in the firm conform to the Rules of Professional Conduct. ERs 5.1 cmt. 2; 5.3 cmt. 2. The size of the firm is relevant in determining what is "reasonable," and in a large firm such as P&A, "more elaborate measures may be necessary." ER 5.1 cmt. 3.

P24 HN2 Go to this Headnote in the case. The rules imposing managerial and supervisory obligations, however, do not provide for vicarious liability for a subordinate's acts; rather, they "mandate an independent duty of supervision." In re Galbasini, 163 Ariz. 120, 124, 786 P.2d 971, 975 (1990). Nor is a supervising attorney of a nonlawyer assistant "required to guarantee that that assistant will never engage in conduct that is not compatible with the professional obligations of the lawyer." In re Miller, 178 Ariz. 257, 259, 872 P.2d 661, 663 (1994).

P25 The Hearing Officer expressly recognized these legal principles in his decision and did not apply an incorrect vicarious liability standard when finding that Phillips violated ERs 5.1(a) and 5.3(a). Although he found on many of the counts that P&A attorneys' and staff members' conduct violated various ethical rules, the supervisory and managerial breaches for which Phillips was found liable under ER 5.1 or 5.3 were independent. For each violation of ER 5.1 or 5.3, the Hearing Officer found that Phillips had personally failed to engage in the required supervision of either lawyers or nonlawyer personnel. Indeed, on a number of counts (for example, Counts 5 and 6), the Hearing Officer found that someone at P&A had violated an ethical rule, but that Phillips had not personally violated the rules requiring supervision. Had the Hearing Officer or the Commission applied a vicarious liability standard, Phillips would have been held liable for those violations as well.

P26 In contesting the findings that he violated ERs 5.1(a) and 5.3(a), Phillips refers to the "mountain of undisputed evidence" adduced at the hearing of P&A's supervisory efforts and the "relatively rare" occurrence of ethical breaches by other P&A employees. But the prior modification of firm policies, made pursuant to the 2002 judgment and order, did not alleviate Phillips's ongoing duty to ensure that his subordinates complied with the revised policies and ethical rules. Because the Hearing Officer clearly understood and correctly applied the law by carefully not conflating vicarious liability with managerial and supervisory liability, we find no error in his determination, adopted by the Disciplinary Commission, that Phillips violated ERs 5.1(a) and 5.3(a).

III. Sanction

P27 We next address Phillips's argument that the recommended six-months and one-day suspension was disproportionate and excessive. HN3Go to this Headnote in the case. We review recommended sanctions de novo. In re White-Steiner, 219 Ariz. 323, 327 ¶ 25, 198 P.3d 1195, 1199 (2009). Although we independently review a recommended sanction, we give "serious consideration to the findings and recommendations" of the Commission. In re Pappas, 159 Ariz. 516, 518, 768 P.2d 1161, 1163 (1988) (citing In re Neville, 147 Ariz. 106, 108, 708 P.2d 1297, 1299 (1985)).

P28 HN4Go to this Headnote in the case. "Attorney discipline serves to protect the public, the legal profession, and the legal system, and to deter other attorneys from engaging in unprofessional conduct." In re White-Steiner, 219 Ariz. at 325 ¶ 9, 198 P.3d at 1197 (citing In re Scholl, 200 Ariz. 222, 227 ¶ 29, 25 P.3d 710, 715 (2001)). Another purpose is to instill public confidence in the Bar's integrity. In re Horwitz, 180 Ariz. 20, 29, 881 P.2d 352, 361 (1994) (citing In re Loftus, 171 Ariz. 672, 675, 832 P.2d 689, 692 (1992)).

P29 HN5Go to this Headnote in the case. In determining sanctions, we are guided by the American Bar Association's Standards for Imposing Lawyer Sanctions (2005). In re Van Dox, 214 Ariz. 300, 303 ¶ 11, 152 P.3d 1183, 1186 (2007). Several factors are relevant in determining the appropriate sanction: (1) the duty violated, (2) the lawyer's mental state, (3) the potential or actual injury caused by the lawyer's conduct, and (4) the existence of aggravating or mitigating factors. *Id.* (citing ABA Standard 3.0). We may also consider any similar cases to assess what sanctions are proportionate to the unethical conduct. *Id.* at 307 ¶ 39, 152 P.3d at 1190.

A. Duty Violated

P30 HN6Go to this Headnote in the case. ABA Standard 7.0 provides sanctions for violations of duties owed as a professional. The Hearing Officer and the Commission concluded that ABA Standard 7.0 governed this case because the violations of ERs 5.1 and 5.3 involved duties owed to the legal profession. Although these violations also implicate duties owed to the client, ABA Standard 7.0 will guide our analysis because we find no error on this point and because Phillips does not challenge the applicability of that standard. See In re Lenaburg, 177 Ariz. 20, 23, 864 P.2d 1052, 1055 (1993) (applying ABA Standard 7.0 to supervisory violations); In re Rice, 173 Ariz. 376, 377, 843 P.2d 1268, 1269 (1992) (same).

B. Mental State

P31 HN7Go to this Headnote in the case. A lawyer's mental state affects the appropriate sanction for ethical violations. Intentional or knowing conduct is sanctioned more severely than negligent conduct because it threatens more harm. In re White-Steiner, 219 Ariz. at 325 ¶ 13, 198 P.3d at 1197.

P32 HN8Go to this Headnote in the case. ABA Standard 7.0 provides the following guidelines with regard to sanctions:

7.1 Disbarment is generally appropriate when a lawyer knowingly engages in conduct that is a violation of a duty owed as a professional with the intent to obtain a benefit for the lawyer or another, and causes serious or potentially serious injury to a client, the public, or the legal system.

7.2 Suspension is generally appropriate when a lawyer knowingly engages in conduct that is a violation of a duty owed as a professional and causes injury or potential injury to a client, the public, or the legal system.

7.3 Reprimand is generally appropriate when a lawyer negligently engages in conduct that is a violation of a duty owed as a professional and causes injury or potential injury to a client, the public, or the legal system.

P33 The Hearing Officer expressly found that both Phillips's and Arentz's violations of ERs 5.1 and 5.3 were "knowing." Although Phillips challenged that finding in his petition for review, we did not grant review of that issue and, therefore, accept as established that Phillips knowingly violated ERs 5.1(a) and 5.3(a).

C. Actual or Potential Injury

P34 The Hearing Officer found actual injury in each of the client-related counts. P&A clients were misled and improperly advised by unqualified lawyers, had difficulty obtaining refunds, and were misinformed about the reasonable objectives of the representation. Clients were also financially harmed, having paid unreasonable fees or retainers without a full understanding of the likely results of the representation. The record supports these findings.

D. Aggravating and Mitigating Factors

P35 Because Phillips's knowing conduct caused actual injury to clients, we agree with the Hearing Officer that the presumptive sanction in this case is suspension. See ABA Standard 7.2. The Hearing Officer and the Commission found the following aggravating and mitigating factors apply to Phillips:

Aggravating Factors:

(1) Prior disciplinary offense
(2) Selfish motive
(3) Multiple offenses
(4) Refusal to acknowledge wrongful nature of conduct
(5) Vulnerability of victim
(6) Substantial experience in the practice of law

Mitigating Factors

(1) Full and free disclosure to the Bar
(2) Delay in disciplinary proceedings
(3) Willingness to remedy practice
(4) Character

P36 We find none of these findings clearly erroneous. And we agree with the Hearing Officer that the aggravating and mitigating factors, in conjunction with Phillips's knowing misconduct, further support suspension as an appropriate sanction. See In re Galbasini, 163 Ariz. at 121, 125-26, 786 P.2d at 972, 976-77 (adopting recommended six-month suspension of attorney for knowingly failing to supervise nonlawyer employees who engaged in debt collection and improperly solicited clients in attorney's name); Davis & Goldberg v. Ala. State Bar, 676 So. 2d 306, 307-08 (Ala. 1996) (upholding two-month suspension of two partners for implementing policies designed to minimize expenses and maximize profits, to clients' detriment, when firm's practices resulted in unmanageable caseloads and permitted non-lawyers to perform legal services); Att'y Grievance Comm'n of Md. v. Kimmel, 405 Md. 647, 955 A.2d 269, 292-94 (Md. 2008) (holding that violations of ethical rules requiring adequate supervision warranted a ninety-day suspension when attorneys had no prior disciplinary record).

E. Proportionality Review

P37 HN9Go to this Headnote in the case. We may consider the sanctions imposed in similar cases "to preserve some degree of proportionality, ensure that the sanction fits the offense, and avoid discipline by whim or caprice." In re Dean, 212 Ariz. 221, 225 ¶ 24, 129 P.3d 943, 947 (2006) (quoting In re Struthers, 179 Ariz. 216, 226, 877 P.2d 789, 799 (1994)). The Hearing Officer cited two cases for comparison purposes, but they are distinguishable and not very helpful. [2] Nor have the parties cited any authorities that bear on whether the recommended length of suspension is appropriate here. Although we have sometimes engaged in comparative analysis, see In re Van Dox, 214 Ariz. at 307-08 ¶¶ 39-42, 152 P.3d at 1190-91, we agree with the Hearing Officer that this case, involving a "consumer law firm" and a high volume practice, is difficult to compare with others. In any event, "[proportionality review ... is 'an imperfect process' that, as here, often provides little guidance. In re Dean, 212 Ariz. at 225 ¶ 24, 129 P.3d at 947 (quoting In re Owens, 182 Ariz. 121, 127, 893 P.2d 1284, 1290 (1995)).

FN2 See In re Lenaburg, 177 Ariz. at 24, 864 P.2d at 1056 (imposing public censure with probation on attorney who negligently violated ER 5.1, causing lack of communication with clients and failure to refund fees in four separate cases); In re Rice, 173 Ariz. at 377, 843 P.2d at 1269 (imposing censure and probation on attorney with no prior disciplinary record who negligently failed to adequately supervise staff during firm's rapid expansion, resulting in sloppy office procedures and mismanagement).

P38 In assessing the duration of Phillips's suspension, however, we must also consider internal proportionality, in particular the length of his suspension in relation to Arentz's. We considered internal proportionality in In re Dean, 212 Ariz. at 225 ¶ 25, 129 P.3d at 947. That case involved a romantic relationship between a prosecutor and a superior court judge. *Id.* at 221 ¶ 2, 129 P.3d at 943. We reduced from one year to six months the Commission's recommended suspension for the prosecutor in part because the judge had not been disciplined. *Id.* at 225 ¶ 25, 129 P.3d at 947. The prosecutor's ethical violations involved the same conduct as the judge's, and we concluded that a reduced sanction for the prosecutor was warranted to avoid a disparity in treatment. *Id.* Without minimizing the seriousness of the attorney's misconduct, we determined that "the interests of justice" required reconsideration of an otherwise suitable sanction. *Id.* Although the judge's immunity from lawyer discipline in that case had resulted inadvertently from this Court's prior action, see *Id.*, the rationale employed there also applies here.

P39 In this case, the Hearing Officer found, and the Commission affirmed, that Arentz had a total of nineteen ethical violations (eighteen of which were found to be knowing), compared to Phillips's twelve violations (eleven of which were found to be knowing). The Hearing Officer consistently found that Arentz, but not Phillips, violated subsection (b) of ERs 5.1 and 5.3 based on Arentz's having had direct supervisory authority of P&A's criminal department. [3] Arentz was also directly involved in approving excessive fees, as alleged in Counts 8, 9, and 12, in violation of ER 1.5. In contrast, as the dissenting Commission members noted, the Hearing Officer did not find that Phillips had direct personal knowledge of any of the specific conduct giving rise to the allegations of ER 5.1 or 5.3 violations until after the conduct occurred. Yet Arentz received a suspension of only sixty days compared to Phillips's six-month and one-day suspension. Neither the Hearing Officer nor the Commission addressed or explained this disparity.

FN3. Ethical Rule 5.1(b) requires that a lawyer having direct supervisory authority over another lawyer make "reasonable efforts to ensure that the other lawyer conforms to the Rules of Professional Conduct." Similarly, ER 5.3(b) requires that a lawyer having direct supervisory authority over a nonlawyer make "reasonable efforts to ensure that the person's conduct is compatible with the professional obligations of the lawyer."

P40 Moreover, a six-month and one-day suspension is not actually completed in that time period.HN10Go to this Headnote in the case. Under Rule 65(a), Arizona Rules of the Supreme Court, any suspension exceeding six months requires the lawyer to go through formal reinstatement proceedings. That process extends the effective length of a suspension considerably. An applicant for formal reinstatement must provide an array of personal and financial information and prove by clear and convincing evidence his or her rehabilitation, compliance with all disciplinary orders and rules, fitness to practice, and competence. See Ariz. R. Sup. Ct. 65(a)-(b).

F. Appropriate Sanction

P41 Although Arentz had more violations than Phillips and was more directly involved in the underlying ethical violations of P&A employees in his department, we conclude Phillips's conduct and disciplinary history warrant a more severe sanction for him than Arentz received. Unlike Phillips, Arentz has no prior disciplinary record. We take Phillips's prior disciplinary record seriously, considering it involved the same type of supervisory shortcomings at issue here. HN11Go to this Headnote in the case.The goal of attorney discipline is to protect the public. In re Rivkind, 164 Ariz. 154, 157, 791 P.2d 1037, 1040 (1990). Neither the Hearing Officer nor the Commission erred in determining that the 2002 discipline did not adequately rehabilitate Phillips and was insufficient to protect P&A clients.

P42 We also recognize that Phillips, as managing partner of a law firm representing more than 10,000 clients per year, was in a position of greater supervisory authority than Arentz. Phillips, not Arentz, had full power and control over P&A's policies and practices. As such, he was better able to effect positive change and insist on full compliance with ethics standards. Conversely, Phillips's lapses in these areas might potentially cause greater harm. Phillips's apparent delegation of responsibility and hands-off approach does not make his policies any less of a danger. Indeed, the decisions he makes directly affect the public, the profession, and the integrity of the legal system.

P43 Although attorney partners and supervisors are not guarantors of their employees' conduct, they must take reasonable steps to ensure that firm practices, not merely policies, actually comply with ethical rules binding all lawyers practicing law in this state. Phillips's failure to do so, particularly in view of his disciplinary history, warrants a significant period of suspension followed by a lengthy probation term with strict conditions.

P44 A longer suspension for Phillips is therefore justified. But we do not believe that a sanction at least six times harsher than Arentz's is proportional in this case. [4] Rather, as the two dissenting Commission members observed when recommending a ninety-day suspension for Phillips, a lesser sanction against him would appropriately address the violations found here while deterring future misconduct and thereby protecting the public. We therefore reduce Phillips's suspension to six months. In doing so, we do not minimize the seriousness of Phillips's misconduct. But we believe a six-month suspension avoids an unjust disparity in treatment between him and Arentz.

FN4. Rule 64(e)(1), Arizona Rules of the Supreme Court, permits a lawyer who has been suspended for more than six months to apply for reinstatement no sooner than ninety days prior to the expiration of the suspension. Rule 65(b)(1), as amended this year and effective to reinstatement proceedings commencing after January 1, 2011, provides that a Bar hearing panel will hold a hearing within 150 days of the filing of the application. Within thirty days after completing the hearing, the hearing panel must file a report with this Court containing findings of facts and recommendations concerning the reinstatement. Ariz. R. Sup. Ct. 65(b)(3). The Court must "promptly" review the report and decide whether the applicant is qualified for reinstatement, a process that typically takes about two months. *Id.* at 65(b)(4). Thus, the reinstatement process for Phillips would, at the very least, last five to six months after his suspension is complete, effectively extending his suspension to a total of twelve months, six times longer than Arentz's suspension.

P45 The Hearing Officer and the Commission recommended that Phillips's two-year probation term and conditions of probation begin and take effect after Phillips's suspension is fully served. We accept that recommendation. Although Phillips is prohibited from practicing law or holding himself out as an active attorney during his suspension, he is permitted and strongly encouraged during that time to work with the Bar to immediately address the issues and rectify the problems that led to the violations of ERs 5.1 and 5.3 in this case. Otherwise, P&A would be left with many of its current problems and no immediate solution during Phillips's period of suspension.

P46 During the suspension, however, Phillips's name may not be used in firm advertisements, letterhead, or other communications. [5] Nor is Phillips entitled to receive any income generated by the firm during his suspension. [6]

FN5. See ERs 5.5(b)(2); 7.1; 7.5(a) and (d); see also State Bar of Ariz. Comm. on Rules of Prof'l Conduct, Formal Op. 02-07 (2002) (concluding that a law firm should not continue to use attorney's name in the firm name, letterhead, business cards, or stationary while the attorney is on disability inactive status, and noting that "a suspended partner's name must be dropped in all communications with the public"); Wash. State Bar Ass'n, Formal Op. 196 (2000) (prohibiting use of suspended lawyer's name in firm name or business communications).

FN6. See ER 5.4(a) [***29] ("A lawyer or law firm shall not share legal fees with a nonlawyer."); Disciplinary Counsel v. McCord, 121 Ohio St. 3d 497, 2009 Ohio 1517, 905 N.E.2d 1182, 1189 (Ohio 2009) (concluding that lawyer's receipt of attorney fees while suspended from practice of law was improper and actionable as ethics violation); Office of Disciplinary Counsel v. Jackson, 536 Pa. 26, 637 A.2d 615, 620 (Pa. 1994) (noting a suspended attorney is a "'non-lawyer' within the meaning of the rules"); Comm. on Prof'l Ethics, State Bar of Tex., Op. 592 (2010) (prohibiting a lawyer from sharing legal fees with suspended attorney); cf. West v. Jayne, 484 N.W.2d 186, 190-91 (Iowa 1992) (allowing lawyer in breach of contract action against fellow associate to collect portion of fee, but suggesting that attorney would not be entitled to fees for any work done after he was suspended from practice of law).

P47 In addition to reducing Phillips's suspension to six months, we remove from the Commission's recommended terms of probation term number 13, which would have permitted the Bar to send at random times unidentified "testers" to P&A to check the firm's compliance with required intake procedures. The Bar did not request that particular term and, at oral argument in this Court, acknowledged that it was not warranted. We adopt the Commission's probation terms in all other respects, as set forth in the appendix, as well as the restitution amounts it ordered.

IV. Conclusion

P48 For the foregoing reasons, we modify the recommended length of Phillips's suspension, but otherwise accept the Commission's recommendations. The probation terms and conditions prescribed by the Commission as set forth in the appendix to this opinion shall apply.

A. John Pelander, Justice

CONCURRING: Rebecca White Berch, Chief Justice

Andrew D. Hurwitz, Vice Chief Justice,

Jon W. Thompson, Judge*

*Pursuant to Article 6, Section 3 of the Arizona Constitution, the Honorable Jon W. Thompson, Judge of the Arizona Court of Appeals, Division One, was designated to sit on this matter.

Appendix

1. Phillips shall refrain from engaging in any conduct that would violate the Rules of Professional Conduct or other rules of the Supreme Court of Arizona.
2. Phillips shall contact the director of LOMAP within from the filing date of this opinion and shall schedule and submit to a LOMAP audit within forty-five (45) days thereafter. Following the audit, the director of LOMAP shall formulate and include recommendations based on the audit in a Probation Contract to be executed and implemented by Phillips. The director of LOMAP shall also monitor the terms of probation.
3. Before entering into any written attorney/client fee agreement for the firm, an Arizona licensed attorney must speak with the client and approve the legal fees to be charged and retention of the firm by the client. The attorney meeting with the potential client must be knowledgeable in the practice area, and issues that relate to the retention and retention decision must be discussed before a decision is made on the retention. Retention attorneys shall review all paperwork and ensure that appropriate information is given to the client even if the client lacks the sophistication or knowledge to ask the right questions.
4. Any nonlawyer personnel conducting initial consultations with clients must clearly and affirmatively identify themselves as nonlawyers to prospective clients.
5. Respondent shall ensure that nonlawyer staff shall not give legal advice to clients and shall not make predictions or guarantees as to the outcome of a case.
6. Standard intake forms including a standard fee agreement shall be utilized. The firm shall participate in fee arbitration whenever it is requested by the client and the firm has been unable to resolve the dispute directly with the client.
7. A standardized training manual for intake procedures shall be provided to each intake employee.
8. Pursuant to ER 5.3, Phillips or other attorneys with supervisory authority in the firm (over whom Phillips has direct control) will be responsible for compliance by all intake personnel and nonlawyer staff with applicable ethical rules.
9. When accepting payment of a client's fees in a form other than cash, the firm shall not accept payment without signed, written consent (which may be evidenced by a check, electronic signature, credit card authorization, or other writing) from the party making the payment.
10. A one-time ethics training program, not to exceed three (3) hours, shall be given to all administrative staff including intake and collection personnel. The program shall be provided by the director of LOMAP

or designee, and shall be given at a time within the first six (6) months of the probationary terms and in a manner that does not disrupt the firm's practice. The program may be repeated or additional programs may be given during the probationary period if needed as determined by the director of LOMAP. The initial program shall be taped and shown to any new personnel hired during the probationary period.

11. A one-time Continuing Legal Education ethics program, not to exceed three (3) hours, shall be given to all attorneys employed by Phillips's firm. The program shall be provided by the director of LOMAP or designee, and shall be given at a time within the first six (6) months of the probationary period and in a manner that does not disrupt the firm's practice. The program may be repeated or additional programs may be given during the probationary period. The initial program shall be taped and shown to any new lawyers hired during the probationary period.

12. The firm shall utilize a fee review process, consistent with In re Swartz, 141 Ariz. 266, 686 P.2d 1236 (1984), and ER 1.5, at the conclusion of all cases in order to determine whether a refund is due. All attorneys and other billable staff members who work on criminal cases [8] shall keep contemporaneous time records to enable the firm to conduct a "backward glance" at the conclusion of a case in order to determine whether a refund is due.

FN8. The record indicates that P&A has sold its criminal department. Assuming that P&A no longer offers services in criminal law, this term and others relating to P&A's criminal department no longer apply.

13. The firm shall provide a written accounting of time spent and fees incurred within fifteen (15) days of request by a client. When a client terminates the firm's representation in a criminal case and the firm has been permitted to withdraw by the court, the firm shall, within fifteen (15) days following receipt of the Order permitting withdrawal, provide to the client a written accounting of time spent, fees incurred, and when appropriate, a refund of any unearned fees.

14. If Phillips's firm uses client testimonials in advertisements, the client must acknowledge in writing that he or she is not receiving any money benefit (or the equivalent) for the appearance.

15. Phillips shall develop a system in which he is promptly advised of all client complaint(s) against the firm or lawyers employed by the firm, which implicate the provisions of ERs 5.1 and 5.3. Phillips shall document, in writing, his or the firm's response to each such complaint, and shall maintain a file of such complaints and responses.

16. Phillips shall make reasonable and good faith efforts to ensure compliance with these probation terms and shall respond directly or through his counsel to inquiries concerning the implementation and compliance with these probationary terms.

17. Before conducting a screening investigation into any new complaint(s) relating to practices covered by these terms and conditions of probation, the State Bar, when appropriate and consistent with its normal practice, will first attempt to resolve the complaint(s) through A/CAP and Central Intake, or will, when appropriate, consistent with its normal practice and pursuant to Rule 54(b)(1), Arizona Rules of the Supreme Court, refer the matter for mediation. Nothing in this paragraph is intended to limit the jurisdiction or power of the State Bar disciplinary agency.

18. Bonuses to legal administrators shall not be based, in whole or in part, on the number of clients retained, the amount of fees generated, the number of clients who cancel, or the amount of fees refunded.

19. The firm shall keep accurate records for all work done on a case.

20. Phillips shall pay all costs incurred as a result of these probationary terms.

21. In the event that Phillips fails to comply with any of the foregoing conditions and the State Bar receives information thereof, bar counsel shall file with the imposing entity a Notice of Non-Compliance, pursuant to Rule 60(a)(5), Arizona Rules of the Supreme Court. The Hearing Officer shall conduct a hearing within thirty (30) days after receipt of said notice, to determine whether the terms of probation have been violated and whether an additional sanction should be imposed. In the event there is an allegation that any of these terms have been violated, the burden of proof shall be on the State Bar of Arizona to prove noncompliance by a preponderance of the evidence.

CONCUR BY: SHELDON H. WEISBERG (In Part)

DISSENT BY: SHELDON H. WEISBERG (In Part)

WEISBERG, Judge, concurring in part and dissenting in part

P49 As the majority explains, the impact of a suspension of six months and one day is a great deal more than the impact of a suspension of only six months. Here, however, even allowing for the subjectivity that creeps into the "imperfect process" when considering proportionality, I must respectfully dissent from the majority's decision to reduce Phillips's suspension from the six months and one day recommended by the Hearing Officer. I do so because, unlike the majority, I conclude that a six-month and one day suspension is internally proportionate to the two-months suspension meted out to Arentz.

P50 The majority's conclusion is understandably not based on a general proportionality review. Not only is that approach no longer favored, but it is of little benefit here because Phillips's firm is a fairly unique "consumer" law firm with accordingly tailored practices. The disciplinary cases referenced by the parties are just not comparable enough to be helpful.

P51 In this case, it is enough that Phillips's violations are the sort for which the relevant ABA Standard mandates a suspension. Specifically, ABA Standard 7.2 provides that "[suspension is generally appropriate when a lawyer knowingly engages in conduct that is a violation of a duty owed as a professional, and causes injury or potential injury to a client, the public, or the legal system." Phillips's conduct clearly falls within that described by the ABA Standard. I therefore consider next whether Phillips's recommended suspension of six months and one day would be proportionate to Arentz's two months. I conclude it would.

P52 To begin, Phillips is not being sanctioned for his second ethics violation. He is being sanctioned for his ethics violations eighteen through twenty-nine. I am not aware of any other attorney in Arizona who has committed twenty-nine violations and received only a six-month suspension for his twenty-ninth. While Arentz was arguably punished too lightly for having committed nineteen violations, and Phillips's latest violations number twelve, Phillips had committed seventeen earlier violations. This comparison alone supports the recommended six months and one day suspension. [7]

FN7. I also note that these most recent twelve violations of Phillips involved separate complaints by nine of P&A's clients, while Arentz's complaints involved only six clients.

P53 Second, Arentz's sanction consisting of a two-month suspension and two years of probation represents his first such sanction. It is to be hoped and presumed that this sanction will be sufficient to prevent further violations by him. Phillips, on the other hand, was punished for his earlier violations and completed that probationary period. Unfortunately, he has reoffended multiple times. Thus, a greater penalty that includes a six-month and one day suspension is both warranted and proportionate.

P54 Finally, Arentz committed his ethical violations while working in a system that was developed, implemented, and supervised by Phillips. It was Phillips's decision as to what P&A resources would be devoted to meet its attorneys' ethical responsibilities to their clients. He clearly did not attach sufficient importance to those ethical responsibilities. As the attorney in sole charge of P&A, his fault was therefore far greater than that of Arentz.

P55 For the foregoing reasons, and although I concur with all else in the majority's opinion, I must respectfully disagree with its decision to reduce the period of Phillips's suspension.

SHELDON H. WEISBERG, Judge*

*Pursuant to Article 6, Section 3 of the Arizona Constitution, the Honorable Sheldon H. Weisberg, Judge of the Arizona Court of Appeals, Division One, was designated to sit on this matter.

Case Review Exercises

1. Discuss the court's reasoning for handling each attorney's suspension differently.
2. Referring to Exhibit 1-13, analyze what the attorneys did correctly and incorrectly in terms of the responsibilities of law firm management.
3. How could the attorneys have corrected their management strategy?
4. What issues did the court address concerning legal administrators?

Helpful Web Sites

Organization	Description	Internet Address
American Association for Paralegal Education	Association for paralegal educators. Contains position papers on the paralegal profession and information on how to find quality paralegal programs to attend.	http://www.aafpe.org
American Bar Association (ABA)	Association for attorneys. The site contains a large amount of information and publications relevant to individuals working in the legal profession.	http://www.americanbar.org/
ABA Law Practice Division	ABA site devoted to law practice management issues and concerns, including management publications, articles, and resources.	http://www.americanbar.org/groups/law_practice
ABA Standing Committee on Paralegals	ABA site devoted to the use of paralegals/legal assistants in legal organizations. Contains publications, articles, and other useful information for paralegals and legal assistants.	http://www.americanbar.org/groups/paralegals
American Bar Association—Legal Profession Statistic	ABA site devoted to links to other sites regarding research, statistics, and information about the legal profession.	http://www.americanbar.org/resources_for_lawyers/profession_statistics
Association of Legal Administrators	National association for legal administrators. Contains resources and information related to law office management and legal administration.	http://www.alanet.org
Findlaw—Find a Lawyer site	Internet legal resource related to finding lawyers. Contains a database and links to attorney and law firm Web sites nationwide.	http://lawyers.findlaw.com
International Practice Management Association	Global association providing resources and education on the management of paralegals and other practice support professionals in the legal profession.	http://www.theipma.org/
Paralegal Today	National magazine for paralegals. The Web site has limited information, but the magazine itself is full of extremely useful and practical information for paralegals.	http://paralegaltoday.com/
National Association of Legal Assistants Paralegals	National association for paralegals. Contains many resources for paralegals students and practicing paralegals. Includes articles, utilization surveys, and other helpful information.	http://www.nala.org
National Federation of Paralegal Associations	National association for paralegals. Contains extensive links for practicing paralegals.	http://www.paralegals.org

Suggested Reading

1. *Law Practice* magazine, published by the American Bar Association Law Practice Management Section http://www.americanbar.org/publications/law_practice_magazine.
2. *Paralegal Today* magazine, published by Conexion International Media, Inc. http://paralegaltoday.com/.
3. *ABA Model Guidelines for the Utilization of Paralegal Services,* American Bar Association, 2012 http://www.americanbar.org/content/dam/aba/administrative/paralegals/ls_prlgs_modelguidelines.authcheckdam.pdf.
4. *National Association of Legal Assistants' [Annual] Utilization and Compensation Survey,* National Association of Legal Assistants http://www.nala.org/Upload/file/PDF-Files/News-Articles/15SEC4.pdf.
5. Munneke, G. A., & Davis, A. E. (2003, 2007, 2010). *The Essential Formbook: Comprehensive Management Tools for Lawyers, Volumes I–IV.* American Bar Association.
6. Grella, T. C., & Hudkins, M. L. (2005). *The Lawyer's Guide to Strategic Planning: Defining, Setting, and Achieving Your Firm's Goals.* American Bar Association.

2

Legal Administration and Technology

Chapter Objectives

After you read this chapter, you should be able to:

- Distinguish between office administration and practice management.
- Identify the functions of legal administration.
- Define total quality management.
- List and explain major federal employment laws.
- Discuss what a staff manual is and why it is important.
- Explain the purpose of strategic planning.
- Describe what disaster planning is.
- Discuss major technology issues in law offices.

Over the past several decades, the legal profession has experienced a dramatic growth, not only with the increased number of lawyers and paralegals entering the profession, but also with technological advances that have revolutionized the practice of law. Now more than ever, effective legal administration is essential to the success of any type of law office structure. For lawyers and law firms to thrive, they must embrace this new technology, integrating it with routine duties, representing clients, drafting legal documents and filing lawsuits, conducting research, and preparing for trials and negotiation settlements. Like many other professions, lawyers know their craft, but often lack the time and/or the skills for management. A strong support team is an integral part of an effective legal administration which is necessary to ensure that lawyers and paralegals successfully compete in today's law practice.

Legal Administration Principles

This chapter covers the full spectrum of law office management and legal administration principles, terms that are used interchangeably, yet in fact, have distinct responsibilities associated with them. Legal administration is complex and broad in scope. Some legal administration topics will be covered in more detail in later chapters while others will only get brief coverage in this chapter.

There was a time, not so long ago, when legal administration was viewed as unimportant. Attorneys viewed oversight responsibilities as something that got in the way of providing legal services to their clients. In truth, some of this view still exist. This is why a competent paralegal, capable of taking over legal administration responsibilities, is a valuable member of the legal team. Today, the highly competitive nature of the legal field and the need to control costs make legal administration an important topic. If a law practice is going to be successful in serving clients as well as providing a quality workplace for its employees, efficient operations and profits for its partners, along with good administration and management practices are a must, regardless of the size or type of law firm.

During the last 30 years, there has been a computer and automation revolution that has forever changed legal administration. Before that, law offices were generally unconcerned with computers, word processing, computerized accounting and billing, mobile computing, the "paperless office," the Internet, e-mail, and much more. Now, virtually every aspect of legal administration is computerized in some way. Law offices have spent hundreds of millions of dollars to implement these new technologies.

Dispelling a Myth

A particular myth about attorneys needs to be dispelled. Many people assume that attorneys automatically make good managers, this is simply not true. Truth be told, law office management and practicing law are not synonymous. Although lawyers have gone to school to learn about practicing law, most have no management skills or training. They may realize that management skills are important, but that does not necessarily mean they are proficient at it. As you read this chapter, keep in mind that many attorneys, practicing today, have never taken a course like this one. There are several national and local bar associations offering some training or education for law office management; because there is a general lack of this type of training, paralegals with good administrative skills can be very useful to law firms.

In today's medium- and large-sized law firms, the situation is alleviated somewhat with the use of professional administrators. Unfortunately, small-sized law firms generally do not have the resources to hire administrators and must rely on attorneys, paralegals, and other staff members to deal with problems as well as their other duties. Given the increasing competitiveness of the legal market, effective legal administration will be a prime concern for law firms for years to come.

The Importance of Legal Administration

Good legal administration affects paralegals, attorneys, and other law office staff alike. The law firms that are unsuccessful in legal administration must close, merge, or even lay off staff. The operating costs of running a law office are extremely high, and paralegals depend on the viability of the law office for their economic survival. Practicing good management is hard; it takes time and teamwork, but it is well worth the effort. Some signs of poor management include frustrated and unhappy staff members and clients, daily "crises," reduced attorney effectiveness, higher costs, low employee job satisfaction, high employee turnover, increased use of employee sick leave, and low staff morale.

Practice Management v. Administrative Management

practice management

Management decisions about how a law office will practice law and handle its cases.

The law office structure basically has two major aspects: practice management and administrative management. **Practice management** (i.e., **substantive or case management**) refers to management decisions about how a law office will practice law and handle its cases (see Exhibit 2-1). Practice management decisions include determining the general types of cases

Exhibit 2-1 Practice Management v. Administrative Management

Practice, Case, or Substantive Management
- What type of cases should we specialize in?
- Which cases should we accept?
- How will case files be organized?
- How will documents for each case be indexed for retrieval later?
- What form files will need to be created for each type of case?

Administrative or Office Management
- Purchasing equipment and supplies for the law office
- Hiring and evaluating law office staff
- Sending out invoices for the law office
- Managing the finances and profitability of the law office
- What administrative structure is the most efficient for the law office?

the law office will specialize in, how many cases the law office should accept in a given area, and which clients should be accepted or rejected. Practice management is sometimes called "case management" or "file management" because this type of management centers on managing and controlling client files and client cases.

The cases and clients a law office takes on directly affect the profitability of the law firm. If a law office undertakes to represent a number of client cases that do not generate any profits because the client does not pay, the contingency case is lost, or the fees received are unexpectedly low, the economic effects on the law office are quite harmful. Also, if law office staff do not manage and organize cases effectively, then there may be poor-quality legal services, reduced profitability, unhappy clients, and ethical complaints.

administrative management

Management decisions relating to operating or managing a law office, including financial and personnel matters.

Administrative management (i.e., **office management**) refers to management decisions relating to operating or managing a law office, including financial and personnel matters. This text largely covers administrative management topics, but some practice management areas are also introduced.

Functions of Legal Administration

management

The administration of people and other resources to accomplish objectives.

Management is the administration of people and other resources to accomplish objectives. In private law practices, the primary objective of management is to provide efficient, high-quality legal services that please clients while earning a reasonable profit for the firm. In a corporate or government legal department, where generating a profit is not applicable, the objective of management is to provide efficient, high-quality legal services to its client at a reasonable cost.

The functions of legal administration (see Exhibit 2-2) include practice management, leadership, controlling, financial management, human resources management, planning, marketing management, organization/policies/systems, facilities management, office services management, and technology or information systems management. Each of these areas will be discussed in this chapter. Two areas, financial management and marketing, have one or more chapters devoted to them later in the text, so they are only introduced in this chapter. All of these functions are essential to successful legal administration regardless of the size of the law office. The people who perform these tasks vary, depending on the management structure of the firm; it could be a sole practitioner, a managing partner with the help of an office manager, committees with the help of professional administrators, or all of the partners or shareholders in a law firm.

Practice Management

As defined earlier, practice management refers to management decisions about how a law firm will practice law and provide legal services to clients. In the end, every law practice must be able to provide their clients with prompt, competent, and courteous legal services that satisfy and add value to the client, and that are priced at a cost that clients are willing to pay. Law firms are service providers, and if clients do not receive quality legal services, they *will* go somewhere else to get them; it is currently easier than ever to do so, given the intense level of competition in the legal marketplace. A firm's lifeblood is the ability of management to prudently choose the type of clients it serves, to keep existing clients, and to gain new clients

Exhibit 2-2 The Functions of Legal Administration

for the future. To do this, law firms must define what practice areas and clients to focus on, what legal services they will provide to those clients, and what practice systems and resources they will need to provide those services to the clients. Every law firm must deal with these types of practice management issues.

Defining the Law Firm's Practice

Every law practice must define who it is they will serve. Exhibit 2-3 shows fundamental questions that every law practice must answer and basic decisions that management will need to make. Most of these questions must be answered by the law firm's owners. None of the questions are easy, and all of them will dramatically affect who the law firm will serve and how it will provide services to its clients. There are two basic and important practice management maxims to understand: (1) the practice of law is so broad that even megafirms with 1000 or

Exhibit 2-3 Practice Management—Defining the Law Firm's Practice

Who are our primary clients (businesses, individuals, governments)?
What market segments will we serve?
What legal services will we provide?
What resources will be needed to provide those services?
What services do our clients need or want? What will we need to add or delete in order to be successful?
What types of cases do we want to take? What is the long-term projection for those cases?
In what legal areas will we specialize? Should we focus on area subspecialties?
How many practice areas will we have? How much can we do well with the resources we have?
Who will champion the practice areas and lead their development?
Should we focus on providing services to an industry?
What geographic area will we serve?
How will we attract clients?
How will we assure that the clients receive quality services?
How will we hold on to the clients (what will be our basis for competition to differentiate our services from the next firm)?

more attorneys cannot possibly practice in all subspecialty areas of law, therefore, specialization is absolutely required and (2) successful law practices do not take all of the clients or cases that come to them. Successful law practices weed out good clients from bad clients and strong cases from poor ones. Not all clients are created equal; some clients are easier to work with than others. Some clients have financial resources to pay for legal services, and some do not. Some clients are honest and trustworthy, and some are not. A successful law firm will decide which clients are right for them. Likewise, some cases have true merit to them and some are frivolous or without legal foundation. Again, successful law firms and attorneys are able to decide which cases are the best for them and which ones to refuse.

Defining the Law Firm's Services

Once a law firm has decided upon areas of practice and which clients to serve, it must decide and define what services will be provided. For example, if a solo practitioner has decided to practice in the general area of decedent estates, that person must decide whether he or she will (1) draft trusts, (2) advise clients on complex tax issues, (3) perform estate planning, (4) draft wills (including whether to write only simple wills or to draft complex wills involving millions of dollars in assets), (5) probate estates, and so forth. The law firm must decide what specific services they are willing to provide and what services they should refer to other attorneys or decline to take because they lack particular expertise. The answers to these questions are important to the practice management of every law firm.

Defining the Law Firm's Practice System Needs

Once the law firm has decided which clients they want to serve and what services they want to provide, the firm must then determine what types of practice systems are needed to provide and implement those services. Law firms have nearly endless choices regarding the types of practice systems and tools they can use to provide legal services to clients. Exhibit 2-4 contains some examples of different practice systems and options that are available. Technology

Exhibit 2-4 Defining The Law Firm's Practice Systems

Practice Systems	Choices
Document preparation	Pen/paper, typewriter, word processor
File/records management	File cabinets, computer/paperless office
Legal research	State or county law libraries, personal collection of books, Westlaw, LexisNexis, CD-ROMs
Docket control	Paper calendars, computer calendars (Outlook), legal docket control, full case management
Specialty-specific software	Word processors and general tools or costly but efficient and sophisticated specialty software
Litigation support	Manual methods, computerized litigation support programs, outsourcing to litigation support vendors, e-discovery
Computer systems	Stand-alone systems, hardwired network systems, wireless networks, the Internet, intranet, extranet, desktop computers, laptop computers, PDAs
Communication systems	Telephone systems, voice mail, mobile phones, e-mail, e-filing

had virtually no role in how law was practiced 30 years ago; at that time, technology mainly impacted "back office" functions, such as timekeeping, billing, and administrative systems. This is no longer the case. Attorneys and paralegals use practice management technology every day in the practice of law. There is almost no area of law practice that has not been profoundly changed by technology. For more than 200 years, lawyers exclusively used files and file cabinets for records management. Now, many law firms have moved to "paperless offices," where all documents coming into or going out of the firm are scanned and saved in an electronic format for later retrieval without a hard copy. Likewise, legal research has taken the same route. Law books that take up large amount of expensive space and quickly become outdated have mostly been replaced with CD-ROMs or electronic services such as Westlaw, LexisNexis, the Internet, and others. Law practices must also provide practice systems that set standards for things such as ethics, internal law practice policies for providing service, and quality. And, of course with a virtual law office, cloud computing provides real-time and file-sharing capabilities for remote collaboration by the members of the legal team.

Quality and Total Quality Management (TQM)

Ensuring that clients receive quality legal services is one of the most important practice management responsibilities of any law firm partner or administrator. There simply is no substitute for having a quality product, particularly in the legal field.

What Is TQM?

Some might say that total quality management (TQM) is outdated and has little to do with a legal organization or a practicing paralegal. Others would say that quality never goes out of style. Because legal organizations must provide quality legal services to stay in business and please clients—whether a megacorporation in litigation, an ordinary person needing a will, or a corporate legal department—that quality must always be the object of focus for a law firm. Legal organizations provide quality legal services through their staff, including their paralegals. There will always be a market for paralegals who look out for the client and provide quality legal services. Quality is what distinguishes poor or average paralegals from exceptional ones. There is also a strong connection between quality and loyalty when it comes to clients. When a client is receiving quality legal services, he or she is usually willing to pay a higher price for those services and has no reason to look elsewhere for a different service provider.

> *Why would a client risk moving his or her business to another law firm (and have to pay to educate that firm on his or her business) when his or her current firm, current attorneys, and current legal assistants provide outstanding quality legal services that always meet or exceed his or her expectations?*

total quality management

Management philosophy of knowing the needs of each client and allowing those needs to drive the legal organization.

Total quality management (*TQM*) is a management philosophy that is based upon knowing the needs of each client and allowing those needs to drive the legal organization at all levels of activity, from the receptionist to the senior partner. From the outset of this book, you have been introduced to the importance of meeting client needs and providing quality legal services to clients. TQM is just an expansion on this basic idea. The TQM philosophy of allowing clients' needs to drive an organization, instead of the other way around, was taught to major Japanese corporations in the 1950s by W. Edwards Deming.

The TQM philosophy focuses on the idea that businesses should compete based on the quality of the service that is provided, as opposed to price or other factors. Exhibit 2-5 shows the difference between management decisions based on client needs and those based on what is easiest for the law practice to provide.

Exhibit 2-5
Product-Centered v. Client-Centered Philosophies in a Law Office

Product-Centered Philosophy	Client-Centered Philosophy
1. Inner forces control the law office.	Client forces control law office decision making.
2. Emphasis is on short-run productivity.	Emphasis is on long-range planning for quality and client satisfaction.
3. Law office decisions are forced upon clients.	Law office decisions are made based on client input and meeting clients' needs.
4. Law office provides services they already have.	Law office develops new services and modifies existing services based on clients' needs.
5. Law office provides services but does not survey clients to ensure satisfaction.	Law office surveys clients before, during, and after services are rendered to ensure client satisfaction and makes appropriate changes based on clients' needs.
6. Law office focuses on short-term profitability and financial success.	Law office focuses on long-range profitability by putting the priority on meeting clients' needs and providing quality legal services.

What Are Specific TQM Philosophies?

TQM has many nuances and subtleties, but there are several main points to the TQM philosophy.

1. **Management has an overriding duty to ensure that the law firm provides quality legal service.** Management must make decisions based on how the decision will affect the quality of the legal services being provided. The distribution of law firm assets, including purchases, contracts, and staff employees, must be viewed from the client's perspective and be based on how these decisions will affect the *quality* of the services the firm provides. Likewise, when a paralegal makes a decision or participates in making a decision about a case, he or she must view that decision in terms of how the decision will affect the quality of legal services, such as deciding what copy service, litigation support bureau, or software to use.
2. **Quality service involves every person in the law firm, and everyone must be involved and committed.** Providing quality services begins and ends with everyone. It encompasses the idea of putting dedication and commitment into everything that is done; it requires integrating quality methods into the daily work routine of every member of the staff; and it begins with every person taking pride in his or her work.
3. **Quality service is based not on management's or our own perception of quality, but on the perceptions of the client.** In the end, the only person who is going to bring business back to the firm, or refer your services to other businesses, is the client. Therefore, only the client's perception of quality is what counts. Because it is the client's opinion that counts, law firms must regularly poll or survey their clients to find out what they are doing right, what they are doing wrong, and how they can provide better services to the client. This can be done by interviewing current clients and mailing out client surveys when matters have been resolved, but it is the client's opinions that motivate the firm to change. For a TQM policy to be effective, the firm must be willing to *listen* to the client and to institute *change* to meet the needs of the client. Keep in mind that client needs are constantly changing, so to keep up, the firm must also be willing to change.

As a practicing paralegal, you do not have to wait until the end of a case or matter to ask a client whether or not he or she is pleased with the services you are providing or if there is anything else you can do to be of assistance. Clients will not always volunteer that kind of information; you may have to ask.

4. **Quality service depends on the individual's, the team's, and ultimately the organization's performance.** In the end, the client will judge the quality of a law firm's job based on his or her experience. Thus, everyone involved must be committed to the idea of quality and must be able to share in the financial or other types of benefits the firm receives. TQM eliminates the "we versus they" mentality and rewards all members of the team who contribute. TQM uses project teams to identify and solve problems and increase efficiency.

As a paralegal, it is crucial that you work as a team member with the other legal professionals on a client's case. If you see another team member struggling, about to make a mistake, or unable to complete a task in a timely fashion, you have to be willing to help.

5. **Improve systems constantly.** Along with assuring high-quality services, there is also a focus on increasing performance and productivity by constantly improving the systems and ways in which services are provided. This may include purchasing technology, rethinking the ways in which work is performed or routed, removing repetitive tasks, or taking further actions that will increase productivity and efficiency. This is a vigorous process that never ends.

What Are the Benefits of the TQM Philosophy?

The TQM philosophy offers many benefits:

- **Increased client satisfaction**—The ultimate benefit is that clients are satisfied beyond their expectations, and, based on this satisfaction, they will entrust all their legal services and refer new clients to the law firm.
- **Unity among the management, attorneys, and staff**—TQM breaks down the barriers among competing groups in a law practice by focusing everyone on the same goal (unity of purpose) and by allowing all involved to share in the profits of the business. This can be done by awarding bonuses, giving awards, or recognizing outstanding performance. The "we versus they" mentality is a thing of the past.
- **Seek to continuously improve performance and productivity**—TQM seeks to improve the quality of legal services to clients by increasing staff efficiency and productivity, not just once or twice a year, but constantly, in order to improve the system. This involves all members of the staff checking the quality of their own work, learning advanced technologies, and doing whatever is necessary to provide the client with the best service.

How Is TQM Implemented?

TQM can be implemented by hiring professional consultants to develop systems for obtaining client feedback and to educate staff members on TQM techniques.

Some law firms include a TQM policy in their staff manual. For example, the American Bar Association publishes a sample manual that includes TQM; it addresses the importance of the entire legal team providing high-quality service to every client throughout the representation in the most cost-effective method.

To a lesser degree, TQM also can be implemented by reading about the subject, by simply accepting the principles of TQM, by being responsive to client needs, and by recognizing the effect management decisions have on the quality of the legal services being provided. In effect, TQM serves as a reminder that quality services are what everything else in the law firm depends on.

Leadership

leadership

The act of motivating or causing others to perform and achieve objectives.

Another function of legal administration is leadership. **Leadership** is the act of motivating or causing others to perform and achieve objectives. Effective leaders inspire others; they set a clear mission, vision, and goals for an organization, and they provide direction and guidance. Good leaders are forward thinking, set clear objectives, measure results, inspire trust, are innovators, and make quality decisions. For any law firm or practice to be truly successful, quality

Exhibit 2-6 Effective Law Office Leadership

Effective Law Office Leadership

Establishes a vision of a positive and successful future for the law practice.
Enlists others in generating the firm's mission statement, goals, and objectives.
Develops a written strategic plan incorporating the input, values, and ideas of others.
Anticipates what can go wrong and acts proactively.
Acts consistently to support the legal team in carrying out the firm's mission.
Stresses goal attainment in day-to-day activities.
Rewards team members based on their achievements of goals and objectives.
Reports and tracks goal attainment data at partnership and law firm meetings.
Shows confidence in and respect for all legal team members.
Defuses rumors by keeping all legal team members informed of matters that are relevant to them or the practice.
Never represents facts or divulges information given in confidence.
Insists that all team members have strong ethics and high integrity.
Is trusted by others in the practice.
Creates a supportive environment for learning, coaching, and developing staff; takes interest in team members as human beings; and is not overly critical of mistakes.
Takes time to listen to others, no matter who they are, and makes a concerted effort to be responsive.
Effectively communicates with team members so that they are given continuous, specific feedback regarding progress toward their goals and clearly know what is expected of them.
Consistently makes difficult decisions without procrastinating and seeks appropriate input from others.

leadership must exist, whether it be from the partnership, a managing partner, legal administrators, committees, or other individuals or groups. Exhibit 2-6 shows a more complete list of effective leadership practices in a law office.

Controlling

controlling

The process of determining whether the law practice is achieving its objectives, holding stakeholders accountable for their goals and making strategy adjustments as necessary so the firm achieves its objectives.

Controlling is the process of determining whether the law practice is achieving its objectives, holding stakeholders accountable for their goals, and making strategy adjustments as necessary so that the law firm achieves the objectives. Management must determine whether the law office is achieving its short- and long-range goals. Management must also make stakeholders accountable for meeting objectives and should assist in adjusting strategies so goals can be met. Exercising control is a fundamental aspect of management; this is done via financial audits, budgets v. actual reporting, operational audits, risk management, analysis of financial reports, and the progress tracking of short- and long-range plans.

Financial Management

financial management

The oversight of a firm's financial assets and profitability to ensure overall financial health.

Financial management is the oversight of a firm's financial assets and profitability to ensure overall financial health. Financial management is important in any business; a business that does not earn a profit will quickly cease to exist. There are many different aspects of the financial management of a law firm. Timekeeping and billing, which include tracking time spent on clients by attorneys and paralegals and billing clients, is a particularly crucial area, as is trust accounting, which entails the ethical responsibilities of keeping track of client monies paid but not yet earned by the firm. Budgeting and tracking firm expenses, revenue, and profitability, as well as making payments (accounts payable) and tracking firm receipts (accounts receivable), are also important to the overall success of the firm. Other areas of financial management include setting billing and hourly rates, purchasing high-quality goods and services at the least expensive cost, tracking the assets of the firm (including equipment and furniture), properly investing firm monies that are not currently being used, having a good relationship with a bank to secure loans as necessary, tracking tax liabilities, and having proper insurance to protect the firm's assets, payroll, and cash flow. Chapters 5 and 6 cover these topics in detail.

Human Resources Management

human resources management

Hiring, evaluating, compensating, training, and directing law office personnel.

Human resources management refers to hiring, evaluating, compensating, training, and directing law office personnel. While law firms use technology to serve clients more efficiently, for the most part, legal services are delivered to clients by a firm's staff. Therefore, the quality management of that staff is of great concern to most law offices. Firms must recruit, select, and hire staff who are trained and competent in their areas of expertise. Managers must also effectively evaluate staff to let them know how they are doing in terms of meeting the expectations of their jobs, and coach and counsel staff if there are performance problems. Firms must provide compensation and benefits that will appropriately reward and motivate staff so that they are able to retain the employees they have. Furthermore, the staff must be trained regarding changes in the law, technology, and client needs. The firm must also direct staff and periodically review its organizational structure, job designs, and how services are provided to clients, in order to make adjustments that ensure effectiveness.

The Hiring Process

At some point in your career, you may be required to hire someone, such as a legal secretary, another paralegal, or a clerk. It is important that you hire the right individual for the job the first time. A poor hiring decision can cost a law office thousands of dollars in wasted salary, training expenses, time, and potential malpractice problems. In addition, if the right person is not hired the first time, the firm must hire another individual and incur the cost of advertising and training all over again.

The hiring process is fairly detailed. Typically, a detailed job description is drafted, ads are placed in newspapers (or recruitment is started), resumes and employment applications are analyzed, candidates are interviewed, references are checked, and a final selection is made.

WRITING JOB DESCRIPTIONS The first step in the hiring process is to write a detailed job description (see Exhibit 2-7) that explains the duties of the position. If an employer does not know what the new hire is going to do, there is no way he or she can recognize the best person for the position. A detailed job description lets the employer match the strengths of candidates to the particular position that is being filled. Job descriptions also help the employee to understand his or her role in the firm and what will be expected. Most job descriptions include a job title, a summary of the position, a list of duties, and minimum qualifications that the new employee must have.

Exhibit 2-7 Sample Litigation Paralegal Job Description

Job Description

JOB TITLE: **PARALEGAL** (Litigation)

EXEMPT:	Non-Exempt	**GRADE LEVEL:**	11
DIVISION:	Legal	**LOCATION:**	Headquarters
DEPARTMENT:	Litigation		
INCUMBENT:			
REPORTS TO:	Attorney		
PREPARED BY:	Angelina Smith	**DATE:**	January 2015
APPROVED BY:	Graham Jones	**DATE:**	January 2015

SUMMARY:

Under supervision of an attorney, provides a broad range of professional and technical duties related to litigation. Performs factual investigations including gathering documents, researching records, and interviewing witnesses/clients. Works with the supervising attorney and client to prepare and answer discovery documents in draft form. Prepares deposition summaries, witness summaries, and case chronologies or timelines. Manages and organizes litigation files and exhibits. Prepares drafts of pleadings and correspondence. Conducts legal research as needed. Manages the computerized litigation support for each case as needed.

ESSENTIAL DUTIES AND RESPONSIBILITIES (and other duties as assigned):

1. Performs factual investigations including gathering, analyzing, and organizing documents such as medical records, police records, birth and death records, motor vehicle records, incorporation records, and other documents using a variety of sources including the Internet, government agencies, and other contacts. Compiles and summarizes data as necessary. Conducts interviews with clients and witnesses as needed. Works with expert witnesses as needed.
2. Performs a variety of tasks related to discovery under the supervision of an attorney including preparing drafts of interrogatories, requests for admissions, and requests for production of documents. Works with the attorney and client to prepare and coordinate drafts of discovery responses. May prepare drafts of deposition questions, coordinate deposition scheduling, and prepare case chronologies and timelines as necessary. Prepares deposition and witness summaries.
3. Organizes and maintains litigation files, prepares trial notebooks, and assists in organizing, maintaining, and indexing trial exhibits. Performs case management, docketing, scheduling, and planning as needed.
4. Conducts drafts of legal research memorandums using the Internet, Westlaw, LexisNexis, CD-ROM databases, and the law library as needed.
5. Prepares drafts of a variety of litigation-related legal documents under the supervision of an attorney including pleadings, motions, discovery documents, and general correspondence.
6. Reviews, analyzes, organizes, and indexes discovery documents and all case-related documents, including managing the computerized litigation support for each case.

MINIMUM EDUCATION AND EXPERIENCE:

Bachelor's degree (B.A.) from four-year college or university (major: paralegal); or one to two years of related experience; and/or training or equivalent work experience.

LICENSES/CERTIFICATIONS REQUIRED:

Paralegal certificate

(continued)

Exhibit 2-7 Sample Litigation Paralegal Job Description *(continued)*

KNOWLEDGE, SKILLS, AND ABILITIES REQUIRED:

Knowledge of the principles and procedures of legal research. Strong interpersonal and communication skills and the ability to work effectively with a wide range of constituencies in a diverse community. Skill in the use of personal computers and related software applications. Ability to draft legal documents, such as pleadings, legal responses, affidavits, position statements, and briefs. Ability to develop and maintain recordkeeping systems and procedures. Database management skills. Ability to gather and organize legal evidence. Knowledge of litigation and civil procedure helpful. Knowledge of planning and scheduling techniques. Skill in organizing resources and establishing priorities. Ability to maintain confidentiality of records and information. Excellent customer service skills required.

REASONING ABILITY:

Ability to define problems, collect data, establish facts, and draw valid conclusions. Ability to interpret an extensive variety of legal instructions in different areas of the law and deal with several abstract and concrete variables.

LANGUAGE ABILITY:

Ability to read, analyze, and interpret legal documents. Ability to write legal documents and legal/ business correspondence. Ability to effectively present information and respond to clients, attorneys, witnesses, opposing counsel, and the general public.

ADVERTISING AND RECRUITING After a detailed and accurate job description is drafted, organizations begin the actual hiring process. This includes either promoting from within the organization or recruiting candidates from outside the organization. The process of recruiting candidates can include the use of newspaper advertisements, candidate interviews at specific schools or institutions, employment agencies and search firms, professional associations, the Internet, or candidate referrals from the organization's own employees.

EMPLOYMENT APPLICATIONS AND RESUMES Once an employer has drafted a detailed job description and advertised the position, the next step is to review the employment applications or resumes received.

In many cases, an organization will receive a resume first and subsequently have the individual fill out a formal application for employment. An application for employment is a good idea, because resumes are inconsistent and may not provide all the information needed to make a quality decision.

Employment applications must comply with legal requirements and may not ask for information that the employer is not entitled to have, such as information regarding race, religion, or age.

INTERVIEWING Once resumes and employment applications have been analyzed and the field of candidates narrowed, the next step is the interview process. The interview is typically the most dynamic part of the hiring process. This is the point where the interviewer decides which applicant is the most qualified and will "fit" with the organization. Below are some general insights regarding interviews.

Screen Applicants to be Interviewed A common problem that occurs during the interview is the discovery that a candidate who looked good on paper is, in fact, a bad "fit" for the organization. In this case, the whole interview is a waste of both the employer's and the applicant's time. One way to avoid this is to conduct a casual phone screen of all applicants. By asking some salient questions over the phone, an interviewer can determine whether it is appropriate to have the applicant come in for a formal interview.

Ensure That All Interviews Are Consistent It is extremely important that all interviews conducted for a position are done consistently. The interviewer must make sure that all candidates are asked the same questions and that all candidates are treated fairly. If interviews are not performed consistently, an interviewer may be giving preference or special treatment to one candidate over another. The more consistent the interview is, the less likely an organization will be susceptible to a discrimination complaint.

The Interviewer Should Talk Less and Listen More The interviewer should talk as little as possible. Any time the interviewer is talking, he or she is giving up the opportunity to hear from the candidate, which is the whole purpose of the interview. Interviewers should avoid filling in pauses or completing sentences for candidates.

Ask Open-Ended and Behavioral-Based Questions Most questions in interviews today are open-ended in that no specific answer is hinted at or suggested by how the interview question is asked. The applicant must decide how to answer the question. For example, a typical open-ended question might be "Can you review your work experience for me and tell me how it prepares you for the position you have applied for?" A behavioral-based question is another type often asked in interviews; this type of question asks the candidate to provide a specific example from his or her past. For example, a typical behavioral-based question is "Can you tell me about a time you had a particularly difficult legal ethics problem and how you handled it?" Many organizations use behavioral-based questions because it is more difficult for an applicant to rehearse these answers beforehand. Good interviewers will ask candidates a variety of open-ended and behavioral-based questions that call for concrete examples relating to the candidate's personality, job history, education, and experience related to the potential job.

Avoid Discriminatory Questions Particular caution should be used when deciding what interview questions to ask. There are many questions that should be avoided because they might be considered discriminatory (see Exhibit 2-8). Exhibit 2-8 is not an all-inclusive list, as many states and local governments have additional antidiscrimination laws. As a rule, if a question is not directly relevant to the position or job performance, an interviewer should not ask it. There is no reason to take unnecessary risks. Personal or family-related questions should be avoided; the problem with most personal questions is that they relate to the applicant's race, color, religion, sex, national origin, age, or disability. Many city statutes and ordinances prevent discrimination on the basis of sexual orientation, so questions related to this should be avoided as well.

REFERENCE CHECKS Once the employer has narrowed the list to two or three final candidates, the only thing left to do is check references. Checking references is an important part of the hiring process and should never be left out. Researchers have found that nearly 30% of all resumes contain exaggerated statements or misstatements about education or employment history. In addition, employers have been held liable for negligent hiring. **Negligent hiring** is when an employer hires an employee without sufficiently and reasonably checking the employee's background. In one case, an apartment complex was found liable after a new manager used a passkey to enter an apartment and rape a tenant. The apartment complex

negligent hiring

Hiring an employee without sufficiently and reasonably checking the employee's background.

Exhibit 2-8 Interview Questions that Should *Not Be* Asked

Race/Color/Religion/Sex
Any question that is related to a candidate's race, color, religion, sex, national origin, age, disability, sexual orientation, or veteran status

Name/Marital Status
- What was your maiden name?
- Have you ever used another name?
- Are you married? (permissible after hiring)

Ancestry
- Where were you born?
- Where does your family come from?

Residence
- How long have you lived at this address?
- Do you own your house?

Family/Personal
- How many children do you have?
- How will you provide child care?
- Are you pregnant?

Credit/Financial
- Have you ever filed for bankruptcy?
- Have your wages been garnished?

Age
- What is your date of birth? (permissible after hiring)
- When did you graduate from elementary or high school?

Organizations
- What organizations do you belong to? (You can ask this if you instruct them to delete organizations related to race, religion, color, disability, age, and so forth.)

Religion
- What church do you belong to?

Medical
- Are you disabled or taking medication regularly? (You can ask whether they have the ability to perform the essential functions of the job.)

had failed to check the new manager's references and reasonably investigate the person's background for felony convictions, fighting, and other criminal activity. Thus, references should always be checked, and gaps in employment and other indicators of problematic behavior should be investigated.

The following are some tips on how to get good information when performing reference checks.

Call Past Employers/Supervisors Typically, the most relevant information an employer can gather is from the candidate's last employer or supervisor. Call these people first. Although some will refuse to give out any information for fear of being sued for defamation if they say something negative, many will still answer your questions. A way around this problem is to ask potential candidates to sign a release or waiver that allows the past employer to talk to you openly and freely without fear of being sued for defamation. Ask specific questions about the candidate's dates of employment, job duties and responsibilities, quality and quantity of work, disciplinary problems, work attitude, communication skills, dependability, ability to be a team player, and reason for leaving. Also ask whether the former employer would rehire the person.

Call Institutions/Schools If a candidate lists graduation from a school or institution, call the school and confirm it. This usually does not take a great deal of time. This is seldom done and many candidates claim that they have finished degrees when, in fact, they have not.

Call Character References Last Candidates only give potential employers character references who will give them a glowing recommendation. Expect this, but ask specific questions as well.

Fair Credit Reporting Act

Federal legislation that governs the use of consumer reports in all employment decisions.

Fair Credit Reporting Act The **Fair Credit Reporting Act** is federal legislation that governs the use of "consumer reports" in all employment decisions. "Consumer reports" are defined very broadly and include reference checks, education checks, credit history reports, and criminal background checks, when an employer hires a third party to conduct these checks. If an employer conducts these checks personally, compliance with the Fair Credit Reporting Act is not required; however, if a third party is used, the organization must comply. The employer must give prior written notice to the applicant before procuring the consumer report, and obtain prior written authorization by the applicant before obtaining the consumer report. Before "adverse action" is taken against the applicant (such as not hiring the applicant based on the consumer report), the applicant must be provided with a copy of the report and notified of his or her legal rights.

Performance Evaluations

Timely performance evaluations are a strong human resource development technique. Employees need to know—on a regular basis—what they are doing right and where they need to improve. Performance evaluations allow employees to know where they stand and help them to grow and progress. A performance evaluation should not be viewed as a heavy object with which to beat or threaten employees, but rather as a part of the process of working toward a common goal.

If done correctly, evaluations can strengthen ties with employees by allowing them to participate in the evaluation process. In the end, a well-defined evaluation process can make the organization more efficient. Employee evaluations should be conducted privately, and, when possible, the evaluation itself should be given to the employee before meeting so that he or she is prepared to talk about the evaluation and its findings. The evaluation should always be performed in writing and should be kept in the employee's personnel file.

EVALUATIONS SHOULD BE DONE REGULARLY Evaluations should be done on a regular basis in order to be effective. Some law offices evaluate employees quarterly, biannually, or annually. Quarterly or biannually evaluations are recommended, because criticism or praise usually has more effect soon after an incident has happened.

EVALUATIONS SHOULD BE OBJECTIVE AND MATCH RATINGS WITH PERFORMANCE Evaluations should be based on objective performance by an employee and not on any personal likes or dislikes of the employer. It is particularly important to match ratings with performance and to always remain fair. It is also important that employers communicate with employees on a regular basis and take a "hands-on" approach to knowing whether or not employees really deserve a certain rating. Using objective criteria and actual examples of the employee's performance will help in this process. Examples of how the employee earned an "excellent" or "average" performance rating will help identify what he or she is doing correctly or incorrectly.

ELICIT OPEN COMMUNICATION AND SET MUTUAL GOALS FOR IMPROVEMENT Any evaluation method must allow the employee to participate in the process by communicating how he or she feels about the evaluation, including what he or she likes or dislikes and what both parties can do to help solve problems. There must be a give-and-take relationship in the evaluation process to make it work. One technique is to ask the employee how he or she feels the year went: what went right or wrong? Let him or her do the talking. This will put the employee at ease and will let the person feel that he or she has taken part in the process. Setting realistic goals to solve any problems also helps to communicate what is expected of the employee in the future. One way of doing this is by having both the employer and the employee set certain goals.

coaching technique

Counseling that focuses on the positive aspects of the employee's performance and explores alternative ways to improve his or her performance.

COACHING TECHNIQUE—ONGOING EVALUATION One way to help an employee succeed in his or her job is to coach and counsel him or her on a daily, ongoing basis. The **coaching technique** focuses on the positive aspects of the employee's performance and explores alternative ways to improve performance. Most people are more willing to listen to advice from a "friend" who is interested in their well-being than from a disinterested and heavy-handed "boss." The coaching technique is borrowed from sports, where a coach works with an individual to overcome deficiencies through counseling and by explaining any problems to the person.

The coaching technique works best when the supervisor has had direct experience in the employee's position. This allows the supervisor to give concrete tips, examples, information, and opinions that the employee can use. Employees typically are more willing to accept advice if the supervisor has been in the same position. When discussing areas that need improvement, try not to be judgmental, but instead give advice on exactly how to correct a deficiency. This technique is especially useful when an employee lacks knowledge about a situation. One of the most positive aspects of the coaching technique is that it does not place blame on the employee; the employee is able to retain his or her self-esteem, which can be lost when an employee is simply reprimanded. Exhibit 2-9 explains how the coaching technique works. The coaching technique is not a substitute for a regular evaluation, but it is a technique for helping an employee to be successful in his or her job.

GENERAL PERFORMANCE EVALUATION FORM Exhibit 2-10 contains a general performance evaluation form that could be used for many law office support jobs. This type of evaluation is straightforward and quick to prepare. However, the checklist is not job specific and does not allow a great deal of interaction on the part of the employee. If possible, the employee should be allowed to make comments and be an active participant in the evaluation process.

Exhibit 2-9
The Coaching Technique

1. Event—Describe exactly what happened; do not be negative, just state the facts.
2. Effect—Describe the impact of the event, including who or what was adversely affected and why; be specific. Let the employee know why the behavior should be changed.
3. Advice—Describe exactly how the employee can improve performance in the future.
4. Remind—Emphasize that you believe the employee is competent and that this was just a lapse.
5. Reinforce—Monitor the employee's performance. If the employee corrects the mistake, let the person know that he or she is doing it right. Reinforce the positive change he or she made.

Exhibit 2-10 Paralegal Performance Evaluation

PARALEGAL
PERFORMANCE EVALUATION

Name: ______________________ Title: ______________________

Evaluation Type: Probation Six-Month Annual Special: ______________

Date: ____________ Evaluation Period: ______________________

Evaluate the staff member's performance using the following rating criteria and make comments as necessary:

Rating:	Description:
5	**Outstanding:** Employee's performance is exceptional and far exceeds normal expectations.
4	**Above Average:** Employee's performance is very good and exceeds expectations.
3	**Average**: Employee performs to normal expectations of the position.
2	**Below Average:** Employee's performance falls below acceptable levels from time to time.
1	**Unacceptable:** Employee's performance is completely unacceptable.

1. Competence in the Law Office

__________ a. Is technically competent in all areas of work.
__________ b. Other staff members have confidence in and trust the employee's work.
__________ c. Continuously strives to learn and expand his/her competence level.

Comments: ____
____
____

2. Quality of Work

__________ a. Is accurate in all work.
__________ b. Is thorough and complete in all work.
__________ c. Takes pride in work.
__________ d. Work is consistently of high quality.

Comments: ____
____
____

(continued)

Exhibit 2-10 Paralegal Performance Evaluation *(continued)*

3. Dependability

__________ a. Highly dependable.
__________ b. Work is always turned on time.
__________ c. Can be counted on in a crisis.
__________ d. Works independently without need of supervision.

Comments: ____________________

4. Work Habits/Attitude

__________ a. Has excellent work habits.
__________ b. Has a positive and enthusiastic attitude.
__________ c. Acts as a team player.
__________ d. Gets along with other staff members and supervisors.

Comments: ____________________

5. Communication/Relationships

__________ a. Treats clients professionally.
__________ b. Treats other staff members professionally.
__________ c. Can write effectively.
__________ d. Has good grammar skills.
__________ e. Listens effectively.
__________ f. Can make self-understood orally.

Comments: ____________________

6. Judgment

__________ a. Makes sound judgment calls.
__________ b. Exercises appropriate discretion.
__________ c. Intelligently arrives at decisions.
__________ d. Thinks through decisions.

Comments: ____________________

7. Initiative

__________ a. Accepts new assignments willingly.
__________ b. Takes on new responsibilities without being asked.

Comments: ____________________

Exhibit 2-10
(continued)

General Comments:____

Employee's Strengths: ____

Areas That Need Improvement: ____________________________________

OVERALL RATING: **Outstanding Above Average Average Below Average Unacceptable**

Employee Comments: ____

Supervisor Signature: ________________ Employee Signature: ________________
Date: ______________ Date: ______________

Employee signature only verifies that this evaluation has been discussed and does not indicate agreement with the evaluation.

EMPLOYEE SELF-APPRAISAL:

A. What were your achievements this year?

B. List any goals you would like to achieve next year.

C. What strengths do you have in performing this position?

D. What areas do you think you can improve upon?

E. What can your supervisor do to help you reach your goals?

F. Overall, how would you rate your own performance level?

management by objectives

A performance program in which the individual employee and the employer agree on goals for the employee.

GOAL SETTING AND MANAGEMENT BY OBJECTIVES (MBO) Another type of performance system is based on goal setting, also commonly referred to as "management by objectives" (see Exhibit 2-11). In a **management by objectives** (MBO) performance program, the employee and employer agree upon the employee's goals at the beginning of the evaluation period. Target dates for reviewing the employee's progress toward the goals, and a determination for how it will be decided if the goals were achieved or not, are also included in the objectives. An accomplishment report is prepared detailing which goals were accomplished, and rewards or incentives are given for meeting the goals. For example, a goal might be to reduce nonbillable hours by 5% or increase billable hours by 50 hours during the fourth quarter.

Compensation and Benefits

Another aspect of human resources management is paying law practice employees and providing them with benefit packages. Most firms set compensation for positions based on the "market salary" for the job in the marketplace. Some firms may be "above market" while others are "below market." To determine the appropriate compensation and benefits for a position, law practices will consider job description and the education and experience requirements, and will use the average market salary as a benchmark (see Exhibit 1-10 for paralegal salary data). According to the 2015 National Utilization and Compensation Survey Report, a paralegal's annual compensation averaged $58,410; paralegals paid bonuses average $4581 annually. Many firms also offer benefit packages to attract and retain paralegals. According to the 2015 survey, 89% received some form of health insurance, 79% received some kind of retirement benefit, 75% received some form of life insurance, 82% had professional association dues paid either entirely or partially by their employer, and 68% received some form of dental coverage.

Training and Development

Some law practices offer training and development opportunities for new professional staff, including paralegals. This is usually offered in large-sized law firms where a structured development program is instituted. Specific learning experiences are planned and progress is measured. In many small- to medium-sized firms, little training is provided, and new paralegals learn through experience. Many firms, of all sizes, offer continuing education programs to staff. Some of these may be offered through in-house training programs within large-sized firms or by sending staff to external continuing education programs at the firms' expense in small- to medium-sized firms.

Exhibit 2-11
Management by Objectives Process

1. Employee and supervisor agree on the employee's major performance objectives for the coming period, including target dates for accomplishing each part of them.
2. Employee and supervisor agree on how the objectives will be measured and how it will be decided if the objectives have been met.
3. Employee and supervisor meet periodically to discuss the employee's progress toward meeting the goals.
4. An accomplishment report is prepared at the end of the period, stating which objectives were met or not met.
5. Awards or incentives are given, depending on whether the objectives were met.

Personnel Policies

personnel handbook

A manual that lists the formal personnel policies of an organization.

One of the most useful things a law office of any type can do to effectively manage its human resources is to create a comprehensive and up-to-date personnel handbook. A **personnel handbook** (sometimes called an employee handbook) lists the formal personnel policies of an organization. Personnel handbooks (1) establish formal policies on personnel matters so staff members will know what to expect of management and what management expects of them regarding personnel issues; (2) establish a standard so that all employees are treated fairly and uniformly; and (3) help to protect the law office if it is involved in litigation regarding personnel matters and to avoid government-compliance problems.

Current Personnel Law Issues

employment-at-will doctrine

Doctrine that states that an employer and employee freely enter into an employment relationship, and that either party has the right to sever the relationship at any time without reason.

Personnel-related issues are highly regulated and often litigated. The following is a sampling of some of the more important areas related to federal personnel/labor law. Exhibit 2-12 contains a summary of federal employment laws.

Employment-At-Will Doctrine

The **employment-at-will doctrine** states that an employer and employee freely enter into an employment relationship, and that either party has the right to sever the relationship at

Exhibit 2-12
Partial List of Federal Employment-Related Laws

Law	Description
Family and Medical Leave Act of 1993	Provides that eligible employees be allowed up to 12 work weeks of unpaid leave within any 12-month period for (1) the birth, adoption, or placement of a child for foster care; (2) the care of a child, spouse, or parent with a serious health condition; and (3) the employee's own serious health condition.
Civil Rights Act of 1991	Relaxes the burden of proof in discrimination claims and allows for greater recovery of damages.
Civil Rights Act of 1964	Prohibits discrimination against employees on the basis of race, color, religion, sex, or national origin. The Equal Employment Opportunity Commission (EEOC) was established to enforce this law.
Americans with Disabilities Act of 1990 (ADA)	Prohibits employers from discriminating against persons with disabilities in several different areas.
Age Discrimination in Employment Act of 1967 (ADEA) (Amended 1978)	Prohibits employers from discriminating against persons age 40 or more on the basis of their age unless age is a bona fide occupational qualification.
Equal Pay Act of 1963	Prohibits employers from basing arbitrary wage differences on gender.
Fair Labor Standards Act of 1938	Sets minimum wage and maximum basic hours of work for employees and requires overtime pay for nonexempt employees.

any time without reason. If an employee is covered by a union collective-bargaining agreement, employment contract, or civil service regulations, the employment-at-will doctrine does not apply, and the employer must comply with the terms of the contract or regulations. Employment-at-will typically happens when an employee works for an employer without any type of written agreement or reference to how long the employee will work. For example, suppose a law office hired a legal secretary in an employment-at-will state. The legal secretary did good work, but the firm subsequently changed its mind and decided that it did not need the extra position and terminated the secretary. This would be perfectly acceptable, and the secretary would have no basis for a lawsuit against the law office. For another example, suppose that the legal secretary gets a better-paying job at another law office and quits without giving notice. This also would be acceptable under employment-at-will status.

Organizations should be careful when drafting their personnel handbook to state that the policies therein are not a contract or that employees will be retained for a certain amount of time. For example, an employer should not include language such as "If you do your work satisfactorily, you will always have a job here." If a court finds that the employer gave the expectation to an employee that he or she would have a job forever (as long as the work were satisfactory), or that the policies in the personnel handbook were a type of contract, this would upset the normal expectation of employment-at-will. Personnel handbooks should contain a simple employment-at-will statement, typically near the front, that states the following:

> *Employment-At-Will*
> *It is understood that these personnel policies and any other firm documents do not constitute a contract for employment, and that any person who is hired may voluntarily leave employment without proper notice, and may be terminated by the firm any time and for any reason.*

In addition, some employers require employees to sign a statement like the one above, or they place the statement on the employment application form.

The employment-at-will doctrine does, of course, have limitations. Courts have found that at-will employees may have legal rights against employers, even though the employer is supposed to be able to terminate the employee without any reason. Instances include when the employer violates public policies, such as firing an employee for filing a workers' compensation claim, firing an employee for refusing to commit perjury, or terminating an employee to avoid paying retirement benefits or sales commissions. Other instances include terminating an employee based on discrimination or terminating an employee when the employer promised to retain the employee as long as the employee does a good job. Thus, although employment-at-will is a doctrine that works in favor of employers, it is by no means absolute. Some states even limit the employment-at-will doctrine by statute, so any organization should be familiar with its own state laws.

When employment-at-will is not in effect, or if there is an employment contract in place, the typical standard is "just cause." An employment contract is a contract between the employer and an employee, setting forth the terms and conditions of the employment relationship. "Just cause" means that before an employer can terminate an employee, the employer must have a just, reasonable cause to do so. Just cause can include many things, such as violating the company's rules and regulations, insubordination, and dishonesty.

The Family and Medical Leave Act of 1993

Family and Medical Leave Act of 1993 (FMLA)

Legislation that allows employees in certain circumstances to receive up to 12 workweeks of unpaid leave from their jobs for family- or health-related reasons.

The **Family and Medical Leave Act of 1993 (FMLA)** applies to employers with 50 or more employees and provides that eligible employees be allowed up to 12 workweeks of unpaid leave within any 12-month period for (1) the birth or adoption of a child or placement of a child for foster care; (2) the care of a child, spouse, or parent with a serious health condition; and (3) the employee's own serious health condition. To be eligible for FMLA, an employee must have one year of service with the organization and have worked at least 1250 hours in the last year. The FMLA requires that an employee granted leave under the act be returned to the same position held before the leave or be given one that is equivalent in pay, benefits, privileges, and other terms and conditions of employment. The employee also is entitled to health-care benefits during the leave. The purpose of the FMLA is to assist workers to better balance the demands of the workplace with the needs of their families.

Fair Labor Standards Act

The Fair Labor Standards Act sets minimum wage and maximum hours of work for employees. It also requires that overtime pay (one- and one-half times their normal rate) be paid to employees who work in excess of 40 hours a week. Employees do not need to be paid overtime if they fall into one of the four "white-collar" exemptions: executive, administrative, professional, or outside sales.

If an employee is exempt, it means that he or she is not required to be paid overtime wages. If an employee is nonexempt, it means that he or she is required to be paid overtime wages. Whether paralegals are exempt or nonexempt is a hotly debated issue (see Chapter 1 for a detailed discussion).

Equal Employment Opportunity

equal employment opportunity

Concept that requires employers to make employment-related decisions without arbitrarily discriminating against an individual.

Civil Rights Act of 1964

Legislation that prohibits employers from discriminating against employees or applicants on the basis of race, color, national origin, religion, or gender.

Americans with Disabilities Act of 1990 (ADA)

Legislation that prohibits employers from discriminating against employees or applicants with disabilities.

Age Discrimination in Employment Act of 1967

Legislation that prohibits employers from discriminating against employees and applicants on the basis of age when the individual is 40 or older.

Equal Pay Act of 1963

Legislation that prohibits employers from paying workers of one sex less than the rate paid to an employee of the opposite sex for work on jobs that require equal skill, effort, and responsibility and that are performed under the same working conditions.

Equal employment opportunity requires employers to make employment-related decisions without arbitrarily discriminating against an individual. This is a statement that is often seen in want ads, employment applications, and other employment-related documents. Federal laws, including the **Civil Rights Act of 1964**, prohibit employers from discriminating against employees or applicants on the basis of race, color, national origin, religion, or gender. The **Americans with Disabilities Act of 1990 (ADA)** prohibits employers from discriminating against employees or applicants with disabilities (see the following section on the ADA). The **Age Discrimination in Employment Act of 1967** prohibits employers from discriminating against employees and applicants on the basis of age where the individual is 40 or older. The **Equal Pay Act of 1963** prohibits employers from paying workers of one sex less than the rate paid to an employee of the opposite sex for work on jobs that require equal skill, effort, and responsibility and that are performed under the same working conditions. There are several other federal laws that legislate in this area. Most of the laws cited here make it unlawful for an employer to arbitrarily discriminate against employees or applicants.

Every personnel handbook should have a policy stating the law office's position on equal employment opportunity, such as:

> *Equal Employment Opportunity Statement*
> *It is the policy of the firm to apply recruiting, hiring, promotion, compensation, and professional development practices without regard to race, religion, color, national origin, sex, age, creed, handicap, veteran status, or any other characteristic protected by law.*

bona fide occupational qualification

An allowable exception to equal employment opportunity, for example, for an employee to perform a specific job, the employee must be of a certain age, sex, or religion.

An exception to equal employment opportunity is when age, sex, or religion is a **bona fide occupational qualification** (BFOQ). A BFOQ means that to perform a specific job adequately, an employee must be of a certain age, sex, or religion. A BFOQ does not apply to race or color; an example of a BFOQ would be for a position as a Catholic priest. The employer could reasonably discriminate against non-Catholics because the candidate must believe in and have knowledge of the Catholic religion in order to qualify. In general, BFOQs have been narrowly construed by most courts, and there are few positions in a law office—if any—that would qualify.

Americans with Disabilities Act

The Americans with Disabilities Act of 1990 (ADA), among other things, makes it unlawful to discriminate in employment against qualified applicants and employees with disabilities. Under the ADA, a person has a "disability" if he or she has a physical or mental impairment that substantially limits a major life activity, such as seeing, hearing, breathing, speaking, walking, performing manual tasks, working, or learning. This does not include a minor impairment of short duration, such as a broken limb, infection, or sprain. An individual with a disability also must be qualified to perform the essential functions of the job, with or without reasonable accommodation; that is, the applicant or employee must be able to satisfy the job requirements, including education, experience, skills, and licenses, and be able to perform the job. The ADA does not interfere with an employer's right to hire the best-qualified applicant but simply prohibits employers from discriminating against a qualified applicant or employee because of his or her disability.

reasonable accommodation

Accommodating a person with a disability, which may include making existing facilities readily accessible, restructuring the job, or modifying work schedules.

The ADA also requires that employers "reasonably accommodate" persons with disabilities. An employer must make **reasonable accommodation** for a person with a disability, which may include making existing facilities readily accessible, restructuring the job, or modifying work schedules. The ADA provides that individuals with disabilities have the same rights and privileges in employment as employees without disabilities. For example, if an employee lounge is in a place inaccessible to a person using a wheelchair, the lounge might be modified or relocated, or comparable facilities might be provided in a location that would enable the individual to take a break with coworkers. Persons who have been discriminated against because of a disability can receive back-pay damages, reinstatement, punitive damages, and other remedies.

Sexual Harassment

sexual harassment

Unwelcome sexual advances, requests for sexual favors, and other verbal or physical conduct of a sexual nature that create an intimidating, a hostile, or an offensive working environment. Exhibit 2-13 contains a sample antiharassment policy.

Sexual harassment includes unwelcome sexual advances, requests for sexual favors, and other verbal or physical conduct of a sexual nature that creates an intimidating, hostile, or offensive working environment.

Many people typically think of sexual harassment as a male supervisor sexually coercing a female subordinate in order for her to keep her position or to be promoted. Sexual harassment is much broader than this, however. Sexual harassment can include unwelcome sexual jokes, inappropriate sexual remarks, inappropriate e-mails, innuendos, insults, leering, subtle forms of pressure for sexual activity, vulgar or indecent language, sexual propositions, displaying sexually oriented photographs, and unwelcome and inappropriate touching, patting, and pinching.

Exhibit 2-13
Antiharassment Policy (Contents)

ANTIHARASSMENT

We have a strong commitment to provide fair employment opportunities and provide a work environment free from all types of discriminatory behavior. Harassment of any persons employed or doing business with us will not be tolerated.

Harassment includes unwelcomed advances of a verbal, physical, or sexual nature by an employee or any individual (including customers, vendors, or suppliers) that shows hostility and aversion or denigrates an employee and/or his or her relatives, friends, or associates because of his or her race, color, sex, religion, age, national origin, handicap or disability, veteran status, sexual orientation, or other status protected by law, and which

1. has the purpose or effect of unreasonably interfering with an individual's work performance,
2. has the purpose or effect or creating an intimidating, a hostile, an abusive, or an offensive working environment,
3. otherwise adversely affects an individual's work performance.

This includes acts that are intended to be "jokes" or "pranks" but that are hostile or demeaning with regard to race, color, religion, gender, national origin, age, handicap or disability, veteran status, sexual orientation, or other status protected by law.

As part of this antiharassment policy, no employee or any other individual (including customers, vendors, or suppliers) may sexually harass any employee. Sexual harassment includes unwelcome sexual advances, sexual jokes or comments, requests for sexual favors, or other unwelcome verbal or physical conduct of a sexual nature. This policy is violated when

1. submission to such conduct is made, either explicitly or implicitly, a condition of employment.
2. submission to or rejection of such conduct is used as a basis for employment-related decisions such as promotion, discharge, performance evaluation, pay adjustment, discipline, work assignment, or any other condition of employment or career development.
3. such conduct otherwise unreasonably interferes with work performance or creates an intimidating, abusive, or offensive working environment, even if it leads to no adverse job consequences.

We encourage any employee who has a question, concern, or complaint of discrimination, including harassment based on race, color, sex, religion, age, national origin, handicap or disability, veteran status, sexual orientation, or other protected status, to immediately notify of his or her supervisor or manager. If for any reason the employee would feel uncomfortable discussing the situation with his or her supervisor or manager, or if he or she feels further discussion is needed, the employee should contact the human resources manager.

All reports of inappropriate conduct will be promptly and thoroughly investigated to ensure that any improper conduct will cease immediately and corrective action will be taken to prevent a recurrence. Any employee who violates this policy will be subject to disciplinary actions, up to and including termination of employment. The complaining employee will be informed concerning resolution of the complaint as appropriate.

Complaints will be treated confidentially to the extent practical for an effective resolution. No adverse employment consequences will be suffered by the employee as a result of making a good faith complaint or taking part in the investigation of a complaint. Any person who knowingly alleges a false claim against a manager, supervisor, other employee or individual will be subject to disciplinary actions, up to and including termination of employment.

Sexual harassment does not have to involve a subordinate and a supervisor; it also can take place between persons at the same job level. Sexual harassment can involve clients as well; it has been reported that clients sometimes sexually harass law office staff. The law office has as a duty to investigate a client harassing a staff member, since the law office may be liable if it does not take appropriate action to protect its employees. Finally, although the majority of sexual harassment cases involve male employees harassing female employees, women also have been accused of sexually harassing male subordinates. Regardless of who is involved, the employer is responsible for taking corrective action. Paralegal managers play a key role in preventing harassment by communicating policies and keeping the door open to complaints

Planning

planning

The process of setting objectives, assessing the future, and developing courses of action to achieve these objectives.

Planning is the process of setting objectives, assessing future needs, and developing a course of action to achieve the objectives. Planning is the road map for meeting the firm's goals. Law firms should have short-range and long-range plans or goals. A short-term plan for a law office might include increasing profitability by 10%, while a long-term plan might include opening additional offices in other cities or expanding the practice into new legal areas. Without a plan, the law office goes about its business with no real direction. Successful law practices only happen with careful planning and the execution of good management decisions.

Why Paralegals Need to Learn to Develop Plans

As a paralegal's career expands, he or she will be given more complex assignments, duties, and tasks. As the complexity of assignments increases, the ability to develop and execute plans is crucial. The following are some plans that paralegals may prepare:

- Budgets for a paralegal department
- Case budgets for a particular case (i.e., how much the law office will expend to bring a case to trial)
- Case plans (in conjunction with a supervising attorney), including which witnesses need to be deposed; which interrogatories, requests for production, and requests for admissions need to be issued, and to whom; which experts need to be hired; which strategies the law office should pursue; what further investigation needs to be conducted, and so forth.
- Large projects, such as developing a litigation-support database in cases that have thousands of documents (paralegals and others must plan how the documents will be entered into the computer, what program, service bureau, or technique will be the most successful, and so forth)
- Administrative projects that require planning, including computerizing a law office's time and billing system from a manual system, implementing a computerized docket control system, or setting up a new filing system or law library
- The office's mission statement and some strategic plans (in small-sized law offices)
- Their own career plans (where they want to be in two to five years and how they are going to get there)

The Mission Statement and Strategic Plans

mission statement

A general, enduring statement of the purpose or intent of the law practice.

A mission statement is a particular type of plan. The **mission statement** is a general, enduring statement of the purpose or intent of the law practice. It is a plan or vision stating what the firm is about and what are its goals and objectives. It puts forth the fundamental and unique purpose that sets it apart from other firms, identifies the firm's scope, and explains why it exists. For examples, see the mission statements in Exhibit 2-14.

All law practices need a vision: they need to know where they have been and where they are going. They need to have a few guiding principles and philosophies that motivate and determine the direction of the firm. The mission statement represents the foundation for priorities and all other plans. If the firm you work for has a mission statement, memorize and use it. Every idea, new client, new employee, equipment purchase—everything you do should be judged by whether it advances the mission of the firm. If it does not advance the mission, then it may not be right for the firm.

Mission statements may include when the firm began, who founded the firm, the philosophy of the founder(s), the nature of the practice (areas of experience and expertise), the geographic service area, the departments in the practice, the philosophies toward costs, income, growth, technology, client services, and personnel, and who the firm's clients are. Mission statements are not static; they should be changed and updated as long as everyone in the firm understands the change. A mission statement is a vision that keeps the firm headed in the right direction. Without one, a law practice may spend a considerable amount of time never knowing where it is headed.

Strategic planning has always been important, but the present circumstances make it imperative for law offices to consider strengths and weaknesses, evaluate the competition, and devise a game plan that will set the course to the future.

Exhibit 2-14 Law Office Mission Statements

Large-sized law firm	*The mission of the Davis, Saunders, & Lavely law firm is to deliver high-quality legal services to business clients nationwide through personalized, value-added service and a strict adherence to the highest ethical standards.*
Corporate law department	*The KGLPE law department seeks to offer the corporation the best legal services available while keeping costs to a minimum. The law department will utilize four divisions: labor, environmental, litigation, and general business. The use of in-house staff will be maximized. Only matters of vital importance to the corporation will be contracted out. The other departments of the corporation will be defined as our **"clients."** Our clients will be given the same high-quality legal services as provided by outside counsel. Our clients will be surveyed on an annual basis, and we will obtain a **90 percent** average approval rating.*
Small-sized law firm	*Woodson and Stetson is a full-service, client-centered law firm. Our goal is to provide outstanding, responsive services to our clients at a reasonable cost. We represent clients as we ourselves would want to be represented. We use a team approach to provide legal services to our clients, including lawyers, paralegals, and office associates to ensure a professional level of response to our clients' needs.*

Exhibit 2-15 Strategic Planning Process

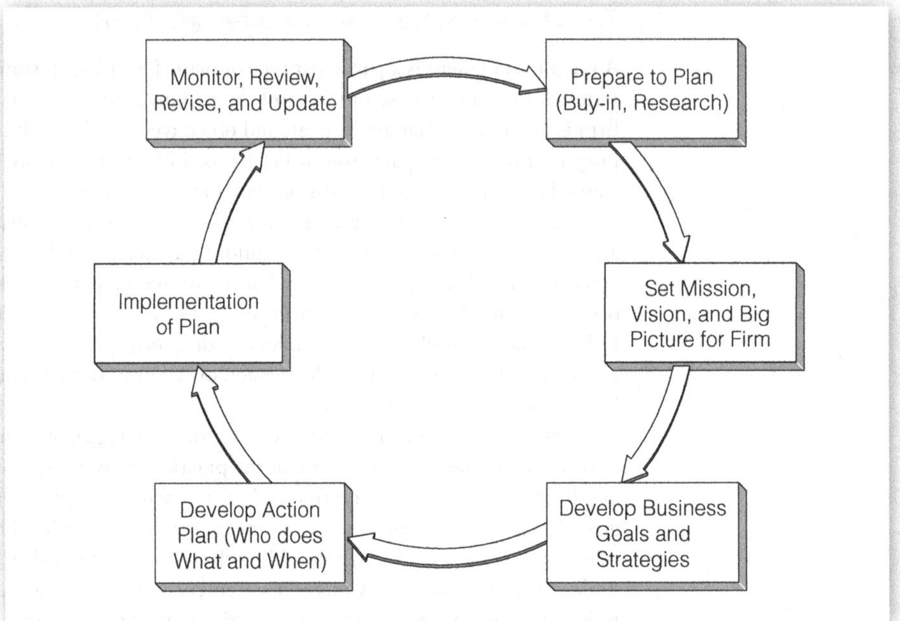

strategic planning

Determining the major goals of a firm and then adopting the courses of action necessary to achieve those goals.

Strategic planning is the process of determining the major goals of a firm and then adapting the courses of action and allocating resources necessary to achieve those goals. Exhibit 2-15 shows a diagram of the strategic planning process. For instance, a strategic plan may include expanding a firm's practice into additional areas of the law, such as adding a tax or labor law department. Before you can sell a legal service to someone, though, you must have a buyer; that is, you should not focus on what you want to sell but rather on what the buyer or the client wants to buy. Strategic plans usually answer the questions contained in Exhibit 2-16.

Ideas on How to Plan Effectively

The following are some ideas on how to plan effectively.

- **Gather timely, relevant information.** It is axiomatic that, without good information, you cannot possibly make an effective plan. Too many times, people make plans based on faulty information. Gathering timely and relevant information is one of the most important things you can do to make sure your plan will succeed. You can gather information from public libraries, law libraries, the Internet, Westlaw, LexisNexis, the American Bar Association (ABA), local, state, and national bar associations, law office surveys, consultants, other firms, and historical records from your own firm. Good information is a key to making good decisions.
- **Write all plans.** Goals and plans should be in writing as constant reminders of where you are supposed to be headed.

Exhibit 2-16 Key Questions a Law Office Strategic Plan Should Answer

Who are our clients and what legal services will we provide? (See all of the questions regarding practice management in Exhibit 2-3.)

Who will manage the firm? Is our governing structure still adequate? Evaluate the current methods used to set and implement firm policy.

Assess the effectiveness of the executive committee, managing partner, planning committee, compensation committee, and legal administrator.

What are the general goals of the firm? Rank them in order of importance.

What new geographic area of the country/world will we enter?

What sources of finance will we use?

Will we rent or purchase office space and equipment?

What kind of technology and systems will we use to provide our legal services to clients?

What marketing channels will we use to attract clients?

How will we achieve continual growth?

What was the firm's growth rate over the past three years? Can the projected growth rate for the next three years be established with any degree of certainty?

Does the firm have established bill rate requirements for legal staff? Are they adequate or should they be revisited?

What is the capability of the firm to meet its future needs within existing practice areas? Which areas need improvement?

What is the culture of the firm? Does it suit the firm well?

What kinds of insurance will we need to purchase (health, disability, life, malpractice)?

How many employees will we need and in what positions?

Should we use alternatives to permanent staff such as temporary workers, contract workers, or should we use outsourcing techniques?

How will we recruit, train, and retain the right people for our firm?

Will the firm merge with another firm to obtain a competitive advantage?

Environmental Analysis—Consider demographic, political, and economic factors when considering strategic planning. How will these factors affect how the firm will serve the clients?

Industry Analysis—Consider the legal environment as a whole, including surveys of other law firms, average profit margins, growth rates, costs, etc. How does the firm compare to industry averages?

Competitive Analysis—Who are the firm's major competitors? What are their strengths and weaknesses? What are your competitors' business strategies?

Internal Analysis—Compare your strategies with those of your major competitors, and compare your strengths and weaknesses to those of your competitors.

Determine Threats and Opportunities—Consider what new markets are the most attractive for the firm and then analyze the firm's competitive position in the marketplace, identify any threats that competitors may have, and identify opportunities resulting from market conditions or a competitor's weakness.

- **Involve everyone in the planning process.** Always ask for comments from anyone who would be affected by the plan. You want to build a consensus so that everyone will have input into the plan and will support it when it comes time to implement it. People promote plans that they perceive as being their own, either in part or as a whole. This is the "ownership" concept. Soliciting input from others opens the lines of communication and allows all firm members to feel that they have a stake in the action, that their thoughts are important, and that they are needed. When you are involving others in the process, do not judge their suggestions; listen to them and consider them. Your job is to facilitate communication and to provide a nonthreatening environment in which everyone can participate.
- **Stick to the plan.** It takes an amazing amount of patience to stick to a plan and follow through with what you started. It does a firm little good to make a detailed and wonderful plan and then scrap it two months later. It takes commitment from everyone involved to give the plan a chance to succeed.
- **Recognize that planning is a continuous process.** Planning is a continuous process of making improvements; it is not a onetime effort in which you develop a plan and then never revisit it. If all you do is make a plan and never follow it up or monitor it, you have wasted the firm's time.
- **Monitor the plan and communicate the results to others.** Always monitor the progress of the plan. One way to do this is to make a timeline or Gantt chart to track the expected progress over time. A **Gantt chart** is a plan or timeline of the projected begin and end dates of a project. A Gantt chart breaks a large project down into specific jobs or items that must be accomplished. As an item is finished, it can be marked completed (see Exhibit 2-17). Gantt charts are also good at simplifying and communicating complicated projects. Most people find charts more reader friendly than straight text.

Gantt chart

A plan or timeline of the projected begin and end dates of a project.

Periodically, you should check the progress of the project to determine whether the plan needs to be revised or completely overhauled to accomplish its objectives. One way to do this is to hold monthly planning meetings or to otherwise communicate the progress of the plan to others by keeping them informed about how the project is going. If possible, you should build into the plan quantifiable means of progress so others can see that the plan is working as expected and resources are not being wasted.

Marketing Management

marketing

The process of educating consumers on the quality legal services that a law office can provide.

Marketing is the process of educating consumers about the legal services the law office provides. It is not enough to simply service existing clients. Law firms, like other businesses in a competitive environment, must continue to bring in new business in order to grow and survive. Marketing has become an important element of management in today's law office. Marketing efforts include market research, discovering and developing a market niche regarding a client need that has previously been unrecognized or unmet, creating a "brand" name for the firm so that it is recognized by potential clients, and advertising efforts through brochures, word-of-mouth/referrals, networking, television, radio, and the Internet. Chapter 7 contains a full chapter on legal marketing.

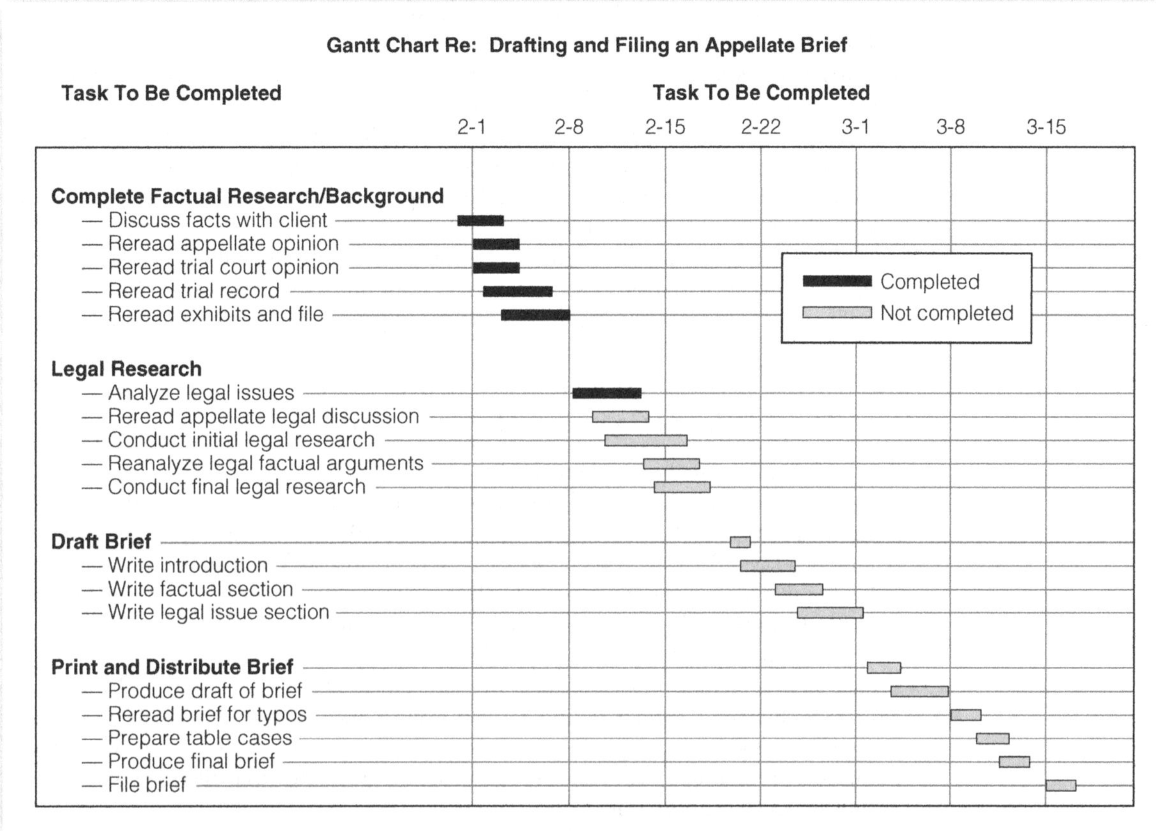

Exhibit 2-17 A Gantt Chart

Organizing, Policies, and Systems

organizing

The process of arranging people and physical sources to carry out plans and accomplish objectives.

system

A consistent or an organized way of doing something.

Organizing is the process of arranging people and physical resources to carry out plans and accomplish objectives. Effective legal administrators create order through setting policy and creating effective systems for accomplishing tasks. A **system** is a consistent or an organized way of doing something. A system allows you to create a set procedure for doing something as opposed to dealing with activities or problems in an ad hoc manner. Without a system, each time a legal service or an administrative function is performed, the person performing the task would rely solely on his or her memory to complete the task. Productivity and accuracy suffer when staff must recreate processes each time a task is done. By developing a system, staff members can take advantage of the experience and expertise of others in the law office. A system collects experience and expertise and passes it on to others. Systems preserve the procedures that have worked successfully in the past, but must be reviewed periodically to allow for future evolution. Systems guarantee quality because the same mistakes are not made twice.

substantive task

A task that relates to the process of actually performing legal work for clients.

administrative task

A task relating to the internal practices and duties involved with operating or managing a law office.

Systems can be used for both substantive tasks and administrative tasks. A **substantive task** is a task that relates to the process of actually performing legal work for clients. An **administrative task** (or a business-related task) is one that relates to the internal practices and duties involved with operating or managing a law office.

Substantive systems include using form files, checklists, and detailed instructions to standardize many types of legal tasks. Certain areas of the law are particularly suitable for systems because of their routine nature, including bankruptcy, divorces, adoptions, probate, estate planning, and workers' compensation.

Administrative tasks such as docket control, timekeeping and billing, purchasing, and human resource management can also be set up using an established system of procedures. A staff manual establishes administrative policies and procedures and documents how things will be accomplished administratively.

Law Practice Policies and Procedures—the Staff Manual

Read and digest any staff manual provided.

One of the main systems is a law office staff manual, also called a policy and procedures manual. The purpose of a staff manual is to set out in writing the standing policies and procedures of a law office. The types of policies covered by the staff manual depend on the law office, but they can range from personnel policies and how files will be maintained to how letters and pleadings will be formatted (see Exhibit 2-18). Staff manuals establish and document an efficient and cost-effective way of handling the day-to-day operations of the firm. The manual allows everyone to operate under the same procedures and to quickly find consistent answers to common questions. Without a staff manual, each person develops his or her own particular method for accomplishing tasks. Law offices need uniformity so that elements are not missed or forgotten. Staff manuals can be used to guarantee each client the same high-quality legal services, every time.

Staff manuals are particularly helpful when training new employees. New employees can immediately get a feel for how the firm operates and what procedures are to be followed just by reading the manual. This makes the orientation process quicker and less difficult. The idea that staff manuals are only needed in large-sized firms is a misconception. Small-sized law offices, legal aid offices, and government and corporate law departments need written procedures as well.

What Systems or Subjects Are Included in the Staff Manual?

Exhibit 2-18 contains a list of systems that are often found in staff manuals. Staff manuals usually cover such items as how the office is organized, ethical and confidentiality policies, personnel-related policies, the use of office equipment, and office procedures for opening new files. Staff manuals can be adapted to the needs of the specific law practice. In general, if management has to reiterate a policy more than once or twice on a matter of importance, the policy should be put in writing.

policy

A specific statement that sets out what is or is not acceptable.

Drafting Policies and Procedures

Staff manuals can contain both policies and procedures. Although the concepts are similar, they also are very different from each other. A **policy** is a specific statement that sets out

Exhibit 2-18
Partial Law Office Staff Manual—Table of Contents

Source: Adapted from Wert, R., & Hatoff, H. (2004). *Office Policy and Procedures Manual* (4th ed., p. iii). American Bar Association.

Part 1

Committees and Departments

1.1 Committees
1.2 Departments Based on Areas of Law

Part 2

Office Policies

2.1 Equal Opportunity Employer
2.2 Diversity
2.3 Policy on Sexual Harassment
2.4 Americans with Disabilities Act of 1990 (ADA)
2.5 The Family and Medical Leave Act of 1993
2.6 Quality Management/Client Relations
2.7 Office Hours
2.8 Overtime
2.9 Weekly Time Report
2.10 Code of Personal and Professional Conduct
2.11 Professional Attitude
2.12 Personal Appearance

Part 3

Personnel Benefits and Policies

3.1 Employee Classifications
3.2 Recruitment and Hiring
3.3 Compensation
3.4 Training
3.5 Probation or Trial Period

Part 4

Preparation of Correspondence, Memoranda, and Legal Documents

4.1 Prepare Letters
4.2 Prepare Memoranda
4.3 Prepare Drafts
4.4 Prepare Legal Opinion Letters
4.5 Legal Documents

Part 5

Office Security and Emergency Procedures

5.1 Data Protection
5.2 Emergency Procedures
5.3 Medical Emergencies, Accidents or Work Injuries
5.4 Disaster Planning and Recovery

Part 6

Financial Management

6.1 Trust Account
6.2 Receipts
6.3 Disbursements
6.4 Petty Cash
6.5 Billing Procedures
6.6 Timekeeping Records

(continued)

Exhibit 2-18
Partial Law Office Staff Manual—Table of Contents *(continued)*

Part 7
File System

7.1 The File Opening Form and Worksheet
7.2 Opening a New File
7.3 Removal of Files from the Record Room
7.4 Returning Files to the Record Room
7.5 Closing Files
7.6 Form Files
7.7 Electronic Files

Part 8
Technology

8.1 Policy on the Use of Technology
8.2 Training
8.3 Dealing with Computer Viruses
8.4 Handling Computer Crashes
8.5 Network
8.6 Word Processing
8.7 Docket/Calendar Software
8.8 Time/Billing Software
8.9 Fax/Modems/Internet
8.10 LexisNexis/Westlaw
8.11 Security

Part 9
Library

9.1 The Function and Use of the Library
9.2 Library Organization and Functions
9.3 The Librarian
9.4 Use by Non-Firm Personnel
9.5 Library Copies of the Firm's Work Product
9.6 Client Charges

procedure
A series of steps that must be followed to accomplish a task.

what is or is not acceptable (see Exhibit 2-13). A **procedure** is a series of steps that must be followed to accomplish a task. Some firms have separate manuals for policies and procedures. All policies and/or procedures should be detailed, accurate, and succinct; procedures should be clearly stated, easy to read, and should assign specific responsibilities, stating *who* is responsible for the tasks. In addition, whenever possible, a due date also is included so that staff members know exactly *when* items are due. When writing policies and procedures, a balance should be struck between having too many details (i.e., overregulating) and having too few. The aim is not to make a bureaucratic, detail-ridden manual, but to have a usable, practical guide.

Staff Manuals from an Ethics Perspective

Staff manuals also are important from an ethical point of view. The manual allows management to draft policies that will deter ethical violations. For instance, a common ethical problem is neglect of client matters. A manual can address this by stating which person is responsible for keeping the calendar, how items will be put on the calendar, and what steps will be taken to avoid missing the deadline. In addition, the staff manual can be used to set out policies on ethical situations, such as the need for strict confidentiality of client information.

Staff Manuals on the Law Office Intranet

intranet

An internal information distribution system used only by a law firm staff.

An **intranet** is an internal information distribution system based on Internet technology. In short, it is a private "Internet" that is used only by law firm staff. When the staff manual is on an intranet, it is immediately accessible to all staff with access to a computer; it can be updated electronically; and it can save thousands of dollars in reduced paper and copying costs.

An intranet can also be used to provide information related to

- Accounting and billing—Access to client time/billing records, firm accounting policies, and accounting forms.
- Law library resources—Access to form files, brief banks, CD-ROM products, Westlaw, LexisNexis, and links to many legal sites on the Internet.
- Human resources and benefits—Human resource information, including job openings, compensation plans, legal postings, benefit plans, and links to benefit-provider sites.
- Continuing legal education—Information related to upcoming CLE seminars and links to local and national bar associations.
- Client tracking—Client directories, matter lists, contact information, matter numbers, and other client-related information.
- Practice areas—Separate pages can be created for each of a firm's departments and specialties. Each specialty can have information specifically related to that area of the law, including Internet links to government regulations and statutes, case law, discussion groups, and resources developed by the firm itself to assist practitioners.

Facilities Management

facilities management

Encompasses planning, designing, controlling, and managing a law office's building or office space.

Facilities management encompasses planning, designing, controlling, and managing a law office's building or office space. Facilities management includes a variety of subject areas, such as property acquisition, moves/construction/remodeling, space planning/office design/furniture, parking, cleaning/maintenance/grounds, common areas, environmental considerations (lighting, electrical, climate, and plumbing), and security/safety/disaster recovery.

Property Acquisition

Property acquisition refers to acquiring space in which the law office will be housed, including purchasing a building/property or leasing office space. Property acquisition is an important and expensive proposition for any law office, whether it is a large-sized law firm looking for a long-term lease for a number of floors in a downtown office building (to be near business clients) or a sole practitioner who concentrates on family law and might purchase a house or small building near a residential area. Depending on the office, the practice may want to be on public transportation routes, accessible from major highways, and other such considerations.

Moves/Construction/Remodeling

Facilities management also includes moving from one location to another, constructing a whole new office from scratch, or constructing/remodeling existing office space to meet new needs or demands. All of these areas include a great deal of planning and organizing.

Space Planning/Office Design/Furniture

Office space is important for many reasons; office space and decor help define the law office's image. The facility should be functional and practical, and it should work for the particular law office's structure and needs.

One of the first aspects of space planning that must be considered is the organization of the law office. Law office management must decide upon the needs of the office. For example, management must decide whether practice groups will be grouped together or apart; whether computers, files, and other equipment will be centralized or decentralized; what types of offices are needed (e.g., number and size of conference rooms, kitchen area, and separate postage and copy areas); and whether the office will need to expand in the near future. An effective way of determining needs is to survey the staff members, ask them what they think they need, and then use that information in the planning process. Some offices, especially medium- to large-sized offices, hire consultants and architects to help with these as well as other issues.

Furniture should not only project an office's image but also provide sufficient work surfaces, be comfortable and usable, and efficiently use the space within the law office. There are thousands of different styles of furniture, including traditional (wood and plastic laminate); contemporary (wood, metal, and laminate); high-tech (glass, wood, and metal); and ergonomic (laminate, wood, and metal).

Many law offices use system furniture or module design, including movable partitions or panels, and work surfaces, file cabinets, and drawers that attach to the partitions instead of interior walls. The panels typically have electric cabling that runs through the bottom of each of the electrical outlets. In this way, law offices can be completely flexible and use their space more wisely than ever before. The major disadvantages of interior landscaping are increased noise and decreased privacy. Interior landscaping has gained in popularity because of the increased cost of office space; minimizing the amount of space a law office uses reduces rent and maintenance costs.

Some studies have shown that the most negative feature of interior landscaping is not the increased noise but the lack of personal privacy, especially when short partitions that allow people to see over the top are used, and when the entryways face out, allowing others to see into the work space.

CORRELATION BETWEEN SPACE AND COST Any law office administrator will tell you that there is a direct correlation between the amount of office space needed and the cost. Office space has become increasingly more expensive, especially in metropolitan areas. Lease payments represent a large overhead expense, which can put pressure on cash flow because it is a fixed cost, meaning that it is incurred every month without relation to whether the office is having a good month, financially speaking. Thus, offices have struggled to become physically smaller and more compact and to use the space they have wisely.

Parking

Adequate parking for both employees and clients should be taken into consideration when choosing office space. Poor parking is a common complaint of the law offices in downtown business districts.

Cleaning/Maintenance/Grounds

Facilities management also includes having the facility cleaned (typically through a cleaning service), repairing or replacing items that break, and being responsible for the office grounds, including lawn care, snow removal, and more.

Common Areas

Facilities management may also include being responsible for common areas in the law office, such as waiting room, kitchen areas, conference rooms, bathrooms, and storage rooms, to name a few.

Environmental Considerations

Environmental considerations include a variety of important topics such as lighting, electrical, climate, and plumbing. Depending on the size of the law office and the number of employees, each of these areas can be extremely technical and involve government standards, and many are operated by sophisticated computer systems. Many law offices hire a facilities management company to provide maintenance and other services regarding environmental matters.

Security and Workplace Violence

Law office security and safety is an extremely important aspect of facilities management. Tragically, violence to attorneys, paralegals, court personnel, and other legal professionals happens quite frequently. Disgruntled clients assault all kinds of law offices all over the country, from the rural solo practitioner to large downtown law firms in skyscrapers.

On December 8, 2006, Joe Jackson, a disgruntled client, forced a security guard at gunpoint to bring him to the 38th floor of a downtown Chicago building and the offices of Wood, Phillips, Katz, Clark & Mortimer. Once inside the firm's offices, he chain locked the entrance doors and began shooting, killing three people before he was killed by a sniper.

There are many ways to provide security, including installing security systems, limiting access to private areas of the law office using locked and secure doors that open only with security cards, installing locking doors with buzzers at reception areas, hiring security guards, installing security cameras, issuing identification and/or building passes, and limiting elevator service after certain hours. Law offices simply cannot afford to ignore the security issues that face them. Exhibit 2-19 lists suggestions for tightening security. The type of security you use depends on the size of the law firm, the type of building, and many other factors.

Exhibit 2-19
Strengthening Law Office Security

- **Never allow free access throughout your office**—The golden rule of security is to **never** allow people free access throughout your office. Access to your office can be limited by restricting points of entry. If you are in a small building, lock the back door and do not allow the public to use it. Require the public to use the front door and have a receptionist there at all times, monitoring the entrance with a panic button that will contact the police or others in the case of an emergency.

  If your office is in a high-rise building, security stations and/or a receptionist can be posted at the entrance to the building or your suite.
- **Limit the public to a waiting room with a locked door to inner offices**—A good way to limit access to your office is to secure your waiting room. Simply put, the door from your waiting room to your inner offices should be locked and have a buzzer installed. By having a locked door to your inner offices, you restrict access and require the visitor to check in with the receptionist. This is similar to many doctor's offices, where a receptionist sits behind a sliding window and sounds a buzzer that enables the visitor to enter the internal part of the office.
- **Issue security badges**—Another way to limit access in large-sized offices is to issue security cards or badges to personnel, and to require visitors to check in and be issued a visitor badge.
- **Use security cards**—Many offices use electronic locked doors that use a keyless entry system. If a person does not have a security card, he or she cannot open the locked door.
- **Monitor entrances**—Entrances to the building or suites should be monitored, when possible, by using security cameras, buzzers, security guards, keyless entry systems, or other such methods.
- **Remind staff about security issues and issue policies**—Always remind staff about the importance of security issues, and draft policies regarding security issues. Always be prepared.
- **Train staff members on security issues**—Whenever possible, staff members should be trained regarding safety awareness and security issues.
- **Large buildings may install metal detectors**—Metal detectors may be installed in large-sized law offices.

Law offices also need formal policies on security and workplace violence issues, such as the following:

Doors

The doors between interoffice access and the reception area should be locked at all times.

Admission of Visitors and Strangers

No persons, other than employees, shall be allowed within the main law firm office area without being escorted by an employee. Any one not authorized in the office area must identify themselves and their purpose for being in the office. Please contact the receptionist if you encountered unauthorized persons in the office, if it is after normal business hours, contact the local police.

Workplace Violence

The firm's policy prohibits any acts or threats of violence by any party against any employee in or about the firm's facilities or elsewhere at any time. There is a zero-tolerance policy regarding any firm. The firm is committed to:

1. *provide a safe and healthy work environment;*
2. *take prompt remedial action against anyone who engages in any threatening behavior or acts of violence or who uses any abusive or threatening language or gestures on the firm's premises or while on firm business;*
3. *take appropriate action when dealing with employees, former employees, or visitors to the firm's facilities who engage in such behavior. Action may include disciplinary action including termination, notifying the police, and prosecuting violators of this policy to the maximum extent of the law;*
4. *prohibit employees, former employees, and visitors, other than law enforcement personnel, from bringing firearms or other weapons onto the firm's premises.*

SAFETY Safety issues include ensuring the building has a sprinkler system, fire alarms, emergency power/lighting, fire escapes, and similar features. All law offices should also have an evacuation plan and policies in their firm's staff manual regarding what to do in case of a fire, earthquake, or bomb threat. A policy should be in place regarding what to do in case of a medical emergency, a work injury, or an accident. It is also prudent for the law office to have safety-related items such as bandages, gauze, and related items on hand. Large-sized law offices may have oxygen and more advanced medical supplies as well. Occasional fire drills (and related drills) are also prudent and advised.

DISASTER RECOVERY PLANNING Disaster recovery planning also tends to fall under the scope of facilities management. All law offices should have a disaster recovery plan in place that can be implemented in the case of a disaster. The **disaster recovery plan** includes information on how the law office will rebuild and recover from a total disaster. Copies of the disaster recovery plan should be kept off-site. It is important to have information and plans in place that can be implemented at a moment's notice.

disaster recovery plan

A disaster recovery plan includes information on how the law office will rebuild and recover from a total disaster.

Typical information contained in a disaster recovery plan would include the following:

- Who is in charge of overseeing implementation of the disaster recovery operation? What key individuals make up the disaster recovery team, and what are their functions and responsibilities? Who will be contacted, and how? Where is the designated meeting place (and an alternative) if the whole facility is unavailable?
- What services/areas/departments have been determined as vital to the recovery operation? What are the steps, components, and alternative strategies for making each area/department operational? What will each department require in terms of resources (computers, minimal office space, desk, chairs, information, etc.) to be operational? All of this must be put in writing, and a copy should be maintained off-site.
- How do firm personnel obtain information and instructions on what to do when a disaster happens?
- Where are important papers and computer backup data located? Important documents should always be maintained off-site in the case of a disaster. These include copies of leases; names, addresses, and phone numbers of all staff; bank account information; copies of insurance policies; a listing of all clients, including contact information for the client and opposing counsel in cases; complete firm-wide inventory list (computers, furniture, art, library books, fixtures, etc.); disaster recovery plans for each department; and computer backup tapes.
- In the case of a disaster, what vendors and companies have been identified in advance who can help to assist with restoration, and who are the contact people for these vendors?

If you wait until the disaster occurs to start planning, it's too late. By that time, you could lose everything. If everything *is* lost, can the firm recover? Can the law office continue as a business? What are the ethical problems with losing everything related to a client's case? If a law office of any size loses everything in a disaster, there is a good chance that it will not be able to recover; that's why disaster recovery planning is so important.

Office Services Management

office services management

It refers to the administration of a number of internal systems and services in a law office. These include mail, copy, fax, and telecommunication services, among others.

Office services management refers to a number of internal systems and services in a law office. Office service responsibilities include management of the mail room, copiers and copy facility, file/records management (discussed in Chapter 9), telecommunications (including telephone systems, voice mail, fax machines, and video conferencing), among others.

Mail Room

Medium- and large-sized law offices have mail rooms that manage and sort incoming mail. They also weigh and place postage on mail with either a postage meter device or electronic means. They may also coordinate overnight delivery services. In small-sized law offices, a clerk, receptionist, or legal secretary may perform these services.

Copy Machines

Copy machines are a staple of every law office, regardless of size or type. Law offices must routinely copy documents for internal files, clients, courts, opposing counsel, and others. While the delivery of documents through electronic means is popular, there is no end in sight for the copier's usage. It is not uncommon, even in a solo practitioner's office, to make tens of thousands of copies a year. Some large-sized law offices have a centralized copy center or department that has its own staff. Other law offices have one or more self-serve copy machines located throughout the office while some have both a centralized department, which handles large documents, and self-serve copy machines for smaller jobs.

As an alternative to the high cost of purchasing and maintaining copy machines, some law offices outsource this function to a vendor. The vendor provides the copy machine, maintenance, supplies, and personnel. In many cases, the vendor is given office space and provides these services on-site.

BILLING FOR CLIENT COPIES Making sure that clients are properly billed for copies made for their case can be problematic, given the large number of cases and copies. Some law offices have staff members complete expense slips detailing which client the copies were made for, how many copies were made, and why. Some copy machines allow the user to enter a client identification number, which then tracks the number of copies to be billed to each client, while other machines use client copy cards to calculate the number of copies.

File/Records Management

Law offices of all types must have an effective file/records management system that allows the practice to store, track, and retrieve information about cases in a logical, efficient, and expeditious manner. File/records management is covered in detail in Chapter 9.

Telecommunications

Telecommunications is a rapidly evolving area that has many aspects important to law offices. Among these are telephone systems, voice mail, fax machines, video conferencing, and voice communications through Internet known as VoIP (Voice over Internet Protocol).

TELEPHONE EQUIPMENT Telephones are vital to any law office because they are the means by which staff members communicate with clients, opposing counsel, courts, witnesses, and one another.

Telephone systems for law offices can cost from $1000 to $100,000 or more, depending on the number of phone stations and outgoing lines needed.

VOICE MAIL Voice mail is a computerized telecommunications system that stores and delivers voice messages. Callers are able to leave a detailed message directly, without going through a secretary or other individual where messages can be distorted or miscommunication can take place. An individual can then retrieve his or her messages—either on-site or off-site—by dialing his other "mailbox." Voice mail is available 24 hours a day, so clients can leave messages for people even when the law office is not open. Voice mail is an integral part of many law offices.

FAX MACHINES Fax machines are used by most law offices. Fax machines allow a user to electronically transmit a document's image to a receiving fax machine at another location, which prints the document that was sent. Fax machines are easy to operate and come in hundreds of styles with many features. Some fax machines work in conjunction with a computer system and allows a user to fax a document, such as a word processing file, from his or her computer.

Faxes have become so accepted in the legal community that many courts allow documents to be faxed if the documents are not more than 10–15 pages long.

FAXES AND CONFIDENTIALITY Faxes should be sent very carefully because an improper or a misdirected fax transmission can lead to breach of client confidentiality, loss of attorney–client privilege, and legal malpractice. All fax cover pages for law offices should have some kind of confidentiality disclaimer on them, such as the following:

> CONFIDENTIALITY NOTICE—*This fax message contains legally confidential and privileged information intended for the sole use of the individual(s) or organizations named above. If you are not the intended recipient of this fax message, you are hereby notified that any dissemination, distribution, or copy of this message is strictly prohibited. If you have received this fax in error, please notify us immediately by telephone and return this fax to us by mail.*

Other precautions that can be taken to ensure fax information stays confidential include assuring that everyone using the fax machine knows how to use it correctly; making sure that everyone operating the fax machine understands that a misdirected fax can destroy client confidentiality and the attorney–client privilege and can result in charges of malpractice; and requiring the sender to check to make sure the material has been received.

TELECOMMUNICATIONS AND CLIENT CONFIDENTIALITY Client confidentiality should always be considered when dealing with phone systems. This is especially true considering the amount of time that paralegals spend on the phone. Users should never broadcast client names over the law office's intercom/paging system; users should also be very careful about who is in the room when a client's case is being discussed on the phone. Conversations on mobile phones, particularly those that include confidential or sensitive information, should be limited, if possible. Some radios/scanners have the ability to pick up these frequencies.

Video Conferencing

Video conferencing allows users in remote sites to see and hear one another via a monitor and speaker using telephone lines, computer equipment, and a camera. Medium- and large-sized law offices may have these internally. Small-sized law offices can use a vendor for video conferencing. Video conferencing may be used internally to connect remote offices for a meeting and, on occasion, may be used for depositions, among other things.

Technology and Information Systems Management

It is difficult to overestimate the impact that technology has had on the practice of law in the last 25 years. Technology, computers, networks, mobile computing, and information systems in general have completely changed the way that legal professionals practice law and run a law office business. There is virtually no aspect of how legal services are delivered to clients and how a law office is operated that has not been affected. While technology has greatly increased productivity and efficiency, enhanced systems for communicating, and made researching and finding information easier and more accessible, all this has come at a price. Many large- and small-sized law offices struggle to keep up with technology advancements and with finding the money and resources to continue to enhance their technology. Recent surveys found that, on average, firms annually spend between $8000 and $17,000 per attorney. The commitment to and reliance on technology at medium- and large-sized firms are substantial.

Most law offices, even small ones, must now have dedicated staff to support the myriad of computer systems in a typical law practice. Most medium- and large-sized firms must have a host of computer professionals including a chief information officer, who are solely responsible for the firm's technology. Exhibit 2-20 shows a partial list of common technology in law offices. The list grows every year as new technology is introduced.

Paralegals and Technology

Paralegals, like attorneys and other members of the legal team use common electronic resources such as e-mail, the Internet, word processing, calendar/docket control, and time and billing programs on a daily basis. Most law offices are equipped with network computers and paralegals, especially those with technology training are consulted concerning technology decisions made at their firms.

Hardware

The selection of currently available computer hardware is overwhelming. Law offices can choose from many different types of computer hardware and manufacturers, depending on

Exhibit 2-20
Partial List of Typical Technology in a Law Office

Hardware (and Software) Used by Technical Staff	Software Used by Legal Professionals or Administrators	Telecommunications
Desktop or laptop computer, monitor, speakers, storage devices, and mouse for every staff member	Word processing	Internet
Networked or stand-alone printer	Spreadsheet	Intranet
Networked or stand-alone color printer	Database	Extranet
Multifunction printer (printer, fax, scanner, copier)	Presentation	Westlaw/LexisNexis/other online service
Local network servers, cards, wireless, etc.	E-mail	Instant messaging
Wide-area network servers	Internet browser	Blogs
Laptop computers	Docket control/calendar	
PDAs (personal digital assistants, handheld computers)	Litigation support	
Mobile phones	Time and billing	
Scanner	Accounting	
Operating system software on every computer, laptop, and handheld device	Case management	
Virus protection software	Document assembly	
Digital projector	Document management	
Digital camera	Electronic discovery	
Digital video camera	Knowledge management	
Portable printer	PDF creation	
Firewall	Scanning/optical character recognition	
Central storage devices	Speech recognition	
Tape backup	Trial presentation	
Digital printers	Legal-specific programs	
Computerized telecommunication equipment	Graphic/illustration programs	
Computerized security systems	Project management	
Web design/development software	Citation checking	
Web site management	Conflict checking	
Document sharing software	Transcript/deposition management	
Portable hard drives	Contact management	
Remote access software		

the type of operation and objectives they have. Options include desktop, laptop, handheld, wireless, and mobile technology. Due to the wide selection of available hardware and the fact that computer technology prices continue to fall, any size law firm has access to adequate technology to operate their office in today's electronic business environment.

Mobile computing is also changing the way legal professionals practice. Paralegals and attorneys have nearly constant access to their firms and information via networks, wireless technology, and the Internet. Legal professionals can access data from the courthouse, their homes, the road, and nearly anywhere in the world. Court-bound lawyers can now take entire cases with them on a laptop, including pleadings, transcripts of arguments and proceedings, court records, depositions, discovery, and millions of documents, all accessible and ready to be retrieved.

Software

Law offices have a wide selection of software that includes general business and productivity programs, general legal programs (such as time and billing), legal programs designed for a specific type of practice (such as software designed for professionals practicing in the area of taxes or bankruptcy) and legal programs designed to perform electronic discovery and trial presentations.

ELECTRONIC MAIL Electronic mail is the single most used software application by legal professionals.

Electronic mail (e-mail) allows users to send and receive messages using a computer. When an Internet account is opened, the user is given an e-mail address and can then send and receive messages. Hundreds of millions of people use e-mail to communicate every day.

There are many advantages to using e-mail such as messages can be sent, almost instantaneously, nearly anywhere in the world; e-mail is very inexpensive (the cost of an Internet account); word processing, sound, and graphic files can be attached to e-mail messages; messages can be sent, read, and replied to at the user's convenience; e-mail prevents telephone tag; messages can be sent to groups of people at the same time; users can get their messages from anywhere; and messages can be saved, tracked, and managed electronically. A common client complaint is that legal professionals are often very busy and hard to reach. E-mail allows legal professionals and clients to communicate with one another quickly and conveniently.

E-Mail in the Legal Environment

E-mail is now a major means of communicating with clients, other attorneys, and courts, and most paralegals use e-mail in their jobs every day. E-mail is being used in legal organizations for everything from routine correspondence to billing, newsletters, and filing court papers. Most clients now demand e-mail access to their lawyers and paralegals. The security of e-mail has long been a concern to legal professionals, but given the dramatic increase with confidential and privileged communications/documents sent via e-mail, security is now critical. The issue of security can be handled in a number of ways, including requiring clients to provide oral or written consent to sending confidential information via e-mail, adding a confidentiality statement at the end of all e-mails, using encryption software, or simply not using e-mail to send confidential documents. In addition, new uses of e-mail arise often; the service of process by e-mail has even been approved by a few courts.

E-Mail Encryption and Digital Signatures

Because e-mail can pass through many network servers before it reaches its destination, it is subject to being read by system administrators, hackers, or others. E-mail is often considered to be more like a postcard than a sealed letter in this respect. Some legal organizations use encryption software to protect confidential e-mails sent to others. Encryption software is used to lock e-mail so that it can be opened only by the intended recipient.

Business E-Mail Etiquette and Tips Most people are familiar with e-mail. However, there is a difference between using e-mail for personal use and business use. In business, you must be very careful about your e-mail usage. The following points provide some important tips for using e-mail in a law office setting.

- *Be succinct and clear, and use short paragraphs*—Whenever possible, keep your e-mails short and to the point. You should be as clear as possible in your messages so that the reader does not have to ask for clarification regarding something you wrote. Use paragraphs liberally. Long paragraphs are hard to read on a computer screen, and it is easy to lose your place, particularly if you have to scroll up and down the message.
- *Spell-check and reread your e-mails*—Most e-mail programs have a spell-check function; use it whenever possible. Many users send e-mails full of spelling and grammar errors that may change the meaning of the message. Before sending your e-mails, reread them to make sure they make sense. Remember, you will be using e-mail to correspond with clients, so it should not be sloppy.
- *Be careful to treat e-mail as business correspondence*—E-mails cannot be retrieved once they are sent. They are written records that are kept by the recipients, so be extremely careful about what you send and make sure that you can live with the message. When in doubt, do not send it. Also, remember that the recipient cannot see your body language or interpret your tone, so be careful how you phrase things.
- *If a message is unclear, ask for clarification*—If you are unsure about a message someone has sent you, ask for clarification and do not assume you know the answer.
- *Be careful of "Reply All"*—Sometimes users get e-mail with 20 other people copied on it. If the user selects "Reply," only the sender of the original e-mail will get a response, but selecting "Reply All" will send a reply to all 20 of the other recipients. Far too often, a user intends to send a personal message to the sender of the e-mail and mistakenly selects "Reply All." Before you select "Reply All," make sure you really want to send your e-mail to everyone on the original message.
- *Do not use e-mail to communicate with clients regarding sensitive information*—Since Internet e-mail can pass through many network servers where the e-mail can be read, it is probably better not to use e-mail at all for communicating with clients about sensitive information; if in doubt, always ask the client first.
- *Double-check the recipient of your e-mail*—Often users intend to send e-mail to one person and accidentally select the wrong person. Always double-check the e-mail address to make sure you entered the correct one.

- *Limit each e-mail message to one topic*—It is difficult to decide where to file multiple-topic e-mails, and it is sometimes difficult to follow-up on them. There could be multiple follow-up actions buried in one e-mail.
- *Always password-protect word processing and other documents sent to clients*—By password-protecting documents, you add some degree of security to the attachment with minimal effort.

Problems with E-Mail While e-mail is inexpensive and convenient, it is not perfect. Keep the following considerations in mind when using e-mail.

- *Do not assume that an e-mail was read just because you sent it*—Like any other form of written communication, e-mail can be lost, unopened, or accidentally deleted.
- *E-mail relies on computer technology that fails from time to time*—E-mail works only if the computer networks, telephone lines or other technology, and the recipient's computer hardware and software are working correctly. If any of these fail, your message will not reach the recipient.
- *Be careful what you say in e-mails, since they can be forwarded to others*—The nature of an e-mail is that it can be easily forwarded to another person. For example, you may send an e-mail to X about Y, and X can immediately forward it to Y.
- *E-mail security can be breached*—As noted before, e-mail is not necessarily confidential, and e-mail security can be breached in many ways, including the following:
  - Leaving confidential e-mails open on your computer screen for others to read over your shoulder
  - Leaving your office for lunch or a break while signed into your e-mail program
  - Printing e-mails that others can find (such as at a network printer)
  - Using a password such as "password" or names of family members that would be easy for others to guess

E-Mail Errors

It is important to be careful when using e-mail. Errors can happen in several different ways and may result in malpractice claims against the lawyer and/or the legal organization. Some common errors include the following:

- *Sending an ill-conceived e-mail to a client or others before it is carefully considered*—Unlike a letter placed in the outgoing mailbox that can be retrieved a few hours later, once the user presses the "Send" button, e-mail is gone.
- *Sending e-mail to unintended parties*—It is easy to use the "Reply All" command to send a private message to a group of people unintentionally, or to click on the wrong e-mail address. Depending on the content of the message, errors like these can damage a client's case, particularly when e-mail is sent to the opposition.
- *Sending the wrong attachments*—Since files can be sent as attachments to e-mails, it is particularly important to ensure that the correct file is attached. It is easy to attach a wrong file to an e-mail that might be devastating to a client's case. This can be avoided by opening the file after it is attached to the e-mail to make sure it is the correct one.
- *Typing errors*—Typing errors, such as leaving words out, can substantially change the meaning of a sentence. For example, in a client e-mail you might intend to type "We don't recommend that you do this," but instead you type "We recommend that you do this." While you have left only one word out, that word could be crucial to how the client proceeds.

E-Mail Confidentiality

As discussed earlier, confidentiality while using e-mail to communicate with clients is an important issue. Attorneys have duty to protect client information pursuant to their respective state's rules of professional conduct, modeled from the *ABA Model Rules of Professional Conduct*. The ABA Ethics Committee looked at the confidentiality of e-mail exchanges between attorneys and clients and concluded that an attorney can communicate with clients over e-mail without encryption. The Ethics Committee stated that e-mail affords users a reasonable standard of expectation of privacy, similar to that of a telephone call, and that unencrypted e-mail could be used to communicate with a client.

However, the ABA also found that an attorney had a duty to consider the sensitivity of the issue being communicated, what it would mean to the client's representation if the communication were disclosed, and the relative security of the contemplated means of communication. Arguably, the ABA wants legal professionals to use a common sense standard when using e-mail or other forms of communication with clients. If communication with a client is highly sensitive, then the legal professional should check with the client about whether a more secure form of communication is warranted.

Practical considerations for using e-mail ethically include the following:

- Having a policy for the legal organization regarding the use of e-mail and how it will be used to communicate with clients
- Consulting clients about what type of information they want to communicate via e-mail, how often the client receives or responds to e-mail, and other information about the particulars of the client's specific e-mail system or habits
- Making sure the e-mail addresses are accurately entered so that client communication is not sent to others by mistake
- Sending a test e-mail to a client to ensure the right e-mail address is being used
- Adding a confidentiality statement to all client e-mails—this is similar to statements accompanying many fax cover pages that state that the information is intended solely for the recipient and any third party who receives it should immediately forward it or destroy it
- Not using e-mail at all for particularly sensitive information

WORD PROCESSING/SPREADSHEETS/DATABASE MANAGEMENT/PRESENTATION SOFTWARE
Word processing, spreadsheets, databases, and presentation software are some of the most commonly used software by legal professionals. They are used to draft documents and correspondence, make financial calculations and projections, track and organize documents, and present information to fact finders.

DOCKET CONTROL/CALENDARING/CASE MANAGEMENT Docket control, calendaring, and case management are covered in detail in Chapter 7; these programs are generally used to track, organize, and manage many appointments and deadlines in a law office.

document management software

Organizes, controls, distributes, and allows for extensive searching of electronic documents, typically in a networked environment.

TIME AND BILLING Timekeeping and billing software automate the process of tracking a timekeeper's billable hours, billing clients, and posting payments to a client's account. Timekeeping and billing is covered in detail in Chapter 5.

DOCUMENT MANAGEMENT **Document management software** organizes, controls, distributes, and allows for extensive searching of electronic documents typically in a networked environment. Document management software allows a legal organization to file documents electronically so they can be found by anyone in the organization, even when there are hundreds of users spread across offices throughout the country. Document management software goes far beyond the file management capabilities in operating system software. It is the electronic equivalent of a filing room with rows and rows of filing cabinets. If a legal organization is going to move to a "paperless office," the office will have to have a document management program to manage the electronic files. Document management software also provides for extensive searching capabilities and allows users to add a profile of every document that can be easily searched on later.

document assembly software

Creates powerful standardized templates and forms

DOCUMENT ASSEMBLY **Document assembly software** creates powerful standardized templates and forms. Instead of having to open an existing client's word processing document and edit it for a new client, it allows the user to create a template than can be used over and over. Document assembly programs have more powerful commands and capabilities than templates found in word processing programs.

LITIGATION SUPPORT Litigation support software organizes, stores, retrieves, and summarizes information that is gathered in the litigation of a lawsuit. Litigation support programs are powerful database management programs that have been designed specifically for litigation. They can store thousands and even millions of records, search for and retrieve the requested records, summarize and track important case information, and much more.

ELECTRONIC DISCOVERY Electronic discovery programs have the ability to store, search, and retrieve electronic documents in a case, such as e-mails, word processing files, spreadsheets, and other attachments and electronic data produced during discovery. For 200 years, documents have been produced as hard copy, but this is no longer the case. In many legal matters, the parties need the ability to search, sort, track, and organize electronic data. People communicate via e-mails, attachments, and electronic files, and legal professionals need a way to search this information to find data that will assist them in representing their clients.

LEGAL-SPECIFIC SOFTWARE Legal-specific software includes programs developed for a legal specialty area. For example, an attorney who practices criminal law might purchase a program that automates and tracks information about criminal cases. The software might track each individual criminal count against a defendant, automate the scheduling of the case, automate the documents in the case (such as witness lists), track restitution, track evidence, and much more.

TRIAL SOFTWARE Trial software assists litigators in preparing for and presenting information to a jury or fact finder. They can work closely with automated courtrooms where judges and juries have computer screens in front of them to receive evidence. The programs typically provide sophisticated presentation graphics features, outline and organize information that will be presented to the fact finder, and include the ability to organize information by legal issue; organize, track, and display trial exhibits; and generate and display complex timelines.

Telecommunications

LAW OFFICE WEB SITES Many law offices now have home pages on the Internet and almost all the U.S. law offices have Web sites. Most offices use the Web site for marketing information, but some are expanding the content to include such things as client intake questionnaires, real-time consulting with prospective clients, and self-help information and research. Some firms have in-house staff and a variety of computer programs to design, develop, and host their own sites, while others outsource these tasks.

INTERNET ACCESS Nearly all law offices provide access to the Internet for a variety of purposes, including factual research, legal research (including access to Westlaw and LexisNexis), purchasing, marketing, communicating with clients, and much more. With this access comes a host of security issues, such as hackers, viruses, spyware, and so forth.

INTRANET As defined earlier, an intranet is an internal distribution system used only by a law firm staff. It disseminates information to internal staff using a Web browser and the look and feel of the World Wide Web. An intranet provides information to internal users in the same way the Internet provides information to the public. Typical information a firm might include on its intranet site includes office policies and procedures, links to law-related Web sites, training material, contact lists, links to form files or brief banks, and much more.

extranet

A network designed to provide, disseminate, and share confidential information with clients.

EXTRANET An **extranet** is a network designed to provide, disseminate, and share confidential information with clients. A client with a Web browser can access the law practice's extranet, go through security and ID/password protections, and access his or her case plans, documents, strategies, billing information, and other data.

LEGAL WEBLOGS A weblog, or "blog," is a Web site with information contained in posts that are arranged in reverse chronological order. Blogs resemble diary or journal entries in a notebook, and they can contain links to other Web sites or articles. There are many law-related blogs on the Internet, including specific blogs on certain type of law, such as immigration or taxes.

Summary

Legal administration is important to the survival of every law practice. Legal administration covers the following subject matters: practice management, leadership, controlling, financial management, human resources management, planning, marketing, organization/policies/systems, facilities management, office services management, and technology or information services management.

Practice management refers to management decisions regarding how a law office will practice law and handle cases. Administrative management refers to management decisions regarding how a firm will operate as a business, such as how it will handle financial or human resources matters.

Practice management decisions include defining the law office's practice (what cases it will take), services, and the practice systems necessary to provide legal services to clients.

Another aspect of practice management is the quality of services that it provides to clients. Quality and TQM is a management philosophy that is based on knowing the needs of each client and allowing those needs to drive the legal organization. This includes the ideas (1) that management has the duty to make sure the firm provides quality legal services to clients; (2) that quality service involves every person in the firm; (3) that clients determine what constitutes "quality services"; (4) that quality depends on individual, team, and organizational performance; and (5) that there is a focus on constantly improving services.

Leadership is the act of motivating or causing others to perform and achieve objectives. Controlling is the process of determining whether the law practice is achieving its objectives, holding stakeholders accountable for their goals, and making strategy adjustment so the firm achieves its objectives. Financial management is the oversight of the firm's financial assets and profitability to ensure overall financial health.

Human resources management refers to hiring, evaluating, compensating, training, and directing law office personnel. Important federal employment laws include the Family and Medical Leave Act, the Fair Labor Standards Act, the Civil Rights Act of 1964, the Americans with Disabilities Act, and the Age Discrimination in Employment Act, among others.

Planning is the process of setting objectives, assessing the future, and developing courses of action to achieve the objectives. Marketing is the process of educating consumers on the quality of legal services that a law office can provide. Organizing is the process of arranging people and physical resources to carry out plans and accomplish objectives. A system is a consistent way of performing a task. A policy is a specific statement that sets out what is or is not acceptable. A procedure is a series of steps that must be followed to accomplish a task. A law office staff manual contains the firm's policies and procedures related to legal and administrative work.

Facilities management includes planning, designing, controlling, and managing a law office's building or office space. Facilities management includes areas such as property acquisition, moves/construction/remodeling, space planning/office design/furniture, parking, cleaning/maintenance/grounds, common areas, environmental considerations (lighting, electrical, climate, and plumbing), security, safety, and disaster recovery planning. Maintaining a secure and safe environment is an extremely important aspect of facilities management. Locked doors, security systems, limited access to interior halls, security passes, and other initiatives help to keep a law office secure. A disaster recovery plan includes information on how the law office will rebuild and recover from a disaster.

Office services management refers to internal systems and services in a law office. The services include management of the mail room, copiers and copy facilities, file/records management, and telecommunications (including telephone systems, voice mail, fax machines, and video conferencing).

Technology has had a large and continual impact on how legal professionals practice law. Law offices have a myriad of choices when it comes to computer hardware and software. Electronic mail is used more by legal professionals on a daily basis than any other application. Other applications that legal professionals use include docket control, time and billing, document management, document assembly, litigation support, electronic discovery programs, and others. Telecommunication services that legal professionals use include law office Web sites, Internet access, intranets, extranets, and legal blogs.

Key Terms

administrative management
administrative task
Age Discrimination in Employment Act of 1967
Americans with Disabilities Act of 1990
bona fide occupational qualification
Civil Rights Act of 1964
coaching technique
controlling
disaster recovery plan
document assembly software
employment-at-will doctrine
document management software
equal employment opportunity
Equal Pay Act of 1963
extranet
facilities management
Fair Credit Reporting Act
Family and Medical Leave Act of 1993
financial management
Gantt chart
human resources management
intranet
leadership
management
management by objectives
marketing
mission statement
negligent hiring
office services management
organizing
personnel handbook
planning
policy
practice management
procedure
reasonable accommodation
sexual harassment
strategic planning
substantive task
system
total quality management

Test Your Knowledge

Test your knowledge of the chapter by answering these questions.

1. ________________ management refers to management decisions related to how a law office practices law and handles its cases.
2. ________________ management refers to management decisions related to operating a law office including financial and personnel matters.
3. Three basic practice management questions that must be considered are (a) what clients will the law office serve? (b) what services will be offered to the client? and (c) ________________.
4. True or false: It is generally recognized that a good law office strategy is to practice in all areas and subspecialties.
5. List the 11 functions of legal administration.
6. ________________ is a management philosophy that is based upon knowing the needs of each client and allowing those needs to drive the legal organization.
7. The quality of provided legal services is best determined by the ________________.
8. What is the act of motivating or causing others to perform and achieve objectives called?
9. What is the process of determining whether the law practice is achieving its objectives, holding stakeholders accountable for their goals, and making strategy adjustments as necessary so the firm achieves the objectives, called?
10. Setting hourly billing rates, tracking firm assets, and budgeting are responsibilities regarding ________________ management.

11. The ________________ technique is taken from sports, focuses on the positive aspects of the employee's performance, and explores alternative ways to improve his or her performance.
12. What employment doctrine states that both the employee and employer are free to enter and sever the employment relationship at any time without reason?
13. What law prohibits employers from discriminating against people with a disability?
14. Define sexual harassment.
15. ________________ is the process of setting objectives, assessing the future, and developing courses of action to achieve these objectives.
16. ________________ is a general, enduring statement of what the purpose or intent of the law practice is about.
17. What is marketing?
18. A manual that governs the policies and procedures of law office is called a ________________.
19. What is the type of management that is responsible for property acquisition, moves, space planning, and design, parking, and security?
20. A plan that describes how the law office will react to a catastrophe is called a ________________.
21. What type of management is responsible for the mail room, copy room, and records/file management?
22. Name three problems or errors that can occur when using e-mail.
23. The "paperless office" is associated with what type of computer program?

On the Web Exercises

1. Compare, contrast, and print out mission statements for three law offices. Some law firms may call them core values, firm philosophy, or a purpose statement while some include their purpose or their mission in a general introductory statement; large-sized law firms typically include this on their Web site. Start by going to a general search engine like http://www.google.com or http://www.yahoo.com and search for "global law firms" or "large law firms." The Findlaw site, http://www.findlaw.com, has features that allow users to search for lawyers and law firm Web sites as well. Research law-related blogs on the Internet. Find five legal blogs including at least one on either law office technology or law practice management or administration. Print a few pages of the blogs that you found and write a paragraph explaining each Web site. Again start by going to a general search engine, such as http://www.google.com or http://www.yahoo.com, and type "legal blog."

2. Using the Web sites listed in the Web Links section of this chapter, or a general search engine, find checklists and helpful Web sites regarding moving a law office.

3. Using the Web sites listed in the Web Links section of this chapter, or a general search engine, find resources, information, and checklists that would assist an attorney in opening a new law practice.

4. Use a general search engine to find job descriptions for a legal secretary, paralegal or legal assistant, attorney, legal administrator, and law librarian.

5. The chapter states that successful law practices do not take all of the clients or cases that come to them, and that they carefully select those that are profitable and right for them. Using the Web sites contained in the Web Links section of this chapter, research articles on how to weed out undesirable clients and cases.

Projects

1. Research and write an in-depth report on disaster recovery plans. Obtain a minimum of five different resources. Information covered in the report should include why they are important, which major sections or areas a disaster recovery plan has, how they are used, and information related to why disaster recovery plans are particularly important in law offices. In addition, write a disaster recovery plan for yourself (e.g., if your apartment or residence has caught fire and everything you had has been destroyed).

2. Assume that you have been asked by an attorney, who is starting a new law practice, to prepare a detailed list of computer hardware and software that he or she might need. The attorney is a general practitioner and employ himself or herself, a legal secretary, and you as the paralegal. Compile a detailed list, including pricing and some background on why each item is necessary.

3. Research and write a detailed report on total quality management. At a minimum, the report should include who is credited with developing it, where it originated and became popular, what specific ideologies it includes, and how it can be implemented in any business, including a law office.

4. Research and write a one-page detailed summary on each of the following federal employment laws: Civil Rights Act of 1964, Family and Medical Leave Act, Americans with Disabilities Act, and Age Discrimination in Employment Act. At a minimum, include why the law was passed, major provisions of the law, what agency is responsible for enforcing it, and other relevant information about it.

5. Research and write a report on law office security and workplace violence. Include some history of the subject, including major tragedies like the 1993 Pettit & Martin shootings and others. Include what law offices can do to limit their exposure to security problems.

6. Group Project: Opening a Law Office

Your group will act as the Law Practice Management Committee of Brayton and James Attorneys at Law, a new firm specializing in corporate and insurance law that expects to begin practicing law this year.

Your job as the Law Practice Management Committee is to put together a strategic management plan for the first year of operation. You need to take great care in preparing the plan, since the plan will guide your firm for the first year of operation and will also be given to your bank to secure financing. You are to submit one copy of the strategic management plan, which will be reviewed for accuracy, completeness, and logic. Each member of your group will receive a grade. You will also evaluate each other regarding the work done on the project.

The Brayton and James law office will have two partners and two associate attorneys. The partners expect to make $100,000 a year, and associates expect to make $70,000 a year. You must determine what other staff will need to be hired and at what pay rate. You have no budgetary constraints.

Your strategic management plan should include the following sections:

A. **Physical location of the building:** You must choose an actual office site for the business. You will need private offices for each of the attorneys and appropriate office space for the other staff. You will also need a reception area, library, and conference room. You must give a narrative description of the office site and include cost (leased or purchased) and justification as to why this site has been chosen.

B. **Layout of the office and furniture:** You must decide how the office interior will be laid out. A layout of the office should be provided, including a narrative description of each office and its accompanying furniture, and an explanation as to why the office was laid out in the particular manner.

C. **Technology/equipment:** Appropriate technology/equipment should be researched. Assume the attorneys want to purchase all new equipment typically found in a law office, including computers, software, printers, Internet access, fax machine, copiers, and so forth. A narrative description of the items to be purchased (and their cost) should be included, as well as the justification for the purchase.

D. **Staff employment:** Explain what additional staff positions will be needed to support the two partners and two associates. Draft job descriptions for each of the positions.

E. **Law library:** An appropriate library for insurance and corporate law must be purchased. Please explain what will be purchased, why, and the cost.

F. **Budget:** A detailed budget should be included for both income and expenses (see Chapter 6). Please indicate the billing rates and hours to be billed for the partners, associates, and any paralegals hired (see Chapter 5). The rates and hours should reflect the common market rates and hours for the area. When considering expenses, do not forget to add 25% to associate and staff salaries to cover fringe benefits. The budget should provide the partners with the income they expect and include the typical expenses found in most law offices.

Practical Applications

1. Interview an attorney and get answers to the following questions: What is the mission of his or her firm? How does he or she define his or her practice? Who are his or her primary clients? What primary services does he or she provide? What practice systems does he or she use to support the legal services provided to clients? Does he or she prefer practice or administrative management?

2. Many business professionals believe that it is easier to find and keep a long-term customer than to constantly find new customers. Think of a product or service to which you are very loyal (brand of car, shoe, computer, printer, bike, clothes, etc.). How long have you been loyal to the brand or product? Why are you loyal to it? Does it have to do with the quality of the product? How much money have you given to the brand or product because of your loyalty? Could you have gone to a competitor? Why did not you go? Can you see how this same philosophy applies to the practice of law? Why is providing quality services to clients important?

3. Assume that you are a new paralegal in a sole practitioner's office. The attorney has asked you to sit in with him or her to interview a legal secretary. He or she has asked you to draft a job description, and 15 interview questions. Use the Internet or other resources to do this. What things would you be looking for in a candidate?

4. Write a mission statement for yourself. What is important to you? What are your goals and objectives? Develop a five-year strategic plan for yourself. Where do you see yourself in five years? What will you have to do to reach your goals and objectives?

Case Review

Bednar et al v. CT Corporation, No. 02-3646 JMR/JSM (D. Minn. filed Sept. 16, 2002)

West's Minnesota Jury Verdict Reports

Thomas Bednar worked for CT Corporation System as a customer specialist. CT is a nationwide legal document service company. The company offers various services to attorneys and law firms and has offices in several states. There are approximately 300 customer specialists employed by CT. Until August of 2002, the customer specialists were compensated on a salary or "exempt" basis, and as such, were ineligible for overtime pay for any hours worked in excess of 40 hours per week. After August 2002, customer service specialists were reclassified as nonexempt. In 2003, Bednar filed a class action complaint again CT in a Minnesota federal district court, alleging the classification of customer specialists as exempt violated the federal Fair Labor Standards Act, 29 U.S.C. 207(a)(1) and various state wage and hour laws. The complaint sought reimbursement for unpaid overtime, liquidated damages, and an award of attorney's fees and costs. The parties agreed to settle the case on December 15, 2003 for a total payment not to exceed $2,825,000, including attorney's fees. Under the terms of the settlement agreement, each member of the class who chose to participate in the settlement would receive back overtime pay based on the actual excess hours that individual worked, in addition to a payment of $4066. The additional payment was deemed to cover any potential state law violations, liquidated damages and various other damages.

Questions

1. Were you surprised that this FLSA violation happened to a company that works in the legal industry and works with attorneys and law firms every day?
2. Notice in this case that it was only *after* the defendants figured out that they had wrongly misclassified the customer service specialists—and, in fact, corrected the matter—that the plaintiffs discovered the error and filed the class action to recover damages when they were misclassified. Is that fair?
3. Notice also that what may have started as one person, Thomas Bednar, having a single claim against the defendant turned into a full-blown class action costing the firm $2.8 million dollars in damages alone. Did it surprise you how much the case was settled for and how quickly it was litigated?

Case Review

Littell v. Allstate Insurance Co., 177 P.3d 1080 (N.M. Ct. App. 2007).

177 P.3d 1080

(Cite as: 177 P.3d 1080)

Court of Appeals of New Mexico,

Patricia LITTELL, Plaintiff-Appellee,

v.

ALLSTATE INSURANCE COMPANY, Defendant-Appellant.

No. 26,268.

November 21, 2007

{1} Defendant Allstate Insurance Co. appeals from a judgment on a jury verdict in favor of Plaintiff Patricia Littell on her claims of hostile work environment sexual harassment and retaliatory constructive discharge. Allstate argues that: (1) the district court abused its discretion in admitting certain, evidence; (2) there was no evidence supporting either of Plaintiff's claims or the jury's award of compensatory damages for alleged emotional injuries; (3) the issue of punitive damages should not have been submitted to the jury; and (4) the award of punitive damages manifested the influence of passion and prejudice and, therefore, violates due process. We affirm. We also remand to the district court the issue of whether Plaintiff is entitled to an award of attorney fees for this appeal.

Background

{2} Plaintiff began work as a paralegal in Allstate's Albuquerque Staff Counsel Office in 1996. In October 1998, Todd Aakhus joined the office as lead counsel. At this point, according to Plaintiff, conditions at the office changed. Aakhus regularly made sexual innuendoes and told dirty jokes that were demeaning to women. Aakhus allegedly engaged in sexual discussions and flirted with female employees, inappropriately touched female employees, commented about other employees' sexual preferences, and tolerated similar conduct by other office employees. When Plaintiff reported these occurrences anonymously to Allstate's hotline for employment disputes, Allstate investigated, but Plaintiff did not feel that Allstate did anything to resolve the situation. Also according to Plaintiff, Aakhus began treating her differently after she complained to the Allstate hotline. He became more aggressive,***1083** disciplined Plaintiff for pretextual reasons, and berated and belittled her publicly. Ultimately, when Aakhus refused to give Plaintiff a leave of absence so that she could deal with a "family crisis," Plaintiff resigned.

{3} Plaintiff sued Allstate and asserted claims for violations of the New Mexico Human Rights Act, intentional infliction "of emotional distress, prima facie tort, retaliatory discharge, and punitive damages. The district court entered summary judgment in favor of Allstate on Plaintiffs claim for intentional infliction of emotional distress and on her claim under the Human Rights Act to the extent it was predicated on retaliation. The case went to trial before a jury, and at the close of Plaintiffs evidence, the district court granted judgment as a matter of law in favor of Allstate on Plaintiffs claim for prima facie tort. After deliberating, the jury returned a verdict in favor of Plaintiff on her claims of hostile work environment sexual harassment and retaliatory discharge. The jury awarded Plaintiff $360,000 in compensatory damages and $1 million in punitive damages. The district court denied Allstate's subsequent motion for judgment notwithstanding the verdict or, in the alternative, for remittitur or a new trial. This appeal followed. We provide additional facts in our discussion.

Discussion

{4} Allstate makes the following arguments on appeal: (1) the district court abused its discretion by admitting evidence of incidents of which Plaintiff was not aware, of Allstate's discipline of Aakhus, and of other matters that occurred after Plaintiff left Allstate's employ; (2) there was no evidence supporting the jury's determinations (a) that Allstate violated the Human Rights Act by allowing a hostile work environment to exist in the office, (b) that. Allstate subjected Plaintiff to retaliatory constructive discharge, And (e) that Plaintiff was entitled to compensatory damages for alleged emotional injuries in the amount of $200,000 to $250,000; (3) the district court should not have allowed the issue of punitive damages to go to the jury because (a) Aakhus was not acting in a managerial capacity or in the scope of employment and (b) Allstate did not authorize, ratify, or participate in Aakhus's misconduct; and (4) the punitive damages award manifested the influence of passion and prejudice, was excessive, and violates due process. We address each argument in turn.

I. The District Court Did Not Abuse Its Discretion in Admitting Evidence

{5} Allstate argues that the district court abused its discretion in admitting two categories of evidence, including: (1) testimony about incidents that Plaintiff was not aware of, and (2) evidence of matters that postdated Plaintiffs employment with Allstate, including Allstate's disciplining and discharge of Aakhus. We review the district court's admission of evidence for abuse of discretion, *Coates v. Wal-Mart Stores, Inc.*, 1999-NMSC-013, ¶ 36, 127 N.M. 47, 976 P.2d 999, and conclude that the district court's admission of this evidence was within the sound exercise of its discretion.

A. Incidents of Which Plaintiff Was Purportedly. Not Aware

{6} Allstate contends that the only evidence admissible on Plaintiffs claim of sexual harassment was evidence regarding incidents of which Plaintiff was aware or made aware during her employment. Allstate further argues that Plaintiff failed to lay a foundation that she was aware of several incidents about which fellow employees Maureen Reed and Margie Lang testified. These incidents included Reed's testimony that Aakhus reported a story in the office concerning a physician putting his hand in a woman's vagina, Reed's testimony regarding a twenty-minute discussion at lunch about a female attorney's breasts, Reed's testimony that a female attorney in the office would squat in her office "with her crotch open to the area," Lang's testimony that Aakhus gave her a book of erotica, and Lang's testimony about a staff meeting at which a female attorney discussed her breasts.

{7} We agree with Allstate that there is case law supporting the view that Plaintiff could rely only on evidence relating to harassment of which she was aware during the time of her employment. See *Hirase-Doi v. U.S. W. Commc*'ns, Inc., 61 F.3d 777, ***1084**782 (10th Cir.1995) (explaining that the plaintiff in a hostile environment sexual harassment suit under Title VII "may only rely on evidence relating to harassment of which she was aware during the time that she was allegedly subject to a hostile work environment"). Consistent with this view, the district court ruled that evidence of events not witnessed by Plaintiff would be admitted if the events "occurred prior to the time of [Plaintiffs] departure, which she learned of essentially contemporaneously." Our review of the trial transcript establishes that sufficient foundation was laid for introduction of the specified testimony.

{8} Reed testified that Plaintiff "knew about" Aakhus's story regarding the doctor putting his hand in a woman's vagina, and that Plaintiff was probably at the lunch where the female attorney talked about her breasts. Lang testified that she told Plaintiff about the book of erotica Aakhus had given her, and that she was sure that Plaintiff was made aware of the staff meeting where the female attorney discussed her breasts. Given this foundational testimony, we cannot say that the district court abused its discretion in admitting the evidence.

B. Evidence of Matters Postdating Plaintiffs Employment with Allstate

{9} Allstate also contends the district court should have excluded evidence of events that occurred after Plaintiff resigned. That evidence consisted of a complaint to Allstate management about Aakhus, Allstate's subsequent investigation of that complaint, and Allstate's disciplining and discharge of Aakhus. Allstate maintains this evidence was inadmissible under Rule 11-407 NMRA. This rule provides:

> When, after an event, measures are taken which, if taken previously, would have made the event less likely to occur, evidence of the subsequent measures is not admissible to prove negligence or culpable conduct in connection with the event. This rule does not require the exclusion of evidence of subsequent measures when offered for another purpose, such as proving ownership, control or feasibility of precautionary measures, if controverted, or impeachment.*Id.*

Allstate further relies on *Spina v. Forest Preserve of Cook County*, No. 98 C 1393, 2001 WL 1491524 (N.D.Ill. Nov.23, 2001) (mem. and order), in which a federal district court, citing Federal Rule of Evidence 407, excluded evidence of the defendant employer's disciplinary actions against the alleged perpetrators of sexual harassment against the plaintiff. *Id.* at *11. We are not persuaded that Rule 11-407 mandated exclusion of this evidence.

{10} Plaintiff offered evidence of post-resignation events for a purpose other than to prove negligence or culpable conduct. Plaintiff argued to the district court that this evidence was relevant to show that Allstate management did nothing substantive in response to Plaintiffs and other employees' complaints of sexual harassment by Aakhus and to show Allstate's state of mind for purposes of punitive damages. The district court agreed with Plaintiff and further noted that the evidence was relevant to Allstate's affirmative defense that it "exercised reasonable care to prevent and correct promptly any sexual harassment in the workplace." Consequently, the evidence fell within the exception contained in the second sentence of Rule 11-407. See 23 Charles Alan Wright & Kenneth W. Graham, Jr., Federal Practice and Procedure § 5290, at 148-49 (1980) ("The list of permissible uses in Rule 407 is illustrative, not exclusive; evidence of subsequent repairs may be admitted for any purpose that does not require an inference to the negligence or culpable conduct of the repairer, whether as an ultimate fact or intermediate inference." (footnotes omitted)).

{11} In addition, we do not consider Spina to be persuasive authority. Although the federal district court in that case excluded evidence of the suspension of the plaintiffs superiors, it did so without any significant analysis and in reliance on *Wanke v. Lynn's* Transportation Co., 836 F.Supp. 587, 595 (N.D.Ind.1993) (mem. and order), which was a wrongful death case, not an employment discrimination case. See Spina, 2001 WL 1491524, at *11. We are similarly unpersuaded by the other cases upon which All-state ***1085** relies. *Maddox v. City of Los Angeles*, 792 F.2d 1408, 1417 (9th Cir.1986), like *Wanke*, did not analyze the issue. *Hull v. Chevron U.S.A., Inc.*, 812 F.2d 584, 587 (10th Cir.1987), was a personal injury action, in which the policy reasons for excluding subsequent remedial measures (i.e., to encourage the undertaking of measures that enhance safety, see *Couch v. Astec Industries, Inc.*, 2002-NMCA-084, ¶ 26, 132 N.M. 631, 53 P.3d 398) have primary significance. In *Jumper v. Yellow Corp.*, 176 F.R.D. 282, 285 (N.D.Ill. 1997) (mem. and order), the federal district court reserved judgment on whether the subsequent measures would be admissible at trial.

{12} We therefore conclude that the district court did not abuse its discretion in admitting evidence of events that occurred after Plaintiff resigned her position.

II. There Was Substantial Evidence to Support Plaintiffs Claims of Hostile Work Environment and Retaliatory Constructive Discharge, and to Support the Jury's Award of Compensatory Damages

{13} Allstate argues that there was no evidence supporting Plaintiffs claims of hostile work environment sexual harassment and retaliatory discharge, and that there was insufficient evidence justifying the jury's award of compensatory damages for Plaintiffs emotional distress. "In reviewing a sufficiency of the evidence claim, this Court views the evidence in a light most favorable to the prevailing party and disregard[s] any inferences and evidence to the contrary." *Weidler v. Big J Enters., Inc.*, 1998-NMCA-021, ¶ 30, 124 N.M. 591, 953 P.2d 1089 (alteration in original) (internal quotation marks and citations omitted). We defer to the jury's determination regarding the credibility of witnesses and the reconciliation of inconsistent or contradictory evidence. *Id.* "We simply review the evidence to determine whether there is evidence that a reasonable mind would find adequate to support a conclusion." *Id.* We reject Allstate's contention that the "clearly erroneous" standard of review, which is employed by the federal courts, applies in this state court action. See *Bovee v. State Highway & Transp. Dep't*, 2003-NMCA-025, ¶ 17, 133 N.M. 519, 65 P.3d 254.

A. Hostile Work Environment

{14} Allstate contends that Plaintiff failed to introduce evidence on the claim of hostile work environment that Aakhus's conduct rose to the level of extreme offensiveness required by the applicable law. Allstate maintains that Plaintiffs evidence demonstrated nothing more than "a smattering of incidents" that occurred over Plaintiff s three-year employment in the office.

{15} Our Supreme Court, interpreting the New Mexico Human Rights Act, NMSA 1978, §§ 28-1-1 to-14 (1969, as amended through 2007), established what constitutes sexual harassment under a hostile work environment theory in *Ocana v. American Furniture Co.*, 2004-NMSC-018, 135 N.M. 539, 91 P.3d 58. Analogizing to federal law regarding a similar cause of action under Title VII, the Court stated that such a claim "is actionable ... when the offensive conduct becomes so severe and pervasive that it alters the conditions of employment in such a manner that the workplace is transformed into a hostile and abusive environment for the employee." *Id.* ¶ 24, 135 N.M. 539, 91 P.3d 58. The fact finder must look at the totality of the circumstances, including the frequency of the discriminatory conduct; its severity; whether it is physically threatening or humiliating, or a mere offensive utterance; and whether it unreasonably interferes with an employee's work performance. The work environment must be both objectively and subjectively offensive—one that a reasonable person would find hostile or abusive and one that the employee did perceive as being hostile or abusive. *Id.* (internal quotation marks and citation omitted). In the present case, the district court instructed the jury in accordance with Ocana.

{16} Plaintiff introduced the following evidence in support of her claim. Plaintiff testified that she was very happy working for Allstate and that there were no discussions of sex or foul language in the office prior to the ***1086** hiring of Aakhus. However, things changed when Aakhus was hired in October 1998. On his second day in the office, Aakhus came into Plaintiff's office, got physically very close to her, and, using profanity, told her a joke about President Clinton, Monica Lewinsky, and oral sex. Plaintiff said she felt shocked and "absolutely terrified" because the joke was so demeaning to women. The next day Plaintiff told Aakhus she did not want him to tell her, that kind of joke again and that what he had done was against Allstate policy.

{17} Plaintiff testified that, while Aakhus never told her a joke again, the sexual behavior never stopped, and Aakhus continued to tell dirty jokes in Plaintiffs presence over the next three years and four months. This behavior occurred almost daily. Most often, the jokes, which were both written and oral, were demeaning to women and frequently referred to sex acts. Aakhus used profanity and made comments about male and female genitalia. At Halloween, Aakhus commented that a witch on a broomstick looked as if she must be male and referred to the broomstick as a male body part. Aakhus also frequently followed Plaintiff closely, pointing at Plaintiff and berating her in public. Although he did not actually touch her, Plaintiff felt assaulted. Aakhus frequently "flip[ped] people off." Once, Aakhus referred to a news reporter as "Dicks Sniffing" and this offended Plaintiff. In addition, Aakhus frequently used the phrase "bite me."

{18} In 1999 Plaintiff complained to Allstate's Resolution Line, which is a hotline for Allstate employees to use to complain anonymously about their job-related concerns. An employee would complain, the complaint would be investigated, and the people investigating would get back to the complaining employee. Soon thereafter other employees began to complain about Aakhus's sexual jokes and comments. A secretary in the office, Lou Wise, told Plaintiff that Aakhus had said that Wise's daughters must be homosexual because they were not married, and this offended Wise.

{19} Plaintiff became more stressed and tried to avoid being alone with Aakhus, and she observed other employees changing their behavior as well. For example, Plaintiff and Wise, who often worked after 5:00, agreed that neither would leave the other alone and that they would stay until both could leave at the same time. Meanwhile, Plaintiff had received nothing in writing regarding her complaint to the Resolution Line. Several times, she called Allstate's employee assistance program, which provided confidential counseling to employees.

{20} Aakhus became more aggressive and gradually more temperamental. Going into 2000, Aakhus's sexual innuendoes and aggressiveness escalated. Employee complaints to the Resolution Line continued. People from Allstate's human resources department showed up at the office, and Plaintiff tried to communicate to them her understanding of the office atmosphere. Plaintiff was still frightened. Every time she called the Resolution Line, she was told to call back, and when she called back, she was told either that the matter was still under investigation or that the case was closed and to call someone else for further assistance. Plaintiff just wanted Aakhus to stop his behavior, but he would not, and no one at Allstate would make him stop.

{21} In 2000, there were several new hires in the office, including a new paralegal and a new secretary. Plaintiff noticed Aakhus flirting with the paralegal, and the two engaged in sexual discussions and told sexual jokes. The new secretary would touch Aakhus at meetings, and the two would leave the office together, which Plaintiff found demeaning and embarrassing. Two of the female employees discussed explicit details of the sexual acts required to conceive babies, the best time of the month to get pregnant, and said they would be meeting their spouses on company time to try to conceive, noting that their return to the office would be delayed because they would have to elevate their legs. Aakhus participated in these discussions, and he used a rubber chicken to demonstrate elevation of the legs. Several of the female employees, "who played along with [Aakhus's] sexualization of the office," dressed provocatively, displaying cleavage and wearing short, tight skirts.***1087**

{22} Plaintiff testified that the office was divided between those who engaged with Aakhus in sexual conversation and those who did not. The people who went along with Aakhus received special privileges and came and went as they pleased.

{23} Secretary Lou Wise testified that when she first began working at the office, Aakhus handed her two to three pages that included content that was "of a sexual nature having to do with oral sex." Wise further testified that "[i]t was constant from Todd Aakhus as far as lewd jokes." Every joke Aakhus told was sexual. Due to the open, area in the office, Wise could hear Aakhus talking dirty and engaging in sexual banter. After Wise objected to Aakhus, his behavior changed. The episodes of a sexual nature increased and Aakhus would raise his voice so that Wise could hear what he was saying, "which was always of a sexual nature." Plaintiff was aware of all of this having occurred.

{24} Wise observed Aakhus hanging over Plaintiffs desk many times, talking in a very loud voice and pointing his finger at her. Wise observed instances of Aakhus's physical presence being very close to Plaintiff, and she saw Aakhus following Plaintiff, right on her heels. Aakhus's sexual talk got worse in 2000, and Wise saw Aakhus approach Plaintiff more often. Aakhus's criticism of Plaintiff intensified, and Wise saw Plaintiff crying or on the verge of tears many times. This affected Plaintiffs work because she seemed to be afraid of what Aakhus would do next.

{25} Wise reported Aakhus's behavior several times to Allstate's human resources department and to Larry Vogel, an Allstate attorney in the Denver office who was Aakhus's boss. According to Wise, Allstate "corporate" was aware of what was going on. Despite these reports to Allstate, Aakhus did not stop his behavior.

{26} Maureen Reed, who worked for eleven years as an attorney in Allstate's Albuquerque Staff Counsel Office, testified that Aakhus got sexual jokes off the Internet and passed them around to people in the office. Everyone was very shocked and upset by this, and this information was imparted to Plaintiff. Reed said that Aakhus's "sexual references never stopped for the whole time he was there." During team meetings each week, Aakhus made "constant sexual references." Reed reported that "[Aakhus's] thing was talking about sex in front of people.... He loved it, couldn't stop himself for some reason. So it was always sex." All of this kind of talk in a professional setting was "demeaning to women." Plaintiff was aware of all of these incidents.

{27} The sex talk continued at office lunches, which generally occurred when Aakhus's boss, Larry Vogel, was present. Reed heard a female attorney talk about her breasts for twenty minutes at one of these office lunches attended by Vogel. Reed thought Plaintiff was probably at this lunch. Reed also recalled that at a team meeting, one of the female attorneys said she had to go get medicine for her "ta-ta."

{28} Reed described the unprofessional conduct she observed, including "sexualizing the office, constant references to sex, either by innuendo, jokes that you tell, jokes that you pass out." Aakhus once told her a story that included "graphic detail about some doctor on the [witness] stand testifying about putting his hand up into some woman's vagina, in graphic detail." Plaintiff knew about this story.

{29} Allstate's human resources department came to the office, and Reed participated in at least two of these' investigations. Following these investigations, Vogel told the employees that Aakhus "might have a few little problems, ... but it's the rest of you's [sic] problem, and you need to take care of yourselves." Aakhus then told the employees that they were not to call Vogel, and that he, Aakhus, "could do whatever he wanted." Reed said that this "was horrible and it was frightening." She testified that there was a division in the office between Aakhus's employee friends whom he had hired and the employees who complained about Aakhus. She said that "at times, you could cut the tension with a knife. I mean, it was very tense and very hostile."

{30} Reed further testified that Plaintiff would become very upset when Aakhus was particularly abusive or did something outrageous. ***1088** "[Plaintiff] was, obviously, under a huge amount of stress." By 2001, Aakhus "was totally angry and totally taking his anger out on the people who he believed were complaining." Plaintiff would tell Aakhus when he did something that she did not think was right, and "[t]his made him crazy with her.... So he was totally angry and abusive to [Plaintiff]." Reed testified that "[a]s things escalated, [Aakhus] was unreasonably trying to manage [Plaintiff's] time, making false accusations ... about her work quality." In addition, Aakhus "followed [Plaintiff] around on her heels out in the open area in front of everyone." He would "hang over those dividers, and that's what he would do, yelling at her, with his face bright purple." Reed said "it was totally, totally scary."

{31} Margie Lang, a senior legal assistant in the office at the time, also testified. She said that Aakhus told blonde jokes and sexual jokes, many of which had to do with women. Shortly after Aakhus started working in the office, he gave Lang a book to read. The book was erotica. When she discovered the nature of the book, Lang gave it back to Aakhus. She told Plaintiff about this. Lang also testified that at one of the office's staff meetings, there was a discussion about the breasts of one of the attorneys. Plaintiff was made aware of this after the meeting. Lang believed that Vogel and human resources were aware of the complaints about Aakhus's behavior, but she did not observe a change in Aakhus's behavior.

{32} Exhibits introduced at trial showed that Allstate had first received complaints about Aakhus making "inappropriate, unprofessional and sexual comments in the office" in 2000. Allstate's investigation confirmed the validity of the complaints and Aakhus received formal counseling in August 2000. Plaintiff knew nothing about this. In May 2002, Allstate placed Aakhus on "Job in Jeopardy" status for making such comments. Allstate then discovered in August 2002 that Aakhus had violated the terms of the Job in Jeopardy notice by continuing to make such comments. Allstate terminated Aakhus on October 3, 2002. Then, in December 2002, Allstate rescinded its termination of Aakhus and reinstated him as an employee.

{33} Considering this evidence in the context of the applicable law, we conclude there was sufficient evidence to support Plaintiff's claim of hostile work environment sexual harassment. We evaluate the evidence with reference to the language of the jury instructions given, which constitute the law of the case. *Atler v. Murphy Enters., Inc.,* 2005-NMCA-006, ¶ 13, 136 N.M. 701, 104 P.3d 1092. The testimony of Plaintiff, Wise, Reed, and Lang established that Plaintiff was "subjected to offensive conduct of a sexual nature" and that "the conduct was unwelcome." In addition, the evidence gave rise to a reasonable inference that "the harassment occurred because of [Plaintiff's] sex." Both Plaintiff and Reed testified that Aakhus's sexual commentary was demeaning to women.

{34} The evidence also supported the conclusion that Plaintiff "perceived the working environment to be abusive or hostile" because she testified that Aakhus's conduct caused her to feel "assaulted" and "frightened." As time went by, she became more stressed and avoided being alone with Aakhus. Wise testified that Aakhus's conduct affected Plaintiff's work because she seemed to be afraid of what Aakhus would do next. Reed testified that Plaintiff "was, obviously, under a huge amount' of stress." In addition, given Wise's testimony that she reported Aakhus's behavior to Allstate several times, Reed's testimony that "you could cut the tension with a knife" in the office, and all the testimony regarding the frequency of profanity and sex-related conversation, a jury could reasonably conclude that "a reasonable wom[a] n in [Plaintiff's] circumstances would consider the working environment to be abusive or hostile."

{35} Allstate argues that the witnesses' generalized and conclusory testimony that Aakhus's comments "never stopped" and were "constant" is insufficient as a matter of law to establish a hostile work environment. In support, Allstate cites several cases, which we do not find persuasive. For example, the issue in *Woodward v. City of Worland,* 977 F.2d 1392 (10th Cir.1992), was limited to the ***1089** question of whether the district court had properly denied the defendants' motion to dismiss on the basis of qualified immunity. *Id.* at 1396. Thus, the court's discussion regarding generalized and conclusory testimony focused on the lack, of time-specific evidence tying the alleged harassment to a time when the law was clearly established that sexual harassment violated equal protection rights. *Id.* at 1398. Allstate's reliance on that case is inapposite. The other cases cited by Allstate are equally unpersuasive. See *Miranda v. Wis. Power & Light Co.*, 91 F.3d 1011, 1018 (7th Cir.1996) (affirming summary judgment against the plaintiff because her assertions of a hostile work environment consisted of vague, conclusory allegations); *Ceasar v. N. Star Steel Tex., Inc.,* 69 F.Supp.2d 858, 867 (E.D.Tex.1999) (granting summary judgment against the plaintiff because her allegations constituted only her subjective perception of discrimination and suggested nothing more than a bad working relationship with her superior); *Leskinen v. Utz Quality Foods, Inc.,* 30 F.Supp.2d 530, 533 (D.Md.1998) (granting summary judgment to the defendant because the plaintiff's generalized statements of harassment did not establish that any violations of Title VII occurred within the limitations period).

{36} Allstate contends that there was no evidence that Aakhus's "conduct was sufficiently severe or pervasive to alter the conditions of [Plaintiffs] employment." In support, Allstate cites to *Baskerville v. Culligan International Co.,* 50 F.3d 428 (7th Cir.1995), where the Seventh Circuit Court of Appeals reversed a jury verdict in favor of the plaintiff on her claim of sexual harassment. In that case, the manager called the plaintiff "pretty girl," made a grunting noise at her, suggested she was "hot," talked about "los[ing] control" around pretty girls, and made a gesture suggesting masturbation. *Id.* at 430. The court stated, "We do not think that these incidents, spread over seven months, could reasonably be thought to add up to sexual harassment." *Id.* The court noted that the manager never touched the plaintiff, never invited her to have sex or a date, and he never threatened her, exposed himself, or showed her a dirty picture. *Id.* at 431. Allstate argues that Aakhus never did any of these things either.

{37} We are not persuaded that this case is like Baskerville. The jury in this case was instructed that [w]hether the environment constituted a sexually hostile work environment is determined by looking at the totality of the circumstances, including the frequency of the discriminatory conduct, the severity of the conduct, whether the conduct was physically threatening or humiliating or a mere offensive utterance, and whether it unreasonably interfered with an employee's work performance. There was evidence that Aakhus's profanity and his sex-related comments and jokes occurred almost daily, that it was "constant" and increased over time, that it occurred at office lunches and staff meetings, and that Aakhus became more aggressive as time passed. Plaintiff, Wise, and Reed testified that Aakhus frequently followed Plaintiff close on her heels, pointed his finger at her, and yelled at her "with his face bright purple," and Reed said that Aakhus "was totally angry and abusive" to Plaintiff. Plaintiff testified that Aakhus became critical of her work and that his criticisms were completely unfounded, that Aakhus told her that he knew she had reported him to management, that Aakhus began sabotaging her computer, and that she was operating at an extremely high stress level.

{38} The jury could reasonably consider the totality of these circumstances and conclude that the environment in the office was hostile. See *Nava v. City of Santa Fe,* 2004-NMSC-039; ¶ 15, 136 N.M. 647, 103 P.3d 571 (holding that there was sufficient evidence of harassment even though each incident by itself "may not have been severe enough to support a hostile work environment claim" but "in their aggregate, the incidents reflect[ed] the severity and pervasiveness of the harassment"). While Allstate presented evidence that could be viewed as inconsistent with such a conclusion, "[t]he question is not whether substantial evidence exists to support the opposite result, but rather whether such evidence supports the result reached." *Las Cruces Prof'l Fire Fighters v. City of****1090** *Las Cruces,* 1997-NMCA-044, ¶ 12, 123 N.M. 329, 940 P.2d 177. We therefore conclude that substantial evidence supported the jury's verdict in favor of Plaintiff on her claim of hostile work environment sexual harassment.

B. Retaliatory Constructive Discharge

{39} Allstate contends the evidence did not support Plaintiff's claim of retaliatory constructive discharge. It makes two arguments on this issue. First, it argues that Plaintiff was not constructively discharged because a reasonable person in Plaintiff s situation would not have felt compelled to resign. See *Ulibarri v. State,* 2006-NMSC-009, ¶ 14, 139 N.M. 193, 131 P.3d 43 (explaining that in order to show constructive discharge, a plaintiff "must show that the employer made working conditions so intolerable, when viewed objectively, that a reasonable person would be compelled to resign" (internal quotation marks and citation omitted)). Second, Allstate asserts that, even if Plaintiff was constructively discharged, she failed to prove that her discharge was in retaliation for an act she performed that public policy would authorize or encourage.

1. Constructive Discharge

{40} Allstate maintains that Plaintiff failed to prove constructive discharge. At most, according to Allstate, Plaintiff presented evidence of (1) a hostile work environment, (2) arguably unfair criticism of her work, (3) being forced to relinquish her private office for a carrel, and (4) an unfounded denial of her request for a leave of absence. According to Allstate, this evidence does not rise to the "extraordinary and egregious" level necessary "to overcome the normal motivation of a competent, diligent, and reasonable employee to remain on the job." *Turner v. Anheuser-Busch, Inc.,* 7 Cal.4th 1238, 32 Cal.Rptr.2d 223, 876 P.2d 1022, 1026 (1994) (in bank), overruled on other grounds in *Romano v. Rockwell Int'l, Inc.,* 14 Cal.4th 479, 59 Cal. Rptr.2d 20; 926 P.2d 1114 (1996).

{41} Again, we assess the sufficiency of the evidence in the context of the jury instructions given. The district court instructed the jury:

> You may consider that [Plaintiff] was constructively discharged from her employment if you find that Defendant Allstate Insurance Company made her working conditions so intolerable, when viewed objectively, that a reasonable person would be compelled to resign, and she had no other choice but to quit. Our review of the transcript convinces us that the jury could have reasonably found that Allstate constructively discharged Plaintiff.

{42} As discussed previously in this opinion, there was substantial evidence supporting the conclusion that Allstate subjected Plaintiff to hostile work environment sexual harassment consisting of pervasive sexual commentary and innuendo. In addition, there was evidence that Aakhus subjected Plaintiff to aggressive, physically intimidating conduct, such as his frequently following her closely on her heels, pointing his finger at her, and shouting at and berating her in public areas of the office. Plaintiff testified that after she reported Aakhus to Allstate's Resolution Line, Aakhus began criticizing her work and that the criticisms were inaccurate and outrageous. Then, in 2000, after Allstate's human resources department conducted an investigation of the various complaints about Aakhus, he told Plaintiff he knew she had reported him, and he became more aggressive. Plaintiff testified that Aakhus began deleting the "ticklers" on her computer. Ticklers were computerized reminders of deadlines in the various cases handled by the office. In 2001, Aakhus formally disciplined Plaintiff by giving her a "requires improvement" notice. Plaintiff testified that the notice was "absolutely full of false accusations." Notably, the evidence of unfair criticism was not solely Plaintiff's testimony of her subjective views. Several witnesses, including two attorneys who worked closely with Plaintiff, testified that Plaintiff was very competent arid her work was excellent.

{43} There was also evidence that Plaintiff and others made many complaints about Aakhus to Allstate, apparently to no avail. ***1091** Plaintiff first complained to the Resolution Line in 1999, and others also complained. Plaintiff received no response to her initial complaint indicating that Allstate had looked at the matter, and she was told that the case was closed. She spoke several times with Allstate's employee assistance program to try to figure out how to get Aakhus to stop his behavior. There were many complaints about Aakhus to the Resolution Line in 2000. Ultimately, Allstate sent two people from human resources to the office, and Plaintiff spoke to them. Allstate disciplined Aakhus, but Plaintiff did not know at the time that this had occurred. Every time she called the Resolution Line she was told to call back on a specific date, but when she did so, she was told the matter was still under investigation and to call back.

{44} In May 2001, Aakhus was very agitated and told Plaintiff she had to move out of her office into a work carrel area, even though there was vacant office space. This exposed her to more of the sexual talk and innuendo. In 2002, Plaintiffs father died, and her 95-year-old, infirm grandfather was "crushed." Plaintiff, who believed she had a leave of absence available to her, asked Aakhus for leave, and he denied it. Plaintiff begged Aakhus because she "was at [her] wits' end." She testified that this "was the worst day of [her] professional life" and that she "had absolutely no alternative but to give [her] notice."

{45} Allstate presented evidence that was inconsistent with Plaintiffs testimony. However, "when there is a conflict in the testimony, we defer to the trier of fact." *Buckingham v. Ryan,* 1998-NMCA-012, ¶ 10, 124 N.M. 498, 953 P.2d 33. The jury apparently found Plaintiffs evidence to be more credible than that submitted by Allstate, and we will not second guess that determination.

{46} Allstate analogizes this case to *Gormley v. Coca-Cola Enterprises,* 2005-NMSC-003, 137 N.M. 192, 109 P.3d 280, in which the Court affirmed summary judgment in favor of the defendant on the plaintiff's claim of constructive discharge because the plaintiff failed to show that his working conditions rose to the necessary level. *Id.* ¶ 1, 137 N.M. 192, 109 P.3d 280. The plaintiff based his claim on criticism of his job performance, loss of overtime, reduction in pay, and loss of a lighter duty position, which the plaintiff contended jeopardized his safety. *Id.* ¶¶ 13, 17, 137 N.M. 192, 109 P.3d 280. The Court held that the plaintiffs claim of criticism was too generalized, in that he had never received any written discipline; that loss of overtime was not material because it did not result in a reduction in base pay; that the reduction in pay was not extreme; and that he failed to provide record support for his claim that his change in duties jeopardized his safety. *Id.* ¶¶ 14-18, 137 N.M. 192, 109 P.3d 280.

{47} We do not agree that the evidence presented in Gormley was equivalent to Plaintiffs evidence in the present case. Plaintiff introduced proof establishing hostile work environment sexual harassment and evidence that her supervisor physically intimidated her, sabotaged her computer, and falsely accused her of inadequate work performance. The actions of the plaintiffs employer in Gormley were not nearly so egregious.

{48} Allstate's additional arguments on this issue in effect ask us to reweigh the evidence. It cites numerous cases for the propositions that criticism is expected by employees, that denial of leave or movement from an office to a carrel are not egregious enough to constitute constructive discharge, and that giving notice of resignation rather than quitting on the spot demonstrates voluntary termination of employment. We are not persuaded. These contentions are more in the nature of closing argument than legal reasons for concluding that the evidence was insufficient. It is not our role to reweigh the evidence or substitute our judgment for that of the jury. *Id.* Consequently, we conclude that the evidence, when considered in its totality, could have reasonably supported the jury's conclusion that Allstate made Plaintiffs working conditions so intolerable that a reasonable person in her position would have been compelled to resign.

2. Retaliation for an Act Public Policy Has Authorized or Encouraged

{49} Allstate argues that, even if Plaintiff proved that she was constructively discharged, ***1092** she failed to prove that her discharge was in retaliation for an act that public policy has authorized or encouraged. It contends that it is unclear what act' Plaintiff claimed was the reason for her discharge, that she failed to prove a causal connection. between the act and the discharge, and that there was no retaliation as a matter of law because the district court granted Allstate's pretrial motion for summary judgment on Plaintiff's claim under the Human Rights Act to the extent it was predicated on retaliation. We disagree.

{50} First, the jury instructions provide the answer with respect to Allstate's claim that the evidence did not establish what act of Plaintiff was authorized or encouraged by public policy. The district court instructed the jury that `lilt is the public policy of the State of New Mexico to prohibit sexual harassment in the work place and to encourage employees to report sexual harassment."

{51} Second, in light of (a) our holding that there was sufficient evidence to support the jury's finding of sexual harassment, (b) Plaintiff's public-policy-sanctioned reporting of that harassment, (c) the evidence that Aakhus indicated that he knew Plaintiff had reported him and that he became more aggressive afterward, and (d) Plaintiff's testimony about what caused her to resign her job, it would be reasonable for the jury to infer that there was a connection between the harassment, the reporting of the harassment, and the discharge.

{52} Third, the district court granted summary judgment to Allstate on Plaintiff s retaliation claims under the version of the Human Rights Act that was in effect at the time because she failed to make her claims within 180 days of each retaliatory act of discipline she alleged. See § 28-1-10(A) (1995) (amended 2005) (requiring complaints of unlawful discriminatory practice to be filed with the human rights division within 180 days after the alleged act was committed). When these claims were argued on summary judgment, they did not include the ultimate claim of retaliatory constructive discharge that ripened on February 15. These statutory claims were distinct from Plaintiffs claim of retaliatory constructive discharge, which is a common law claim. See Gormley, 2005-NMSC-003, ¶ 9, 137 N.M. 192, 109 P.3d 280 (explaining that "constructive discharge is a doctrine that permits an employee to recast a resignation as a de facto firing, depending on the circumstances surrounding the employment relationship and the employee's departure"). We fail to see how the untimely filing of specific statutory claims under the Human Rights Act translates into the substantive failure of Plaintiff's claim of retaliatory discharge, and the district court did not rule that the facts surrounding the ultimate retaliatory discharge claim were untimely because that matter was not before it.

C. Compensatory Damages for Alleged Emotional Injuries

{53} The jury awarded Plaintiff $360,000 in compensatory damages after being instructed that, if it found in favor of Plaintiff, it should calculate the amount of damages by considering:

[(1) t]he benefits Plaintiff would have earned, less the amount Plaintiff could through exercise of reasonable diligence have earned, in the time made available as a result of the conclusion of her employment with Allstate, from employment of the same quality as her employment with

Allstate[,] . . . [and (2) an amount of money that will reasonably and fairly compensate her for any emotional distress caused by the violation.

Allstate surmises that the portion of the total damages awarded that is attributable to Plaintiff's economic damages is between $105,000, which was the amount Plaintiffs counsel requested in closing argument as compensation for loss of pension benefits, and $159,349, which was the amount Plaintiff s expert economist testified was the total amount of pension benefits lost. Consequently, Allstate continues, the remaining amount of damages—between $200,651 and $255,000—must be attributable to Plaintiff's emotional injuries. Allstate claims that this amount is excessive and that the district court should have granted remittitur because Plaintiff offered no corroborating evidence in ***1093**the form of medical diagnosis or treatment, or in the form of testimony that Plaintiff missed work or looked' for another job while Aakhus was employed at Allstate.

{54} Allstate's argument is partly that there was insufficient evidence supporting the damages award, and to that extent we employ the substantial evidence standard of review recited earlier in this opinion. Allstate also argues that the district court should have ordered remittitur. In determining whether a jury verdict is excessive, we do not reweigh the evidence but determine whether the verdict is excessive as a matter of law. The jury's verdict is presumed to be correct. When a [district] court denies a motion for a remittitur, we defer to the trial court's judgment. *Ennis v. Kmart Corp.*, 2001-NMCA-068, ¶ 27, 131 N.M. 32, 33 P.3d 32 (citations omitted).

{55} We first observe that Allstate may be wrong about the amount the jury attributed to Plaintiff's economic damages. Plaintiffs expert economist based the present value of Plaintiffs lost pension on the assumption of a normal life expectancy of age 81. It is possible that the jury concluded that Plaintiff would live longer than age 81.

{56} More importantly, Allstate has not cited any authority for the proposition that a plaintiffs testimony of emotional distress' must be corroborated before the plaintiff is entitled to be compensated for such distress. Allstate relies on the Nava case to support its position, and points to language in that sexual harassment case emphasizing that the plaintiff had not presented any "evidence of concrete damages, such as counseling expenses or lost time from work." 2004-NMSC-039, ¶ 18, 136 N.M. 647, 103 P.3d 571. However, in that case our Supreme Court was reviewing a district court's order granting remittitur. *Id.* ¶ 3, 136 N.M. 647, 103 P.3d 571. The Court properly deferred to the district court's determination, just as we must defer to the district court's denial of remittitur in the present case. See *Id.* ¶ 20, 136 N.M. 647, 103 P.3d 571.

{57} There was substantial evidence upon which the jury could base an award of damages for emotional distress. Plaintiff and her co-employees testified about the stress Plaintiff suffered as a result of the sexual atmosphere in the office and the conduct of Aakhus. Plaintiff testified that she was frightened for her job, that she feared being alone with Aakhus and took steps to avoid such a scenario, and that Aakhus publicly belittled and berated her. Her co-workers testified that Aakhus sometimes followed Plaintiff closely and yelled at her and that they saw Plaintiff crying or on the verge of tears many times. Aakhus formally disciplined Plaintiff after she complained about him, and several witnesses testified that Plaintiffs work was exemplary.

{58} Allstate has failed to meet its burden of establishing "that the verdict was infected with passion, prejudice, partiality, sympathy, undue influence, or some corrupt cause or motive." *Ennis*, 2001-NMCA-068, ¶ 27, 131 N.M. 32, 33 P.3d 32 (internal quotation marks and citation omitted). We will not reweigh the evidence and substitute our judgment for that of the jury.

III. The District Court Properly Allowed the Jury to Consider Punitive Damages

{59} Allstate argues that the district court should have granted its motion for directed verdict on the issue of punitive damages because Allstate did not have the culpable mental state that is a prerequisite to an award of such damages. See *Allsup's Convenience Stores, Inc. v. N. River Ins. Co.*, 1999-NMSC-006, ¶ 53, 127 N.M. 1, 976 P.2d 1 (explaining that an award of punitive damages must be based on "a culpable mental state indivisible from the conduct constituting liability" (internal quotation marks omitted)). When we review a district court's ruling on a motion for directed verdict, "any conflicts in the evidence or reasonable interpretations of it are viewed in favor of the party resisting the directed verdict." *Hedicke v. Gunville*, 2003-NMCA-032, ¶ 9, 133 N.M. 335, 62 P.3d 1217. "The sufficiency of evidence presented to support a legal claim or defense is a question of law for the trial ***1094** court to decide. This

Court reviews questions of law de novo." *Id.* (internal quotation marks and citations omitted).

{60} Allstate advances two sub-arguments: (1) that Allstate cannot be vicariously liable for the acts of Aakhus because Aakhus was not acting within the scope of employment when he was engaged in sexually harassing conduct and because Aakhus was not employed in a managerial capacity; and (2) that Allstate did not authorize, ratify, or participate in Aakhus's misconduct. See *Weidler*, 1998-NMCA-021, ¶ 42, 124 N.M. 591, 953 P.2d 1089 (listing two methods of holding a principal liable for punitive damages: by establishing that "the principal has in some way authorized, ratified, or participated in the wanton, oppressive, malicious, fraudulent, or criminal acts of its agent" or by establishing that "the agent was employed in a managerial capacity and was acting in the scope of his employment" (internal quotation marks and citation omitted)): We need not address the first sub-argument because we conclude that the evidence supported the view that Allstate authorized, ratified, or participated in Aakhus's misconduct. See *Atler*, 2005-NMCA-006, ¶ 16, 136 N.M. 701, 104 P.3d 1092 ("When the jury instructions provide two alternative bases for awarding punitive damages, we will uphold the jury verdict if there is substantial evidence in the record to support either.").

{61} There was testimony at trial that Aakhus's boss, Larry Vogel, was present for some of the "sex talk" that occurred in the office and apparently did nothing to stop it. Although Allstate reprimanded Aakhus for "unprofessional behavior" in August 2000, the employees in the office did not know this, and it appeared that the reprimand had no effect because Aakhus's behavior never improved. On the contrary, it worsened, despite numerous complaints to Allstate over the three-year period when Plaintiff's employment overlapped with Aakhus's. Indeed, Reed testified that Vogel told employees that Aakhus "might have a few little problems ... but ... you need to take care of yourselves." When others in Allstate management wanted to impose additional discipline on Aakhus, Vogel resisted because he did not think there was sufficient evidence for such discipline and because the Albuquerque office was performing well.

{62} Viewing the reasonable interpretations of this evidence in favor of Plaintiff, see *Hedicke,* 2003-NMCA-032, ¶ 9, 133 N.M. 335, 62 P.3d 1217, we conclude there was sufficient evidence to submit the issue of punitive damages to the jury. We agree with the district court that Vogel's failure to act after observing Aakhus's misconduct firsthand "could constitute authorization, participation in, or ratification. There's also a question for the [j]ury as to whether the disciplinary actions taken were adequate or whether they represent in some way authorization of ... Aakhus's conduct."

IV. The Punitive Damages Award Did Not Violate Due Process

{63} Allstate contends the punitive damages award reflects passion and prejudice and, consequently, violates due process. See *Aken v. Plains Elec. Generation. & Transmission, Coop., Inc.*, 2002-NMSC-021, ¶ 17, 132 N.M. 401, 49 P.3d 662 (explaining that punitive damages awards are reviewed under a de novo standard "as a matter of federal constitutional imperative"). We conduct an independent, de novo assessment of the award. *Id.* ¶ 19, 132 N.M. 401, 49 P.3d 662. In effect, we are reviewing the award for reasonableness. *Chavarria v. Fleetwood Retail Corp.*, 2006-NMSC-046, ¶ 36, 140 N.M. 478, 143 P.3d 717. In undertaking this review we consider three criteria: (1) the reprehensibility of the defendant's conduct, or the enormity and nature of the wrong; (2) the relationship between the harm suffered and the punitive damages award; and (3) the difference between the punitive damages award and the civil and criminal penalties authorized or imposed in comparable cases. *Id.*

{64} With respect to the first criterion, the reprehensibility of the conduct, Allstate argues that there was no evidence that Allstate engaged in a pattern of threatening employees with their jobs if they reported sexual harassment, or that Allstate "persisted **1095** in a course of conduct after it had been adjudged unlawful on even one occasion, let alone repeat occasions." Our Supreme Court in Aken noted that in retaliatory discharge cases "evidence of repeated engagement in prohibited conduct knowing or suspecting it is unlawful is relevant support for a substantial award." 2002-NMSC-021, ¶ 21, 132 N.M. 401, 49 P.3d 662 (internal quotation marks and citation omitted).

{65} Plaintiff presented evidence that, even after Allstate privately reprimanded Aakhus in August 2000 for what it called "unprofessional behavior," Aakhus's misconduct intensified, and employees continued to make complaints to Allstate's Resolution Line and its human resources department. Although Allstate management investigated these complaints, it did nothing further about Aakhus until nearly two years later, in May 2002. There is no question that Allstate knew that sexual harassment, and specifically Aakhus's conduct, was unlawful, because it distributed to its employees a pamphlet stating that "[i]t is [Allstate's] policy to maintain a working environment free from discrimination and sexual advances or harassment which may affect an employee's terms or conditions of employment." That pamphlet cited, as an example of sexual harassment, "[w]ritten material, photos and/or any other items of a sexual nature." Given this and the testimony of various employees that they reported Aakhus's misconduct many times over a period of years, we conclude that the jury reasonably could have found that Allstate demonstrated consciousness of wrongdoing. See *Id.* (finding support for award of punitive damages in light of evidence showing that "[the defendant's] behavior exhibited consciousness of wrongdoing"). And, like the Court in Aken, "we conclude that a substantial award was necessary to meet the goal of punishing [Allstate] for its conduct and deterring it, and others similarly situated in the future, from engaging in such conduct." *Id.*

{66} As for the second criterion for assessing the reasonableness of the award, the relationship between the harm suffered and the award, we must consider whether the amount of the award is "so unrelated to the injury and actual damages proven as to plainly manifest passion and prejudice rather than reason or justice." *Id.* ¶ 23, 132 N.M. 401, 49 P.3d 662 (internal quotation marks and citation omitted). Although the United States Supreme Court has suggested that due process is most likely satisfied if there is "a single-digit ratio between punitive and compensatory damages," *State Farm Mut. Auto. Ins. Co. v. Campbell*, 538 U.S. 408, 425, 123 S.Ct. 1513, 155 L.Ed.2d 585 (2003), the Court has also indicated the need for a flexible approach. *Id.* Here, the ratio of punitive damages to compensatory damages is 3.6 to 1. This is within the range deemed by the Supreme Court to be consistent with due process. See *Id.*

{67} Allstate contends that the punitive damages award is in some ways duplicative of the compensatory damages awarded for emotional distress because both awards derive from the outrage and humiliation suffered by Plaintiff. This argument is somewhat speculative, and "[a]ny doubt in the mind of the appellate court concerning the question of what appropriate damages may be in the abstract, or owing to the coldness of the record, should be resolved in favor of the jury verdict." *Aken,* 2002-NMSC-021, ¶ 19, 132 N.M. 401, 49 P.3d 662.

{68} The third criterion, comparing the punitive damages award to civil and/or criminal penalties imposed for comparable Misconduct, "has been criticized as ineffective and very difficult to employ." *Id.* ¶ 25, 132 N.M. 401, 49 P.3d 662. This is in part because there may be some categories of conduct for which there is no significant statutory guidance as to what sanctions should be imposed for the conduct. *Id.* As a result, our Supreme Court has characterized this criterion as "the least important indicium." *Id.* We can find no legislative guidance as to the civil or criminal sanctions that might be imposed for sexual harassment or retaliatory discharge. We doubt that Aakhus's misconduct could be characterized as any type of crime, but this does not render his behavior less reprehensible. On the civil side, the legislature, via the Human Rights Act, has clearly condemned discrimination, but it has not attempted to place a monetary valuation on recovery for violations of the Act. See § 28-1-7 ***1096** (listing the various forms of discrimination that are deemed unlawful); § 28-1-11(E) (permitting human rights commission to award "actual damages"); § 28-1-13(D) (permitting district court to award "actual damages"). This does not signify to us that discriminatory behavior is considered to be minimally sanctionable. To the contrary, it indicates the legislature's willingness to leave the assessment of reasonable compensation to the fact finder, whether the fact finder is the human rights commission or a court of law. Consequently, we deem the third criterion to be neutral. Because the other two criteria convince us of the reasonableness of the punitive damages award, we affirm the award.

V. Plaintiff's Request for Attorney Fees

{69} Pursuant to Rule 12-403 NMRA (permitting appellate court to award attorney fees where allowed by law) and Section 28-1-13(D) (allowing award of attorney fees to prevailing party in an appeal under the Human Rights Act), Plaintiff asks us to award attorney fees for this appeal, or to remand to allow the district court to make this determination. We remand this issue to the district court to determine whether to make such an award and, if so, in what amount.

Conclusion

{70} For the foregoing reasons, we affirm the judgment of the district court.

{71} IT IS SO ORDERED. WE CONCUR: LYNN PICKARD and JAMES J. WECHSLER, Judges.

Exercises

1. If the Allstate employee, in fact, made repeated sexual advances and comments about others to the paralegal, do you believe this constitutes sexual harassment?
2. Based on the facts of the case, do you believe the defendants discharge was a retaliatory?
3. Did you agree with the court that the work environment was hostile? Explain your answer.
4. Did you generally agree or disagree with the decision?

Helpful Web Sites

Organization	Description	Internet Address
ABA Law Practice Today	ABA site devoted to law practice management and legal administration.	http://www.abanet.org/lpm
ABA Legal Technology Resource Center	ABA site devoted to technology. Includes resources and articles.	http://www.abanet.org/tech/ltrc/home.html
Alabama State Bar—Law Office Management Assistance Program	Articles on a variety of law office management topics, including a disaster recovery kit.	http://www.alabar.org/
Association of Legal Administrators	National association for legal administrators. Contains resources and information related to law office management and legal administration.	http://www.alanet.org
Law Technology News	Excellent periodical for legal technology issues.	http://www.lawtechnews.com
Maryland State Bar Association—Law Practice Management Assistance	The site has a wide variety of law office management topics, including a number of articles and excellent resources.	http://www.msba.org/
New Jersey State Bar Association—Law Office Management Articles	Articles on a variety of law office management topics.	http://www.njsba.com/
	The site is extremely in-depth and has a collection of some of the best law office management-related articles and information on the Internet. The articles are also arranged by folders according to subject matter.	http://www.nysba.org/
South Carolina Bar—Practice Management Section	The site has a wide variety of law office management topics, including a number of articles and excellent resources.	http://www.scbar.org/
State Bar of Georgia—Law Practice Management Articles	Articles on a variety of law office management topics.	http://www.gabar.org/
State Bar of New Mexico—Law Office Management Site	Miscellaneous law office management and legal administration topics and links.	http://www.nmbar.org/

Suggested Reading

1. American Bar Association. (2004). *American Bar Association Legal Technology Surveys.*
2. Schultz, S. S. & Schultz, J. S. (2005). *The Complete Guide to Designing your Law Office.* American Bar Association.
3. Wert, R. C. & Hatoff, H. I. (2004). *Law Office Policy & Procedures Manual* (4th ed.). American Bar Association.
4. *Law Practice* magazine, published by the American Bar Association Law Practice Management Section [http://www.abanet.org/lpm].
5. *Law Technology* News periodical [http://www.lawtechnologynews.com].
6. Grella, T. C. & Hudkins, M. L. (2005). *The Lawyer's Guide to Strategic Planning: Defining, Setting, and Achieving Your Firm's Goals.* American Bar Association.
7. Munneke, G. A., & Davis, A. E. (2003, 2007, 2010). *The Essential Formbook: Comprehensive Management Tools for Lawyers, Volumes I–IV.* American Bar Association.

3

Ethics and Malpractice

Chapter Objectives

After you read this chapter, you should be able to:

- Define what the unauthorized practice of law is and list factors that are used to determine whether a paralegal is "practicing law."
- Discuss the voluntary ethical codes established by national paralegal and legal assistants associations.
- Explain the attorney–client privilege and to whom it applies.
- List guidelines that will prevent paralegals from accidentally revealing confidential client information.
- Explain what a conflict of interest is and what a law office can do to limit conflict of interest problems.
- Discuss what an "Ethical Wall" is and when it applies.

The Johnson & Smith law firm primarily handled bankruptcy cases. The firm employed two attorneys, several paralegals, and clerical staff. The bankruptcy trustee considered the firm to be a "high-volume filer," filing an average of 77 cases per month (nearly 1000 per year). The firm's standard practice in handling cases was for a paralegal to:

- Hold an initial consultation meeting with the client, without an attorney present.
- Discuss with the client the bankruptcy chapters available.
- Assist the client in deciding which, if any, chapter proceedings should be filed.
- Consult an attorney if a client had a question he or she could not answer and relay the attorney's response back to the client.
- Ask the client to complete a questionnaire.
- Review the questionnaire.
- Prepare the bankruptcy papers to be filed.
- Meet with the client again (without an attorney present) for the purpose of having the client sign the papers.

In most instances, unless the client specifically requested to meet with an attorney, the client's first contact with the attorney was at the meeting of creditors. The court found that the paralegals performed many services that constituted the unauthorized practice of law. Adapted from *In re Pinkins*, 213 B.R. 818 (Bankr. E.D. Mich. 1997), included at the end of this chapter.

Why Are Ethics and Malpractice Important?

The importance of high ethical standards and of following your state's ethical rules cannot be overemphasized. Clients and attorneys must have total confidence that a paralegal understands the many ethical problems that might arise in the practice of law and that the paralegal's ethical judgment is clear. Ethical problems routinely encountered by paralegals include unauthorized practice of law questions, conflict of interest problems, and confidentiality problems. Unethical behavior of a paralegal can cause an attorney to lose a case, destroy client confidence in the entire law office, or lead a client to dismiss the attorney. Unethical behavior on the part of a paralegal could lead to sanctions, fines, and disciplinary action against the attorney, and can cost a paralegal his or her job. It also could result in damaging publicity for the law office and may even lead to criminal charges being filed against the attorney. Consequently, paralegals must know how to work through and solve tough ethical problems.

A paralegal must perform careful, high-quality work in everything he or she does. An error can be very costly and can subject an attorney or a law office to a malpractice claim. Malpractice occurs when an attorney's or a law office's conduct does not meet the professional standard for the area and injures a client. Malpractice claims can result in a law office being liable for thousands of dollars of damages to injured clients. Paralegals must clearly understand how malpractice occurs and how it can be prevented.

Legal Ethics and Professional Responsibility

Legal ethics is an increasingly important and difficult topic for paralegals in every type of law practice. There are many treatises that cover this topic in depth. This section will cover ethics only from a paralegal's perspective and will give insight into common ethical problems likely to arise.

Ethics is an important topic, not only because a law office or an attorney can be disciplined for violating ethical rules, but also because legal ethics bears on whether quality legal services are being provided to clients. If a law office or its employee engages in unethical conduct, the reputation of the office will be affected and clients will lose confidence in it. The unethical behavior does not necessarily have to be directly detrimental to the client or the client's case. If a client senses that the attorney or paralegal is acting unethically toward an adversary, the client may suspect that the attorney or paralegal could be guilty of the same type of practice toward him or her. The issues of trust and ethics are closely related and bear directly upon the attorney–client relationship.

When clients lose confidence, they may move their business to another law office, cease referring new clients to the law office, or even sue. Nearly 70% of all new business a law office receives comes from referrals. When a client takes business elsewhere, it has an immediate as well as a long-term effect on the firm, since that source of revenue is also gone for future years. In short, legal ethics has a direct bearing on the law office's bottom line and on the long-term success of the firm. Thus, paralegals and attorneys have both an incentive and a duty to act ethically and to develop systems that stress the importance of legal ethics on a daily basis.

Ethical Standards for Attorneys

ethical rule

A minimal standard of conduct.

An **ethical rule** is a minimal standard of conduct. An attorney may not fall below the standard without losing his or her good standing with the state bar. Attorneys who violate ethical rules may be disciplined; discipline for unethical conduct may include permanent disbarment from practicing law, temporary suspension from practicing, public censure, private censure, or an informal reprimand. Exhibit 3-1 shows a procedural example of ethical rules at work. The client initiates the inquiry in most instances of attorney misconduct, typically by sending a letter of complaint to the state's disciplinary administrator. The state disciplinary administration is in charge of enforcing the state's professional licensing standards for attorneys.

Ethics has had a long-standing place in the American legal system. In 1908, the American Bar Association (ABA), a voluntary association of attorneys, adopted the Canons of

Exhibit 3-1 Example of Ethical Violation and Subsequent Ethical Proceedings Against an Attorney

The facts:	An attorney represented a client who was selling a piece of real estate. It was agreed that the attorney's fees would be $6500. After completing the sale, the proceeds of the sale were placed into the attorney's trust account (i.e., a holding account for client funds). The attorney paid some proceeds to the client, withdrew $14,000 for himself, would not provide an accounting of the funds to the client, and would not respond to many messages left by the client.
The client:	The client, becoming increasingly frustrated with the attorney, calls the local courthouse and asks how to complain about the conduct of the attorney. The client is told to send a letter of complaint to the state's disciplinary administrator in the state's judicial branch. The client is told that the letter should clearly explain who the attorney was and exactly what happened. The client then sends the letter.
The disciplinary administrator:	The state's disciplinary administrator receives the client's letter. The administrator determines that if everything the client says is true, the attorney may have violated Supreme Court Rule 4-1.5 for his state, which says that "an attorney shall not charge an illegal or clearly excessive fee." The administrator sends a letter to the attorney asking for his side of the story but never receives a reply.
Investigation:	The disciplinary administrator then refers the matter to the State Bar's Investigation Committee, which investigates the matter, including interviews with both the client and the attorney. The Committee, after a full investigation, recommends that formal charges be filed before the state's bar court to discipline the attorney.
State's bar court/state's supreme court:	The disciplinary administrator files formal charges and prosecutes the attorney for the ethical violations before the state's bar court, an arm of the state's supreme court. A hearing or trial is held where both sides present their evidence. The bar court determines that the attorney violated Rule 4-1.5 and disciplines the attorney by suspending him from the practice of law for two years, and orders him to pay restitution to the client.

Model Code of Professional Responsibility/Model Rules of Professional Conduct

Self-imposed ethical standards for ABA members, but they also serve as a prototype of legal ethics standards for state court systems.

Professional Ethics. In 1969, the ABA updated and expanded the canons into the ***Model Code of Professional Responsibility***. The *Model Code* was updated in 1983 and is now called the ***Model Rules of Professional Conduct***.

In the late 1990s, the ABA convened the Ethics 2000 Commission on evaluation of the rules of professional conduct to undertake a comprehensive review and rewrite of the *Model Rules;* in 2002, the ABA adopted the newly revised *Model Rules* after several years of work and 50 days of open meetings, including numerous public hearings and free debate. The ABA's last revision was in 2008.

Today, nearly all states base their ethical rules on the ABA *Model Rules*. Attorneys in each state are regulated by their individual state bar association and state court system. Although state courts are free to create their own rules of conduct for attorneys, most simply modify either the ABA *Model Code* or ABA *Model Rules* to reflect the specific ethical conditions in their own states. For this text, the ABA *Model Rules* is most often referenced, even though some states still model their ethical/disciplinary rules on the older ABA *Model Code*.

Attorney Ethical Rules Not Directly Applicable to the Paralegal

State canons of ethics, the *Model Code of Professional Responsibility*, or the *Model Rules of Professional Conduct* do not apply directly to paralegals, but to attorneys only. However, attorneys can be disciplined for the acts of their staff members, including paralegals, because attorneys have the duty to adequately supervise their staff as shown in Exhibit 3-2, illustrating Louisiana's Rule 5.3 (identical to the *ABA's Rule 5.3*).

This section of the *Model Rules* is important to paralegals because it requires attorneys to ensure that their staff members operate within the bounds of these rules. Exhibit 3-3 illustrates

Exhibit 3-2 State Example: Louisiana's Rules of Professional Conduct, Rule 5.3

Source: State of Louisiana.

RULE 5.3 RESPONSIBILITIES REGARDING NONLAWYER ASSISTANTS

With respect to a nonlawyer employed or retained by or associated with a lawyer:

(a) a partner, and a lawyer who individually or together with other lawyers possesses comparable managerial authority in a law firm shall make reasonable efforts to ensure that the firm has in effect measures giving reasonable assurance that the person's conduct is compatible with the professional obligations of the lawyer;

(b) a lawyer having direct supervisory authority over the nonlawyer shall make reasonable efforts to ensure that the person's conduct is compatible with the professional obligations of the lawyer; and

(c) a lawyer shall be responsible for conduct of such a person that would be a violation of the Rules of Professional Conduct if engaged in by a lawyer if:

  (1) the lawyer orders or, with the knowledge of the specific conduct, ratifies the conduct involved; or

  (2) the lawyer is a partner or has comparable managerial authority in the law firm in which the person is employed, or has direct supervisory authority over the person, and knows of the conduct at a time when its consequences can be avoided or mitigated but fails to take reasonable remedial action.

Exhibit 3-3 Attorneys Liable for Unethical Acts of Paralegal

Source: See Asphalt Engineers, Inc. v. Galusha, 770 P.2d 1180 (160 Ariz. 134, 1989).

In April, the owners of Asphalt Engineers met with Robert Walston, a legal assistant with Lee and Peggy Galusha, doing business as Galusha, Ltd., a private law firm. Asphalt Engineers told Walston that they wanted to file liens against real property involved in three construction jobs for which they had not been paid. They also requested that lawsuits foreclosing those liens be filed, if necessary. At trial, the owners of Asphalt Engineers testified that they believed Walston was an attorney. Walston requested and received a retainer payment from Asphalt Engineers. A lien was filed on one of the projects, but not on the other two. The project where the lien was filed was settled.

In June of the same year, Walston requested and received an additional retainer fee. Although Walston indicated that liens had been filed on the remaining two projects, none actually were. The time for filing both liens expired. Before Asphalt Engineers discovered that the two liens had not been filed, they brought forth another project for Walston to file a lien on; again, no lien was filed.

The court found that neither of the Galushas had ever met with Asphalt Engineers and that the Galushas allowed Walston, a nonlawyer, to provide legal advice to Asphalt Engineers, failed to file and foreclose liens, failed to adequately supervise Walston, and failed to prevent Walston from actually practicing law, among other things. Subsequently, a jury awarded Asphalt Engineers more than $75,000 in actual damages, attorneys' fees, and punitive damages against the Galusha law firm. In addition, Lee Galusha faced ethical proceedings for failing to adequately supervise the legal assistant and for failing to adequately perform legal work for a client. Lee Galusha was subsequently suspended from the practice of law and eventually was disbarred.

a case summary where a law office was sued for malpractice and the attorney was suspended from practice because of the unethical acts of a paralegal. If a paralegal is found to be acting unethically, especially when there is a pattern and practice of doing so, the attorney has an affirmative duty to remedy the situation, even if that means terminating the paralegal's employment. Thus, there are many incentives for paralegals to act ethically and to comply with the same rules as attorneys. In addition, this section of the rule ensures that an attorney cannot avoid the ethical rules and accomplish an unethical act by delegating or allowing a staff member to do it.

So, although a paralegal cannot be disciplined by state regulatory bodies for violating state ethical rules, he or she would be held accountable by the attorney who hired or supervised him or her. Paralegals must understand and abide by any ethical rules governing the conduct of attorneys.

Voluntary Ethical Codes Established by Paralegal Associations

Paralegals remain largely unregulated. There are, however, self-imposed, *voluntary* ethical standards set out by national or local paralegal and legal assistants associations. Both the National Association of Legal Assistants Paralegals (NALA) and the National Federation of Paralegal Associations (NFPA) have adopted ethical canons for their members. Exhibits 3-4 and 3-5 show the codes of ethics for both associations. Paralegals cannot be disciplined for not following such voluntary codes. However, following such a code will help the paralegal avoid ethical problems.

Criminal Statutes Regarding the Unauthorized Practice of Law

There are criminal statutes in nearly every state that provide sanctions for nonlawyers who engage in "practicing law," which usually includes providing legal advice to the public or representation of a client in a court of law.

There is no direct regulation of paralegals, but they are indirectly regulated through state ethical standards for attorneys, nonbinding paralegal association ethical standards, and criminal statutes barring non-attorneys from practicing law.

The Unauthorized Practice of Law

Most states have a criminal statute that prohibits a layperson from practicing law. The reason behind such a statute is to protect the general public from individuals who are not qualified to give legal advice because they do not have the proper educational training, have not passed the bar exam, or are not fit to practice law. In Florida for example, an unauthorized practice violation results in a third-degree felony charge and up to a $5000 fine.

Besides criminal prohibitions, there are ethical prohibitions as well. Rule 5.5 regarding the rules of professional conduct prohibits an attorney from assisting a person who is not a member of the bar in an activity that would constitute the unauthorized practice of the law. This rule draws a line that paralegals cannot cross. A paralegal is permitted to assist an attorney as long as the activity does not, in itself, constitute "practicing law."

Exhibit 3-4
National Association of Legal Assistants—Paralegals Code of Ethics and Professional Responsibility

NALA Code of Ethics and Professional Responsibility

A paralegal must adhere strictly to the accepted standards of legal ethics and to the general principles of proper conduct. The performance of the duties of the paralegal shall be governed by specific canons as defined herein so that justice will be served and goals of the profession attained. (*See Model Standards and Guidelines for Utilization of Legal Assistants, Section II.*)

The canons of ethics set forth hereafter are adopted by the National Association of Legal Assistants, Inc., as a general guide intended to aid paralegals and attorneys. The enumeration of these rules does not mean there are not others of equal importance although not specifically mentioned. Court rules, agency rules and statutes must be taken into consideration when interpreting the canons.

Definition: Legal assistants, also known as paralegals, are a distinguishable group of persons who assist attorneys in the delivery of legal services. Through formal education, training and experience, legal assistants have knowledge and expertise regarding the legal system and substantive and procedural law which qualify them to do work of a legal nature under the supervision of an attorney.

In 2001, NALA members also adopted the ABA definition of a legal assistant/paralegal, as follows:

A legal assistant or paralegal is a person qualified by education, training or work experience who is employed or retained by a lawyer, law office, corporation, governmental agency or other entity who performs specifically delegated substantive legal work for which a lawyer is responsible. (Adopted by the ABA in 1997)

Canon 1. A paralegal must not perform any of the duties that attorneys only may perform nor take any actions that attorneys may not take.

Canon 2. A paralegal may perform any task which is properly delegated and supervised by an attorney, as long as the attorney is ultimately responsible to the client, maintains a direct relationship with the client, and assumes professional responsibility for the work product.

Canon 3. A paralegal must not: (a) engage in, encourage, or contribute to any act which could constitute the unauthorized practice of law; and (b) establish attorney-client relationships, set fees, give legal opinions or advice or represent a client before a court or agency unless so authorized by that court or agency; and (c) engage in conduct or take any action which would assist or involve the attorney in a violation of professional ethics or give the appearance of professional impropriety.

Canon 4. A paralegal must use discretion and professional judgment commensurate with knowledge and experience but must not render independent legal judgment in place of an attorney. The services of an attorney are essential in the public interest whenever such legal judgment is required.

Canon 5. A paralegal must disclose his or her status as a paralegal at the outset of any professional relationship with a client, attorney, a court or administrative agency or personnel thereof, or a member of the general public. A paralegal must act prudently in determining the extent to which a client may be assisted without the presence of an attorney.

Canon 6. A paralegal must strive to maintain integrity and a high degree of competency through education and training with respect to professional responsibility, local rules and practice, and through continuing education in substantive areas of law to better assist the legal profession in fulfilling its duty to provide legal service.

Canon 7. A paralegal must protect the confidences of a client and must not violate any rule or statute now in effect or hereafter enacted controlling the doctrine of privileged communications between a client and an attorney.

Canon 8. A paralegal must disclose to his or her employer or prospective employer any pre-existing client or personal relationship that may conflict with the interests of the employer or prospective employer and/or their clients.

Canon 9. A paralegal must do all other things incidental, necessary, or expedient for the attainment of the ethics and responsibilities as defined by statute or rule of court.

Canon 10. A paralegal's conduct is guided by bar associations' codes of professional responsibility and rules of professional conduct.

Exhibit 3-5
NFPA Model Code of Ethics and Professional Responsibility

Courtesy of National Federation of Paralegal Associations.

NATIONAL FEDERATION OF PARALEGAL ASSOCIATIONS, INC.
MODEL CODE OF ETHICS AND PROFESSIONAL RESPONSIBILITY
AND GUIDELINES FOR ENFORCEMENT

PREAMBLE

The National Federation of Paralegal Associations, Inc. (NFPA) is a professional organization comprised of paralegal associations and individual paralegals throughout the United States and Canada. Members of NFPA have varying backgrounds, experiences, education and job responsibilities that reflect the diversity of the paralegal profession. NFPA promotes the growth, development and recognition of the paralegal profession as an integral partner in the delivery of legal services.

In May 1993 NFPA adopted its Model Code of Ethics and Professional Responsibility (*Model Code*) to delineate the principles for ethics and conduct to which every paralegal should aspire.

Many paralegal associations throughout the United States have endorsed the concept and content of NFPA's *Model Code* through the adoption of their own ethical codes. In doing so, paralegals have confirmed the profession's commitment to increase the quality and efficiency of legal services, as well as recognized its responsibilities to the public, the legal community, and colleagues.

Paralegals have recognized, and will continue to recognize, that the profession must continue to evolve to enhance their roles in the delivery of legal services. With increased levels of responsibility comes the need to define and enforce mandatory rules of professional conduct. Enforcement of codes of paralegal conduct is a logical and necessary step to enhance and ensure the confidence of the legal community and the public in the integrity and professional responsibility of paralegals.

In April 1997 NFPA adopted the Model Disciplinary Rules (*Model Rules*) to make possible the enforcement of the Canons and Ethical Considerations contained in the NFPA *Model Code*. A concurrent determination was made that the *Model Code of Ethics and Professional Responsibility*, formerly aspirational in nature, should be recognized as setting forth the enforceable obligations of all paralegals.

The *Model Code* and *Model Rules* offer a framework for professional discipline, either voluntarily or through formal regulatory programs.

§1. NFPA MODEL DISCIPLINARY RULES AND ETHICAL CONSIDERATIONS

1.1 A PARALEGAL SHALL ACHIEVE AND MAINTAIN A HIGH LEVEL OF COMPETENCE.

1.2 A PARALEGAL SHALL MAINTAIN A HIGH LEVEL OF PERSONAL AND PROFESSIONAL INTEGRITY.

1.3 A PARALEGAL SHALL MAINTAIN A HIGH STANDARD OF PROFESSIONAL CONDUCT.

1.4 A PARALEGAL SHALL SERVE THE PUBLIC INTEREST BY CONTRIBUTING TO THE IMPROVEMENT OF THE LEGAL SYSTEM AND DELIVERY OF QUALITY LEGAL SERVICES, INCLUDING PRO BONO PUBLICO SERVICES AND COMMUNITY SERVICE.

1.5 A PARALEGAL SHALL PRESERVE ALL CONFIDENTIAL INFORMATION PROVIDED BY THE CLIENT OR ACQUIRED FROM OTHER SOURCES BEFORE, DURING, AND AFTER THE COURSE OF THE PROFESSIONAL RELATIONSHIP.

1.6 A PARALEGAL SHALL AVOID CONFLICTS OF INTEREST AND SHALL DISCLOSE ANY POSSIBLE CONFLICT TO THE EMPLOYER OR CLIENT, AS WELL AS TO THE PROSPECTIVE EMPLOYERS OR CLIENTS.

1.7 A PARALEGAL'S TITLE SHALL BE FULLY DISCLOSED.

1.8 A PARALEGAL SHALL NOT ENGAGE IN THE UNAUTHORIZED PRACTICE OF LAW.

The real question is: at what point does one actually "practice law"? The ABA, as well as most states, have been unwilling to give a specific definition of exactly what the "practice of law" is, preferring to consider the matter on a case-by-case basis.

While what constitutes the practice of law is established by each jurisdiction, Exhibit 3-6 explains what types of actions are typically referred to in court decisions as the "practice of law;" Exhibit 3-6 also defines "other work" in a law office. Notice in Exhibit 3-6 that there are many other professional duties that a paralegal can perform that do not constitute the practice of law.

Giving Legal Advice

Paralegals may not directly advise a client regarding a legal matter. Throughout the years, courts have used several methods to distinguish between giving legal advice and simply

Exhibit 3-6
The "Practice of Law" Versus "Other Work" in a Law Office

"Practice of Law"	"Other Work" in a Law Office
Giving legal advice	Obtaining facts from a client
Representing clients in court	Communicating information to the client
Proceedings	Interviewing witnesses
Performing legal analysis and preparing legal documents	Performing limited legal research to assist an attorney with legal analysis
Evaluating a case and selecting an appropriate course of action	Obtaining documents. Preparing drafts of requests for production of a document
Accepting or rejecting a case	Preparing drafts of interrogatories
Setting a fee	Preparing drafts of responses to requests for production of documents
Sharing a fee with an attorney	Preparing drafts of responses to interrogatories
	Preparing drafts of pleadings
	Preparing correspondence
	Organizing documents and evidence
	Preparing case chronologies
	Preparing deposition summaries
	Preparing exhibit lists
	Organizing and tracking deadlines
	Conducting factual research on the Internet
	Designing/entering litigation support database
	Working w/e-discovery requests/software
	Preparing presentations

providing legal information. The purpose for this is to protect the public from unethical people that prey on unsuspecting individuals. In determining what constitutes legal advice, the court focuses on the context in which the advice is given:

- **Was a particular legal skill or knowledge used for the advice given?** The issue here is whether the information given was based on specific advice involving the operation of law or the process regarding a legal matter.
- **Was a specific direction involving the individual's rights or consequences provided for the advice given?** The issue here is whether the advice given explained legal rights or the law as it pertains to the issue? Although it is clearly understood that paralegals may not give legal advice, most courts do recognize a properly supervised paralegal is not practicing law when they convey the attorney's answer to a client's legal question; the paralegal may not convey their own opinion regarding the attorney's answer.

  For example, in *In re Houston*, 127 N.M. 582, 985 P.2d 752 (N.M. 1999), clients came to an attorney's office when a van they had recently purchased had serious mechanical problems that the dealer refused to repair. The firm filed a lawsuit against the dealer. Approximately 18 months later, the car dealer filed for bankruptcy. The law firm received the bankruptcy notice, but never told the clients. The clients discovered the bankruptcy from someone else and called the law firm. The attorney's legal assistant handled the call and told the clients that the bankruptcy would not affect the case. The clients were never told that their claim could be lost if a discharge was entered in bankruptcy without an objection to discharge being granted for their claim. After the bankruptcy was closed, the district court dismissed the clients' claim as barred by the discharge in bankruptcy. At no time, from when the clients initially came to the law firm until just before the case was dismissed, did the clients meet with an attorney. The legal assistant gave legal advice specifically related to the effect of bankruptcy on the clients' case. The advice required legal skill and knowledge, arguably included advising the clients of their rights (the conclusion that the clients did not need to do anything because the bankruptcy would have no effect). In addition, the court found that having a legal assistant conduct all meetings with the clients, during which the clients' objectives and the means for pursuing them were discussed and decided, raised serious questions regarding the unauthorized practice of law. The attorney was suspended for 18 months. In another case, the Oregon state attorney general's office is presuming a $25,000 fine for an unauthorized practice of law validation of a paralegal. The unauthorized practice of law violation is for "continued possession of immigration law materials in his business office, representation to consumers of expertise of special knowledge about immigration matters, and use of the Internet to provide information related to immigration matters to consumers."
- **Was the advice given considered an action by the nonlawyer that would be outside the scope of normal business activity?** There are several professions such as real estate agents, financial advisors, accountants, and engineers that provide legal related advice as it pertains to conducting their business. It generally will not constitute practicing law.

Misrepresentation of Status

Another factor sometimes at issue regarding the giving of legal advice is whether or not the person giving the information to the client or third party clearly identified himself or herself as a paralegal. Unless otherwise told, a client may rightly assume that he or she is talking to an attorney when, in fact, he or she is not. In such instances, the client may rely on the information from the paralegal as legal advice. To avoid misunderstandings, paralegals should always disclose their status as a paralegal and nonlawyer. NALA Code of Ethics and Professional Responsibility, Canon 5, speaks to this issue noting that paralegals should always disclose their position as a "paralegal" when dealing with any of the parties (including the general public) concerning client representation or affiliation with lawyers and law firms (*see* Cannon 5; Exhibit 3-4).

Representing Clients in Court Proceedings

Paralegals generally cannot appear in federal or state courts or legal proceedings, such as a deposition, on behalf of a client; the rights and interests of the parties are more fully safeguarded with licensed attorneys who have extended training. However, some administrative agencies do allow a paralegal to appear on behalf of a client. Some federal and state agencies require nonlawyers to satisfy certain requirements before appearing before them, while others do not. Some jurisdictions allow paralegals to make limited appearances, such as in uncontested matters and small claims court. A paralegal should carefully check the rules of his or her jurisdiction before making an appearance in a proceeding.

Performing Legal Analysis and Preparing Legal Documents

Paralegals cannot draft legal documents such as wills, briefs, motions, pleadings, or contracts without the supervision of an attorney. Paralegals routinely draft these types of documents; the distinction is that they do so properly under the direction and supervision of a member of the bar. The attorney is ultimately responsible for the legal documents; legal documents affect the legal rights of clients and parties and therefore require the oversight of an attorney. As long as a paralegal is actively working under the supervision of an attorney, and the attorney maintains a relationship with the client, the paralegal may interview witnesses or prospective clients, perform legal research, draft pleadings and briefs, and investigate the facts of cases without being accused of the unauthorized practice of law.

Evaluating a Case, Selecting or Rejecting a Case, and Selecting an Appropriate Course of Action

The act of evaluating a fact pattern, applying it to the law, considering possible courses of action based on that factual and legal analysis, and working with the client to strategize the best outcome for the client is reserved exclusively for an attorney. It is a fundamental duty of practicing law for an attorney to perform these functions. Paralegals may, of course, participate in this process, but they must do so under the auspices of an attorney. Also, the act of accepting or rejecting the representation of a client is usually reserved by an attorney, because the process includes the evaluation of the case and the potential giving of legal advice to the client. In *Cincinnati Bar Association v. Bertsche*, 84 Ohio St.3d 170, 702 N.E.2d 859 (Ohio 1998), an attorney allowed a paralegal to operate a satellite office without adequate supervision. The paralegal interviewed clients, obtained information, prepared documents, operated bank accounts, secured signings of bankruptcy petitions and other documents, and presumably (though not specifically stated) accepted cases (given that it was a satellite office). From time to time, the attorney would visit the office, interview clients, and oversee the signing of documents. The court concluded that the attorney's delegation of such matters to the paralegal and his lack of supervision over that assistant violated a disciplinary rule regarding a lawyer not neglecting an entrusted legal matter.

Setting a Fee and Sharing a Fee

The attorney is the only person allowed to establish fees with the client; a paralegal may not set fees. Additionally, the attorney may not share fees with anyone other than another attorney; a paralegal may not share fees with an attorney. A paralegal can provide information regarding fees to a client at the attorney's direction, but the paralegal should be careful to explain that the setting of the fee was done by the attorney. Rule 5.4 regarding the rules of professional conduct specifically addresses fee setting and fee sharing.

In *In re Soulisak*, 227 B.R. 77 (E.D. Va. 1998), a lawyer and a nonlawyer worked together to provide legal services in bankruptcy cases. In addition, they agreed to split the legal fees. The agreement was to charge bankruptcy clients \$650; \$400 was paid to the attorney, and \$250 was paid to the nonlawyer to cover paralegal, clerical, and operating expenses. The court found that the nonlawyer provided many of the services to the clients, thereby committing a UPL violation. The court also found the fee agreement to be improper fee sharing.

Legal Technicians, Freelance Paralegals, and the Unauthorized Practice of Law

legal technicians
People who market their legal services directly to the public.

Recently, a new class of paralegals, sometimes called "legal technicians," has emerged. What separates **legal technicians** from paralegals is that they market their services directly to the public and do not work under the supervision of an attorney. Bar associations across the country have argued that since legal technicians do not work under the supervision of a licensed attorney but represent clients directly, they dearly violate criminal statutes regarding the unauthorized practice of law. Legal technicians argue that they simply provide forms that have been written by attorneys and help the clients fill in the forms. However, as mentioned in Chapter 1, Limited Licensed Legal Technician (LLLT) laws were passed in Washington State, and other states have contemplated allowing non-attorneys, with specialized training and certification to practice law in a limited capacity. For now, decisions regarding this issue are being decided on a case-by-case basis, with many courts limiting or greatly restricting what services legal technicians can provide.

Freelance paralegals were defined in Chapter 1 as self-employed paralegals who market and sell their services to law offices on a per-job basis. Freelance paralegals are less likely to be accused of the unauthorized practice of law, since they are supposed to be acting under the supervision of an attorney. However, in instances where the freelance paralegal is removed from the attorney, and where supervision is limited or nonexistent, unauthorized practice of law problems can occur.

How to Avoid the Unauthorized Practice of Law

- **A supervising attorney should always approved the paralegal's work.** No matter how routine a legal document is, an attorney should always review it. Remember, a paralegal can do many types of activities as long as they are done under the supervision of an attorney, so take advantage of this and get everything approved. A paralegal should never let an attorney approve his or her work without reading it. If the attorney says, "I do not have time to review it; I'll sign it and you just send it out, I trust you," bring the document back at another time or find a tactful way to suggest to him or her that the document needs to be approved the right way.
- **Never let clients talk you into giving them legal advice**. Most paralegals never intend to give a client legal advice, however, it is easy to do when a client presses for information. This is usually because the attorney is unavailable and the client "needs an answer now." Legal advice might include telling the client what he or she should or should not do, answering a legal or statutory question, or telling the client what defense or legal argument he or she should make. Tell the client that you are a paralegal and cannot give legal advice, but that you will either have the attorney call the client directly or you will talk to the attorney and call the client with the attorney's advice. If a paralegal does give legal advice and things go wrong, for any reason, many clients will not hesitate to turn on you and say that they relied on your advice; this is why this issue is so critical. What a paralegal can do is provide general broad information or the procedural aspects of the matter and suggest that the client seek the advice of an attorney.
- **Never begin a sentences with "You should" or "I think."** When on non-attorney hears themselves say "You should" or "I think," they should immediately stop and realize that they are probably about to give legal advice. Again, it's not worth the risk.
- **Always clearly identify yourself as a paralegal**. When you talk to clients or send letters out on law office or company letterhead, *always* identify yourself as a paralegal. It is very easy for a client to say "Well I thought he was an attorney" to a disciplinary administrator or in a malpractice case.

  Never represent to others, either directly or indirectly, that you are an attorney. Paralegals are allowed to have business cards and sign letters on the law practice letterhead in many states, as long as the title of "paralegal" or "legal assistant" is included.
- **Management should develop ethical guidelines and rules**. From a management perspective, law office managers should publish rules regarding the unauthorized practice of law, tell staff members what they can and cannot do, and provide a policy on the responsibilities of supervising attorneys.
- **Management should make periodic checks of ethical standards**. It is not enough to simply establish rules and then never monitor them to see if they are being followed. Occasionally, management must monitor its staff regarding compliance with law practice rules and state guidelines to ensure compliance. Management should keep staff members up-to-date on changes or clarifications in ethical standards by circulating recent ethical opinions. Publications of paralegal associations also report on recent ethical opinions. When appropriate, these should be called to the attention of management for general circulation. Another option is for law office management to hold workshops or seminars on ethics. Attorneys, paralegals, and staff members should be constantly reminded about ethics.

Competence and Diligence

Attorneys and paralegals must perform legal services in a competent and diligent manner. Rule 1.1 regarding the rules of professional conduct speaks to the issue of competence. As noted throughout the text, nearly every state's rules of professional conduct are modeled after the *ABA's Model Rules of Professional Conduct*. Exhibit 3-7 illustrates Minnesota's Rule 1.1 (identical to the *ABA's Rule 1.1*), which states that an attorney must be competent in order to represent the client; that is, he or she must reasonably know the area of law that the client needs representation in and, assuming the attorney does know the area of law, that he or she takes the preparation time to become familiar with the case in order to represent the client adequately.

The purpose of this rule is to ensure that an attorney does not undertake a matter that he or she is not competent in, and to ensure that the attorney has had "adequate preparation." The amount of adequate preparation depends on the type of legal matter the client has; major litigation will require far more preparation time than, say, the amount of time it takes to prepare a will. A legal professional should not undertake to represent a client if he or she does not have the skill or preparation time necessary to do so. Paralegals must have a basic understanding of the law in each area in which they are working. Additionally, they must be able to analyze, organize, and prepare the factual and legal data obtained to perform their job competently.

Rule 1.3 regarding the rules of professional conduct requires that an attorney act with a reasonable degree of diligence and promptness in pursuing the client's case. Further insight is found in Comment [3] of the rule. It notes that attorneys should carry through to conclusion all legal matters undertaken for a client unless the relationship is properly and clearly terminated. The purpose of this rule is to ensure that attorneys put forth reasonable effort and diligence in representing a client. Attorneys and paralegals cannot adequately represent the interests of clients if they ignore the case, if they are lazy and do not work the case, or if they negligently handle the case.

Attention to detail is an extremely important skill for a paralegal to possess. Exhibit 3-8 provides examples of how paralegals failed to perform competently—not by failing to know the law, but rather by being disorganized or failing to pay attention to details.

Confidentiality and the Attorney–Client Privilege

client confidentiality

Keeping information exchanged between a client and law office staff confidential.

Another basic ethical concept is that of client confidentiality. **Client confidentiality** refers to the need to keep information exchanged between a client and law office staff, including attorneys and paralegals, confidential. In addition to the ethical rules of maintaining client confidences, there is a rule of evidence, generally called the attorney–client privilege, that an attorney or a paralegal may invoke to avoid revealing the secrets of a client. The purpose of both the privilege and the ethical rules is to ensure that clients can consult with their attorneys without the fear that such statements will be passed to others or used against them later. If clients knew that what they told their attorney could be repeated to others, clients would be reluctant to tell their attorneys the truth. The attorney–client privilege and the ethical rules on confidentiality complement one another to achieve the same end.

Exhibit 3-7 State Example: Minnesota's Rules of Professional Conduct—Rule 1.1

Source State of Minnesota.

RULE 1.1 COMPETENCE

A lawyer shall provide competent representation to a client. Competent representation requires the legal knowledge, skill, thoroughness and preparation reasonably necessary for the representation.

Comment:

Legal Knowledge and Skill

[1] In determining whether a lawyer employs the requisite knowledge and skill in a particular matter, relevant factors include the relative complexity and specialized nature of the matter, the lawyer's general experience, the lawyer's training and experience in the field in question, the preparation and study the lawyer is able to give the matter and whether it is feasible to refer the matter to, or associate or consult with, a lawyer of established competence in the field in question. In many instances, the required proficiency is that of a general practitioner. Expertise in a particular field of law may be required in some circumstances.

[2] A lawyer need not necessarily have special training or prior experience to handle legal problems of a type with which the lawyer is unfamiliar. A newly admitted lawyer can be as competent as a practitioner with long experience. Some important legal skills, such as the analysis of precedent, the evaluation of evidence, and legal drafting, are required in all legal problems. Perhaps the most fundamental legal skill consists of determining what kind of legal problems a situation may involve, a skill that necessarily transcends any particular specialized knowledge. A lawyer can provide adequate representation in a wholly novel field through necessary study. Competent representation can also be provided through the association of a lawyer of established competence in the field in question.

[3] In an emergency a lawyer may give advice or assistance in a matter in which the lawyer does not have the skill ordinarily required where referral to or consultation or association with another lawyer would be impractical. Even in an emergency, however, assistance should be limited to that reasonably necessary in the circumstances, for ill-considered action under emergency conditions can jeopardize the client's interest.

[4] A lawyer may accept representation where the requisite level of competence can be achieved by reasonable preparation. This applies as well to a lawyer who is appointed as counsel for an unrepresented person. See also Rule 6.2.

Thoroughness and Preparation

[5] Competent handling of a particular matter includes inquiry into and analysis of the factual and legal elements of the problem, and use of methods and procedures meeting the standards of competent practitioners. It also includes adequate preparation. The required attention and preparation are determined in part by what is at stake; major litigation and complex transactions ordinarily require more extensive treatment than matters of lesser complexity and consequence. An agreement between the lawyer and the client regarding the scope of the representation may limit the matters for which the lawyer is responsible. See Rule 1.2(c).

Maintaining Competence

[6] To maintain the requisite knowledge and skill, a lawyer should keep abreast of changes in the law and its practice, engage in continuing study and education and comply with all continuing legal education requirements to which the lawyer is subject.

Exhibit 3-8
Paralegals/Legal Assistants Failing to Act Competently and Diligently

Paralegal/Legal Assistant's $92 Million Dollar Error

A paralegal/legal assistant at Prudential mistakenly left off the last three zeros on a mortgage used to secure a $92,885,000 loan made by Prudential to a company that filed for bankruptcy. Because of the mistake, Prudential had a lien for only $92,885; the error left Prudential's lien $92,792,115 short.

Prudential Ins. v. Dewey, 170 A.D.2d 108 (N.Y. App. Div. 1991)

Paralegals/Legal Assistants Sued for Negligence

Unsupervised paralegals engaged in the unauthorized practice of law:

When she represented three clients regarding their auto accident claims, the paralegal's negligence was the proximate cause of clients' injuries, and attorneys and paralegal were jointly and severally liable for damages.

Tegman, et al., v. Accident Medical Investigations, Inc., 107 Wn.2d. 102, 75 P.3d 497 (2003).

Paralegal/Legal Assistant Fails to File Document, Leads to Dismissal of Case

See *Ortiz v. Gavenda*, 590 N.W.2d 119 (Minn. 1999).

Israel Ortiz was severely injured on September 24, 1993 when the motorcycle he was driving collided with a truck driven by Bryan Gavenda and owned by Gavenda's employer, Frito Lay, Inc. Israel Ortiz died from those injuries on December 11, 1993. On June 6, 1995, his widow, Frances Ortiz (Ortiz), served a complaint on Gavenda and Frito Lay (collectively Gavenda) asserting a wrongful death claim and seeking damages as the trustee for the heirs of Israel Ortiz. Gavenda's answer to the complaint denied liability and alleged that Ortiz's claim "failed to comply with the provisions of Chapter 573 of Minnesota Statutes"—the chapter governing wrongful death actions.

On November 15, 1995, Ortiz signed a petition to have herself appointed trustee for the next of kin of her deceased husband as required by Minn. Stat. § 573.02, subd. 3 (1998). Although the petition and an accompanying consent and oath form were properly signed and duly notarized, a legal assistant for Ortiz's attorney inadvertently failed to submit the documents to the court and, as a consequence, Ortiz was not appointed trustee. The mistake went unnoticed when Ortiz's complaint was filed with the Anoka County District Court on December 6, 1995. The oversight came to light and Ortiz filed her petition to be appointed trustee on January 8, 1997, but by then more than three years had elapsed since her husband's death. The Minnesota Supreme Court dismissed the action due to the document not being filed on time by the legal assistant.

The Attorney–Client Privilege Rule of Evidence

attorney–client privilege

A standard that precludes the disclosure of confidential communications between a lawyer and a client by the lawyer.

Generally, the **attorney–client privilege** precludes the disclosure of confidential communications between a lawyer and a client by the lawyer. Thus, if a criminal defendant confessed a crime to his attorney, the attorney–client privilege prevents the prosecutor from calling the attorney to the stand to testify about the confession. In addition, courts have applied the attorney–client privilege to paralegals. For the privilege to be invoked, the communication must have been made in confidence between the client and the attorney for the purpose of obtaining legal advice.

Ethical Prohibitions on Revealing Client Communications

There are several ethical rules that address attorneys preserving client communications, including Rule 1.6 regarding the rules of professional conduct. Rule 1.6 states that an attorney cannot reveal information relating to the representation of a client unless the client has consented to the release of that information.

Canon 7 of the NALA *Code of Ethics and Professional Responsibility* (see Exhibit 3-4) and Section 1.5 of NFPA's *Model Code of Ethics and Professional Responsibility* (see Exhibit 3-5), although not enforceable, prohibit paralegals from revealing client confidences.

Again, the purpose of these ethical rules is to encourage clients to be completely honest with their attorneys. Note that there are many nuances regarding the attorney–client privilege and ethical rules, however, including some exceptions to the rules.

Paralegals have an absolute duty to preserve the confidences and communications of clients. All information must be kept confidential and should not, under any circumstances, be revealed in casual conversations with anyone outside the workplace. In addition to the moral and ethical reasons for not disclosing client communications, there also is the issue of quality service to the client. If a client learns that his or her communications have been revealed to outside sources, by whatever means, even if it is by accident, the client may lose confidence in the entire firm. If a client cannot trust his or her attorney, the client will quickly move on to another firm. If confidential information gets out, it could actually compromise the client's case.

How to Avoid Confidentiality Problems

- **Resist the temptation to talk about what goes on in the office, whether or not it is client related.** There is always a temptation to talk about office politics and other office matters with people outside the firm. Resist this temptation. If you do this, it will only make it easier to talk about client-related matters. Consider that you are a professional and that both your firm and your clients demand anonymity.
- **Only talk about client matters to office personnel on a need-to-know basis.** Never go around your office talking about a client's case to employees who do not have a reason to know about it. You must get in the habit of keeping information to yourself. Why tell someone about client-related matters, even if it is a fellow employee, unless he or she needs to know for some legitimate reason? Even if you are talking to someone who has a need to know, avoid doing so in public places, such as waiting rooms, elevators, and restaurants, where your conversation can be overheard.
- **Never discuss the specific facts or circumstances of a client's case with anyone, not even friends or relatives.** There is a specific temptation to talk with friends and relatives about interesting cases you have worked on, because you trust them. However, many client secrets have been unwittingly revealed by friends and relatives who have repeated information they never should have been told. The statement "I promise I won't tell anyone" does not work. People do tell. Former girlfriends or boyfriends may reveal knowledge you told them in order to spite you. Mothers, fathers, brothers, sisters, or friends may inadvertently reveal a confidence you told them that gets back to the client, adverse party, or a member of your law office. When this happens, you will hear about it one way or another, and the repercussions can be severe. Do not take the chance; it is simply not worth losing a client or a job. You should not even reveal the fact that an individual is or may be a client of your law office.
- **Always clear your desk of other case files when meeting with clients.** If case files are left in the open, other clients can read the files and access confidential information. Be very careful with any case files taken away from the law office.
- **Do not take phone calls from other clients when meeting with a client.** Taking phone calls from other clients while a client is in your office can expose confidential information. Be aware of who is in your office when talking about confidential information on the phone, and, when possible, keep your door closed when meeting or talking with clients.

Exhibit 3-9
Law Office Confidentiality Policy

Confidential Nature of Client Matters

All matters relating to any clients or office matters are completely confidential. Nothing that occurs in the office should be discussed with family, friends, other clients, or anyone else. Particular care should be taken with papers that are transmitted in the office. Papers should not be examined and matters should not be discussed in public places such as restaurants, lobbies, or elevators, where other persons can peruse such papers or overhear conversations. Particular care should be exercised in commuter trains, buses, or any public area where much law office talk still continues to be overheard on a daily basis. Even after a case has become a matter of public notice by virtue of its having been filed in court or reported in the press, assume that it is still confidential and do not discuss it publicly.

Staff members should be careful, even in the office, not to leave confidential papers in open or public areas, nor should they leave computer monitors on in places where they can be easily seen by passersby. It is the policy of the firm not to use a client's name for the purpose of surveys or in materials that are prepared to describe the firm without the permission of the billing lawyer(s).

The paper shredder located in ______________________ should be used for confidential material that must be destroyed; however, such material should not be destroyed without the prior approval of the billing lawyer(s). The use of a confidentiality notice on facsimile (telecopier) transmissions should also be considered as appropriate. Likewise, care must be exercised in dealing with all computer disks, tapes, and other media that contain privileged material.

Care should be taken when dealing with vendors as well. A confidentiality agreement may exist between the firm and a vendor or potential vendors making proposals to the firm.

- **Management must create policies and systems to ensure confidentiality.** Law office managers also have a duty to create systems that ensure confidentiality. Some of these systems may include locking file cabinets that contain client files, limiting access to client files on a need-to-know basis, requiring files to be checked out, having law office policies on client confidentiality, and developing procedures to ensure that the confidential information of clients is maintained (see Exhibit 3-9). Most law offices limit staff members from revealing to persons outside the office that a particular individual is being represented; even revealing the names of clients can give the appearance that the law office does not take confidentiality seriously. Although there is an affirmative ethical duty to maintain client confidentiality, there is also the potential for malpractice liability for firms that violate confidentiality. Under a legal malpractice theory, if a law office (through its employees) reveals client confidences, accidentally or intentionally, it could be legally liable to the client for damages that result.
- **Be careful when responding to discovery requests.** Many times, paralegals are involved in responding to discovery document requests. It is important that all confidential files (including electronic files) are labeled and identified appropriately, that each piece of documentation that is to be submitted to the opposing party is carefully reviewed to ensure that confidential client information is not given out, and that such information is discussed with the supervising attorney.
- **Be particularly careful when using fax machines, e-mail, mobile telephones, and related services.** There have been many instances where confidential information conveyed over these media has been inadvertently revealed to others. It is particularly easy to accidentally reveal confidential information via fax machine and e-mail.

Faxes should be sent very carefully. An improper or a misdirected fax transmission can lead to breach of client confidentiality. All fax cover pages for law offices should have some kind of confidentiality disclaimer on them. The confidentiality of e-mail is also a concern. From the client's perspective, there are many advantages to using e-mail to communicate with legal professionals. The problem with e-mail was addressed in Chapter 2.

Conflict of Interest

conflict of interest

A competing personal or professional interest that would preclude an attorney or a paralegal from acting impartially toward the client.

Conflict of interest problems are an important ethical concept. A **conflict of interest** occurs when an attorney or a paralegal has competing personal or professional interests with a client's case that would preclude him or her from acting impartially toward the client.

Conflict of interest problems typically occur when:

- The attorney or paralegal has a personal, financial, or other interest in a case.
- The attorney or paralegal is a substantial witness in the case.
- The law office, attorney, or paralegal sometime in the past represented a client who is now an adverse party in a current case.
- The attorney and a client enter into business together.
- When the attorney is asked to advocate a position on behalf of a client that is contrary to the position of another of the firm's clients (an issue conflict).
- When law firm mergers or acquisitions occur.
- When legal professionals change jobs/firms.

If, for instance, an attorney represented a husband and wife in a legal action and then, several years later, the husband approaches the attorney to sue the wife for divorce, the attorney has a conflict of interest problem because he had at one time represented both parties. Not only would he have a question as to which client he should be loyal to, but the attorney may have during the first representation been privy to confidences and secrets of the wife that could be used in the divorce case against her.

Rule 1.7 regarding the rules of professional conduct speaks to conflicts of interest, whereby an attorney would be unable to represent a client when a conflict exists. According to Rule 1.7, a conflict exists if an attorney's representation of one client directly and adversely affects another client. The rule allows the attorney to represent the clients where the attorney is able to provide competent representation of each client, it is not prohibited by law, both clients give informed written consent, and the attorney is not representing both parties in the same litigation where the parties are asserting claims against each other.

Most case law in this area presumes that if a firm has represented both parties in the past, there is an actual conflict of interest. It is not necessary to prove that confidences and secrets were exchanged during the first representation. Usually, but not always, when an actual conflict of interest occurs, the whole firm, not just the attorney involved, is prohibited from entering the case.

Rule 1.8 regarding the rules of professional conduct speaks to the conflict of interest issue. It states, among other things, that attorneys cannot enter into business transactions with a client that is adverse to the client unless a number of specific conditions are met. Rule 1.8 also prohibits an attorney from using information related to the representation of a client to the disadvantage of the client unless the client has given informed consent. Under the rule, generally, attorneys cannot solicit substantial gifts from clients as well.

Exhibit 3-10 Conflict of Interest Examples

- Using Client Information to Harm the Client
  An ambitious associate attorney regularly defends the X insurance company. Client comes into attorney's office and wants to sue X insurance company for a major personal injury claim, not knowing that the attorney has represented the company before. Attorney, in an effort to help X insurance company, intentionally lets the statute of limitations run and then pays the client $2500 from his own pocket, telling him that the insurance company settled. Attorney had a clear duty to tell the client of his conflict of interest. Attorney was disbarred and the law firm was sued for malpractice.
- Financial Interest
  Attorney is an employee of the county government's water district. Attorney uses his position of authority to influence the water board's decision to purchase a piece of land that he owns through a partnership. Attorney also delays $300,000 of sewer connection fees to another of his pieces of land until after the sale of land is completed to a third party. Attorney had a clear conflict of interest in both cases. Attorney was suspended for two years for the practice of law and pled guilty to using his official office to influence a governmental decision.

Attorneys and paralegals should be loyal to their clients and have no alternative motives that might influence their independent professional judgment to represent the clients. Exhibit 3-10 provides a few more examples of conflict of interest problems.

As noted before, there are different types of conflicts, including an issue conflict. In an issue conflict, an attorney or a firm takes different positions on the same issues for different clients. The *Model Rules* generally prohibits this; however, if each client gives an informed consent, then the firm can most likely continue representing the clients. Also, if the legal matters are in different jurisdictions and the firm reasonably believes neither party will be adversely affected, then most likely the firm can continue representing the clients.

Conflict Checking

Because law offices and attorneys typically represent a large number of clients, it is often difficult for them to remember every client. As a result, it is possible for an attorney to have a conflict of interest but simply not remember the former client. Thus, it becomes the responsibility of management to ensure that before new cases are taken, a conflicts check takes place. A written policy regarding conflict checking is prudent.

Many law offices maintain a list of all their former clients and adverse parties so that when a new case is being considered as to whether it should be accepted, the firm will routinely check this list to ensure that there are no conflict of interest problems.

Most law firms now use a computer program to search for conflicts; some firms use a computerized database program to do conflict checking. A database program is application software that stores, searches, sorts, and organizes data. When using a database, it is advantageous to include the client's date of birth or social security number, otherwise a misspelled name may not be picked up by the program. Some accounting, billing, docket control, and case management programs can also be used to perform conflicts checking. Exhibit 3-11 shows some case-specific conflict of interest designs. If a firm practices in a certain area, a more specific design would be beneficial.

Exhibit 3-11 Fields to Track in a Case-Specific Conflict of Interest Check

Type of Legal Matter	Fields to Track
Administrative law	• Adverse party • Counsel • Investigator • Witnesses
Bankruptcy	• Debtor(s) • Creditor(s) • Other interested parties • Counsel
Corporate	• Owner(s) • Officers • Partners • Shareholders • General counsel • Affiliates/subsidiaries
Criminal	• Defendant(s) • Prosecutor • Victim(s) • Witnesses • Experts
Estates, trusts, probate	• Testator • Heirs • Children • Spouse • Trustee • Conservator • Power of attorney • Personal representative • Beneficiaries • Counsel
Family law	• Spouse • Children • In-laws • Counsel • Guardian
Litigation	• Client • Adverse parties • Witnesses • Expert • Insurer
Real estate	• Buyer • Seller • Agent • Counsel
Workers' compensation	• Client • Employer • Insurer • Health-care provider
Other	• Firm lawyers • Firm paralegals/legal assistants • Spouses/parents/siblings • Employees • Current/past clients • Prospective clients

Exhibit 3-12 A Case Upholding the Ethical Wall Theory

Source: Lamb v. Pralex, 333 F.Supp.2d 361 (2004 D. Virgin Islands).

The plaintiff in this case is represented by Lee J. Rohn (Rohn) of the Law Offices of Lee J. Rohn. Defendants are represented by Kevin Rames, Esq. (Rames) of the Law Offices of Kevin Rames. This motion revolves around Eliza Combie (Combie), who worked as a paralegal at the Rames law office from October 30, 2000 to March 26, 2004. Her work at Rames' office involved working with several litigation matters, including this case. On March 26, 2004, Combie began work with the Rohn law firm. During Combie's interview with Rohn, they discussed the possible conflicts raised by Combie's possible employment. Combie was told should she accept employment with the Rohn firm, she would be barred from contact with those cases. Rohn states that on Combie's first day of work with Rohn, she submitted the list of cases. The list was circulated to all employees and a memo informing employees to refrain from discussing those cases in her presence was circulated and posted in common areas of the office. Combie and Rohn state that no one in the office has discussed any of the relevant matters with Combie. They also state that Combie is locked out of the electronic files and does not work in close proximity to them or to Rohn.

Rames invokes ABA Rules of Professional Conduct 5.3, 1.9, 1.16, and 1.10 to argue that Rohn and the entire law firm must be disqualified because during Combie's previous employment with Rames, she obtained confidential information regarding pending matters which she may divulge to Rohn. The Court is satisfied that the procedures employed by Rohn's office to shield Combie from the files supports a finding that any information obtained at the Rames law firm will not be disclosed. It is important that nonlawyer employees have as much mobility in employment opportunity consistent with the protection of clients' interests. To so limit employment opportunities that some nonlawyers trained to work with law firms might be required to leave the careers for which they have been trained would disserve clients as well as the legal profession.

In light of the foregoing, disqualification is not warranted. In addressing ethical problems created by nonlawyers changing employment from a law firm representing one party to a law firm representing an adverse party, courts must fashion rules which strike a balance between the public policy of protecting the confidentiality of attorney–client communications and a party's right to representation by chosen counsel. Accordingly, any restrictions on the nonlawyers' employment should be held to the minimum necessary to protect confidentiality of client information. The Court finds that plaintiff's counsel has rebutted the presumption of improper disclosure by presenting evidence of the "Chinese Wall" ["or Ethical Wall"] implemented in that regard. Accordingly, disqualification is not warranted and the defendants' motion will be denied at this time.

Some insurance companies that issue malpractice insurance to attorneys also require that, before the policy is written, the firm must have and consistently use a conflict-checking device.

The Ethical Wall

Although it is the general rule that courts tend to disqualify a whole firm when a conflict of interest problem arises, some courts have carved out an alternative to disqualification. The alternative is called the **Ethical Wall**, which occurs when a firm effectively isolates the paralegal or attorney with a conflict of interest from having anything whatsoever to do with the case, thus creating an Ethical Wall around him or her (see excerpts of the *Lamb v. Pralex* opinion in Exhibit 3-12). This is typically done by instructing staff members not to talk to the attorney in question about the case, not to disclose any information acquired at the previous firm, and limiting any access the attorney might have to the files of the case by locking file cabinets and placing passwords on computer files.

Ethical Wall

Term for a technique used to isolate the paralegal or attorney with a conflict of interest from having anything to do with a case.

If the Ethical Wall is erected and the court agrees, it will limit disqualification to the paralegal or attorney. Not all courts accept the Ethical Wall theory. Again, it would be the duty of management to ensure that the office locks up the files, and to segregate the attorney or paralegal with the conflict from the rest of the staff. Law offices must also effectively limit access to computers and client data files to build an effective Ethical Wall.

Paralegal Conflict of Interests

Many courts have extended the conflict of interest issue to paralegals as well as attorneys. Conflict of interest problems usually occur when a paralegal changes employment. For instance, in *In re Complex Asbestos Litigation*, a paralegal worked for a law firm defending major asbestos litigation claims. He worked with discovery documents, was a part of the defense team for three years, and attended defense strategy meetings. Subsequently, he was hired by a firm representing asbestos plaintiffs. The defendants moved to disqualify the plaintiff's attorney because of the paralegal's conflict of interest (he had knowledge of confidential information gained over several years). The motion was granted by the court.

Paralegals should be ready to answer questions about their previous employers when interviewing for jobs to avoid conflict of interest problems. The ABA Committee on Ethics and Professional Responsibility issued an opinion regarding this matter. It pointed out that effective screening of nonlawyers, such as a paralegal, could help to avoid disqualification, when a paralegal might have worked on a common case at their previous law firm employment. The paralegal's diligence in providing potential conflict information to the new law firm employer is the key to avoiding the problems associated with disqualifications.

The paralegal should be alert to situations that might present a potential conflict of interest as a result of information gained in past employment and should disclose any questionable situation to the employer.

How Paralegals Can Avoid Conflicts of Interest

- **When changing jobs, bring up the issue of potential conflicts in the interview.** Tell the firm whom you have worked for and what types of cases you have worked on. It is better to deal with potential conflict problems up front than for an employer to hire you and then find out there are problems.
- **Be absolutely honest about your past.** Do not hide or deceive employers about potential conflict of interest problems. Honesty is always the best policy.
- **If you later find out you may have a conflict, immediately inform your supervising attorney or paralegal manager and do not have anything to do with the case.** If you find out after you have been hired by a new firm that you may have a conflict problem, immediately raise the issue with your supervising attorney. Do not volunteer information to the new firm regarding the matter. If you can, approach your former employer and ask for an informed and express written waiver giving consent for you to work for the other firm. Verbal consent is hard to prove, so get it in writing.
- **Management must ensure that conflict of interest problems are checked.** It is also the duty of management to ensure that employees are not hired who have substantial conflict of interest problems, or if they do have such problems, that the firm knows about them up front. For instance, management might want to add a question to its employment form that asks potential employees to state any conflict problems, in addition to establishing the conflict-checking system mentioned earlier.

Resolving Ethical Problems

There is nothing easy about resolving an ethical problem. Typically, ethical issues are complex and messy; they are rarely "black and white." However, the following ideas can help you deal with ethical problems.

- **Talk to your paralegal manager or supervising attorney regarding ethical problems.** When you encounter an ethical problem, the first thing you should do is to talk to someone else about it to get a different perspective. Typically, this will be your paralegal manager or supervising attorney. However, this is sometimes hard to do when the supervising attorney is the one asking you to do something you think is unethical or if the attorney is him- or herself doing something unethical. One way to approach the issue is to discreetly ask the attorney if he or she thinks this might be a problem; it is important not to be accusatory, but to simply inquire into the issue and to present your point as objectively as possible. You always have the option, no matter how difficult, to say no to the attorney if he or she asks you to do something that you know is unethical. Also, be sure to check your firm's personnel policy manual. Ethical problems and procedures for handling them are sometimes covered in this type of manual.
- **Talk to another attorney or paralegal in the firm regarding ethical problems.** If you have a hard time talking to your supervising attorney about an ethical problem, talk to another attorney, paralegal, or ethics committee, if the firm has one. It is important when dealing with ethical problems to take counsel with others, to bounce ideas off others, and to talk about them. Other people may have more experience than you might have previously dealt with a similar situation. When talking to another attorney in the firm, use the same non-accusatory approach. Be sure that you are talking to a person you can trust for sincere advice on how to handle the situation; you do not want to be perceived as spreading rumors or stirring up trouble. In large-sized firms, you also have the option of asking to be transferred.
- **Join a professional paralegal association.** Professional associations offer a good way to share information and experiences with others, including information about ethical problems. Most professional paralegal organizations provide guidance on ethical concerns. Use these resources to help you solve your ethical problem.
- **Be familiar with the ethical rules of your state.** It is always a good idea to have a copy of the ethical rules used in your jurisdiction and to review them from time to time.
- **Subscribe to paralegal periodicals that cover ethical issues.** Many national paralegal publications routinely carry articles on ethical concerns. Some even have a regular column on the issues of ethics. This kind of timely information can be helpful when dealing with ethical problems.
- **Report ethical violations to the state bar association as a last resort.** If you have tried to work out an ethical problem to no avail, you always have the option of reporting the violation to the state bar association. This is a very difficult decision to make because you may lose your job as a result. Ethical problems are not easy to deal with, and you must be able to live with whatever decision you make.
- **When considering ethical questions, think conservatively.** When you are faced with a hard ethical question, be conservative and do what you know is right, no matter how much it may hurt. Exhibit 3-13 contains a list of ethical "commandments" that may guide you in this direction.

Exhibit 3-13
What Paralegals Should Know About Ethics

1. You should always know the rules of professional conduct for attorneys; if you know the standards expected by attorneys, you can help prevent mistakes that lead to disciplinary actions.
2. You should know the professional rules for paralegals; these standards maintain the integrity of the paralegal profession.
3. You should know what constitutes giving legal advice; make sure to avoid any pressure to provide advice under any circumstance.
4. You should make sure that everyone knows your position as a paralegal/legal assistant; always clarify to anyone you come in contact with that you are not an attorney.
5. You should know to never sign your name to anything unless you are certain that the law permits a paralegal to sign.
6. You should know to never contact other parties associated with a dispute without permission form the supervising attorney.
7. You should know to never discuss any matters that you are working on with anyone outside of the legal team; this means anyone.
8. You should know to always report time accurately.
9. You should know never perform a task when you feel uncomfortable about the work; make sure to clarify the task to ensure your performance is appropriate.

- **Do not ignore the ethical problem.** A common way to handle ethical problems is to simply ignore them and hope they will go away. Unfortunately, this approach rarely works. In many instances, it simply makes the situation worse. For example, if you see a staff person charging time to a client's case when he or she is not working on that case, it is better to bring the issue to the forefront right away than wait for him or her to do the same to 20 clients. Ethical problems are better handled when they first occur as opposed to letting them fester and become far more complicated.

Answers to Common Paralegal Ethical Questions

The following are answers to other common paralegal/legal assistant ethical questions. The answers are based on general statements of law, but an answer may be different depending on your particular jurisdiction.

- **May paralegals have business cards and may their names appear on law firm stationery?** In many states, the answer is yes. For business cards, care must be taken to ensure that the nonlawyer status of the cardholder is displayed prominently on the card. Regarding firm stationery, the name of the paralegal(s) must be set apart from the lawyers' names, and the paralegal's title must be shown clearly. Some firms print lawyers' names on one side of the stationery and print paralegals names on the other.
- **May a paralegal sign letters prepared on firm stationery?** Yes, provided (1) the letter contains no direct legal advice or opinions, and (2) the paralegal's status is shown clearly. The best practice is to include the title "Paralegal" or "Legal Assistant to X" directly below the typed name in the signature block of the letter.

- **May a paralegal discuss fee ranges with a client on a preliminary basis, leaving the final discussion and decision to the supervising attorney?** All discussions related to fees must be deferred to the attorney. Even when a firm uses an internal fee schedule, it generally serves as a guideline only. It is solely the attorney's responsibility to measure the situation presented by each case and to set the fee.
- **How often and in what way must a paralegal identify his or her nonlawyer status?** There is no single, correct way to identify the paralegal's status. It seems prudent to do so at the beginning of all telephone conversations and at the beginning of every initial conference with a client or witness. For example, regarding a telephone call, one might say, "Hello. This is Jack Samson, Jane Mitchell's paralegal." If it appears that the other party thinks the paralegal is a lawyer, that impression should be corrected right away. The issue is not how often identity must be clarified to comply with the rules, it is how often identity should be clarified to protect the paralegal from charges related to the unauthorized practice of law.
- **May a paralegal counsel a close friend or a relative about a legal matter when the friend or relative knows that the paralegal is not a lawyer and when the paralegal is not paid for the advice?** Other than suggesting that the friend or relative see a lawyer, the paralegal cannot give advice or comment in any way that may be taken as a legal opinion. The problem arises most frequently at family dinners, parties, and other social events. Friends and relatives can create an extremely uncomfortable situation. Whether the paralegal is paid or not is irrelevant; legal advice cannot be given by the paralegal under any circumstances.

Malpractice and Malpractice Prevention

legal malpractice

Possible consequence when an attorney's or a law office's conduct falls below the standard skill, prudence, and diligence that an ordinary lawyer would possess or that is commonly available in the legal community.

Legal malpractice occurs when an attorney's or a law office's conduct in representing a client falls below the standard skill, prudence, and diligence that an ordinary lawyer would possess or that is commonly available in the legal community.

Exhibit 3-14 lists the most common types of errors that result in a malpractice claim being filed. Notice in Exhibit 3-14 that substantive errors account for 47% of malpractice claims and that failure to know or properly apply the law represented the most common reason for all malpractice claims.

Exhibit 3-15 also provides some excellent suggestions for helping to avoid costly malpractice claims. Engagement and disengagement letters are another way to avoid malpractice claims. Clients sometimes think attorneys are representing them when, in fact, they are not. Law offices should always send an engagement letter or a contract that clearly sets out when a case is taken, what the firm is going to do, and on what the fees will be based.

In addition, law offices should routinely send out disengagement letters for any type of case or legal matter, even if the only thing the law office did was to meet with the client in an initial interview (see Exhibit 3-16). The purpose of the disengagement letter is to clearly set out in writing that the attorney–client relationship was not formed or has ended. A client may not understand that the firm, is not pursuing the matter, then come back months or even years later claiming that the attorney committed malpractice against him or her by not following up on the case.

Exhibit 3-14 Profile of Legal Malpractice Claims

Source: 2004–2007, 2000–2003 American Bar Association Standing Committee on Lawyers' Professional Liability.

Type of Alleged Error	2000–2007	2000–2007
ADMINISTRATIVE	**NUMBER**	**PERCENTAGE**
Failure to calendar properly	2825	6.7
Procrastination in performance/follow-up	2490	5.9
Failure to file document (no deadline)	3636	8.6
Failure to react to calendar	1609	3.8
Clerical error	1226	2.9
Lost file/document evidence	222	0.5
SUBSTANTIVE		
Failure to know/properly apply law	4770	11.3
Failure to know/ascertain deadline	2782	6.6
Inadequate discovery/investigation	3719	8.8
Conflict of interest	2218	5.3
Planning error (procedure choice)	3737	8.9
Error in public record search	1491	3.5
Failure to understand/anticipate tax	666	1.6
Error in mathematical calculation	323	0.8
CLIENT RELATIONS		
Failure to obtain consent/inform client	2293	5.4
Failure to follow client's instruction	1832	4.4
Improper withdrawal of representation	1054	2.5
INTENTIONAL WRONG		
Malicious prosecution/abuse of process	1593	3.8
Fraud	2113	5.0
Libel or slander	774	1.8
Violation of civil rights	705	1.7

Exhibit 3-15 Tips to Prevent Legal Malpractice

1. Gather factual information from the client to determine the basis of any legal claim and immediately determine and track when the statute of limitations takes effect.
2. Give the client a copy of the written fee agreement specifying the terms of employment and the basis of the attorney's fees in the case.
3. Conduct a thorough conflict of interest check before the client's case is accepted and immediately notify the client in writing if a conflict or a potential conflict is discovered.
4. Investigate the facts of the client's case and the law regarding the case diligently and promptly.
5. Keep the client informed regarding the status of his or her case by providing routine status reports; always inform the client of all developments that might affect the client's rights; and ask for his or her participation throughout the case.
6. Charge a reasonable and fair fee for services performed and provide the client with clear and detailed accounting of the basis for the fees charged.
7. Carefully and thoroughly proofread all documents and e-mails before they go out for mistakes and, whenever possible, send a copy of the document to the client for his or her approval and review.
8. Immediately tell the client of problems or mistakes as they happen and offer solutions.
9. Do not overestimate the firm's capacity to take on cases outside its expertise and always determine whether there is sufficient time to handle the matter properly.
10. Provide the client with written notice upon the attorney's withdrawal from representation (obtain court approval in matters involving litigation) and promptly provide the client with his or her file and other property he or she is entitled to.

Exhibit 3-16
Disengagement Letters

Example 1: Disengagement Letter—New Client Where Case Was Not Accepted

Subject: Potential Claim of Client v. Smith

Dear Client

Thank you for coming in to our office on Thursday, February XX, 201, regarding your legal matter. We are interested in your concerns and appreciated the opportunity to meet with you. However, after further consideration we have decided to decline representation of your interests in the captioned matter.

We have not made a legal opinion as to the validity or merits of your case. You should be aware that any action in this matter must be filed within the applicable statute of limitations. We suggest that you consult with another attorney concerning your rights in this matter.

Again, we will not be representing you in the captioned matter and are closing our file.

Thank you again, and we wish you the best.

Kindest Regards,

Example 2: Disengagement Letter Following Representation

Subject: *Client v. Smith*

Dear Client

Thank you for allowing us the opportunity to serve you regarding the captioned matter. The case is now closed and we are removing the case from our active file status. We will be archiving the file shortly. If you would like evidence or other material that you have provided to us returned, please give me a call so I can get it to you.

We are interested in knowing how you feel about the quality of legal services you received from our firm. We would appreciate it if you would complete the enclosed client survey questionnaire. We are always interested in knowing how we can serve you better in the future.

Again, the captioned case is now closed, and we greatly enjoyed representing your interests.

If you have any questions, please feel free to give me a call.

Kindest Regards,

Summary

An ethical rule is a minimal standard of conduct. An attorney may not fall below the standard without losing his or her good standing with the state bar. The *Model Rules of Professional Conduct* are ethical rules for attorneys that are promulgated by the American Bar Association. Ethical rules for attorneys do not apply directly to paralegals. However, attorneys can be disciplined for the acts of their staff, including paralegals. In addition, paralegals themselves can lose their jobs and face criminal charges and fines for practicing law without a license, among other things, so it is important that paralegals act in an ethical manner.

Attorneys are directly responsible for the acts of their paralegals/legal assistants and under the *Model Rules* must make reasonable efforts to ensure that their conduct is compatible with the ethical rules. Paralegals and legal assistants have two national associations that they may belong to, the National Association of Legal Assistants–Paralegals and the National Federation of Paralegal Associations. Both associations have voluntary model codes of ethics for paralegals/legal assistants.

All states have statutes regarding the unauthorized practice of law by nonlawyers. Paralegals that "practice law" can be criminally charged under these statutes. Paralegals are prevented from giving legal advice. The factors involved in making this determination include (1) whether advice given requires legal skill or knowledge, (2) whether the person was advised of his or her legal rights, and, (3) whether the advice is not normally given by a nonlawyer as part of another business or transaction (such as a tax consultant). A paralegal also may not misrepresent his or her status so that others believe that he or she is an attorney; the paralegals must clearly state his or her title and that he or she is not an attorney. Paralegals may not represent clients in court proceedings, perform legal analysis and prepare legal documents (without supervision of an attorney), set or share a fee, or evaluate a case regarding whether to accept or reject it.

Attorneys—and, therefore, paralegals—are required to act in a competent manner for their clients. They must reasonably know and understand the area of the law they are working in and they must adequately prepare for the representation of the client. Attorneys and legal professionals must also act diligently, including acting promptly and without undue delay.

Attorneys and paralegals are required to maintain client confidentiality. The duty of confidentiality is an important part of the client–attorney relationship; the attorney–client privilege is a part of that relationship. The privilege precludes the disclosure of confidential communications between a lawyer and a client by the lawyer. The privilege also extends to paralegals.

Attorneys and paralegals are prohibited from representing a client where they have a conflict of interest. A conflict of interest is a competing personal or professional interest that would preclude an attorney or a paralegal from acting impartially toward the client. An "Ethical Wall" is a technique used to isolate the paralegal with a conflict of interest from having anything to do with a case; the Ethical Wall can sometimes be erected so that an entire firm does not have to be disqualified from representing a client because of the conflict with one staff member, such as a paralegal.

Legal malpractice occurs when an attorney's conduct in representing a client falls below the standard skill, prudence, and diligence that an ordinary lawyer would possess or that is commonly available in the legal community.

Key Terms

ABA *Model Code of Professional Responsibility*
ABA *Model Rules of Professional Conduct*
attorney–client privilege
client confidentiality
conflict of interest
ethical rule
Ethical Wall
legal malpractice
legal technicians

Test Your Knowledge

Test your knowledge of the chapter by answering these questions.

1. Explain what the ABA *Model Rules of Professional Conduct* are.
2. True or false: An attorney can be disciplined for the acts of his or her paralegal/legal assistant.
3. True or false: Paralegals/legal assistants must comply with the model codes of ethics from the two major national paralegal associations.
4. True or false: In most states, you can go to jail for the unauthorized practice of law.
5. List five things that a paralegal/legal assistant cannot do without being accused of the unauthorized practice of law: __________, __________, __________, __________, and __________.
6. What are three factors that are considered in determining whether a paralegal/legal assistant gave legal advice to a client?
7. What does "competent representation" require, according to the *Model Rules?*
8. The standard that precludes the disclosure of confidential communications between a lawyer and a client by the lawyer is called the __________.
9. A conflict of interest occurs when __________ __________.
10. True or false: Even if a conflict of interest exists, if the affected clients give informed consent, confirmed in writing, the attorney can represent the parties (subject to the provision in the rule).
11. A technique used to isolate a paralegal/legal assistant or attorney with a conflict of interest from having anything to do with a case is called an __________.
12. When an attorney's conduct in representing a client falls below the standard skill, prudence, and diligence that ordinary attorney would possess, it is called __________.

Practical Applications

1. You are a paralegal in the real estate section of a corporate law department. Your company is a large retailer that owns thousands of small retail outlets across the country. You process the leases, review the contracts, and coordinate lease payments with the accounts payable department to make sure the proper lease payments will be made. By the time the lease gets to you, the contract has been reviewed by the attorneys. Typically, you assume that the description of the property is accurate, even though you could pull the full file to confirm the description. This is the way that it has always been done. What are your thoughts regarding the adequacy of the description of the property? Is this a good policy? What is the risk if the property description is not accurate? Does it change your answer if your supervising attorney thinks that you are in fact reviewing the contract for accuracy and completeness?

2. You are a paralegal at a law firm that is representing a company in the process of negotiating a deal to merge with a competitor. You inadvertently mention the possibility of the merger to your father. Without your knowledge, your father purchases a large sum of stock in the company you represent, knowing that when the merger becomes public, the price of the stock will substantially rise. Several months after the transaction, your father gives you a check for $5000 and explains how he made the money. He tells you that he only did it for your benefit. Disregarding the criminal statutes that have been violated, how would you handle the situation and how could the problem have been avoided?

3. You work for a government agency and are responding to a plaintiff's request for production of documents. One of the requests specifically asks for any notes or memoranda arising out of the facts of the case. In one of the boxes of material the agency has collected on the matter, you find a particularly incriminating memorandum that will virtually win the case for the plaintiffs if it is produced. What do you do?

Assume you go to your supervising attorney about the matter. The attorney responds that he or she will take care of the matter and thanks you for your diligent work. Several months go by and you are now working on preparing the case for trial. You quickly realize that the document was never produced to the plaintiffs. How would you resolve this situation?

4. You are working on a client's case when the client's accountant calls and asks you for information about the client. You have worked with this particular accountant before and know the accountant is trustworthy. Is there any problem with revealing the information to the accountant? How would you handle it?

5. Your law office just signed an agreement to represent a famous athlete in contract negotiations with his team. A reporter from *Sports Illustrated* calls and asks if your firm is representing the athlete. You read *Sports Illustrated* all the time and are impressed that one of its reporters called your firm. In fact, you are caught off guard by the question. Being typically honest and forthright, you begin to answer. What is your answer?

6. You are a new paralegal right out of school. You take the first job offered to you, at a small-sized firm that is poorly run and not very well respected in the legal community. You work at the firm for only a month and quit. You apply for another position at a different firm and decide not to mention the employment of the small-sized firm, as it was for only a month. You sign the employment application form knowing that it says if you are found to have lied on the application form, you could be terminated. You are subsequently hired by the new firm. Later, you find out the two firms have a highly publicized case they are litigating against each other. What would you do?

7. As a paralegal in a medium-sized law office, you have access to all the resources of the firm, including copy machines, telephones, e-mail, and the postage meter. While the firm's staff manual states that the firm's equipment will only be used for firm business, you notice that the other paralegals frequently use the copier, envelopes, and postage machine for personal use. When you ask one of the other paralegals in the firm about it, the paralegal says, "Don't worry about it. Everyone does it." How would you handle the situation?

8. Your law office represents a nonprofit corporation. The executive director of the nonprofit corporation calls you when your supervising attorney is out of the office. The executive director states that an employee is demanding overtime pay, since she has worked for more than 40 hours last week, and is saying that if she is not paid overtime, she will immediately file a wage-and-hour complaint with the appropriate state agency. The attorney will not be in the office the whole week but may call in. You recollect from previous experience that the Fair Labor Standards Act generally states that employees should receive overtime pay for hours worked in excess of 40 hours a week, though you are not sure about exceptions to the rule. The executive director presses you and says that he absolutely has to have an answer immediately and that if your firm cannot respond to emergencies, then maybe he will take his business elsewhere. How would you resolve the situation? Give options.

9. As a paralegal for a legal aid office, one of your jobs is to screen clients. You routinely see new clients and report the facts of each client's case to one of the attorneys. The attorneys then decide for which cases they have time to take on. On Monday, a client comes into your office. The client has no money but appears to need an attorney. The client advises you that she has been sued and needs legal counsel to represent her for a hearing in the state district court on Friday at 10:00 A.M. before the Judge Smith. From your experience, you are sure the attorneys do not have the time to accept this case. After listening to the client, you respectfully tell her that you do not think the office will be able to represent her. The client then leaves and you prepare a memo to the attorneys. The attorneys subsequently decide not to handle the matter and file is closed.

On Friday at 10:15 A.M., the office receives a phone call from Judge Smith. Judge Smith tells your receptionist that an attorney from your office has five minutes to get over to her courtroom to represent the client or she (Judge Smith) will hold the office/attorneys in contempt of court and levy a fine against the office. Apparently, the client told Judge Smith that she had met with a representative from the legal aid office and had told the representative about the hearing. It was the client's understanding that an attorney from the legal aid office would represent her. Explain how this matter could have been avoided.

10. You notice one of your fellow paralegals at the legal aid office where you work routinely using fake names and misrepresenting herself when tracking down witnesses or trying to serve subpoenas. Is this unethical or just uncouth? Analyze the situation using either the NALA or NFPA code of ethics.

11. You are a paralegal for a sole practitioner. You have been working on a motion that has to be filed by 4:30 P.M. At 4:10 P.M., you handover the completed motion to the attorney. The attorney signs the motion and handovers it back to you and asks you to copy it and file it. How would you handle this situation? List your options.

On the Web Exercises

1. Start by going to the search engines, such as http://www.google.com or http://www.yahoo.com; search for all of the lawyer disciplinary agencies for the 50 states. A number of them have Web sites. Visit five of the Web sites and compare what kind of information is available to clients that are having difficulty with an attorney.

2. Visit three state bar association Web sites on the Internet and compare the information on ethics for each one. Several Web sites are listed in the Web Links section of this chapter and also of Chapter 2. Alternatively, you can search for state bar associations using http://www.google.com or http://www.yahoo.com. Most of the disciplinary administrator Web sites found in Exercise 1 use the state bar association Web sites as well, so if you completed that assignment, you should have already found most of them.

3. Visit the NALA and NFPA Web sites on ethics that are listed in the Web Links section of this chapter. What kind of information do they offer, and is it helpful?

4. Visit several state bar association Web sites and find articles on conflicts of interest, confidentiality, malpractice, and competence.

Projects

1. Write a comprehensive report that compares and contrasts the NALA and NFPA codes of ethics. In the report, explain which code you thought was better, and why. Also discuss how the sections on confidentiality and conflict of interests compare with the ABA's *Model Rules*. Were the sections similar to the *Model Rules* or not?

2. Write a report regarding paralegal/legal assistants and the unauthorized practice of law; use a minimum of four resources. Discuss what paralegal/legal assistants can and cannot do, and why. You may want to begin your research with state bar associations as well as NALA and NFPA.

Case Review

Tegman v. Accident & Medical Investigations, 107 Wash. App. 868, 30 P.3d 8 (Wash.App.Div.1 08/13/2001).

Court of Appeals of Washington, Division 1.

Maria TEGMAN, Linda Leszynski and Daina Calixto, Respondents,

v.

ACCIDENT & MEDICAL INVESTIGATIONS, INC., a Washington corporation, Richard McClellan and Jane Doe McClellan, individually and as husband and wife, and the marital community composed thereof; Joy A. Brown and John Doe Brown, individually and as husband and wife, and the marital community composed thereof; Michael D. Hoyt and John Doe Hoyt, individually and as husband and wife, and the marital community composed thereof; James P. Bailey and Jane Doe Bailey, individually and as husband and wife, and the marital community composed thereof; Camille H. Jescavage and John Doe Jescavage, individually and as husband and wife, and the marital community composed thereof, Defendants,

Deloris M. Mullen and John Doe Mullen, individually and as husband and wife, and the marital community composed thereof; Lorinda S. Noble and John Doe Noble, individually and as husband and wife, and the marital community composed thereof, Appellants.

Nos. 45837-0-I, 45885-0-I, 45886-8-I, 46085-4-I.

Aug. 13, 2001.

PUBLISHED IN PART

BECKER, A.C.J.

When a paralegal performs legal services with knowledge that there is no supervising attorney responsible for the case, the paralegal will be held to an attorney's standard of care. Attorneys have a duty to keep ***872** their clients informed about material developments in their cases. The trial court found that Deloris Mullen, a paralegal, and Lorinda Noble, an attorney, while employed by a nonlawyer who represented accident victims, breached this duty and caused harm to the plaintiffs when they failed to advise them of the risk involved with allowing a nonlawyer to settle their cases. We affirm the judgments.

The trial court's findings of fact present the following account of the events surrounding this dispute. Between 1989 and 1991, plaintiffs Maria Tegman, Linda Leszynski, and Daina Calixto were each injured in separate and unrelated automobile accidents. After their accidents, each plaintiff retained G. Richard McClellan and Accident & Medical Investigations, Inc. (AMI) for legal counsel and assistance in handling their personal injury claims. McClellan and AMI purported to represent each plaintiff in seeking compensation from insurance companies for their injuries. Each plaintiff signed a contingency fee agreement with AMI, believing that McClellan was an attorney and AMI a law firm. McClellan has never been an attorney in any jurisdiction.

McClellan and AMI employed Camille Jescavage and Lorinda Noble, both licensed attorneys. ****12** Jescavage and Noble learned that McClellan entered into contingency fee agreements with AMI's clients and that McClellan was not an attorney. They settled a number of cases for AMI, and learned that McClellan processed settlements of AMI cases through his own bank account. Noble resigned from AMI in May 1991, after working there approximately six months. In July 1991, McClellan hired Deloris Mullen as a paralegal. Mullen considered Jescavage to be her supervising attorney though Jescavage provided little supervision. Jescavage resigned from AMI in the first week of September 1991. McClellan told Mullen that her new supervising attorney would be James Bailey. Mullen did not immediately contact Bailey to confirm that he was her supervising attorney. He later told her he was not. While at AMI, Mullen worked on approximately 50–60 ***873** cases, including those of plaintiffs Tegman, Leszynski, and Calixto. Mullen was aware of some of McClellan's questionable practices and knew that there were substantial improprieties involved with his operation. Mullen stopped working at AMI on December 6, 1991, when the situation became personally intolerable to her and she obtained direct knowledge that she was without a supervising attorney. When she left, she did not advise any of the plaintiffs about the problems at AMI. After Mullen left, McClellan settled each plaintiff's case for various amounts without their knowledge or consent, and deposited the funds in his general account by forging their names on the settlement checks. In 1993, Calixto, Leszynski, and Tegman each individually sued McClellan, AMI, Mullen, and Jescavage. Tegman also sued Noble. Their complaints sought damages on various theories. The cases were consolidated. Discovery took place between 1993 and 1998. In the interim, McClellan pleaded guilty to mail fraud in United States District Court in 1997 and was sentenced to two years imprisonment. Also, this court affirmed a judgment by the same trial court in another case where McClellan settled a client's case without authorization and stole the proceeds. *Bullard v. Bailey*, 91 Wash. App. 750, 959 P.2d 1122 (1998). That judgment apportioned 20-percent fault to attorney James Bailey who, like Noble and Jescavage, had associated himself with AMI and failed to warn his clients of McClellan's improprieties. In the present matter, the court entered summary judgment against McClellan and AMI on the issue of liability. After a six-day trial, the court held Mullen, Noble, and Jescavage liable for negligence and legal negligence, and awarded damages. Only Mullen and Noble appealed. Their appeals have been consolidated.

STANDARD OF REVIEW

[1] An appellate brief must include argument in support of issues presented for review, together with citations to ***874** legal authority. *See* RAP 10.3(a)(5). Assignments of error not argued in a brief are deemed abandoned. *Valley View Industrial Park v. City of Redmond*, 107 Wash.2d 621, 630, 733 P.2d 182 (1987); *Pappas v. Hershberger*, 85 Wash.2d 152, 153, 530 P.2d 642 (1975). Accordingly, we review only those assignments of error that are supported by argument in appellants' briefs. [2] Our review of a trial court's findings of fact and conclusions of law is a two-step process. We first determine whether the trial court's findings of fact were supported by substantial evidence in the record. *Landmark Development, Inc. v. City of Roy*, 138 Wash.2d 561, 573, 980 P.2d 1234 (1999). Substantial

evidence is evidence which, viewed in the light most favorable to the party prevailing below, would persuade a fair-minded, rational person of the truth of the finding. *State v. Hill*, 123 Wash.2d 641, 644, 870 P.2d 313 (1994). If the findings are adequately supported, we next decide whether those findings of fact support the trial court's conclusions of law. *Landmark Development*, 138 Wash.2d at 573, 980 P.2d 1234.

PARALEGAL NEGLIGENCE

[3] Mullen, a paralegal, contends the court erred in finding her negligent. To establish the elements of an action for negligence, a plaintiff must show: (1) the existence ****13*** of a duty owed, (2) breach of that duty, (3) a resulting injury, and (4) a proximate cause between the breach and the injury. *Iwai v. State*, 129 Wash.2d 84, 96, 915 P.2d 1089 (1996). [4] Nonattorneys who attempt to practice law will be held to the same standards of competence demanded of attorneys and will be liable for negligence if these standards are not met. *Bowers v. Transamerica Title Insurance Company*, 100 Wash.2d 581, 586-89, 675 P.2d 193 (1983); *Hogan v. Monroe*, 38 Wash. App. 60, 65, 684 P.2d 757 (1984) (realtor who drafted addendum that substantially altered the rights of property buyers held to the standard of care of a reasonably prudent attorney). ***875*** In *Bowers*, sellers sold property to buyers who had persuaded a nonattorney escrow agent to prepare an unsecured promissory note in favor of the sellers. After the deed was delivered to the buyers, the sellers learned the significance of the fact that the note was unsecured. They discovered that the buyers had departed for places unknown after using the property as security for a substantial loan. The sellers sued the escrow agent and obtained summary judgment on liability for negligence. Our Supreme Court affirmed, holding the escrow agent to an attorney's standard of care. The escrow agent breached a duty to inform the sellers of the advisability of obtaining independent counsel. *Bowers*, 100 Wash.2d at 590, 675 P.2d 193. That duty was owed because the escrow agent, by preparing the closing documents, was engaging in the practice of law. [5] The "practice of law" clearly does not just mean appearing in court. In a larger sense, it includes "legal advice and counsel, and the preparation of legal instruments and contracts by which legal rights are secured." *In re Droker and Mulholland*, 59 Wash.2d 707, 719, 370 P.2d 242 (1962). *See also Bowers*, 100 Wash.2d at 586, 675 P.2d 193; *Washington State Bar Assn v. Great West. Union Fed. Savings & Loan Assn*, 91 Wash.2d 48, 54, 586 P.2d 870 (1978); *State v. Hunt*, 75 Wash. App. 795, 801–02, 880 P.2d 96 (1994). [6] Mullen contends that her status as a paralegal precludes a finding that she was engaged in the practice of law. She argues that a paralegal is, by definition, someone who works under the supervision of an attorney, and that it is necessarily the attorney, not the paralegal, who is practicing law and owes a duty to the clients. Her argument assumes that she had a supervising attorney. The trial court's determination that Mullen was negligent was dependent on the court's finding that Mullen knew, or should have known, that she did not have a supervising attorney over a period of several months while she was at AMI. "Had Mullen been properly supervised by an attorney at all times during her employment with AMI, plaintiffs presumably ***876*** would have no case against her. Rather, her supervising attorney would be responsible for any alleged wrongdoing on her part." [FN1]

FN1. Court's Memorandum Decision Following Trial, at 24.

[7] [8] We agree with the trial court's observation. The label "paralegal" is not in itself a shield from liability. A factual evaluation is necessary to distinguish a paralegal who is working under an attorney's supervision from one who is actually practicing law. A finding that a paralegal is practicing law will not be supported merely by evidence of infrequent contact with the supervising attorney. As long as the paralegal does in fact have a supervising attorney who is responsible for the case, any deficiency in the quality of the supervision or in the quality of the paralegal's work goes to the attorney's negligence, not the paralegal's. In this case, Mullen testified that she believed James Bailey was her supervising attorney after Jescavage left. The court found Mullen was not justified in that belief. Mullen assigns error to this finding, but the evidence supports it. Mullen testified that she had started to distrust McClellan before he informed her that Bailey would be her supervising attorney. Mullen also testified that she did not contact Bailey to confirm that he was supervising her. Bailey testified at a deposition that he did not share Mullen's clients and she did not consult him regarding any of her ongoing cases. He also said that one of the only conversations he remembers having with ****14*** Mullen with respect to AMI is one where he told her that he was not her supervising attorney after she raised the issue with him. This testimony amply supports the trial court's finding that Mullen was unjustified in her

belief that Bailey was her supervising attorney. [9] In *Hunt*, a paralegal appealed a criminal conviction for the unauthorized practice of law based on his conduct in running a claim settlement company. Among other things, Hunt failed to inform his clients of his activities, did not inform clients of the full amount of settlements, reached ***877*** settlements without consulting his clients, and filed incomplete or improper documents in court. In a constitutional challenge to the unauthorized practice of law statute, RCW 2.48.180, Hunt argued that his status as a paralegal prevented a finding that he was engaged in the practice of law. The Court of Appeals disagreed and affirmed his conviction: "It is the nature and character of the service performed which governs whether given activities constitute the practice of law, not the nature or status of the person performing the services." *Hunt*, 75 Wash. App. at 802, 880 P.2d 96 (citing in part, *WSBA*, 91 Wash.2d at 54, 586 P.2d 870). As in *Hunt*, Mullen's status as a paralegal did not preclude the trial court from concluding that Mullen had engaged in the practice of law. [10] Contrary to Mullen's argument, such a conclusion does not require evidence that the paralegal called herself an attorney, entered appearances, or charged fees. Mullen testified that she negotiated settlements on behalf of the plaintiffs. She sent a letter rejecting, without Tegman's knowledge, a settlement offer made to Tegman. She continued to send out demand and representation letters after Jescavage left AMI. Letters written by Mullen before Jescavage's departure identify Mullen as a paralegal after her signature, whereas letters she wrote after Jescavage's departure lacked such identification. Even after Mullen discovered, in late November 1991, that Bailey was not her supervising attorney, she wrote letters identifying "this office" as representing the plaintiffs, neglecting to mention that she was a paralegal and that no attorney was responsible for the case. This evidence substantially supports the finding that Mullen engaged in the practice of law. [11] Mullen contends that she cannot be held liable for negligence because the statute that prohibits the unauthorized practice of law was not in effect at the time she worked for AMI. The trial court dismissed the plaintiffs' claims that were based on the alleged statutory violation, but this does not prevent Mullen from being liable on the negligence claim. Under *Bowers*, the duty arises from the ***878*** practice of law, not from the statute. [12] Mullen points out that an attorney-client relationship is an element of a cause of action for legal malpractice. *Daugert v. Pappas*, 104 Wash.2d 254, 704 P.2d 600 (1985). The trial court did not find that she had an attorney-client relationship with any of the plaintiffs, and she contends that as a result it is illogical to hold her to the standard of care of an attorney. Mullen, because she is not an attorney, could not have attorney-client relationships. Nevertheless, as *Bowers* demonstrates, a layperson can logically be held to the standard of care of an attorney in a negligence action. The duty arises from the attempt to engage in the practice of law rather than from the professional status of the defendant. The trial court, covering all bases, held Mullen liable both for negligence and legal negligence. While the "legal negligence" label may have been incorrect, any such error is immaterial because the negligence theory produces the same result and, as the trial court observed, for practical purposes the allegations are the same. [13] Accordingly, we conclude the trial court did not err in following *Bowers* and holding Mullen to the duty of an attorney. The duty of care owed by an attorney is that degree of care, skill, diligence, and knowledge commonly possessed and exercised by a reasonable, careful, and prudent lawyer in the practice of law in Washington. *Hizey v. Carpenter*, 119 Wash.2d 251, 261, 830 P.2d 646 (1992). [14] Mullen challenges, as unsupported by the evidence, the trial court's key finding ****15*** as to the duties that Mullen owed and breached. The court found that the standard of care owed by an attorney, and therefore also by Mullen, required her to notify the plaintiffs of: (1) the serious problems concerning the accessibility of their files to persons who had no right to see them, (2) the fact that client settlements were not processed through an attorney's trust account, but rather McClellan's own account, (3) the fact that McClellan and AMI, as nonlawyers, had no right to enter ***879*** into contingent fee agreements with clients and receive contingent fees, (4) the fact that McClellan was, in fact, engaged in the unlawful practice of law, and that, generally, (5) the clients of McClellan and AMI were at substantial risk of financial harm as a result of their association with AMI. Mullen breached her duty to her clients in all of these particulars. [FN2]

FN2. Finding of fact 101. This same finding was made under number 80 in the Leszynski and Calixto cases.

The finding rests on the testimony of attorney Charles Nelson Berry III, an expert witness for the plaintiffs. The trial court found Berry's testimony to be "thoughtful and well-considered" and significantly, unrebutted. [15] [16] Mullen argues that the finding must be stricken because Berry improperly derived the standard of care from the Rules of Professional Conduct. In testifying that an attorney's conduct violated the legal standard of care, an expert witness may base an opinion on an attorney's failure to conform to an ethics rule, and may testify using language found in the Rules of Professional Conduct, as long as the jury is not led to believe that the ethical violations were actionable. *Hizey*, 119 Wash.2d at 265, 830 P.2d 646. Berry's testimony, phrased in terms of breach of the standard of care, stayed within this constraint. We conclude the finding is supported by substantial evidence. Accordingly, the trial court did not err in concluding that Mullen was negligent. [17] [18] The trial court's findings on damages, unchallenged by Mullen on appeal, are verities. *See Cowiche Canyon Conservancy v. Bosley*, 118 Wash.2d 801, 808, 828 P.2d 549 (1992). Mullen does, however, challenge the trial court's findings on proximate cause. Like the defendant attorney in *Bullard v. Bailey*, 91 Wash. App. 750, 959 P.2d 1122 (1998), she essentially contends this element is unsupported because McClellan's improper settlement of the cases would have caused the plaintiffs' damages regardless of her failure to warn them. She emphasizes that by the time she left AMI, the plaintiffs had already signed invalid contingency fee agreements with McClellan and that he was well on his way to converting their funds. [19] [20] ***880** Proximate cause consists of two elements: cause in fact and legal causation. *Bullard*, 91 Wash. App. at 755, 959 P.2d 1122. Cause in fact is the "but for" consequence of the injury. Bullard, 91 Wash. App. at 755, 959 P.2d 1122 (citing *Seattle v. Blume*, 134 Wash.2d 243, 251, 947 P.2d 223 [1997]). It is a matter of what has in fact occurred and is generally for the trier of fact to decide. *Bullard*, 91 Wash. App. at 755, 959 P.2d 1122. As in *Bullard*, we conclude the trial court did not err in its determinations of proximate cause. All three plaintiffs testified that they hired McClellan and AMI to legally represent them and believed that McClellan was an attorney whom they trusted and relied upon to handle their respective claims. They found out that he was not an attorney only after their claims had been settled. Mullen did not advise any of the plaintiffs that McClellan was not a lawyer; that AMI was not a law firm; that she, as a paralegal, had no real supervision; or that client funds did not go through a trust account. These omissions by Mullen sufficiently link her to the plaintiffs' later injury to establish cause in fact. *See Bullard*, 91 Wash. App. at 757, 959 P.2d 1122. It was reasonable for the trial court to infer that if Mullen had properly advised the plaintiffs of the problems at AMI, more likely than not they would have withdrawn their cases from AMI in time to avoid being harmed by McClellan's fraudulent acts. *****16*** [21] [22] Legal causation turns on a policy question of how far the consequences of a defendant's acts should extend. *Blume*, 134 Wash.2d at 252, 947 P.2d 223. Whether legal liability adheres depends on "mixed considerations of logic, common sense, justice, policy, and precedent." *Hartley v. State*, 103 Wash.2d 768, 779, 698 P.2d 77 (1985). Mullen contends that her connection to the plaintiffs' injuries is too remote because she did not render direct legal advice and that it is unjust to hold her, an employee paralegal, responsible for the criminal, intentional acts of her employer. The *Bullard* court rejected a similar argument asserted by Bailey, an attorney who allowed himself to become associated with McClellan: ***881** Under the circumstances presented, particularly McClellan's financial difficulties, unlawful legal practice, and Bailey's failure to correct Bullard's misapprehensions, ordinary human experience should have led Bailey to expect Bullard would suffer some harm at McClellan's hands, regardless whether it was the precise harm suffered. *Bullard*, 91 Wash. App. at 759, 959 P.2d 1122. Although Mullen was a paralegal, she is held to an attorney's standard of care because she worked on the plaintiffs' cases during a period of several months when she had no supervising attorney. The fact that she did not render legal advice directly does not excuse her; in fact, her failure to advise the plaintiffs of the improper arrangements at AMI is the very omission that breached her duty. Under these circumstances it is not unjust to hold her accountable as a legal cause of the plaintiffs' injuries. As all the elements of negligence have been established, we affirm the judgment against Mullen.

JOINT AND SEVERAL LIABILITY

[23] The trial court entered judgment against Mullen and Noble, McClellan, and AMI jointly and severally for compensatory damages. These amounts were $15,067.25 for Tegman, $27,362 for Leszynski, and $25,000 for Calixto. The court entered judgment against McClellan and AMI for substantial additional sums, including attorney fees, for criminal profiteering and Consumer Protection Act violations. Mullen and Noble object to being held jointly liable for the compensatory damages. They ask that the judgments be revised so that they are responsible for only that portion of the compensatory damages corresponding to the

percentages of fault the trial court attributed to them. The trier of fact, in all "actions" involving fault of more than one "entity", must "determine the percentage of the total fault which is attributable to every entity which caused the claimant's damages". RCW 4.22.070(1). Citing ***882** this statute, the trial court determined that Mullen was 10 percent at fault in each of the three cases; attorney Jescavage was 10 percent at fault in each of the three cases; and Noble was five percent at fault in Tegman's case. The court determined that McClellan and AMI had the remaining percentages in each case. The court then concluded that each of the plaintiffs was not at fault, and held all defendants jointly as well as severally liable in accordance with the statute: (b) If the trier of fact determines that the claimant or party suffering bodily injury or incurring property damages was not at fault, the defendants against whom judgment is entered shall be jointly and severally liable for the sum of their proportionate shares of the claimants total damages. RCW 4.22.070(1)(b). [24] Mullen and Noble argue that under this statute, the court should not have apportioned their fault with McClellan under this statute because he was an intentional tortfeasor and the term "fault" in the statute does not include intentional conduct. They rely on *Welch v. Southland Corp.*, 134 Wash.2d 629, 952 P.2d 162 (1998). In *Welch*, an unknown assailant robbed the plaintiff as he was leaving a convenience store owned by defendant Southland. The complaint alleged that Southland was negligent in failing to maintain a safe premises for its business invitees. The store asserted, as an affirmative defense, that under RCW 4.22.070(1) any ****17** fault on the store's part should be apportioned with the intentional acts of the unknown assailant. The trial court ruled that a negligent defendant is entitled to the benefit of the comparative fault statute, and that the jury would be permitted to attribute comparative fault to the unknown assailant—an "empty chair" entity. The potential effect of this ruling, as Southland readily acknowledged, was to make Southland liable for only its own percentage of the damages instead of being held jointly liable for all the damages. This was because the assailant was not a defendant, and joint liability arises only among defendants "against whom judgment is entered." RCW 4.22.070(1)(b). The ***883** Supreme Court reversed, holding that intentional acts are not included in the statutory definition of "fault" in the contributory and comparative fault statutes, and, thus, a negligent tortfeasor is not entitled to apportion liability to an intentional tortfeasor. Intentional torts are "part of a wholly different legal realm" from the apportionment mechanism provided in RCW 4.22.070(1). Welch, 134 Wash.2d at 635, 952 P.2d 162 (quoting *Price v. Kitsap Transit*, 125 Wash.2d 456, 464, 886 P.2d 556 [1994]). The judgment as entered by the trial court in this case did not violate the statute or *Welch*, because the court treated the action against McClellan and AMI as functionally separate from the action against Mullen, Noble, and Jescavage. The court held McClellan solely liable on the causes of action alleging intentional conduct. The court held Mullen, Noble, and Jescavage solely liable on the causes of action alleging negligence. Because the plaintiffs were free of fault, the court properly held the three negligent tortfeasors jointly as well as severally liable for the total compensatory damages caused by their negligence. That joint liability by the three negligent tortfeasors was the correct result is indicated by the result in *Welch*, which left Southland exposed to liability for the entire damage sustained by the plaintiff. The difference from *Welch* is that in this case, the plaintiffs did make the intentional tortfeasor a defendant in the same suit, and did obtain entry of a judgment against him. This is not a distinction that leads to diminished liability for the negligent tortfeasors. The trial court's apportionment of "fault" to the intentional tortfeasor did not lead to a different result for Mullen and Noble as far as their joint liability is concerned than if the plaintiffs had sued them in a completely separate lawsuit, and it did not have any effect on the recovery of the fault-free plaintiffs. At most it affected the percentages of fault as between the defendants, an issue we need not evaluate as it has not been raised. Any error in the court's decision to apportion "fault" to McClellan has caused no prejudice so far as the issue of ***884** joint liability is concerned, and therefore is not reversible. Noble argues that reversal is necessary because the trial court failed to segregate the damages between the intentional tort and negligence claims. She relies on *Honegger v. Yoke's Washington Foods*, 83 Wash. App. 293, 921 P.2d 1080 (1996). *Honegger* was a personal injury case brought by a shoplifter who was injured when the store's employees aggressively pursued him and committed assault and battery. The trial court refused the plaintiff's request to segregate damages caused by the employees' intentional conduct from damages caused by negligence, including the plaintiff's contributory negligence. The plaintiff appealed from a relatively small judgment. A new trial was found necessary because there had been no allocation of damages between intentional tort and negligence claims. As a result, it was not possible to determine on what basis the jury reached the amount awarded as damages: The verdict could have been an award for damages sustained solely as the result of the assault and battery, or could reflect other injuries. The jury could have concluded all the damages resulted from the employees' actions, since Mr. Honegger was trying to escape further injury. Since we do not know the basis of the award and how it may have been compromised by the contributory negligence instruction, the entire matter needs to be retried. *Honegger*, 83 Wash. App. at 298-99, 921 P.2d 1080. The problem identified by the *Honegger* court does not exist in this case. The judgment separately sets forth the awards to the ****18*** plaintiffs arising from McClellan's criminal profiteering and Consumer Protection Act violations, and holds only McClellan and his firm responsible for these sums. [FN 3] Mullen and Noble are jointly liable with McClellan only for compensatory damages. The trial court measured ****885*** the compensatory damages caused by Mullen and Noble's negligence in exactly the same way as the compensatory damages caused by McClellan's intentional conduct: the value of the settlements the plaintiffs would have received if their claims had been handled by a competent attorney. Noble has not pointed out any basis upon which the trial court, as finder of fact, could have segregated the damages with greater precision.

FN 3. The judgment summary in Tegman's case, for example, provides in pertinent part as follows:

"Name of Plaintiff/ Judgment Creditor:		Maria **Tegman**
"Attorney for Judgment Creditor:		Gregory D. Lucas Lucas & Lucas, P.S.
"Judgment Debtors:		Deloris Mullen Lorinda Sue Noble Camille Jescavage G. Richard McClellan and **Accident & Medical Investigations, Inc.** ("AMI")
"Base Judgment Amount:	$15,067.25	(All defendants)
"Criminal Profiteering:	50,000.00	(McClellan & AMI only)
"Consumer Protection Damages:	10,000.00	(McClellan & AMI only)

"Judgment Amount:	$75,067.25	

"Interest Rate: 12% per annum from the date hereof until paid.

"Statutory Attorneys' Fees	$ 125.00	(All defendants)
"Attorneys' Fees:	$79,218.50	(McClellan & AMI only)"

The judgments are affirmed.

NOTE: This decision was appealed to the Supreme Court of Washington, en banc, see 150 Wash. 2d 102, 75 P.3d 497 (2003). The Court held that the attorney was not jointly and severally liable for the intentional acts of the others.

Case Review Exercises

1. Did it surprise or bother you that the attorneys and the paralegal were all working for a non-attorney?
2. Why did the court find that Mullen, the paralegal, was not working under the supervision of an attorney? What did Mullen do wrong and what should she have done? What difference did it make in this case?
3. The court was very critical of the paralegal. Why was the court so disturbed by the behavior and actions of the paralegal? Do you think it was justified?
4. What did Mullen specifically do that the court found was the unauthorized practice of law?
5. Were you surprised that Mullen, as a paralegal, was held to an attorney's standard of care once she began the authorized practice of law?
6. Why was the plaintiff able to pursue the claim against Mullen?

Case Review

In re Pinkins, 213 B.R. 818 (Bankr. E.D. Mich.1997),

213 B.R. 818
(Cite as. 213 B.R. 818)
United States Bankruptcy Court,
E.D. Michigan,
Southern Division.

In re Darain PINKINS, Walterine Jones, Charles & Shirley Daberkoe, Angela Hall, Pamela Fields, Maretta Roberson, Glenn Peeples, Rahman & Chantay

Harmon, Sabrina Sanders, Phyllis Dunson, Tammy Trombley, Barbara Ellis, Darris

Finney, D'Anyai Asaki, Luis & Denise Sierra, Lashawn & Angela Taylor, Theresa

Singletary, Sandra Asberry, Ralph Knox, Leon Smith, Junotia Robertson, Debtors.

Bankruptcy Nos. 97-40722, 97-40965, 97-42032, 97-42576, 97-42719, 97-42790,

97-42791, 97-42885, 97-43062, 97-43162, 97-13353, 97-43356, 97-43414, 97-43419,

97-43494, 97-43661, 97-43664, 97-44060, 97-44160, 97-44241, 97-44564.
Oct. 14. 1997.

***819** Julie Lesser, Royal Oak, MI, for Debtors.

David Wm. Ruskin, Southfield, MI, Trustee

MEMORANDUM OPINION

STEVEN W. RHODES, Chief Judge.

This matter is before the Court on the Chapter 13 Trustee's objections to fee applications submitted by the Castle Law Office of Detroit, P.C. in 21 cases. The Court conducted a hearing on the objections on August 21, 1997. Because most of the objections relate to all of the fee applications, the Court will address them in one consolidated opinion.

I. Introduction

The Castle Law office ("Castle") handles primarily Chapter 13 bankruptcy cases. The firm employs attorneys Julie Lesser and Terri Weik, and several legal assistants and clerical staff members. The Trustee's office considers Castle a "high volume filer," filing an average of 77 cases per month since January 1997. (Transcript of August 21, 1997 hearing [Tr.] at 36.) Castle's standard practice [FN1] in handling initial consultations with clients was that the client met with a legal assistant, who discussed with the client the available chapters and assisted the client in deciding which, if any, chapter proceedings the client should file. If the client had a question and requested an answer from an attorney, the legal assistant would personally ask the attorney and relate the answer back to the client. The client would not meet with ***820** an attorney. The assistant gave a questionnaire to the client to fill out and return. The assistant then reviewed the questionnaire and prepared the papers to be filed. The client then returned to sign the papers, again meeting with a legal assistant, rather than an attorney. In most instances, unless the client had specifically requested to meet with an attorney, the client's first contact with the attorney was at the meeting of creditors.

FN1. The Court is aware that the law firm has since modified some of its procedures. However, this opinion addresses the procedures in effect at the time the fees in question were generated.

The Trustee's primary fee objection is that the firm's clients did not meet with an attorney prior to the meeting of creditors. The Trustee's concern in this respect is that the legal assistant is giving legal advice and acting without direct supervision of an attorney. The Trustee also objects to the similarity of time entries on the fee applications and the lack of detail. The Trustee raises further objections in specific cases in which the fees charged exceed the agreed-upon fees, and in cases which were dismissed at or before confirmation and Castle submitted an application for the full amount of the fees.

II. Unauthorized Practice of Law

A.

[1] Michigan law governs whether Castle legal assistants engage in the unauthorized practice of law. *In re Bright*, 171 B.R. 799, 802 (Bankr.E.D.Mich.1994) (no federal law regulating the extent to which nonlawyers may appear before the bankruptcy court; Michigan law applies). Mich. Comp. Laws Anno. § 600.916 provides in pertinent part:

> It is unlawful for any person to practice law, or to engage in the law business, or in any manner whatsoever to lead others to believe that he is authorized to practice law or to engage in the law business, or in any manner whatsoever to represent or designate himself as an attorney and counselor, attorney at law, or lawyer, unless the person so doing is regularly licensed and authorized to practice law in this state.

M.C.L.A § 600.916; M.S.A. 271A.916.

[2][3] The statute does not identify the activities that constitute the practice of law. Accordingly, "[t]he formidable task of constructing a definition of the practice of law has largely been left to the judiciary." *State Bar v. Cramer*, 399 Mich. 116, 132, 249 N.W.2d 1 (1976) (citing Comment, *Lay Divorce Firms and the Unauthorized Practice of Law*, 6 J.L. Reform 423, 426 [1973]). The courts should construe the term with the purpose of the statute in mind, which is to protect the public. *Cramer*, 399 Mich, at 134, 249N.W.2d 1.

In Cramer, the issue before the court was whether a nonlawyer selling "Do-It-Yourself Divorce Kits" was engaged in the unauthorized practice of law. The court held that it does not constitute the unauthorized practice of law for a nonlawyer to provide or sell standard forms and general instructions for completing the forms, or to provide typing services. *Cramer*, 399 Mich, at 136, 249 N.W.2d 1. However, the court stated, "[t]o the extent that defendant provides personal advice peculiar to [the client's particular legal situation], she is engaged in the 'unauthorized practice of law." *Id.* at 138, 249 N.W.2d 1.

In Bright, the bankruptcy court addressed whether the services provided by a paralegal constituted the unauthorized practice of law. The paralegal specialized in preparing divorce kits, but also assisted debtors in preparing Chapter 7 bankruptcy forms. The practice of the paralegal in that respect was to collect data from the debtor, decide where information should be placed on the forms, and add language to the standard forms not dictated by the debtor. The paralegal also stated that she responded to questions from debtors regarding the interpretation and definition of terms, referred debtors to specific pages of reference books in response to questions, and provided information about local procedures and requirements. She also consulted an attorney when a legal question arose and related the response back to the debtor. *Bright*, 171 B.R. at 800–01. The court noted that there had been no cases in Michigan specifically dealing with the unauthorized practice of law in the bankruptcy setting and looked to bankruptcy cases in other jurisdictions that have attempted to define what constitutes the unauthorized practice of law in the bankruptcy context. *Id.* at 802. Courts have held that the following activities constitute the practice of law in other jurisdictions:

> ***821** (I) Determining when to file bankruptcy cases. *In re Herren*, 138 B.R. 989, 995 (Bankr.D.Wy0.1992).
>
> (2) Deciding whether to file a Chapter 7 or a Chapter 13. *Arthur*, 15 B.R. at 54[6] [*In re Arthur*,15 B.R. 541 (Bankr.E.D.Pa.1981)].
>
> (3) Filling out or assisting debtors in completing forms or scheduled. *In re Glad*, 98 B.R. 976, 978 (9th Cir. BAP 1989); *In re McCarthy*, 149 B.R. 162, 166 (Bankr.S.D.Cal.1992); *Herren*, 138 B.R. at 993–4; *In re Webster*, 120 B.R. 111, 113 (Bankr.E.D.Wis.1990); *In re Bachmann*, 113 B.R. 769, 773–4 (Bankr.S.D.Fla.1990); *In re Calzadilla*, 151 B.R. 622, 625 (Bankr. S.D. Fla. 1993).
>
> (4) Solicitation of financial information and preparation of schedules. *Herren*, 138 B.R. at 994; *In re Grimes*, 115 B.R. 639, 643 (Bankr. D.S.D.1990).
>
> (5) Providing clients with definitions of legal terms of art. *Herren*, 138 B.R. at 995.
>
> (6) Advising debtors which exemptions they should claim. *McCarthy*, 149 B.R. at 166–7; *Herren*, 138 B.R. at 995; Webster, 120 B.R. at 113.
>
> (7) Preparing motions and answers to motions. *McCarthy*, 149 B.R. at 166; *Webster*, 120 B.R. at 113.
>
> (8) Advising debtors on dischargeability issues. *Arthur*, 15 B.R. at 54 [6].
>
> (9) Advising debtors concerning the automatic stay. *Arthur*, 15 B.R. at 54 [6].
>
> (10) Habitual drafting of legal instruments for hire. *Arthur*, 15 B.R. at 54[6].

(11) Correcting "errors" or omissions on bankruptcy forms. *In re Calzadilla*, 151 B.R. at 625.

(12) Advising clients as to various remedies and procedures available in the bankruptcy system. *In re Calzadilla*, 151 B.R. at 625.

Bright, 171 B.R. at 802-03.

[4] This Court finds that the legal assistants of Castle perform many services that constitute the unauthorized practice of law. First, legal assistants explain to prospective clients the difference between Chapter 7 and Chapter 13. (Tr. at 15.) They are thus defining and explaining concepts and legal terms of art.

Second, Lesser stated that approximately 33 percent of prospective clients who come to their office for an initial consultation are given other suggestions as to how to resolve their problems without filing bankruptcy. (Tr. at 15.) Because these prospective clients meet only with a legal assistant at the initial consultation, the Court infers that the legal assistant makes the determination that bankruptcy is not the best choice for this particular individual and advises the client of other options. The rendering of advice peculiar to a client's particular situation is specifically prohibited by *Cramer*, 399 Mich, at 138, 249 N.W.2d I.

Third, it appears that the assistant helps the client determine whether to file Chapter 7 or Chapter 13. Although Lesser testified that the client makes the choice (Tr. at 151), Lesser also later stated that the decision "by the client and the initial consultant" (Tr. at 16) is immediately reviewed by an attorney. Regardless of that review, the assistant's participation in this important decision constitutes the prohibited practice of law.

Fourth, if the legal assistant is not comfortable answering a specific question, or if the client is not comfortable with the advice given by the legal assistant, the legal assistant asks the attorney what the advice should be and relates that information back to the client. (Tr. at 17.) The primary concern with this practice is that the legal assistant uses his or her own judgment to decide which questions to refer to an attorney and which questions to attempt to answer themselves. There is also a chance that the assistant will not properly phrase the question to the attorney or will not communicate the advice properly to the client. Moreover, and most importantly, the client is entitled to the professional judgment of the attorney.

Lesser stressed that the legal assistants employed by the Castle law firm are very well trained, and that the legal services, although not provided by an attorney, are of the highest quality. (Tr. at 20.) This argument misses the point. Legal assistants are not authorized to practice law.

***822 B.**

A number of the Michigan Rules of Professional Conduct provide further guidance on this issue. Michigan Rules of Professional Conduct 5.5 states in part:

> A lawyer shall not:
>
> ****
>
> (b) assist a person who is not a member of the bar in the performance of activity that constitutes the unauthorized practice of law.

The Comment to Rule 5.5 states, "[l]imiting the practice of law to members of the bar protects the public against rendition of legal services by unqualified persons."

Michigan Rules of Professional Conduct 5.3—Responsibilities Regarding Nonlawyer Assistants—states in part:

> With respect to a nonlawyer employed by, retained by, or associated with a lawyer:
>
> (a) a partner in a law firm shall make reasonable efforts to ensure that the firm has in effect measures giving reasonable assurance that the person's conduct is compatible with the professional obligations of the lawyer;
>
> (b) a lawyer having direct supervisory authority over the nonlawyer shall make reasonable efforts to ensure that the person's conduct is compatible with the professional obligations of the lawyer; ...

The Comment to Rule 5.3 stresses that the "measures employed in supervising nonlawyers should take account of the fact that they do not have legal training and are not subject to professional discipline."

Michigan Rules of Professional Conduct 1.1 states:

> A lawyer shall provide competent representation to a client. A lawyer shall not:
>
> (a) handle a legal matter which the lawyer knows or should know that the lawyer is not competent to handle, without associating with a lawyer who is competent to handle it;
>
> (b) handle a legal matter without preparation adequate in the circumstances; or
>
> (c) neglect a legal matter entrusted to the lawyer.

Michigan Rules of Professional Conduct 2.1 states:

> In representing a client, a lawyer shall exercise independent professional judgment and shall render candid advice. In rendering advice, a lawyer may refer not only to the law, but to other considerations such as moral, economic, social and political factors that may be relevant to the client's situation.
>
> The Comment to Rule 2.1 indicates that the "client is entitled to straightforward advice expressing the lawyer's honest assessment."
>
> [5] An issue similar to the one before the Court was addressed in State Bar of Michigan Ethics Opinion RI-128, April 21, 1992. [FN2] There, an attorney inquired as to whether his legal assistant could meet with a prospective client, collect information from the client, and forward the information to the attorney, at which point the attorney would prepare the required documents for signing without ever meeting with the client. The Standing Committee on Professional and Judicial Ethics examined the rules cited above and stated,
>
> FN2. Although ethics opinions are not binding on state or federal courts, they do provide guidance in resolving issues of professional responsibility. *Upjohn Co. v. Aetna Cas. & Sur. Co.*, 768 F. Supp. 1186, 1214 (W.D. Mich. 1990).

Taken as a whole, the recurrent theme found in these [ ] rules and comments is that a lawyer's expertise and judgment are an integral part of the service provided to a client. While legal assistants may behave in a very professional manner while interacting with clients and carrying out the multitude of other duties they perform on a regular basis, the fact of the matter is that a legal assistant has not received the extensive, in-depth legal training which is required of a lawyer. Without such training, it is possible, perhaps even likely, that a legal assistant, having the only interaction with the client, may not spot an issue or issues that could make a difference in the drafting or representation provided.

RI-128. The Committee further stated that "it is impossible to see how the legal assistant, being the only contact with the law office, could refrain from giving legal advice. ***823** Certainly, any client will have questions regarding legal advice, and if the lawyer is not directly interacting with the client, any advice must be delivered through the legal assistant." RI-128.

[6] Michigan Rules of Professional Conduct 1.4(b), which provides that a "lawyer shall explain a matter to the extent reasonably necessary to permit the client to make informed decisions regarding representation," also infers that it is the lawyer who is communicating with the client. In most instances, clients of the Castle law firm did not meet with an attorney until the meeting of creditors. An attorney cannot adequately represent a client consistent with the Michigan Rules of Professional Conduct without meeting with the client before filing the case.

C.

In *Bright*, the court stated that under the Michigan Rules of Professional Conduct, a lawyer is not adequately supervising a nonlawyer if:

> (1) the lawyer does not know of the existence or content of meetings between the nonlawyer and the client;
>
> (2) the lawyer relies solely on the nonlawyer as intermediary, neglecting to meet directly with the client; or
>
> (3) the lawyer fails to use his independent professional judgment to determine which documents prepared by the nonlawyer should be communicated outside the law office.

Bright, 171 B.R. at 805.

[7] Lesser stressed that an attorney reviews the file at every step. Specifically, after the initial consultation, an attorney reviews the initial consultation paperwork and determines if the appropriate chapter has been selected. (Tr. at 16.) The attorney reviews the petition and plan. The attorney selects the exemptions. (Tr. at 19.) After the client signs the petition, the attorney makes a final review of the papers and signs them. However, even if the attorney is as personally involved with the file as Lesser suggests, this does not obviate the need for direct client contact. Although it is not improper for attorneys to delegate certain matters to nonlawyer members of their staff, lack of contact or a direct relationship with the client precludes proper delegation. *In re Stegemann*, 206 B.R. 176, 179 (Bankr. C.D. 111.1997).

[8] A further problem arises from Castle's practice of having the legal assistant sign client retention letters. The agreement is purportedly entered into by the client and the attorney. However, the attorney does not sign the client retention letter. (See Ex. I.) This issue was addressed by the Standing

Committee on Professional and Judicial Ethics in Op 113. There, the lawyer was prohibited from allowing a nonlawyer employee to sign a client retention letter. The Committee reasoned that since court rules (MCR 2.114) require a lawyer to sign all pleadings, and retention letters are equally important, a nonlawyer may not handle retention letters. See Ethics and Legal Assistants, 71 Mich. BJ. 826 (August 1992).

D.

[9] Various sanctions are available in situations, such as this, involving the unauthorized practice of law. Courts have enjoined the unauthorized practice of law, disgorged fees, denied fees, fined the service provider, and ordered the service provider to pay the bankruptcy trustee's reasonable attorney fees. See *Bright,* 171 B.R. at 807 (citations omitted). The Court finds under the circumstances of these bankruptcy cases that it is appropriate to deny all fees for the work of legal assistants. The Court cannot award fees for unauthorized and unlawful services.

III. Fees Charged in Excess of Fee Agreement

[10] The Trustee raised objections in the following cases where the amount of the fee application was: greater than the agreed upon fees: Darain Pinkins, 97-40722; Tammy Trombley, 97-43353; Charles & Shirley Daberkoe, 97-42032; and Barbara Ellis, 97-43356. Lesser explained that the initial fee agreement covered only limited services and, in certain circumstances, additional services were required. The retainer agreement states that the $1,200 fee covers: 1) prefiling consultations, 2) creditor calls, 3) preparation and filing of original petition, 4) attorney representation at meeting of creditors, and 5) attorney representation at one confirmation ***824** hearing. The retainer does not include attorney representation in any court action filed in conjunction with the petition, including adversary proceedings and motions. (See Ex. 1.) Following a review of the fee applications, the Court is satisfied that Castle has charged additional fees only in situations where services were provided that were not included in the initial fee agreement. Accordingly, this objection is overruled.

IV. Fees for Dismissed Cases

[11] The Trustee objects to Castle charging the full fee in the following cases that were dismissed at or before confirmation: Walterine Jones, 97-40965; Angela Hall, 97-42576; D'Anyai Asaki, 97-3419; and Darain Pinkins, 97-40722. The Trustee questioned whether there was a benefit to the estate in light of the fact that the cases were dismissed. Lesser argued that the dismissals in question were the fault of the debtor and in such instances the law firm should be compensated for the services they provided.

Section 330(a)(3) provides that in determining the amount of reasonable compensation, all relevant factors are to be considered, including:

> (C) whether the services were necessary to the administration of, or beneficial at the time at which the service was rendered toward the completion of, a case under this title.

11 U.S.C. § 330(a) (3) (C).

The Trustee has focused on the subsequent dismissal of the case in his objection to these fees, without identifying any specific charges which he considers objectionable. Because the standard for determining reasonableness considers the fees "at the time at which the service was rendered," it is not appropriate to merely object to the total amount because the case was subsequently dismissed. Lesser argues that in each case in question, the dismissal was the result of actions of the debtor. If any actions by the attorney had contributed to the dismissal, then a reduction in fees would be warranted. However, the Court finds no indication of that in these cases and accordingly this objection is overruled.

V. Services of Clerical Personnel

[12] Castle included in its fee applications expenses for the services of clerical personnel, including the following: Opening of file (file preparation/organization of paperwork, entering client into system); Court preparation for filing; Filing of petition; and Copying of plan/POS to creditors and Trustee. These charges should not be billed separately to clients, but should be included in office overhead. As noted by this Court in *In re Woodward East Project, Inc.*, 195 B.R. 372 (Bankr. E.D. Mich. 1996), "it is the normal practice of attorneys in this district that the expenses of ... clerical services are part of an attorney's office overhead, and are not billed separately to clients." *Id.* at 377; see also *In re Westwood Asphalt*, 45 B.R. 111 (Bankr. E. D. Mich. 1984); *In re Bank of New England Corp.*, 134 B.R. 450 (Bankr.D.Mass.1991), aff'd. 142 B.R. 584 (D.Mass.1992). Accordingly, expenses for clerical services are not permitted and are disallowed.

VI. Similarity of Time Entries and Insufficiency of Detail

The Trustee objected that each of the 21 fee applications stated the same amount of time for the same type of service.

Lesser stated that the firm did not keep contemporaneous time records, and that the fee applications were reconstructed from memory and from reviewing the files. (Tr. at 22–23.)

The Trustee also objected to the lack of specificity of the time records. This lack of specificity necessarily resulted from Castle's initial failure to keep contemporaneous time records and the reconstruction of time records after the fact.

[13] The failure to maintain contemporaneous time records affects the reliability of the records, *In re Dawson*, 180 B.R. 478, 480 (Bankr. E.D.Tex. 1994), and, although it does not automatically result in the denial of all fees, it does justify a reduction in the fees requested, *In re Evangeline Refining Co.*, 890 R2d 1312, 1326–27 (5th Cir.1989). Without an opportunity to review actual time records, it is impossible for the Court to determine whether any particular time entry is reasonable.

[14][15][16] Additionally, the description of services provided in the reconstructed fee applications is lacking in detail, making it difficult for the Court to determine if the fees requested are reasonable. Local Bankruptcy ***825** Rule 3.03(a)(12)(C) requires the time statement to "describe with particularity the services rendered." Entries such as "Signing Appointment 45 min." or "Phone call to client re: insurance 15 min." fail to adequately describe the services rendered. A fee application which sets forth with specificity the exact nature of the services rendered, the time expended, and the expenses incurred is a prerequisite to making a determination that the services were necessary and reasonable. *In re Meyer*, 185 B.R. 571, 574 (Bankr. W.D. Mo. 1995). The Court "will not indulge in extensive labor and guesswork to justify a fee for an attorney who has not done so himself." *In re Taylor*, 66 B.R. 390,393 (Bankr.W.D.Pa.1986); see also *J. F. Wagner's Sons Co.*, 135 B.R. 264, 267 (Bankr.W.D. Ky.1991). The Court finds that a 20-percent reduction in remaining fees is warranted due to Castle's failure to keep contemporaneous time records and resultant lack of detail in their reconstructed time records.

VII. Conclusion

In summary, the Court denies all fees requested for the services of legal assistants and clerical personnel. The Court further reduces the remaining fees for the services of the attorneys by 20 percent. After those deductions, the allowable fees in each case are as follows:

Case Name	Case Number	Amount Requested	Amount allowed
Pinkins	97-40722	$1,500.00	$863.32
Jones	97-40965	$1,200.00	$730.00
Daberkoe	97-12032	$1,500.00	$706.66
Hall	97-42576	$1,200.00	$550.00
Reids	97-42719	$1,200.00	$573.34
Roberson	97-42790	$1,200.00	$436.67
Peeples	97-42791	$1,200.00	$610.00
Harmon	97-42885	$1,200.00	$526.66
Sanders	97-43062	$1,200.00	$570.00
Dunson	97-43162	$1,200.00	$573.34
Trombley	97-43353	$1,400.00	$740.00
Ellis	97-43356	$1,600.00	$806.67
Finney	97-43414	$1,200.00	$516.00
Asaki	97-43419	$1,200.00	$580.00
Sierra	97-43494	$1,200.00	$563.34
Taylor	97-43661	$1,200.00	$566.67
Singletary	97-43664	$1,200.00	$490.00
Asberry	97-44060	$1,200.00	$493.33
Knox	97-44160	$1,000.00	$506.66
Smith	97-44241	$1,200.00	$616.66
Robertson	97-44564	$1,200.00	$466.66

An order regarding the allowed fees will be entered in each case.

END OF DOCUMENT

Case Review Exercises

1. What were the main factors listed by the court that persuaded them that the services performed by the legal assistants violated the unauthorized practice of law statutes?
2. Regarding the decision of a client to either file under Chapter 7 or Chapter 13 bankruptcy, suppose the legal assistants argued that they were simply giving information to the client that the client could have gotten from the Internet, in a book, or at the bankruptcy clerk's office, and that therefore their conduct did not violate UPL statutes. Evaluate their argument.
3. The attorney for the Castle Law Office argued that the legal assistants were very well trained, and that, while they were not attorneys, their legal services were of the highest quality. Is this a strong argument? How much legal analysis did the court spend on this argument?
4. The attorney for the Castle Law Office argued that, even though an attorney did not meet with clients directly, an attorney did, in fact, review every legal document that each legal assistant prepared and therefore there could be no UPL violation. How did the court handle this argument? Whose argument did you find more persuasive: the court's or the Castle Law Office's? Why?
5. The court concluded that the legal assistants should not have been allowed to sign the client retention letter (i.e., the letter agreeing to represent the client) for the Castle Law Office. What issues are raised by this fact? How did the court handle the matter?
6. For each issue raised by the court regarding the unauthorized practice of law by the legal assistants, what new procedural system would you put in place in the Castle Law Office to allow for correction?

Helpful Web Sites

Organization	Description	Internet Address
American Bar Association (ABA) Center for Professional Responsibility	The Web site has a number of excellent resources regarding ethics, including the full version of the *Model Rules of Professional Conduct*, summaries of ABA ethical opinions, and more.	http://www.americanbar.org
ABA Standing Committee on Paralegals	ABA Web site devoted to the use of paralegals in legal organizations. Contains publications, articles, and other useful information for paralegals, including the ABA *Model Guidelines for the Utilization of Paralegal Services.*	http://www.americanbar.org/groups/paralegals.html
California State Bar	State bar Web site with a number of state and national resources related to ethics.	http://www.calbar.ca.gov (http://ethics.calbar.ca.gov/)
Colorado Bar Association—Ethics area	State bar Web site with a number of state and national resources related to ethics.	http://www.cobar.org
FindLaw—Ethics and Professional Responsibility practice area	The Web site has a number of resources, articles, and links to a variety of ethics issues.	http://www.findlaw.com

Paralegal Today	National magazine for paralegals. The Web site has limited information but the magazine itself is full of useful articles, including ethical issues related to paralegals.	http://paralegaltoday.com
LegalEthics.com	An excellent Web site for updated cases and information related to legal ethics.	http://www.legalethics.com
Michigan State Bar	State bar Web site with a number of state and national resources related to ethics.	http://www.michbar.org (http://www.michbar.org/opinions/ethicsopinions)
National Association of Legal Assistants Paralegals	National association for legal assistants–paralegals. Contains many resources for paralegals/legal assistants, including ethics-related articles and model ethics rules.	http://www.nala.org
National Federation of Paralegal Associations	National association for paralegals. Contains many resources for paralegals/legal assistants, including ethics-related articles and model ethics rules. The Web site also has a page related to ethics.	http://www.paralegals.org

Suggested Reading

1. *The Paralegal's Guide to Professional Responsibility* (3rd ed.), American Bar Association, 2011.
2. *Model Guidelines for the Utilization of Paralegal Services*, American Bar Association, 2012. http://www.americanbar.org; direct link to guidelines is currently http://www.americanbar.org/content/dam/aba/administrative/paralegals/ls_prlgs_modelguidelines.authcheckdam.pdf.
3. *Annotated Model Rules of Professional Conduct*, American Bar Association (Sixth Edition, 2007).
4. Kaufman, K. (2014). *Legal ethics*, 3rd ed. Clifton Park, NY: Cengage Learning.
5. *Model Code of Ethics and Professional Responsibility*, National Federation of Paralegal Associations. http://www.paralegals.org.
6. *NALA Code of Ethics and Professional Responsibility*, published by the National Association of Legal Assistants · Paralegals. http://www.nala.org.
7. *NALA Model Standards and Guidelines for Utilization of Paralegals*, published by the National Association of Legal Assistants–Paralegals. http://www.nala.org.
8. Schneeman, A. (2000), *Paralegal ethics*. St. Paul, MN: West Publishing Group.
9. *The Ethical Wall—Its Application to Paralegals*, The National Federation of Paralegal Associations, 2009 http://www.paralegals.org. Direct link is currently http://www.paralegals.org/associations/2270/files/THE_ETHICAL_WALL.pdf.

Hands-On Exercises
Clio—Conflict of Interest Checking

Basic Lessons

Number	Lesson Title	Concepts Covered
Lesson 1*	Part A—Introduction to Clio Part B—Set Up Law Firm Profile	Understanding the Clio Platform Details for Firm descriptions
Lesson 2	Entering Contacts	Adding new contacts
Lesson 3	Conflict of Interest Searching	Using search features in Clio to perform search queries and conflict searches.

*NOTE: Lesson 1—Introduction to Clio is the same for every subject matter. If you completed Lesson 1 in an earlier tutorial, you do not need to repeat it.

Welcome to Adams & Lee

Welcome to Adams & Lee! We are an active and growing law firm with six attorneys and three paralegals. As you know, you have been hired as a paralegal intern. We are very happy to have you on board; we can certainly use your help.

At Adams & Lee we use computer systems extensively, so it is necessary that you have a basic understanding of our system. We currently use Clio, a comprehensive, yet easy-to-use cloud-based law practice management software. Clio automates the practice and management side of operating a law firm. Clio has powerful features to manage cases, clients, documents, bills, appointments, time-tracking, reporting, and accounting.

In this lesson, you will focus on entering new contacts into Clio and learn how to do basic conflict of interest checking. We pride ourselves on being an extremely ethical firm; before we take any new matter we run an extensive conflict of interest search, so it is important that you know how to do this. We know you want to begin using Clio immediately and learning the office case management system will help you gain the skills needed to maintain the client services we deliver. You should review the "Getting Started" guide to help you become familiar with Clio.

Getting Started

Introduction

Throughout these exercises, information you need to type into the program will be designated in several different ways.

- Keys to be pressed on the keyboard will be designated in brackets, in all caps and bold type (e.g., press the [**ENTER**] key).

- Movements with the mouse/pointer will be designated in bold and italics (e.g., ***point to File on the Menu Bar and click the pointer)***.
- Words or letters that should be typed are designated in bold (e.g., type **Training Program**).
- Information that is or should be displayed on your computer screen is shown in bold, with quotation marks (e.g., **"Press ENTER to continue"**).

Clio Installation (Appendix A)

Clio is not a downloaded program; it is accessed from the Web site. You may be invited by your instructor to join as a nonlawyer (paralegal) in a hypothetical law firm through your e-mail. ***Click the hyperlink or copy and paste it into your Internet browser. Follow the on-screen instructions for providing your name and creating a password.*** You will now have access to Clio and the hypothetical law firm.

Your instructor may have you create a Clio account and work independently. In that case, see Appendix A for installation instructions.

LESSON 1: Part A (Appendix B)

You should become familiar with the Clio Platform and its essential functions before you begin any of the lessons. *Note*: If you are already logged in, you will skip Steps 1 and 2.

1. Start your Internet browser. Type **www.goclio.com** in the Internet browser and press the **[ENTER] key**.
2. On the Clio Home page, ***click Log In. On the next screen, enter the e-mail address and password you provided in Clio and click SIGN IN. If you check the box next to KEEP ME SIGNED IN, you will be able to skip this step in the future.***
3. Clio will open in the hypothetical law firm on the PRACTICE page. At this point you are ready to explore the Clio platform and its essential functions. There are 11 tabs available in Clio. We will start with the PRACTICE tab.
4. ***Click*** **PRACTICE**. Your screen should now look like Clio Exhibit 1A-1. This is the Clio dashboard which provides a quick look at the agenda, calendar, and billing information. You will now explore the other 10 tabs.

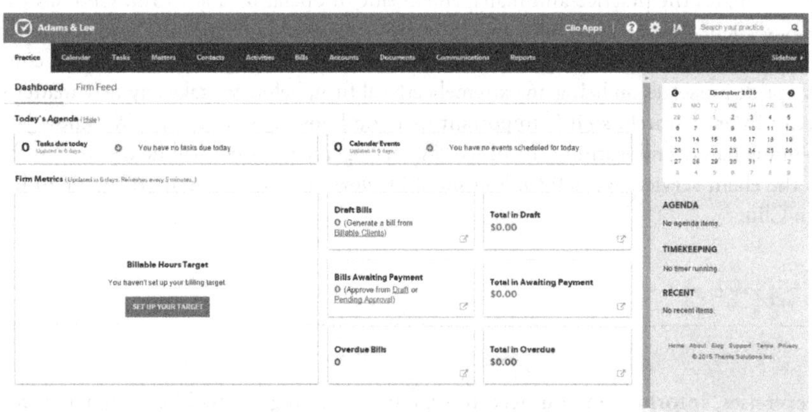

Clio Exhibit 1A-1 Practice Tab

Source: Themis Solutions, Inc.

5. ***Click* CALENDAR.** You may need to scroll down to see the entire page. You can change the view to see your Agenda, or Day, Week, Month, or Year views. You can view your personal calendar, the firm calendar or both.
6. To create a calendar entry, while in the Week view, ***select the Wednesday of that current week and double-click on the 10:00 am time slots.*** The Create Calendar Entry will open. See Clio Exhibit 1A-2. If you ***click Add Event***, the date will default to the current date.

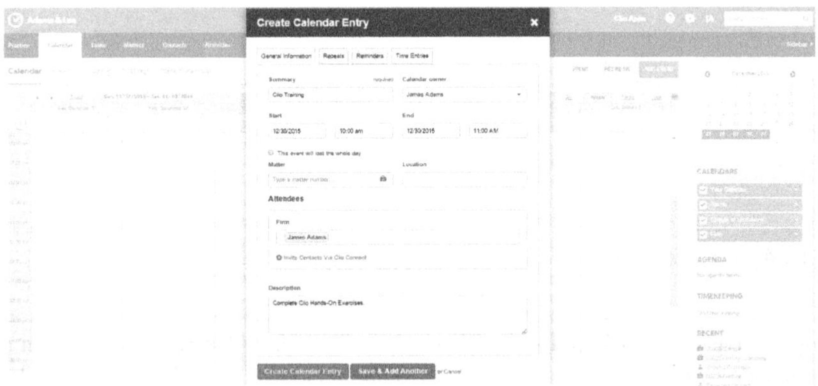

Clio Exhibit 1A-2 Create Calendar Entry

Source: Themis Solutions, Inc.

Under Summary, type **Clio Training**. Under **Start**, type **10:00 AM** and under **End** type **11:00 AM**. Leave Matter and Location "**blank**," and under Description, type **Complete Clio Hands-On Exercises.** ***Click Create Calendar Entry.*** When adding multiple entries, ***click Save & Add Another.*** After the entry is complete, it will appear in the calendar. ***Place your cursor over the new calendar entry*** to see the description. Your calendar should look like Clio Exhibit 1A-3. You can now move to the "Tasks" tab.

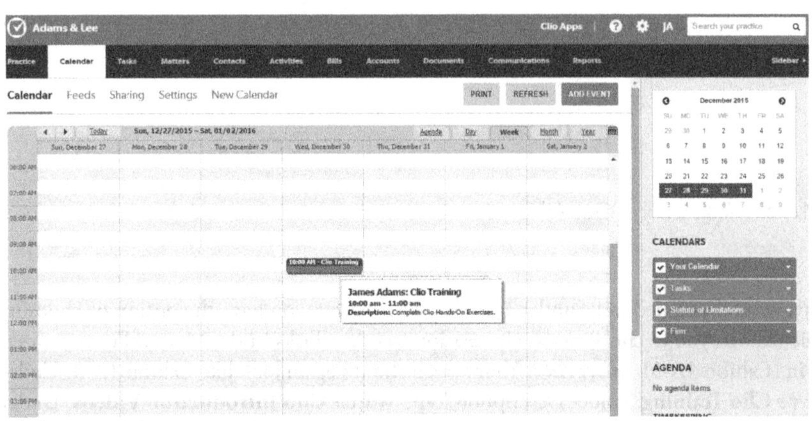

Clio Exhibit 1A-3 Calendar Entry - View

Source: Themis Solutions, Inc.

7. ***Click* TASKS.** This is where specific tasks can be assigned to specific individuals or groups. To create a new Task, ***click Add***. See Clio Exhibit 1A-4. Under Task Name, type **Clio Training.**

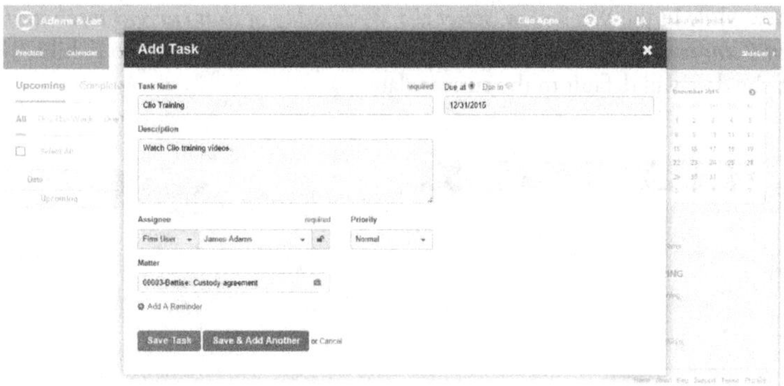

Clio Exhibit 1A-4 Add Task – "Due At"

Source: Themis Solutions, Inc.

Under Description, type **Watch Clio training videos**. Under Due: the radial button will default to **"Due at"** when there are no other tasks associated. ***Click the box under "Due At,"*** and a calendar will appear. ***Select Thursday of the current week***. Under Assignee, ***select Firm User and then choose yourself.*** Under Priority, ***select Normal.*** Under Matter, ***type 00003-Battise: Custody Agreement*** (the case will appear in the list as you begin typing the number). Then ***click Save Task***. When adding multiple tasks, ***select Save and Add Another***. At this point you will be on the ***"tasks" under 00003-Battise***. See Clio Exhibit 1A-5.

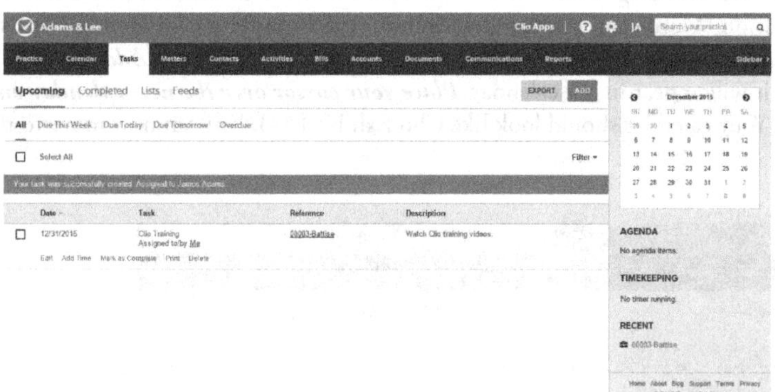

Clio Exhibit 1A-5 Task Entry – "Due At"

Source: Themis Solutions, Inc.

8. When you have several assigned tasks under a specific case matter, you have the option of choosing **"Due in"** which allows you to choose a date in relation to other Tasks in the Matter. From your current position in (Exhibit 1A-5), ***select Add***. Your screen should again look like Exhibit 1A-3. Under Task Name, type **Clio Training**. Under Description, type **Watch Clio Introduction Videos**. Under Assignee, ***select Firm User and then choose yourself.*** Under Priority, ***select Normal.*** Under Matter, ***type 00003-Battise: Custody Agreement*** (the case will appear in the list as you begin typing the number).Then ***select 00003Battise: Custody Agreement.*** Under Due: the radial will default to

"Due at," however; you now have the option to choose **"Due in."** ***Select "Due in,"*** and a dialogue box will appear. See Clio Exhibit 1A-6.

Clio Exhibit 1A-6 Add Task – "Due In"

Source: Themis Solutions, Inc.

ENTER **"1"** in the box marked with a 0. ***Select Calendar Weeks*** under the drop-down menu in the next box, ***Select before*** under the drop-down menu in the next box. Then ***select Clio Training*** under the radial button. ***Click Save Task.*** The second task will now appear listed on the Tasks page. See Clio Exhibit 1A-7.

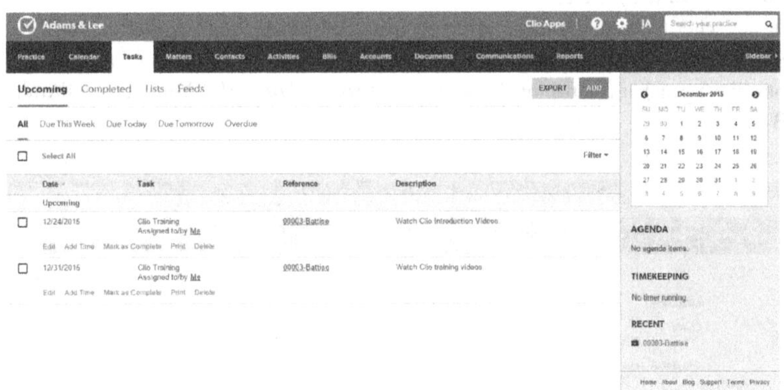

Clio Exhibit 1A-7 Upcoming Task Entries

Source: Themis Solutions, Inc.

9. ***Click*** **MATTERS**. Matters are what Clio calls for cases or files. Clio allows you to associate, or connect, matters with clients, tasks, bills, etc. In later exercises you will see how that works and you will create several new matters.
10. ***Click*** **CONTACTS**. Contacts are people and corporations that you do business with (clients, other attorneys, court reporters, etc.).
11. ***Click*** **ACTIVITIES**. "Activities" is what Clio uses for both time and billing entries as well as expense entries. Time entries can be billed as a flat rate or as an hourly rate. In later exercises you will create several new billing activities.

12. ***Click* BILLS**. Here, you can create a new bill, review a client's billing history, and create bill themes (designs) among other bill-related issues. In later exercises you will create several new bills.
13. ***Click* ACCOUNTS**. Here you can view and manage the various bank accounts of a law firm.
14. ***Click* DOCUMENTS**. Here you can view and manage the documents maintained in Clio.
15. ***Click* COMMUNICATIONS**. Here you can send and receive e-mails, maintain communication logs, interact with colleagues and Clio-connected users, as well as limit permissions between groups for file-related communications.
16. ***Click* REPORTS**. Here you can create reports on a variety of topics (billing client, mater, productivity, and revenue).
17. To end this Clio session, ***click your initials at the top of the screen. Click Sign Out and then close your Internet Browser.***

This concludes the introduction lesson on Clio's platform and essential functions review.

LESSON 1: Part B (Appendix C)

In this lesson, you will set up the firm profile in the hypothetical law firm, establish billing rate, create an activity description, set up bank accounts and establish the matter-numbering protocol.

Note: If you are already logged in, you will skip Steps 1 and 2.

1. Start your Internet browser. Type www.goclio.com in the Internet browser and press the **[ENTER] key**.
2. On the Clio Home page, ***click Log In. On the next screen, enter the e-mail address and password you provided in Clio and click SIGN IN. If you check the box next to KEEP ME SIGNED IN, you will be able to skip this step in the future.***
3. Before you enter new clients, contacts and matters in Clio, details for the hypothetical law firm should be entered. First, you will set up the account information for your hypothetical law firm. ***Click the "settings" icon*** (looks like a gear) at the top of the screen next to the "***initials***." Your screen should look like Clio Exhibit 1B-1.

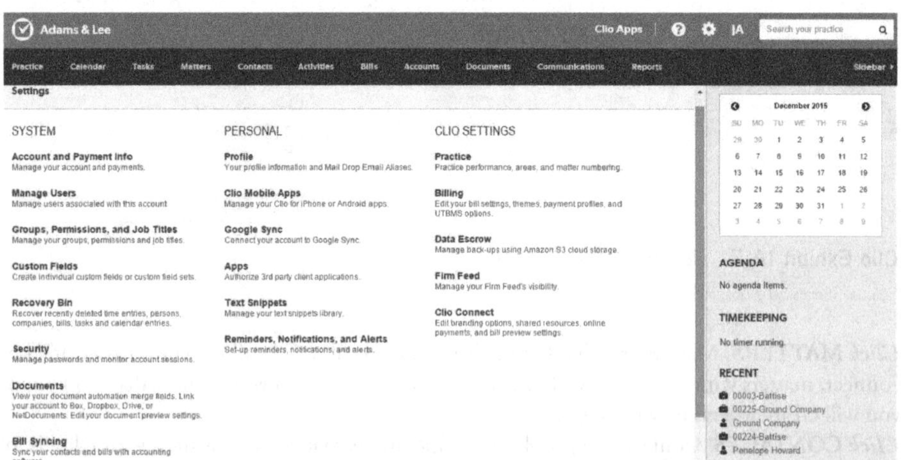

Clio Exhibit 1B-1 Clio Settings Screen

Source: Themis Solutions, Inc.

4. ***Click Account and Payment Info.*** The name of your hypothetical law firm will be established by your instructor (i.e., Adams & Lee) or your First and Last name if you create your own individual account (i.e., Law Office of "First name" "Last name" that you entered). Note: Free accounts do not have access to payment info.
5. ***Type the name, address, and contact information of your firm*** (i.e., sample check from Exhibit 6-1 (Chapter 6), instructor provided, or create your own).
6. Next, ***click the drop-down menu under Date format. Select*** the option that resembles ***12/31/2015.*** Then, ***click the drop-down menu under Time format. Select*** the option that resembles ***11:59 pm. Click Save New Information.***
7. You will now update profile and establish a billing rate. ***Click*** the "settings" icon (looks like a gear) at the top of the screen next to the "initials." Your screen should look like Clio Exhibit 1B-1. ***Click Profile*** and scroll down to **Billing Rate**. ***Type 175.00 next to $/Hr. Click Save New Information.*** See Clio Exhibit 1B-2.

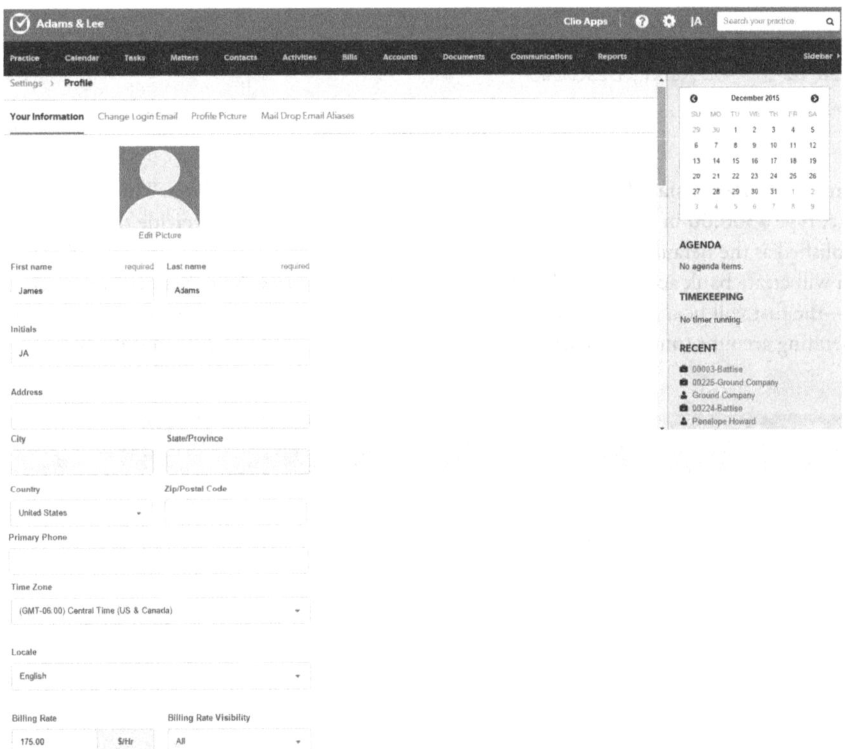

Clio Exhibit 1B-2 Update Profile – Billing Rate

Source: Themis Solutions, Inc.

8. Next, you will create an Activity Description. These are used to ensure a consistent description of commonly used time entries across a law firm. It can also be used as a shortcut—you can save text in the Activity Description and when you enter in a time entry, it will populate this text for you. Activity Descriptions can be shared across a law firm so that everyone in the firm can use them. ***Click the Activities tab, then click Activity Descriptions, then click Add.*** See Clio Exhibit 1B-3.

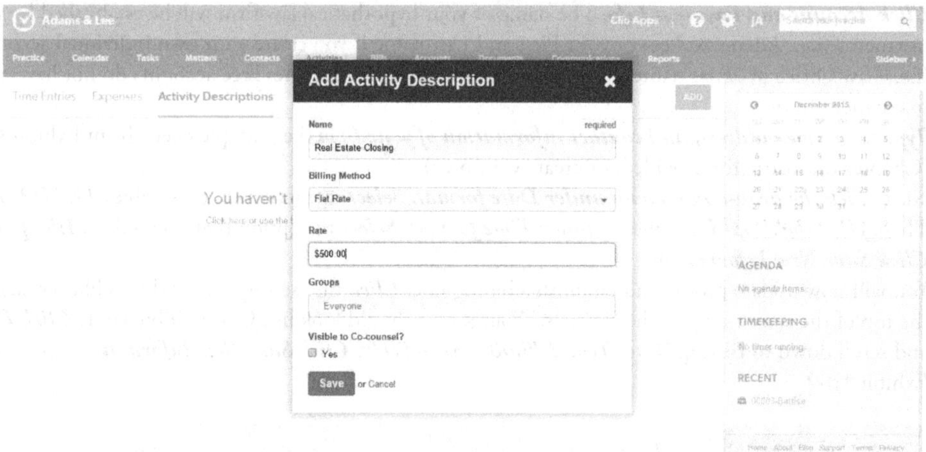

Clio Exhibit 1B-3 Add Activity Description

Source: Themis Solutions, Inc.

Under Name, type **Real Estate Closing**. Under Billing Method, ***select Flat Rate***. This opens a text box called Rate; type **$500.00** in the text box, ***Click Save***. This flat rate fee will override the $175.00 per hour established as the default rate.

9. Next, you will create bank accounts. ***Click the Accounts tab***, then ***click New***. You will set up two accounts—the first will be a Trust Account (one that contains only client money) and the second will be an Operating account (one that ***should not*** contain client money). See Clio Exhibit 1B-4.

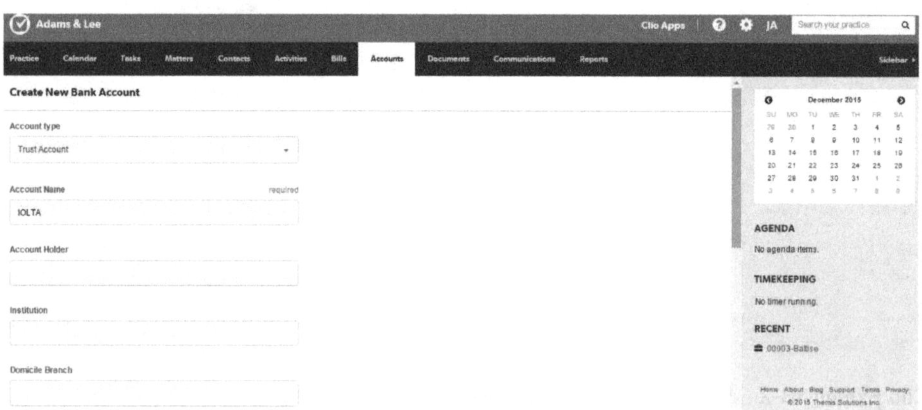

Clio Exhibit 1B-4 Create New Bank Account

Source: Themis Solutions, Inc.

10. Under Account type, ***select Trust Account.*** Under Account name, type **IOLTA** (this stands for Interest on Law Office Trust Account, commonly used for Trust accounts). It is not necessary, nor is it required, to complete the remainder of this form (although you are welcomed to do so). However, you should leave the Balance 0.0. ***Click Create New Bank Account.*** The screen will refresh (showing the new IOLTA account) so additional accounts may be created.
11. Now create the Operating Account. ***Click New,*** then under Account type, ***select Operating Account.*** Under Account name, type **Law Firm Account**. It is not necessary, nor is it required, to complete the remainder of this form (although you are welcomed to do so). However, you should leave the Balance 0.0. ***Click the box next to Default Account.*** (The default account will show up first on the Transactions tab found when a client file is opened under Matters.) ***Click Create New Bank Account.***
12. You will now create the matter-numbering protocol for the hypothetical law firm. ***Click the "settings" icon*** (looks like a gear) at the top of the screen next to the "***initials.***" Your screen should look like Clio Exhibit 1B-1. ***Click Practice,*** and then ***click Matter Numbering.*** See Clio Exhibit 1B-5. ***Under Select***

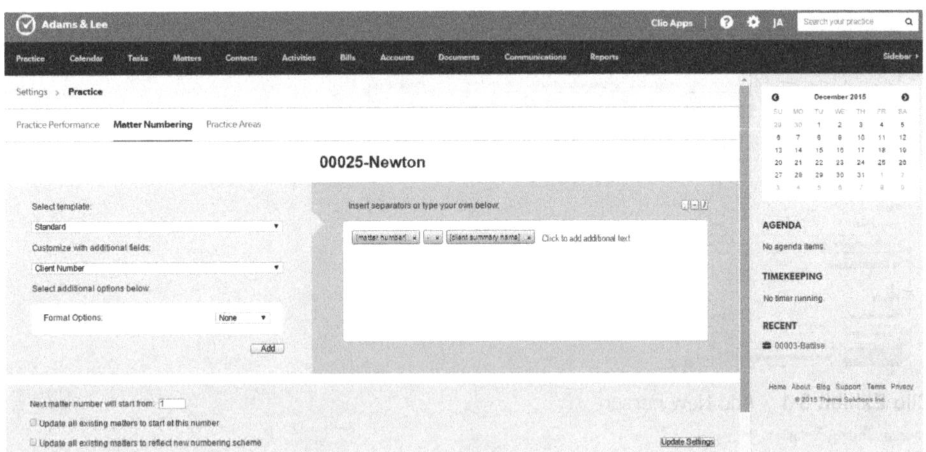

Clio Exhibit 1B-5 Matter Numbering

Source: Themis Solutions, Inc.

Template: click the drop-down menu arrow and click on each of the available options. As you do, notice how the sample matter number (00025-Newton) changes. Use the default (matter number—client summary name), then ***select Standard.*** Under ***Customize with additional fields, select Client Number. Click Update Settings.***

13. To end this Clio session, ***click on your initials*** at the top of the screen. ***Click Sign Out, and then close your Internet browser.***

This concludes the lesson on law firm profile and setup.

LESSON 2: Entering Contacts

In this lesson, you will enter several new contacts into Clio.

Note: If you are already logged in, you will skip Steps 1 and 2.

1. Start you Internet browser. Type www.goclio.com in the Internet browser and press the [**ENTER**] **key**.
2. On the Clio Home page, ***click Log In. On the next screen, enter the email address and password you provided in Clio and click SIGN IN. If you check the box next to KEEP ME SIGNED IN, you will be able to skip this step in the future.***
3. Clio opens in the PRACTICE tab. ***Click the Contacts tab, then click New Person.***
4. At this point you are ready to enter all the details available for the new contact. ***Enter the following information in the "Add New Person" form.*** See Clio Exhibit 3-1.

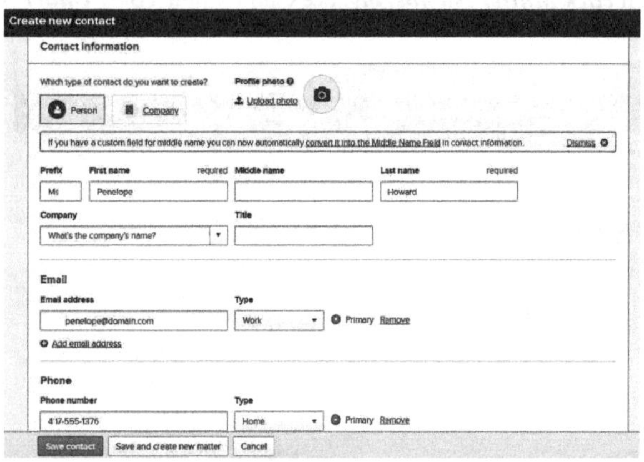

Clio Exhibit 3-1 Add New Person

Source: Themis Solutions, Inc.

Prefix	**Ms.**
First Name	**Penelope**
Last Name	**Howard**

You may skip the company and title information

Email	penelope@domain.com (make sure this is the Home email and click the button to make this the Primary Email address
Phone number	(417) 555-1376 (make sure this is the Home Phone number and click the button to make it the Primary Phone Number)

You may skip the Web site and instant messenger information.

Address

Street	6 Minden Circle
City	Savannah
State/Province	GA
ZIP	30209
Country	United States
Type	Home

You may skip the LEDES and Contact Billing information.

5. ***Click Save New Person.*** At this point your screen should look like Clio Exhibit 3-2:

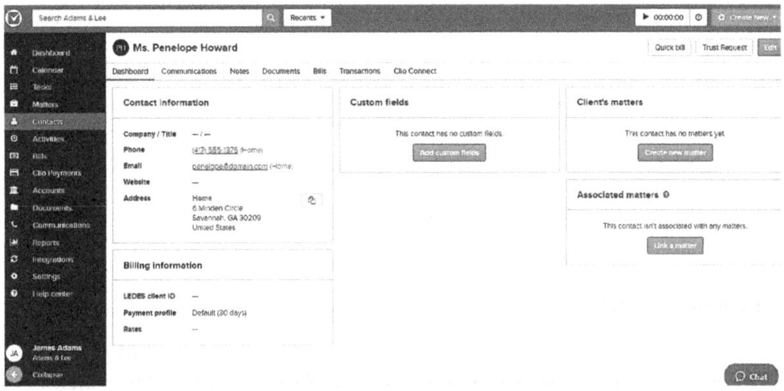

Clio Exhibit 3-2 New Person Entry

Source: Themis Solutions, Inc.

Clio has several additional features to include with adding a new contact. You can exchange documents and billing electronically through LEDES.org (requires an account). Clio also allows you to customize your rates for individual clients.

6. You are now ready to enter some additional contacts on your own. Enter the following contact information:

Field	Data to be Entered
Prefix	**Hon.**
First Name	**Jane**
Last Name	**Hobbs**
Company	**St. Tammany County Courthouse**
Title	**Judge**
E-mail	**jhobbs@vacourthouse.gov**
Phone Number	**(202) 462-6347**
Address	**6300 Main Avenue** **Covington, VA 70005** **Work**

This concludes Lesson 2 on entering new contacts in Clio.

LESSON 3: Conflict of Interest Searching

In this lesson, you will create a field to indicate a conflict check was performed and conduct conflict of interest searches in Clio. *Note:* If you are already logged in, you will skip Steps 1 and 2.

1. Start you Internet browser. Type www.goclio.com in the Internet browser and press the **[ENTER] key**.
2. On the Clio Home page, ***click LOG IN. On the next screen, enter the email address and password you provided in Clio and click SIGN IN. If you check the box next to KEEP ME SIGNED IN, you will be able to skip this step in the future.***
3. Clio opens on the PRACTICE tab. Go to the ***search your practice*** field located in the top right corner of the Clio page. You are now ready to conduct a conflict of interest search across the entire Clio system. In this field, ***type Battise, and then* ENTER**. The search query returned three areas where the name appears. See Clio Exhibit 3-3 (Note: Battise may appear as "00003")

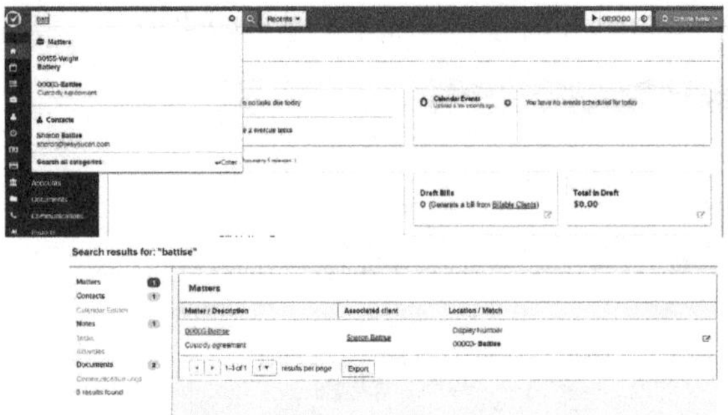

Clio Exhibit 3-3 Conflict of Interest Search

Source: Themis Solutions, Inc.

4. Return to the ***search your practice*** field ***type Linda Blunder, and then*** **ENTER**. The search resulted in no matches. Since there is no conflict, you could proceed to enter this individual as a new client.
5. To Confirm a Conflict Check has been performed, it is helpful to create a custom field. ***Click on Settings at the top of the screen.***
6. ***Click Custom Fields, then under Matter Custom Fields: Individual Custom Fields, click Add.*** Then under name field, *type* ***Conflict check performed?*** Then, under the Type field, ***select checkbox*** from the drop-down menu. Make sure to ***select "Default"*** so that this field will appear automatically for new matters. Then, ***click Save***. See Clio Exhibit 3-4.

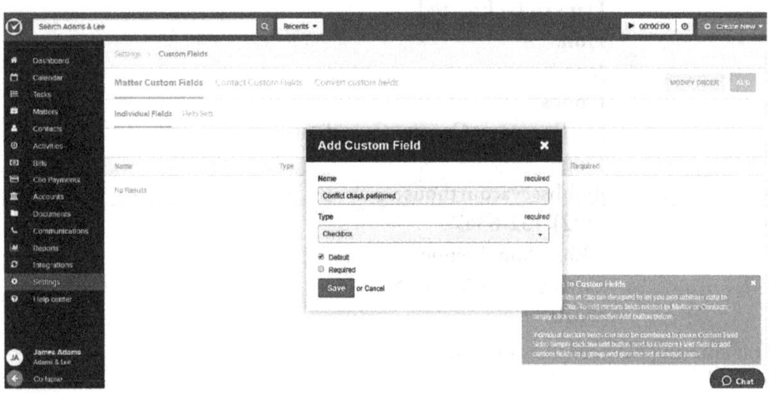

Clio Exhibit 3-4 Add Custom Field

Source: Themis Solutions, Inc.

7. Return to the ***search your practice*** field ***type Joe Smith, and then*** **ENTER**. The search resulted in one match. This may or may not be a problem since "Joe Smith" is a common name and it may not be the same person; however, finding a conflict in the system is a significant issue that would need further follow-up before adding the new contact to Clio.

This concludes Lesson 3 on Conflict of Interest Checking in Clio.

This concludes the Clio Chapter 3 Conflict of Interest Checking Hand-On Exercises.

4

Client Relations and Communication Skills

Chapter Objectives

After you read this chapter, you should be able to:

- Discuss factors that will promote effective client relationships.
- Discuss ways to communicate effectively.
- Identify communication barriers.
- Explain the importance of good listening skills.
- Identify the pros and cons of using groups to make decisions.
- Discuss the characteristics of a leader.

A poorly served client often feels neglected and disrespected. The client expects to receive some evidence of work performed when they have paid the attorney for services. Constant unreturned phone calls by the attorney along with no correspondence or copies of prepared documents is frustrating, not to mention unethical. The client sought a qualified attorney (one authorized to practice—registered with the state bar association) because the law is complicated and most laypersons lack the ability to adequately represent themselves. That said, the attorney's failure to communicate leaves a client in the worst fear—the attorney is not doing their job; they are most likely they are correct. The client's recourse is to file a complaint which now will involve disciplinary actions from the bar association. Poor client communications create poor client relations which may lead to disciplinary actions against the attorney.

***

On the other hand, a well-served client will generally appreciate the efforts put forth by the attorney, even if the outcome is not in his or her favor. A reasonable client wants to be informed concerning his or her case status and receive a fair and honest projection regarding the outcome of the case. When the attorney along with the members of the legal team stays in contact with the clients, providing them with copies of the relevant documents, billing details for services performed and prompt communications about hearings, negotiations, and rulings, the client feels respected. In turn, the client will generally respect the hard work performed by the attorney and his or her staff. Good communications make for good client relations.

Why Do Paralegals Need to Foster Good Client Relationships and Communicate Effectively?

Fostering positive client relationships and communicating effectively with others is an important aspect of practice management and is an absolute necessity for paralegals to be successful. Customer service and satisfaction are very important to the practice of law, especially considering the number of law offices and the fierce competition that exists. Paralegals who mishandle client relationships by not putting the client first will cause clients to go elsewhere for legal services. Nearly every task a paralegal performs, requires communication skills such as writing correspondence, drafting briefs, interviewing clients and witnesses, and legal research/writing. The ability to effectively exchange ideas and information with others is an essential part of being a paralegal.

This section will present an overview of ethical duties to clients and a basic but practical explanation of communication, and it will give you some ideas for how communication skills can be improved. Also included in this section are related communication topics, such as leadership qualities, the advantages and disadvantages of working with groups, and how to conduct client interviews.

Ethical Duty to Communicate with Clients

Although much of this chapter covers how to provide clients with excellent customer service as it relates to providing quality legal services, there is also a strong ethical duty regarding the need to regularly communicate with clients. Keeping a client informed about his or her case, keeping him or her abreast of changes, developing strategy with him or her, and keeping him or her involved in the progress of a case—including communicating settlement offers—is fundamental to the practice of law. Attorneys and paralegals are bound by this ethical duty. Clients cannot make informed decisions about their cases if they do not know what is happening.

Rule 1.4, regarding the rules of professional conduct, requires an attorney, within reason, to promptly comply with the client's requests for information, to keep the client informed about the status of their legal matter(s), to consult with the client, and to provide the client with an explanation of their matter(s) so that the client can make informed decisions.

Rule 1.4 specifically requires the attorney to act "reasonably" with the client when it comes to explaining general strategies, providing information and consulting about their legal matters. The "reasonableness" of the situation will depend on the facts and circumstances of the particular case.

The comment to *Rule 1.4* discussing the guiding principle for a lawyer to consider in fulfilling the client's expectation in a reasonable manner that would be consistent with the duty to act in the client's best interests, and the client's overall requirements as to the character of representation.

Clients become extremely frustrated when they pay for legal services and the attorney or paralegal refuses to take their calls, answer their letters, or otherwise communicate with them in any way.

The duty to communicate derives in part from the attorney's fiduciary duty of utmost good faith to the client. Exhibit 4-1 explains the specific duties of an attorney to communicate with clients as decided by case law.

Client communication includes a duty of an attorney to:

- Routinely inform a client concerning the status of their case.
- Promptly inform a client about important information.
- Never cover up a matter if the attorney failed to carry out the client's instructions.
- Notify a client if he or she is stopping work on a client's case, leaving a firm, or quitting the practice of law.
- Explain the law as well as the benefits and risks of alternative courses of actions for a client.
- Promptly notify and communicate settlement offers to a client.

Exhibit 4-1 Duties of an Attorney to Communicate with a Client

DUTY TO TIMELY RESPOND TO A CLIENT'S REQUEST FOR INFORMATION There is an absolute duty for an attorney to respond to reasonable requests for information. Although this seems basic, many attorneys still do not return client phone calls, respond to client letters, respond to client e-mails, or show up for client appointments. There are thousands of state bar disciplinary opinions where attorneys have been reprimanded, suspended, and disbarred for failing to respond in a timely fashion to their clients.

DUTY TO PROMPTLY INFORM A CLIENT ABOUT IMPORTANT INFORMATION An attorney may not withhold important information that affects a legal matter without telling the client. For example, cases have held that an attorney has a duty to promptly tell a client that the client was named as a defendant in a civil action; an attorney cannot wait for six months to tell an incarcerated defendant that the attorney had been appointed to represent the client; and an attorney had to tell a client that a case was set for docket and later dismissed for failure to prosecute.

DUTY TO NEVER COVER UP A MATTER IF THE ATTORNEY FAILED TO CARRY OUT THE CLIENT'S INSTRUCTIONS If an attorney fails to carry out the instructions of a client by either neglect or design, the attorney has a duty to be up front and communicate this to the client. Many attorney discipline cases have been filed because an attorney agreed to file a claim and then did not, either due to negligence or because the attorney later changed his or her mind and then told the client the case was, in fact, filed. This type of behavior is also prohibited by Rule 1.4.

DUTY TO NOTIFY A CLIENT IF HE OR SHE IS STOPPING WORK ON A CLIENT'S CASE An attorney cannot cease working on a client matter without affirmatively telling the client, because doing so without the client's consent or knowledge could injure the client's legal interests. The withdrawal from a client matter should preferably be in writing, in the form of a letter to the client. If formal representation has been made in court, the attorney must file a motion to withdraw.

DUTY TO NOTIFY A CLIENT IF AN ATTORNEY IS LEAVING THE FIRM OR QUITTING THE PRACTICE OF LAW An attorney has a duty to tell a client that he or she is leaving the firm and, therefore, representation of the client's case will be handled by someone else. The same holds true if the attorney is going to stop practicing law. The client needs to be made aware of this fact so that he or she can get his or her file returned and secure other counsel.

DUTY TO EXPLAIN THE LAW AS WELL AS THE BENEFITS AND RISKS OF ALTERNATIVE COURSES OF ACTION An attorney has a duty to help the client make an informed decision about the client's matter. This may include explaining legal theories to the client, explaining the effects of contracts and other documents, advising a client on the consequences of accepting one alternative over another, and generally giving advice and counseling the client regarding the legal matter.

DUTY TO PROMPTLY NOTIFY AND COMMUNICATE SETTLEMENT OFFERS TO A CLIENT An attorney has a duty to notify a client of all settlement offers, including explaining the terms and conditions of the offer and the ramifications to the client. An attorney cannot ordinarily, without the prior direction of the client, unilaterally decline or accept a settlement offer.

THE PARALEGAL'S ROLE IN COMMUNICATING WITH CLIENTS Paralegals can play an active role in communicating with clients. Paralegals are often more accessible to clients than attorneys and therefore may have many opportunities to work with clients and to keep them informed. This is admirable and encouraged as long as the attorney is actively involved with the case, is reviewing all documents prepared by the paralegal, is the only party giving legal advice to the client, and meets with the client as needed.

Client Relationships

A fundamental aspect of law office management is the commitment to provide quality legal service to clients. This is true whether you work in a private law firm or legal aid office with many clients, or in a corporation or government practice where you have only one client; service is the key. Providing quality legal services begins with a good working relationship with each client, and this relationship is not just for attorneys. Everyone in the office, including paralegals, should be committed to this. Remember, the client always comes first; he or she is the one paying your salary in the end. Clients may not have the legal background to know whether or not they are receiving good legal representation. However, clients do know whether their phone calls are being returned, whether documents in their cases are poorly written and have typographical errors, whether deadlines are missed, or whether they are being treated respectfully. Merely providing good technical legal skills is not enough to please clients. Most clients are referred to attorneys and law offices by previous clients; if you provide poor service to existing clients, you will be depriving your firm of the best way to expand the practice.

Fostering Positive Client Relationships

Exhibit 4-2 shows a list of things that clients like and dislike about attorneys and law office staff. These likes and dislikes determine whether a client will come back for future business or refer others to the firm. Notice that the issue of winning or losing a case is not included in either list.

Exhibit 4-2 What Clients Like and Dislike

What Clients Like	What Clients Dislike
Friendliness	Being talked down to
Competence	Arrogance
Promptness	Staff acting bored or uninterested
Being able to reach attorneys/staff on the first try	Impatience
Excellent follow-up	Rudeness
Not being billed for every two minute phone call	Calls and e-mails not returned
Attorneys/staff taking extra time to explain the legal process in layperson's terms	Incorrect billings
Listening and paying attention to what the client has to say	Being forgotten, treated as unimportant, or taken for granted
Demonstrating genuine interest in the client's problems and concerns year in and year out	Confidentiality breaches
Honesty	Errors
Good financial stewardship	Poor-quality work
Completing work on time	Multiple staff billing for the same event
	Waiting in the waiting room when they have an appointment and they are on time

It is important to note that many of the items listed next are the opinions of how a client perceives the legal professionals.

- Does the client see you as friendly and willing to help, or inattentive and impersonal?
- Do you come across to the client as prompt and businesslike, or indifferent?
- Do you show common courtesy to the client, or do you come across as rude?
- Are you respectful of the client and what he or she is going through, or do you have a superior and condescending attitude?
- Do you, at every possible opportunity, let the client know what is going on with his or her case and establish a feeling of trust and cooperativeness, or is the client ignored?

Each of these areas is critical to the success of the client relationship. Fail in any of these areas, and the relationship is undermined. This section will provide you with some ideas about how to foster excellent client relationships (see Exhibit 4-3).

Exhibit 4-3 Fostering Positive Relationships with Clients—"Clients for Life"

Description	Behavior
Know your client	• When dealing with the client, take into account his or her emotional/mental/physical state (consider how you would feel in the same circumstances), understand that many clients are anxious or nervous about seeing a legal professional and, based on this, respond and ask questions appropriately. • Establish basic trust in the relationship at every opportunity by listening to their needs, being honest, and being respectful. • Ask your client what his or her concerns are about the matter. • Ask the client what his or her business is about. • Do your own research about the client's business and industry. • Ask how the client prefers to be communicated with (in person, e-mail, telephone, or voice mail). • Ask the client how often he or she wants to be communicated with. • Ask how you can serve them better periodically.
Treat each client as if he or she is your only client	• When you meet with a client, only have that person's file on your desk. • Never take another call when meeting with a client, and let others know not to disturb you. • Never talk about how busy you are or about other cases to clients. • Particularly with new clients, it is important that the initial meeting go well and that law office staff is immediately available after a referral is made. • Particularly with new clients, be sure to mention whether the firm has handled similar cases in the past. Clients like to know that the firm is experienced regarding the subject matter of their case.

Exhibit 4-3 *(continued)*

Description	Behavior
Send copies of all documents to clients	• Always send copies of documents to the client. This lets them know what you have been working on and keeps them informed. If the document is not particularly sensitive, attach it to an e-mail to the client; it's cheaper and faster.
Do not use legalese	• Talk to clients in layperson's terms and refrain from using jargon.
Return all phone calls and reply to e-mails and voice mails immediately	• Always return phone calls, e-mails, and voice mails immediately, no later than the end of the day.
Be courteous and professional	• Always be courteous, professional, and empathetic with clients. This is extremely important to most clients. • Dress professionally.
Respond to clients' requests and keep promises	• Always respond to client requests in a timely manner; if you make a promise to get something to a client, make sure you get it done on time and contact the client to let him or her know the status.
Give periodic updates	• Be proactive and periodically give updates to a client on the status of his or her case, whether or not the client specifically asked for it.
Never share personal problems or complain to clients	• Avoid sharing personal problems with clients. Clients are there to receive a service. • Do not complain to clients at all, especially about how hard you are working on their case. They are paying the firm a significant fee.
Preserve client confidences	• Maintaining client confidentiality is critical to maintaining the foundation of trust in the relationship.
Survey clients	• Use formal client surveys to find out what clients think about your services.
Management must help promote good client relations	• Work with management to let them know how to better support positive client relationships.
Publish a client manual	• Publish a client manual to help clients understand what to expect from the law office and how the judicial system functions regarding their type of case.
Take conflicts of interests seriously and be ethical	• Ask yourself who the client is, if there is more than one person in your office. • Always do careful conflicts checks, disclose any issues whatsoever, and get any consents to conflicts in writing after full disclosure. • If a client sees you being unethical in any way, that client may assume that you are not ethical with him or her.
Do not procrastinate	• Do not put things off or delay communicating with clients, even when you do not have good news or when work has not been completed. Be honest and up front.

Know Your Client

Knowing your client and your client's individual needs is extremely important. Each client has a unique set of needs, worries, and desires related to his or her legal matter. Firms with outstanding client relations discover what those specific needs are for each client, and then systematically deliver on each need.

Before you can understand a client and his or her needs, it is helpful to understand why a client comes to a legal professional. Like any other relationship, the client relationship is based on trust. Clients come to legal professionals because they need help. Whenever possible, take the client's emotional, mental, and physical state into consideration and empathize with him or her.

By showing the client that you understand and recognize his or her situation and concerns, you establish trust, which is the foundation of the relationship. Another way to establish trust is by being respectful and honest with the client at all times.

Once a relationship of trust is established with the client, it is important to know specifics about that individual, such as what his or her business is, what his or her concerns are about the legal matter, and what you can do to serve his or her needs.

Do not assume that you know what the client needs or wants. You may or may not be right, but you will know for sure if you ask. Because communication is vitally important, ask the client how he or she wants to receive communication. Are office visits the most convenient? Is e-mail the best? Does the client prefer telephone or voice mail? Again, the trick is to ask and then deliver services based on the client's needs.

TREAT EACH CLIENT AS IF HE OR SHE IS YOUR ONLY CLIENT Every client should be treated individually. Behave as if that client's case is the only thing you are working on and as if the case is the most important one. Everyone at the firm needs to put the client at ease. When you meet with a client, have only his or her file on your desk and give the client your undivided attention. Never take a call when meeting with a client, and let others know not to disturb you. This is a good idea not only because it shows the client that you are interested in his or her case, but also because the confidentiality of your other clients must also be maintained.

Never tell the client how busy you are or how many other cases you are working on; the client's case is the only one he or she is concerned about and the only one you should be talking to him or her about. If a client calls and asks if you are busy, say something such as "I'm never too busy to take a call from a good client" (even if you are swamped). If a client comes in for an appointment, never make him or her wait in the waiting room. A good law practice makes prompt, *personal* service a high priority. Take a personal interest in the client's affairs and be empathetic. It is always best to be personable with clients because this fosters good working relationships that will continue for years to come.

SEND COPIES OF ALL DOCUMENTS TO CLIENTS As a matter of practice, it should be the policy of the law office to always send copies of all letters, memos, pleadings, and documents to the client. In nearly all cases, the client will appreciate this, and it will increase his or her confidence, satisfaction, and trust; even though this might be just another case to you, this matter is of particular importance to the client. Although many people focus on the results of a case, the documents are a large piece of the product for which the client is paying. Even if the client does not understand everything sent, it still allows him or her to know what is happening in the case and how difficult the theories and complexities of the case are, and it lets the client know that you are actively working on the case. The cost of the copies can be charged to the client's account, so there is no real reason not to do it. Also, if the client has e-mail and the document is not particularly sensitive, attach it to an e-mail and send it directly to the client. Clients are usually more willing to pay their attorney's fees when they have seen the work done on the case and may be frustrated if they do not know what is happening and then receive a bill.

DO NOT USE LEGALESE Do not use legalese or legal jargon when talking with clients. Many clients do not understand legal jargon, and it is confusing and frustrating to them. Some clients may be too intimidated to ask what the terms mean. Try to explain legal concepts in words that a layperson could understand.

RETURN CLIENT PHONE CALLS IMMEDIATELY It is essential that you return client phone calls immediately. If that is not possible, at least return the calls on the same day when they are made. It is not uncommon for clients to call paralegals. Usually, paralegals are easier to reach than attorneys, and paralegals often work with clients quite closely, depending on the type of case. Because paralegals typically are very busy and may be working on many projects at once, you will be inclined to put client calls off, but do not do this. Always return a client's call first and then finish the job at hand. If you do not reach the client on the first try, continue to try to reach the client rather than letting the client call back for you.

BE COURTEOUS, EMPATHETIC, AND PROFESSIONAL AT ALL TIMES Some clients may be abusive at times. Do not take client comments personally. Never become impatient with a client, "snap" at a client, or act rudely. If you have a problem with a client treating you abusively, mention it to your supervising attorney or paralegal manager and let him or her handle it. Act professionally in all situations.

Finally, never allow a secretary or receptionist to let a client stay on hold after calling for you. If you are on another call and cannot get to the client immediately, have the receptionist tell the client you will return the call as soon as you get off the phone, then follow up and call the client. If the client leaves a voice mail, return it as soon as possible.

RESPOND TO CLIENT REQUESTS IN A TIMELY FASHION AND KEEP YOUR PROMISES It is not enough to simply return client phone calls. When clients request you to answer their questions, send letters, or need things from you, you must respond as quickly as possible. If you tell the client that you will have something to him or her by a particular time or date, keep your promise. If an emergency comes up and you cannot make the deadline, always contact the client and let him or her know and set a new deadline that you can meet.

GIVE CLIENTS PERIODIC STATUS REPORTS Some cases can be sitting on appeal for months, waiting for a motion to be ruled on, or facing other things that make them lie in a dormant state. This always frustrates clients, who like quick remedies to their problems. On a weekly or not less than a monthly basis, review your cases, and, with the approval of your attorney, write or e-mail clients letting them know what is happening in their cases. E-mail and word processors can be configured to make this a very quick process by having form letters on file for different situations. If the case is waiting for some kind of action, you should still write the client and let him or her know that you are waiting and have not forgotten the case. If you do not review the case periodically, the case could very well sit for months with no contact with the client. Keeping in touch with the client never hurts; it reiterates that his or her business is important to you.

DO NOT SHARE PERSONAL OR OFFICE PROBLEMS WITH CLIENTS Always keep your personal problems to yourself and never make comments that are derogatory about your supervising attorney, firm, or other staff members. Clients need to know that their legal matters are in good hands and that everything is under control. Also, never complain to a client regarding how hard you are working on his or her case. After all, that is what he or she is paying for.

PRESERVE CLIENT CONFIDENCES Preserving client confidence is very important and cannot be overemphasized. Apart from the ethics question, you should keep in mind that if a release of client information gets back to the client, the relationship is most likely finished.

THE USE OF CLIENT SURVEYS A client survey is a way to find out exactly what your clients think of your services (see Exhibit 4-4). Most client questionnaires are given at the conclusion of a case. Anytime you get information directly from a client, you should

Exhibit 4-4 Sample Questionnaire

Thank you for participating in the questionnaire and prompt return for our review. It is through your responses that we may continue to provide excellent service to our clients and the community.

With our kindest regards,

1. Case type: ______
2. Attorney or paralegal: ______
3. Were you previously represented by the firm or an attorney located with the firm?
   ______
   If you answered yes, please provide details (month/date/year) ______
4. For what reason(s) did you chose the attorney and/or the firm? ______
5. Were you informed about the basis of our charges for legal services at the beginning of the case?
   ______
6. Did you ever wait for an extended period of time in the waiting room before the attorney or paralegal met with you? ______
   If yes, how many times? ______
7. Did members of the legal team and the law firm treat you with courtesy? ______
8. Did the attorney or paralegal provide you with timely notices regarding the case progress?
   ______
9. Do you feel the fee charged was reasonable? ______
10. Do you feel the results obtained in the case were to your satisfaction? ______
    If no, why not? ______
11. Would you recommend our law firm? ______
    If yes, why? ______
    If no, why not? ______
12. How would you rate the quality of services provided by the firm (please select).
    ______
    (Excellent, Very Good, Good, Fair, Poor) ______
13. Please provide comments below: ______
    ______
    ______
    ______

take it to heart. Most firms allow the client to remain anonymous in completing the questionnaire to ensure truthfulness, and it is usually short, not more than a page long, to make completion as easy as possible.

MANAGEMENT MUST HELP PROMOTE GOOD CLIENT RELATIONSHIPS Management also has a duty to promote good client relationships. Exhibit 4-5 contains a sample client-centered policy that would be found in a law office staff manual.

Exhibit 4-5 Sample Service Policy for Clients

Part One: Basic Client Representation Goals

The attorneys and all members of the legal team will strive to focus on client representation in the following manner:

- Maintain a communicative process of client representation.
- Clients are not numbers; clients should be treated individually and personably.
- All members of the legal team should display a sincere concern for the clients' issue(s) when contacting them.
- Priority should be given in responding to client contacts.
- All members of the legal team should maintain a consistent mindset that the client is the focus.

Part Two: Correspondence

Communications may include written correspondence (letters, memos), faxes, or e-mail messages and in some situations text messages or instant messaging (IM).

- Clients should receive copies of all documents and pleadings, along with a letter explaining the included paperwork in a promptly manner.
- Client e-mails and/or text messages should mostly be used for brief messages, avoiding confidential or privilege information unless communications have security (encryption) to protect the transmitted information.
- Client updates should be received at least monthly unless other arrangements are agreed to by the client.

Part Three: Telephone Communications

Communications should be consistent with the established agreements between the client and the attorney during the client representation meeting.

- Client communication should meet the client's needs and expectations.
- Clients should receive information concerning important changes or events promptly; bad news should be communicated immediately.
- Returning client phone calls should be done within a reasonable time frame. If not by the attorney, then by a member of the legal team explaining the delays and attempting to help the client if immediate attention is needed.
- Attorneys should return phone calls within the same day, which means clients might be called back late into the evening.

Part Four: Billing Process and Communications

The billing process is an effective client communication tool that provides details regarding the attorney's services through billing invoices.

- Monthly bills along with a cover letter briefly describing the services performed by the attorney and future plans should be sent in order to maintain routine status for the client.
- Time entries should provide information concerning substantive work performed for the client on their case.

Exhibit 4-5 Sample Service Policy for Clients *(Continued)*

Part Five: Handling Client Expectations

Throughout the entire representation, the client's expectations must be handled.

- The client should be informed as soon as possible if there are significant changes in the case plan or course of the matter.
- During the course of the matter, the case plan and any fee estimate should be easily accessed and referenced.
- All members of the legal team should work together to manage a case plan within the client's expectation.
- When preparing monthly billings, attorneys should refer to the fee estimates.
- If the attorneys are unable to meet the fee estimates established, they should adjust the methods for handling the case or contact the client about adjusting the estimates.
- If the monthly bill is higher than the client expected, the attorney should contact them immediately to avoid surprising the client.

Part Six: Recovery

When the client conveys dissatisfaction or a problem concerning the services provided, the situation must be addressed immediately.

- High priority should be given in returning phone calls expressing dissatisfaction with some aspect of services provided.
- Members of the legal team should ensure that messages from clients expressing dissatisfaction should be communicated to the attorney immediately.
- There should be no delays returning a dissatisfied client's phone call either by the attorney or members of the legal team.

PUBLISH A CLIENT MANUAL Some law offices publish a manual for their clients, which explains what to expect from a law office, such as how attorney fees are calculated, how the attorney–client relationship works, what discovery is, how to prepare for a deposition, and what to expect at trial. This type of manual is very beneficial and will save the attorney and paralegal from answering the same questions over and over for different clients.

TAKE CONFLICTS SERIOUSLY AND BE ETHICAL Conflicts of interest must be taken seriously, and a careful conflicts check should be done before a case or client is accepted. If there are any possible conflicts found, they should be fully disclosed to the client and the client should consent in writing. It is also important to always act in an ethical manner to clients, *in everything you do.* If a client sees you being dishonest, he or she will infer that you are dishonest to him or her as well.

DO NOT PROCRASTINATE A law office is no place for people who procrastinate; procrastination always causes problems and never solves them. Handle client problems when they occur. Deliver bad news to clients or admit that a deadline was missed up front. That way, clients can at least respect you for being honest. Honesty is the best and only policy when it comes to dealing with clients. The whole attorney–client relationship is based on trust; if that fails, the attorney–client relationship will fail as well.

Resolving Client Dissatisfaction

Resolving client dissatisfaction is not an easy task and may not be up to the paralegal to resolve at all. Client dissatisfaction can have many roots, including personality conflicts with the legal staff, disagreement on strategy, misunderstandings, lack of knowledge about the law or facts, or frustration with the legal system. Here are some ideas for how to resolve client dissatisfaction.

LISTEN TO THE COMPLAINT; DO NOT INTERRUPT AND DO NOT ARGUE When a client has a complaint, the first thing to do is to listen carefully and patiently. Listen with empathy and do not react. Avoid interrupting or arguing with the client; this is rude. In some instances, clients just want to vent about something they do not agree with, they see as unfair, or they believe was a mistake. The client may be fully satisfied simply by finding someone who will listen patiently and react in a courteous, professional manner. If the client is satisfied with this, thank him or her for the call, let him or her know that you or the firm will try to correct this in the future, and then pass along the information to the appropriate parties who can prevent the problem from recurring.

EMPATHICALLY LISTEN When speaking with a client regarding a complaint, it helps to acknowledge what he or she is saying and reaffirm that you are listening by saying "Yes" or "Hmmmm" or "I see." Responses like these show that you are actively listening.

DO NOT OVERSTEP YOUR BOUNDS OR PROMISE SOMETHING YOU CANNOT DELIVER A client may try to extract a promise from you to do something that you do not have the authority to do. Do not let a client force you into doing something you are not comfortable with or that you do not have the authority to do. In those instances, say something like, "I will talk to my supervising attorney and get back to you as soon as possible, hopefully by X." Telling the client an exact time you will get back to him or her should alleviate fears that the complaint will be ignored.

TAKE NOTES Always take careful notes so that you can recount exactly what the complaint is about, including the fine details. This will allow you to relay it to others for the purpose of resolving the matter.

FORWARD ALL COMPLAINTS TO YOUR SUPERVISING ATTORNEY AND BE HONEST All complaints should be immediately referred to your supervising attorney. If a client is calling to complain about a mistake you made and you know it is a mistake, be honest, admit the mistake to your supervising attorney, generate possible solutions to the problem, and put procedures in place to keep it from happening again.

DO NOT IGNORE THE COMPLAINT If you receive a client complaint, never procrastinate or ignore it. If a client believes he or she has been ignored or his or her comments summarily disregarded, he or she will only become more angry. Resolving the matter as quickly as possible is the best thing to do.

RECOGNIZE THAT SOME CLIENTS WILL ALWAYS COMPLAIN Some clients are seemingly never happy and always have a complaint to make. Hopefully, the number of clients like this is very small, but nonetheless they do exist. Treat the client as considerately as you can and talk to your supervising attorney. In extreme cases, a firm may decide to simply terminate the relationship and move on.

WORK THROUGH PERSONALITY CONFLICTS Some client complaints may be the result of personality conflicts. In most instances, you should work through personality conflicts; in severe instances, you may be able to request that another staff member handles the matter. This should be asked for as a last resort. You may have to handle the matter anyway, either because there is no one else to take over or there is no one else with your experience regarding that client or the legal/factual issues involved.

Clients and Technology

Clients are demanding technology-based solutions. They demand access to their attorney and law office by e-mail; they want documents to be e-mailed to them immediately, instead of waiting for days before they arrive in the mail; they want law offices to use the same basic software programs they have, so they can access documents of all types, from word processing to spreadsheet to presentation files; and they want electronic access to documents so they can edit them in real time. They want their law offices to offer slick technological solutions from practice-based computer programs; they want everything from electronic discovery to the automated tracking of exhibits on a laptop for trial; they want online billing, so that they can receive their bills immediately and in a format *they* want; they want electronic access to *their* files and information via extranets and other services that are available at all times; and they want their attorney's and paralegal's mobile phone numbers so that they can reach them when *they* have an emergency. It is important, when working with a new client, to understand exactly what the client's expectations for technology are and then meet those expectations. Clients mostly want these things because they result in direct access to their legal professionals; however, some clients demand these things, knowing that more technology means greater efficiency and lower hourly bills.

How to Lose Clients

Losing clients is easy; keeping them for life is hard. Losing a client may result from missing an urgent phone call, making an inappropriate or unprofessional remark, losing an important document, giving legal advice that is not well thought out, lacking trust, or making him or her think that you overbilled or that he or she was not treated ethically. There are many reasons why clients leave legal professionals and law offices; the goal is to keep this from happening. The legal professionals who retain their clients year in and year out keep their "eye on the ball" and on what is important to the clients at all times.

Dealing with Difficult Clients

Not all clients are created equal. It was noted in Chapter 2 that successful attorneys and law practices are able to distinguish bad clients and cases from good ones. Some clients may be extremely difficult to work with; some have completely unreasonable expectations about their case; some may have mental impairments; some may be vengeful; some may be violent; some may be dishonest; some may not be able to pay for legal services, and so on. It is up to the attorney to select what kind of clients and cases he or she will accept and work with. Once these decisions are made, it is up to the paralegal to work with the client to the best of his or her ability, even if the client proves difficult.

- **Stay calm and maintain professionalism** Always stay calm when working with a difficult client, no matter what the client does. Maintain a professional demeanor, and never react to a client's outburst with one of your own. If possible, ratchet down the dialogue and try to find common ground with the client. If a client becomes upset or abusive, which is very rare, immediately leave the area and inform the attorney. Some difficult clients are harder on staff than the attorney. It is important that you let the attorney know about the situation.

- **Document conversations** Protect yourself from difficult clients by carefully documenting your conversations with them—e-mail is a great tool for this. It never hurts to send the client an e-mail or a letter confirming an important instruction, just to be sure that all parties are on the same page. Some case management programs provide a place in the program to document all conversations with clients. No matter what tool you use, always save it for future reference.
- **Be courteous, but maintain an arm's-length relationship** Always be courteous to clients, but consider treating a difficult client a little more at "arm's length." You do not need to be "chummy" or friends with clients in order to do your job. Be professional, be competent, and do not let your guard down. You also do not need to share personal information with clients, even if they ask for it. If a client asks for advice or wants to know how you would make a decision regarding something related to his or her case, do not provide an answer—these are decisions that the client must make.
- **Keep the attorney fully informed** It is important, when dealing with a difficult client, to always keep the attorney fully informed of all of your conversations or correspondence with the client. Copying or blind copying the attorney on e-mails to the client is an effective way to keep the attorney informed. Also, do not fail to let the attorney know if a client shows any unprofessional behavior toward you. It is the attorneys' job to prevent clients from abusing staff.

Communication Skills

Possessing good communication skills is necessary in most professional jobs, but it is especially important in a law office. Paralegals must communicate with clients, opposing counsel, supervising attorneys, office staff, court clerks, and witnesses on a daily basis regarding complex and important matters. Good communication skills also bear directly on the effectiveness of law office management. Communication is an important part of management because, without it, management cannot plan, organize, control, or direct the business. Thus, having good communication skills bears directly on both legal services to clients and law office management.

General Communication

communication

The transfer of a message from a sender to a receiver.

communication barrier

Something that inhibits or prevents the receiver from obtaining the correct message.

noise

Any situation that interferes with or distorts the message being communicated.

feedback

Information sent in response to a message.

Professionals, such as paralegals and attorneys, typically spend three-fourths of each day communicating. **Communication** is the transfer of a message from a sender to a receiver. Although communication can be quickly defined, it is more difficult to explain why there is so much poor communication in the world.

A **communication barrier** inhibits or prevents a receiver from obtaining the correct message from a sender. These barriers include situations where the sender and receiver have different cultural backgrounds, perceptions, understandings, and ages. The abundance of communication barriers help to explain why some messages are never properly received. Noise is also a communication barrier; **noise** interferes with or distorts the message being communicated. A good example of noise is when one person is trying to listen to several senders at one time—the messages are distorted because the receiver cannot understand all of the messages at the same time.

Feedback is an important part of effective communication. **Feedback** is information sent in response to the sender's message. There is no way for the sender to know whether his or her information has been properly received without feedback. Feedback allows the receiver to state his or her understanding of the message, and also allows the sender to evaluate the effectiveness of the message and to clarify misunderstood points. Feedback does not have to be verbal; it can be as simple as a puzzled look on the receiver's face.

Nonverbal Communication

Communication is much more than just speech. There are many nonverbal communicators, such as eye contact, facial expressions, posture, appearance, clothing, tone of voice, and gestures. All of these nonverbal means of communication have a hand in determining whether or not a message is properly received.

Improving Your Communication Skills

LISTENING Listening is one of the most important features of communicating effectively, and although it sounds easy to do, often it is not. The average person forgets 50% of what was said to him or her within just a few minutes. We have all caught ourselves in the middle of conversations thinking about something unrelated to the conversation. We become "lazy listeners," only minimally listening. Exhibit 4-6 contains some excellent rules on listening. A common problem that attorneys and paralegals are guilty of is that, instead of listening

Exhibit 4-6 The 10 Commandments to Effective Listening

1. **YOU MUST QUIT SPEAKING.**
   If you are speaking, you are not listening.
2. **YOU MUST MAKE THE SPEAKER FEEL COMFORTABLE.**
   Let the person know he or she can speak freely.
3. **YOU MUST LET THE SPEAKER KNOW YOU ARE LISTENING.**
   Do not read text messages on your phone while someone is speaking. Pay attention and listen attentively.
4. **YOU MUST RELATE TO THE SPEAKER.**
   It is important to recognize the speaker's viewpoint(s).
5. **YOU MUST NOT BE DISTRACTED.**
   Do not read text messages or organize papers. Put your phone on private, silence and shut the office door if possible.
6. **YOU MUST CONTROL YOUR TEMPER WITH THE SPEAKER.**
   If you are upset, it is easy to misunderstand what the speaker said.
7. **YOU MUST BE PATIENT WITH THE SPEAKER.**
   Do not interrupt someone while he or she speaks, begin packing your briefcase, or checking the clock.
8. **YOU MUST NOT ARGUE WITH OR CRITICIZE THE SPEAKER.**
   If the speaker gets defensive, he or she will stop talking. If you argue with the speaker, you do not get anything accomplished.
9. **YOU MUST ASK THE SPEAKER QUESTIONS.**
   When you ask questions, the speaker knows you are listening and helps address additional issues.
10. **YOU MUST QUIT SPEAKING.**
    It is important to reinforce the silence because all other commandments rely on your ability to listen. Human beings have twice as many tools for listening as they do for speaking and should consider that a hint for developing proper listening behaviors.

to what another person is saying, they formulate arguments and prepare for when they will speak. This effectively takes the listener out of good listening, and the listener may miss the total message.

KEEP IT SIMPLE AND TO THE POINT Most people understand more of a message when the sender uses short, direct sentences rather than long, complex ones. You can explain complex issues to others just by using words and phrases they understand. Avoid jargon and legalese when dealing with clients. In the same vein, research has shown that short letters are read sooner than are long ones, and the reader actually remembers the message of the short letter more accurately.

CONSIDER YOUR NONVERBAL SIGNALS Realize that when you are communicating with people, they look at you and your message as a total package. They notice how you are dressed, if you are nervous, if you are fidgeting, if you have your hands in your pockets, and if you have confidence in yourself.

DO NOT BECOME EMOTIONAL Try not to be emotional when communicating. Try to be objective and calm, without being cold and distant.

MAKE EYE CONTACT Make eye contact with everyone you are talking to, since it conveys honesty and interest. Juries, for instance, often cite the lack of eye contact as a reason that they did not believe a witness.

BE AWARE OF YOUR BODY LANGUAGE Crossed arms usually mean you are feeling defensive, scared, or cold about something; poor posture is sometimes interpreted as lazy or slothful. One kind of body language that is more important than anything else for setting a positive tone is a simple smile. A smile relaxes both your audience and you.

BE PRECISE AND CLEAR Always try to be as precise as possible when communicating with others. How often have you heard someone say, "Well, I thought you meant. . . ." Speak clearly and do not leave anything to the imagination. For example, if you tell a delivery person you need something filed at the courthouse, be sure you are precise and tell him or her whether you need it filed at the federal courthouse, the local courthouse, or the state courthouse. These subtle differences can be very important in a law office, so be absolutely clear when you communicate. Look for feedback. If someone has a puzzled look on his or her face, explain your message again or ask him or her to repeat it to you.

CONSIDER YOUR AUDIENCE Always tailor your communication to the specific audience with which you are communicating. You can have the best message in the world, but if you are delivering it to someone who does not care about it, you have wasted your effort. If possible, find out what is important to your audience, what concerns it has, and then tailor everything you say to address these concerns.

CONSIDER THE TIMING AND CONTEXT Timing is everything; a good communicator must know when to communicate his or her message. Be patient and wait until the time is right. Time your message so that noise and barriers are kept to a minimum. You may want to wait until the receiver is in a good mood or has just heard good news. Communication is an art; people will react to the same message in different ways depending on the timing. You must consider the context in which the communication is being made for your message to be effective. Is the receiver having a bad day? Where is the communication taking place: in a crowded hallway or in a private office? What type of relationship have you had with the receiver? Do you respect each other, dislike each other, or distrust each other?

Try to consider the other person's perception of your communication. Consider this, when you find yourself in a disagreement with someone, are you more likely to believe that *your behavior is motivated by context* (e.g., you had a bad day, you are tired, and you are stressed out) while you believe that the *other person's behavior is motivated not by context, but by something personal* (e.g., spite, revenge, meanness, or unreasonableness)? This is a normal reaction. Consider the context and the environment in which the other person is viewing your communication; look at it from his or her point of view and be aware of your own biases. This will improve your ability to communicate with others.

AVOID NEGATIVES AND DO NOT BE JUDGMENTAL Do not start with negative or judgmental comments such as "That probably will not work." This will only make your audience defensive. Try to be positive and explore the conversation in a positive light. If you do not think an idea will work, ask a question about why you think it might not work, such as "Well, have you considered what would happen if this occurred . . .? Will your idea still be successful?" This allows the other person to consider your side but in a positive, constructive light.

ASK QUESTIONS Never assume something based on unsupported evidence. It is very easy for people to misread or assume things about other people. Instead of assuming something incorrectly, ask questions and talk about it. This will allow you to verify whether or not your initial assumptions were accurate.

REPHRASE IDEAS If you are not sure whether you truly understand what someone has told you, try rephrasing. **Rephrasing** is a technique of telling the sender your understanding of the conversation. It allows the sender to clarify information that might not have been understood clearly.

rephrasing

A technique used to improve communication by repeating back to a person your understanding of the conversation.

RECOGNIZE THE IMPORTANCE OF GOOD COMMUNICATION WITH THIRD PARTIES A paralegal deals with many types of people, including witnesses, court personnel, outside agencies, libraries, businesses, and other law offices. You must be professional at all times and have good relationships with these third parties, since they may provide information that will help you to perform your job. When possible, cultivate these relationships.

Use Proper Telephone Techniques

Poor telephone techniques abound in many law offices. Here are some examples of what not to do:

- Office staff: "Law offices."
  Client: "May I speak to Mr. Smith?"
  Office staff: "Sure, just a sec."
- Office staff: "Law offices."
  Client: "May I speak to Mr. Smith?"
  Office staff: "He's yakking on the other line, you want to hold?"
- Office staff: "Law offices."
  Client: "May I speak to Mr. Smith?"
  Office staff: "He's not in. Why don't you call back this afternoon?"

Good telephone techniques are important in any legal organization. Most legal professionals spend a great deal of time on the phone and need courteous telephone skills.

ALWAYS COMMUNICATE IN A BUSINESSLIKE, PROFESSIONAL TONE Because callers cannot see your body language and facial expressions on the phone, the words you say and the tone you use are very important. Always be calm and professional when talking on the phone. If you have a million things to do and you are flustered or might get short with the caller, then do not answer the phone. Call back when you are calm.

PUT THE CALLER AT EASE Listen carefully and make appropriate responses that puts the caller at ease whenever possible. You gain nothing by offering quick responses that may alienate the caller.

REFER TO THE CALLER BY NAME When the caller tells you his or her name, call the person by that name: "Mr. Smith, I'll page her immediately." This puts the caller at ease and lets him or her know that you remember who he or she is. It also communicates personal service.

WHEN TAKING A MESSAGE, ALWAYS OBTAIN THE TELEPHONE NUMBER OF THE CALLER Callers often say that the person whom they are calling already has their number. Obtain a callback number from the caller anyway, just in case the number has been changed recently or has been lost, the caller has a new number, or just because it is more convenient for the person who will return the call.

WHEN TAKING A CALLER'S NAME OR PHONE NUMBER, ALWAYS REPEAT BACK THE INFORMATION By repeating the information back to the caller, you confirm that you have received the message correctly and that the name and number are accurate. Think how frustrated you get when someone takes a message and does not record the information accurately.

ALWAYS IDENTIFY YOURSELF AS A PARALEGAL/LEGAL ASSISTANT If you are taking a call from a client, an attorney, or a third party regarding a case, always identify yourself as a paralegal/legal assistant early in the conversation.

WHEN TAKING A MESSAGE, GET A GENERAL "FEEL" FOR THE SUBJECT It is important to get a general "feel" for what the caller needs when taking a message, because you might be able to handle the matter yourself. If you cannot, then do not ask for too much information, from clients in particular. Some clients do not like to give out details about their problems.

BE WARY OF MOBILE PHONES Be careful that the conversation is not about sensitive client matters when speaking on a mobile phone. Although mobile phones are becoming more secure, it is still prudent to be careful.

WHEN TAKING A MESSAGE, EXPLAIN BRIEFLY WHY THE INDIVIDUAL CALLED IS NOT IN Giving a short explanation as to why someone cannot take a call, such as "Susan is in court this morning," lets the caller know that the person is not ducking his or her call. Avoid saying that the person is "unavailable."

TRY TO ANSWER YOUR PHONE WHEN YOU ARE NOT WITH A CLIENT In the era of e-mail and voice mail, sometimes clients want to talk to a person to discuss a matter. Try to answer your phone instead of letting it roll to voice mail whenever possible. Clients can become quite frustrated when they cannot reach someone on the phone, particularly when the client has an emergency.

The following is a client maxim to think about:

- I needed the help of a lawyer or paralegal.
- I could not reach you.
- I reached a competing law office.
- I no longer need you.

DO NOT KEEP CALLERS ON HOLD EXCEPT FOR A VERY SHORT PERIOD OF TIME Nothing is more frustrating to a caller than to be indefinitely put on hold. If you must place a caller on hold, do so for only a very short period of time. Continually update the caller as to the status of his or her call.

Leadership and Communication

Being a leader takes a special type of communication skill. Leadership was described in Chapter 1 as the act of motivating or causing others to perform and achieve objectives. Leaders give us direction, vision, and motivation. Leadership is an important part of any organization or department. Paralegals need to take leadership roles, and there are opportunities for paralegals who have leadership skills; for instance, paralegals can be paralegal managers or law office administrators. Paralegal "leaders" can take on projects and cases that need innovation and have never been done before. Paralegals with leadership characteristics are sought after and are important to growing law offices.

HOW DO I BECOME A LEADER? Having determined that leadership qualities are essential for the paralegal, the next question is: "How does one become a leader?" This has been a hotly debated issue over the years. Early leadership theories said that only exceptional people were capable of assuming the leadership role (i.e., you either were or were not born with it). But current research overwhelmingly shows that leaders are not born, they are made. The following are some suggestions on how to become a leader:

1. **Be an expert.** Effective leaders are experts in what they do. They know precisely what they are talking about. People around them have confidence in their abilities and rely upon their knowledge and judgment. They are inventive and ingenious and are able to plan, organize, and manage resources to solve problems. Before they give opinions, they do research and master the subject they are talking about. Leaders must be competent, make good decisions, and be able to evaluate situations and act accordingly.
2. **Be honest.** Effective leaders have a reputation for being extremely honest and forthright and for possessing a high degree of integrity. These are important qualities; subordinates must respect leaders and be motivated, inspired, and willing to follow their directives.
3. **Stay calm.** Good leaders stay cool and collected, even when they are "under fire." They have confidence in their own abilities and are not shaken by disagreement or challenge. Instead, they rise to the occasion.
4. **Trust and support those under you.** Good leaders choose effective and competent subordinates and then support them in their efforts. Subordinates know that they are trusted and that their abilities and skills are appreciated, and thus work even harder for the leader.

5. **Take risks and do not be afraid of failure.** Effective leaders take calculated risks. They focus on the positive and refuse to think about failure. Failures and mistakes are steps in the learning process and are to be expected. Leaders have the ability to make bold decisions and to stand by them when others are backpedaling.
6. **Encourage honest opinions from others.** Effective leaders encourage subordinates to be honest and to articulate their opinions, even if those opinions are in disagreement with the leader's opinions. Debate sharpens the decision-making process so that all alternatives are considered and evaluated based on their merits. This is the only way situations can be properly evaluated. Leaders encourage others around them to cooperate and communicate with one another by listening to everyone's ideas and opinions.
7. **Set goals and visions.** Effective leaders set goals and have specific visions for the future. The goals and visions inspire and empower others to accomplish the goals and to work toward the common dream.
8. **Be respectful.** Good leaders respect, get along with, and care for other people. They foster meaningful personal and professional relationships with the people around them.

Communication is at the center of leadership. Leaders emerge when a new crisis arises or when a new challenge surfaces. Leaders are able to put together a solution, empower their subordinates to support it, reshape and retool their resources, and come up with a package that meets the new challenge and solves the problem.

Group Communication

Communicating in groups involves a whole different set of variables than communicating one on one. Paralegals must routinely work with groups (including attorneys and paralegals) on trials and similar projects, and with clients and attorneys on cases. Additionally, they serve on committees and associations. The following are some commonly known advantages and disadvantages of group work:

- Groups tend to make more accurate decisions than do individuals. As the adage says, "Two heads are better than one"; that is, there are more points of view to be heard and considered and a greater number of solutions offered and analyzed in a group.
- Once a group has arrived at a decision, there is an increase in the acceptance of the final choice because group members were involved in the process.
- Group members can communicate and explain the group's decision to others because they were included.
- Once a decision has been made by a group, implementation is easier because the group members were involved in the process and have a "stake in the action."
- Decisions by groups take up to 50% longer to make than do decisions by individuals.
- Group decisions are often compromises between different points of view rather than the most appropriate alternative.
- Group decisions can sometimes result in groupthink. **Groupthink** occurs when the desire for group cohesiveness and consensus becomes stronger than the desire for the best possible decision.
- Groups sometimes make more risky decisions than do individuals, especially when there is no one individual responsible for the consequences of the group decision.
- Groups are sometimes dominated by one or more individuals who rank higher in status within the organization.

groupthink

Term for when the desire for group cohesiveness and consensus becomes stronger than the desire for the best possible decision.

Communication in Interviewing Clients, Witnesses, and Third Parties

Interviewing clients, witnesses, and third parties is a specialized communication skill that you need to possess. In many firms, interviews are conducted by experienced paralegals or attorneys. However, new paralegals sit in interviews with an experienced paralegal or attorney to learn good interviewing skills.

The initial client interview is very important, because it is usually the first real contact the client has with the firm. The purpose of the interview is to relax the client, to convince the client that he or she has come to the right firm, and to gather enough information to decide whether your firm and responsible attorney are interested in representing the client or at least finding out more about the case. The following are some suggestions for handling each part of the interview and what you should do when you encounter difficulties. Exhibit 4-7 is an evaluation sheet to assess your interviewing skills. While Exhibit 4-7 is specifically geared toward a client interview, many of the same principles apply to all interviews.

PREPARE FOR THE INTERVIEW One of the simplest things you can do to make sure that an interview goes well is to prepare for it. Always try to get as much initial information as possible before the interview. Establish a checklist of questions you want to ask and specific information you want to gather. You must establish what the purpose or goal of the interview is, and then steer the interview toward the direction of the goal. For example, if you routinely interview clients regarding workers' compensation claims, there is certain information that you must have. Establish exactly what information you need and then draft a checklist and an agenda to ensure that you obtain the information.

Many law offices also have an intake form on which the client generally describes why he or she has come to the firm. All this information will help you to prepare for the interview. Whoever is setting up the interview should, in addition, always ask the client to bring in any documentation that may be relevant.

BREAK THE ICE The beginning of any interview brings apprehension both for the interviewer and interviewee. Ways to break the ice include meeting the client in the waiting room, offering your hand for a handshake, accompanying the client back to your office, and talking to the client about the weather or other neutral topics. Always wear a smile and be warm and friendly. Another interesting way to break the ice is to ask the client or witness about his or her family. This allows you to gain some background information. Some people may think this is nosy; you may tell the person that the questions are not meant to embarrass him or her, but simply to understand who he or she is and to get the "big picture." You also may explain about the confidentiality of everything that he or she tells you.

ALWAYS INFORM THE PERSON YOU ARE INTERVIEWING OF YOUR STATUS AS A PARALEGAL Once the client is relaxed and is ready to talk about why he or she is there, indicate your status as a paralegal. Do not make a prolonged speech, which may demonstrate your lack of confidence; simply state, "I am a paralegal, and I work for Ms. Smith, who is an attorney here." You should also tell the person what you will be doing and what the attorney is going to do: "I will initially be talking to you about your case. I will take down the facts of your case and then prepare a memo to the attorney about it. The attorney will then contact you to discuss it in more depth." Once you have done that, you are ready to begin the interview. Many people begin with an open-ended statement, such as, "Tell me why you are here. Start at the beginning."

Exhibit 4-7 Client Interviewing Techniques

Client Interview Basics

I. **Preparing for the client interview**
   i. Common factors in preparing the basic client interview:
      (a) What is the effective time allocation for an initial interview?
      (b) What is the best meeting arrangement?
      (c) What information should the client receive?
      (d) What can be done to limit interruptions during the interview?
      (e) What attire should be worn during the interview?
   ii. Common factors in preparing for a specific client interview:
      (a) A conflict check should be performed.
      (b) A preliminary review and legal research should be performed.
      (c) Determine the necessary documents the client should bring for the interview.
         (1) Possibly provide a questionnaire for the client to prepare and provide during the interview.
      (d) Determine a checklist for investigating the areas relative to the client's issue(s).
   iii. Consider what resources should be gathered to properly prepare for the client interview:
      (a) Form books
      (b) Checklists
      (c) Questionnaires

II. **Effective interview skills**
   i. Methods for building client rapport:
      (a) Allow the client to feel comfortable and speak openly.
      (b) Listen with attention and interest to the client while avoiding being emotional or involved connection to the issue(s).
      (c) Be receptive to the client and avoid judgmental attitude.
      (d) Avoid interrupting the client, accept when necessary
      (e) Use active listening responses and language that the client understands.
      (f) Be cognizant of communication blocks.
      (g) Encourage client questions.
      (h) Be respectful and avoid condescension to clients.
      (i) Make sure to offer client support
   ii. Methods to effectively gather information:
      (a) Obtain a detailed factual account of the issue(s).
      (b) Identify additional subjects during the interview process.
      (c) Focus on subjects that will produce relevant information.
      (d) Develop questions in a pattern starting with general to specific or using the opposite approach.
      (e) Use leading and open-ended questions when appropriate.
      (f) Avoid diagnosing client issue(s) prematurely.
      (g) Make sure the client understands the questions and the interviewer understands the client's answers.
   iii. Methods for evaluating and improving interviewing skills:
      (a) Attend CLE seminars that focus on interviewing skills improvements.
      (b) Transcribe and review interview transcripts.
      (c) Review current interviewing skills articles.

III. **Recording and documenting interviews**
   i. Method to preserve information gathered from interviews:
      (a) Take accurate notes during the interview.
      (b) Immediately record interview details.
      (c) Provide abundantly clear details for other reviewers to quickly and accurately understand the interview information.
      (d) Prepare for file follow-up and client follow-up, if necessary.

LISTEN CAREFULLY Listening carefully to the client's story is sometimes hard to do. The client may ramble, talk about events out of sequence, and talk about matters that may be irrelevant to the legal problem. However, refrain from leading the conversation, at least during the first part of the interview. Be patient and let the client tell the whole story in his or her own way. Then go back and fill in the details by asking questions. Do not take too many notes during the first part of the interview. You should give the client your undivided attention and try to make eye contact. Clients need to be reassured that you are interested in their case. As you listen, determine whether the client's story makes sense and think of what facts the client may be leaving out.

COMMUNICATE SINCERITY For any interview to be successful, you must communicate that you are sincerely interested in the client's problem. Characteristics such as dominance or defensiveness are counterproductive to establishing sincerity. One of the best ways you can communicate sincerity is to show you are really listening to what the person is saying by asking thoughtful questions. Avoid appearing as if you are "grilling" a client.

BE EMPATHETIC Be empathetic with the client, letting him or her know that you feel for him or her and for the situation he or she is in. Empathy is distinguished from sympathy, which is feeling sorry for the individual. However, be sure to keep your objectivity. Sometimes the client may have to describe very personal, traumatic, or embarrassing information. In that case, you need to be extra sensitive and inform the client that everything said is confidential and is necessary so that you understand what happened.

ORGANIZE THE INFORMATION Once you have listened to the client tell his or her story the first time through, you are ready to organize the information. A common way to organize the client's story is to build a chronology of events that starts at the beginning of the problem and works forward. This helps the client relive the facts in a particular order and may cause the client to remember more exact details. However, be aware that clients seldom remember things in exact order, so it usually takes several times through before your chronology is accurate.

ASK APPROPRIATE QUESTIONS When you want to get detailed information about a particular event, remember to ask who, what, when, and where questions. Do not ask leading questions that might suggest a particular answer, such as, "You saw the traffic light as you were going through and it was green, right?" Ask your questions carefully. A better approach might be to say, "Describe the intersection before the accident."

In addition, avoid compound questions that ask the client to answer two or more questions; for example, "How many cars were in the intersection and when was the first time you saw the blue car?" Ask your questions one at a time.

DO NOT BE JUDGMENTAL Never be judgmental toward a client. Saying things like "You really need to get a grip on yourself," "You are acting like a child," or "You can't mean that" is the opposite of being empathetic, which is what you ideally want to be. Avoid questions that begin with "Why did you . . . ?" This type of question might be viewed as judgmental and may make the client feels defensive.

NEVER SAY "YOU HAVE A GREAT CASE" Be very careful about judging the client's case. Do not make any promises to the client and never tell the client what a great case he or she has, since this may be bordering on giving legal advice. At this stage you do not have enough information to make that determination. Lawsuits are usually too complex for this type of statement.

LEAVE FEE DISCUSSIONS TO THE ATTORNEY Discussions regarding whether the firm is going to take the case and discussions about the amount of the fee should be left to the attorney.

CLOSE THE INTERVIEW APPROPRIATELY Do not close the interview too quickly. Before you close, be sure to do the following:

- Get copies of all the documentation that the client brought.
- Instruct the client not to discuss the case with anyone else.
- Reassure the client by telling him or her exactly what your office will be doing and when it will be done. For example: "I will draft a memo to the attorney, our office will do some preliminary legal research, and this will be completed by Friday. Our office will call you on Friday to set up an appointment for early next week." Never tell the client that "the attorney will get back to you as soon as he can." Clients want to know exactly what is going to happen and when it is going to happen.
- Get the client's e-mail address.
- Review your checklist to make sure you have obtained all the information you need.
- Have the client sign any release or authorization you might need to get information, such as a medical release for the client's files from a doctor or hospital.
- List everything the client did *not* bring with him or her. Give a copy of the list to the client with a self-addressed return envelope.
- Thank the client for coming into the office, reassure the client that you will be in contact with him or her shortly, and instruct him or her that, if he or she remembers anything else that is important, to be sure to give you a call. Give the client your business card.

Summary

Attorneys have an ethical duty to communicate with their clients, and paralegals can play an active role in this process. This duty includes informing client of the status of his or her case, responding to a client's request for information in a timely manner, explaining the law and benefits and risks of alternative courses of action, and notifying and communicating settlement offers, among other things.

Attorneys and paralegals must also foster positive relationships with clients. This includes knowing your client, treating each client like he or she is your only client, sending copies of documents to clients, responding to client phone calls immediately, being courteous and professional to clients, giving clients periodic status reports, and preserving client confidences. When resolving client complaints, a paralegal should listen to the client and forward complaints to the attorney.

Clients are also demanding the use of technology in how legal services are provided. This includes e-mail, attachments, extranets, electronic billing, and more. In dealing with difficult clients, a paralegal should stay calm and maintain professionalism, document conversations with the client, be courteous but maintain an "arm's-length" posture, and keep the attorney informed.

Paralegal work is largely based on communication; communication is the transfer of a message from a sender to a receiver. Anytime you communicate, you must be prepared to work through communication barriers, such as noise, terminology differences, background differences, different competence levels, and many other factors. In enhancing communication, a person should consider the timing and the context of the message, do not be judgmental, use rephrasing, and ask questions.

Paralegals must also work in group settings. Communicating in a group is different from communicating one on one with another person. Groups take longer to make decisions, tend to make better quality decisions, but can also fall into groupthink, where the desire for group cohesiveness and consensus becomes stronger than the desire for the best possible decision.

Paralegals often must interview clients. Strategies for conducting a good client interview include preparing for the interview in advance, using an icebreaker to open the interview, clearly informing the client that you are a paralegal, listening carefully, taking notes and organizing the information, asking appropriate questions, and closing the interview.

Key Terms

communication
communication barrier
feedback
groupthink
noise
rephrasing

Test Your Knowledge

Test your knowledge of the chapter by answering these questions.

1. Based on *Rule 1.4* regarding rules of professional conduct, list at least four things an attorney must do regarding client communication.
2. True or false: if an attorney is leaving a firm, he or she does not have to contact the client if another attorney at the firm will be taking over the case.
3. True or false: an attorney must notify and communicate all settlement offers to a client.
4. Name three types of conduct that clients typically dislike.
5. Name five strategies for fostering positive relationships with clients.
6. True or false: technology has yet to play a large role in client relations.
7. What is the number one reason that clients leave law offices or attorneys and take their business elsewhere?
8. Name two strategies for dealing with difficult clients.
9. List four barriers to communication.
10. Name 5 of the 10 commandments of good listening.
11. When the desire for group cohesiveness becomes stronger than the desire for the best possible solution, it is called ________________.

Practical Applications

1. You are a paralegal working for an attorney in a large law firm. A general counsel from one of the corporations you work with calls you and tells you that he had just read the legal arguments regarding a Motion for Summary judgment that the firm prepared and that you worked on. He tells you that the legal analysis is extremely weak. You can tell by his voice that he is unhappy. What would you do next?

2. You are a paralegal for a sole practitioner. The attorney represents a client named Betty Johnson in a probate matter that has dragged on for years. Ms. Johnson calls to inquire about the status of her case. She says that she has not heard from the attorney in over a year, and that she has no idea what is going on in the case. You know that the attorney has long since quit working the case and has closed his file. The file takes up three file drawers in the file room.

You tell the attorney about Ms. Johnson's call and he says not to worry about it. What is your analysis of the matter? What would you do next?

3. You are a paralegal in a legal aid office. The executive director calls you into his office to let you know that he has received complaints from clients regarding paralegals being less than courteous on the phone and in person. The executive director gives you one week to begin turning this situation around. He mentions on his way out the door that, in addition to a short-term solution, he wants a long-term solution to the problem. How would you proceed?

4. Over the years, you have become friends with one of your law office's best clients. The client likes you and believes in your ability as a competent paralegal. Recently, you have spent many hours, including evenings and weekends, working on the client's case. The client comes in for an appointment to see you about his case. The client notices that you look very tired and ragged. You tell the client how many hours you have been working on the case to let him know about the hard work that the law office is doing. The client responds by saying that he is going to the lead attorney on the case to demand that you be given an increase for all the extra time you have spent on the case. You are flattered that a client would think of your interest and you could certainly use the money. How would you handle this situation?

5. You are a paralegal at a medium-sized law office. The executive committee thinks that the law office needs to put more emphasis on client services. You are a respected part of the firm and the committee thinks you interact with clients exceptionally well. The committee has approved the development of a client manual that will be given to all of its clients. The committee has chosen you to be in charge of developing the manual in the initial stages.

Your task is to prepare a client manual that will be presented to the executive committee within 30 days. In addition, once the committee approves the manual, you also will be in charge of implementing its use. The committee is giving you control over researching and developing the manual.

Assume you have never heard of or developed a client manual before. Assume you can choose to either accept the task or not. Would you accept the assignment? Why or why not? How would you develop the client manual? Would you choose to use a work group or not? What sections or key points would you include in the manual? Give reasons for your answers.

6. As a paralegal in a busy office, you try your best to talk to clients when they call and to pass along information from the client to your supervising attorney, but sometimes you forget. On one such occasion, a client called you because she was unable to talk to the attorney. The client called with vital information that the attorney needed regarding an important aspect of the case. Unfortunately, you failed to pass the information along. Discuss from an ethics and malpractice standpoint the importance of communication skills.

7. Think about a group or committee that you have worked on. Write down the dynamics of how the group interacted. Who emerged as the leader, and why? Looking back, do you see any evidence of groupthink? Did the group members communicate with each other effectively? Was the group successful at accomplishing its purpose? Why or why not? Did you feel like an active member of the group? Why or why not? If you could have changed one thing about the group, what would that have been?

On the Web Exercises

1. Go to the ABA Center for Professional Responsibility, find the *ABA Model Rules of Professional Conduct*, and read and print out Rule 1.4 Communication and the accompanying comment.

2. Go to a general search engine, such as http://www.google.com or http://www.yahoo.com, and search for state bar association Web sites (or go to state bar association Web sites listed in the Helpful Web Sites sections of Chapters 2, 3, and 4). Find three articles on issues related to client relations, print them out, and read them.

3. Go to a general search engine, such as http://www.google.com or http://www.yahoo.com, and search for Web sites related to improving communication skills. Review a number of Web sites and write a one-page article summarizing the best articles or information you found.

Projects

1. Write an article that compares and contrasts three state bar association rules regarding client communication and include how each compares to Rule 1.4 regarding rules of professional conduct.

2. Go to state bar association Web sites, find one of the several client relation handbooks. Summarize the major points in the handbook.

Case Review

35 P.3d 670 (Colo. 2001)

Office of the Presiding Disciplinary Judge of the Supreme Court of Colorado.

The PEOPLE of the State Of Colorado, Complainant.

v.

Karen S. MILNER, Respondent.

Nos. 99PDJ030, 99PDJ093.

Aug. 7, 2001.

I. Findings of Fact and Conclusions of Law

A. Case No. 99PDJ030

Claim I: The Aldridge Matter

On April 4, 1998, Milner [respondent] entered her appearance on behalf of Nancy Aldridge in a child support and visitation matter. Between April and June 1998, the client paid Milner fees and costs in the amount of $735. A hearing was scheduled regarding visitation issues and subsequently rescheduled. Milner failed to notify the client of the new hearing date. One week prior to the rescheduled hearing, Milner contacted the client and demanded that she pay fees in the amount of $385 or Milner threatened to withdraw. The client paid the fees. At the hearing, the client expressed concern to Milner about her visitation rights while her children were with their father for a six-week period. Milner assured her she would be allowed visitation. Subsequent to the hearing on July 16, 1998, the client left numerous messages for Milner but Milner did not return her calls. The client spoke to Milner's paralegal, Matthew Kemp ("Kemp"), who stated that a motion to clarify the issue of visitation would be filed with the court. Milner failed to file any such motion. Milner agreed to obtain a wage assignment from the client's ex-husband's employer and file it with the court. Subsequently the client, who was not receiving child support, attempted to contact Milner to determine whether the wage assignment had been submitted to the court. For approximately six weeks, Milner failed to respond. Finally, the client spoke with Kemp who promised that the papers would be filed. They were not. After numerous phone calls, the client contacted Kemp in October 1998 who assured her that the wage assignment documents had been sent to opposing counsel; he stated he would contact opposing counsel and advise the client of the status of the assignment. The client had no further contact with Milner after July 1998 and none with Kemp after October 1998. Milner did no further work on the case and did not file a motion to withdraw.

[1] [2] [3] Milner's failure to act on behalf of her client resulted in harm to the client: Aldridge was not able to obtain visitation while her children were with their father; she was forced to seek an alternative method to obtain a wage assignment; and her frustration and concern caused by Milner impacted her work performance. Milner did not refund any of the funds to the client. Milner's failure to return the client's phone calls and her failure to communicate with the client constituted a violation of Colo. RPC 1.4(a) (lawyer shall keep a client reasonably informed about the status of a matter and promptly comply with reasonable requests for information); her failure to notify the client of the change in hearing date, her **677* failure to file a motion concerning the client's visitation rights; and her failure to file a wage assignment on behalf of her client constitutes neglect in violation of Colo. RPC 1.3. Milner's paralegal, Kemp,

misrepresented the status of the matter to the client. Milner failed to adequately supervise Kemp to assure that he did not make such misrepresentations. Her failure to do so constitutes a violation of Colo. RPC 5.3(b) (lawyer having direct supervisory authority over the nonlawyer shall make reasonable efforts to ensure that the person's conduct is compatible with the professional obligations of the lawyer).

Claim II: The Cordova Matter

On September 22, 1998, Darlene Cordova met with Kemp and Milner to determine whether to retain Milner in the client's divorce action. The client was advised that the initial consultation was free. Milner was not present for most of the meeting. Kemp told the client that she would be charged a fee of $75 per hour or a flat fee of $1,500 but he did not say which, and the client was not provided with a written fee agreement. The client paid $400. Milner billed the client $100 per hour rather than the $75 per hour rate which the client had been quoted, and she charged for the initial consultation which she represented at the time of the meeting would be free of charge.

Milner met with the client to discuss service upon the client's husband. Milner stated that the husband would be served on October 12, 1998. The client received no response to her calls on October 12 and 13 to determine if service had been completed. Service was effected the following day. Milner met with the client on October 17, 1998 and stated that the petition for dissolution of marriage would be filed on October 20, 1998, and that the client would be contacted immediately thereafter. The petition was not filed on October 20, 1998; it was filed the following day. On October 26, 1998, the client went to Milner's office to retrieve her file. Kemp was abusive toward her and threatened to call the police.

[4] [5] Milner failed to adequately communicate the basis of her fee to the client before or within a reasonable time after commencing her representation in violation of Colo. RPC 1.5(b) (lawyer shall communicate the basis or rate of the fee within a reasonable time after commencing representation). The Amended Complaint charged a violation of Colo. RPC 1.4(a), which requires a lawyer to keep a client reasonably informed about the status of a matter and promptly comply with reasonable requests for information. The PDJ and Hearing Board cannot find by a clear and convincing standard that Milner violated Colo. RPC 1.4(a) in the Cordova matter. Milner and/or Kemp spoke with Cordova within a reasonable time on each occasion the client called. Accordingly, the alleged violation of Colo. RPC 1.4(a) in claim two of Case No. 99PDJ030 is dismissed. Milner failed to adequately supervise Kemp to ensure that Kemp's conduct was compatible with the professional obligations of a lawyer in violation of Colo. RPC 5.3(b) (failure to adequately supervise nonlawyer).

Claim III: The Wilhelm Matter

Milner met with Mr. Wilhelm and entered into an attorney-client relationship with him to collect monies owed pursuant to a promissory note. At the meeting, Milner obtained the original or a copy of the promissory note. Subsequently, Milner did not take any action regarding the case. Despite the client's attempts to communicate with her and his requests that she return the promissory note to him, she failed to do so, and failed initially to provide it when the Office of Attorney Regulation Counsel ("OARC") requested it. Eventually, she provided OARC with a copy of the note.

[6] [7] Milner's failure to return the original or a copy of the client's promissory note upon the client's request constitutes a violation of Colo. RPC 1.15(b) (a lawyer shall promptly deliver to the client any funds or other property that the client is entitled to receive and render a full accounting regarding such property). Her failure to respond to the client's telephone calls and failure to communicate with him regarding the status of the matter constitutes a violation of Colo. RPC 1.4(a) (failure to communicate). Milner's failure to take any action on behalf of the client after agreeing to represent him ***678** constitutes neglect in violation of Colo. RPC 1.3 (lawyer shall act with reasonable diligence and promptness in representing a client and shall not neglect a legal matter entrusted to the lawyer).

Claim IV: The Chavez Matter

On March 31, 1998, Milner and Kemp met with Cherry Chavez regarding a divorce action. The client paid Milner $600 for fees and costs to represent her in the divorce. The client was told that if she and her husband could agree on settlement, Milner could complete all the paperwork. Kemp offered to assist the client and her husband as a mediator. The client and her husband met with Milner and Kemp again on April 11, 1998 to discuss their divorce, and agreed on all matters except child support. Milner stated that she would prepare a petition for dissolution of marriage and, in the meantime, the husband would consider the issue of child support. Thereafter, the client heard nothing from Milner, but was able to contact Kemp on several occasions, who indicated that the delay in preparing the petition for dissolution was caused by the client's husband's failure to cooperate. In fact, Kemp never attempted to speak with the client's husband. On June 22, 1998, a meeting was scheduled with the client and her husband to review the petition for dissolution. When the client and her husband arrived, both Milner and Kemp were unavailable. Milner's secretary reviewed the documents and stated that they would be filed with the court within the next few days. The client thereafter attempted to contact Milner regarding the status of the case but received no response until late August, when Milner stated that the petition would be filed on or before September 1. Thereafter, Chavez again had difficulty contacting Milner, but spoke to Kemp. Kemp was abusive to Chavez and said he was not aware of the status of the case. On September 24, 1998, the client successfully contacted Milner who stated that the petition had been filed. The client contacted the court clerk's office in early October and was told that no petition had been filed. After the client contacted OARC, Milner filed the petition for dissolution on behalf of Chavez. Milner's failing to file the petition in a timely fashion delayed the divorce.

[8] [9] [10] Milner's failure to communicate with the client regarding the status of the case despite repeated attempts by the client constituted a violation of Colo. RPC 1.4(a) (failure to communicate). Milner's failure to timely file the petition constitutes neglect in violation of Colo. RPC 1.3 (neglect of a legal matter). Milner's statement to the client that she had filed the petition when in fact she had not was conduct involving misrepresentation when, at the time, she knew it had not been filed, was a violation of Colo. RPC 8.4(c) (conduct involving dishonesty, fraud, deceit, or misrepresentation).

[11] Kemp's knowing misrepresentation to Chavez that the delay in filing the divorce action was caused by the husband when it was not is conduct which would not be tolerated if undertaken by a lawyer. As a paralegal to Milner, it was Milner's responsibility to take reasonable efforts that his conduct was compatible with her professional responsibilities. She did not take such steps. Consequently, Milner failed to adequately supervise Kemp in violation of Colo. RPC 5.3(b) (failure to supervise a nonlawyer).

Claim V: The Fisher Matter

In April 1998, Jana Fisher retained Milner in connection with a divorce and to secure a temporary restraining order. In August 1998, Milner represented the client at a permanent orders hearing. The court ordered Milner to submit the permanent orders within 30 days of the hearing. Milner did not do so. The court issued an Order to Show Cause why Milner should not be sanctioned for failure to timely file the permanent orders. A hearing on the Order to Show Cause was set for November 24, 1998. Milner did not provide the client with a copy of the Show Cause Order. Milner filed the permanent orders on November 23, 1998, and the Show Cause Order was vacated. Thereafter, Fisher tried on several occasions to contact Milner because the permanent orders required her to refinance her house within 120 days. She needed a copy of the permanent orders to refinance the house. Unable to reach Milner, ***679** the client spoke with Kemp who told her to "stop calling and bitching." Milner did not provide the client with a copy of the permanent orders.

[12] [13] [14] [15] Milner's failure to timely submit an order to the court regarding the terms of the permanent orders violated Colo. RPC 1.3 (neglect of a legal matter). Milner's failure to communicate with the client following the permanent orders hearing despite the client's repeated attempts to reach her constituted a violation of Colo. RPC 1.4(a) (failure to communicate). By failing to timely submit an order to the court regarding the terms of the permanent orders, Milner knowingly disobeyed obligations under the rules of a tribunal in violation of Colo. RPC 3.4(c) (knowingly disobeying an obligation under the rules of a tribunal), resulting in prejudice to the administration of justice in violation of Colo. RPC 8.4(d) (engaging in conduct prejudicial to the administration of justice). With regard to the alleged violation of Colo. RPC 5.3(b) (failure to adequately supervise a nonlawyer), that allegation is premised solely upon Kemp's outburst with Fisher to "stop calling and bitching." Although lacking in tact, not conducive to a harmonious attorney/client relationship and certainly below the level of professionalism to which the profession must aspire, the PDJ and Hearing Board do not conclude that a single impolite outburst toward a client constitutes conduct incompatible with the professional obligations of a lawyer. Accordingly, the charged violation of Colo. RPC 5.3(b) in claim five is dismissed.

Claim VI: The Abrahamson Matter

In April 1998, Norma Abrahamson retained Milner to assist her in recovering payment of a loan. The parties verbally agreed that Milner would be paid $250 out of the proceeds. Not having heard from Milner, Abrahamson contacted her in June to inquire into the status of the case. Milner admitted she had forgotten the matter, and would take action to proceed at that time. Despite several attempts, it was not until late August that the client was able to speak again with Milner, and Milner informed her that an injunction had been ordered. In October, the client attempted to speak with Milner and instead spoke with "Matthew" of Milner's office, who was unable to give her any information on the case. The client thereafter sent a letter to Milner inquiring about the status of the case. Between October 1998 and January 1999 the client called Milner on six occasions and Milner neither returned her calls nor responded to the letter.

[16] [17] Between April 1998 and June 1998, Milner "forgot" about the case and took no action on it. By agreeing to represent a client in a dispute and then failing to take those ministerial steps necessary to ensure that the matter is not "forgotten," Milner violated Colo. RPC 1.3. The facts reveal repeated failures to communicate with the client regarding the status of the case and therefore establish a violation of Colo. RPC 1.4(a) (failure to communicate). Milner is also charged with violating Colo. RPC 1.16(d) and Colo. RPC 1.15(b) based upon these facts. Colo. RPC 1.16(d) provides:

Upon termination of representation, a lawyer shall take steps to the extent reasonably practicable to protect a client's interests, such as giving reasonable notice to the client, allowing time for employment of other counsel, surrendering papers and property to which the client is entitled and refunding any advance payment of fee that has not been earned. The lawyer may retain papers relating to the client to the extent permitted by law.

The opening phrase of Colo. RPC 1.16(d) requires "[u]pon termination of representation. . . ." No evidence was presented that Milner's representation was terminated, nor is there an allegation of abandonment. Consequently, the PDJ and Hearing Board conclude that the charge under Colo. RPC 1.16(d) in claim six in Case No. 99PDJ030 was not established and is therefore dismissed. Colo. RPC 1.15 provides:

Safekeeping Property: Interest-Bearing Accounts to be Established for the Benefit of the Client or Third Persons or the Colorado Lawyer Trust Account Foundation: Notice of Overdrafts; Record Keeping. (b) Upon receiving funds or other property in which a client or third person has an ***680** interest, a lawyer shall, promptly or otherwise as permitted by law or by agreement with the client, deliver to the client or third person any funds or other property that the client or third person is entitled to receive and, upon request by the client or third person, render a full accounting regarding such property.

[18] The People contend that Milner violated Colo. RPC 1.15(b) by virtue of her failure to return the promissory note and other documents to Abrahamson. There is no evidence, however, that the representation of the case was concluded, or the client had requested the return of documents. The only evidence presented was that Milner told Abrahamson that an injunction had been ordered. [FN1] Although it is possible to surmise that Milner did not undertake the requisite efforts necessary to obtain recovery on the note in light of the remaining facts in other claims of the Amended Complaint, surmise is not proof by clear and convincing evidence. Absent some evidence establishing a termination of the representation, the conclusion of the case, or a request by the client, the PDJ and Hearing Board cannot conclude that Milner violated Colo. RPC 1.15(b) by failing to return documents and the promissory note prior to the end of January 1999. Accordingly, the alleged violation of Colo. RPC 1.15(b) in claim six in Case No. 99PDJ030 is dismissed.

FN1. Although the issuance of an injunction in a promissory note case seems curious, that statement by Milner suggests that a case was filed.

Claim VII: The Spargo Matter

In June 1998, Sherry Spargo retained Milner to represent her in a divorce. The client paid Milner a total of $800 in fees and $124 in costs. Thereafter, Spargo had minimal contact with Milner. Milner failed to notify the client of the permanent orders hearing date until a few days prior to the hearing. Pursuant to the permanent orders, Milner agreed to submit a wage assignment for child support to the employer of the client's husband and failed to do so. The client attempted to contact Milner regarding the wage assignment, but Milner did not return her phone calls. Milner filed the wage assignment after the client made a request for investigation with the OARC.

[19] [20] Milner's failure to communicate adequately with the client regarding the status of the matter and timely notify the client of the scheduled permanent orders hearing constitutes a violation of Colo. RPC 1.4(a) (failure to communicate). Milner's failure to timely notify the client of the permanent orders hearing, and her failure to file a wage assignment for child support until after the client had contacted OARC constitutes neglect of a legal matter in violation of Colo. RPC 1.3 (neglect).

Claim VIII: The Boroos Matter

June Hallinan died on September 18, 1998. In Hallinan's will, Mr. and Mrs. Boroos were named as Ms. Hallinan's sole beneficiaries and Milner was designated as the personal representative of the estate. On the date of death, Hallinan's trailer home was sold for $3,800. Hallinan also owned an automobile at the time of her death. Milner advised the beneficiaries that she had taken the automobile to her home for safekeeping. The beneficiaries discussed selling the vehicle to Milner, but did not finalize any agreement. Subsequently, they conducted a title search and learned that title to the car had been transferred to Milner's husband on October 20, 1998.

In December 1998, one of the beneficiaries met with Milner and requested a listing of the estate's assets. Milner failed to provide one. In January 1999, the beneficiaries met with Milner to discuss and close the estate. However, Milner had not prepared for the meeting nor did she provide to the beneficiaries a list of expenses and assets or any written statement concerning the amount of the final distribution under the estate. She did not show the beneficiaries any bills or bank statements and was not sure of the amounts she provided verbally. Milner scheduled a subsequent meeting in January. By letter, the beneficiaries requested a written statement summarizing the disposition of ***681** assets of the estate. Milner did not respond to the letter. In January, the beneficiaries called Milner several times but Milner did not return their calls. On at least one occasion, the beneficiaries spoke to Kemp, who informed them that the estate was not completed because other claims were being filed against it. This statement was false; there were no other claims filed against the estate. In February 1999, the beneficiaries contacted the court and learned that the will of the deceased had not yet been filed. Thereafter, despite numerous requests by the beneficiaries, Milner failed to provide an accounting of the estate assets and failed to distribute the proceeds of the estate to its beneficiaries. The beneficiaries hired an attorney who wrote to Milner and requested information regarding the status of the estate and demanded the estate files. Milner neither responded nor provided the files to the beneficiaries' attorney. Thereafter, the beneficiaries obtained an order of court removing Milner as personal representative of the estate and appointing one of the beneficiaries as successor personal representative. The order directed Milner to provide all bank account records, all funds or property of the estate, records of Milner's law office trust account, the original will, the estate files, and records relating to the transfer of the vehicle. Milner did not provide the documents ordered by the court. The successor personal representative obtained the deceased's personal bank records and the estate's bank records himself. In April or May 1999, after the beneficiaries had made a request for investigation with the OARC, Milner made a distribution from the estate in the amount of $8,000, but did not provide any documentation or explanation for the $8,000. Milner eventually paid all but $1,071 owed to the beneficiaries.

[21] [22] [23] [24] Milner's actions resulted in harm to the beneficiaries resulting in an attempt to deprive them of their inheritance, causing them extreme stress and expenditure of time and research and requiring that they hire counsel. Milner's failure to promptly deliver to the beneficiaries of the estate funds or other property that the beneficiaries were entitled to receive and, upon request by the beneficiaries, render a full accounting with regard to such property constitutes a violation of Colo. RPC 1.15(b) (lawyer shall promptly deliver to the client or third person any funds or other property the client or third person is entitled to receive and, upon request, render a full accounting). Milner retained property and funds belonging to the beneficiaries long beyond any period of time justifiable by virtue of her position as personal representative. Milner's conduct in acquiring the deceased's vehicle without finalizing a purchase agreement, transferring title of the vehicle to her husband and failing to disclose her actions in the face of requests to do so by the beneficiaries constitutes conduct involving dishonesty, fraud, deceit and misrepresentation in violation of Colo. RPC 8.4(c). The Amended Complaint charged Milner with a violation of Colo. RPC 8.4(h) (engaging in conduct

that adversely reflects on the lawyer's fitness to practice law). Colo. RPC 8.4(h) requires proof that the lawyer engaged in conduct, the totality of which reflects that she lacked the personal or professional moral and/or ethical qualifications required of those authorized to practice law. Conduct involving violence, lack of honesty, violation of trust, serious interference with the administration of justice, criminal endeavors, or comparable misconduct is required to establish a violation of Colo. RPC 8.4(h). *See People v. Cleland*, No. GC98B118, slip op. at 9, 10 (Colo. PDJ September 17, 1999) 28 Colo. Law. 127, 128–129 (November 1999); *People v. Theodore*, 926 P.2d 1237, 1242–43 (Colo.1996) (holding that attorney's engaging in conduct involving dishonesty amounts to conduct that adversely reflects on his fitness to practice law). Viewing the totality of Milner's misconduct in the context of acting as personal representative of an estate as a serious violation of trust, the PDJ and Hearing Board find that such misconduct constitutes a violation of Colo. RPC 8.4(h).

[25] The remaining charge in this claim, [FN2] Colo. RPC 1.3 (a lawyer shall act with reasonable ***682** diligence and promptness in representing a client) requires the existence of an attorney/client relationship. No evidence was presented to establish that Milner acted in any capacity other than as the personal representative of the estate. Such a capacity does not, in and of itself, create an attorney/client relationship. Consequently, the charged violation of Colo. RPC 1.3 in claim eight in Case No. 99PDJ030 is dismissed.

FN2. Upon the People's motion at the closing of the sanctions hearing, the alleged violation of Colo. RPC 1.4(a) in claim eight was dismissed with prejudice.

Claim IX: The Machina Matter

In November 1998, Anisa Machina hired Milner to represent her in a divorce proceeding. The client paid Milner an advance fee of $1,200. In January 1999, Kemp told the client that he had personally delivered papers to the client's husband and provided copies to him by certified mail. The client asked for proof of service on her husband and Kemp said he could not provide her with copies of the certified mail acceptance. The client made an appointment to meet with Milner and asked that she be provided with her husband's acceptance of certified mail. Milner stated that she would provide the client with receipt of the certified mail at the meeting. On January 30, 1999, the client met with Milner and again requested a copy of the receipt of certified mail. It was not provided to her. Milner said she would mail it to the client, and failed to do so. Thereafter, the client heard nothing more from Milner concerning the divorce proceeding.

Machina attempted to contact Milner on several occasions after January 30, 1999, to determine the status of her case and the date of the hearing. Milner did not return her calls. Finally, Machina successfully contacted Milner and told her she wished to terminate her services, and demanded a refund of a portion of the funds paid to Milner. Milner told Machina she could only refund $600 to $800 due to the service fees encountered in serving the husband in the dissolution case. Milner did not, however, refund the $600 to $800 as requested. Indeed, Milner made no refund to Machina until April 1999 after a request for investigation had been filed with the OARC.

[26] The client paid Milner $1,200 for her professional services regarding the client's divorce action. The client terminated Milner's services and requested a refund of a portion of the fees she had paid to Milner. Upon such a request it is the obligation of the attorney to promptly refund any unearned fees. Milner failed to do so. Milner delayed making any refund for approximately two months and did so only after a request for investigation had been filed. Milner's failing to promptly provide a refund upon request by the client constituted a violation of Colo. RPC 1.15(b) (lawyer shall promptly deliver to the client any funds or other property that the client is entitled to receive). Milner's failure to return Machina's phone calls after January 30, 1999, constituted a failure to keep the client reasonably informed about the status of a matter and promptly comply with reasonable requests for information in violation of Colo. RPC 1.4(a).

B. Case No. 99PDJ093

Claim I: The Nelson Matter

In June 1998 Milner entered into an attorney/client relationship with Jannette Nelson who sought her assistance regarding the investigation into the death of her brother. The client paid Milner $2,000 and provided Milner with complete copies of the police file, medical reports, and the names and addresses of those who might have relevant information. Milner promised to investigate the death thoroughly, and told the client that she would schedule a meeting with the Denver District Attorney and the Denver Police Department. Milner and Kemp both assured the client that they would keep her informed of the status of the case.

A meeting was scheduled with the client, Milner and other individuals whom Milner had allegedly involved in the investigation. When the client went to the meeting, only Kemp was present, who told the client the meeting would have to be rescheduled. At the end of October 1998, Milner told the client that she had scheduled a meeting with the Denver Police Department and the Denver District Attorney for November 12, 1998, and that all the necessary work for the meeting had been done. Milner later admitted that she had never arranged such a meeting ***683** with the Denver District Attorney and other parties. Milner promised to call the client but failed to call. When the client inquired about the scheduled meeting, she was told that none had been scheduled. Milner spoke to the client shortly thereafter and said that a report was being prepared regarding the case. From the second week of November 1998, to the third week of March 1999, the client repeatedly contacted Milner, who said that she was revising the report. Milner scheduled meetings with the client and later cancelled them. The client decided to terminate Milner and told Milner's secretary that she wanted to pick up her file. Milner then told the client that the report would be sent to her and to the Denver District Attorney by courier. The client did not hear from Milner again despite many attempts to reach her. Milner never sent a report to the client. The client requested by letter that Milner return the $2,000 in fees she had paid to her. Milner never responded to the client.

[27] [28] [29] [30] [31] Milner agreed to represent the client and investigate her brother's death and thereafter took no action on the case from June 1998 to March 1999. Her neglect of the client's matter constituted a violation of Colo. RPC 1.3. Milner's failure to keep appointments with the client, and failure to return the client's phone calls from June 1998 to March 1999, constituted a violation of Colo. RPC 1.4(a) (failure to communicate). Milner's taking $2,000 as payment for her professional services and failing to take any action from June 1998 through March 1999 on behalf of the client constituted the charging of an unreasonable fee in violation of Colo. RPC 1.5(a) (a lawyer's fee shall be reasonable). Milner's failure to return the file and the client's funds to the client upon request constituted a violation of Colo. RPC 1.15(b) (a lawyer shall promptly deliver to the client any funds or property that the client is entitled to receive). Milner's failure to take steps to the extent reasonably practicable to protect the client's interests upon termination, and failure to surrender papers and property to which the client was entitled including refunding any advance payment of fee that has not been earned constitutes a violation of Colo. RPC 1.16(d) (upon termination of representation, a lawyer shall take steps to protect a client's interests, including surrendering papers or property to which client is entitled).

[32] Milner's misrepresentations to the client that she had: sent a letter to a possible witness on the client's behalf; scheduled numerous meetings and drafted a report when she had not; as well as her failure to return the client's funds when she performed none of the professional services for which she was paid from June 1998 to March 1999 constituted dishonesty in violation of Colo. RPC 8.4(c).

Claim II: The Biggers Matter

In May 1999 Cindy Biggers went to Milner's law office seeking professional help with a bankruptcy and divorce. She met with Milner, Kemp, and a woman named "Patti." Milner stated that she would charge the client $1,000 to handle both her bankruptcy and her divorce. The client paid Milner $969. Milner stated that Kemp would be working on the client's matters. Milner prepared and filed a petition for dissolution of marriage, but took no further action in the divorce proceeding on behalf of the client. Milner took no action whatsoever in the bankruptcy matter.

[33] [34] Milner entered into an attorney/client relationship with the client and accepted $969 for both the divorce and bankruptcy proceeding. Taking into account the nature of professional services to be provided, neglect may justify a finding of abandonment under circumstances where an attorney neglects a client's matter and fails to communicate with the client. In both the divorce and the bankruptcy matter, Milner agreed to take action on behalf of the client. Having created the false expectation that she would do so, Milner completed minimal work in the divorce matter, took no action in the bankruptcy matter, and thereafter failed to communicate with the client. Milner's agreement to perform the services and her failure to do so taken together with her failure to communicate with the client established serious

neglect, which justifies a finding of abandonment in violation of Colo. RPC 1.3 (neglect of a legal matter). Milner's failure to communicate ***684** with the client despite the client's numerous attempts to contact Milner constituted a violation of Colo. RPC 1.4(a) (failure to communicate). By her continued retention of the client's funds, Milner converted the client's funds, in violation of Colo. RPC 8.4(c) (conduct involving dishonesty, fraud, deceit, or misrepresentation). *See People v. Varallo*, 913 P.2d 1, 12 (Colo.1996).

[35] [36] [37] [38] Milner's failure to perform any services with regard to the bankruptcy and failure to take action on behalf of the client in the divorce proceeding beyond the filing of the petition while retaining the $969 in client funds constituted the charging of an unreasonable fee in violation of Colo. RPC 1.5(a) (charging an unreasonable fee). The Complaint alleges a violation of Colo. RPC 1.15(b) (upon receiving funds or other property in which a client or third person has an interest, a lawyer shall promptly deliver to the client any funds or other property that the client is entitled to receive and, upon request by the client, render a full accounting). By failing to perform the work requested by the client while retaining a portion of the client's funds which had not been earned, after effectively abandoning the client, Milner violated Colo. RPC 1.15(b). Milner's abandonment of the client effectively terminated the attorney/client relationship, triggering the provisions of Colo. RPC 1.16(d), requiring Milner to refund any advance payment of fees that had not been earned. Milner failed, upon termination, to take steps to the extent reasonably practicable to protect the client's interests, including failing to refund the advance payment of fee that had not been earned, in violation of Colo. RPC 1.16(d).

[39] The Complaint alleges that Milner violated Colo. RPC 5.5(b) (assisting a person who is not a member of the Colorado Bar in the performance of an activity that constitutes the unauthorized practice of law) by assisting Kemp in the unauthorized practice of law. There is no evidence that established Kemp engaged in the unauthorized practice of law with regard to the Biggers matter. Accordingly, the alleged violation of Colo. RPC 5.5(b) is dismissed.

Claim III: The Stephens Matter

[40] [41] Milner represented Gale Marie Stephens in a bankruptcy proceeding. United States Bankruptcy Judge Sidney B. Brooks dismissed the matter due to Milner's failure to cure deficiencies in the original filing despite an order to do so. Milner took no further action in the case following the court's dismissal. The client, through new counsel, filed a motion to reconsider the dismissal of Stephens' bankruptcy petition, which the court granted. Thereafter, on two separate occasions, the Court ordered Milner to attend a hearing on Milner's mismanagement of the case, the reasonableness of her fees, and whether sanctions should be entered against her. On both occasions, Milner failed to appear. Milner's failing to cure the deficiencies in the original bankruptcy filing constituted a failure to provide competent representation to the client in violation of Colo. RPC 1.1 (a lawyer shall provide competent representation to a client). The failure to timely cure the filing deficiencies also constitutes neglect under Colo. RPC 1.3. Taking into account the nature of the professional services to be provided and the time frame within which those services were required, the level of neglect may justify a finding of abandonment under circumstances where an attorney neglects a client's matter and fails to communicate with the client. Under the circumstances in this case, the facts establish that Milner deserted, rejected, and/or relinquished her professional responsibilities owed to the client. *See People v. Carvell*, No. 99PDJ096 (Colo. PDJ September 11, 2000), 29 Colo. Law 136, 138 (November 2000), 2000 Colo. Discipl. LEXIS 26 (holding that to find abandonment rather than merely neglect, there must be proof that the attorney—during a given time period—was required to accomplish specific professional tasks for the client, failed to accomplish those tasks, and failed to communicate with the client). The level of neglect in the Stephens matter rises to the level of abandonment in violation of Colo. RPC 1.3.

[42] [43] Milner knowingly disobeyed an obligation under the rules of a tribunal on two separate occasions, constituting two separate violations of Colo. RPC 3.4(c) (knowingly ***685** disobeying an obligation under the rules of a tribunal). Milner's conduct violated Colo. RPC 8.4(d) (conduct prejudicial to the administration of justice) by causing the bankruptcy court to dismiss and then reconsider the dismissal of the case, set and reset several hearings. Milner's conduct resulted in harm to the client and to the bankruptcy court: the client's wages were garnished resulting in an arrearage in her house payments, and the bankruptcy court expended unnecessary court time attempting to resolve the difficulties arising from Milner's misconduct.

Claim IV: The Venner Matter

[44] Milner represented Cobe and Sharon Venner who were debtors in a bankruptcy matter. The United States Trustee filed a motion questioning the reasonableness of the fees paid to Milner and questioning whether Milner was sharing fees with nonlawyers. The court ordered Milner to file an accounting for all fees and expenses charged in the case. Milner did not respond to the court's order. On three separate occasions, the court issued an order requiring Milner to appear at hearings, and to show cause why sanctions should not be imposed and/or any monies she received be disgorged for her failure to properly provide representation to her clients. Milner did not appear.

Milner knowingly disobeyed an obligation under the rules of a tribunal by failing to provide an accounting when ordered to do so, and by failing to appear at court-ordered hearings in violation of Colo. RPC 3.4(c) (knowingly disobeying the rules of a tribunal). By causing the court to schedule additional hearings on its docket, Milner engaged in conduct prejudicial to the administration of justice in violation of Colo. RPC 8.4(d) (engaging in conduct prejudicial to the administration of justice). [FN3]

> FN3. Default was denied on the alleged violation of Colo. RPC 1.1 and Colo. RPC 1.3 in claim four in Case No. 99PDJ093, and the People moved to dismiss the charges, which were dismissed by the court on June 6, 2000.

Claim V: The Schmidt Matter

In July 1998, David Schmidt went to Milner's office and spoke with Kemp regarding Schmidt's divorce. Schmidt wanted custody of his two minor children. Kemp, Milner's paralegal, agreed that Milner would accept the case and took $420 from Schmidt. The client paid a total of $595 for Milner's representation. Kemp told Schmidt that Milner would be contacting him. Thereafter, Kemp called Schmidt and told him that Milner would meet with him on the morning of his court appearance date. When Schmidt met with her, Milner was completely unfamiliar with Schmidt's case. Schmidt explained to Milner that his wife was involved in drugs and mentally unstable, and that he wanted custody of the children. At the hearing scheduled that day, Milner arrived late. Moreover, Milner did not inform the court of Schmidt's intent to seek custody. The court ordered a subsequent hearing so that the wife could obtain counsel.

At the next hearing in August 1998, Milner again failed to inform the court of Schmidt's intent to seek custody of his children; on the contrary, she advised the court that the current visitation schedule was working for her client. Milner did not raise any concerns about the welfare of the children. A few days later, Schmidt learned that his estranged wife's boyfriend had beaten her and threatened Schmidt's children with bodily harm. The client called Milner and left a message and Kemp returned his call, stating that they could seek permanent orders in 8 to 12 months, that they could not seek temporary custody, and insisting that Schmidt not contact social services. At no time during the representation of Schmidt did Milner or Kemp inform Schmidt of the availability of court-ordered parenting programs. Schmidt was unable to learn from Milner where he could attend parenting class because Milner did not return his calls nor respond to his letters.

Schmidt wrote to Milner and terminated the representation, asking for the return of his file. Milner did not respond. Months later, on December 28, 1998, Schmidt left a message on Milner's voice mail stating that unless he heard back from her and she returned his file, he and his friends would picket outside her office. The next day he ***686** received a certified letter from Milner's office stating that she would no longer represent him based upon his threats to Milner and to his wife. The letter stated that the police had been notified. Schmidt had never made any threats concerning his wife. The next day, the client received another certified letter from Milner's office containing a court order dismissing his divorce. The client learned from the court that Milner had not taken proper action in his case.

Schmidt's estranged wife saw the letter from Milner's office claiming that he had threatened both his wife and Milner. She notified social services of the alleged threats and the department took action. Schmidt was served with a temporary restraining order preventing him from contacting his children or his ex-wife unless supervised. The statements in the letter regarding threats to his wife were not true.

Despite the client's prior requests, Milner did not return the file to him. The client hired successor counsel. Kemp told successor counsel that he had received information directly from Schmidt's ex-wife about the threats to her and to his children, and claimed that Kemp himself had heard Schmidt make threats regarding Schmidt's children and the ex-wife. None of Kemp's statements were true.

[45] [46] Milner's failure to be apprised of Schmidt's case prior to the hearing, her failure to arrive on time at the hearing, her failure to advocate her client's interests regarding child custody at the hearings, her failure to advise the client that he could seek temporary custody of his children, combined with her failure to advise the client regarding court-ordered parenting classes, constituted a failure to provide competent representation to the client in violation of Colo. RPC 1.1 (failure to provide competent representation) and neglect in violation of Colo. RPC 1.3 (neglect of a legal matter). Milner's failure to adequately communicate with the client despite his repeated efforts to discuss his case with her constituted a violation of Colo. RPC 1.4(a) (failure to communicate). Schmidt terminated Milner's representation, triggering the obligations of Colo. RPC 1.16(d), which required Milner to surrender papers and property to which the client was entitled. Milner failed to return Schmidt's file to him when requested and therefore violated Colo. RPC 1.16(d).

[47] The Complaint alleges a violation of Colo. RPC 5.5(b) (a lawyer shall not assist a person who is not a member of the Colorado bar in the performance of activity that constitute the unauthorized practice of law). Kemp met with the client for an initial interview without Milner's oversight and accepted legal representation of Schmidt. Kemp, also without supervision by Milner, advised Schmidt against seeking temporary custody of the client's children, and advised Schmidt against discussing the children's welfare with social services, all of which constitutes the unauthorized practice of law in violation of Colo. RPC 5.5(b).

[48] The Complaint alleges a violation of Colo. RPC 5.3(b), which provides "a lawyer having direct supervisory authority over the nonlawyer shall make reasonable efforts to ensure that the person's conduct is compatible with the professional obligations of the lawyer." Milner failed to adequately supervise Kemp in Kemp's initial meeting with Schmidt and in subsequent conversations with him; she failed to supervise Kemp when he falsely informed successor counsel that Schmidt had made threats regarding the client's wife and children. By failing to restrict Kemp's ability to act inappropriately with regard to Schmidt, Milner violated Colo. RPC 5.3(b).

II. Analysis of Discipline

These two disciplinary proceedings consist of 14 separate matters. In two matters, Milner violated Colo. RPC 1.1 by failing to provide competent legal advice to the client. In four matters, Milner violated Colo. RPC 1.15(b) by failing to deliver to the client or third person any funds or other property that the client or third person was entitled to receive, and upon request, provide a full accounting regarding such property. In three matters, Milner violated Colo. RPC 1.16(d) by taking reasonable steps to protect the client's interests upon termination. In 10 separate matters, Milner violated ***687** Colo. RPC 1.3 by failing to act with reasonable diligence and promptness in representing the client, and by neglecting legal matters entrusted to her. In 11 separate matters, Milner violated Colo. RPC 1.4(a) by failing to keep her clients reasonably informed about the status of their matters and failed to promptly comply with reasonable requests for information. In two matters, Milner violated Colo. RPC 1.5(a) by charging an unreasonable fee. In one matter, Milner failed to comply with the requirements of Colo. RPC 1.5(b) requiring that she communicate the basis or rate of her fee in writing before or within a reasonable time after commencing the representation of the client. In three matters, Milner knowingly disobeyed an obligation under the rules of a tribunal. In four matters, Milner violated Colo. RPC 5.3(b) by acting as a lawyer having direct supervisory authority over a nonlawyer and failing to make reasonable efforts to ensure that the person's conduct is compatible with the professional obligations of the lawyer. In one matter, Milner violated Colo. RPC 5.5(b) by assisting a person who is not a member of the Colorado bar in the performance of an activity that constitutes the unauthorized practice of law. In four matters, Milner violated Colo. RPC 8.4(c) by engaging in conduct involving dishonesty, fraud, deceit, or misrepresentation. In three matters, Milner violated Colo. RPC 8.4(d) by engaging in conduct prejudicial to the administration of justice. In one matter, Milner violated Colo. RPC 8.4(h) by engaging in conduct that adversely reflects on the lawyer's fitness to practice law.

[49] [50] [51] [52] In the Biggers matter, Milner converted funds belonging to the client. Milner's retention of Biggers' funds for an extended period of time, coupled with her lack of communication with the client, and her failure to account for or return the unearned funds for a significant period of time, constitutes willful and knowing conduct. Knowing conversion of clients' funds warrants disbarment. *See People v. Silvola*, 915 P.2d 1281, 1284 (Colo.1996) (finding that misconduct that occurred over an extended period of time must be deemed to be willful); *People v. Bradley*, 825 P.2d 475, 476–77 (Colo.1992) (lawyer's inaction over a period

of two years deemed willful misconduct); People v. Williams, 824 P.2d 813, 814 (Colo.1992) (continued and chronic neglect over extended periods of time must be considered willful); *People v. Elliott*, 99PDJ059, slip op. at 8 (consolidated with 99PDJ086) (Colo. PDJ March 1, 2000), 29 Colo. Law. 112, 114, 115 (May 2000) (disbarring attorney for his accepting advance fees from two clients, performing some but not all of the services for which he was paid, retaining the fees for one year in one matter and two years in another matter, and abandoning the clients). Milner abandoned her clients in both the Biggers and Stephens matters. Abandonment of clients, absent significant mitigating circumstances, warrants disbarment. *See* ABA *Standards for Imposing Lawyer Sanctions* (1991 & Supp.1992) ("ABA *Standards*") 4.41(a)(providing that disbarment is generally appropriate when a lawyer abandons the practice and causes serious or potentially serious injury to a client). Disbarment is also the appropriate sanction for the extent of neglect and other rule violations demonstrated in these 14 separate client matters. *See* ABA *Standards* 4.41(c) (stating that disbarment is generally appropriate when a lawyer engages in a pattern of neglect with respect to client matters and causes serious or potentially serious injury to a client); People v. Murray, 887 P.2d 1016, 1021 (Colo.1994) (lawyer disbarred for knowingly failing to perform services for clients in 10 separate matters, constituting a pattern of neglect and causing potentially serious harm to clients); People v. Dulaney, 785 P.2d 1302, 1306 (Colo.1990) (lawyer disbarred for chronic neglect of client matters and use of deceit to cover the neglect).

The charges concerning Milner's failure to supervise Kemp, her paralegal, and her assisting him in the unauthorized practice of law are of particular concern and warrant a serious sanction. *See* People v. Felker, 770 P.2d 402, 406–407 (Colo.1989) (disbarring attorney for misrepresenting to a client that the legal assistant was a lawyer and permitting a nonlawyer to render legal advice to the client). Two prior Colorado disciplinary cases resulted in sanctions arising in part from an attorneys' failure to supervise the same paralegal, Matthew Kemp, and aiding ***688** him in the unauthorized practice of law. In People v. Reynolds, 933 P.2d 1295, 1305 (Colo.1997), the respondent attorney was suspended for three years and 30 days for 11 separate violations alleged in two complaints, with conditions upon reinstatement. As in this case, the respondent was found to have repeatedly neglected numerous client matters, engaged in dishonesty, misused client funds, and assisted a nonlawyer in the unauthorized practice of law. In People v. Stewart, 892 P.2d 875, 879 (Colo.1995), an attorney was suspended for three years with conditions placed upon reinstatement for making unauthorized charges to her law firm's credit card, aiding a nonlawyer in the unauthorized practice of law, and neglecting client matters after clients paid retainer fees to the nonlawyer assistant. The Supreme Court decided on the sanction of suspension rather than disbarment due to certain mitigating factors, including the fact that during the relevant time period, the respondent was suffering from depression and other physical and emotional problems.

The PDJ and Hearing Board find that Milner's misconduct, while similar to the misconduct in *Reynolds* and *Stewart*, is considerably worsened by her conduct before the United States Bankruptcy Court in the Venner and Stephens matter. Milner's failure to comply with the bankruptcy judge's orders that she appear, finally resulting in the issuance of a bench warrant for her arrest, demonstrates a flagrant disregard for the court system. Milner's conduct resulted in considerable waste of judicial resources and resulted in the Court making written findings in both matters that Milner's conduct on behalf of her clients was unprofessional, incomplete, and irresponsible, that she failed to disgorge fees despite being ordered to do so, and that she failed to pay sanctions ordered by the court. *See* the Commentary to ABA *Standards* 7.1 (providing that "[d]isbarment should be imposed in cases when the lawyer knowingly engages in conduct that violates a duty owed to the profession with the intent to benefit the lawyer or another, and which causes serious injury or potentially serious injury to a client, the public, or the legal system").

Milner's actions resulted in harm to her clients. Aldridge has been unable to modify visitation rights with her children. In the Chavez divorce, the rapport between the parties worsened as a result of Kemp's incorrectly blaming Milner's delay in the case on the unwillingness of the client's husband to cooperate. Chavez eventually represented herself in her divorce and was unable to obtain child support. In the Schmidt matter, Milner's and Kemp's actions resulted in Schmidt's divorce being dismissed for failure to prosecute, Schmidt's wife obtaining a temporary restraining order against him and his visitation rights were restricted. Nelson, who sought assistance investigating the death of her brother, was a particularly vulnerable client at the time she engaged Milner. The beneficiaries of the estate Milner was appointed to administer were required to obtain an attorney to appoint a successor personal representative and suffered considerable stress as a result of Milner's mishandling of the estate.

In addition to the private harm, the public has been harmed by Milner's misconduct and her failure to supervise Kemp and provide assistance to him in the unauthorized practice of law. Such misconduct causes a heightened sense of public distrust in lawyers and their legal assistants.

[53] The PDJ and Hearing Board considered matters in mitigation and aggravation pursuant to ABA *Standards* 9.32 and 9.22 respectively. In mitigation, Milner has had no prior discipline, *see id. at* 9.32(a); however, the absence of prior discipline, standing alone, is insufficient to justify a sanction less than disbarment. *See* People v. Steinman, 930 P.2d 596, 600 (Colo.1997). Milner was inexperienced at the time of the conduct in question, having been admitted to the bar of Colorado in 1992, *see id. at* 9.32(f), and she has demonstrated remorse for her actions, *see id. at* 9.32(l).

[54] Milner testified in mitigation that the facts giving rise to these proceedings were caused, at least in part, by Kemp. She stated that she was unaware of Kemp's unprofessional conduct with clients, and unaware of the number of cases Kemp had accepted on her behalf. However, Milner, as Kemp's employer and as the supervising lawyer, ***689** was accountable for his interactions with clients. Milner's lack of awareness regarding Kemp's activities cannot be considered a mitigating factor. It is incumbent upon the supervising lawyer to ensure that his or her paralegal adheres to the professional obligations of the lawyer. Ignorance of the paralegal's activities is no excuse. In aggravation, Milner acted with a selfish motive, *see id. at* 9.22(b); she demonstrated a patter of misconduct, *see id. at* 9.22(c); she committed multiple offenses, *see id. at* 9.22(d); she failed to cooperate in the disciplinary proceedings, *see id. at* 9.22(e); several of her clients were vulnerable, *see id. at* 9.22(h); and she exhibited indifference to making restitution, *see id. at* 9.22(j).

The People recommend a three-year suspension to disbarment in Case No. 99PDJ030, and disbarment in Case No. 99PDJ093. The PDJ and Hearing Board find that disbarment is the appropriate sanction considering Milner's chronic neglect in multiple client matters, knowing conversion of client funds, abandonment of two clients, multiple instances of failing to adequately supervise a nonlawyer, aiding another in the unauthorized practice of law, and complete disregard of court orders. The PDJ and Hearing Board further find that Milner must pay restitution to the parties set forth herein within one year of the date of this Order.

III. Order

It is therefore Ordered:

1. That KAREN S. MILNER, attorney registration number 21384 is DISBARRED from the practice of law effective 31 days from the date of this Order, and her name shall be stricken from the roll of attorneys licensed to practice law in this state;
2. Milner shall pay or make arrangements to pay the following amounts in restitution to the following clients within 12 (twelve) months of the date of this Order:
   A. Jannette Nelson $2,000;
   B. Cindy Biggers $484.50;
   C. David Schmidt $595; and
   D. Mr. and Mrs. Boroos $1,071.
3. As a condition of readmission, Milner must demonstrate that she has fully complied with Judge Brooks' Orders in the Stephens and Venner matters, paying $2,000 to Gale Marie Stephens, and paying $2,000 to Cobe and Sharon Venner.
4. Milner is ORDERED to pay the costs of these proceedings; the People shall submit a Statement of Costs within 15 (fifteen) days of the date of this Order. Respondent shall have 10 (ten) days thereafter to submit a response thereto.

Colo.O.P.D.J.,2001.

People v. Milner

35 P.3d 670

END OF DOCUMENT

Case Review Exercises

1. Were you surprised at the number and depth of the violations with which Milner was charged?
2. What role did Kemp play in Milner's office? What did Kemp specifically do wrong?
3. Is it fair that Milner was disbarred but nothing was done to Kemp?

Helpful Web Sites

Organization	Description	Internet Address
Alabama State Bar—Law Office Management Assistance Program	Articles on a variety of law office management topics, including a manual on how to keep clients.	http://www.alabar.org
American Bar Association (ABA)	Association for attorneys. The Web site has a large amount of information and publications relevant to individuals working in the legal profession.	http://www.abanet.org
ABA Law Practice Management	ABA Web site devoted to law practice management issues and concerns, including management publications, articles, and resources.	http://www.abanet.org/lpm
Paralegal Today	National magazine for paralegals. The Web site has limited information but the magazine itself is full of useful articles, including ethical issues related to paralegals.	http://www.paralegaltoday.com
Maryland State Bar Association—Law Practice Management Assistance	The Web site has a wide variety of law office management topics, including using client surveys, tips for enhancing client relations, how to select clients, and much more.	http://www.msba.org
Mississippi State Bar Association	The Web site has a wide variety of law office management topics, including a handbook on client relations.	http://www.msbar.org
National Association of Legal Assistants—Paralegals	Contains many resources for legal assistants and paralegals.	http://www.nala.org
National Federation of Paralegal Associations	National association for paralegals. Contains many resources for paralegals.	http://www.paralegals.org

Suggested Reading

1. Munneke, G. A., & Davis, A.E. (2003, 2007, 2010). *The Essential Formbook: Comprehensive Management Tools for Lawyers, Volumes I–IV.* American Bar Association.
2. *Law Practice* magazine, published by the American Bar Association Law Practice Management Section. http://www.abanet.org.
3. *Paralegal Today* magazine, published by Conexion International Media, Inc. http://www.paralegaltoday.com.
4. Foonberg, J. (2004). *How To Start and Build a Law Practice*. American Bar Association.
5. Ewalt, H. (2002). *Through the Client's Eyes*. American Bar Association.

Hands-On Exercises
Clio—Client Relationship management

Basic Lessons

Number	Lesson Title	Concepts Covered
Lesson 1*	Part A: Introduction to Clio Part B: Set Up Law Firm Profile	Understanding the Clio Platform Details for Firm descriptions
Lesson 2	Entering New Matters/Cases	Entering a new client matter
Lesson 3	Retrieving and Printing Matters Reports	Preparing for review status and upcoming events to monitor.
Lesson 4	Entering Notes for Matters	Entering case matter notes
*NOTE: Lesson 1—Introduction to Clio is the same for every subject matter. If you completed Lesson 1 in an earlier tutorial, you do not need to repeat it.		

Welcome to Adams & Lee

Welcome to Adams & Lee! We are an active and growing law firm with six attorneys and three paralegals. As you know, you have been hired as a paralegal intern. We are very happy to have you on board; we can certainly use your help.

At Adams & Lee we use computer systems extensively, so it is necessary that you have a basic understanding of our system. We currently use Clio, a comprehensive, yet easy-to-use cloud-based law practice management software. Clio automates the practice and management side of operating a law firm. Clio has powerful features to manage cases, clients, documents, bills, appointments, time-tracking, reporting, and accounting.

In the following lessons, you will focus on entering new cases or matters into Clio. You will learn how to retrieve and print client reports and learn how to enter case matter notes into the system. Delivering outstanding legal services to our clients is what our firm is about, and the computer skills you learn in the tutorial will help you do that. We know you want begin using Clio immediately and learning the office case management system will help you gain the skills needed to maintain the client services we deliver. You should review the "Getting Started" guide to help you become familiar with Clio.

Getting Started

Introduction

Throughout these exercises, information you need to type into the program will be designated in several different ways.

- Keys to be pressed on the keyboard will be designated in brackets, in all caps and bold type (e.g., press the **[ENTER]** key).

- Movements with the mouse/pointer will be designated in bold and italics (e.g., ***point to File on the Menu Bar and click the pointer).***
- Words or letters that should be typed are designated in bold (e.g., type **Training Program**).
- Information that is or should be displayed on your computer screen is shown in bold, with quotation marks (e.g., **"Press ENTER to continue"**).

Clio Installation (Appendix A)

Clio is not a downloaded program; it is accessed from the Web site. You may be invited by your instructor to join as a nonlawyer (paralegal) in a hypothetical law firm through your e-mail. ***Click the hyperlink or copy and paste it into your Internet browser. Follow the on-screen instructions for providing your name and creating a password.*** You will now have access to Clio and the hypothetical law firm.

Your instructor may have you create a Clio account and work independently. In that case, see Appendix A for installation instructions.

LESSON 1: Part A (Appendix B)

You should become familiar with the Clio Platform and its essential functions before you begin any of the lessons. *Note*: If you are already logged in, you will skip Steps 1 and 2.

1. Start your Internet browser. Type **www.goclio.com** in the Internet browser and press the **[ENTER] key**.
2. On the Clio Home page, ***click Log In. On the next screen, enter the e-mail address and password you provided in Clio and click SIGN IN. If you check the box next to KEEP ME SIGNED IN, you will be able to skip this step in the future.***
3. Clio will open in the hypothetical law firm on the PRACTICE page. At this point you are ready to explore the Clio platform and its essential functions. There are 11 tabs available in Clio. We will start with the PRACTICE tab.
4. ***Click*** **PRACTICE**. Your screen should now look like Clio Exhibit 1A-1. This is the Clio dashboard which provides a quick look at the agenda, calendar, and billing information. You will now explore the other 10 tabs.

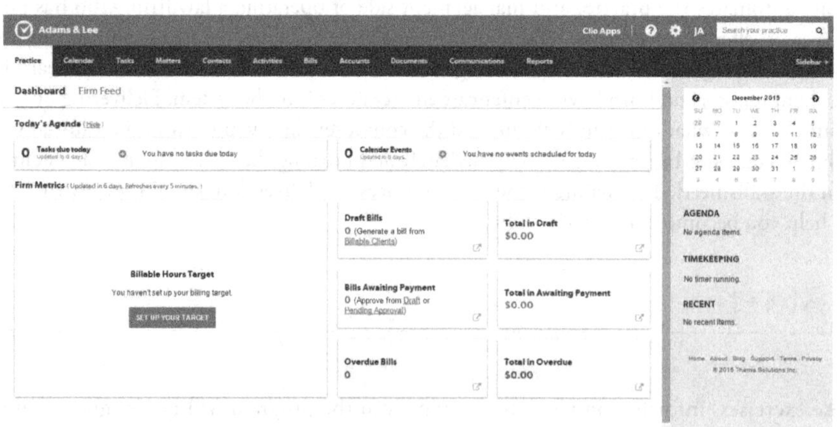

Clio Exhibit 1A-1 Practice Tab

Source: Themis Solutions, Inc.

5. ***Click* CALENDAR.** You may need to scroll down to see the entire page. You can change the view to see your Agenda, or Day, Week, Month, or Year views. You can view your personal calendar, the firm calendar or both.
6. To create a calendar entry, while in the Week view, ***select the Wednesday of that current week and double-click on the 10:00 am time slots.*** The Create Calendar Entry will open. See Clio Exhibit 1A-2. If you ***click Add Event***, the date will default to the current date.

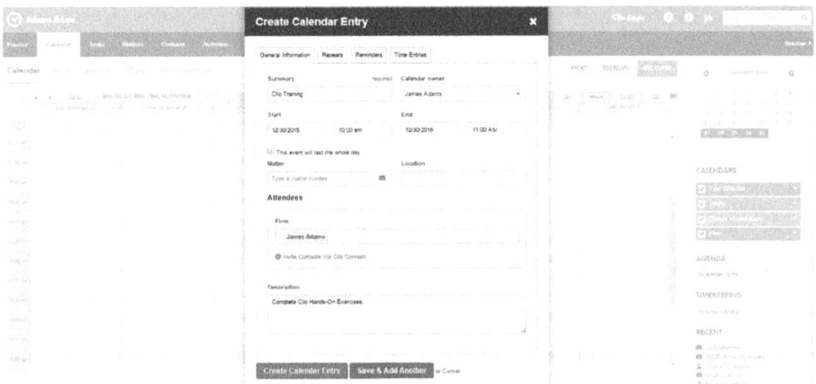

Clio Exhibit 1A-2 Create Calendar Entry

Source: Themis Solutions, Inc.

Under Summary, type **Clio Training**. Under **Start**, type **10:00 AM** and under **End** type **11:00 AM**. Leave Matter and Location "**blank**," and under Description, type **Complete Clio Hands-On Exercises.** ***Click Create Calendar Entry***. When adding multiple entries, ***click Save & Add Another***. After the entry is complete, it will appear in the calendar. ***Place your cursor over the new calendar entry*** to see the description. Your calendar should look like Clio Exhibit 1A-3. You can now move to the "Tasks" tab.

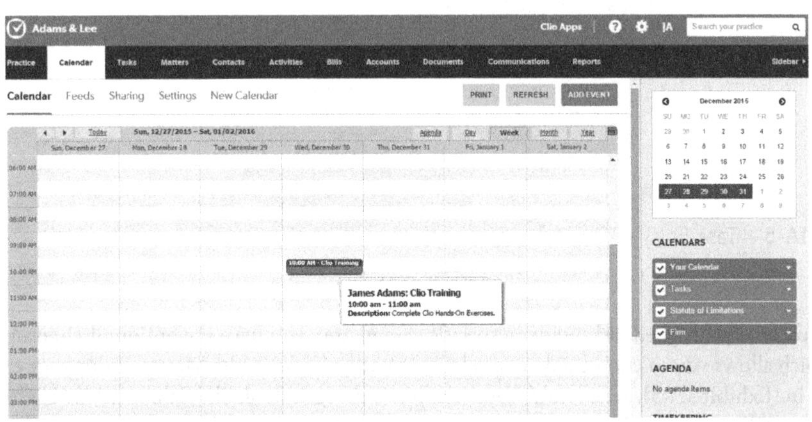

Clio Exhibit 1A-3 Calendar Entry

Source: Themis Solutions, Inc.

7. ***Click* TASKS**. This is where specific tasks can be assigned to specific individuals or groups. To create a new Task, ***click Add***. See Clio Exhibit 1A-4. Under Task Name, type **Clio Training**.

Clio Exhibit 1A-4 Add Task – "Due At"

Source: Themis Solutions, Inc.

Under Description, type **Watch Clio training videos**. Under Due: the radial button will default to **"Due at"** when there are no other tasks associated. ***Click the box under "Due At,"*** and a calendar will appear. ***Select Thursday of the current week***. Under Assignee, ***select Firm User and then choose yourself***. Under Priority, ***select Normal***. Under Matter, ***type 00003-Battise: Custody Agreement*** (the case will appear in the list as you begin typing the number). Then ***click Save Task***. When adding multiple tasks, ***select Save and Add Another***. At this point you will be on the ***"tasks" under 00003-Battise***. See Clio Exhibit 1A-5.

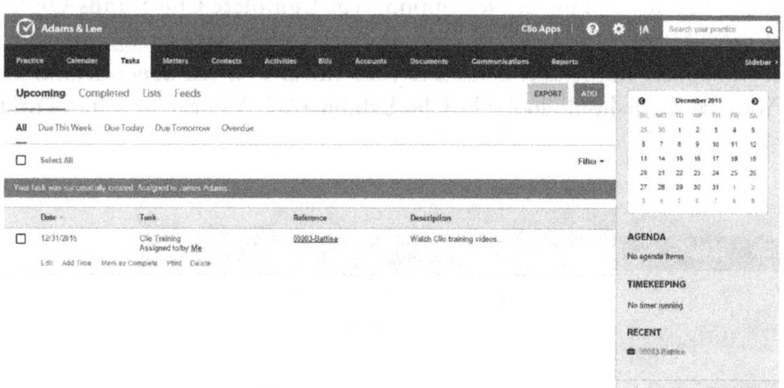

Clio Exhibit 1A-5 Task Entry – "Due At"

Source: Themis Solutions, Inc.

8. When you have several assigned tasks under a specific case matter, you have the option of choosing **"Due in"** which allows you to choose a date in relation to other Tasks in the Matter. From your current position in (Exhibit 1A-5), ***select Add***. Your screen should again look like Exhibit 1A-3. Under Task Name, type **Clio Training**. Under Description, type **Watch Clio Introduction Videos**. Under Assignee, ***select Firm User and then choose yourself***. Under Priority, ***select Normal***. Under Matter, ***type 00003-Battise: Custody Agreement*** (the case will appear in the list as you begin typing the number).Then ***select 00003Battise: Custody Agreement***. Under Due: the radial will default to

"Due at," however; you now have the option to choose **"Due in."** ***Select "Due in,"*** and a dialogue box will appear. See Clio Exhibit 1A-6.

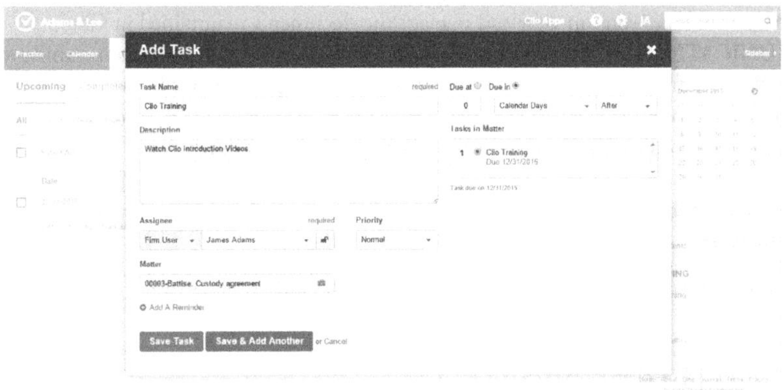

Clio Exhibit 1A-6 Add Task – "Due In"

Source: Themis Solutions, Inc.

ENTER **"1"** in the box marked with a 0. ***Select Calendar Weeks*** under the drop-down menu in the next box, ***Select before*** under the drop-down menu in the next box. Then ***select Clio Training*** under the radial button. ***Click Save Task.*** The second task will now appear listed on the Tasks page. See Clio Exhibit 1A-7.

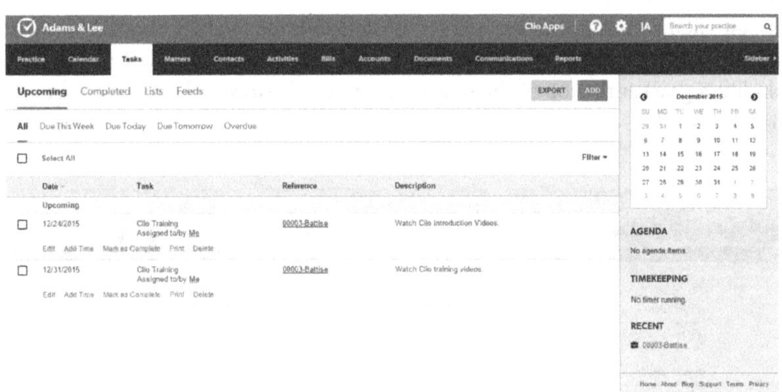

Clio Exhibit 1A-7 Task Entry – "Due In"

Source: Themis Solutions, Inc.

9. ***Click*** **MATTERS**. Matters are what Clio calls for cases or files. Clio allows you to associate, or connect, matters with clients, tasks, bills, etc. In later exercises you will see how that works and you will create several new matters.
10. ***Click*** **CONTACTS**. Contacts are people and corporations that you do business with (clients, other attorneys, court reporters, etc.).
11. ***Click*** **ACTIVITIES**. "Activities" is what Clio uses for both time and billing entries as well as expense entries. Time entries can be billed as a flat rate or as an hourly rate. In later exercises you will create several new billing activities.

12. ***Click* BILLS**. Here, you can create a new bill, review a client's billing history, and create bill themes (designs) among other bill-related issues. In later exercises you will create several new bills.
13. ***Click* ACCOUNTS**. Here you can view and manage the various bank accounts of a law firm.
14. ***Click* DOCUMENTS**. Here you can view and manage the documents maintained in Clio.
15. ***Click* COMMUNICATIONS**. Here you can send and receive e-mails, maintain communication logs, interact with colleagues and Clio-connected users, as well as limit permissions between groups for file-related communications.
16. ***Click* REPORTS**. Here you can create reports on a variety of topics (billing client, mater, productivity, and revenue).
17. To end this Clio session, ***click your initials at the top of the screen. Click Sign Out and then close your Internet Browser.***

This concludes the introduction lesson on Clio's platform and essential functions review.

LESSON 1: Part B (Appendix C)

In this lesson, you will set up the firm profile in the hypothetical law firm, establish billing rate, create an activity description, set up bank accounts and establish the matter-numbering protocol.

Note: If you are already logged in, you will skip Steps 1 and 2.

1. Start your Internet browser. Type www.goclio.com in the Internet browser and press the **[ENTER] key**.
2. On the Clio Home page, ***click Log In. On the next screen, enter the e-mail address and password you provided in Clio and click SIGN IN. If you check the box next to KEEP ME SIGNED IN, you will be able to skip this step in the future.***
3. Before you enter new clients, contacts and matters in Clio, details for the hypothetical law firm should be entered. First, you will set up the account information for your hypothetical law firm. ***Click the "settings" icon*** (looks like a gear) at the top of the screen next to the "***initials***." Your screen should look like Clio Exhibit 1B-1.

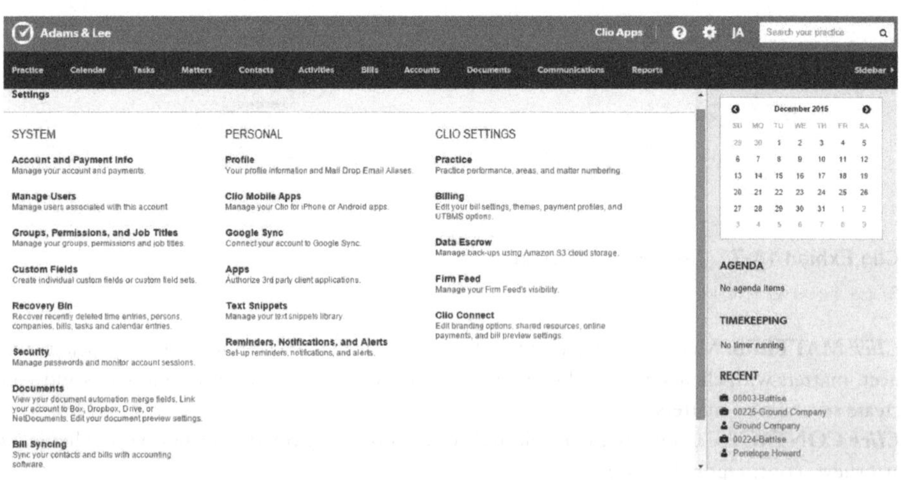

Clio Exhibit 1B-1 Clio Settings Screen

Source: Themis Solutions, Inc.

4. ***Click Account and Payment Info.*** The name of your hypothetical law firm will be established by your instructor (i.e., Adams & Lee) or your First and Last name if you create your own individual account (i.e., Law Office of "First name" "Last name" that you entered). Note: Free accounts do not have access to payment info.
5. ***Type the name, address, and contact information of your firm*** (i.e., sample check from Exhibit 6-1 (Chapter 6), instructor provided, or create your own).
6. Next, ***click the drop-down menu under Date format. Select*** the option that resembles ***12/31/2015.*** Then, ***click the drop-down menu under Time format. Select*** the option that resembles ***11:59 pm. Click Save New Information.***
7. You will now update profile and establish a billing rate. ***Click*** the "settings" icon (looks like a gear) at the top of the screen next to the "initials." Your screen should look like Clio Exhibit 1B-1. ***Click Profile*** and scroll down to **Billing Rate**. ***Type 175.00 next to $/Hr. Click Save New Information.*** See Clio Exhibit 1B-2.

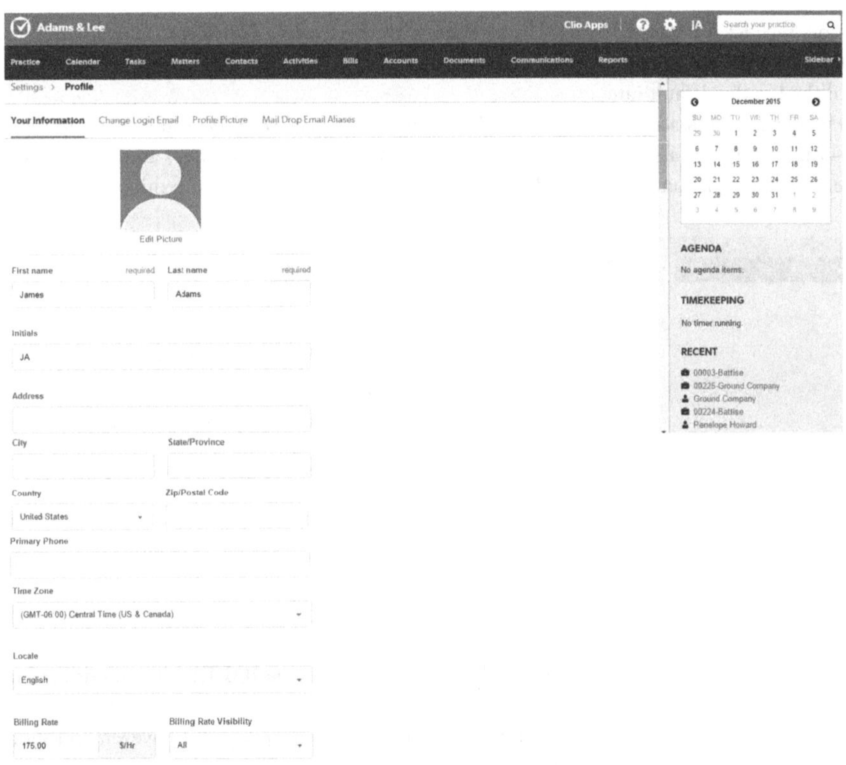

Clio Exhibit 1B-2 Update Profile – Billing Rate

Source: Themis Solutions, Inc.

8. Next, you will create an Activity Description. These are used to ensure a consistent description of commonly used time entries across a law firm. It can also be used as a shortcut—you can save text in the Activity Description and when you enter in a time entry, it will populate this text for you. Activity Descriptions can be shared across a law firm so that everyone in the firm can use them. ***Click the Activities tab, then click Activity Descriptions, then click Add.*** See Clio Exhibit 1B-3.

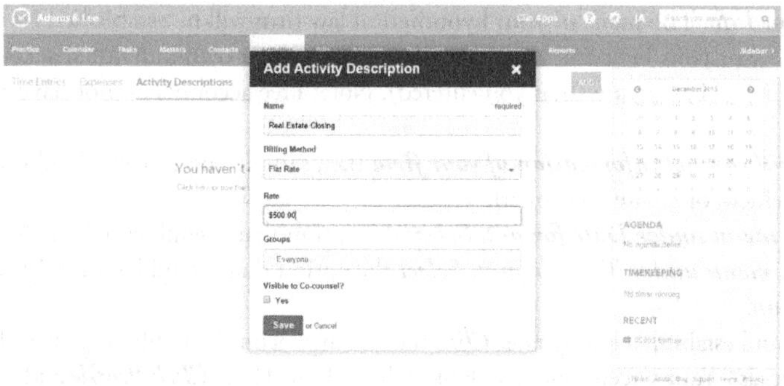

Clio Exhibit 1B-3 Add Activity Description

Source: Themis Solutions, Inc.

Under Name, type **Real Estate Closing**. Under Billing Method, ***select Flat Rate***. This opens a text box called Rate; type **$500.00** in the text box, ***Click Save***. This flat rate fee will override the $175.00 per hour established as the default rate.

9. Next, you will create bank accounts. ***Click the Accounts tab***, then ***click New***. You will set up two accounts—the first will be a Trust Account (one that contains only client money) and the second will be an Operating account (one that ***should not*** contain client money). See Clio Exhibit 1B-4.

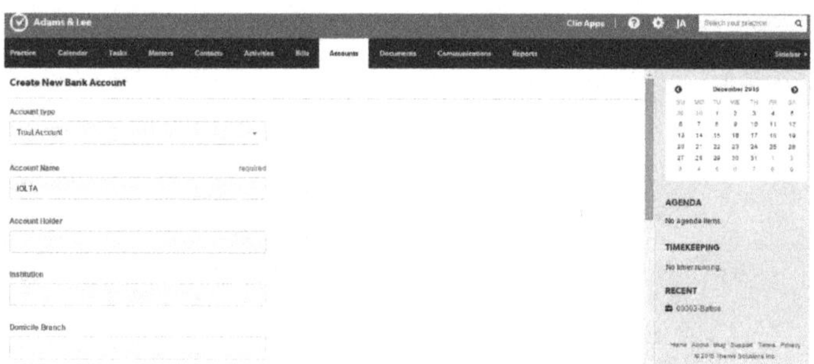

Clio Exhibit 1B-4 Create New Bank Account

Source: Themis Solutions, Inc.

10. Under Account type, ***select Trust Account***. Under Account name, type **IOLTA** (this stands for Interest on Law Office Trust Account, commonly used for Trust accounts). It is not necessary, nor is it required, to complete the remainder of this form (although you are welcomed to do so). However, you should leave the Balance 0.0. ***Click Create New Bank Account***. The screen will refresh (showing the new IOLTA account) so additional accounts may be created.
11. Now create the Operating Account. ***Click New***, then under Account type, ***select Operating Account***. Under Account name, type **Law Firm Account**. It is not necessary, nor is it required, to complete the remainder of this form (although you are welcomed to do so). However, you should leave the Balance 0.0. ***Click the box next to Default Account***. (The default account will show up first on the Transactions tab found when a client file is opened under Matters.) ***Click Create New Bank Account***.

12. You will now create the matter-numbering protocol for the hypothetical law firm. ***Click the "settings" icon*** (looks like a gear) at the top of the screen next to the "***initials***." Your screen should look like Clio Exhibit 1B-1. ***Click Practice***, and then ***click Matter Numbering***. See Clio Exhibit 1B-5.

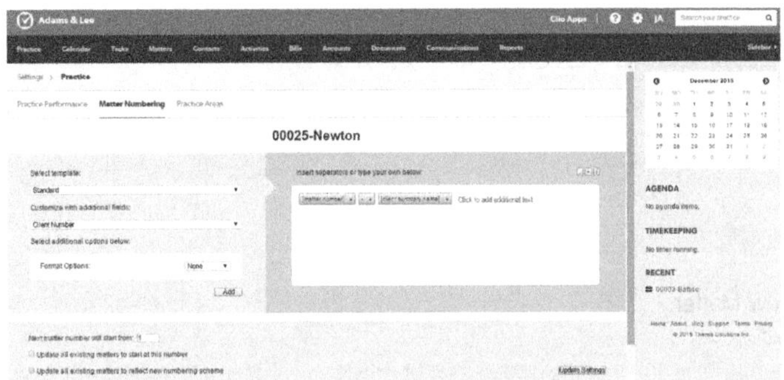

Clio Exhibit 1B-5 Matter Numbering

Source: Themis Solutions, Inc.

Under Select Template: click the drop-down menu arrow and click on each of the available options. As you do, notice how the sample matter number (00025-Newton) changes. Use the default (matter number—client summary name), then ***select Standard***. Under ***Customize with additional fields, select Client Number. Click Update Settings.***

13. To end this Clio session, ***click on your initials*** at the top of the screen. ***Click Sign Out, and then close your Internet browser.***

This concludes the lesson on law firm profile and setup.

This concludes Lesson 1 on introduction and setup in Clio.

You are now ready to enter new matters/cases into Clio and add notes.

LESSON 2: Entering New Matters/Cases

In this lesson, you will enter a new matter/case into Clio.

Note: If you are already logged in, you will skip Steps 1 and 2.

1. Start your Internet browser. Type www.goclio.com in the Internet browser and press the **[ENTER] key**.
2. On the Clio Home page, ***click Log In. On the next screen, enter the e-mail address and password you provided in Clio and click SIGN IN. If you check the box next to KEEP ME SIGNED IN, you will be able to skip this step in the future.***
3. Clio opens in the Practice tab. ***Click the Matters tab, then click New.***
4. At this point you are ready to enter all the details available for the new matter/case. We will use the client ***Sharon Battise*** for this exercise. Under **Find Client**, begin typing her name. You will notice that Clio suggests choices. From the list, locate and select ***Sharon Battise.*** See Clio Exhibit 4-1.

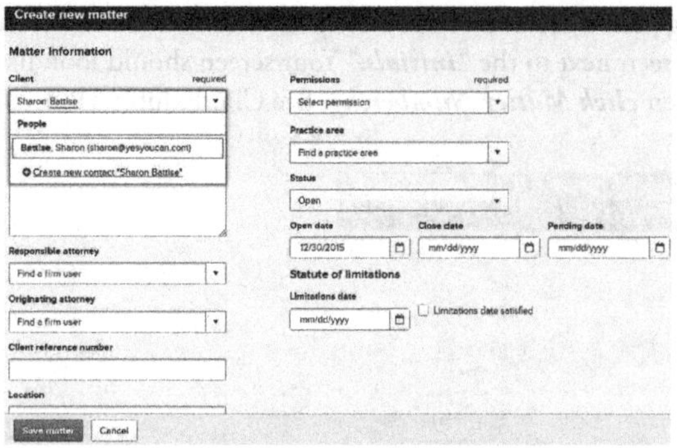

Clio Exhibit 4-1 Create New Matter

Source: Themis Solutions, Inc.

5. Under Matter Information, ***enter the following information:***

Description	Real Estate Closing
Open Date	Use current date (will be shown by default)
Status	Open
Practice Area	Conveyance (Purchase)

You may skip the Client Reference Number.

Responsible Attorney	Use create a name unless the attorney name was provided by the instructor.
Originating Attorney	Use the same information from above.

You may skip the location, Assign Task Lists, Custom Fields, and Statutes of Limitations.

Matter Permissions	Select Everyone
Matter Billing	Check the box so this item is billable. Click the button next to Flat Rate. A text box will open, ***select the name you created (or attorney name provided by the instructor).*** Skip the description box and fill in the Rate box with a $500.00 fee.

6. ***Click Save New Matter.*** At this point your screen should look like Clio Exhibit 4-2. (Note: The new Matter number may vary.)

Clio Exhibit 4-2 New Matter Entry

Source: Themis Solutions, Inc.

7. You will now enter two new matters for new clients in Clio. You will need to return to the MATTERS tab.
8. ***Click the Matters tab***, then ***click New.*** We will Add "**Ground Company**." Under Matter Client, ***select Add A Company, then type "Ground Company,"*** and ***click Create. Enter the following new matter information.***

Description (Matter Information)	Short v. NTT Environmental Company
Open Date	Use current date (will be shown by default)
Status	Open
Practice Area	Civil Litigation (You will notice that Clio suggests choices).

You may skip the Client Reference Number.

Responsible Attorney	Use your name unless the attorney name was been provided by the instructor.
Originating Attorney	Use the same information from above.

You may skip the location, Assign Task Lists, Custom Fields, and Statutes of Limitations.

Matter Permissions	Select Everyone
Matter Billing	Check the box so this item is billable. Click the button next to Flat Rate. A text box will open, ***select your name (or attorney name provided by instructor).*** Skip the description box and fill in the Rate box with a $1000.00 fee.

9. ***Click Save New Matter.*** At this point your screen should look like Clio Exhibit 4-3. (Note: the new matter number may vary.)

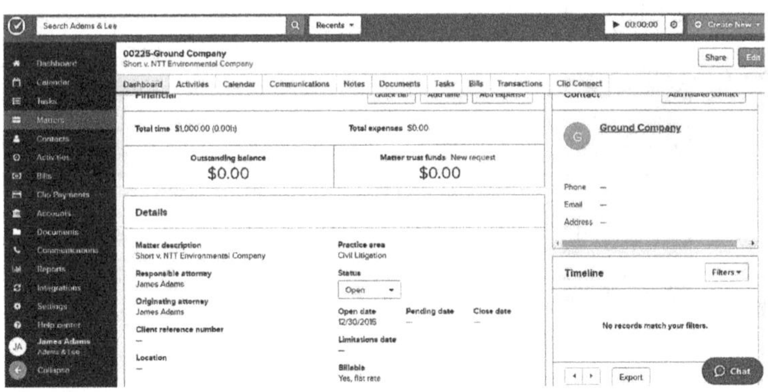

Clio Exhibit 4-3 Ground Company Matter

Source: Themis Solutions, Inc.

You may now enter additional contact information associated with the Ground Company and the new matter ***Short v. NTT Environmental Company.***

10. ***Click the Client tab under Matters,*** and then ***click "edit."*** Ground Company will appear in the ***Name*** box under Company Details. Enter the following address information:

(use info for new person/company)	39381 Policy Avenue Brownsville, SD 37047 Phone: 610-977-9302

Then ***select Update Company.*** See Clio Exhibit 4-4.

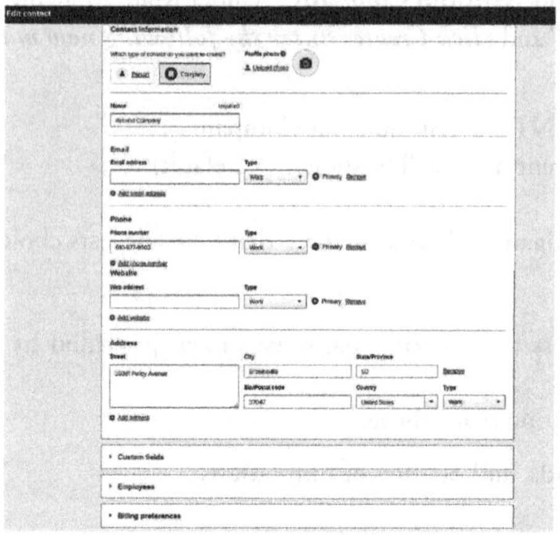

Clio Exhibit 4-4 Update Matter - Company Information

Source: Themis Solutions, Inc.

You will see the matter Ground Company at the bottom of the screen below the updated information screen. From here, you may ***click on*** the matter to add additional contacts.

11. ***Click Ground Company.*** The matter will display several tabs. ***Click the Contacts tab***, and the ***click Add.*** Under Add Relationship, enter the name ***Robert Short.*** Under Relationship, ***add Owner.*** Then, ***click Save.*** Robert Short will be added with the new matter ***Short v. NTT Environmental Company under Ground Company.*** See Clio Exhibit 4-5.

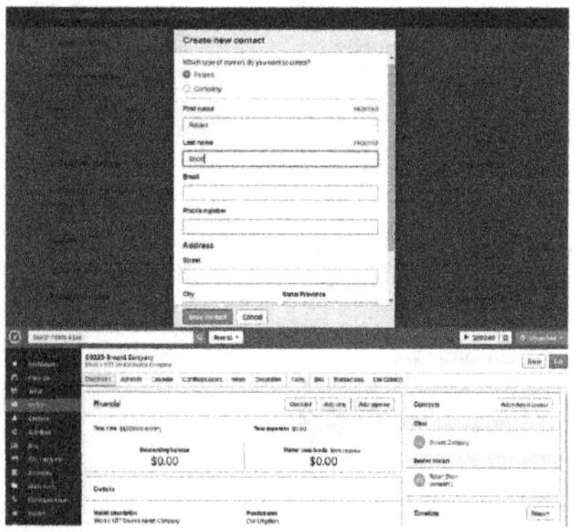

Clio Exhibit 4-5 Update Matter – Contact Information

Source: Themis Solutions, Inc.

12. To end this Clio session, ***click the drop-down menu by your initials at the top of the screen. Click sign out and then close your Internet Browser.***

This concludes Lesson 2 on entering new Matters/Cases in Clio.

LESSON 3: Retrieving and Printing Matters Reports

In this lesson, you will retrieve and print a matter report.

Note: If you are already logged in, you will skip Steps 1 and 2.

1. Start your Internet browser. Type www.goclio.com in the Internet browser and press the **[ENTER] key**.
2. On the Clio Home page, ***click Log In. On the next screen, enter the email address and password you provided in Clio and click SIGN IN. If you check the box next to KEEP ME SIGNED IN, you will be able to skip this step in the future.***
3. ***Click the Reports tab.*** From the list under Matter Reports ***select Matters.*** For the purpose of this exercise we will generate a report for all existing matters. Under Select Attorneys, ***select All Attorneys***, under Select Originating Attorneys, ***select All Attorneys***, and under Clients, ***select All Clients.*** Under Group Results by, ***select Client.*** Under Select Practice Area, ***select All.*** Under Select Open Date Range, ***select This Month.*** The Output Format gives you the option to select a PDF, a CSV or a Web format. For this exercise, ***select Web, then click Generate Report.*** At this point you will see all information of contacts and matters alphabetically listed. See Clio Exhibit 4-6.

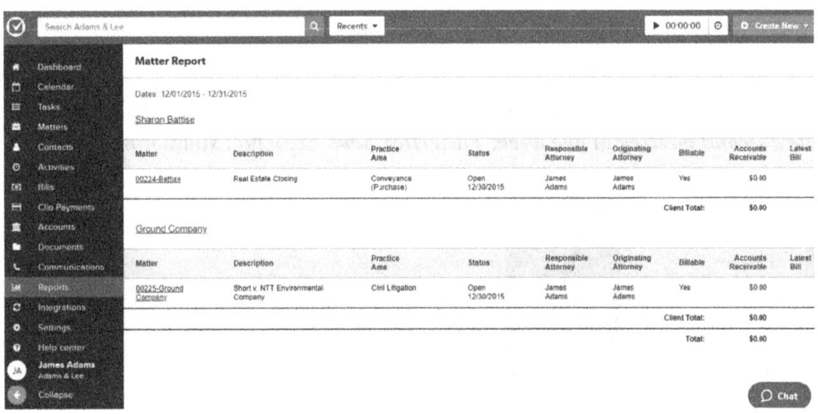

Clio Exhibit 4-6 Matter Report

Source: Themis Solutions, Inc.

4. To end this Clio session, ***click the drop-down menu by your initials at the top of the screen. Click sign out and then close your Internet Browser.***

This concludes Lesson 3 on printing and retrieving Matter reports in Clio.

LESSON 4: Entering Notes for Matters

In this lesson, you will learn to enter notes for Matters in Clio. This is very convenient for recording any notes in the case. Notes allow you to document exactly what took place on client phone calls or mental impressions concerning meetings. Notes are used in many areas throughout the Clio system.

Note: If you are already logged in, you will skip Steps 1 and 2.

1. Start your Internet browser. Type www.goclio.com in the Internet browser and press the **[ENTER] key.**
2. On the Clio Home page, ***click Log In. On the next screen, enter the email address and password you provided in Clio and click SIGN IN. If you check the box next to KEEP ME SIGNED IN, you will be able to skip this step in the future.***
3. ***Click the Matters tab, then select 00003-Battise.**** At this point you have accessed the matter which opens on the INFO tab. Within each matter, new tabs are available to record details for a matter. See Clio Exhibit 4-7.

Clio Exhibit 4-7 Matter Tabs

Source: Themis Solutions, Inc.

4. ***Click the Notes tab***, then ***click Add.*** At this point you are ready to enter notes. Under Subject, type ***Client Initial Interview.*** Under Date, ***use current date.*** Under Note, ***enter the following information: Schedule a second meeting in one week.*** Then ***click Save.*** See Clio Exhibit 4-8

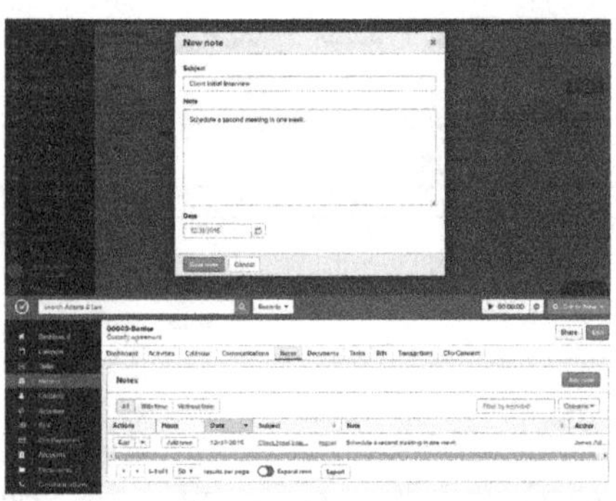

Clio Exhibit 4-8 Add Notes

Source: Themis Solutions, Inc.

5. At this point you can create a PDF report of your notes by ***clicking Export To File.***
6. To end this Clio session, ***click the drop-down menu by your initials at the top of the screen. Click sign out and then close your Internet Browser.***

This concludes Lesson 4 on entering notes for Matters in Clio.

This concludes the Clio Chapter 4 Client Relationship Hands-On Exercises.

5

Legal Fees, Timekeeping, and Billing

Chapter Objectives

After you read this chapter, you should be able to:

- Differentiate between timekeeping and billing.
- Recognize major types of legal fee agreements.
- Know the difference between billable and nonbillable time.
- Explain the concept of value billing.
- Discuss how the billing process works and what it entails.
- Differentiate between an earned and an unearned retainer.

When a New York-based law firm submitted its bill of $675,000 in fees, the client refused to pay. The law firm was hired to handle bankruptcy matters involving one of the client's companies. Despite being disqualified to represent the bankruptcy entity due to a conflict of interest, the law firm continued to work behind the scenes and charged the client fees of $675,000 for additional services. When the firm sued the client, he filed a counterclaim alleging he had overpaid and was overbilled for services that were unnecessary, duplicative, and wasteful.

***

During discovery, incriminating e-mails were uncovered that reflected the law firm's bill churning practice. Among those e-mails was the infamous "Churn that bill, baby!" e-mail that was acknowledged by the law firm. The counterclaim filed by the client requested return of the previous fee payment in the amount of $776,000.00 and punitive damages of $22.5 million against the law firm for their alleged wrongdoings. A confidential stipulation was reached.

Source: *DLA Piper, LLP (US) v. Adam Victor*, Index #650374/2012, State of New York, County of New York (filed February 9, 2012).

The Difference Between Timekeeping and Billing

timekeeping

The process of tracking time for the purpose of billing clients.

billing

The process of issuing invoices for the purpose of collecting monies for legal services performed and being reimbursed for expenses.

In the legal environment, **timekeeping** is the process of tracking time for the purpose of billing clients. The obvious reason private attorneys and paralegals keep track of their time is to bill clients. However, many corporate, government, and legal services/aid practices also keep time records for other reasons. Timekeeping can be used to manage and oversee what cases attorneys and paralegals are working on and whether they are spending too much or too little time on certain cases; it can be used to evaluate the performance of attorneys and paralegals and to help determine promotions and raises; and it also can be used to evaluate what types of cases are the most beneficial and profitable for the office.

Billing is the process of issuing invoices for the purpose of collecting monies for legal services performed and being reimbursed for expenses. The lifeblood of any organization depends on its ability to raise cash and be paid for the services it renders. In most cases, private law practices must be able to generate billings on at least a monthly basis to generate the cash they need to meet their expenses, such as rent, utilities, and salaries. Attorneys and paralegals in corporate and government practices also need to know about billing to ensure that when they hire outside counsel (private law firms), the corporation or government gets the most for its money.

Why Do Paralegals Need to Know Timekeeping and Billing?

There are several reasons why paralegals need to know about timekeeping and billing. In most private law practices, paralegals are required to track their time so it can be charged to the case(s) on which they are working. Many law practices require paralegals to bill a minimum number of hours a year. It is important to remember that private law firms are fundamentally businesses, and like any business, their function is to make money, operate at a profit, and earn money for their owners. Therefore, the billing of time to a firm's clients is crucial to its operations and success as a business. A recent survey of paralegals found that paralegals were most often expected to bill between 26 and 40 hours a week (1352 and 2080 annually). Thus, it is necessary for paralegals to understand how timekeeping and billing works. Paralegals are sometimes discharged from their jobs because they fail to bill the required number of hours. The issue of tracking time and billing a minimum number of hours is very important in many offices.

In addition, paralegals are sometimes put in charge of actually running the timekeeping and billing system, including managing the timekeeping process and generating bills. This usually occurs in smaller law offices. In those cases, it is important for paralegals not only to know the process but also to know how to actually run and operate the system. Timekeeping and billing are important issues because the survival of law offices depends on their ability to track and bill time. However, before exploring the fundamentals of timekeeping and billing in depth, you first need a background in legal fee agreements, legal expenses, and trust accounts.

Kinds of Legal Fee Agreements

Legal fees can be structured in many different ways. The kind of legal fee depends on the type of case or client matter, the specific circumstances of each particular client, and the law practice's preference toward certain types of fee agreements. Fee agreements can be hourly rate fees, contingency fees, flat fees, retainer fees, and others.

Hourly Rate Fees

hourly rate fee

A fee for legal services that is billed to the client by the hour at an agreed-upon rate.

An **hourly rate fee** is a fee for legal services that is billed to the client by the hour, at an agreed-upon rate. For example, suppose a client hires an attorney to draft a business contract. The client agrees to pay $250 for every hour the attorney spends drafting the contract and advising the client. If the attorney spent four hours working on the contract, the client would owe the attorney $1000 ($250 × four hours equals $1000).

One of the frustrations for clients regarding legal professionals billing by the hour is that a client has no idea what the total cost of the matter will be. Exhibit 5-1 contains a fee projection worksheet for a case in litigation. Using a tool like this at the beginning of a matter, a client can get an idea what the total cost will be.

Hourly rate agreements can be complicated. Law offices have several specific types of hourly rate contracts, including the following:

- Attorney or paralegal hourly rate
- Client hourly rate
- Blended hourly rate fee
- Activity hourly rate

Some law practices use a combination of these to bill clients.

attorney or paralegal hourly rate

Fee based on the attorney's or paralegal's level of expertise and experience in a particular area.

ATTORNEY OR PARALEGAL HOURLY RATE The **attorney or paralegal hourly rate** is based on the attorney's or paralegal's level of expertise and experience in a particular area; Exhibit 5-2

Exhibit 5-1 Fee Projection Worksheet

Based on: Calloway & Robertson (2002). Winning alternatives to the billable hour (p. 214). American Bar Association.

Adams & Lee Law Firm **Worksheet—Fee Projection (Civil Litigation)**

Date: ______________________

Case: ______________________

	Partner	Associate	Paralegal
Billing Rate	$350	$250	$90

No.	Activity Description	Partner Hours	Associate Hours	Paralegal Others
A.	Preliminary Work			
B.	Factual Investigation			
C.	Strategy Conference			
D.	Initial Legal Research			
E.	Complaint/Answer/Counterclaim			
F.	Motions (Nondiscovery)			
G.	Witness Interviews			
H.	Discovery			
	i. Drafting Interrogatories			
	ii. Answering Interrogatories			
	iii. Drafting Discover Requests			
	iv. Reviewing Produced Documents & E-Discovery			
	v. Responding to Document Requests			
	vi. Opposing Party Depos			
	vii. Our Depos			
I.	Discovery Motions			
J.	Additional Legal Research			
K.	Motions (Substantive)			
L.	Pretrial Memoranda/Conference			
M.	Settlement Conference			
N.	Trial (includes preparation days and actual trial days)			
O.	Miscellaneous phone calls/strategy			
	Total Hours			
	TOTAL PROJECTED FEES			

is an example of this type of contract. If a partner or shareholder worked on a case, his or her hourly rate charge might be considerably more than that of an associate or a paralegal's hourly rate charge. Partners typically can earn from $200 to $500 per hour. Paralegals typically charge from $60 to $100 per hour. The difference in price is based on the expertise of the individual working on the case and on locally acceptable rates. In this type of fee

HOURLY RATE CONTRACT FOR LEGAL SERVICES

This contract for legal services is entered into by and between H. David Green (hereinafter "Client") and Adams & Lee (hereinafter "Attorneys") on this ________________ day of December, 201_. The following terms and conditions constitute the entirety of the agreement between Attorneys and Client and said agreement supersedes and is wholly separate and apart from any previous written or oral agreements.

1. Client hereby agrees to employ Attorneys and Attorneys hereby agree to represent Client in connection with a contract dispute in Shelby County District Court of Clients claim against North Train Manufacturing.
2. Client agrees to pay a retainer fee of **$5,000.00**, which will be held in Attorney's trust account until earned.
3. Client agrees to pay associate attorneys at **$250** per hour, partners at **$350** per hour, paralegals at **$80** per hour and senior paralegals at **$100** per hour for legal services rendered regarding the matter in paragraph one. Attorneys are not hereby obligated to take an appeal from any judgment at the trial court level; if an occasion for an appeal arises, Attorneys and Client hereby expressly agree that employment for such an appeal must be arranged by a separate contract between Attorneys and Client.
4. Client agrees to reimburse Attorneys for all expenses incurred in connection with said matter; and Client agrees to advance all expenses requested by Attorneys during the duration of this contract. Client understands that he is ultimately responsible for the payment of all expenses incurred in connection with this matter.
5. Client understands that Attorneys will bill Client periodically (usually on a monthly or quarterly basis, depending on how quickly the case moves through the system) for copying costs at the rate of $.25 cents per copy, postage and handling costs, long-distance telephone costs, travel costs, and other costs, and that Client is obligated to make payments upon said billing for said fees and expenses described at paragraphs (2), (3), and (4) above, or otherwise satisfy said fees and expenses. Attorneys will also bill Client for all deposition costs incurred and Client is solely responsible for said deposition costs and Client will be required to advance the sum of $2,500 (or more as necessary) for trial costs (including subpoenas, travel costs, and preparation costs) once the case is set for trial.
6. Client understands and agrees that this litigation may take two to five years or longer to complete and that he will make himself available for Attorneys to confer with and generally to assist Attorneys in said matter. Client agrees he will not discuss the matter of his litigation with any unauthorized person at any time or in any way. Client understands and agrees that Attorneys may withdraw from representation of Client upon proper notice. Client further understands that he can apply for judicial review and approval of this fee agreement if he so desires.
7. Client agrees that associate counsel may be employed at the discretion of Attorneys and that any attorney so employed may be designated to appear on Client's behalf and undertake Client's representation in this matter and such representation shall be upon the same terms as set out herein. **Client understands that Attorneys cannot and do not guarantee any particular or certain relief and expressly state that they cannot promise or guarantee Client will receive any money damages or money settlement.**

The undersigned hereby voluntarily executes this agreement with a full understanding of same and without coercion or duress. All agreements contained herein are severable and in the event any of them shall be deemed to be invalid by any competent court, this contract shall be interpreted as if such invalid agreements or covenants were not contained herein. Client acknowledges receiving a fully executed copy of this contract.

________________ ____

Date

________________ ____

Date ADAMS & LEE

NOTE: THIS IS ONLY AN EXAMPLE AND IS NOT INTENDED TO BE A FORM; CHECK WITH YOUR STATE BAR FOR A PROPER FORM.

Exhibit 5-2 Attorney/Paralegal Hourly Rate Contract

agreement, it is possible for a client to be billed at several different rates in a given period if several attorneys or paralegals work on a matter, because they all may have different rates.

client hourly rate

Fee based on one hourly charge for the client, regardless of which attorney works on the case and what he or she does on the case.

CLIENT HOURLY RATE The **client hourly rate** method is based on one hourly charge for the client, regardless of which attorney works on the case and what he or she does on the case. For example, if an insurance company hires a law practice to represent it, the insurance company and the law practice might negotiate a client hourly charge of $225 for attorneys and $85 for paralegals. This means that no matter which attorney or paralegal works on the case, whether the attorney or paralegal has 1 year or 20 years of experience, and regardless of what the attorney or paralegal does (e.g., making routine phone calls or appearing in court), the insurance company would be charged $225 per hour for attorney time or $85 per hour for paralegal time.

blended hourly rate fee

An hourly rate that is set taking into account the blend or mix of attorneys working on the matter.

BLENDED HOURLY RATE FEE A **blended hourly rate fee** is an hourly rate that is set taking into account the blend or mix of law office staff working on the matter. The "blend" includes the mix among associates, partners, and (sometimes) paralegals working on the matter. Some states only allow the "blend" to include associates and partners, while other states allow paralegals to be included. Billing is simpler, because there is one rate for all paralegals and attorneys time spent on the case. The bill is thus easier for the law office to produce and easier for the client to read. Some states will allow paralegals to have their own "blend" and have one rate for all paralegals, whether experienced or inexperienced.

activity hourly rate

Fee based on the different hourly rates, depending on what type of service or activity is actually performed.

ACTIVITY HOURLY RATE An **activity hourly rate** is based on the different hourly rates, depending on what type of service or activity is actually performed. For example, offices using this approach might bill attorney time to clients as follows:

Court appearances	$300 per hour
Legal research by attorneys	$225 per hour
Drafting by attorneys	$200 per hour
Telephone calls by attorneys	$150 per hour
Legal research by paralegals	$85 per hour
Drafting by paralegals	$80 per hour

This is sliding-scale hourly fee based on the difficulty of an activity. Hourly rate agreements, no matter what the type, are the most common kind of fee agreement.

Contingency Fees

contingency fee

Fee collected if the attorney successfully represents the client.

A **contingency fee** is a fee that is collected if the attorney successfully represents the client. The attorney is entitled to a certain percentage of the total amount of money awarded to the client. If the client's case is not won, and no money is recovered, the attorney collects no legal fees but is still entitled to be reimbursed for all expenses incurred (see Exhibit 5-3). Contingency fees are typically used in representing plaintiffs in personal injury cases, workers' compensation cases, employment cases, medical malpractice, and other types of cases in which monetary damages are generated. The individual who would like to bring the lawsuit usually has little or no money to pay legal fees up front. Contingency fees typically range from 20% to 50%.

Exhibit 5-3
Contingency Fee Contract

CONTINGENCY FEE CONTRACT FOR LEGAL SERVICES

Date:

Name: D.O.B.

Address: Phone:

1. I hereby employ **Adams & Lee** (hereinafter "attorneys") to perform legal services in connection with the following matter as described below:
   Personal injury claims arising out of an automobile accident which occurred January 15, 2015, on Interstate I-55.
2. I agree to pay a nonrefundable retainer fee of $2,500 plus
3. I agree attorneys will receive 25% of any recovery, if prior to filing suit.
   I agree attorneys will receive 25% of any recovery, if prior to pretrial conference.
   I agree attorneys will receive 33% of any recovery, if after first trial begins.
   I agree attorneys will receive 40% of any recovery, if after appeal or second trial begins.
   Attorneys are not hereby obligated to take an appeal from any judgment at the trial court level; if an occasion for an appeal arises, attorneys and client hereby expressly agree that employment for such an appeal will be arranged by a separate contract between these parties. Further, I agree that attorneys will be entitled to the applicable above-mentioned percentage of recovery minus whatever a court may award, if I am a prevailing party and the court awards fees following my request therefor.
4. As to the expenses of litigation, I agree to reimburse attorneys for all expenses incurred in connection with said matter, and any expenses not fully paid as incurred may be deducted from my portion of any recovery. I agree to advance any and all expenses requested by attorneys during the duration of this contract. I agree to make an advance of expenses upon execution of this contract in the amount of $1,500. I understand that these litigation expenses do not pertain to the retainer fee or percentage of any recovery, and I am ultimately responsible for the payment of all litigation expenses.
5. I understand that attorneys will bill client periodically, and that client is obligated to make payments upon said billing for said fees and expenses described at paragraphs (2) and (4), or otherwise satisfy said fees and expenses.
6. I understand and agree that this litigation may take two to five years (or longer) to complete, and that I will make myself available for attorneys to confer with, and generally to assist attorneys in said matter. I will not discuss the matter of my litigation with an unauthorized person at any time in any way. I understand and agree that attorneys may withdraw from representation of client at any time upon proper notice.
7. I agree that associate counsel may be employed at the discretion of ADAMS & LEE, and that any attorney so employed may be designated to appear on my behalf and undertake my representation in this matter and such representation shall be upon the same terms as set out herein. Attorneys have not guaranteed, nor can they guarantee, any particular or certain relief.

The undersigned herewith executes this agreement with a full understanding of same, without coercion or duress, and understands the same to be the only agreement between the parties with regard to the above matter, and that if any other terms are to be added to this contract, the same will not be binding, unless and until they are reduced to writing and signed by all parties to this contract. I acknowledge receiving a fully executed copy of this contract. Further, the undersigned Client understands that said Client is entitled to apply for judicial review and approval of this fee agreement, if Client so desires.

________________ ______________________________

Date

________________ ______________________________

Date ADAMS & LEE

NOTE: THIS IS ONLY AN EXAMPLE AND IS NOT INTENDED TO BE A FORM; CHECK YOUR STATE BAR FOR A PROPER FORM.

For example, suppose a client hires an attorney to file a personal injury claim regarding an automobile accident the client was in. The client has no money but agrees to pay the attorney 20% of any money that is recovered (plus legal expenses) before the case is filed, 25% of any money that is recovered after the case is filed but before trial, and 33% of any money recovered during trial or after appeal. Suppose the claim is settled after the case is filed but before trial for $10,800. Suppose, also, that the legal expenses the attorney incurred were $800. Under most state laws, legal expenses are paid first and then the contingency fee is calculated. The attorney would deduct the expenses off the top and the remaining $10,000 would be divided according to the contingency fee agreement. Because the suit was settled after the case was filed but before the trial, the attorney would be entitled to receive 25% of any recovery. The attorney would be entitled to $2500 and the client would be entitled to 75%, or $7500 (see Exhibit 5-4).

Contingency fee agreements must be in writing. Exhibit 5-3 contains a sample contingency fee contract. Some states put a cap or a maximum percentage on what an attorney can collect in areas such as workers' compensation and medical malpractice claims; for example, some states prevent attorneys from receiving more than a 25% contingency in a workers' compensation case. Contingency fees, by their nature, are risky—if no money is recovered, the attorney receives no fee. However, even if no money is recovered, the client must still pay legal expenses, such as filing fees and photocopying. Contingency fees and hourly fees also may be used together; some offices reduce their hourly fee and charge a contingency fee.

Exhibit 5-4
Contingency Fee Example

Written Contingency Fee Agreement Provisions

Attorney receives

- 25% of any money recovered (plus legal expenses) before case is filed.
- 33% of any money recovered (plus legal expenses) after case is filed or during trial.
- 40% of any money recovered (plus legal expenses) after trial or second trial begins.

Settlement

Case is settled for $10,800 after case is filed, but before trial.
Attorney has $800 worth of legal expenses.

Calculation of Contingency Fee

1. Legal expenses are paid first.		
Settlement of		$10,800
Minus legal expenses		-800
Balance		$10,000
2. Contingency fee is calculated as follows:		
Total recovery minus legal expenses		$10,000
Attorney's 25% contingency fee ($10,000 × 25% = $2500)		-2500
	TOTAL TO CLIENT	$7500
3. Total fees and expenses to attorney		
Reimbursement of legal expense		$800
Contingency fee		$2500
	TOTAL TO ATTORNEY	$3300

Flat Fee

flat fee

A fee for legal services that is billed as a flat or fixed amount.

A **flat fee** is a fee for legal services that is billed as a flat or fixed amount. Some offices have a set fee for handling certain types of matters, such as preparing a will or handling an uncontested divorce, a name change, or a bankruptcy (see Exhibit 5-5). For example, suppose a client agreed to pay an attorney a flat fee of $500 to prepare a will. No matter how many hours the attorney spends preparing the will, the fee is still $500. Flat fee agreements are usually used when a legal matter is simple, straightforward, and involves few risks.

Exhibit 5-6 shows a comparison of different methods of billing for drafting a routine or standard will. Flat rates will typically be the least expensive for the client in routine matters. In addition, flat rates and the blended methods are typically the easiest types of bills to both prepare and read.

Retainer Fees

The word "retainer" has several meanings in the legal environment. Generally, retainer fees are monies paid by the client at the beginning of a case or matter. However, there are many types of retainers. When an attorney or a paralegal uses the term "retainer," it could mean a retainer for general representation, a case retainer, a pure retainer, or a cash advance. In addition, all retainer fees are either earned or unearned.

PRICE LIST

Initial Consultation with Branch Lawyer............$100.00

REAL ESTATE

Divorce - Uncontested.................................1000.00
Domestic contracts and family litigation vary according to time involved.

REAL ESTATE

Purchase or Sale of House............................1000.00
Each Mortgage—Additional...........................300.00
Each Discharge of Mortgage—Additional.........200.00
Refinancing..700.00

WILLS & ESTATES

Basic Will..500.00
Estates, administrations, and estate litigation vary according to time involved

BUSINESS

Consultation..200.00
Incorporation..2000.00
We provide many other business services, including:

- *Commercial Leases*
- *Purchase and Sale of Businesses*
- *Trade Marks & Copyright*

ADDITIONAL SERVICES

Collection—demand letter..............................200.00
Notarization (per signature).............................20.00
Power of Attorney / Promissory Note.................50.00

PAYMENT POLICY

We require a retainer before commencing work on your behalf, which amount is paid into trust. We then draw checks on the retainer to pay out-of-pocket expenses made on your behalf and our fees.

We will advise you of completion of our services to you and ask you to come in and pick up the documentation involved and pay any balance owing at the same time.

In real estate transaction the balance must be paid prior to closing. In litigation and criminal matters, any outstanding account and the estimated fee for the appearance must be paid prior to the court appearance.

ETHICAL NOTE: Even if the firm has a price list, legal assistants should leave the matter of fees to the attorney.

Exhibit 5-5 Flat Fee Price List

Activities Provided:

1. Paralegal interviews client (office conference) regarding the law office drafting a will for client. Paralegal gets background information including financial holdings, heirs, family tree, etc. .... 1.50 hours
2. Paralegal drafts memo to associate attorney, itemizing the conference with client .... 0.25 hours
3. Associate attorney reads the paralegal's memo and talks with client on the telephone .... 0.25 hours
4. Associate attorney conducts legal research and prepares a draft of the will that meets the expectations of the client .... 0.50 hours
5. Associate confers with senior partner regarding the will .... 0.50 hours
6. Client reviews will, holds office conf. with associate attorney, associate attorney discusses client's changes to the will, makes client's changes to the will, and the will is executed, witnessed, and notarized .... 1.0 hours

TOTAL HOURS .... 4.0 hours

- **CLIENT HOURLY RATE**

Assume attorney agrees to charge the client to prepare the will for his/her time as follows:

- $275 per hour for all attorney's time
- $90 per hour for his/her paralegal's time

TOTAL COST $845.00

(Paralegal 1.75 hours × $90 = $157.50; Attorney 2.50 × $275 per hour = $687.50; $157.50 + $687.50 = $845.00)

- **ATTORNEY/PARALEGAL HOURLY RATE**
- Assume the senior partner's normal hourly rate is $350.
- Assume the associate attorney's normal hourly rate is $250.
- Assume the paralegal's normal hourly rate is $80.

TOTAL COST $752.50

(Paralegal 1.75 hours × $80 per hour = $140; Associate attorney 1.75 hours × $250 per hour = $437.50; Senior partner 0.50 hour × $350 per hour = $175; $140 + $437.5 + $175 = $752.50)

- **BLENDED (Attorneys and Paralegal) HOURLY RATE**
- Assume blended hourly rate for all attorney and paralegal time is $175 per hour.

TOTAL COST $700 (4 hours × $175 per hour = $700).

ACTIVITY HOURLY RATE

Assume:

- Paralegal office conference rate is $70 per hour and for attorney is $200 per hour.
- Paralegal time for drafting memo is $80 per hour and for attorney is $225 per hour.
- Attorney time for phone conferences is $150 per hour.
- Attorney time for drafting pleadings, will, legal research, and conferring with other partners is $225 per hour.

TOTAL COST $587.50

1.5 × $70 = $105; 0.25 × $80 = $20; 0.25 × $150 = $37.50; 0.50 × $225 = $112.5; 0.50 × $225 = $112.50, 1.0 × $200 = $200; Total $587.50

FLAT FEE RATE

Assume attorney and client agree on a flat rate of $500 to prepare the will.

TOTAL COST $500.00

CONTINGENCY RATE $0.00 (No monetary recovery—not applicable)

Exhibit 5-6 Comparison Legal Fees to Prepare a Will

earned retainer

Term for the money the law office or attorney has earned and is entitled to deposit in the office's or attorney's own bank account.

EARNED V. UNEARNED RETAINERS There is a very important difference between an earned retainer and an unearned retainer. An **earned retainer** means that the law office or attorney, who has earned the money, is entitled to deposit it in the office's or attorney's own bank account, and can use it to pay the attorney's or law office's operating expenses, such as salaries, immediately upon deposit.

For example, suppose an attorney agrees to take a products liability case on a contingency fee basis, but requires that the client pay a nonrefundable (earned) retainer of $2000. The attorney drafts a contract and both parties sign it; the contract clearly states that the $2000 is nonrefundable. The earned, nonrefundable retainer is an incentive for the attorney to accept the case on a contingency basis. The attorney may deposit the $2000 in his or her law office checking account and pay operating expenses out of it. This is an example of a case retainer, which is discussed in more detail later in this section.

unearned retainer

Monies that are paid up front by the client as an advance against the attorney's future fees and expenses. Until the monies are actually earned by the attorney or law office, they belong to the client.

An **unearned retainer** is money that is paid up front by the client as an advance against the attorney's future fees and expenses as a kind of down payment. Until the monies are actually earned by the attorney or law office, they belong to the client. According to ethical rules, unearned retainers may not be deposited in the attorney's or law office's normal operating checking account; unearned retainers must be deposited into a separate trust account and can be transferred into the firm account as it is earned.

For example, suppose a business client wants to sue his or her insurance company for failing to pay a claim submitted by the business. The business signs a contract with the attorney to pay a (unearned) retainer of $10,000. The contract states that the $10,000 will be held in trust and paid to the attorney as the attorney incurs fees and properly bills the client. This is an example of a cash advance retainer, which is covered in more detail in the next section.

trust or escrow account

A separate bank account, apart from a law office's or an attorney's operating checking account, where unearned client funds are deposited.

A **trust or escrow account** is a separate bank account, apart from a law office or an attorney's operating checking account, where unearned client funds are deposited. Client trust accounts are covered in detail in Chapter 6. As an attorney or a law office begins to earn an unearned retainer by providing legal services to the client, the attorney can then bill the client and move the earned portion from the trust account to his or her own law office operating account.

The written contract should set out whether the retainer is earned or unearned. However, in some instances the contract may be vague on this point. Typically, when a contract refers to a "nonrefundable retainer," this means an earned retainer.

Additionally, flat fee rates, as discussed earlier, are said to be "nonrefundable" in many contracts, and thus are treated as earned. However, some state ethical rules regulate this area heavily and hold that all flat fees are a retainer, have been unearned, and must be placed in trust until they are earned. Whether a retainer is earned or unearned will depend on your state's ethical rules and on the written contract.

cash advance

Unearined monies that are the advance against the attorney's future fees and expenses.

CASH ADVANCE RETAINER One type of retainer is a **cash advance**, unearned monies that act as an advance against the attorney's future fees and expenses. Until the cash advance is earned by the attorney, it actually belongs to the client. The cash advance is a typical type of unearned retainer.

Suppose a client wishes to hire an attorney to litigate a contract dispute. The attorney agrees to represent the client only if the client agrees to pay $200 per hour with a $2500 cash advance against fees and expenses. The attorney must deposit the $2500 in a trust account. If the attorney deposits the cash advance into his or her own account (whether it is the firm's account or the attorney's own personal account), the attorney has violated several ethical rules. As the attorney works on the case and bills the client for fees and expenses, the attorney will write himself or herself a check out of the trust account for the amount of the billing. The attorney must tell the client that he or she is withdrawing the money, and keep an accurate balance of how much the client has left in trust. If the attorney billed the client for $500, the attorney would write himself a check for $500 from the trust account, deposit the $500 in the attorney's or the firm's own bank account, and inform the client that there was a remaining balance of $2000 in trust. If the case ended at this point, the client would be entitled to a refund of the remaining $2000 in trust. Look closely at the payment policy in Exhibit 5-5; the firm described requires a cash advance before it will take any case.

retainer for general representation

Retainer typically used when a client such as a corporation or entity requires continuing legal services throughout the year.

RETAINER FOR GENERAL REPRESENTATION Another type of retainer is a **retainer for general representation.** This type of retainer is typically used when a client such as a corporation or entity requires continuing legal services throughout the year. The client pays an amount, typically up front or on a prearranged schedule, to receive these ongoing services. For example, suppose a small school board would like to be able to contact an attorney at any time with general legal questions. The attorney and school board could enter into this type of agreement for a fee of $5000 every six months; the school board could contact the attorney at any time and ask general questions; and the attorney would never receive more than the $5000 for the six-month period. Retainers for general representation allow the client to negotiate and anticipate what his or her fee will be for the year. This type of agreement usually only covers general legal advice and would not include matters, such as litigation (see Exhibit 5-7). Depending on the specific arrangements between the client and the attorney, and on the specific ethical rules in your state, many retainers for general representation are viewed as being earned because the client can call at any time and get legal advice. Retainers for general representation resemble a flat fee agreement. The difference is that, in a flat fee agreement, the attorney or law office is contracted to do specific work for a client, such as prepare a will or file a bankruptcy. In the case of a retainer for general representation, the attorney is agreeing to make himself or herself available to the client for all nonlitigation needs.

case retainer

A fee that is billed at the beginning of a matter, is not refundable to the client, and is usually paid at the beginning of the case as an incentive for the office to take the case.

CASE RETAINER Another type of retainer is a **case retainer**, which is a fee that is billed at the beginning of a matter, is not refundable to the client, and is usually paid to the office at the beginning of the case as an incentive for the office to take the case. As an example, say that a client comes to an attorney with a criminal matter. The attorney agrees to take on the case only if the client agrees to pay a case retainer of $2000 up front plus $200 per hour for every hour worked on the case. The $2000 is paid to the attorney as an incentive to take the case and, thus, is earned. The $200 per hour is a client hourly basis charge. Because the case retainer is earned, the attorney can immediately deposit it in the office's own bank account.

A case involving a contingency fee presents another example of a case retainer. Suppose a client comes to an attorney to file a civil rights case. The attorney agrees to accept the case only if the client agrees to a 30% contingency fee and a nonrefundable or case retainer of $2000.

Exhibit 5-7
Retainer for General Representation Agreement

Ms Erin Smith, Chairperson
Shelby School District
No. 354 School Board

Subject: General Representation of the SSD No. 354 School Board

Dear Ms Smith:

Thank you for your letter informing us that the School Board would like to place our law firm on a general retainer of $____________ for the coming year. We will bill on a quarterly basis for the retainer plus any expenses incurred.

The retainer will include general advice concerning business operations, personnel questions, legislative initiative, and attendance at all board meetings. It will not cover litigated matters requiring appearances at boards or commissions, court, or state administrative agencies. Should any of the excluded services appear to be necessary, we shall be happy to discuss the cost of these services with you.

It is our hope that the knowledge that we are ready to serve you under the retainer will provide you with regular advice to avoid any serious problems or litigation. Please sign this letter and return it to us. If you have any questions, please feel free to give me a call.

Kindest Regards,

James Adams
ADAMS & LEE

Accepted for Shelby School District No. 354 School Board by:

____

Erin Smith, Chairperson

Again, the earned retainer is an incentive for the attorney to take the case and can be deposited in the attorney's or the office's own bank account.

pure retainer

A fee that obligates the office to be available to represent the client throughout the time period agreed upon.

PURE RETAINER A rather rare type of retainer is a **pure retainer**; a pure retainer obligates the law office to be available to represent the client throughout the agreed-upon time period. The part that distinguishes a pure retainer from a retainer for general representation is that the office typically must agree to not represent any of the client's competitors or to undertake any type of adverse representation to the client.

Retainers for general representation, case retainers, and pure retainers are usually earned retainers; a cash advance is an unearned retainer. However, the language of the contract will determine whether amounts paid to attorneys up front are earned or unearned. The earned/unearned distinction is extremely important, and it is one reason all fee agreements should be in writing.

Court-Awarded Fees

Court-awarded fees are another type of fee agreement. In certain federal and state statutes, the prevailing party (i.e., the party that wins the case) is given the right to recover from the opposing side reasonable attorney's fees. The amount of the attorney's fees is decided by the court; thus, these are called **court-awarded fees**. Court-awarded fees are provided for in civil rights law, antitrust, civil racketeering, and in many other instances and statutes as well. The prevailing party must submit to the court, detailed time records showing specifically how much time was spent on the case. If the prevailing law office does not keep such records, the court will not award fees. The purpose of court-awarded fees is to encourage potential plaintiffs in public interest issues to pursue legitimate claims while discouraging frivolous claims. For example, if an employee brings a sexual harassment suit against an employer and subsequently wins the suit, the employee's attorneys would be entitled to receive reasonable attorney's fees from the defendant.

court-awarded fees

Fees given to the prevailing parties pursuant to certain federal and state statutes.

Prepaid Legal Services

A prepaid legal service plan is another type of fee agreement. **Prepaid legal service** is a plan that a person can purchase, which entitles the person to receive legal services (as enumerated in the plan) either free or at a greatly reduced rate. In some cases, corporations or labor unions, for example, provide a prepaid legal service plan to their employees as a fringe benefit. For instance, if a person who is a member of a prepaid legal service plan needs a will drafted, that person would go to either an attorney employed by the prepaid plan—or a private attorney with whom the prepaid plan contracted—and get the will drafted free of charge or at a greatly reduced rate.

prepaid legal service

A plan that a person can purchase that entitles the person to receive legal services either free or at a greatly reduced rate.

Value Billing

Over time, there have been plenty of discussions about why private law practices should stop billing by the hour and use a different billing method instead. The arguments for the change from hourly billing include the following:

- During any stage of the work, the client never knows the total amount they will be charged for legal fees.
- Clients sometimes avoid calling paralegals and attorneys, even it is a simple phone call, because they know they will be charged for the time.
- Clients have trouble seeing the relationship between what is performed by the paralegal or attorney and the enormous fees that can be generated.
- Hourly billing encourages lawyers and paralegals to be inefficient (i.e., the longer it takes to perform a job, the more revenue they earn).
- Many law offices force attorneys and paralegals to bill a quota number of hours a year, which puts a tremendous amount of pressure on the individual paralegal and attorney.

So what is value billing? The **value billing** concept represents a type of fee agreement that is based not on the time required to perform the work but on the basis of the perceived value of the services to the client. Value billing typically provides that the attorney and client reach a consensus on the amount of fees to be charged. Because of increased competition in the legal environment and because of the power of the client as a buyer, clients are demanding that they have a say in how much they are going to pay for legal services, what type of service will be provided, and what the quality of the legal notice services will be for the price.

value billing

A type of fee agreement that is based not on the time spent to perform the work but on the basis of the perceived value of the services to the client.

The Ethics of Timekeeping and Billing

There are more timekeeping- and billing-related ethical complaints filed against attorneys and law offices than all other types of complaints; thus, paralegals should completely understand the ethics of timekeeping and billing. In past years, timekeeping and billing complaints were viewed simply as "misunderstandings" between the client and the law office. Recently, state bars have viewed timekeeping and billing disputes as having major ethical implications for attorneys; that is, such disputes were simply not misunderstandings, but law offices were sometimes flagrantly violating ethical rules regarding money issues.

Billing from the Corporate and Government Perspective

outside counsel

Term referring to when corporate and government law practices contract with law offices (i.e., outside of the corporation or government practice) to help them with legal matters, such as litigation, specialized contracts, stock/bond offerings, and so forth.

Corporate and governmental law practices sometimes hire outside counsel (private law offices). **Outside counsel** refers to when corporate and government law practices contract with private law offices (i.e., outside of the corporation or government practice) to help them with legal matters, such as litigation, specialized contracts, stock/bond offerings, and so forth. Thus, corporate and government law practices are purchasers of legal services and tend to look at billing from a different perspective.

Corporate and government law practices are concerned with limiting the costs of legal fees. Many corporate clients will state that they will not pay more than a certain amount—perhaps $200 per hour—for any attorney, regardless of experience. If the office wants to maintain the particular client, it will agree to the terms. Because corporations and governments have access to large sums of money and typically are good-paying clients, many offices will reduce their price to get and keep the business.

Corporate and government clients usually require very detailed bills to control costs and what is being done on the case; in some cases, corporations and governments use a competitive bidding process to select outside counsel. Thus, summary billings are usually not accepted. They also will typically limit the type and cost of expenses that are billed to them. For instance, some corporations require that computerized legal research (Westlaw, LexisNexis, etc.), postage, fax costs, and similar expenses be borne by the office.

It is not uncommon for a corporate law practice to publish policies and guidelines covering exactly what outside counsel will charge, when it will charge, how payments will be made, how much and what type of legal expenses will be reimbursed, and so on. Exhibit 5-8 shows the top 10 reasons corporate law departments fail to pay private law offices.

Timekeeping and billing complaints by clients can lead not just to ethical complaints against attorneys, but may also turn into criminal fraud charges filed against attorneys and paralegals.

Ethical Considerations Regarding Legal Fee Agreements

There are several important ethical considerations that need to be stressed about fee agreements. The first is that all fee agreements should be in writing, especially when a contingency fee is involved. Second, contingency fees should not be used in criminal- or domestic-relation matters.

Fee Agreements Should Be in Writing

It is highly recommended that, as a matter of course, all fee agreements be in writing. The days of a handshake cementing an agreement between an attorney and a client are long over.

Exhibit 5-8 Reasons Why Corporate Law Departments and Government Legal Departments Sometimes Refuse to Negotiate on Legal Bills

Reason	Explanation
Legal services are below standard	The legal services provided were below standard or did not meet the needs of the corporate client. Corporate law departments typically attempt to negotiate down the fees. In these instances, the corporate law department staff must take the time to correct the problems, even though they paid to have it done correctly.
Too many attorneys and paralegals working the case	When multiple timekeepers attend the same deposition or bill for the same work provided, the costs rise quickly. Many corporate law departments try to set limits on the number of timekeepers working on a case at one time. Also, if the attorneys or paralegals, who are working on the case, change, the client must pay for the new attorneys or paralegals to get up to speed.
Billing lacks detail	Most law departments want to see detailed reports of how timekeepers spent their time and not just "for legal services provided."
Billing is incomplete	A bill does not include previous payments made or is otherwise incomplete.
Billing has numerical errors	The bill does not add up, or wrong billing rates are used.
Sticker shock	The corporate law department expects a bill for $5000 and receives a bill for $25,000.
Attorneys and paralegals conferencing with each other frequently	It is frustrating for a client to receive a bill where attorneys and paralegals are frequently meeting to discuss strategy or otherwise, because this greatly increases the client's bill. This is particularly frustrating for the client when the bill does not say why the staff members working on the case were meeting.
Billing sent to the wrong person	Sending the bill to the wrong person can be frustrating in a large corporation. The bill can literally get lost inside the corporation unless the bill is sent to the correct person.
Billing every little thing	Clients strongly dislike being billed for every five-minute phone call, being billed for the time it takes to prepare the bill itself, or other items that—in the big picture—do not amount to much.
Being billed for another case	Occasionally, a client is billed for time spent on another case. This undermines the whole billing process.
Billing is received late	Corporate clients become frustrated when they receive a bill for services that were delivered five months ago. Not only is the billing late, but it is difficult to remember that far back as to the details of the service.

There is no substitute for reducing all fee agreements to writing. If the firm and the client have a dispute over fees, the document will clarify the understanding between the parties.

Rule 1.5(b) regarding the rules of professional conduct states that an attorney is required to provide a client with the rate for fees and expenses along with the basis for charging those rates and communicate the scope of representation. The rule recommends, but does not require the communication be written.

Although the rules of professional conduct state that the agreement should "preferably" be in writing, nearly every authority on this subject, as well as most attorneys will tell you that the agreement absolutely should be in writing to protect both the attorney and the client. Legal fee agreements should be in writing for the following reasons:

1. Clients file more ethical complaints against attorneys and law offices for fee disputes than for any other type of complaint.
2. The client and the attorney may (will) forget what the exact fee agreement was, unless it is reduced to writing.
3. In a factual dispute regarding a fee between a client and an attorney, the evidence is typically construed in the light most favorable to the client.

CONTINGENCY FEE AGREEMENT MUST BE IN WRITING When a contingency fee is involved, most jurisdictions state that the agreement *shall* be in writing for the office to collect the fee. *Rule 1.5(c)* regarding the rules of professional conduct state that the contingency fee agreement must be in writing, state the contingency fee arrangement, along with client responsible expenses and how the expenses will be deducted and the client must sign the agreement. It also requires the attorney to give the client a final written statement specifically explaining the recovery amount, how it was determined and the allocation of the monies received.

Even the *Model Rules* makes a distinction between contingency agreements and other types of fee agreements, and requires that contingency agreements be in writing. It must be in writing because, in many cases, large sums of money are recovered, and the difference between 20% and 30% may be tens of thousands of dollars. Contingency agreements are risky for the attorney, and they simply must be reduced to writing so that the client and the attorney know what the proper percentage of fees should be. It is also important that the contingency agreement state, and the client understand, that even if there is no recovery in the case, the client must still pay for expenses.

NO CONTINGENCY FEES IN CRIMINAL AND DOMESTIC-RELATION PROCEEDINGS IN SOME JURISDICTIONS Many jurisdictions prohibit contingency fees in criminal and domestic-relation proceedings as a matter of public policy. *Rule 1.5(d)* regarding the rules of professional conduct specifically states that an attorney shall not enter into a contingency fee arrangement regarding domestic relations or criminal matters. For example, suppose that an attorney agrees to represent a client in a criminal matter. The client agrees to pay the attorney $10,000 if the client is found innocent, but the attorney will receive nothing if the client is found guilty. This is an unethical contingency fee agreement; contingency fees in these types of cases appear to be against the public policy and should be prohibited.

Only a "Reasonable" Fee Can Be Collected

No matter what the contract or legal fee agreement is with a client, it is important to keep in mind that attorneys and paralegals can only receive a "reasonable" fee. Unfortunately, there is no absolute standard for determining reasonableness, except that reasonableness will be determined on a case-by-case basis.

Rules 1.5 regarding the rules for professional conduct along with cases on the subject have provided numerous factors to consider in determining reasonableness regarding fees. These factors include the following:

- the amount of time and labor required;
- the novelty or difficulty of the issues raised;
- the skill required to perform the legal services;
- the acceptance of the case and whether it would preclude the attorney from taking other cases;
- the local "going rate" or fee customarily charged in the area for the services performed;
- the end result of the case (how successful the representation was);
- the time limitations imposed by the client or by the circumstances;
- the professional relationship with the client, including past dealings or history with the client;
- the experience of the attorney;
- the attorney's reputation and/or the ability of the lawyer (or lawyers) performing the services;
- the type of fee agreement, including whether the fee was fixed or contingent.

Notably, courts have found certain fee amounts unreasonable, such as a $22,500 fee, pursuant to a written agreement for a real estate matter that was not unduly complex and involved very little time for the attorney.

For many years, it was thought that overbilling and stealing from clients by attorneys was only done by sole practitioners and attorneys in small firms. However, court rulings on this subject indicate these practices happen at all levels.

> *In John Grisham's modern classic,* The Firm, *Avery Tolar advises the young lawyer Mitchell McDeere on how to charge clients, explaining that the client should be charged for "every minute spent even thinking about a case." It was this philosophy that got the legal team into trouble. Unethical billing practices do not only exist in legal novels like* The Firm *but have been a pervasive problem in law firms across the country.*
>
> *James Dougherty, a Florida attorney was disbarred for five years after turning in padded bills for an insurance investigation and overcharging a client by more than $2 million. The Court found that Dougherty overbilled by $300,000 for his own work, by $1.2 million for the work of his associates, and by over $1.2 million for expenses. The court held that "[f]ederal felony convictions for wire fraud by overbilling [the] client ... warranted disbarment for five years.*
>
> *—The Florida Bar v. Dougherty,* 769 So.2d. 1027 (Fla. 2000).

Many State Bars' Rules Provide for Oversight/Arbitration on Fee Issues

One of the ways that state bar associations and courts have dealt with the abundance of fee disputes is to provide for immediate and informal review/arbitration of fee disputes. Many state ethical and court rules provide that clients have the right, at any time, to request that the judge in the case or an attorney representing the state bar review the reasonableness of the attorney's fees. The attorney is required to inform the client of this right in many states; in those states, the judge or attorney hearing the matter has the right to set the fee and determine what is reasonable under the particular facts and circumstances of the case.

Fraud and Criminal Charges

Intentionally overbilling clients for work not done is called "fraud." You can be criminally prosecuted by government officials and civilly prosecuted by your clients.

Charging an unreasonable fee is no longer simply a matter of ethics. Recently, attorneys and paralegals have been criminally charged with fraud for intentionally recording time and sending bills for legal services that were never provided. **Criminal fraud** is a false representation of a present or past fact made by the defendant, upon which the victim relies, resulting in the victim suffering damages.

criminal fraud

A false representation of a present or past fact made by a defendant.

Criminal charges for fraud are not filed against attorneys and paralegals when there is simply a disagreement over what constitutes a reasonable fee. Criminal charges are filed when an attorney or a paralegal acts intentionally to defraud clients. This usually happens when the attorney or paralegal bills for time when he or she did not really work on the case, or in instances in which the office intentionally billed a grossly overstated hourly rate far above the market rate.

Interestingly, many of the most recent criminal cases being brought are against well-respected large and small law offices specializing in insurance defense and corporate work. Some insurance companies and corporations, as a matter of course when a case has been concluded, hire an audit firm or independent attorney to go back and audit the firm's billing and files to be sure they were billed accurately. In some instances, these audits have concluded that intentional criminal fraud has occurred and have been referred to prosecutors where criminal charges have been filed. No matter what type of firm is involved, intentionally overstating bills can lead to very big problems.

Ethical Problems

There are several difficult ethical problems with no definite solutions regarding timekeeping and billing that need to be explored. The rule in answering ethical questions such as these is to use your common sense and notions of fairness and honesty.

BILLING MORE THAN ONE CLIENT FOR THE SAME TIME, OR "DOUBLE BILLING" A situation happens from time to time in which a paralegal or an attorney has the opportunity to bill more than one client for the same time period. For instance, while you are monitoring the opposing side's inspection of your client's documents in case A, you are drafting discovery for case B. Another example, while traveling to attend an interview with a witness in case A, you work on case B.

If you were the client, would you think it fair for the attorney to charge full price for travel time related to your case while billing another case? A reasonable approach is to bill only the case on which you are actively working on, split the time between the cases, or bill the case you are actively working on at the regular hourly rate and bill the case you are inactively working on at a greatly reduced rate. Be fair and honest; your clients, as well as judges and others looking at the time, will respect you for it.

WHEN BILLING BY THE HOUR, IS THERE AN ETHICAL OBLIGATION TO BE EFFICIENT? DOES THE FIRM HAVE TO HAVE A FORM FILE IN LIEU OF RESEARCHING EACH DOCUMENT EACH TIME? MUST AN OFFICE USE A COMPUTER TO SAVE TIME? These types of ethical questions are decided on a case-by-case basis. Billing by the hour rewards people who work slowly, since the more slowly they work, the more they are paid.

Common sense says that if you were the client, you would want your legal staff to be efficient and not to "milk" you for money. The real issue is whether the attorney or paralegal acted so inefficiently and charged so much—when compared with what a similar attorney or paralegal with similar qualifications would charge in the same community—that the fee is clearly unreasonable. When a judge rules on the reasonableness of fees, there is no doubt that he or she will consider what a reasonably efficient attorney or paralegal in the same circumstances would have charged. Use your common sense and be honest and efficient, because someone in your office might have to justify your time and charges someday.

SHOULD YOU BILL FOR CLERICAL OR SECRETARIAL DUTIES? Law offices cannot bill clients for clerical or secretarial tasks, because these tasks are viewed as overhead costs or are considered a normal part of doing business. An easy but unethical way to bill more hours is for a paralegal to bill time to clients for clerical functions such as copying documents or filing material. Paralegals clearly should not bill for these types of clerical tasks; paralegals bill time for professional services, not for clerical functions.

This issue was addressed in the United States Supreme Court case of *Missouri v. Jenkins*, 491 U.S. 274, 109 S.Ct. 2463, 105 L.Ed. 2d 229 (1989). The Court found that when paralegals perform professional level work, these hours are recoverable as "attorney's fees," but services that are merely clerical or secretarial cannot be billed. The Court held

> It has frequently been recognized in the lower courts that paralegals are capable of carrying out many tasks, under the supervision of an attorney that might otherwise be performed by a lawyer and billed at a higher rate. Such work might include, for example, factual investigation, including locating and interviewing witnesses; assistance with depositions, interrogatories, and document production; compilation of statistical and financial data; checking legal citations; and drafting correspondence .... Of course, purely clerical or secretarial tasks should not be billed at a paralegal rate, regardless of who performs them. (p. 288)

If you are unsure about whether a task is clerical, ask your supervising attorney or record the time initially, point it out to the supervising attorney, and let him or her decide.

SHOULD YOU BILL FOR THE MISTAKES OF THE LAW OFFICE? This is another tough problem. People make mistakes all the time. Clients generally feel that they should not have to pay for mistakes, since the reason they went to an attorney was to get an expert to handle their situation. This is a decision that should be left to every law office to decide, but generally the practice of billing for mistakes should be discouraged.

MUST A TASK BE ASSIGNED TO LESS EXPENSIVE SUPPORT STAFF WHEN POSSIBLE? Common sense and efficiency will tell you that tasks should be delegated as low as possible. Clients should not have to pay for attorney time when the task could be completed by an experienced paralegal. In addition, this practice is more profitable to the law office because higher paid persons are free to do tasks for which they can bill clients at their normal rates.

Legal Expenses

In addition to recovering for legal fees, law practices are also entitled to recover from the client reasonable expenses incurred by the office in representing the client. For example, in Exhibit 5-9, the office needed to make copies of a motion to compel and mail them to opposing counsels. The cost of making the copies of the motion and mailing them out is directly related to the case, so the office is entitled to be reimbursed from the client for this expense. In most offices, it is important that the client is billed for the expense either through manual records, as in Exhibit 5-9, or some type of computerized or automated system. Such expenses typically include the costs of photocopying documents, postage, long-distance telephone calls, or travel expenses (see Exhibit 5-10).

The expenses alone can run into the tens of thousands of dollars in cases involving litigation. Therefore, the careful tracking of expenses is no trivial matter. Consider the revenues that would be generated if you billed copies at 25 cents and the office made 80,000 copies a year directly related to clients; this would be $20,000. Consider also the additional overhead an office would have if it did not bill clients for the copies.

As a paralegal, you may be required to pay expenses for a case out of your own pocket from time to time. If this happens, be sure to ask for receipts. It also helps to know in advance what specific expenses the office will reimburse you for before they are incurred.

Exhibit 5-9
Expense Slip

Adams & Lee
Expense Slip

Expense Type & Code			
1 Photocopies	4 Filing Fees	7 Facsimile	10 Travel
2 Postage	5 Witness Fees	8 Lodging	11 Overnight Delivery
3 Long Distance	6 Westlaw/LexisNexis	9 Meals	12 Other _______________

Exhibit 5-10
Expenses Typically Billed to Clients

Court reporter fees (deposition transcripts)
Delivery charges (FedEx, etc.)
Expert witness fees
Facsimile costs
Filing fees
Long-distance phone calls
Photocopying
Postage
Travel expenses
Westlaw/LexisNexis
Witness fees

Timekeeping

Timekeeping is the process of tracking what attorneys and paralegals do with their time. Although this might seem like an incredibly easy task, it is not. Timekeeping is a necessary evil in most law practices. Keeping careful time records is important both for managerial reasons and for producing income.

From a managerial perspective, time records (1) provide the office with a way to monitor the progress of a case, who is working on the case, and/or who is responsible for the matter; (2) allow the office to determine which cases are the most profitable; and (3) allow office management to monitor the efficiencies of law practice staff.

From an income-producing perspective, time records (1) allow offices to bill their time to clients and (2) allow the office to document its fees in probate matters and in cases where legal fees will be decided by a court.

Notice that managerial reasons could apply to any type of law practice, including corporate, government, or legal services/aid. It is also not uncommon for corporate, government, and legal services/aid practices to be given court-awarded attorney's fees from time to time.

time sheet or time slip

A record of detailed information about the legal services professionals provide to each client.

Exhibit 5-11 is an example of a manual time sheet. A **time sheet** or **time slip** is where legal professionals record detailed information about the legal services they provide to each client. Timekeeping entries must contain information, such as the name of the case, the date the service was provided, and a description of the service.

Manual Timekeeping

There are many different types of manual timekeeping methods that can be purchased from most legal law office supply catalogs. The time slips are recorded chronologically and are completed by different billing people within the office for a variety of different cases. At some point, typically once a week, the time slips are turned in to the billing department by everyone in the office. Each individual slip can be separated and is often designed with adhesive on the back. Each slip is separated and stuck to each client's time-slip page (see Exhibit 5-12); this provides a convenient method for tracking time for each client. All clients' time-slip pages can be stored in a three-ring notebook in alphabetical order by client name, or stored in each individual client's accounting file.

It is important to point out that time records do not automatically get charged to clients. The supervising attorney in the case typically reviews the time records turned in and determines whether they will be charged as is, or whether the time should be adjusted upward or downward. It should also be noted that it is common to have clients with more than one matter pending. Separate records need to be kept for each matter, and typically, separate invoices are generated. Most manual timekeeping systems are being replaced with computerized methods, even in very small law firms.

Computerized Timekeeping

Nearly all timekeeping and billing computer programs can provide assistance in keeping track of time. In some programs, the user enters what case is being worked on and whether the

PC—Phone Conference
LR—Legal Research
L—Letter
D—Dictation

R—Review
OC—Office Conference
T—Travel
CT—Court Hearing

Time Conversion

6 Minutes = .1 Hour	36 Minutes = .6 Hour
12 Minutes = .2 Hour	42 Minutes = .7 Hour
15 Minutes = .25 Hour	45 Minutes = .75 Hour
18 Minutes = .3 Hour	48 Minutes = .8 Hour
24 Minutes = .4 Hour	54 Minutes = .9 Hour
30 Minutes = .5 Hour	60 Minutes = 1.0 Hour

Date	Client/Case	File No.	Services Performed	Attorney	Time Hours & Tenths	
6-18-15	Jones v. United Sales	18294	Summarized 6 depositions; Client; Δ (Defendant) Heler; Δ Barnes, Δ Rosalie; Witness Forham & Johns	JBD	6.	5
6-19-15	Marcel v. Green Oil	18003	PC w/Client Re: Settlement offer; Discussions w/Attorney; Memo to file Re: offer	JBD	.	3
6-19-15	Jolly v. State	18118	PC w/Client's Mother, PC w/Client; LR Re: Bail; Memo to file; R correspondence	JBD	.	75
6-19-15	Potential claim of Walters v. Leslie Nursery	Not Assigned Yet	OC w/Client; (New client); Reviewed facts; Received medical records Re; accident; Conf. w/atty	JBD	1.	50
6-19-15	Jones v. United Sales	18294	Computerized searches on depositions for attorney	JBD	.	75
9-5-15	Jay Mahoney Bankruptcy	18319	PC w/Creditor, Capital One; Memo to file; Client; LJ to Client	JBD	.	3
9-5-15	Potential Claim of Walters v. Leslie Nursery	—	LR Slip & Fall cases generally; Standard of care	JBD	1.	00
9-5-15	Marcel v. Green Oil	18003	Conf. w/atty. & Client Re: Settlement; Drafted & prepared LJ to Δ's Re: Settlement offer	JBD	1.	10
9-5-15	Jay Mahoney Bankruptcy	18319	Drafted Bankruptcy petition; OC w/Client; List of Debts; Fin. Stmt; Conf. w/atty	JBD	1.	00
9-5-15	Jones v. United Sales	18294	Drafted and prepared depo notice to Witness Autumn	JBD	.	25
9-5-15	Seeley Real Estate Matter	18300	Ran amortization schedule to attach to 'Contract for Deed'	JBD	.	25

Exhibit 5-11 Typical Manual Time Slip/Time Record Form

Time Records for Case Name: *Jones v. United Sales* Case No: *18294*

6-19-15	Jones v. United Sales	18294	Summarized 6 depositions; Client; Δ(Defendant) Heler; Δ Barnes, ΔRosalie; Witness Forham & Johns	JBD	6.	5
6-19-15	Jones v. United Sales	18294	Computerized searches on depositions for attorney	JBD	.	75
9-5-15	Jones v. United Sales	18294	Drafted and prepared depo notice to Witness Autumn	JBD	.	25

Exhibit 5-12 Time Sheet Record for a Case

time is billable or nonbillable and then turns the "meter" on. The computer keeps track of the time until the user is completed with the project for that client. The computerized time slip is then stored in the program until a bill is generated. When a bill is generated, the computerized time slip is automatically calculated and included in the client's bill. Exhibit 5-13 is an example of a computerized time slip.

Billable v. Nonbillable Time

billable time

Actual time that a paralegal or an attorney spends working on a case and that is directly billed to a client's account.

nonbillable time

Time that cannot be directly billed to a paying client.

One of the basics of timekeeping is the difference between billable and nonbillable time. **Billable time** is actual time that a paralegal or an attorney spends working on a case and that is directly billed to a client's account. Any activity that an attorney or a paralegal performs further to a client's case, other than clerical functions, is usually considered billable time, including interviewing witnesses, investigating a case, serving subpoenas, performing legal research, drafting, and so forth. **Nonbillable time** is the time that cannot be directly billed to a paying client. Nonetheless, it should still be tracked.

There are typically three types of nonbillable time:

(1) general firm activities
(2) personal time
(3) pro bono work

pro bono

Legal services that are provided free of charge to a client who is not able to pay for the services.

General firm activities refer to time spent on personnel materials, planning, marketing, client development, staff/committee meetings, library maintenance, and professional development. Personal time refers to taking breaks, cleaning and organizing, and taking sick/vacation days. **Pro bono** work is legal services that are provided free of charge to a client who is not able to pay for the services. Pro bono may be required by your firm or by some state bars. Typically, pro bono cases are taken to generate goodwill in the community for the office or to provide a community service. Although handling pro bono cases is a morally proper thing to do, it is still counted as nonbillable time.

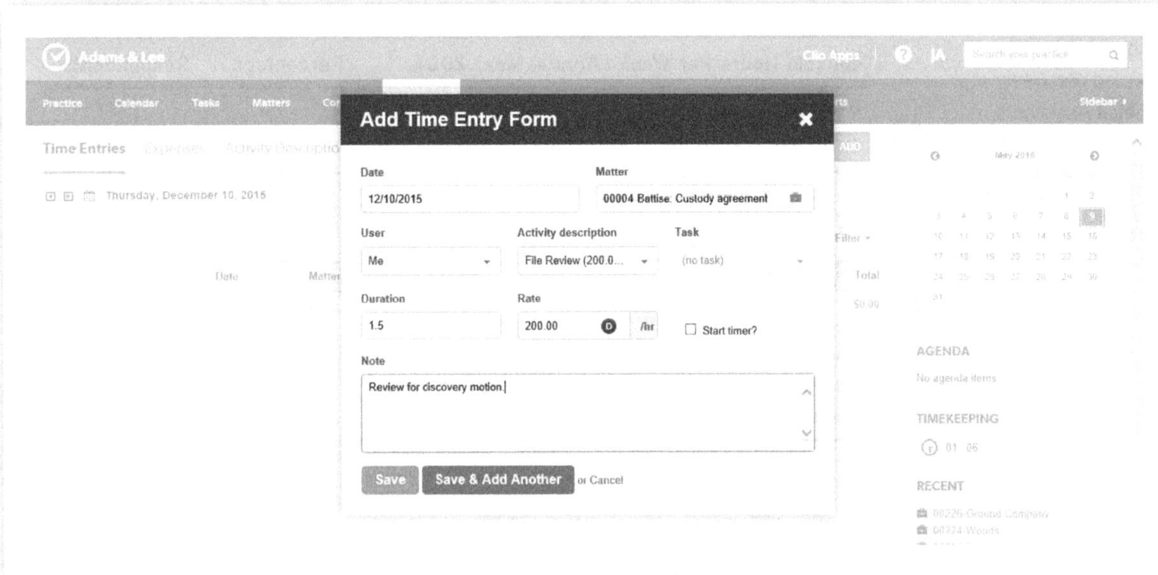

Exhibit 5-13 Computerized Time Slip

Source: Themis Solutions, Inc.

overhead

General administrative costs of doing business, including costs such as rent, utilities, phone, and salary costs for administrators.

Nonbillable time is sometimes referred to as "overhead" or "office hours" because the cost of nonbillable time must be paid for by the office. **Overhead** refers to general administrative costs of doing business; they are incidental costs regarding the management and supervision of the business. Overhead includes costs such as rent, utilities, phones, office supplies, equipment, and salary costs for administrators who manage the business and others. Overhead costs are sometimes defined as any cost not directly associated with the production of goods or services.

Timekeeping for Paralegals

Many law offices have a preoccupation with the billable hour concept and set billable hour quotas that paralegals must meet (see Exhibit 5-14). During the past decade the average number of annual billable hours for paralegals ranges from 520 to more than 2340; most paralegals must bill between 1400 and 1800 hours annually. Historically, this was not the case. In the early 1960s, 1300 billable hours was thought to be realistic. The minimum number of billable hours depends greatly on the location and size of the law office and on the types of cases it handles. In 2015, the survey related to billable hours found that most paralegal work 40 hours per week and are expected to bill about 30 hours per week. When accepting a job, you should understand exactly what the expectation is regarding the billable hours. There is obviously a big difference in the quality of life between billing 1400 hours and 1800 hours.

Exhibit 5-14
Billable Hours Expected per Week for Legal Assistants

Source: National Association of Paralegals, 2015 National Utilization and Compensation Survey Report, Table 3.2, Billable Hours Expected Per Week, Data.

Billable Hours Per Week (Annual Max) 2004	Percentage	Respondents
6–10 hours (520 hours)	1%	2
11–15 hours (780 hours)	1%	2
16–20 hours (1040 hours)	4%	15
21–25 hours (1300 hours)	9%	33
26–30 hours (1560 hours)	31%	111
31–35 hours (1820 hours)	31%	112
36–40 hours (2080 hours)	17%	61
41–45 hours (2340 hours)	1%	3
More than 45 hours	7%	25
Billable Hours Per Week (Annual Max) 2015: 26-35 hours (1560–1820 hours)	25%	125

Recording Time

There are several different ways to actually record or track your time. One method is to bill time in tenths of an hour, with 0.5 being a half-hour and 1.0 being an hour. Every six minutes is a tenth of the hour, so you would be billing on six-minute intervals. Billing in tenths works out as follows:

0–6 minutes = 0.1 hour
7–12 minutes = 0.2 hour
13–15 minutes = 0.25 hour
16–18 minutes = 0.3 hour
19–24 minutes = 0.4 hour
25–30 minutes = 0.5 hour
31–36 minutes = 0.6 hour
37–42 minutes = 0.7 hour
43–45 minutes = 0.75 hour
46–48 minutes = 0.8 hour
49–54 minutes = 0.9 hour
55–60 minutes = 1.0 hour

As an alternative, some offices will bill using a quarter of an hour as the basis, as follows:

0–15 minutes = 0.25 hour
16–30 minutes = 0.50 hour
31–45 minutes = 0.75 hour
46–60 minutes = 1.0 hour

Although the quarterly basis is easier to use, it is not as accurate as the tenth-of-an-hour system. Suppose you took a five-minute phone call from a client and your average billing rate is $80 per hour. Using the tenth of an hour system, the fee for the phone call would be $8 (0.1 hour × $80 equals $8). However, using the quarterly system, the fee for the phone call would be $20.00, since 0.25 is the smallest interval (0.25 × $80 equals $20.00), or more than twice as much.

It is important that you include as much detail as possible when completing your time records, that the language be clear and easily understood, and that the time record itself be legibly written. Clients are usually more willing to pay a bill when they know exactly what service was performed for them. For example, compare these general bill statements.

1. "Telephone conference—0.50 hour $40.00."
2. "Telephone conference with client on Plaintiff's Request for Production of Documents regarding whether or not client has copies of the draft contracts at issue—0.50 hour $40.00."

Which of these statements would you rather receive?

Many clients would prefer the latter, since they are able to see, and hopefully remember, exactly what specific services they received.

Timekeeping Practices

If the average paralegal is required to bill between 1400 and 1800 hours a year, it is very important that he or she take the timekeeping function extremely seriously. The following are some suggestions to consider regarding keeping track of time.

- *Find out how many hours you must bill annually, monthly, and weekly up front, and track where you are in relationship to the quota*—one of the first things you should do when you start a new paralegal job is to find out how many billable hours you must have. If the office requires that you bill 1400 hours a year, budget this on a monthly and weekly basis, and keep track of where you are so that you will not have to try to make it all up at the end of the year.
- *Find out when time sheets are due*—Another thing you should do when starting a new position is to find out exactly what day time sheets are due so that you can submit them on time.
- *Keep copies of your time sheets*—Always keep a copy of your time sheet or know how to access them electronically for your own file, in case the original is lost or misplaced. Having a record also allows you to go back and calculate your number of billable hours.
- *Record your time contemporaneously on a daily basis*—One of the biggest mistakes you can make is to not record your time as you go along during the day. If you wait until the end of the day to try to remember all the things you did, there is absolutely no way that you will be able to accurately reconstruct everything. In the end, you will be the one suffering, doing work you did not get credit for. So be sure to keep a time sheet handy and fill it out as you go along.
- *Record your actual time spent; do not discount your time*—Do not discount your time because you think you should have been able to perform a job faster. If it took you four hours to finish an assignment and you worked the whole four hours, there is no reason to discount the time. *If the supervising attorneys think a discount is warranted, they can decide that, but it is not up to you to do that.* However, if you made a mistake or had a problem that you do not think the client should be billed for, tell your supervising attorney, and let him or her help you to make the decision.

> *A daunting task for bankruptcy trustees is preparing a Trustee's Final Account. As a new trustee, it was hard to recall at the end of the day or that week, the time spent on the cases. Things happen quickly and I am certain that early on, billable time was left out and not compensated. I immediately realized the value of recording time as you go and developed daily time sheets that could later be entered into the computer system to track time and expenses. That is the only way to be accurate.*
> —Cynthia Traina Donnes

- *Be aware if billable hours are related to bonuses or merit increases*—Be aware of how billable hours are used. In some law offices, billable hours are used in distributing bonuses and merit increases and can be used in performance evaluations, so know up front how they will be used.

- *Be ethical*—Always be honest and ethical in the way you fill out your time sheets. Padding your time sheets is unethical and simply wrong. Eventually, wrongdoing regarding timekeeping, billing, or handling client funds will become apparent.
- *Be aware of things that keep you from billing time*—Be aware of things that keep you from having a productive day, such as:
  - People who lay their troubles at your feet or who are constantly taking your attention away from your work. An appropriate approach is to say, "I would really like to hear about it at lunch, but right now I am really busy."
  - Wasted time spent trying to track down other people or trying to find information you need.
  - Constant interruptions, including phone calls. If you really need to get something done, go someplace where you can get the work done, and tell others to hold your calls. However, check in every once in a while to return client phone calls. Clients should have their phone calls returned as soon as possible.

Billing

To generate the necessary income to operate the firm, special attention must be paid to billing, the process of issuing bills for the purpose of collecting monies for legal services performed and for being reimbursed for expenses.

Billing for Paralegal Time and Profitability

Many law offices bill for paralegal time as well as for attorney time. Clients often prefer this because the paralegal hourly rates are much lower than attorney hourly rates. Exhibit 5-15 shows the average hourly rates for paralegals in different regions of the country.

For example, assume an associate attorney and a paralegal can both prepare discovery documents in a case and that the task will take seven hours. Assuming the paralegal bills at $80 per hour and the associate bills at $175 per hour, the cost to the client if the paralegal does the job is $560, and the cost if the associate drafts the discovery is $1225. Thus, the client will have saved $665 by simply allowing the paralegal to do the job. The client would still have to pay for the attorney's time to review the paralegal's discovery, but the cost would be minimal. This represents substantial savings to clients.

Exhibit 5-15 Average Legal Assistant Billing Rate by Region

Source: National Association of Paralegals, 2015 National Utilization and Compensation Survey Report, Table 3.4, Hourly Billing Rates By Region Data.

Paralegal 2014 Region	Average Billing Rate
Region 1: New England/Mideast	$111
Region 2: Great Lakes	$116
Region 3: Plain States	$114
Region 4: Southeast	$128
Region 5: Southwest	$127
Region 6: Rocky Mountains	$109
Region 7: Far West	$133

As mentioned earlier, the question of whether law offices can bill for paralegal time was considered by the United States Court in *Missouri v. Jenkins*, 491 U.S. 274 (1989). In that case, the plaintiff was successful on several counts in a civil rights lawsuit and was attempting to recover attorney's fees from the defendant under a federal statute. The statutory language provided that the prevailing party could recover "reasonable attorney's fees" from the other party. The plaintiff argued for recovery for the time that paralegals spent working on the case as well as for the time attorneys spent. The defendant argued that paralegal time was not "attorney's fees." Alternatively, the defendants argued that if they did have to pay something for paralegal time, they should only have to pay about $15 per hour, which represents the overhead costs to the office for a paralegal.

The court found that paralegals carry out many useful tasks under the direction of attorneys and that "reasonable attorney's fees" referred to the reasonable fee for work produced, whether by attorneys or paralegals. The court also found that, under the federal statute, paralegal time should not be compensated as overhead costs to the office but should be paid at the prevailing market rates in the area for paralegal time. The court noted that the prevailing rate for paralegals in that part of the country at that time was about $40 per hour and held that the office was entitled to receive that amount for paralegal hours worked on the case. Thus, it is clear that offices can bill for paralegal time if they choose to do so.

Leveraging and How Hourly Billing Rates Are Determined

leveraging

The process of earning a profit from legal services that are provided by law office personnel (usually partners, associates, and paralegals).

Leveraging is an important concept in law office billing. **Leveraging** is the process of earning a profit from legal services that are provided by law office personnel (usually partners, associates, and paralegals). Leveraging allows the office not only to recover the cost of an attorney or a paralegal's salary but also to pay overhead expenses and even make a profit on each such person. Thus, paralegals are also a profit center for law firms. It is a win–win situation; clients pay lower fees for paralegals over attorneys, and law firms still generate a profit on paralegal time.

Functions of a Successful Billing System

An oft-forgotten aspect of any billing system is that the system must please the firm's customers or clients. A good billing system is determined by whether or not the firm's clients are satisfied with the billings and whether or not they are paying the bills that are sent to them. One quick way a firm can lose a good client is by mishandling the client's money in some way, by overbilling the client, or by giving the client the impression that her or his money is being used unjustly or unfairly. In addition, mishandling a client's money is a top reason that attorneys are disciplined. A good billing system, whether computerized or not, must do several things, including accurately tracking the client's account, providing regular billings, and providing clients with an itemization of the services performed.

ACCURATELY TRACK HOW MUCH A CLIENT HAS PAID THE FIRM A successful billing system must be able to accurately track how much clients have paid the firm and whether the payments are made in cash, through a trust account, or otherwise. Although this may seem easy, often it is not. Consider how you feel when a creditor has either lost one of your payments or misapplied it in some manner. This is especially important for a law firm because, in many instances, large sums of money are involved. Payments can be lost, not entered into the system, or even applied to the wrong client. The firm must take great care with regard to what goes in and out of the billing system and must ensure that the information is accurate.

SEND REGULAR BILLINGS Nearly all clients like to receive timely billings. We all expect to receive regular billings for routine things, such as credit cards, utilities, and so forth. Likewise, most clients like to receive billings that are at least monthly. Imagine the frustration of a client who receives a quarterly billing that is four or five times more expensive than expected. Regular billings alert the client on how he or she is being billed and how much needs to be budgeted. In addition, if a client sees timely bills that are more expensive than were planned for, he or she can tell the firm how to proceed so as to limit future bills before costs are incurred. This at least gives the client the option of cutting back on legal services instead of getting angry at the firm for not communicating the charges on a timely basis.

PROVIDE CLIENT BILLINGS THAT ARE FAIR AND RESPECTFUL Billings that are fair and courteous are essential to a good billing system. If a client believes that the firm is overcharging for services or that the billings are curt and unprofessional, the client may simply not pay a bill or may hold payment. If you ever must speak to a client regarding a bill, always be courteous and respectful, and try to understand the situation from the client's point of view. If a dispute arises, simply take down the client's side of the story, relay the information to the attorney in charge of the matter, and let the attorney resolve the situation.

PROVIDE CLIENT BILLINGS THAT IDENTIFY WHAT SERVICES HAVE BEEN PROVIDED When a client receives a billing, it is important that the client knows what services were received. Bills that simply say "For Services Rendered" are, for the most part, a thing of the past. Although the format of bills depends on the client, it is recommended that you indicate exactly what service was performed, by whom, on what date, for how long, and for what charge. If a client can see exactly what the firm is doing and how hard the staff are working, the client may be more willing to pay the bill.

PROVIDE CLIENT BILLINGS THAT ARE CLEAR Finally, billings should be clear and without legalese. They should be easy to read and should provide the information that a client wants to see. Payments on billings that are complicated and hard to read are often held up while a client tries to decipher a bill.

In short, a billing system should satisfy your customers so that they are willing to make payments on time.

Manual Billing Systems

Before legal billing software was widely available, billings were generated manually, using typewriters or word processors and time sheets. Law practices typically would store the time sheets in the accounting file of each case and then periodically send a statement. Although a few offices may still produce billings manually, manual systems have certain inherent limitations. Manual billings typically are slow and cumbersome, are prone to mathematical errors, and can take a great deal of overhead time to generate the bill. Thus, manual billings are sent out less frequently than most offices would like, which can cause cash-flow problems. In addition, management reports on manual systems are burdensome to produce. Computerized billing systems automatically produce management reports that show who is billing the most hours, which clients pay the best, and which types of cases generate the most money.

Computerized Billing Systems

Computerized billing systems solve many of the problems associated with manual systems. Generally, timekeepers still must record what they do with their time on a time slip or time sheet, or record the entry directly into the program. If the time slips are completed manually, then they must be entered into the legal billing software, usually on a daily or weekly basis. It is common for offices using computerized billing systems to produce monthly or even biweekly bills according to the wishes of the client. In addition to solving cash-flow problems, most legal billing software programs produce reports that can help the office make good management decisions (this is covered in more detail later in the chapter). Computerized timekeeping and billing also produces billings that are more accurate than manual methods because all mathematical computations are performed automatically by the computer. Because legal timekeeping and billing software prices have plunged several hundred dollars, nearly any office can afford these types of programs.

The Computerized Timekeeping and Billing Process

Timekeeping and billing software packages differ greatly from one another. However, the computerized timekeeping and billing process for most billing packages is as shown in Exhibit 5-16.

1. **The Client and the Attorney Reach an Agreement on Legal Fees** An attorney can bill for services in many different ways. At the outset of most cases, the client and the attorney reach an agreement regarding how much the attorney will charge for her or his services. Preferably, the agreement is in writing in the form of a contract. After the legal fee has been agreed on, the new matter is set up in the computerized billing package by entering information, including the client's name and address, the type of case it is, and the type of legal fee that has been agreed upon.
2. **The Attorney and Paralegal Perform Legal Services and Prepare Time Slips** When attorneys or paralegals perform work on a legal matter for a client, they fill out a time slip to track the exact services (either using a manual time slip form or entering the information directly into the computer). Many timekeeping and billing programs also support data entry from a handheld personal digital assistant (PDA).
3. **Time Slips and Expense Slips Are Entered into the Computer** If manual time slips are used, they must be entered into the computer. The information is typed into the computer in roughly the same format as it appears on the time slip. It is essential that the information be accurately entered into the computer. In addition, expense slips are also entered into the computer to track the expenses a firm incurs on behalf of a client.

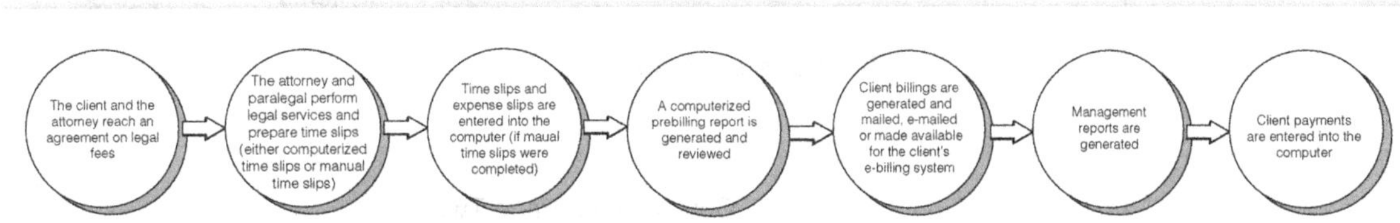

Exhibit 5-16 Computerized Timekeeping and Billing Cycle

prebilling report

A rough draft version of billings.

4. **A Prebilling Report Is Generated and Reviewed** After legal services have been performed and recorded in the time and billing software, the next step is for a prebilling report to be generated. This is done before the final client bills are generated. A **prebilling report** is a rough draft of billings that eventually will be sent to clients (see Exhibit 5-17). The prebilling report is given to the attorney in charge of the case for review or to a billing committee to make sure the billing is accurate.

Adams & Lee

12/15/2015 Prebilling Report Page 1

Power Systems, Inc.	Corporate Matters
Miscellaneous Corporate Matters	Monthly
Case Number: Corp 1002	Trust Balance: $3,825
P.O. Box 83001	Case Rate: $125
500 South Peters Street	Case Attorney: JBD
Malibu, CA 90014	
Phone: (213) 553-9342	

Previous Bill Owed $470.20

—Legal Fees—

Date	Atty	Description	Time	Amount
12/10/15	JBD	Telephone conference with Stevenson re: November minutes	.50 hr	$62.50
12/13/15	JBD	Preparation of November minutes; prepared for review at next meeting of the board of directors	1.00 hr	$125.00 MJB
12/14/15	JBD	Conference with Schorr at home	.25 hr	none
		Total Legal Fees	**1.75 hr**	**$187.50 MJB**

—Costs Advanced—

Date	Atty	Description	Rate	Amount
12/13/15	JBD	Photocopy documents; October 2010 minutes (for board meeting)	$.25 ea 100 items	$25.00
		Total Costs Advanced		**$25.00**

Continued on Page Two

Exhibit 5-17 Prebilling Report

Attorneys may choose to discount bills for a variety of reasons, including thinking the task should have taken less time than it actually did. Discounts also are used for good customers, because of the client's hardship, for professional courtesy or for friends, or because the billing looks unreasonable. This can, however, be very frustrating to a paralegal who has his or her time cut back. Typically, only the amount that is actually billed is counted against the target or minimum billable number of hours.

5. **Client Billings Are Generated and Mailed** Formal client billings are generated by the computer (see Exhibit 5-18). Most timekeeping and billing software can produce many different billing formats. The computer automatically prints the bills, and they are subsequently mailed to the clients.
6. **Management Reports Are Generated** Most computerized timekeeping and billing programs have a wide variety of management reports available. Management reports are not used for billing clients; they are used to evaluate the effectiveness of a firm. For example, most programs generate a report that shows how much time is nonbillable (i.e., not chargeable to clients). If a firm has a lot of nonbillable time, it might indicate that the firm is not productive and is losing valuable time from its timekeepers.

   Management reports can also be used to make management decisions, such that particular types of cases are no longer profitable, the firm needs to raise hourly rates, or other types of decisions.
7. **Client Payments Are Entered into the Computer** Finally, payments made as a result of billings must be recorded or entered into the computer, giving clients proper credit for the payments.

Bill Formats

Generating bills is the most important aspect of any timekeeping and billing program. There is no uniform way that all law offices bill clients; the look and format of billings depend on the law office, its clients, the type of law it practices, and so forth. Thus, it is important that any timekeeping and billing system is used, whether manual or computerized, be flexible in the number of client billing formats that are available. For example, some bill formats contain only general information about the services provided, while others show greater detail. In many computerized systems, the format of the bill is set up when the client's case is first entered into the system.

Historically, many offices did not itemize their billing, simply stating "For Services Rendered $XXX" on the bill. Although each client is different, most clients like to receive detailed billings of exactly what services are being provided. This allows the client to see what he or she is paying for. This also is beneficial to the office, since clients are more willing to pay the bill when they know what it is for. Producing detailed bills takes work. It requires timekeepers to make accurate, current time slips of what services they have provided. Although this seems enough, it is not. It is very hard to persuade timekeepers to write down each service they perform (e.g., 12/22/15, Telephone call to Larry Jones, witness, regarding statement given 10/10/15........15 minutes). Yet, the whole point of billing is to be paid. So, if an office produces a bill that is not itemized and, therefore, the client does not pay it, nothing has been gained. Although itemized billings are sometimes inconvenient for the timekeeper and take longer to produce, the extra work has paid off if the bill is paid in the end.

Adams & Lee
11 Canal Street, Suite 2B
New Orleans, Louisiana 70115
(212) 585-2342

Sara Autumn
Power Systems, Inc.
P.O. Box 83001
500 South Peters Street

Malibu, CA 90014

Billing Date: 01/03/16

Account # 00237
Previous Bal. in Trust
$3,825.00

RE: Power Systems, Inc. Miscellaneous Corporate Matters

DATE	PROFESSIONAL SERVICES	INDIV.	TIME	
12/10/15	Telephone conference with Schorr re: November minutes	JBD	.50	$62.50
12/13/15	Preparation of November minutes: prepared for review at next meeting of the board of directors	JBD	1.00	$125.00
12/14/15	Conference with Schorr at home	JBD	.25	$-0-
TOTAL FOR THE ABOVE SERVICES			**1.75**	**$187.50**

DATE	EXPENSES	
12/13/15	Photocopy documents; November minutes (for board meeting)	$25.00
TOTAL FOR ABOVE EXPENSES		**$25.00**
TOTAL BILLING		**$212.50**
CURRENT BALANCE IN TRUST		**$3,612.50**

Exhibit 5-18 Final Client Billing

Management Reports

management reports

Reports used to help management analyze whether the office is operating in an efficient and effective manner.

Almost all timekeeping and billing software packages produce a wide variety of management reports (see Exhibit 5-19). **Management reports** are used to help management analyze whether the office is operating in an efficient and effective manner. Management reports can be used to track problems an office may be experiencing and to help devise ways to correct the problems. The following are explanations of some common management reports and how they are used by offices.

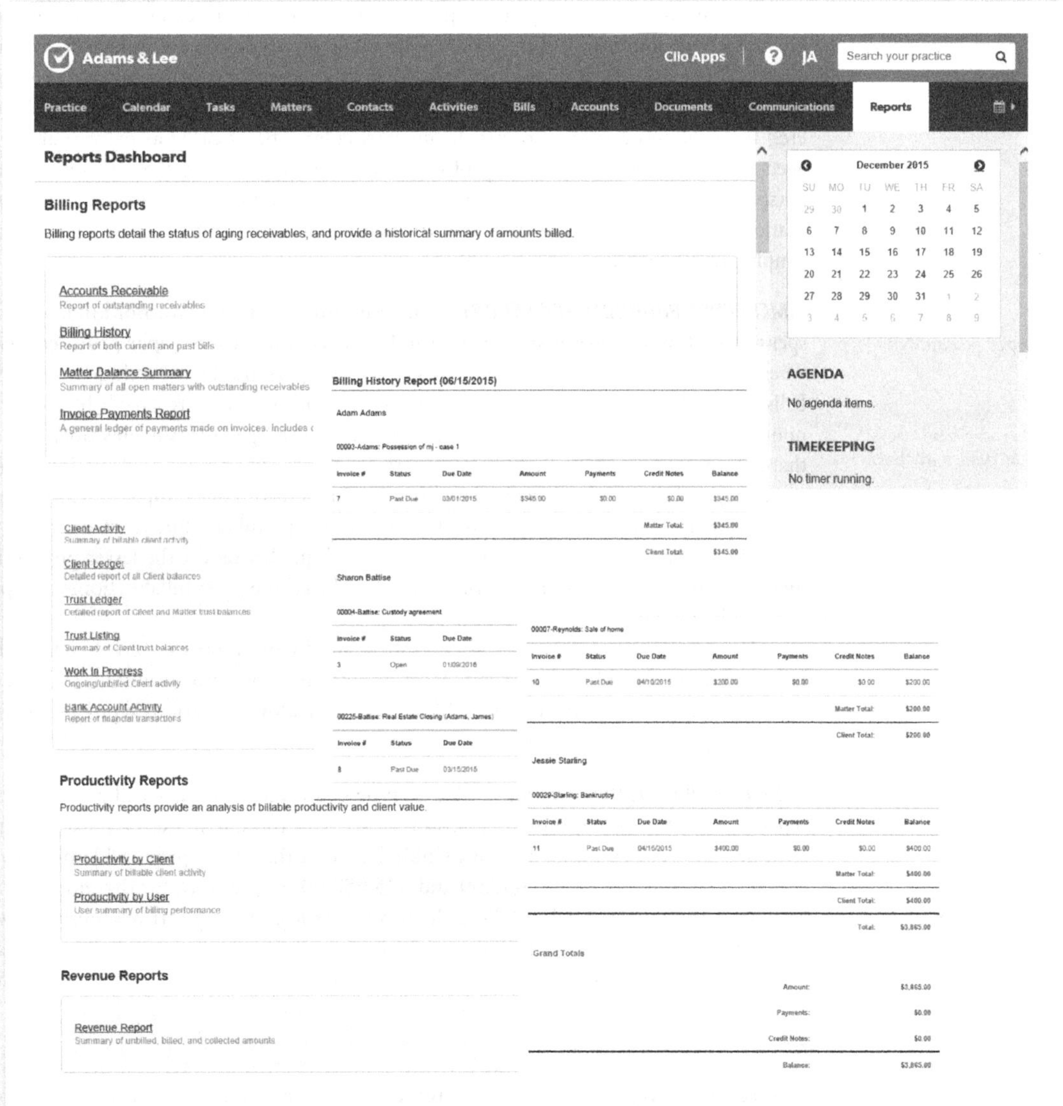

Exhibit 5-19 Time & Billing—Management Reports

CASE/CLIENT LIST Most billing packages allow the user to produce a case or client list. A list of all active cases an office has is very important in trying to effectively manage a large caseload. Most reports list not only the client names but also the appropriate account number (also called the "client identification number" by some programs). This is useful when trying to locate a client's identification number.

aged accounts receivable report

A report showing all cases that have outstanding balances due and how long these balances are past due.

AGED ACCOUNTS RECEIVABLE REPORT An **aged accounts receivable report** shows all cases that have outstanding balances due to the office and how long these balances are past due. These reports break down the current balances due and the balances that are 30, 60, and more than 90 days past due. Using this type of report, management can clearly see which clients are not paying and how old the balances are. The report is also helpful for following up on clients who are slow in paying their bills. Most programs allow the report to run according to the type of case. Thus, management can also see what types of cases (criminal, divorce, tax, etc.) have the most aged accounts. If one particular type of case has more than its share of aged accounts, it might be more profitable to stop taking that type. So, from a management perspective, this can be a very important report. It should be noted that aged account information should not appear on bills sent to clients. Bills that are more than 30 days old should simply say "past due."

timekeeper productivity report

A report showing how much billable and nonbillable time is being spent by each timekeeper.

TIMEKEEPER PRODUCTIVITY REPORT The amount of billable and nonbillable time being spent by each timekeeper is shown and can be reflected in a **timekeeper productivity report.** These reports can be used to identify which timekeepers are the most diligent in their work. It lists the billable hours, the total amount billed and payments received. It also reflects the nonbillable or nonchargeable hours, amount that are charged off (uncollectible) and amount that are on hold (not billed). This information helps to determine the deviation between the standard rate billed and the realized rate for the time billed. For example, if team member "A" billed a total of only 77.75 hours for the month of September while team members "B" and "C" billed more than 100 hours, the report would quickly reflect the lesser productive team member. Also, notice that "Byron B. Brown" produced the most billable hours and payments received by the office.

Along with reflecting each team members' production, most programs reflect the office billable and nonbillable information. Most importantly, the report should reflect the amount billed against the payments received. Most programs allow for various reporting periods (i.e., monthly, quarterly, annually, etc.).

case type productivity report

A report showing which types of cases (e.g., criminal, personal injury, bankruptcy, etc.) are the most profitable.

CASE TYPE PRODUCTIVITY REPORT A **case type productivity report** will generally show case types (criminal, personal injury, bankruptcy, etc.) and those that are the most profitable (see Exhibit 5-20). For example, note in Exhibit 5-20 that the bankruptcy and family law areas of the law office brought in $36,050.00 and $25,050.00, respectively, for the month of September, 2015 or 24.74% and 17.19% of the income earned. This report obviously shows which types of cases are the most profitable and which types are the least profitable. Management will use this type of report to decide which areas to concentrate on to become more profitable.

Electronic Billing

electronic billing

When law firms bill clients using electronic means, such as the Internet.

Electronic billing is when law firms bill clients using electronic means, such as the Internet. Many large clients—such as Fortune 1000 and other businesses—are demanding that law firms bill them using electronic means. The Legal Electronic Data Exchange Standard

ADAMS & LEE

Productivity Report by Case Type

September 30, 2015

CASE TYPE	BILLABLE HOURS	BILLED FEES	PAYMENTS	FEE INCOME % TOTAL	HOURS % TOTAL
Admiralty	95.75	$10,053.75	$7,550.75	5.18	6.75
Bankruptcies	245.00	$55,125.00	$36,050.00	24.74	17.26
Civil Matters	128.50	$12,850.00	$8,350.50	5.73	9.05
Corporate Matters	80.75	$12,112.50	$10,112.50	6.94	5.69
Estate Planning	58.75	$14,687.50	$10,487.50	7.20	4.14
Family Law	220.50	$33,075.00	$25,050.00	17.19	15.53
Insurance Defense	108.25	$13,531.25	$9,785.00	6.71	7.63
Labor Law	150.75	$16,582.50	$11,500.00	7.89	10.62
Litigation	125.50	$13,805.00	$10,805.00	7.41	8.84
Personal Injury	25.75	$3,862.50	$2,850.00	1.96	1.81
Taxation Matters	180.00	$19,800.00	$13,200.00	9.06	7.61
September Totals	1,419.50	$205,485.00	$145,741.25		

Exhibit 5-20 Time and Billing—Productivity Report

specifies a uniform output for law firm time and billing systems to export to e-billing systems. Many of the e-billing vendors are application service providers (ASPs), third-party vendors that set up the e-billing part of the system, receive data from law firms, and operate the software over the Internet. Clients are able to see bills (from any law firm they use) in a standard format and then customize the reports to meet their particular needs. For large clients, electronic billing is a big enhancement over traditional paper billing.

Summary

Timekeeping is the process of tracking time for the purpose of billing clients. Billing is the process of issuing invoices for the purpose of collecting monies for legal services performed and being reimbursed for expenses.

There are several different kinds of legal fee agreements. An hourly rate fee is a fee for legal services that is billed to the client by the hour at an agreed-upon rate. An attorney or a paralegal hourly rate is based on the attorney's or paralegal's level of expertise and experience in a particular area. A client hourly rate is based on an hourly charge for that particular client; no matter what level of attorney (associate, partner, etc.) works on a case, the client is billed one rate. Similarly, no matter what level of paralegal works on a case (entry level, senior level, etc.) the client is billed one rate. A blended hourly rate is an hourly rate that takes into account the blend or mix of office staff working on the matter. Depending on the state, a "blend" may include paralegals. If a law office charges $175 for all staff (paralegals, associates, senior partners, etc.), this would be a blend. An activity hourly rate means that different hourly rates are charged depending on the type of activity, for example, $150 for telephone calls, $200 for office conference, and $250 for legal research and drafting.

A contingency fee is a fee that is collected if the attorney successfully represents a client. The attorney is entitled to a certain percentage of the money that is recovered. If the client's case is not won, and no money is recovered, the attorney collects no legal fees but is still entitled to recover expenses. Contingency fee agreements must be in writing. A flat fee is a fee for legal services that is billed as a flat or fixed amount, no matter how much time is actually spent on the matter.

An earned retainer means that the money has been earned and can be deposited in the law office's or attorney's operating bank account. An unearned retainer means that the money has not yet been earned and is placed in trust as an advance against the attorney's future fees and expenses. As the money is earned by the law office, the money is removed from the trust and placed in the law office's or attorney's operating account. A trust or escrow bank account is a separate bank account, apart from a law office's or attorney's operating checking account, where unearned client funds are deposited. A cash advance retainer is an unearned retainer.

A retainer for general representation is used when a client such as a corporation requires continuing legal services (not including litigation) throughout the year. The client pays a retainer and is entitled to the legal services without any additional fees. In many states, a retainer for general representation is an earned retainer, because the client can call at any time and receive legal services. A case retainer is a fee paid at the beginning of a matter, is nonrefundable, and is paid as an incentive for the attorney to take the case. Case retainers are earned retainers. A pure retainer obligates the office to be available to represent a client throughout a certain time period, and the firm agrees to not represent any of its competitors. A pure retainer is typically an earned retainer.

Court-awarded attorney fees are given to prevailing parties pursuant to certain federal and state statutes. Value billing is a type of fee agreement that is based on the perceived value of the services to the client.

The rules of professional conduct require that the basis or rate of the fee and expenses for a matter should be communicated to the client, preferably in writing, and that any fee charged should be reasonable. Whether a fee is reasonable depends on a number of factors, including the time and labor required, the novelty and difficulty of the issues raised, the fee customarily charged, the results obtained, the nature and length of the professional relationship, and the experience and reputation of the attorney, among other things.

Attorneys and law offices can charge and be reimbursed for reasonable legal expenses. Billable time is time that a legal professional can directly bill to a client's account. Nonbillable time cannot be billed to a client and includes pro bono work (services that are provided free of charge) and overheard costs such as general management, supervision, client development, and other activities. Paralegals are allowed to bill for their time as long as the work is professional and not clerical in nature. Leveraging is the process of earning profit from legal services that are provided by paralegals and attorneys.

A successful billing system, whether computerized or manual, accurately tracks how much clients have paid, can send out regular billings, and provides clients with fair, respectful, and detailed bills.

The computerized timekeeping and billing process includes a client and an attorney reaching a fee agreement, legal services being provided, times and expense slips entered into the computer, a prebilling report generated, a final bill generated, management reports run, and client payment recorded. Most computerized time and billing systems can produce management reports, including case/client list, aged accounts receivable, timekeeper productivity, and case type productivity reports, among others. Electronic billing is when law offices bill clients using electronic means, such as the Internet.

Key Terms

activity hourly rate
aged accounts receivable report
attorney or paralegal hourly rate
billable time
billing
blended hourly rate fee
case retainer
case type productivity report
cash advance
client hourly rate
contingency fee
court-awarded fees
criminal fraud
earned retainer
electronic billing
flat fee
hourly rate fee
leveraging
management reports
nonbillable time
outside counsel
overhead
prebilling report
prepaid legal service
pro bono
pure retainer
retainer for general representation
timekeeper productivity report
timekeeping
time sheet or time slip
trust or escrow account
unearned retainer
value billing

Test Your Knowledge

Test your knowledge of the chapter by answering these questions.

1. What is the difference between timekeeping and billing?
2. Name four types of hourly rates: ________________, ________________, ________________, and ________________.
3. When a lawyer takes a percentage of the recovery of the case, it is called a ________________ fee.
4. True or false: it is strongly recommended that all fee arrangements be in writing.
5. True or false: a flat fee agreement must be in writing.

6. A retainer that can be deposited in the firm's or attorney's operating checking account is called an __________________ retainer.
7. True or false: an account where unearned client monies are deposited is called a trust account.
8. A retainer for general representation is an __________________ retainer.
9. A case retainer is an __________________ retainer.
10. A cash advance retainer is an __________________ retainer.
11. A plan that can be purchased that entitles the person to receive legal services either free or at a greatly reduced price is called ______________________.
12. A legal billing arrangement that is similar to the type used when you get your car fixed is called ______________________ billing.
13. For what activity do clients file the most ethical complaints against lawyers?
14. What must the attorney do at the end of a case where a contingency fee or an agreement was used?
15. True or false: a contingency agreement can be used in all kinds of cases.
16. True or false: if a client signs a contract with an attorney and the fee turns out to be clearly excessive, it does not matter because a contract was signed and the contract prevails.
17. Name four of the eight factors that courts use to determine if a fee is unreasonable.
18. Define criminal fraud.
19. True or false: paralegals can bill for time spent copying and other clerical duties.
20. Legal services that are provided free of charge are called __________________ work.
21. True or false: paralegals represent a profit center at most law firms (i.e., they bill more to clients than they are paid in salary and benefits).
22. What is e-billing?

Practical Applications

1. You are a new paralegal and have worked for a medium-sized law office for three months. It has been a tremendous learning experience for you. It has taken time to learn how the office does business, its policies and procedures, what type of service you are expected to give to clients, and where resources are and how to use them (such as the office's computer systems, law library, copy machines, and form files). Although it has taken time for you to learn these things, you also have been productive and have received several compliments on the quality of your work.

One day, you read in the office's staff manual that all paralegals are required to bill 1500 hours annually or face possible discipline. You immediately contact your supervisor and ask whether, as a new paralegal, you will be expected to bill this amount. Your supervisor responds, "Of course. You were told that when you were hired." You immediately begin gathering copies of your time sheets to compile your total. You also request that the billing department send you the total numbers of hours you have billed to date. When you get the report from billing, you panic; you have billed only 300 hours. You are 75 hours behind where you should be (1500 divided by four [i.e., one-fourth of the way through the year] equals 375). What would you do now, and how could you have avoided this unfortunate situation?

2. On April 1, a billing goes out to John Myers, one of the clients whose cases you have been working on. Mr. Myers calls you a few days later and complains about the amount of time shown on the bill. He is extremely rude and discourteous. Mr. Myers flatly states that he thinks he is being overbilled. How would you handle the phone call?

3. Your office is on the same side of the city as a major manufacturing plant. You notice that many of the plant's employees come to your office for routine legal services, such as wills, adoptions, and name changes. Although the office has been charging these clients on an hourly basis, you think that there might be alternatives. You talk to one of the partners, and she suggests that you look into the alternatives. Prepare a memorandum to the partner discussing billing options for this situation.

4. You are interviewing a new client. The client wants to hire your office to help negotiate the purchase of a small business. The seller has offered $20,000. The new client would be willing to pay this amount, although she thinks it is a bit high, but does not feel comfortable negotiating with the seller and would rather have an attorney involved in the deal for her protection. The new client is suspicious of paralegals and attorneys and is especially concerned about how much her case will cost. You inform the client that the attorney will be the one who actually talks to her about the fee issue, but that typically this type of case is taken on an hourly basis and that the attorney will only be able to give her a very broad estimate of what the total matter will cost. The client states that this would be unacceptable to her because she does not have a lot of money to pay overpriced attorneys. The client also states that she would like this matter to get settled as soon as possible. You must prepare a memorandum to the attorney outlining the facts of the case. What type of fee arrangement would you suggest to the attorney? Please keep in mind the client's anxieties and her particular needs.

5. Recently, your office has found a niche in representing spouses collecting on past-due child support. In most cases, your clients have little money with which to pay you and are financially strapped, as they no longer have the income of their former spouses to support their children and have not received child support. In some cases, large amounts of money are owed, but finding the former spouses has proved difficult. Your supervising attorney decides that the best way to handle these types of cases is on a one-third contingency basis. Your supervising attorney asks for your comments. How do you respond?

6. You work for a firm with 17 attorneys. The firm has always done well financially, but recently it has begun to struggle. There is a great deal of pressure for you to meet your billing requirements of 1800 hours, even if no one has work for you to do. The firm will not accept the answer, "No one is giving me any work." You are being encouraged to go to each attorney's office and drum something up. Discuss the ethical situation in which you are being placed and how you might handle it.

7. You and another paralegal, Jonathan, were hired in a medium-sized law office approximately three months ago. You work very hard at your job, record your hours honestly, and always receive compliments on the quality of your work. However, your supervising attorney constantly compares you with Jonathan, who consistently bills more hours than you do. You suspect that Jonathan is padding his time. How do you handle the matter?

8. A client contacts your law office for representation regarding the routine sale of a piece of property. The client appears to be fairly wealthy. Your supervising attorney charges the client what amounts to be about double what the firm regularly charges. You know this because the office uses an internal fee schedule to help the attorneys set a proper fee. Discuss the ethical considerations. How would you handle the situation?

9. You work in a relatively small-sized law office. The office is having a cash-flow problem and has requested that the staff members bill as much as they can and work on cases in which the firm may be able to solve some of its cash-flow problem. The office manager comes to you and tells you that a client on whose case you are working has several thousands of dollars in the trust account. Although not telling you directly, the office manager lets you know that she wants you to bill some hours to this client so the firm can get some of the money in the trust account. Discuss the ethical problems associated with this. Assume you bill the client when, in fact, no hours were worked on the case. What problems arise?

10. You have just finished a hectic morning. Before you go to lunch, you fill out your timekeeping report for the day. Although you wanted to record your time earlier, you just could not get to it. Please record your time on a blank piece of paper or a spreadsheet; have columns set up for the date, client/case name, timekeeper, services rendered, billable or nonbillable, and the amount of time spent on the matter (see Exhibit 5-11). For each activity listed, decide whether it is billable or not billable. Record your time, using tenths of hours. You should also fill out expense slips for items that should be charged back to clients. Record the expenses on a blank piece of paper and include date, client/case name, your name, type of expense, and cost. Please total the cost of each expense slip. The firm charges 25 cents each for copies and 50 cents per page to send a fax. Assume long-distance phone calls cost 25 cents a minute.

As best you can recall, this is how your day went:

8:00 A.M. to 8:12 A.M.	Got a cup of coffee, talked to other law office staff members, reviewed your schedule/things to do for the day, and reviewed your e-mail inbox.
8:13 A.M. to 8:25 A.M.	Talked to your supervising attorney (Jan Mitchell) about some research she needs to be done on the standards necessary to file a motion to dismiss in *Johnson v. Cuttingham Steel.* Ms. Mitchell also asked you to find a bankruptcy statute she needs for *Halvert v. Shawnee Saving & Loan.*
8:26 A.M. to 8:37 A.M.	A paralegal from another office calls to remind you that the paralegal association you belong to is having a meeting at noon, and that you are running the meeting.
8:38 A.M. to 8:40 A.M.	One of your least favorite clients, John Hamilton, calls to ask you when he is supposed to be at your office to prepare for his deposition tomorrow. You access the weekly schedule electronically and read him the information he needs.
8:41 A.M. to 8:50 A.M.	You find the information you need re: the motion to dismiss in *Johnson v. Cuttingham Steel* in a motion in another case you helped prepare last month. The research is still current, so Ms. Mitchell will be pleased you found it so fast. You note that it took you two hours to research this issue when you did it the first time. You copy the material Ms. Mitchell needed (five pages), put it in her box, and send it to her electronically.
8:51 A.M. to 9:30 A.M.	You get hold of a witness you have been trying to contact in *Menly v. Menly.* The call was long-distance. The call lasted 15 minutes, and the memo to the file documenting the call took 20 minutes.
9:31 A.M. to 9:54 A.M.	Ms. Mitchell asks you to contact the attorney in *Glass v. Huron* regarding a discovery question. You spend 10 minutes on hold. The call is long-distance but you get an answer to Ms. Mitchell's question.
9:55 A.M. to 10:45 A.M.	One of the secretaries informs you that you must interview a new client, Richard Sherman. The person who was supposed to see Mr. Sherman got delayed. Mr. Sherman comes to your office regarding a simple adoption. However, in talking to Mr. Sherman, you find out that he also needs someone to incorporate a small business that he is getting ready to open. You gladly note that your office has a department that handles this type of matter. You take the basic information down regarding both matters. You tell the client that you will prepare a memo regarding these matters to the appropriate attorney and one of the office's attorneys will contact him within two days to further discuss the matter. You also copy 10 pages of information that Mr. Sherman brought.
10:46 A.M. to 10:54 A.M.	One of the secretaries asks you to cover her phone for her while she takes a quick break. Because the secretary always helps you when you ask for it, you gladly cover the phone for a few minutes. Ms. Mitchell asks you to send a fax in *Stewart v. Layhorn Glass,* so you use this time to send the six-page fax.
10:55 A.M. to 12:00 P.M.	You were given the job of organizing some exhibits in *Ranking v. Siefkin* yesterday by Ms. Mitchell. You finally have some free time to organize the exhibits.
12:01 P.M. to 1:00 P.M.	You attend the paralegal association lunch.

1:01 P.M. to 2:00 P.M.	You work on a pro bono criminal case that Ms. Mitchell is representing on appeal. In an effort to become familiar with the case, you read some of the transcripts from the trial.
2:01 P.M. to 5:30 P.M.	Ms. Mitchell hands you a new case. Ms. Mitchell says that the office will be representing the defendant. She asks you to read the petition and client file, analyze the case, and draft interrogatories to send to the plaintiff. You spend the rest of the day working on this case.

11. You have just been hired by a private law practice. You begin to get a little worried because your employers say you should "hold on" to your paycheck for an extra day to make sure it will clear the bank. You notice that many times staff members "forget" to fill out slips for charging expenses back to the clients, that bills are usually done on a quarterly basis, and that many expenses (such as copying) are included in the overhead of the office and not billed to the clients at all. Please identify what the problems are with the office and give a detailed answer on how you would go about addressing the problems.

12. You work for an insurance company. The head of the legal department asks you to begin drafting some billing guidelines for private law practices that represent your interests. The department currently reviews bills at varying hourly rates from firm to firm, and law offices are passing on to your office all types of expenses that they should not be including. Please draft a set of guidelines as requested.

13. Assume for this exercise that you can bill for all activities that relate to learning. Keep a detailed record of all your activities for one day, from when you wake up until you go to sleep. Record your time in tenths (i.e., in six-minute intervals). At the end of the day, calculate the amount due based on your time sheet.

Your law office recently began representing a client who had been defrauded in a security scam at a national brokerage firm. The client signed a 40% contingency contract. You know that the only thing your office has done on the case is to meet with the client several times, do some general research regarding the case, and prepare a demand letter to the brokerage firm setting out the facts of the case. The brokerage firm does not want bad publicity and has agreed to settle the claim for $1.2 million dollars. The client is going to accept the offer. Discuss the ethical implications. What should the law firm do?

On the Web Exercises

1. Go to the ABA Center for Professional Responsibility at http://www.americanbar.org, find the *ABA Model Rules of Professional Conduct*, and read and print out *Rule 1.5* Fees and the comment.

2. Visit five state bar association Web sites and find three articles on legal timekeeping, billing, or legal fees. The following link will take you to a Web site that connects to all state bar sites:

3. Go to the Georgia Bar Association Web site at http://www.gabar.org/committeesprogramssections/programs/lpm/forms.cfm and find a sample contingency fee agreement. Go to several other state bar association Web sites and try to find another sample contingency fee or hourly rate contract agreements.

4. Go to http://www.findlaw.com and print out and read the United States Supreme Court case of *Missouri v. Jenkins*, 491 U.S. 274 (1989). ***Click*** "Visit Our Professional Site," then ***click*** "Cases and Codes." Scroll down to US Courts of Appeal – Opinions and Resources and ***click*** "United States Supreme Court," then ***click*** "Search by Docket Number or Citation." You should then be able to enter the citation of the case—491 U.S. 274.

5. Visit the National Association of Paralegals Web site at http://www.nala.org and review the latest NALA National Utilization and Compensation Survey Report. Read and print out the section related to paralegal billing rates. If you have difficulty finding it, try using the "Search" feature on the Web site. If you still have trouble finding it, go to http://www.google.com and search for the full title.

6. Go to the ABA Law Practice Management Section home page at http://www.americanbar.org and find timekeeping, billing, fees, and finance-related articles.

Projects

1. Using a general search engine, such as http://www.google.com or http://www.yahoo.com, search for legal value billing. Alternatively, go to a library or visit state bar association Web sites and write a detailed paper on value billing. Your paper should cover how it works and what are the positive and negatives of value billing.

2. Research and write a paper on computerized timekeeping and billing systems. Visit the American Bar Association Legal Technology Resource Center [http://www.americanbar.org] and state bar association Web sites, as well as other legal technology sites, and review helpful articles and materials that you find. Next, go to the timekeeping and billing Web sites in the Helpful Web Sites section of this chapter. Compare and contrast some of the different products that are available. Which one were you most impressed with, and why?

3. Using a law library, the Internet, and other resources, write an in-depth paper on the subject of legal billing. There are many, many resources available regarding the subject. Your paper should address why clients do not pay legal bills and what can be done to improve this. Your paper should include research from at least five different resources.

Case Review

Eureste v. Commission for Lawyer Discipline 76 S.W. 3d. 184 (Tex. App. - Houston [14th Dist.] 2002, no pet.)

76 S.W.3d 184 (2002)
Court of Appeals of Texas,
Houston (14th Dist.).

Bernardo EURESTE, Appellant,
v.
COMMISSION FOR LAWYER DISCIPLINE, Appellee.
No. 14-01-00311-CV.
April 18, 2002.

Opinion

I. Background

Eureste is an attorney licensed to practice law in Texas since 1990. During the relevant time period, his practice consisted almost entirely of representing claimants in workers' compensation matters. At the peak of his practice in 1996 and 1997, he had offices in 13 cities across Texas, over 60 employees, and approximately 1200 clients. The Texas Workers' Compensation Fund ("the Fund") [FN1] and Juan Granado, a former client, filed complaints against Eureste with the State Bar of Texas ("State Bar"). The basis of the Fund's complaint was Eureste's billing practices and resulting attorney's fees in workers' compensation cases. Granado's complaint arose from Eureste's allegedly deficient representation in a workers' compensation case. A brief overview of workers' compensation laws regarding attorney's fees is in order.

FN1. The Fund is a state-created entity that provides workers' compensation insurance and investigates cases of workers' compensation fraud in conjunction with the Texas Workers' Compensation Commission.

Texas Workers' Compensation Attorney's Fees

Section 408.221 of the Texas Labor Code governs the award of attorney's fees to the workers' compensation claimant's attorney. *See* Tex. Lab.Code Ann. § 408.221 (Vernon Supp.2002). Section 408.221 provides that the attorney's fees must be approved by the Texas Workers' Compensation Commission ("TWCC") or the court. *Id.* § 408.221(a). The fees are "based on the attorney's time and expenses according to written evidence presented to the commission or court." *Id.* § 408.221(b). The fees are paid from the claimant's recovery and may not exceed 25 percent of that recovery. *Id.* § 408.221(b), (i). The TWCC or the court shall consider the following factors in approving attorney's fees: (1) the time and labor required; (2) the novelty and difficulty of the questions involved; (3) the skill required to perform the legal services properly; (4) the fee customarily charged ***189** in the locality for similar legal services; (5) the amount involved in the controversy; (6) the benefits to the claimant that the attorney is responsible for securing; and (7) the experience and ability of the attorney performing the services. *Id.* § 408.221(d). Section 408.221 requires that the TWCC provide guidelines for maximum attorney's fees for specific services in accordance with these provisions. *See id.* § 408.221(f).

The TWCC rules set forth additional requirements for the submission and approval of attorney's fees. The TWCC rules reiterate that any fee approved by the commission "shall be limited to 25 percent of each weekly income benefit payment to the employee, up to 25 percent of the total income benefits allowed, and shall also be based on the attorney's time and expenses." 28 Tex. Admin. Code § 152.1(c) (2001). To claim a fee, an attorney must submit Form TWCC 152 entitled "Application and Order for Attorney's Fees," with "time, hourly rate, and expenses itemized separately for the attorney and for any paralegal." *Id.* § 152.3(a). On Form TWCC-152, the attorney must list the category of service rendered, the date of the service, the person who provided the service, the actions performed, the recipient of the action, and the hours requested. The TWCC has also established guidelines for the approval of attorney's fees that include a list of a maximum number of hours allowed per month for various legal services. *See id.* § 152.4(c). The TWCC automatically approves a fee for legal services without justification from the attorney if the number of hours for the services is within the guidelines. *See id.* § 152.3(b); Form TWCC-152. The guidelines also set the maximum hourly rate for an attorney at $150, and the maximum hourly rate for a paralegal at $50. *See* 28 Tex. Admin. Code § 152.4(d). Once the fees are approved, the TWCC issues an order for payment. *Id.* § 152.3(b). The fees, up to the cap of 25 percent, are then deducted from the client's monthly income benefit checks and paid directly to the attorney. *Id.* § 152.1(c).

Eureste's Billing Practices

There was no dispute at trial regarding the method used by Eureste to submit attorney's fees to the TWCC. His office submitted a Form TWCC-152 for each client on a monthly basis. At the time of trial, Eureste had submitted approximately 200,000 TWCC-152 forms. Eureste did not account for actual time spent by him or his employees on the forms. Rather, he always reported he had personally worked a number of hours that, when multiplied by the statutory attorney rate of $150, resulted in a fee that was at least 25 percent of his clients' monthly income benefit. Eureste acknowledged that during the year and a half before August 1997, when the State Bar complaint arose, his policy was to bill the maximum allowed by the guidelines on every file. Some of the activities he billed for included opening the client's file and preparation and attendance at hearings. On most files, even though actual activities performed and time spent varied from client to client, he billed each client 2.5 hours per month (resulting in a fee of $375) for "file review" under the "Communications" category. This is the maximum time allowed for "Communications" under the TWCC guidelines. *See* 28 TEX. ADMIN. CODE § 152.4(c). His Form TWCC-152 submissions did not arouse any suspicion and were always automatically approved because they were always within the guidelines. At trial, Elliott Flood, an attorney and vice-president of special investigations for the Fund, referred to this practice as billing "beneath the radar."

***190** Eureste testified that on many of the cases, he was not spending the number of hours he billed every month. During the peak of his practice, he spent 80 percent of his time on administrative matters and 20 percent of his time on individual client's cases. Yet, he billed all time on the client's file under his name and at the attorney rate. He admitted that most of the attorney time he billed during the period before August 1997 was performed by nonattorneys or attorneys other than himself. Eureste estimated that only 25 percent of the work billed was performed by attorneys, while 75 percent of the work billed was performed by nonattorneys. [FN2] The nonattorney time was billed by Eureste at the higher attorney rate of $150. Eureste never billed paralegal time at the paralegal rate.

> FN2. Eureste's offices were staffed primarily by nonattorney caseworkers who conducted the "intake" of new clients, explained the workers' compensation system and attorney's fees procedures to clients, and "worked up" the clients' files.

At trial, Flood testified Eureste's case was unique because no other situation approached the number of hours that Eureste billed for each day on his Form TWCC-152s. Eureste's fees, approved by the TWCC from June 1, 1995, to May 31, 1996, totaled $2,330,376.32, while the next highest attorney's approved fees totaled $935,582.50. Flood testified Eureste billed an average of 80 to 90 hours per day. A summary of Eureste's TWCC attorney's fees orders from December 1, 1995, to November 30, 1996, reveals he billed as his own time more than 24 hours almost daily and on many days, Eureste billed more than 100 hours. Eureste did not dispute that he billed in excess of 24 hours per day of his own time. Rather, he testified it would have been too burdensome to base his billings on actual time. In support of that claim, he referred to a one-day test accounting in which he instructed his employees to account for every activity they performed during that one day and the time spent on the activity. [FN3] Ordinarily, Eureste's employees input a description of the activities they performed on a case into the computer file for that case, but did not detail the time required to perform those activities. Based on the results of his one-day test, Eureste concluded it would be too onerous for him to submit bills based on actual time expended because that would require a larger number of entries per month.

FN3. Eureste also performed another one-day test accounting, but the results were not entered into evidence.

Granado Complaint

On November 15, 1995, Granado fell from a tractor while on the job and injured both shoulders. On May 9, 1996, he retained Eureste's Amarillo office because he was experiencing difficulties advancing his workers' compensation claim. Granado signed a contract, which provided that Eureste would represent him in connection with his claim for workers' compensation benefits and that attorney's fees would be in an amount governed by the workers' compensation laws of Texas.

Before Granado retained Eureste, he had been classified as having a 10 percent Maximum Medical Improvement. Eureste's office successfully negotiated with the carrier and obtained a 20 percent Maximum Medical Improvement. This increase made Granado eligible for additional benefits. Furthermore, when Granado retained Eureste, the workers' compensation carrier had accepted his left shoulder injury as a compensable injury, but had refused to accept the right shoulder injury. An attorney from Eureste's office attended two Benefit ***191** Review Conferences on Granado's behalf and secured an agreement establishing Granado's right shoulder injury as a compensable injury. Notwithstanding that agreement, the carrier denied payment for surgery to the right shoulder maintaining the surgery was not "reasonable and necessary." Granado testified that his physician, Dr. Brooker, repeatedly told him he could not treat his right shoulder because of the carrier's denials and that his lawyer would have to assist him further.

Eureste did not submit any letters or forms to obtain Medical Review for Granado regarding the denials of payment. *See* Tex. Lab.Code Ann. § 413.031 (Vernon Supp. 2002). He testified that he does not represent claimants during the Medical Review process because he cannot bill for that representation. Eureste maintained it is a doctor's responsibility to pursue Medical Review to obtain authorization for a particular treatment.

On April 8, 1997, Granado wrote a letter to Eureste expressing dissatisfaction with the handling of his case. Granado relayed his inability to work and the "agonizing pain" he experienced due to numerous delays and denials of benefits. He complained he had only met with a lawyer twice and that, despite numerous calls to Eureste's office, he still had received no treatment for his right shoulder. He implored Eureste to take immediate action on his case. Four months later, on August 29, 1997, Granado wrote another letter to Eureste complaining that his right shoulder still had not been treated, despite having had Eureste as his attorney for over a year. Granado stated he "called time after time and right now I've exhausted my income and my cabinets are bare."

Granado further testified that all he had received from Eureste during the time he needed surgery were charges for reviewing his file. Eureste billed at his hourly rate and under his name for the intake of Granado's file, although the intake was performed by nonattorney employees in the Amarillo office. He also billed at his rate and in his name for attending Granado's Benefit Review Conferences, although another attorney actually attended the conferences. As with his other clients, Eureste billed Granado's file two and a half hours for "file review" with a resulting fee of $375 per month from May of 1996 until November of 1997. Granado testified that although he rarely spoke with Eureste, he did speak to the ladies in his office for 15 to 20 minutes per month. Eureste admitted that neither he nor his staff had reviewed Granado's file for two and one-half hours every month. Eureste billed a total of $7,875 on Granado's file, of which he collected $5,753.38.

Shortly before Granado's benefits ran out in November 1997, he discovered that Eureste's Amarillo office was being closed. At that time, a staff person informed Granado that Eureste planned to withdraw as his attorney. On January 13, 1998, Eureste sent a letter to Granado withdrawing as his attorney. Eureste testified he withdrew because he was closing his Amarillo and Lubbock offices due to State Bar complaints. After Eureste withdrew, Granado continued on his own to pursue the treatment he needed. He requested a Medical Review hearing in Austin, drove from his home near Amarillo to the hearing, and appeared at the hearing opposite an attorney representing the insurance carrier. He was eventually successful in the Medical Review process and obtained approval for the surgery. He had the surgery in October of 1999, more than three years after he retained Eureste.

Trial Court Proceedings

After State Bar grievance panels conducted hearings and recommended discipline, ***192** Eureste exercised his right to trial de novo in district court. *See* Tex.R. Disciplinary P. 2.14, *reprinted in* Tex. Gov't Code Ann., tit. 2, subtit. G app. A 1 (Vernon 1998). The Commission for Lawyer Discipline ("CFLD") brought this attorney disciplinary action alleging violations of multiple provisions of the Texas Disciplinary Rules of Professional Conduct. The Supreme Court of Texas appointed Judge David Brabham of the 188th District Court of Gregg County to preside over Eureste's disciplinary action in the 152nd District Court of Harris County. *See* Tex.R. Disciplinary P. 3.02, 3.03; Tex. Gov't Code Ann. § 74.057 (Vernon 1998). After a bench trial, the trial court found Eureste had violated Texas Disciplinary Rules of Professional Conduct 1.01(b), 1.03(a), 1.03(b), 1.04(a), 1.15(d), 8.04(a)(1) and 8.04(a)(3). *See* Tex.R. Disciplinary Prof'l Conduct, *reprinted* in Tex. Gov't Code Ann. tit. 2, subtit. G app. A (Vernon 1998). The trial court then imposed sanctions that included a two-year active suspension and a one-year probated suspension. The court also ordered Eureste to pay restitution in the amount of $3,000 to Granado, and to reimburse the CFLD's attorney's fees in the amount of $18,310.

Sufficiency of the Evidence Issues

Eureste challenges the legal and factual sufficiency of the evidence to support the trial court's conclusions regarding his violations of the Texas Disciplinary Rules of Professional Conduct.

1. Standard of Review

[5] [6] In reviewing a challenge to the legal sufficiency of the evidence, a reviewing court must consider only the evidence and reasonable inferences therefrom, which, when viewed in the most favorable light, support the findings of the fact finder. *Southwestern Bell Mobile Sys., Inc. v. Franco,* 971 S.W.2d 52, 54 (Tex.1998); *Foye v. Montes,* 9 S.W.3d 436, 438 (Tex.App.-Houston [14th Dist.] 1999, pet. denied). We must disregard all evidence and inferences which are contrary to the findings. *Franco,* 971 S.W.2d at 54; *Foye,* 9 S.W.3d at 438. If the evidence is legally ***195** sufficient when viewed in this light, then we may not reverse the trial court's judgment. *Franco,* 971 S.W.2d 52, 54; *Harris County Dist. Attorney's Office v. M.G.G.,* 866 S.W.2d 796, 797–98 (Tex.App.-Houston [14th Dist.] 1993, no writ).

[7] [8] When reviewing a challenge to the factual sufficiency of the evidence, we examine the entire record, considering both the evidence in favor of, and contrary to, the challenged finding. Plas-Tex, Inc. v. U.S. Steel Corp., 772 S.W.2d 442, 445 (Tex.1989); *Mayes v. Stewart,* 11 S.W.3d 440, 450 (Tex.App.-Houston [14th Dist.] 2000, pet. denied). We shall set aside the verdict only if it is so contrary to the overwhelming weight of the evidence as to be clearly wrong and unjust. *Ortiz v. Jones,* 917 S.W.2d 770, 772 (Tex.1996); *Mayes,* 11 S.W.3d at 450–51. The trier of fact is the sole judge of the weight and credibility of the witnesses' testimony. *Mayes,* 11 S.W.3d at 450–51; *Knox v. Taylor,* 992 S.W.2d 40, 50 (Tex.App.-Houston [14th Dist.] 1999, no pet.). The appellate court may not substitute its own judgment for that of the trier of fact, even if a different answer could be reached on the evidence. *Knox,* 992 S.W.2d at 50; *Mayes,* 11 S.W.3d at 450. The amount of evidence necessary to affirm a judgment is far less than that necessary to reverse a judgment. *Mayes,* 11 S.W.3d at 450–51; *Knox,* 992 S.W.2d at 50.

2. Eureste's Fees

In his second issue, Eureste challenges the trial court's conclusions regarding his billing practices and resulting fees. Specifically, the trial court found Eureste violated Texas Disciplinary Rules of Professional Conduct 1.04(a) and 8.04(3).

a. Rule 1.04(a)—Illegal or Unconscionable Fees

Texas Disciplinary Rule of Professional Conduct 1.04(a) provides that a lawyer shall not enter into an arrangement for, charge, or collect an illegal or unconscionable fee. Tex.R. Disciplinary P. 1.04(a). Eureste contends there was no evidence at trial that his fees were illegal because they were not prohibited by statute. In support, he argues that "time and labor required" is only one of several factors enumerated by the Labor Code that the TWCC must consider in approving attorney's fees. He further argues the Labor Code does not specify that fees must be billed in a certain manner. We disagree.

[9] Although Section 408.221 of the Labor Code does list certain factors to be considered in approving a fee, only one of which is the time and labor required, Section 408.221 clearly requires that the fees be based on the attorney's actual time. *See* Tex. Lab.Code Ann. § 408.221(b). The TWCC rules also require that fees be based on actual time. 28 Tex. Admin. Code § 152.1(c).

[10] Eureste further contends his fees were not illegal because only the TWCC rules require that time be itemized separately for attorneys and paralegals, and this requirement is not included in the more general provisions of the Labor Code. This contention is without merit. Eureste apparently maintains that because the Labor Code mentions only attorneys, and not paralegals, it does not prohibit him from billing paralegal's time at the attorney's rate. Although paralegals are not specifically mentioned by Section 408.221 of the Labor Code, nothing in Section 408.221 of the Labor Code authorizes Eureste to submit paralegal time as attorney time. *See* Tex. Lab.Code Ann. 408.221. Furthermore, the Labor Code should be read together with the TWCC rules. *See* 28 Tex. Admin. Code 152.4(a) (providing that guidelines outlined in Rule 152.4 shall be considered by TWCC along with factors and maximum ***196** fee limitations set forth in Section 408.221 of Labor Code). The Labor Code provides that fees must be approved by the TWCC, and allows the TWCC to promulgate guidelines for maximum attorney's fees for specific services. *See* Tex. Lab.Code Ann. 408.221(a), (f). The TWCC rules are more specific than, but do not conflict with, Section 408.211 of the Labor Code. The TWCC rules address paralegals, and allow their time to be billed, but separately and at a different rate than attorney time. *See* 28 Tex. Admin. Code § 52.3(a). Additionally, the instructions accompanying Form TWCC-152 could not be more direct in requiring itemization of each individual's actual time. *See* Form TWCC-152.

[11] Eureste acknowledged he submitted fees that were not based on actual time expended in many cases. He also testified he charged paralegal time at the higher attorney rate and billed other attorneys' time as his own. Although Eureste urges on appeal that his fees were not prohibited by law, he, in effect, has admitted to submitting fees prohibited by law. The practical effect of his billing method was that his fees would equal 25 percent of the client's recovery irrespective of actual time spent on the case. Twenty-five percent is the maximum an attorney may bill, not an amount that should be billed regardless of actual time expended. Eureste's billing practices clearly controverted the mandated time based billing system. *See* Tex. Lab.Code Ann. §?408.221; 28 Tex. Admin. Code § 152.1.

[12] Eureste also challenges the court's finding that his fees were unconscionable. Rule 1.04 of the Texas Disciplinary Rules of Professional Conduct provides that a fee is unconscionable if a competent lawyer could not form a reasonable belief that the fee is reasonable. Tex. Disciplinary R. Prof'l Conduct 1.04(a). Rule 1.04(b) lists certain factors that *may* be considered in determining the reasonableness of a fee, *but not to the exclusion of other relevant factors. Id.* Eureste complains the trial court focused almost exclusively on his billing practices, which are not an enumerated factor for determining reasonableness under Rule 1.04, when it should have focused on the fees themselves. The gist of Eureste's argument is that if the trial court had focused on the actual fees instead of his billing practices, the court would have concluded his fees were reasonable. This argument is based on Eureste's contention that the amounts he billed were less than he would have billed had he completed the Form TWCC 152s differently and submitted all billable hours by person and by rate.

The evidence does not support Eureste's contention that his fees were reasonable because he would have billed more had he billed actual activities performed. The only evidence offered by Eureste in support of this contention was Eureste's very general testimony. Although some of Eureste's TWCC fee orders were entered into evidence, there were no corresponding client files in the record showing the work justified the fee award in every case. [FN8] Eureste's logic results in grossly disproportionate billing for those clients who had very little work done on their files. Because the factors enumerated in Rule 1.04(a) are not exclusive, the trial court could consider all relevant evidence, including evidence regarding Eureste's billing ***197*** practices, to determine whether the resulting fees were reasonable. One of the enumerated factors in determining reasonableness under Rule 1.04 is the amount involved and the results obtained. *See* Tex. Disciplinary R. Prof'l Conduct 1.04(b)(4). If a client who had very little work performed on her file is billed the same as every other client, the amount of that fee cannot be considered reasonable in relation to the work performed.

> FN8. The record contains an exhibit prepared by Eureste showing that the total amount of his actual fees billed in July of 1997 was less than the fees would have been if all employees had billed 40 hours per week at the rates set forth in the TWCC rules. However, this report relates to his total billings and not his billings for each client. Moreover, the report only covered one month.

On the other hand, there was evidence that Eureste billed more than he would have billed by using the prescribed method. In fact, the computer file for one particular client reflects that Eureste continued to bill two and one-half hours for file review every month for almost a year after the client's death although the only activity during that entire period consisted of three telephone calls to the decedent's mother. Additionally, Flood calculated that Eureste would have billed approximately $900,000 instead of approximately $2,300,000 during the period from June 1, 1995, to May 31, 1996, had he billed actual time for each file. Assuming that 50 percent of the billings were collected, which is the usual percentage based on Flood's experience, Eureste earned approximately $700,000 above and beyond a reasonable fee.

Moreover, Eureste's argument that his fees were reasonable because they conformed with the TWCC fee guidelines is without merit. Flood testified that the presumption that a fee is reasonable if it does not exceed the guidelines is a rebuttable presumption based on actual time spent by the attorney. Clearly, the guidelines are just that: guidelines. They are the maximum amount that the TWCC will automatically approve for various activities, not the maximum amount an attorney may bill regardless of actual time expended. *See* 28 TEX. ADMIN. CODE § 152.3(b), 152.4(b).

The record reflects it was possible for Eureste to accurately account for his and his employees' time, but it would have cut into his profits to do so because of the size of his practice. He candidly admitted he could not ask an employee to whom he paid $7–8 per hour to keep track of time in the manner prescribed by the TWCC rules. However, Flood testified all other law firms keep track of actual time and that he also kept track of actual time when he represented workers' compensation claimants. Eureste was aware that numerous law firms, including large law firms, bill attorney time at $150 per hour and use elaborate computer accounting programs to keep track of time. Nevertheless, he chose to employ a system whereby he billed every one of his clients (including Granado) $375 per month regardless of the amount of work actually performed. The result was that he billed and collected payment for legal services that were not rendered. That his excessive fees came directly out of his clients' benefit checks is particularly disturbing. Comment 8 to Rule 1.04 states that overreaching by a lawyer, particularly of a client who is unusually susceptible to overreaching, may indicate that a fee is unconscionable. Tex. Disciplinary R. Prof'l Conduct 1.04 cmt. 8. Comment 8 further explains that a fee arrangement with an uneducated or unsophisticated individual having no prior experience in such matters should be more carefully scrutinized for overreaching. *Id.* According to Flood, many of Eureste's clients did not speak English, were not educated, could not read or write, and were not sophisticated. Yet, many of them were penalized as a result of Eureste's billing practices. Accordingly, we hold the evidence is legally and factually sufficient to support the finding that Eureste charged illegal and unconscionable fees. The trial court did ***198*** not err in concluding that Eureste violated Rule 1.04(a).

b. Rule 8.04(a)(3)—Conduct Involving Dishonesty, Fraud, Deceit, or Misrepresentation

[13] Rule 8.04(a)(3) of the Texas Disciplinary Rules of Professional Conduct provides that a lawyer shall not engage in conduct involving dishonesty, fraud, deceit, or misrepresentation. Tex. Disciplinary R. Prof'l Conduct 8.04(a)(3). Fraud is defined under the rules as conduct having a purpose to deceive and not merely negligent misrepresentation or failure to apprise another of relevant information. Tex. Disciplinary R. Prof'l Conduct terminology. Eureste contends he did not commit fraud because there is no evidence he intended to deceive the TWCC, the Fund, or his clients

as to the legal representation provided. However, he ignores the fact that fraud is not the only conduct prohibited by Rule 8.04(a)(3). Any conduct involving dishonesty, deceit, or misrepresentation is also prohibited by Rule 8.04(a)(3). *See* Tex. Disciplinary R. Prof'l Conduct 8.04(a)(3).

Eureste testified he approved the placement of his facsimile signature on each Form TWCC-152 generated by his office. He understood that by approving the placement of his signature on the forms, he was certifying that "every statement, numerical figure, and calculation contained herein is within my personal knowledge and is true and correct, that it represents services, charges, and expenses provided by me or my paralegal under my supervision." The record, however, demonstrates that in many instances, Eureste's forms contained false information. Eureste's testimony reflects that he was aware of the requirement that the fees be itemized for attorneys and paralegals and that they be based on actual time. Notwithstanding his knowledge of those requirements, he made a conscious decision to submit false information and disregard the requirement. Most significantly, he submitted the bills in such a manner that the inaccuracies would not be detected. The trial court could infer an intent to deceive from Eureste consistently billing "beneath the radar." Thus, the record supports the conclusion that his conduct constituted fraud, in addition to dishonesty, deceit, and misrepresentation.

Eureste next contends his representations, even if false, were immaterial because no one was misled since he did not submit fees that were greater than they would have been had he properly completed the forms. However, Rule 8.04(a)(3) does not contain a requirement that the representations be material to constitute a violation. *See* Tex. Disciplinary R. Prof'l Conduct 8.04(a)(3). Eureste cites *Curtis v. Commission for Lawyer Discipline*, 20 S.W.3d 227, 234 (Tex. App.-Houston [14th Dist.] 2000, no pet.) as holding that a misrepresentation under Rule 8.04(a)(3) must be material and have been knowingly made by the attorney with the goal of misleading the party to whom the representation was made. In *Curtis*, the court found that a lawyer had violated Rule 7.02(a)(1), which prohibits a lawyer from making a material representation about his qualifications or services. *Id.* Although the *Curtis* court also considered a separate Rule 8.04(a)(3) violation, it did not establish a requirement of materiality for a Rule 8.04(a)(3) violation. *See id.* Nevertheless, the record reveals that Eureste's fraud was material because as previously discussed, it resulted in some clients being billed for work that was not performed. Some clients were misled because their contracts provided they would be billed in accordance with the workers' compensation laws, but the falsified forms ensured they were not billed in accordance with the workers' compensation ***199** laws. The TWCC was misled because the fees were billed in such a manner that the falsifications would not be detected.

We find the evidence is both legally and factually sufficient to show that Eureste engaged in conduct involving dishonesty, fraud, deceit, or misrepresentation. The trial court did not err in finding that Eureste violated Rule 8.04(a)(3).

3. Issues Regarding Representation of Granado

In his third issue, Eureste challenges the trial court's conclusions regarding his representation of Juan Granado. Specifically, the trial court found Eureste violated Texas Disciplinary Rules of Professional Conduct 1.01(b), 1.03(a) and (b) and 1.15(d).

a. Rule 1.01(b)—Adequacy of Representation

[14] Rule 1.01(b) prohibits a lawyer from neglecting a legal matter entrusted to the lawyer or frequently failing to carry out completely the obligations that the lawyer owes to a client. Tex. Disciplinary R. Prof'l Conduct 1.01(b). As used in the rule, "neglect" means inattentiveness involving a conscious disregard for the responsibilities owed to a client. Tex. Disciplinary R. Prof'l Conduct 1.01(c). Comment 6 to Rule 1.01 explains that having accepted employment, a lawyer should act with competence, commitment, and dedication to the interest of the client and with zeal in advocacy upon the client's behalf. Tex. Disciplinary R. Prof'l Conduct 1.01 cmt. 6. Granado's complaints against Eureste center on Eureste's failure to assist Granado in obtaining surgery on his right shoulder. In essence, Eureste argues he adequately represented Granado because there was nothing more for him to do when he withdrew. Eureste's contract with Granado provided that Eureste would represent Granado in connection with his "claim for workers' compensation benefits." Eureste contends the contract did not impose a duty to represent Granado in pursuing the surgery through Medical Review because Medical Review is not a benefit but a forum for resolving medical disputes after benefits have attached.

[15] There are four types of benefits available to injured workers under the Texas Workers' Compensation Act:

medical, income, death, and burial. *Continental Cas. Insur. Co. v. Functional Restoration Assocs.*, 19 S.W.3d 393, 396 (Tex.2000). Medical Review is the "dispute resolution procedure for certain types of medical benefits disputes." *Id.* Eureste's contract did not specify that Eureste's representation would be limited or would not encompass Medical Review.

[16] The record reflects that the statements and actions of Eureste and his staff led Granado to believe Eureste felt an obligation to assist him in obtaining the right shoulder surgery. The contractual relationship between an attorney and client, whereby the attorney agrees to render professional services for the client, may be express or implied from the parties' conduct. *Byrd v. Woodruff*, 891 S.W.2d 689, 700 (Tex.App.-Dallas 1994, writ denied). Although Eureste contends he repeatedly informed Granado that he could not represent him in Medical Review, the record contains evidence that neither Eureste nor his staff replied to Granado's requests for assistance with a statement that they could not assist him further. Instead, during the time Granado inquired about the surgery, Eureste told him to "be patient" because these matters "take time." The notes in Granado's file reflect that on November 4, 1997, Granado called Eureste's office and inquired if his shoulder was going to be treated. A staff ***200** person responded that she would talk to the attorney and "find out what we can do." Eureste admitted that one could conclude from Granado's August 29, 1997, letter requesting Eureste's assistance that Granado thought Eureste had a duty to help him get his operation. Moreover, Eureste provided conflicting testimony regarding the extent of his duties. At trial, he denied he had a duty to represent claimants in Medical Review. However, he previously testified by deposition that "[m]aybe we have a duty, even though we cannot be compensating [sic] to continue to represent people at that level."

Finally, Eureste's contention that he had no duty to further assist Granado in obtaining surgery is controverted by his own withdrawal letter. Eureste wrote, "[p]lease attempt to seek the services of another attorney to represent you in your case. While having an attorney to represent you in workers' compensation claims in Texas is not required, I am convinced that legal representation in these matters is important." At that time, obtaining surgery to the right shoulder was the only benefit left to obtain in Granado's case. The letter acknowledges there was further work for an attorney to perform on Granado's case.

Therefore, the record contains sufficient evidence from which the trial court could conclude Eureste did not take appropriate steps to obtain Medical Review for Granado or otherwise assist him through that process.

We hold the evidence is both legally and factually sufficient to show neglect and failure to completely carry out Eureste's obligations to Granado. The trial court did not err in finding that Eureste violated Rule 1.01(b).

b. Rules 1.03(a) and (b)—Communications with Granado

[17] Rule 1.03(a) requires a lawyer to keep a client reasonably informed about the status of a matter and promptly comply with reasonable requests for information. Tex. Disciplinary R. Prof'l Conduct 1.03(a). Rule 1.03(b) requires a lawyer to explain a matter to the extent reasonably necessary to permit the client to make informed decisions regarding the representation. Tex. Disciplinary R. Prof'l Conduct 1.03(b). Comment 2 to Rule 1.03 illustrates that it is not the quantity, but the quality and content of the communications that shows compliance with Rule 1.03. *See* Tex. Disciplinary R. Prof'l Conduct 1.03 cmt. 2. According to Comment 2, the guiding principle is that the lawyer should reasonably fulfill client expectations for information consistent with the duty to act in the client's best interests and the client's overall requirements as to the character of representation. *Id.*

As Eureste notes, the record shows numerous telephone conversations between Granado and Eureste's office. Eureste contends the only evidence of inadequate communication with Granado was Granado's testimony that he did not believe Eureste communicated with him enough. However, Granado assailed the quality as well as the quantity of Eureste's communication with him. It is clear from Granado's testimony that his expectations were not met. Granado testified that when he tried to call Eureste at his office, he was told Eureste was not there or was unavailable. Then, the staff in the Amarillo office became angry at Granado and told him: "You are supposed to come to us before you talk to him." However, the staff never explained to Granado what they were doing to help him. Instead, Granado testified the staff told him: "You are just going to have to talk to Mr. Eureste. He is your lawyer." According to Granado, Eureste called him about four times, but Eureste ***201** never told Granado what he was doing to help him obtain the operation. Most importantly, the communications between Granado and Eureste or his office led Granado to believe Eureste had an obligation to help him obtain the surgery. Granado was clearly left with the expectation that Eureste would help him obtain the surgery.

We find the evidence is both legally and factually sufficient to show Eureste failed to keep Granado reasonably informed. The trial court did not err in finding that Eureste violated Rule 1.03(a) and Rule 1.03(b).

c. Rule 1.15(b)—Withdrawal from Representation

[18] Rule 1.15(d) provides that upon termination of representation, a lawyer shall take steps to the extent reasonably practicable to protect a client's interests, such as giving reasonable notice to the client, allowing time for employment of other counsel, surrendering papers and property to which the client is entitled, and refunding any advance payments of unearned fees. Tex. Disciplinary R. Prof'l Conduct 1.15(d). Eureste contends his withdrawal complied with the requirements of Rule 1.15 in that he gave reasonable notice both verbally and in writing, allowed time for employment of other counsel, and returned Granado's file. He also contends that because Granado did not ask for the return of any unearned fees, he was in full compliance with Rule 1.15. We disagree with Eureste's contention that he complied with Rule 1.5.

There is evidence from which the trial court could reasonably infer that Eureste abruptly withdrew when there were no more benefits from which to extract attorney's fees. Eureste's withdrawal corresponded with the time that Granado's benefits ran out. Granado testified he did not even know the Amarillo office was being closed until he called the office and was informed he had reached the Houston office instead. He was also not informed that Eureste planned to withdraw until he was informed by a staff person that "Bernardo Eureste is going to drop you."

We find the evidence is legally and factually sufficient to show that Eureste failed to take reasonable steps to protect Granado's interests when Eureste withdrew. The trial court did not err in finding that Eureste violated Rule 1.15(b).

d. Rule 8.04(a)(1)—General Violations

[19] [20] In his fourth issue, Eureste challenges the legal and factual sufficiency of the evidence supporting the trial court's finding that he violated Rule 8.04(a)(1). Rule 8.04(a)(1) is a general rule that prohibits a lawyer from violating, or knowingly assisting, inducing, or acting through another to violate the Texas Disciplinary Rules of Professional Conduct. Tex. Disciplinary R. Prof'l Conduct 8.04(a)(1). All that is necessary to establish a violation of Rule 8.04(a)(1) is a violation of another rule. *See id.* We conclude that because the evidence is legally and factually sufficient to support the trial court's finding that Eureste violated Rules 1.01(b)(1), 1.01(b)(2), 1.03(a), 1.03(b), 1.04(a), 1.15(d) and 8.04(a)(3), the evidence is legally and factually sufficient to support the trial court's finding that Eureste violated Rule 8.04(a)(1).

C. Sanctions

[21] [22] [23] [24] Eureste contends in his fifth and final issue that the trial court abused its discretion when it ordered the sanction of suspension. Sanctions for professional misconduct may include disbarment, resignation in lieu of disbarment, indefinite disability suspension, suspension for a certain term, probation of suspension, interim suspension, ***202** public reprimand, and private reprimand. Tex.R. Disciplinary P. 1.06(T). A trial court has broad discretion to determine the consequences of professional misconduct. *Love v. State Bar of Texas*, 982 S.W.2d 939, 944 (Tex.App.-Houston [1st Dist.] 1998, no pet.); *State Bar of Texas v. Kilpatrick*, 874 S.W.2d 656, 659 (Tex.1994); *Curtis*, 20 S.W.3d at 234–35. However, the judgment of a trial court in a disciplinary proceeding may be so light or heavy as to amount to an abuse of discretion. *Love*, 982 S.W.2d at 944; *Kilpatrick*, 874 S.W.2d at 659. An appellate court should only reverse the trial court's decision if an abuse of discretion is shown. *Love*, 982 S.W.2d at 944. A court abuses its discretion only when it acts in an unreasonable and arbitrary manner, or when it acts without reference to any guiding principles. *Furr's Supermarkets, Inc. V. Bethune*, 53 S.W.3d 375, 379 (Tex.2001); *Love*, 982 S.W.2d at 944. The court must consider the following factors in determining the appropriate sanction: (1) the nature and degree of the professional misconduct for which the respondent is being sanctioned; (2) the seriousness of and circumstances surrounding the professional misconduct; (3) the loss or damage to clients; (4) the damage to the profession; (5) the assurance that those who seek legal services in the future will be insulated from the type of professional misconduct found; (6) the profit to the attorney; (7) the avoidance of repetition; (8) the deterrent effect on

others; (9) the maintenance of respect for the legal profession; (10) the conduct of the respondent during the course of the Committee action; (11) the trial of the case; and (12) other relevant evidence concerning the respondent's personal and professional background. Tex.R. Disciplinary P. 3.10; *Kilpatrick*, 874 S.W.2d at 659; *Curtis*, 20 S.W.3d at 235.

We find that in imposing the sanctions, the trial court did not act in an unreasonable and arbitrary manner or without reference to any guiding principles. To the contrary, the record shows the trial court considered the relevant factors outlined in Texas Rule of Disciplinary Procedure 3.10. In particular, the trial court found: (1) Eureste's actions were of a serious nature and degree; (2) the loss to Eureste's clients from their workers' compensation benefits was great; (3) the legal profession had been badly damaged by Eureste's conduct; (4) it is important to insulate future workers' compensation claimants and other clients from the risk of Eureste's billing practices; (5) Eureste profited greatly from his fraudulent billing scheme; and (6) other attorneys should be deterred from similar actions regarding their billing practices.

Eureste argues the sanction of suspension is unduly harsh because he has assisted many clients and his streamlined office procedures may have maximized client benefits. Eureste cites cases in which attorneys who committed allegedly more egregious conduct than Eureste received lighter sentences. However, the trial court had broad discretion in balancing the evidence in this case and applying it in terms of the statutory factors. [FN9] Considering the range of sanctions available to the court, the conduct at issue, and the trial ***203** court's reasoning, we conclude the trial court did not abuse its broad discretion in imposing the sanction of suspension upon Eureste.

FN9. The trial court, in fact, specifically found Eureste genuinely believed his method of practicing was a means and manner to help people although he did so in the wrong way and that Eureste was cooperative during the disciplinary process. However pure Eureste's intentions may have been, the result of his conduct was that he greatly profited at the expense of his clients whose workers' compensation checks were reduced by his illegal and unconscionable fees. One of his clients, Granado, suffered personally from Eureste's lack of adequate representation, while Eureste overbilled and profited from his case.

Case Review Exercises

1. How did the attorney manipulate the TWCC rules regarding not having to justify bills?
2. Did you feel the attorney's internal policy of billing the maximum amount possible complied with the TWCC's rules of billing actual time spent?
3. Were you surprised that this billing "beneath the radar" scheme was so effective?
4. Did the attorney commit fraud?
5. What did you think of the attorney's practice of billing paralegal time as attorney time?
6. What was the attorney's rationale for billing more than 24 hours in a day for himself? Was it credible?
7. Do you suppose that for a very small part of the $2.3 million the attorney billed in one year, he could have secured computers and a state-of-the-art timekeeping and billing system that could have tracked actual time spent?
8. Did the attorney earn the hours he billed for in the Granado case?
9. Did you find it unconscionable that the attorney billed 2.5 hours a month for almost a year after a client had died?
10. What did you think of the trial court's decision to give the attorney a two-year active suspension, a one-year probated suspension, and restitution in the amount of $3,000 to Granado, and to reimburse the CFLD's attorney's fees of $18,310? Did you agree with their reasoning? How much money did the investigator find that the attorney received beyond what was a reasonable fee?

Case Review

Committee for Public Counsel Services v. Lookner, 47 Mass.App.Ct. 833, 716 N.E. 2d 690 (Mass. App. 1999)

(Cite as: 47 Mass.App.Ct. 833, 716 N.E.2d 690)

Appeals Court of Massachusetts, Suffolk.

COMMITTEE FOR PUBIC COUNSEL SERVICES

v.

Norman S. LOOKNER.

No, 97-P-2138.

Argued April 8, 1999.

Decided Sept. 29, 1999.

Mary Murphy-Hensley, Boston, Assistant Attorney General, for the plaintiff.

Present: LAURENCE, SMITH, & SPINA, JJ.

LAURENCE, J.

Norman S. Lookner is an attorney licensed to practice in the Commonwealth. As part of his practice, he was certified to, and did, accept paid assignments from the Committee for Public Counsel Services (committee) (see G.L. c. 211D) to represent indigent clients in cases involving custody of children, delinquency charges, and termination of parental rights. In early 1995, he was the subject of an audit by the committee, which investigated his billing practices (see G.L. c. 211D, § 12).

A committee auditor found that Lookner had overbilled the committee $18,445 in fiscal year 1994 by billing at least .25 hours for each task, such as a short telephone call, as opposed to billing the actual time worked in a given day rounded off to the nearest quarter of an hour. In addition, Lookner's time sheets did not record the actual amount of time spent on billable***834** tasks or explain the nature of the work performed. Lookner had billed the committee 2,327 hours over 364 days of the fiscal year and was paid $79,022.63 for fiscal year 1994 services. The auditor recommended to the committee's executive committee that Lookner repay $18,445 in overbillings within 24 months.

Lookner appealed the auditor's recommendation and requested a hearing. On November 1, 1995, pursuant to the procedures set forth in Section E of the committee's Manual for Counsel Assigned Through the Committee for Public Counsel Services—Policies and Procedures (June 1995) (manual), a hearing officer conducted a hearing at which Lookner was represented by an attorney. The manual, which is binding upon all "[a]ttorneys who accept ****692** assignments of cases through the Committee," expressly provides that "[t]he action of the Executive Committee Hearing Officer shall be final." On February 28, 1996, the hearing officer issued his findings and final decision, concurring with the auditor's findings but reducing the overbilled amount to $11,130, payable within 12 months on terms to be mutually agreed upon by Lookner's attorney and the committee's audit staff.

After a hearing on the committee's motion to dismiss the complaint on August 16, 1996, a judge of the Superior Court ruled that the time for seeking relief under G.L. c. 249, §4, had expired but that Lookner's count for declaratory relief had been timely asserted. After a further hearing, on December 19, 1996, a second Superior Court judge allowed the committee's motion to dismiss, not only on the ground that it was untimely, [FN1] but also because Lookner's claim for declaratory relief could not be maintained against the judiciary department (see G.L. c. 231A, § 2), of which the committee is a part. We conclude that the dismissal of Lookner's certiorari count was correct on this record. [FN2]

Case Review Exercises

1. Do you think Mr. Lookner expected the Committee for Public Counsel Services to conduct an audit of his billings?
2. Do you think a court would take into account the types of clients Lookner would be representing and the fact that the Committee is a nonprofit/governmental entity?

3. What do you think of the auditor's conclusion that the Committee had been overbilled by Lookner's rounding tasks to .25 hours instead of billing for the actual time incurred?
4. What if Lookner had argued that in some instances he billed .25 when the service was actually .30 or .35, that he actually rounded down, and that it "all came out in the wash" and was, in fact, reasonably fair? Is this argument compelling to you?
5. Lookner failed to keep detailed records of exactly what he did on cases, but did record the amount of time he spent. Why was this not enough to please the auditors? What other fact concerned the auditors and led them to question even the amount of time that he recorded?
6. Did Lookner's billing practices violate the *Model Rules?* Why?

Helpful Web Sites

Organization	Description	Internet Address
Alabama State Bar—Law Office Management Assistance Program	Articles on a variety of law office management topics, including billing-related articles and information.	https://www.alabar.org/programs-departments/practice-management-assistance-program-pmap/
American Bar Association (ABA)	Association for attorneys. The site has a large amount of information and publications relevant to individuals working in the legal profession.	http://www.americanbar.org
ABA Law Practice Today	ABA site devoted to law practice management issues, including timekeeping and billing issues.	http://www.americanbar.org/groups/law_practice.html
ABA Legal Technology Resource Center	ABA site devoted to technology. Includes resources and articles.	http://www.americanbar.org/groups/departments_offices/legal_technology_resources.html
Association of Legal Administrators	National association for legal administrators. Contains resources and information related to law office management and legal administration.	http://www.alanet.org
Georgia State Bar Association	Articles on a variety of law office management topics, including billing-related articles and information.	http://www.gabar.org
Law Technology News	Excellent periodical for legal technology issues. Good white papers on technology issues.	http://www.msba.org/practicemanagement/default.aspx
Maryland State Bar Association—Law Practice Management Assistance	Articles on a variety of law office management topics, including billing-related articles and information.	http://www.msbar.org
Mississippi State Bar Association	Articles on a variety of law office management topics, including billing-related articles and information.	
National Association of Paralegals	National association for paralegals. Contains many resources for paralegals.	http://www.nala.org
National Federation of Paralegal Associations	National association for paralegals. Contains many resources for paralegals.	http://www.paralegals.org
New Jersey State Bar Association—Law Office Management Articles	Articles on a variety of law office management topics, including billing-related articles and information.	http://www.njsba.com/
New York State Bar Association	Articles on a variety of law office management topics, including billing-related articles and information.	http://www.nysba.org/
South Carolina Bar—Practice Management Section	Articles on a variety of law office management topics, including billing-related articles and information.	http://www.scbar.org/Bar-Members/Practice-Management-PMAP

Timekeeping and Billing Software

Organization	Product/Service	Internet Address
Abacus Data Systems	Abacus Law—accounting and billing program	http://www.abacuslaw.com/
ADC Legal Systems, Inc.	Practice Perfect—billing and accounting	http://www.adclegal.com
Clio	Web-based accounting and Billing program	http://www.goclio.com
Journyx, Inc.	Journyx Timesheet/e-billing	http://www.journyx.com
LexisNexis	PCLaw Legal timekeeping and billing software Juris—Legal timekeeping and billing software	http://www.lexisnexis.com/law-firm-practice-management/pclaw/
Sage Software, Inc.	Timeslips legal timekeeping and billing software	http://na.sage.com/us/sage-timeslips
Thomas Reuters Elite	ProLaw legal timekeeping and billing software.	http://www.elite.com
TimeSolv	Easy Time and Billing Software	http://www.timesolv.com/

Suggested Reading

1. Morgan, J. H. & Foonberg, J. (2003). *How to Draft Bills Client Rush to Pay.* (2nd ed.). American Bar Association.
2. Foonberg, J. (2004). *How To Start and Build a Law Practice.* (5th ed.). American Bar Association. (6th ed. available in e-book only).
3. *Law Practice* magazine, published by the American Bar Association Law Practice Management Section http://www.lawpracticetoday.org/.
4. *Paralegal Today* magazine, published by Conexion International Media, Inc. http://www.paralegaltoday.com.
5. Munneke, G. A., & Davis, A. E. (2003, 2007, 2010). *The Essential Formbook: Comprehensive Management Tools for Lawyers, Volumes I–IV.* American Bar Association.
6. Greene, A. G. (2012). *The Lawyer's Guide to Increasing Revenue, E-Book.* (Second Edition). American Bar Association.
7. Robertson, M. A., & Calloway, J. A. (2008). *Winning Alternatives to the Billable Hour.* (Third Edition). American Bar Association.

Hands-On Exercises:
Clio—Timekeeping and Billing

Training Manual Outline

Number	Lesson Title	Concepts Covered
Lesson 1*	Part A: Introduction to Clio Part B: Set Up Law Firm Profile	Understanding the Clio platform Details for firm description
Lesson 2	Creating Time Records	Making time entries into Clio
Lesson 3	Using the Timer Feature and Entering Expense Slips	Making expense entries into Clio and using the timer feature to automatically track and record time
Lesson 4	Producing Prebills, Final Bills, and Reports	Producing prebill reports, final bills, and other timekeeping and billing reports

*Note: Lesson 1—Introduction to Clio is the same for every subject matter. If you completed Lesson 1 in an earlier tutorial, you do not need to repeat it.

Welcome to Adams & Lee

Welcome to Adams & Lee! We are an active and growing firm with six attorneys and three paralegals. As you know, you have been hired as a paralegal intern. We are very happy to have you on board; we can certainly use your help.

At Adams & Lee, we put an emphasis on providing quality legal services to our clients. We bill our clients on a regular basis for these quality services, typically on a monthly basis, depending on the needs of our clients. We strive to make sure our billings are timely and without errors. Because billings and fee disputes are some of the most common types of ethical complaints filed against lawyers, we require that all staff members understand the billing process. In addition, we want our staff members to have many job skills and to be flexible enough to enter their own time entries into the computer. All staff members are required to have at least minimal training in our billing system. We have developed this training manual to help you learn our system.

We currently use Clio, a comprehensive, yet easy-to-use cloud-based law practice management software. Clio automates the practice and management side of operating a law firm. Clio has powerful features to manage cases, clients, documents, bills, appointments, time-tracking, reporting, and accounting.

During the training exercise you will enter information as a non-attorney. We know you want begin using Clio immediately and learning the office case management system will help you gain the skills needed to maintain the client services we deliver. You should review the "Getting Started" guide to help you become familiar with Clio.

Getting Started

Introduction

Throughout these exercises, information you need to type into the program will be designated in several different ways.

- Keys to be pressed on the keyboard will be designated in brackets, in all caps and bold type (e.g., press the **[ENTER]** key).
- Movements with the mouse/pointer will be designated in bold and italics (e.g., ***point to File on the Menu Bar and click the pointer).***
- Words or letters that should be typed are designated in bold (e.g., type **Training Program**).
- Information that is or should be displayed on your computer screen is shown in bold, with quotation marks (e.g., **"Press ENTER to continue"**).

Clio Installation (Appendix A)

Clio is not a downloaded program; it is accessed from the Web site. You may be invited by your instructor to join as a nonlawyer (paralegal) in a hypothetical law firm through your e-mail. ***Click the hyperlink or copy and paste it into your Internet browser. Follow the on-screen instructions for providing your name and creating a password.*** You will now have access to Clio and the hypothetical law firm.

Your instructor may have you create a Clio account and work independently. In that case, see Appendix A for installation instructions.

LESSON 1: Part A (Appendix B)

You should become familiar with the Clio Platform and its essential functions before you begin any of the lessons. *Note*: If you are already logged in, you will skip Steps 1 and 2.

1. Start your Internet browser. Type **www.goclio.com** in the Internet browser and press the **[ENTER] key**.
2. On the Clio Home page, ***click Log In. On the next screen, enter the e-mail address and password you provided in Clio and click SIGN IN. If you check the box next to KEEP ME SIGNED IN, you will be able to skip this step in the future.***
3. Clio will open in the hypothetical law firm on the PRACTICE page. At this point you are ready to explore the Clio platform and its essential functions. There are 11 tabs available in Clio. We will start with the PRACTICE tab.
4. ***Click*** **PRACTICE**. Your screen should now look like Clio Exhibit 1A-1. This is the Clio dashboard which provides a quick look at the agenda, calendar, and billing information. You will now explore the other 10 tabs.

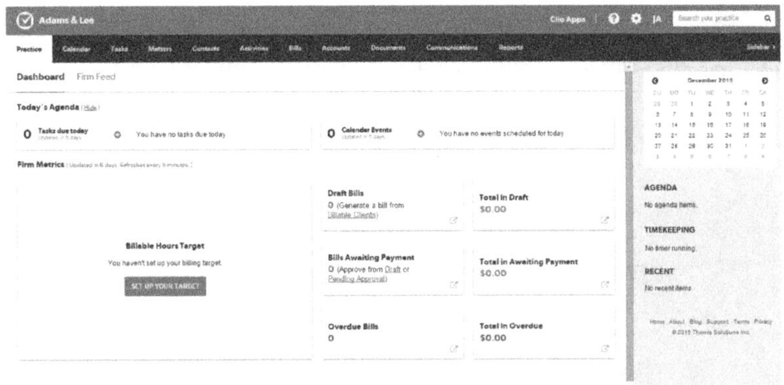

Clio Exhibit 1A-1 Practice Tab

Source: Themis Solutions, Inc.

5. ***Click* CALENDAR.** You may need to scroll down to see the entire page. You can change the view to see your Agenda, or Day, Week, Month, or Year views. You can view your personal calendar, the firm calendar or both.
6. To create a calendar entry, while in the Week view, ***select the Wednesday of that current week and double-click on the 10:00 am time slots.*** The Create Calendar Entry will open. See Clio Exhibit 1A-2. If you ***click Add Event,*** the date will default to the current date.

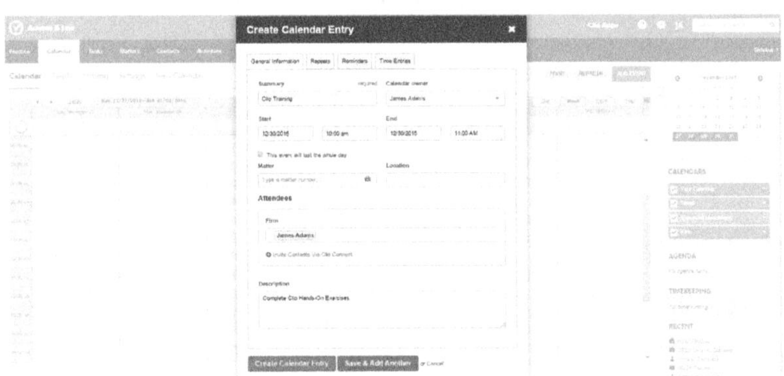

Clio Exhibit 1A-2 Create Calendar Entry

Source: Themis Solutions, Inc.

Under Summary, type **Clio Training**. Under **Start**, type **10:00 AM** and under **End** type **11:00 AM**. Leave Matter and Location "**blank**," and under Description, type **Complete Clio Hands-On Exercises.** ***Click Create Calendar Entry.*** When adding multiple entries, ***click Save & Add Another.*** After the entry is complete, it will appear in the calendar. ***Place your cursor over the new calendar entry*** to see the description. Your calendar should look like Clio Exhibit 1A-3. You can now move to the "Tasks" tab.

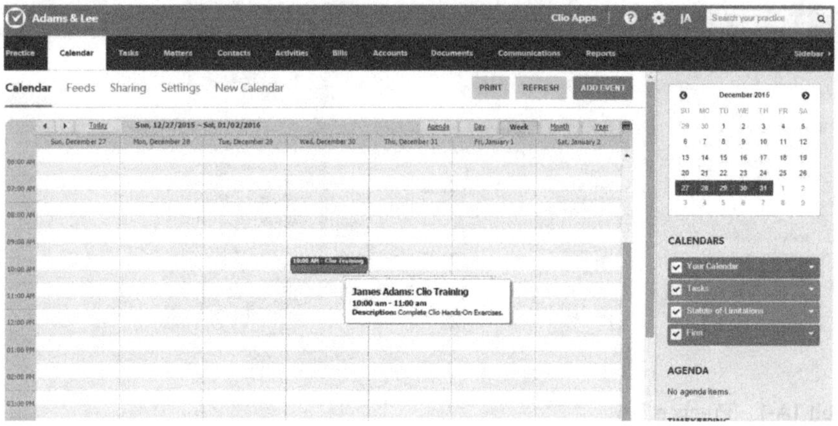

Clio Exhibit 1A-3 Calendar Entry

Source: Themis Solutions, Inc.

7. ***Click* TASKS**. This is where specific tasks can be assigned to specific individuals or groups. To create a new Task, ***click Add.*** See Clio Exhibit 1A-4. Under Task Name, type **Clio Training**.

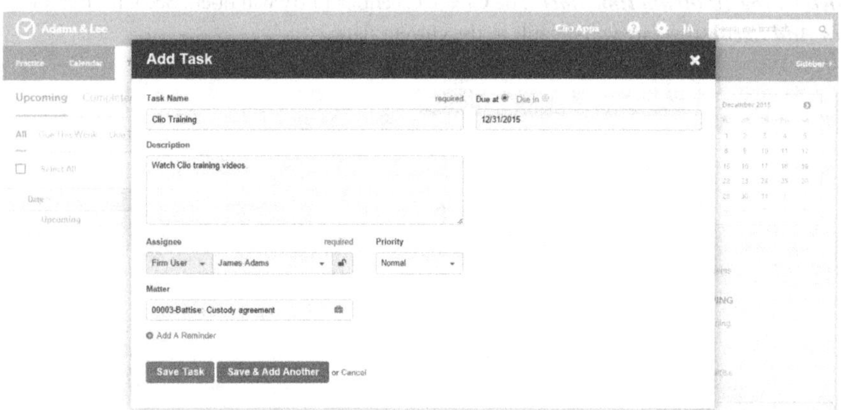

Clio Exhibit 1A-4 Add Task – "Due At"

Source: Themis Solutions, Inc.

Under Description, type **Watch Clio training videos**. Under Due: the radial button will default to **"Due at"** when there are no other tasks associated. ***Click the box under "Due At,"*** and a calendar will appear. ***Select Thursday of the current week.*** Under Assignee, ***select Firm User and then choose yourself.*** Under Priority, ***select Normal.*** Under Matter, ***type 00003-Battise: Custody Agreement*** (the case will appear in the list as you begin typing the number). Then ***click Save Task.*** When adding multiple tasks, ***select Save and Add Another.*** At this point you will be on the ***"tasks" under 00003-Battise.*** See Clio Exhibit 1A-5.

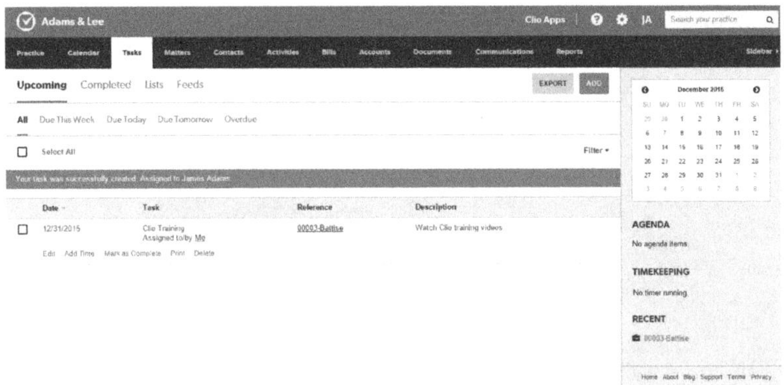

Clio Exhibit 1A-5 Task Entry – "Due At"

Source: Themis Solutions, Inc.

8. When you have several assigned tasks under a specific case matter, you have the option of choosing **"Due in"** which allows you to choose a date in relation to other Tasks in the Matter. From your current position in (Exhibit 1A-5), ***select Add***. Your screen should again look like Exhibit 1A-3. Under Task Name, type **Clio Training**. Under Description, type **Watch Clio Introduction Videos**. Under Assignee, ***select Firm User and then choose yourself***. Under Priority, ***select Normal***. Under Matter, ***type 00003-Battise: Custody Agreement*** (the case will appear in the list as you begin typing the number).Then ***select 00003Battise: Custody Agreement***. Under Due: the radial will default to **"Due at,"** however; you now have the option to choose **"Due in."** ***Select "Due in,"*** and a dialogue box will appear. See Clio Exhibit 1A-6.

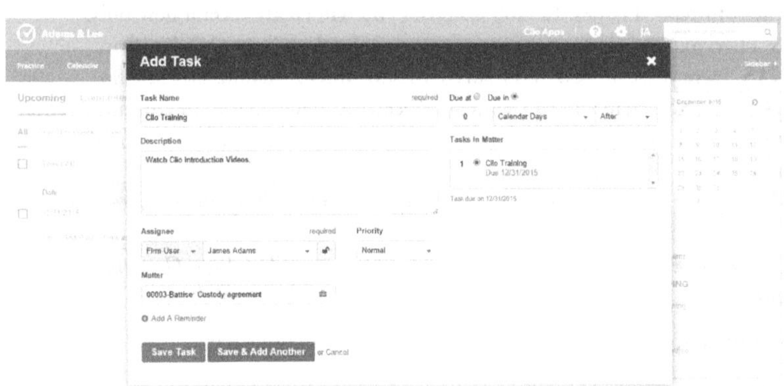

Clio Exhibit 1A-6 Add Task – "Due In"

Source: Themis Solutions, Inc.

ENTER **"1"** in the box marked with a 0. ***Select Calendar Weeks*** under the drop-down menu in the next box, ***Select before*** under the drop-down menu in the next box. Then ***select Clio Training*** under the radial button. ***Click Save Task***. The second task will now appear listed on the Tasks page. See Clio Exhibit 1A-7.

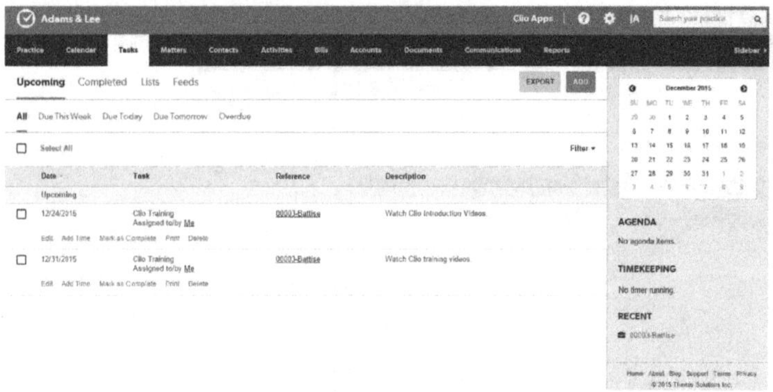

Clio Exhibit 1A-7 Task Entry - "Due In"

Source: Themis Solutions, Inc.

9. ***Click* MATTERS**. Matters are what Clio calls for cases or files. Clio allows you to associate, or connect, matters with clients, tasks, bills, etc. In later exercises you will see how that works and you will create several new matters.
10. ***Click* CONTACTS**. Contacts are people and corporations that you do business with (clients, other attorneys, court reporters, etc.).
11. ***Click* ACTIVITIES**. "Activities" is what Clio uses for both time and billing entries as well as expense entries. Time entries can be billed as a flat rate or as an hourly rate. In later exercises you will create several new billing activities.
12. ***Click* BILLS**. Here, you can create a new bill, review a client's billing history, and create bill themes (designs) among other bill-related issues. In later exercises you will create several new bills.
13. ***Click* ACCOUNTS**. Here you can view and manage the various bank accounts of a law firm.
14. ***Click* DOCUMENTS**. Here you can view and manage the documents maintained in Clio.
15. ***Click* COMMUNICATIONS**. Here you can send and receive e-mails, maintain communication logs, interact with colleagues and Clio-connected users, as well as limit permissions between groups for file-related communications.
16. ***Click* REPORTS**. Here you can create reports on a variety of topics (billing client, mater, productivity, and revenue).
17. To end this Clio session, ***click your initials at the top of the screen. Click Sign Out and then close your Internet Browser.***

This concludes the introduction lesson on Clio's platform and essential functions review.

LESSON 1: Part B (Appendix C)

In this lesson, you will set up the firm profile in the hypothetical law firm, establish billing rate, create an activity description, set up bank accounts and establish the matter-numbering protocol.

Note: If you are already logged in, you will skip Steps 1 and 2.

1. Start your Internet browser. Type www.goclio.com in the Internet browser and press the **[ENTER] key**.
2. On the Clio Home page, ***click Log In. On the next screen, enter the e-mail address and password you provided in Clio and click SIGN IN. If you check the box next to KEEP ME SIGNED IN, you will be able to skip this step in the future.***
3. Before you enter new clients, contacts and matters in Clio, details for the hypothetical law firm should be entered. First, you will set up the account information for your hypothetical law firm. ***Click the "settings" icon*** (looks like a gear) at the top of the screen next to the "***initials.***" Your screen should look like Clio Exhibit 1B-1.

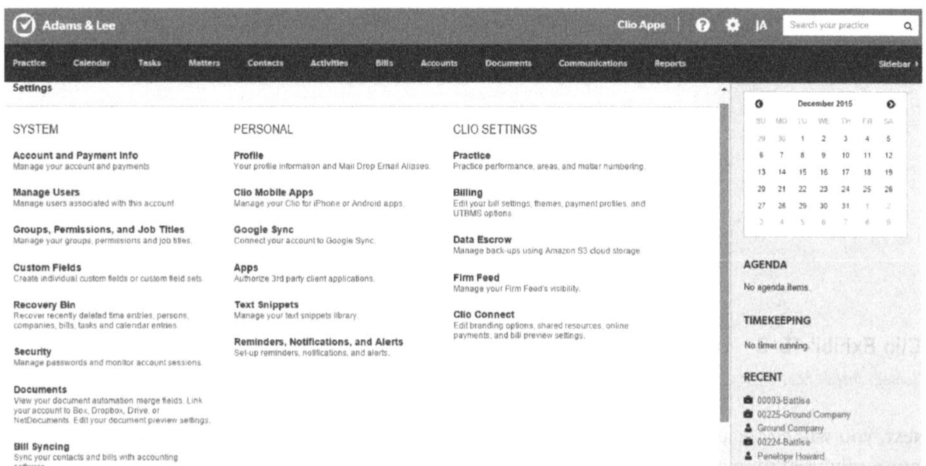

Clio Exhibit 1B-1 Clio Settings Screen

Source: Themis Solutions, Inc.

4. ***Click Account and Payment Info.*** The name of your hypothetical law firm will be established by your instructor (i.e., Adams & Lee) or your First and Last name if you create your own individual account (i.e., Law Office of "First name" "Last name" that you entered). Note: Free accounts do not have access to payment info.
5. ***Type the name, address, and contact information of your firm*** (i.e., sample check from Exhibit 6-1 (Chapter 6), instructor provided, or create your own).
6. Next, ***click the drop-down menu under Date format. Select*** the option that resembles ***12/31/2015.*** Then, ***click the drop-down menu under Time format. Select*** the option that resembles ***11:59 pm. Click Save New Information.***
7. You will now update profile and establish a billing rate. ***Click*** the "settings" icon (looks like a gear) at the top of the screen next to the "initials." Your screen should look like Clio Exhibit 1B-1. ***Click Profile*** and scroll down to **Billing Rate**. ***Type 175.00 next to $/Hr. Click Save New Information.*** See Clio Exhibit 1B-2.

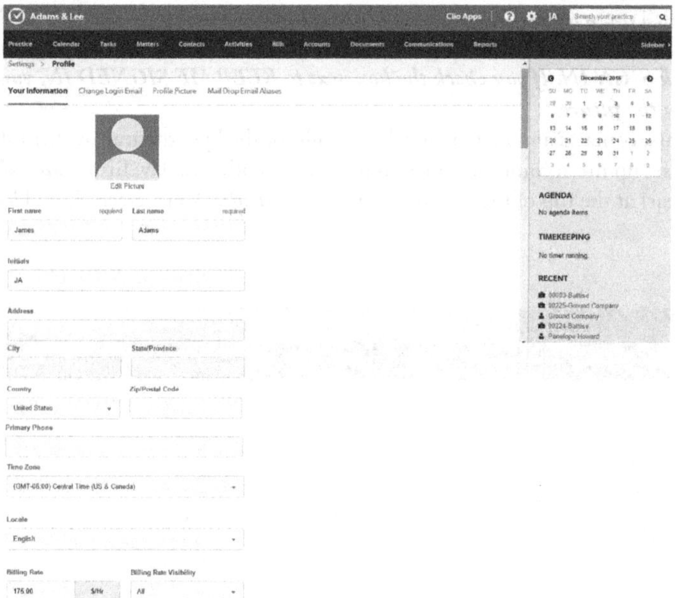

Clio Exhibit 1B-2 Update Profile – Billing Rate

Source: Themis Solutions, Inc.

8. Next, you will create an Activity Description. These are used to ensure a consistent description of commonly used time entries across a law firm. It can also be used as a shortcut—you can save text in the Activity Description and when you enter in a time entry, it will populate this text for you. Activity Descriptions can be shared across a law firm so that everyone in the firm can use them. ***Click the Activities tab, then click Activity Descriptions, then click Add.*** See Clio Exhibit 1B-3.

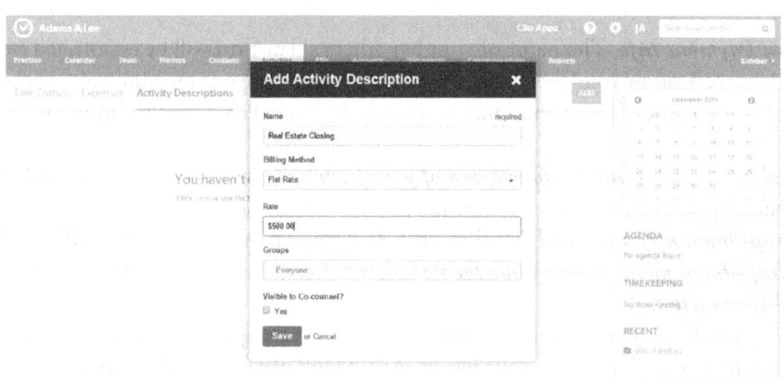

Clio Exhibit 1B-3 Add Activity Description

Source: Themis Solutions, Inc.

Under Name, type **Real Estate Closing**. Under Billing Method, ***select Flat Rate***. This opens a text box called Rate; type **$500.00** in the text box, ***Click Save.*** This flat rate fee will override the $175.00 per hour established as the default rate.

9. Next, you will create bank accounts. ***Click the Accounts tab***, then ***click New***. You will set up two accounts—the first will be a Trust Account (one that contains only client money) and the second will be an Operating account (one that ***should not*** contain client money). See Clio Exhibit 1B-4.

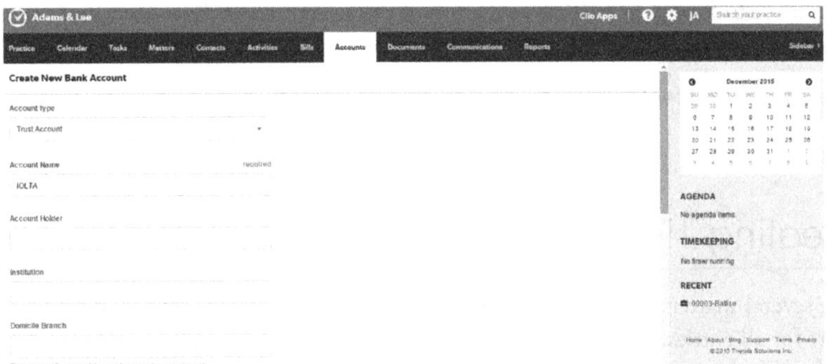

Clio Exhibit 1B-4 Create New Bank Account

Source: Themis Solutions, Inc.

10. Under Account type, ***select Trust Account***. Under Account name, type **IOLTA** (this stands for Interest on Law Office Trust Account, commonly used for Trust accounts). It is not necessary, nor is it required, to complete the remainder of this form (although you are welcomed to do so). However, you should leave the Balance 0.0. ***Click Create New Bank Account***. The screen will refresh (showing the new IOLTA account) so additional accounts may be created.
11. Now create the Operating Account. ***Click New***, then under Account type, ***select Operating Account***. Under Account name, type **Law Firm Account**. It is not necessary, nor is it required, to complete the remainder of this form (although you are welcomed to do so). However, you should leave the Balance 0.0. ***Click the box next to Default Account***. (The default account will show up first on the Transactions tab found when a client file is opened under Matters.) ***Click Create New Bank Account***.
12. You will now create the matter-numbering protocol for the hypothetical law firm. ***Click the "settings" icon*** (looks like a gear) at the top of the screen next to the "***initials***." Your screen should look like Clio Exhibit 1B-1. ***Click Practice***, and then ***click Matter Numbering***. See Clio Exhibit 1B-5.

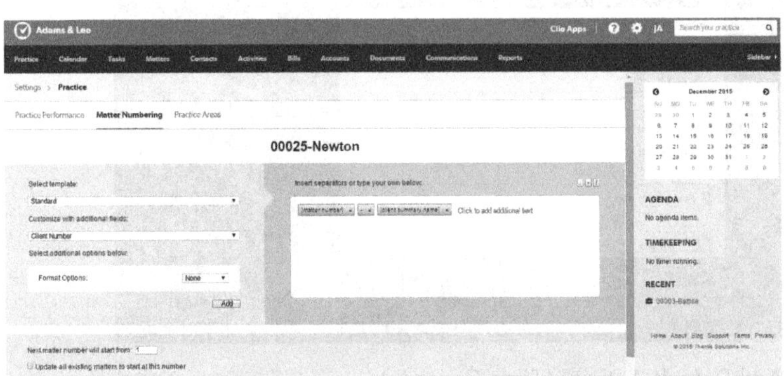

Clio Exhibit 1B-5 Matter Numbering

Source: Themis Solutions, Inc.

Under Select Template: click the drop-down menu arrow and click on each of the available options. As you do, notice how the sample matter number (00025-Newton) changes. Use the default (matter number—client summary name), then ***select Standard.*** Under ***Customize with additional fields, select Client Number. Click Update Settings.***

13. To end this Clio session, ***click on your initials*** at the top of the screen. ***Click Sign Out, and then close your Internet browser.***

This concludes the lesson on law firm profile and setup.

LESSON 2: Creating Time Records

In this lesson, you will use several matters from the preloaded lists to enter time records into Clio. You will use the current month and date for all entries.

Note: If you are already logged in, you will skip Steps 1 and 2.

1. Start your Internet browser. Type www.goclio.com in the Internet browser and press the **[ENTER] key**.
2. On the Clio Home page, ***click Log In.*** On the next screen, ***enter the e-mail address and password*** you provided in ***Clio*** and ***click SIGN IN. If you check the box next to "KEEP ME SIGNED IN," you will be able to skip this step in the future.***
3. Clio opens into the **PRACTICE** tab and will display the **"Dashboard"** with **Today's Agenda** that includes **Tasks, Calendar Events, Bills,** and **Timekeeping**. ***Click*** the **ACTIVITIES** tab.
4. You will notice that there are several categories under **ACTIVITIES**. Before you begin entering time, you should create some default activity descriptions for common use and consistency. From the **ACTIVITIES** tab, ***click Activity Descriptions***, then ***click* Add**. Under **Name, type: File Review**. Under **Billing Method**, *click* the ***drop-down menu*** and ***click "User Default Rate."*** Under **Groups**, it should reflect **"Everyone."** ***Click box* "Yes"** for **"Visible to Co-counsel?,"** then ***click Save*** (see Clio Exhibit 5-1).

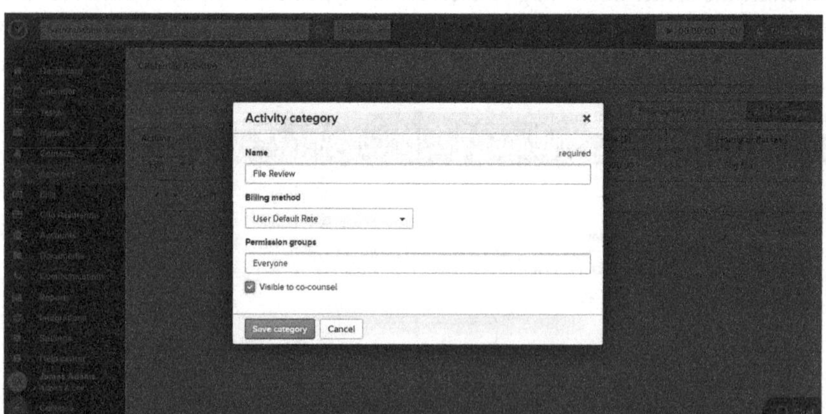

Clio Exhibit 5-1 Add Default Activity (Time Records)

Source: Themis Solutions, Inc.

5. At this point your instructor may provide additional descriptions to add or have you incorporate UTBMS (Uniform Task Based Management System) utilized by Clio. ***Click the "Settings" icon*** (looks like a gear) at the top of the screen next to the ***"initials."*** Then ***click*** **Billing** under **Clio Settings** where you should see several subcategories. ***Click*** **UTBMS Codes**, then ***click all the boxes to add a "check mark."*** Then ***click*** **Update UTBMS Settings** (see Clio Exhibit 5-2). You will now have standardized legal codes to select from during the exercise.

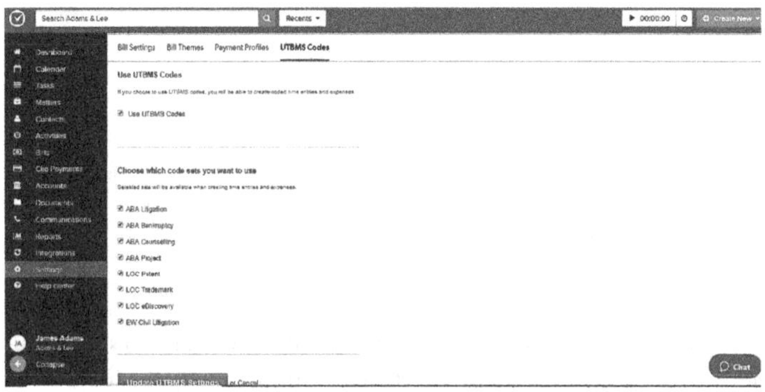

Clio Exhibit 5-2 Add UTBMS Codes (Time Records)

Source: Themis Solutions, Inc.

6. Under the **Activities** tab, ***click Time Entries***, then ***click Add***. This is where you record time spent on matters for tracking and billing purposes. We will use the **Battise** matter for this exercise.
7. Use the default **Date** and under **Matter**, begin ***typing the first few letters of the last name (Battise)***. You will notice **00003-Battise: Custody agreement** appear in the choices; ***click Battise***. Then ***click*** **User**. Your instructor may have you select the attorney or use the default **Me**. Under **Activity Description**, ***click File Review***. Notice the **Task** is grey colored and you are unable to enter information. Under **Duration type 1.5** and the rate should show the default (blue letter "D"). If the rate is missing or you want to customize the rate, enter a different amount (i.e., 100). Do not check **Start Timer?** Under Notes, **type, Review for discovery motion**, then ***click Save*** (see Clio Exhibit 5-3).

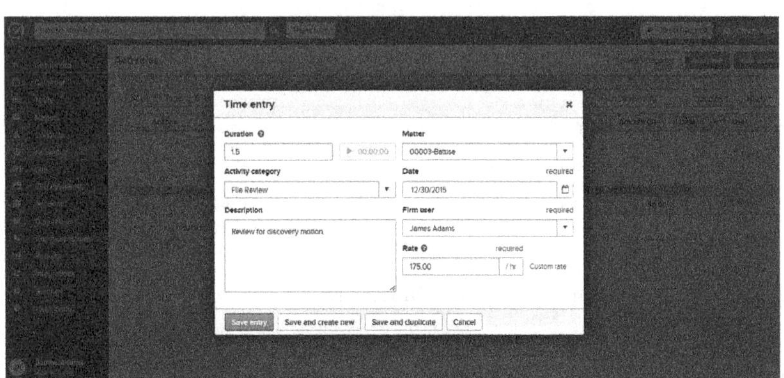

Clio Exhibit 5-3 Add Time Entry - No Timer

Source: Themis Solutions, Inc.

8. The time entry reflected includes the total amount to bill for that activity (i.e., 1.5 hours @ $175.00 per hour = $262.50) (see Clio Exhibit 5-4).

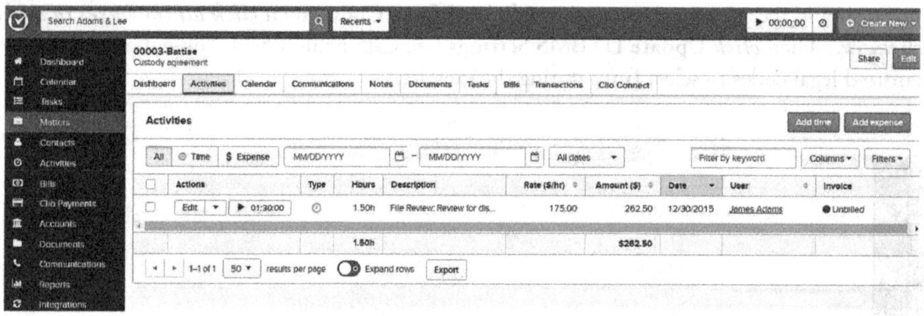

Clio Exhibit 5-4 Time Entry - No Timer

Source: Themis Solutions, Inc.

9. We will now create a time entry using UTBMS Codes. While still in the **Time Entries** subtab under the **Activities** tab, ***click Add***. Use the default Date and under Matter, begin typing the first few letters of the last name (McFly). You will notice that **00133-McFly: Destruction of Property** appears in the choices; ***click McFly***. Then ***click*** to select User. Your instructor may have you select the attorney or use the default Me. Under Activity Description scroll down to choose from the UTBMS codes and ***click A105 Communicate (in firm)***.
10. Notice with UTBMS codes, you are required to enter a **Task**. ***Click L-110, Fact Investigation***. Under "**Duration**," **type: .50**. The Rate should show the default (blue letter "D"). If the rate is missing or you want to customize the rate, enter a different amount (i.e., 100). Under **"Notes," type: Strategy meeting**, then ***click Save***.
11. The time entry reflected includes the total amount to bill for that activity (i.e., .5 hours @ $175.00 per hour = $87.50).
12. Continue to ***Add*** the following entries (use default date and the same user with the previous entries):

Note: When entering multiple entries use the "**Save and Enter Another**" feature.

Entries for 00133 -McFly: Destruction of Property

Activity Description	Task Code	Duration	Notes
A101—Plan and prepare for	L-110 Fact Investigation	2	Prep for deposition of defendant
A104—Review/analyze	L-110 Fact Investigation	.50	Letter from counsel
A105—Communicate (in firm)	L-110 Fact Investigation	1	Strategy meeting with partner re: defendant's deposition

This concludes Lesson 2 (Time Records) of the Clio Hands-On Exercises.

LESSON 3: Using the Timer Feature and Entering Expense Slips

In this lesson, you will learn how to use the timer feature and enter expense entries into Clio. You will use the preloaded lists to enter time records and the current month and date for all entries.

Note: If you are already logged in, you will skip Steps 1 and 2.

1. Start your Internet browser. Type www.goclio.com in the Internet browser and press the **[ENTER] key**.
2. On the Clio Home page, ***click Log In***. On the next screen, ***enter the e-mail address and password*** you provided in ***Clio*** and ***click SIGN IN. If you check the box next to "KEEP ME SIGNED IN," you will be able to skip this step in the future.***
3. Clio opens into the **PRACTICE** tab and will display the "**Dashboard**" with **Today's Agenda** that includes **Tasks**, **Calendar Events**, **Bills**, and **Timekeeping**. ***Click*** the **ACTIVITIES** tab, and under the ***Time Entries*** tab, ***click Add.***
4. We will use UTBMS Codes to record time. Under "**Matter**," begin typing the first few letters of the last name (McFly). You will notice that **00133-McFly: Destruction of Property** appears in the choices; ***click McFly***. Then ***click*** "**User**." Your instructor may have you select the attorney or use the default Me. Under "**Activity Description**" scroll down to choose from the UTBMS codes and ***click A106 Communicate (with client)***.
5. Notice with UTBMS codes, you are required to enter a **Task**. ***Click L-110, Fact Investigation***. Skip "**Duration**," and ***click the box*** next to "**Start Timer?**" Under **"Notes" type: Setup meeting for deposition review**, then ***click Save***.
6. At this point you will no longer see the play record icon, you will see a clock icon. The Default rate is reflected, but no total appears (see Clio Exhibit 5-5).

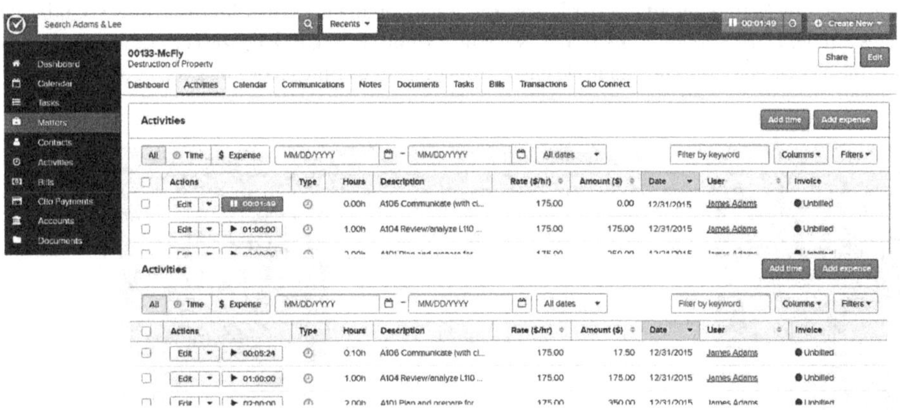

Clio Exhibit 5-5 Recorded Time Entry - Timer Clock Feature

Source: Themis Solutions, Inc.

The time is currently measuring the time length for the listed activity in Clio Exhibit 5-5. ***Click Stop Timer***, and a "dollar" amount will immediately appear, based on the amount of time, in the Total column.

7. Notice the difference with the two entries in Clio Exhibit 5-5. The first record, which has an undetermined time duration, has a "clock" icon, along with **Stop Timer** listed below. The second record, which has a determined time duration, has a record/play icon (looks like a circle with an arrow in the middle) along with **Start Timer** listed below. Clio allows the user to have continuous time or add a running time feature for a time record already entered.
8. In Clio Exhibit 5-5, the right-hand side of the screen shows the Timekeeping feature (currently "No timer running"). Clio also has a feature that allows the user to create time entries simultaneously with the activity and use the timer's start/stop option to reflect ongoing time with exact time spent.
9. ***Move the pointer over the*** "**Timekeeping**" area and ***click***. A screen will appear that allows you to start the timer. Notice there are no entries. Then ***click Create a time entry***. At this point you may create a time record and it will automatically begin registering time (See Clio Exhibit 5-6).

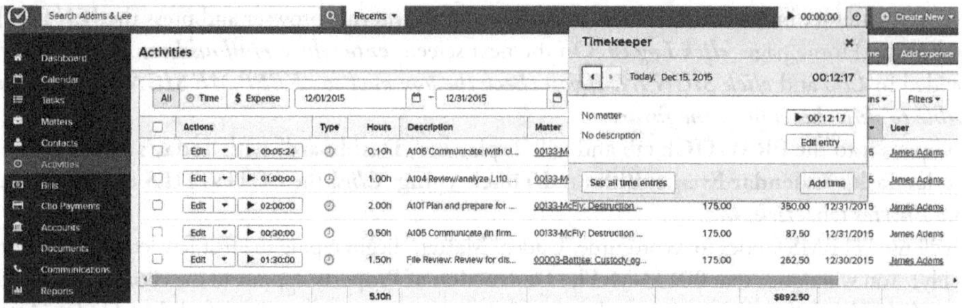

Clio Exhibit 5-6 Time Activity – Timekeeper Feature

Source: Themis Solutions, Inc.

10. ***Click on the* Update** icon (looks like a pencil). A screen will appear to "Update an Entry." Under **Matter**, begin ***typing the first few letters of the last name (McFly)***. You will notice **(00133)-McFly: Destruction of Property** appear in the choices; ***click McFly***. Under **Date**, use the default date, Under **Activity Description**, ***click the drop-down menu and click* A102 Research**. Under **Task**, ***click* L140 Document/File Management**. Under **Duration**, leave out an entry (it will be on timer). Under **Notes**, **type: Westlaw**. ***Click Update Time Entry***. (see Clio Exhibit 5-7). ***Clicking the*** [+] in the right-hand corner allows the Timekeeper to record multiple entries for continuous time recording over a period of time.

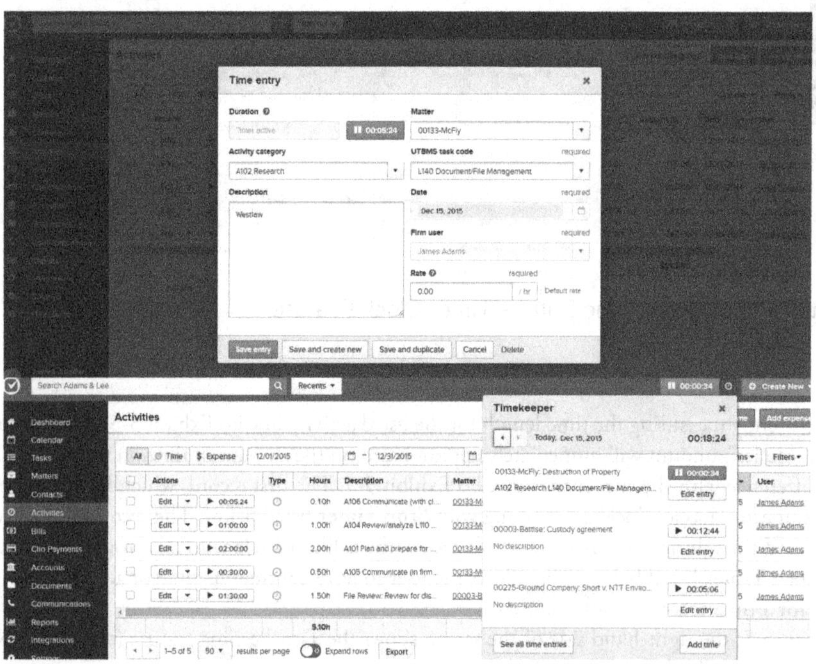

Clio Exhibit 5-7 Timekeeper Entry

Source: Themis Solutions, Inc.

11. You are now ready to enter some client expenses. ***Click*** **Activities**, then ***click*** **Expenses**, and then ***click Add***.
12. Under **Matter**, begin ***typing the first few letters of the last name (McFly)***. You will notice **(00133)-McFly: Destruction of Property** appears in the choices; ***click McFly***. Then ***click*** **User**. Your instructor may have you select the attorney or Use the default **Me**. Under **Date**, use the default date. Under **Expense Code**, ***click the drop-down menu*** and ***click*** **E102 Outside printing**. Under **Amount type: 20.00**. Under **Notes type: copy services**, then ***click*** *Save* (see Clio Exhibit 5-8).

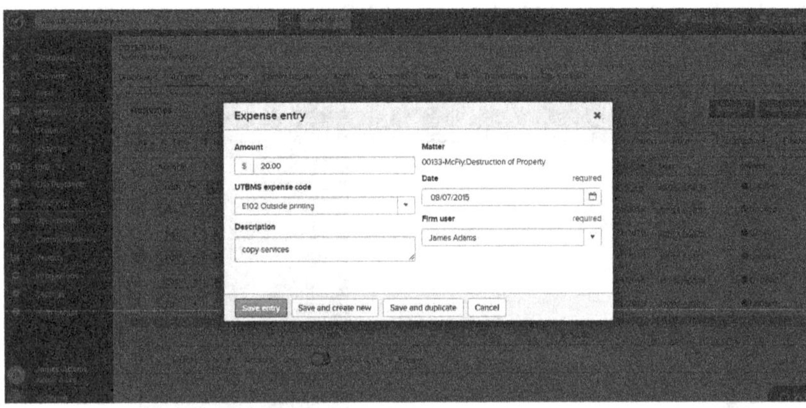

Clio Exhibit 5-8 Add Expense Entry

Source: Themis Solutions, Inc.

13. ***Enter the following additional expense entries in the McFly Matter:***
Note: When adding multiple entries, ***click*** **Save & Add Another**.

Expense Entries for 00133 McFly—Destruction of Property

Date	Expense Code	Amount	Notes
08/11/2015	E101—Copying	25.00	100 Photocopies of PreTrial Questionnaire @.25 each
08/25/2015	E108—Postage	2.50	Letter to counsel re: interrogatories
08/25/2015	E108—Postage	.49	Letter to client
10/26/2015	E105—Telephone	5.00	Long-distance charges (charges for call to expert witness)

14. This concludes Lesson 3 (Timer and Expense Records) of the Clio Hands-On Exercises.

LESSON 4: Producing Prebills, Final Bills, and Reports

In this lesson, you will review several stages of a bill and print a pre-bill, a final bill, and some additional reports. You will use the current month and date for all entries.

Note: If you are already logged in, you will skip Steps 1 and 2.

1. Start your Internet browser. Type www.goclio.com in the Internet browser and press the **[ENTER] key**.
2. On the Clio Home page, ***click Log In***. On the next screen, ***enter the e-mail address and password*** you provided ***Clio*** and ***click SIGN IN. If you check the box next to "KEEP ME SIGNED IN," you will be able to skip this step in the future.***
3. Clio opens into the **PRACTICE** tab and will display the "**Dashboard**" with **Today's Agenda** that includes **Tasks**, **Calendar Events**, **Bills**, and **Timekeeping**. ***Click*** the **BILLS** tab.
4. You will notice several categories under **BILLS:** ***Billable Clients; Drafts; Pending Approval; Awaiting Payment; Paid.*** For this exercise, ***click*** "**Billable Clients.**" From the list, you will choose the two matters from Lesson 2 and Lesson 3 (**Battise** and **McFly**), then ***click*** **Generate** (a new screen will appear). You can leave the default information unchanged and ***click Generate Bills.*** see Clio Exhibit 5-9.

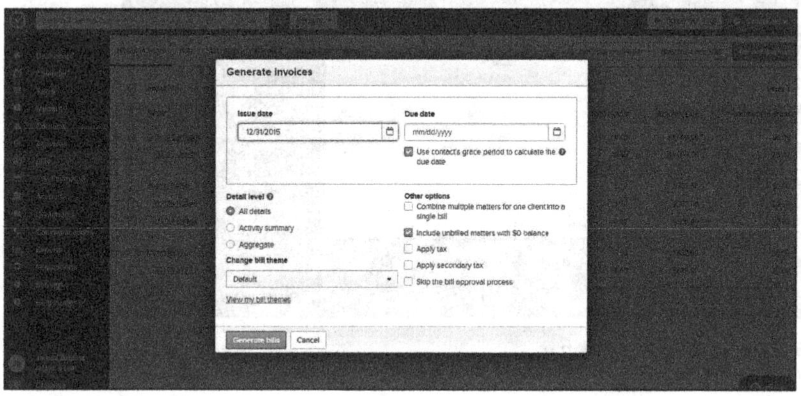

Clio Exhibit 5-9 Generate Bills - Draft

Source: Themis Solutions, Inc.

5. Under the **Bills** tab, the number "2" will appear next to the **Draft** subtab. ***Click Draft***, then ***click the box next to the Battise and McFly***. Under **Action**, ***click the drop-down menu***, which will reveal several options; ***select Approve***. Then ***click Apply***. Under the **Bills** tab, you will notice that the number "2" now appears next to **Awaiting Payment** subtab (see Clio Exhibit 5-10).

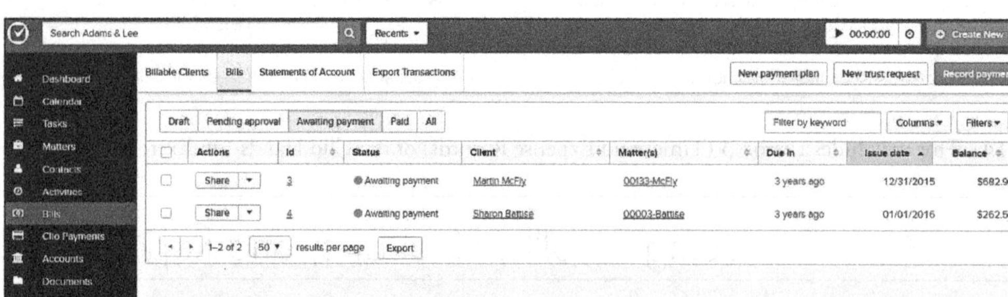

Clio Exhibit 5-10 Bills - Awaiting Payment

Source: Themis Solutions, Inc.

6. As Clio Exhibit 5-10 reflects, a bill could be created in various stages. With most programs, once a bill "approved," it may not be altered. If the bill is not ready for approval, choose another option to create a bill.
7. ***Click*** **Draft** if you are not ready to submit the bill and would like to make changes or add to the bill.
8. ***Click*** "**Submit for Approval**" to allow a supervising attorney, administrator or managing partner to review the bill before it is sent to the client. This is the most common practice to ensure accuracy with client bills. It ensures that a responsible party in the law firm inspects the bills.
9. Once "approved," the bill may be generated, and then sent to the client. For example, ***click*** **View** Battise to produce the actual bill sent to the client (see Clio Exhibit 5-11).

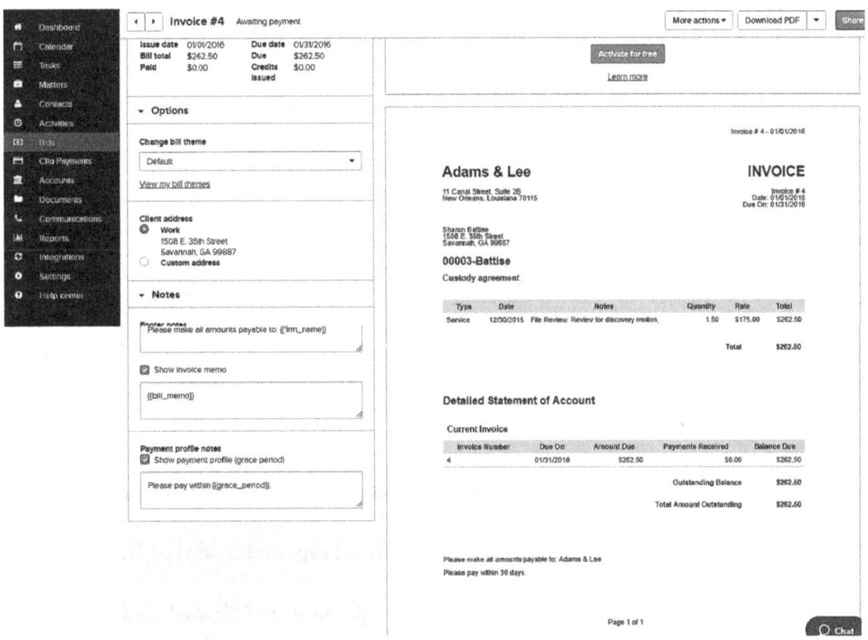

Clio Exhibit 5-11 Bills - Client Invoice

Source: Themis Solutions, Inc.

This concludes Lesson 4 Producing Prebills, Final Bills, and Reports. To exit Clio, ***Click on the "initials"*** (right hand corner), then ***click*** **SIGN OUT**.

This concludes the Clio Exercises for Chapter 5.

Hands-On Exercises
Microsoft Excel

Basic Lessons

Number	Lesson Title
Lesson 1	Creating a Client Settlement Worksheet
Lesson 2	Creating a Fee Projection Worksheet

Getting Started

Overview

Microsoft Excel is a powerful spreadsheet program that allows you to create formulas, "what-if" scenarios, graphs, and much more.

Introduction

Throughout these lessons and exercises, information that you need to operate the program will be designated in several different ways:

- Keys to be pressed on the keyboard will be designated in brackets, in all caps and bold type (e.g., press the **[ENTER]** key).
- Movements with the mouse will be designated in bold and italics (e.g., ***point to File and click***).
- Words or letters that should be typed will be designated in bold (e.g., type **Training Program**).
- Information that is or should be displayed on your computer screen is shown in bold, with quotation marks: (e.g. "**Press ENTER to continue.**")

Overview of Excel

I. Worksheet

A. *Entering Commands: The Ribbon*—The primary way of entering commands in Excel 2013 is through the ribbon. The ribbon is a set of commands or tools that change depending on which ribbon is selected. There are seven ribbon tabs: Home, Insert, Page Layout, Formulas, Data, Review, and View (see Excel Exhibit 5-1). Each tab has a group of commands. For example, on the Home tab, the Font Group contains a group of commands that govern font choice, font size, bold, italics, underling, and other attributes (see Excel Exhibit 5-1).

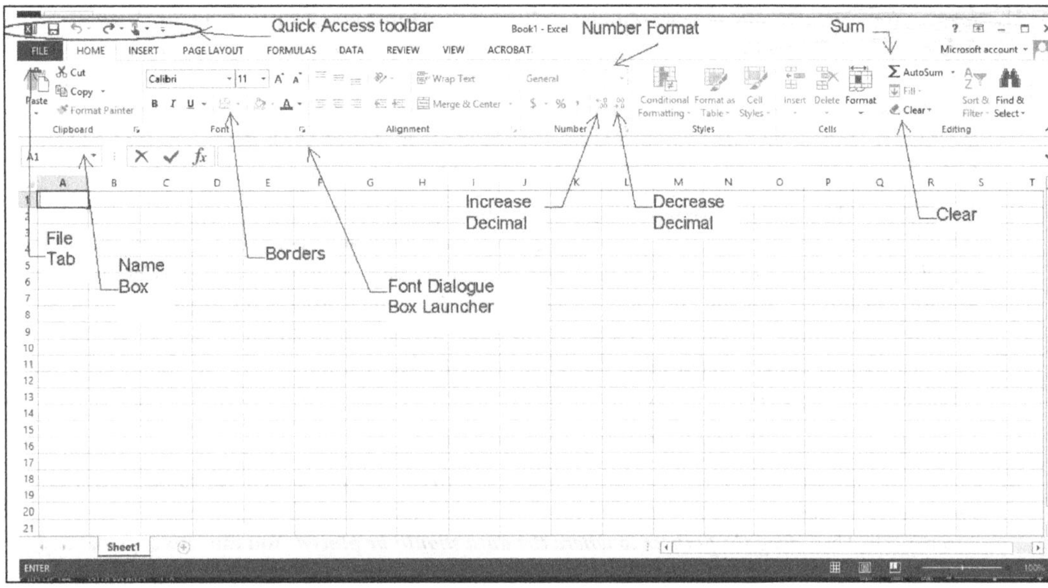

Excel Exhibit 5-1 Excel Interface

Used with permission from Microsoft.

B. *File tab*—The file tab is where a user accesses commands such as New, Open, Save, and Print. The File tab replaces the Office button used in Excel 2007.

C. *Entering Data*—To enter data, **type**: the text or number in a cell, and ***press*** the **[ENTER]** key or one of the arrow (cursor) keys.

D. *Ranges*—A range is a group of contiguous cells. Cell ranges can be created by ***clicking and dragging the pointer*** or holding the **[SHIFT]** key on and using the arrow (cursor) keys.

E. *Format*—Cells can be formatted, including changing the font style, font size, shading, border, cell type (currency, percentage, etc.), alignment, and others by ***clicking*** the **Home** ribbon tab, then ***clicking "one of the dialog box launchers"*** in the **Font** group, **Alignment** group, or **Number** group. Each of these dialog box launchers brings up a similar "Format Cells" window. You can also enter a number of formatting options directly from the Home tab.

F. *Editing a Cell*—You can edit a cell by ***clicking in the cell*** and then ***clicking in the formula bar***. The formula bar is directly under the ribbon and just to the right of the "fx" sign. The formula bar shows the current contents of the selected cell, and it allows you to edit the cell contents. You can also edit the content of a cell by ***clicking in the cell*** and then pressing the **[F2]** key.

G. *Column Width/Row Height*—You can change the width of a column by ***clicking the line to the right of the column heading***. (This is the line that separates two columns. When you point to a line, the cursor changes to double-headed vertical arrows.) Next, ***drag the pointer to the right or to the left*** which will increase or decrease the column width, respectively. Similarly, you can change the height of a row by ***clicking and dragging the horizontal line separating two rows***. You can also change the width of a column or height of a row, by ***clicking*** the **Home** tab, and then ***clicking*** **Format** in the **Cells** group.

H. *Insert*—You can insert one row or column by ***clicking*** the **Home** tab, then ***clicking the down arrow below the*** "**Insert**" ***icon*** in the **Cells** group, and ***clicking*** either "***Insert Sheet Rows***" ***or*** "***Insert Sheet Columns.***" You can also insert a number of rows or columns by ***dragging the pointer over the number of rows or columns you want to add, clicking*** the **Home** tab, ***clicking the down arrow below the*** "**Insert**" ***icon*** in the **Cells** group, and then ***clicking*** either "***Insert Sheet Rows***" ***or*** "***Insert Sheet Columns.***" Finally, you can ***right-click*** and select ***Insert from the menu.***

I. *Erase/Delete*—You can erase data by ***dragging the pointer over the area*** and then pressing the **[DELETE]** key. You can also erase by ***dragging the pointer over the area, clicking*** the **Home** ribbon tab, ***clicking the down arrow***, next to the **Clear icon** in the **Editing** group, and then ***clicking Clear All.*** You can also delete whole columns or rows by ***pointing and clicking in a column or row, then clicking*** on the **Home** ribbon tab, ***clicking on the down arrow*** next to ***Delete*** in the **Cells** group, and then ***clicking either*** "***Delete Sheet Rows***" ***or*** "***Delete Sheet Columns.***" You can also delete whole columns or rows by ***pointing in the column or row*** and then ***right-clicking*** and selecting ***Delete.***

J. *Quit*—To quit Excel, ***click on the File tab***, then ***click Close.***

K. *Copy*—To copy data to adjacent columns or rows, ***click in the cell you wish to copy and then select the AutoFill command***, which is accessed from the small black box at the bottom right corner of the selected cell. Then ***drag the pointer to where the data should be placed.*** You can also copy data by ***clicking in the cell***, then ***right-clicking***, and ***clicking*** "**Copy**," then ***clicking at the location where the information should be copied***, and pressing the **[ENTER]** key. Finally, data can also be copied by ***clicking and dragging to highlight the information that will be copied, clicking*** the **Home** tab, then ***clicking*** "**Copy**" in the "**Clipboard**" group. Then go to the location where the information should be copied, ***click*** the **Home** tab, and ***click*** "**Paste**" in the "**Clipboard**" group.

L. *Move*—Move data by ***clicking on the cell***, then by ***right-clicking***, select "**Cut**," and then ***click in the location where the information should be inserted***, and ***press*** the **[ENTER]** key. Data can also be moved by ***highlighting the information to be moved***, and from the **Home** tab, ***click on Cut*** (looks like a pair of scissors) ***in the Clipboard group.***

M. *Saving and Opening Files*—Save a file by ***clicking*** the **File** tab, then ***click*** **Save** *or* **Save As**, and typing the file name. You can also save a file by ***clicking*** the "**Save**" **icon** (it looks like a floppy disk) on the "**Quick Access**" toolbar (see Excel Exhibit 5-1). Open a file that was previously saved by ***clicking*** the **File** tab, then ***click*** **Open**, and then, type (or ***click***) the name of the file to be opened.

N. *Print*—To print a file, ***click the File tab***, then ***click Print***, and then ***click Print.***

II. Numbers and Formulas

A. *Numbers*—To enter a number in a cell ***click in the cell***, type the number and press the **[ENTER]** key or an arrow (cursor) key.

B. *Adding Cells (Addition)*—You can add the contents of two or more cells by three different methods:

1. To add the contents of a range of two or more cells,
   - **a.** ***Click in the cell where the total should be placed*** (you choose).
   - **b.** From the **Home** tab, under the **Editing** group, ***click the AutoSum icon*** (see Excel Exhibit 5-1). The Sum icon looks like the Greek letter "Sigma." (*Note:* to see the name of an icon, point at the icon for a second and the name of the icon will be displayed.)
   - **c.** Excel guesses which cells you want to add. Press **[ENTER]** if the correct range is automatically selected, or select the correct range by highlighting it (i.e., ***clicking and dragging until the range of cells to be added is highlighted).*** Then press **[ENTER]** key.

2. To add the contents of two cells, which need not consist of a range:
   a. ***Click in the cell where the total should be placed*** (you choose).
   b. ***Press*** = (the equal sign).
   c. **Type:** the address of the first cell to be added (e.g., C4), or ***click in that cell.***
   d. ***Press*** + (the plus sign).
   e. Enter the address of the second cell to be added (e.g. C5) or ***click in that cell.***
   f. Press the **[ENTER]** key. (e.g., to add the values of C4 and C5, the formula would read = C4 + C5).
3. To add the contents of a range of two or more cells:
   a. ***Click in the cell where the total should be placed*** (you choose).
   b. **Type:** = **SUM(**
   c. **Type:** the address of the first cell to be added (e.g., C4), or ***click in that cell.***
   d. ***Press*** **:** (a colon)
   e. **Type:** the address of the second cell to be added (e.g., C5), or ***click in that cell.***
   f. ***Press*** **)** [a closing parenthesis].
   g. ***Press*** the **[ENTER]** key. (e.g., to add the values of C4 and C5, the formula would read "**=SUM(C4:C5)**").

C. *Subtracting Cells*—To subtract the contents of one or more cells from those of another:
   1. ***Click in the cell where the total should be placed*** (you choose).
   2. ***Press*** = (the equal sign).
   3. **Type:** the first cell address (e.g., C4), or ***click in that cell.***
   4. ***Press*** – (the minus sign).
   5. **Type:** the second cell address (e.g., C5), or ***click in that cell.***
   6. ***Press*** the **[ENTER]** key. (e.g., to subtract the value of C4 from the value of C5, the formula would read "**=C5-C4**").

D. *Multiplying Cells*—To multiply the contents of two (or more) cells:
   1. ***Click in the cell where the total should be placed*** (you choose).
   2. ***Press*** = (the equal sign).
   3. **Type:** the first cell address (e.g., C4), or ***click in that cell.***
   4. ***Press*** * (hold the **[SHIFT]** key and **[8]** key).
   5. **Type:** the second cell address (e.g., C5), or ***click in that cell.***
   6. ***Press*** the **[ENTER]** key. (e.g., to multiply the value in C4 times the value in C5, the formula would read "**=C5*C4**").

E. *Dividing Cells*—To divide two cells,
   1. ***Click in the cell where the total should be placed*** (you choose).
   2. ***Press*** = (the equal sign).
   3. **Type:** the first cell address (e.g., C4), or ***click in that cell.***
   4. ***Press*** "/" (the forward slash).
   5. **Type:** the second cell address (e.g., C5), or ***click in that cell.***
   6. ***Press*** the **[ENTER]** key. (e.g., to divide the value in C4 by the value in C5, the formula would read "**=C4/C5**").

*Please note: depending on the version of Excel you are using, the toolbars, icons, and menus may look slightly different than the figures, but the differences should be minor. You are now ready to begin Lesson 1 of Chapter 5.

III. BASIC LESSONS

Lesson 1: Creating a Client Settlement Worksheet

This lesson shows you how to build the spreadsheet in Excel Exhibit 5-2—Excel Tutorial Spreadsheet. Keep in mind that if you make a mistake at any time during this lesson, you can simply press **[CTRL][Z]** to undo what you have done.

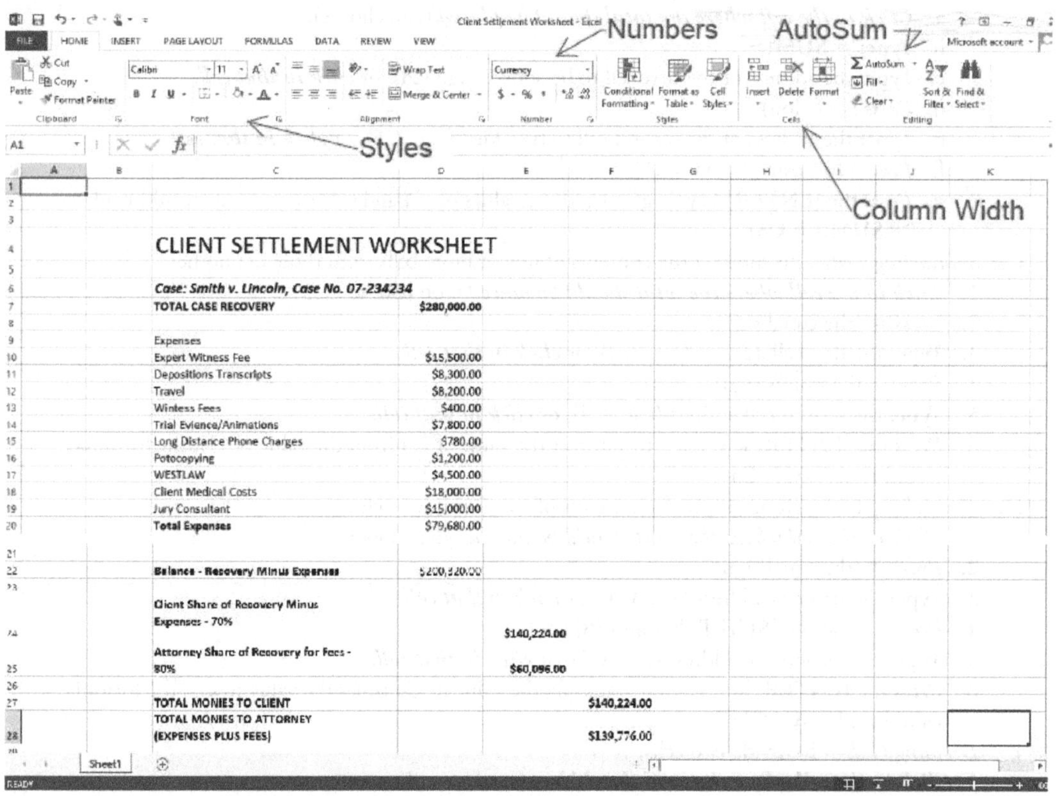

Excel Exhibit 5-2 Excel Tutorial Spreadsheet

Used with permission from Microsoft.

1. Open Windows. Then, ***double-click on the Microsoft Office Excel 2013 icon on the desktop*** to open the program. Alternatively, ***click on the "Start" button, point to "Programs" or "All Programs," point to Microsoft Office, and then click Microsoft Excel 2013***. You should be in a clean, blank workbook. If you are not in a blank workbook, ***click the File tab*** (see Excel Exhibit 5-1), ***click on New***, and then ***click Blank Workbook***.
2. Notice that the cell pointer is at **cell A1** and the current cell indicator (also called the name box by Excel) shows **A1**. The "name" box is just under the ribbon and all the way to the left (see Excel Exhibit 5-1). Also notice that you can move the pointer around the spreadsheet using the cursor keys. Go back to cell A1 by pressing the **[CTRL][HOME]** keys.

3. Go to cell C4 by ***moving the pointer on cell C4 and pressing the left mouse button once***. The name box should now show cell C4.
4. Change the width of column C to 45 by ***clicking the column heading (the letter C)*** at the top of the screen. ***Move your pointer to the right edge of the column***. The pointer should then change to a double-headed vertical arrow. ***Drag the pointer to the right until the column width is 45***. Alternatively, change the cell width by ***placing the cell pointer anywhere in column C***. From the **Home** tab, ***click Format*** in the **Cells** group, then ***click Column Width***. Then type **45** and ***click OK***.
5. ***Click in cell C4***. **Type CLIENT SETTLEMENT WORKSHEET.** ***Drag the pointer across cell C4 so that the entire cell is highlighted***. From the **Home** tab, under the **Font** group, ***click*** the ***Font size*** (number next to the font style), then ***click the drop-down menu*** and ***click*** "**24.**" Alternatively, you can ***click in cell C4***, then ***right-click on the mouse/pointer***. A dialogue box will appear which includes the **Font** option. ***Click the drop-down menu*** and ***click*** "**24.**"
6. ***Click in cell C6 and type: Case: Smith v. Lincoln, Case No. 07-234234 and press the*** **[ENTER]** ***key. Drag the pointer across cell C6 so that the entire cell is highlighted***. From the **Home** tab, ***click the Font size*** under **Font** group, then ***click "I"*** (for Italics), ***click "B"*** (for Bold) and under ***the drop-down menu, click*** "**14.**" Alternatively, you can ***click in cell C4***, then ***right-click on the mouse/pointer***. A dialogue box will appear which includes the **Font** option. ***Click "I"*** (for Italics), ***click "B"*** (for Bold) and under the ***drop-down menu, click*** "**14.**"
7. You will now select an area in the worksheet and make it all 12-point type. ***Click in cell C7 and drag the pointer*** (with the white plus sign) ***to cell F28*** so that the entire cell range is highlighted. From the **Home** tab, under the **Font** group, ***click the Font size*** (number next to the font style), then ***click the drop-down menu*** and ***click*** "**12.**" Alternatively, while the area is still highlighted, you can ***right-click on the mouse/pointer***. A dialogue box will appear which includes the **Font** option. ***Click the drop-down menu*** and ***click*** "**12.**"
8. ***Click in cell C7 and type: Case: TOTAL CASE RECOVERY and press the [ENTER] key. Drag the pointer across cell C7 so that the entire cell is highlighted***. From the **Home** tab, ***click the Font size*** under **Font** group, then ***click "B"*** (for Bold).
9. You will now increase the width of columns D, E, and F. ***Click to cell D7 with the pointer*** (showing white plus sign), ***drag the pointer to cell F7*** (cells D7, E7, and F7 should now be highlighted). From the **Home** tab, under **Cells**, ***click Format*** then ***click Column Width***. A dialogue box will appear. **Type 15** and ***press*** **[ENTER]**. Notice that the width of columns D, E, and F were expanded.
10. With the pointer, ***click in cell D7 and type:*** **280000** ***and press the*** **[ENTER]** ***key***. Do not press the dollar sign or a comma.
11. You will now change the formal of cells D7 through F28 to currency. ***Point and click on cell D7***, then ***drag the pointer*** (with the white plus sign) ***to cell F28*** so that the entire cell is highlighted. From the **Home** tab, under the **Number** group, ***click the drop-down menu***, then ***click Currency***.
12. ***Click on cell D7***. From the **Home** tab, under the **Font** group, ***click "B"*** (for Bold).
13. You should now be ready to enter information. Enter the following information into the cells indicated:

    —**Expenses** in C9

    —**Expert Witness Fee** in C10

    —**Deposition Transcripts** in C11

    —**Travel** in C12

    —**Witness Fee** in C13

    —**Trial Evidence/Animation** in C14

    —**Long Distance Phone Charges** in C15

    —**Photocopying** in C16

    —**Westlaw** in C17

—**Client Medical Costs** in C18
—**Jury Consultant** in C19
—**TOTAL EXPENSES** in C20 (this is **bold**)
—**Balance—Recovery Minus Expenses** in C22 (this is bold)
—**Client Share of Recovery Minus Expenses—70%** in C24 (this is bold)
—**Attorney Share of Recovery for Fees—30%** in C25 (this is bold)
—**TOTAL MONIES TO CLIENT** in C27 (this is bold)
—**TOTAL MONIES TO ATTORNEY (EXPENSES PLUS FEES)** in C28 (this is bold)

14. Notice that some of the longer text may flow into the next cell. We will wrap the text to fix this. ***Point and click on cell C24***, then ***drag the pointer*** (with the white plus sign) ***to cell C28*** so that the entire cell is highlighted. From the **Home** tab, under the **Alignment** group, ***click Wrap Text.*** The text should now be wrapped so it fits within the cell.
15. Enter the following information into the cells indicated:
—**15500** in D10
—**8300** in D11
—**8200** in D12
—**400** in D13
—**7800** in D14
—**780** in D15
—**1200** in D16
—**4500** in D17
—**18000** in D18
—**15000** in D19
16. You are now ready to enter formulas into the worksheet. ***Click in cell D20.*** From the **Home** tab, under the **Editing** group, ***click AutoSum*** (looks like a Greek letter). Notice that "dashed lines" will rotate around D10–D19; ***press the*** **[ENTER]** ***key***. The completed formula should read: =SUM(D10:D19). ***Note:*** you can select cell D20 to see the formula in the formula bar at the top of the screen. The correct amount of $79,680.00 should be displayed in cell D20. ***Click in cell D20*** and from the **Home** tab, under the **Font** group, ***click "B"*** (for Bold).
17. ***Click in cell D22.*** **Type: =D7-D20** and then ***press the*** **[ENTER]** ***key. Note:*** you can select cell D22 to see the formula in the formula bar at the top of the screen. The formula subtracts D20 (Total Expenses) from D7 (Total Case Recovery). The correct amount of $200,320.00 should be displayed in cell D22. ***Click in cell D22*** and from the **Home** tab, under the **Font** group, ***click "B"*** (for Bold).
18. ***Click on cell E24.*** **Type: = D22*.70** and then press the **[ENTER]** ***key. Click on cell E24*** and from the **Home** tab, under the **Font** group, ***click "B"*** (for Bold).The formula calculates the client's share of the recovery (which is 70% after expenses are paid). The correct answer of $140,224.00 should be displayed in E24.
19. ***Click on cell E25.*** **Type: =D22*.30** and then press the **[ENTER]** ***key. Click on cell E25*** and from the **Home** tab, under the **Font** group, ***click "B"*** (for Bold). The formula calculates the attorney's share of the recovery for fees (which is 30% after expenses are paid). The correct answer of $60,096.00 should be displayed in cell E25.
20. ***Click on cell F27.*** **Type: *+E24*** and then press the **[ENTER]** ***key. Click on cell F27*** and from the **Home** tab, under the **Font** group, ***click "B"*** (for Bold). Since the client receives no monies other than 70% of the recovery after expenses, this is the total amount the client gets. The correct answer of $140,224.00 should be displayed in F27.

21. ***Click on cell F28.*** Type: ***+D20+E25*** and then press the **[ENTER]** ***key. Click on cell F28*** and from the **Home** tab, under the **Font** group, ***click "B"*** (for Bold). This formula adds the total amount of expenses for which the attorney must pay, together with the attorney's contingency fee of 30%, and adds them together for the total amount of the settlement the attorney will receive. The correct answer of $139,776.00 should be displayed in cell F28.
22. You will next print out your spreadsheet on one page. ***Click File, then click Print.*** Under **Settings,** you will need to choose the last group of selections (scaling). ***Click on the drop-down menu and click "Fit Sheet on One Page,"*** then ***click Print.*** This will compress everything in the print area to one page.
23. To save the document, ***click on File***, then ***click Save, or Save As*** and **type Client Settlement Worksheet** under File name, then ***click Save.***
24. To quit Excel, ***click the File tab***, then ***click Close.***

This concludes Lesson 1.

Lesson 2: Creating a Fee Projection Worksheet

This lesson shows you how to build the fee projection worksheet shown in Excel Exhibit 5-3—Excel Tutorial Spreadsheet. This lesson assumes you have successfully completed Lesson 1. Keep in mind that if at any time you make a mistake in this lesson, you can simply press **[CTRL][Z]** to undo what you have done.

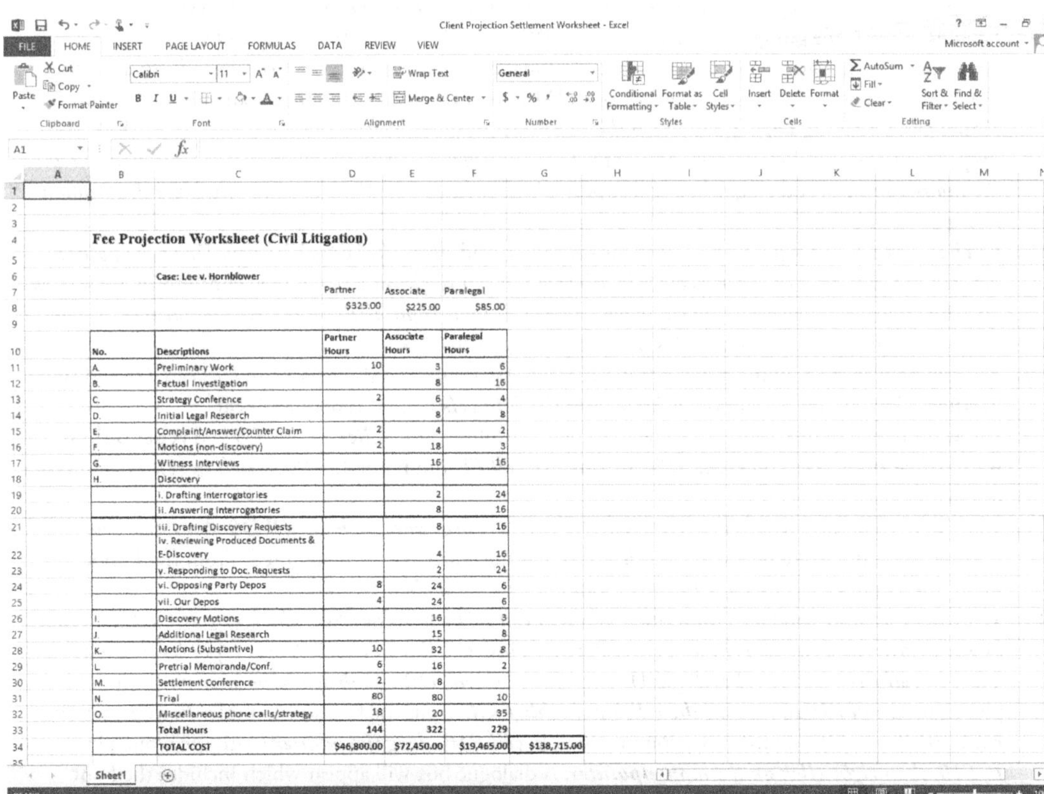

Fee Projection Worksheet (Civil Litigation)

Case: Lee v. Hornblower

		Partner	Associate	Paralegal	
		$325.00	$225.00	$85.00	
No.	**Descriptions**	**Partner Hours**	**Associate Hours**	**Paralegal Hours**	
A.	Preliminary Work	10	3	6	
B.	Factual Investigation		8	16	
C.	Strategy Conference	2	6	4	
D.	Initial Legal Research		8	8	
E.	Complaint/Answer/Counter Claim	2	4	2	
F.	Motions (non-discovery)	2	18	3	
G.	Witness Interviews		16	16	
H.	Discovery				
	i. Drafting Interrogatories		2	24	
	ii. Answering Interrogatories		8	16	
	iii. Drafting Discovery Requests		8	16	
	iv. Reviewing Produced Documents & E-Discovery		4	16	
	v. Responding to Doc. Requests		2	24	
	vi. Opposing Party Depos	8	24	6	
	vii. Our Depos	4	24	6	
I.	Discovery Motions		16	3	
J.	Additional Legal Research		15	8	
K.	Motions (Substantive)	10	32	8	
L.	Pretrial Memoranda/Conf.	6	16	2	
M.	Settlement Conference	2	8		
N.	Trial	80	80	10	
O.	Miscellaneous phone calls/strategy	18	20	35	
	Total Hours	**144**	**322**	**229**	
	TOTAL COST	**$46,800.00**	**$72,450.00**	**$19,465.00**	**$138,715.00**

Excel Exhibit 5-3 Excel Tutorial Spreadsheet

1. Open Windows. Then, ***double-click on the Microsoft Office Excel 2013 icon on the desktop*** to open the program. Alternatively, ***click on the "Start" button, point to "Programs" or "All Programs," point to Microsoft Office, and then click Microsoft Excel 2013.*** You should be in a clean, blank workbook. If you are not in a blank workbook, ***click the File tab*** (see Excel Exhibit 5-1), ***click on New***, and then ***click Blank Workbook.***
2. Notice that the cell pointer is at **cell A1** and the current cell indicator (also called the name box by Excel) shows **A1**. The "name" box is just under the ribbon and all the way to the left (as seen in Excel Exhibit 1). Also notice that you can move the pointer around the spreadsheet using the cursor keys. Go back to cell A1 by pressing the **[CTRL][HOME]** keys.
3. Go to cell B4 by ***moving the pointer on cell B4 and pressing the left mouse button once.*** The name box should now show cell B4.
4. In cell B4 **type: Fee Projection Worksheet (Litigation)**. *Drag the pointer across cell B4 so that the entire cell is highlighted.* From the **Home** tab, under the **Font** group, ***click*** the ***Font size*** (number next to the font style), then ***click the drop-down menu*** and ***click*** "**14**." Alternatively, you can ***click in cell B4***, then ***right-click on the mouse/pointer***. A dialogue box will appear which includes the **Font** option. ***Click the drop-down menu*** and ***click*** "**14**."
5. Change the width of column C to 30 by ***clicking the column heading (the letter C)*** at the top of the screen. ***Move your pointer to the right edge of the column.*** The pointer should then change to a double-headed vertical arrow. ***Drag the pointer to the right until the column width is 30.*** Alternatively, change the cell width by ***placing the cell pointer anywhere in column C.*** From the **Home** tab, ***click Format*** in the **Cells** group, then ***click Column Width...*** Then type **30** and ***click OK.***
6. You will now select an area in the worksheet and make it all 10-point type. ***Click in cell B6 and drag the pointer*** (with the white plus sign) ***to cell G34*** so that the entire cell range is highlighted. From the **Home** tab, under the **Font** group, ***click the Font size*** (number next to the font style), then ***click the drop-down menu*** and ***click*** "**10**." Alternatively, while the area is still highlighted, you can ***right-click on the mouse/pointer.*** A dialogue box will appear which includes the **Font** option. ***Click the drop-down menu*** and ***click*** "**10**."
7. ***Click in cell C6*** and **type: Case: Lee v. Hornblower**, and ***press the* [ENTER] *key. Drag the pointer across cell C6 so that the entire cell is highlighted.*** From the **Home** tab, under **Font** group, then ***click "B"*** (for Bold). Alternatively, you can ***click in cell C6***, then ***right-click on the mouse/pointer.*** A dialogue box will appear which includes the **Font** option. ***Click "B"*** (for Bold).
8. You will now create a billing category for a Partner, Associate, and Paralegal. ***Click in cell D7*** and **type: Partner**; ***Click in cell E7*** and **type: Associate**; ***Click in cell F7*** and **type: Paralegal.**
9. You will provide information regarding each person's billing rate. ***Click in cell C8*** and **type: Billing Rate**. ***Click in cell D8*** and **type: 325.00**; ***Click in cell E8*** and **type: 225.00**; ***Click in cell F8*** and **type: 85.00.**
10. You will need to format cells D8–F8 to currency style. ***Point and click on cell D8***, then ***drag the pointer*** (with the white plus sign) ***to cell F8*** so that the entire cell is highlighted. From the **Home** tab, under the **Number** group, ***click the drop-down menu***, then ***click Currency.***
11. You will now create several column titles: ***Click in cell B10*** and **type: No.**; ***Click in cell C10*** and **type: Description**; ***Click in cell D10*** and **type: Partner Hours**; ***Click in cell E10*** and **type: Associate Hours**; ***Click in cell F10*** and **type: Paralegal Hours**. ***Click on cell B10*** and ***drag the pointer*** (with the white plus sign) ***to cell F10 so that all the cells are highlighted.*** From the **Home** tab, under **Font** group, then ***click "B"*** (for Bold). Alternatively, you can ***click in cell B10, drag the pointer*** (with the white plus sign) ***to F10, then right-click on the mouse/pointer.*** A dialogue box will appear which includes the **Font** option. ***Click "B"*** (for Bold).

12. Notice that some of the longer text may flow into the next cell. We will wrap the text to fix this. ***Point and click on cell D10***, then ***drag the pointer*** (with the white plus sign) ***to cell F10*** so that all those cells are highlighted. From the **Home** tab, under the **Alignment** group, ***click Wrap Text***. The text should now be wrapped so it fits within the cell.
13. You should now be ready to enter information. Enter the following information into the cells indicated: if the cell is not listed, there is no information to enter (it should be blank).
    —**I** in B11 – **Preliminary Work** in C11 – **10** in D11 – **3** in E11 – **6** in F11
    —**II** in B12 – **Factual Investigation** in C12 – **8** in E12 – **16** in F12
    —**III** in B13 – **Strategy Conference** in C13 – **2** in D13 – **6** in E13 – **4** in F13
    —**IV** in B14 – **Initial Legal Research** in C14 – – **8** in E14 – **8** in F14
    —**V** in B15 – **Complaint/Answer/Counter Claim** in C15 – **2** in D15 – **4** in E15 – **2** in F15
    —**VI** in B16 – **Motions (non-discovery)** in C16 – **2** in D16 – **18** in E16 – **3** in F16
    —**VII** in B17 – **Witness Interviews** in C17 – –**16** in E17 – **16** in F17
    —**VIII** in B18 – **Discovery** in C18 –
    A. Drafting Interrogatories in C19 – – **2** in E19 – **24** in F19
    B. Answering Interrogatories in C20 – – **8** in E20 – **16** in F20
    C. Drafting Discovery Requests in C21 – – **8** in E21 – **16** in F21
    D. Reviewing Produced Documents & E-Discovery in C22 – – **4** in E22 – **16** in F22
    E. Responding to Doc. Request in C23 – **2** in E23 – **24** in F23
    F. Opposing Party Depos in C24 – **8** in D24 – **24** in E24 – **6** in F24
    G. Our Depos in C25 – **4** in D25 – **24** in E25 – **6** in F25
    —**IX** in B26 – **Discovery Motions** in C26 – **16** in E26 – **3** in F26
    —**X** in B27 – **Additional Legal Research** in C27 – **15** in E27 – **8** in F27
    —**XI** in B28 – **Motions (Substantive)** in C28 – **10** in D28 – **32** in E28 – **8** in F28
    —**XII** in B29 – **Pretrial Memoranda/Conf.** in C29 – **6** in D29 – **16** in E29 – **2** in F29
    —**XIII** in B30 – **Settlement Conference** in C30 – **2** in D30 – **8** in E30 –
    —**XIV** in B31 – **Trial** in C31 – **80** in D31 – **80** in E31 – **10** in F31
    —**XV** in B32 – **Miscellaneous phone calls/strategy** in C32 – **18** in D32 – **20** in E32 – **35** in F32
14. You will notice that text in cell C22 flows into the next cell. ***Point and click on cell C22***, then ***drag the pointer*** (with the white plus sign) so that the entire cell is highlighted. From the **Home** tab, under the **Alignment** group, ***click Wrap Text***. The text should now be wrapped so it fits within the cell.
15. ***Click in cell C33*** and **type: Total Hours**, and ***press the* [ENTER] *key***. Your cursor should now be in ***cell C34***. **Type: TOTAL COST**, and ***press the* [ENTER] *key***. ***Drag the pointer across cell C33 and C34 so that the cells are highlighted***. From the **Home** tab, under **Font** group, then ***click "B"*** (for Bold).
16. The following formulas should be entered:
    —**=SUM(D11:D32)** in cell D33 (this cell is in **bold**)
    —**=SUM(E11:E32)** in cell E33 (this cell is in **bold**)
    —**=SUM(F11:F32)** in cell F33 (this cell is in **bold**)
    —**=D33*D8** in cell D34 (this cell is in **bold**)
    —**=E33*E8** in cell E34 (this cell is in **bold**)
    —**=F33*F8** in cell F34 (this cell is in **bold**)
    —**=SUM(D34:F34)** in cell G34 (this cell is in **bold**)
17. To add borders around the cells, ***click on cell B10, then drag the pointer*** (using white plus sign) ***to cell F34***. From the Home tab, ***click the drop down menu on the "Borders" icon under Font*** (looks like "four squares"), then ***click* "All Borders."**

18. To put a heavy border around cell G34, ***click on cell G34***. From the Home tab, ***click the drop down menu on the "Borders" icon under Font*** (looks like "four squares"), then ***click* "Thick Box Borde."**
19. You will next print out your spreadsheet on one page. ***Click File, then click Print***. Under **Settings**, you will need to choose the last group of selections (scaling). ***Click on the drop down menu and click "Fit Sheet on One Page,"*** then ***click Print***. This will compress everything in the print area to one page.
20. To save the document, ***click on File***, then ***click Save, or Save As*** and **type Fee Projection Worksheet** under File name, then ***click Save***.
21. To quit Excel, ***click the File tab***, then ***click Close***.

This concludes Lesson 2 and the Excel tutorials for Chapter 5.

6

Client Trust Funds and Law Office Accounting

Chapter Objectives

After you read this chapter, you should be able to:

- Understand the purpose and importance of trust/escrow accounts.
- Discuss the ethics rules regarding safeguarding client funds.
- Explain the budgeting process.
- Identify strategies for maintaining strong financial internal controls.

Some 18 months prior to the Office of Disciplinary Counsel's investigation, a lawyer was informed by his partner that proceeds on a claim he settled without the clients' knowledge had been misappropriated and that $1,695,000 owed to clients, Mr. and Mrs. A, was missing from the trust account. The lawyer took no action and instead executed a promissory note to Mr. and Mrs. A, agreeing to pay $12,000 a month until the debt was satisfied. This was one of the several cases where client funds where misappropriated; the exact manner this occurred varied from case to case. The Lawyers' Fund for Client Protection (Lawyers' Fund) received more than $1,286,000 in claims from respondent's clients and more than $3,800,000 in claims from partner's clients. The attorneys and other firm staff members routinely signed client names to settlement documents and endorsed client names on settlement checks. Many clients were unaware that their cases were settled, discovered that medical bills went unpaid and their credit had been damaged. The lawyer was disbarred for misappropriating client funds by settling cases without the respective clients' knowledge or consent and allowing attorneys and other staff members of the firm to routinely sign the names of clients to settlement documents and endorsed their names on checks.

(Source: *In re Rivers*, 409 S.C. 80, 761 S.E.2d 234 (S.C., 2014).)

Why Paralegals Need a Basic Understanding of Law Office Accounting

Paralegals need to have a basic understanding of law office accounting for several reasons. One reason is that paralegals either directly or indirectly work with trust/escrow accounts on a regular basis; they need to understand what a trust account is and how they work. Another reason is that financial decisions drive the law office. It is important to understand how and why a law office operates and to know some basic accounting concepts. In smaller law offices, paralegals may actually have some bookkeeping or accounting responsibilities. Finally, paralegals help prepare office or department budgets in some firms; thus, it is important to have at least a basic knowledge of how to prepare a budget.

Client Funds—Trust/Escrow Accounts

A trust account, sometimes called an "escrow account" or a "client account," is an important part of how law practices manage money. A trust or escrow account is a bank account, separate from a law office's or attorney's business or operating checking account, where unearned client funds are deposited. Nearly all private law practices have at least two checking accounts,

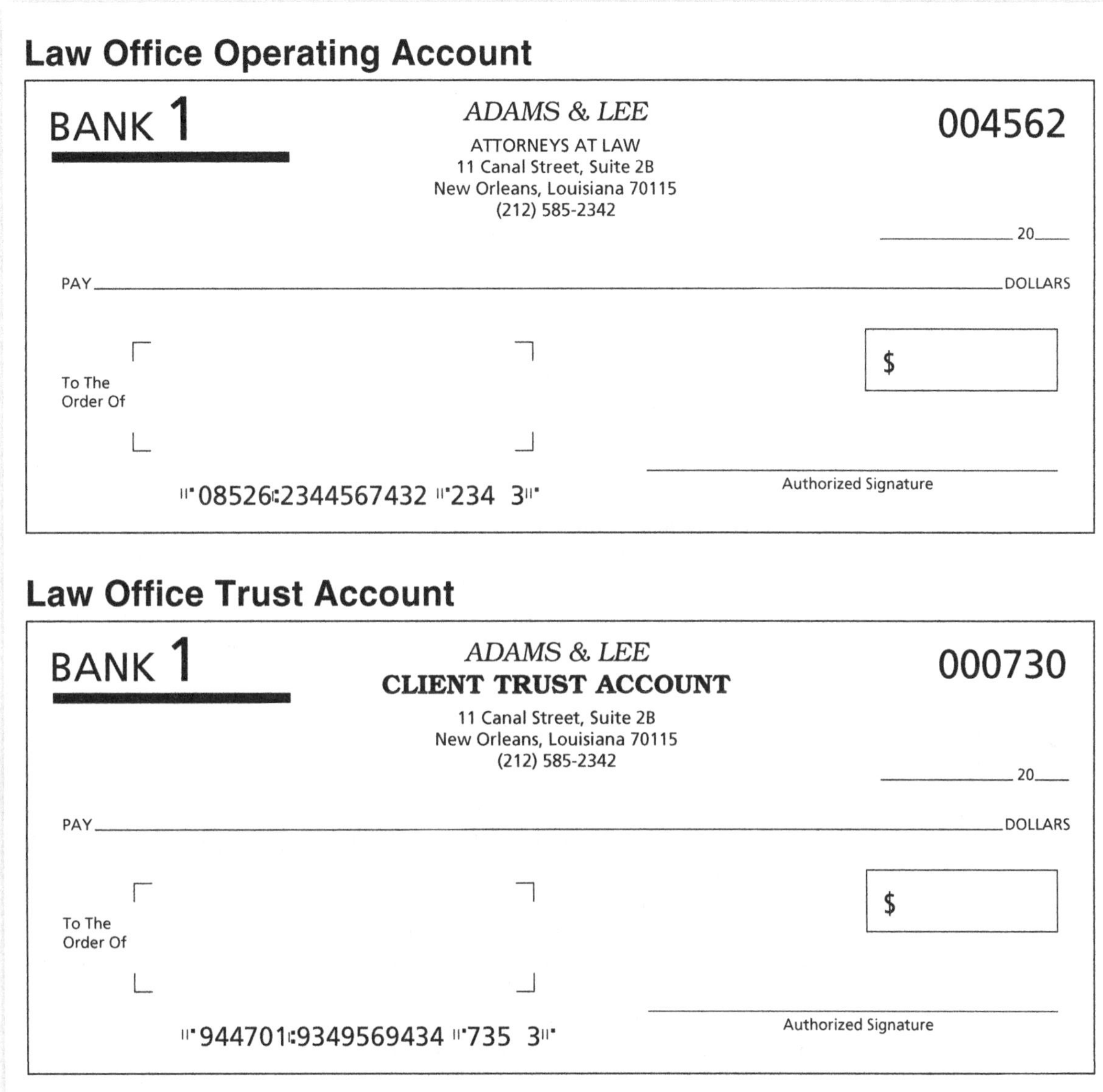

Exhibit 6-1 Operating and Trust Checks

one account from which normal business deposits and expenses are paid and a separate trust account, typically a checking account as opposed to a savings account, where only client funds are kept (see Exhibit 6-1). Checks used with the trust/escrow account will carry the title of "Trust Account," "Client Trust Account," or "Escrow Account." Deposit slips also will have this designation, and a separate bank statement will be received for the trust account.

No Commingling of Client and Law Office Funds

Ethical rules prohibit the commingling of client funds and law office funds in the same account. This rule cannot be overemphasized, and there is virtually no flexibility regarding it.

Examples of How a Trust Account Is Used

There are times when clients pay a cash advance or an unearned retainer to an office to apply against future fees and expenses. Until the office has actually earned these monies, it must keep these funds in the trust account. The reason is simple: if client funds are commingled in the same bank account with general law practice funds, creditors could seize these funds to repay debts of the law practice.

settlement

A mutual agreement to resolve a dispute on specified terms.

The cash advance is just one way that the trust account is used. Trust accounts also are used in other ways, such as for distributing settlement checks. A **settlement** occurs when both parties in a dispute mutually agree to resolve the dispute on specified terms, such as for one party to pay to the other party a certain sum of money.

For example, suppose that an attorney represented a client in a personal injury case and the matter was settled out of court for $10,000. Suppose that the defendant issued a $10,000 check made payable to both the attorney and the client, and that the attorney was entitled to $2000 and the client to $8000. The proper way to dispose of the monies would be for both the attorney and the client to endorse the settlement check. Then, the attorney would deposit the $10,000 settlement check in the trust account and subsequently write an $8000 check from the trust account to the client and a $2000 check from the trust account to the law office.

Ethics and Trust Accounts

Trust Funds and Office Operating Funds Cannot Be Commingled

Every state bar's ethical rules prohibit the commingling of client and law office funds. *Rule 1.15* regarding the rules of professional conduct provides that an attorney must hold the property of a client (such as unearned monies) in a separate account from the attorney's own operating account. An attorney must also maintain complete and accurate records regarding the client's property or monies, and such records must be maintained for five years after termination of the representation. According to the rule, the only time an attorney can deposit the attorney's own money in the trust account is to pay for bank service charges on the trust account. An attorney can only withdraw monies from the trust account as they are earned or actual expenses incurred. An attorney also has an ethical duty under the rule to promptly deliver to a client monies that are owed to the client and to render to the client a full accounting of the monies in the matter.

It is permissible to use one trust account for all client funds as long as there is sufficient record-keeping to know how much each client has in the trust account. Law practices do not have to have separate trust accounts for every client. In fact, many law offices have only one trust account for all client monies. Large-sized offices may choose to have several trust accounts to help organize and control the large numbers of cases they have.

For example, suppose Attorney A has 25 clients who have monies deposited in one trust account, and each client has differing amounts. This is perfectly acceptable, as long as Attorney A knows—and has records to prove—exactly how much each client has in the trust

Adams & Lee Law Firm
Trust Account Checkbook Register

Check No.	Date	Payee or Deposit Source	Check Amount	Deposit Amount	Balance
	01/01/15	Balance from Previous Month			$10,000.00
	01/02/15	Roy Smith v. Vancouver Steel		$2000.00	$12,000.00
	01/16/15	Chance Efron Tax Matter		$2000.00	$14,000.00
2001	01/23/15	Dist Ct. – Filing Fee – Smith v. Steel	$100.00		$13,900.00
2002	01/23/15	Process Server Inc.– Smith v. Steel	$200.00		$13,700.00
2003	01/23/15	Court Reporting Inc.– Smith v. Steel	$700.00		$13,000.00
2004	01/24/15	Adams Law Firm – Fees – Efron Tax	$500.00		$12,500.00
2005	01/25/15	Brown & Koehn CPAs – Efron Tax	$500.00		$12,000.00
2006	01/31/15	Adams Law Firm – Fees – Smith v. Steel	$500.00		$11,500.00

Trust Account Client Subsidiary Ledger Page
Roy Smith v. Vancouver Steel
Case No. 00084

Check No.	Date	Description of Transaction	Funds Paid	Funds Received	Balance
	01/02/15	Cash Advance Retainer		$2000.00	$2000.00
2001	01/23/15	Filing Fee	$100.00		$1900.00
2002	01/23/15	Service of Process	$200.00		$1700.00
2003	01/23/15	Court Reporter Fees	$700.00		$1000.00
2006	01/31/15	Attorney's Fees	$500.00		$500.00

Trust Account Client Summary Ledger Page
Balance as of 01/31/2015

Client	Balance as of 1/31/15
Roy Smith	$500.00
Chance Efron	$1000.00
Bertrand Shoemaker	$5000.00
John Page	$5000.00
TOTAL BALANCE IN TRUST ACCOUNT	$11,500.00

Exhibit 6-2 Trust Account Ledgers

account and maintains a running ledger to show what money was taken out check by check and deposited for each client (see Exhibit 6-2). This is why good record-keeping regarding trust accounts is crucial. Law offices must know to the penny how much each client has in the trust account so that when it comes time to give the money back to the client, the money will be there. Most state bars require that the bank statement for the trust account be reconciled every month, showing exactly which clients have what amounts in the trust account. A failure of the law office to keep detailed records can result in a finding by the state bar that the attorney is subject to disciplinary action.

TRUST ACCOUNTS CANNOT BE USED TO PAY LAW OFFICE OR PERSONAL EXPENSES Ethical rules also prohibit attorneys from using trust funds to pay for general office expenses. For example, if an attorney had client money in the trust account but did not have enough money in law office checking account to cover his rent, the attorney would be absolutely prohibited from writing the rent check on the trust account.

Sometimes attorneys will say that they are simply "borrowing" money from the trust fund and will pay it back. This, too, is a violation of the ethical rules, even if the money is in fact repaid to the trust account within the same day. Client funds simply cannot be used in any way for the personal use of the law office or attorney.

Under *Rule 1.15(d)* regarding the rules of professional conduct, once the client is entitled to receive monies held in trust, the attorney must deliver the monies promptly. For example, if a client's case is concluded and the client still has money left in trust from a cash advance, the attorney has a duty to promptly return the funds.

Commingling of Client Funds is a Common Problem

The commingling of client funds with attorney or law office funds is not a trivial or uncommon matter (see Exhibit 6-3). Hundreds of attorneys are disbarred or suspended from practice every year for commingling client funds. In nearly every issue of every state's bar association journal, one can read about an attorney being disciplined for commingling client monies. Funds that *must* be held in a client trust account include:

- client funds
- third-party funds
- funds that belong partly to a client and partly to an attorney (such as settlement funds)
- retainers for legal services that are unearned and that are the client's property until they are earned

Funds that *cannot* be held in a client trust account include:

- personal funds of the attorney or staff
- business funds of the law firm
- investment funds of the law firm
- earned fee payments that have become the property of the attorney or law firm

State disciplinary authorities have taken notice of the problem of attorneys commingling client and business funds and attorneys stealing from their clients. Many jurisdictions now have rules in place that require a bank or financial institution to contact the state disciplinary authorities when any attorney trust account has checks returned as insufficient. When this happens, state disciplinary authorities conduct an audit of the law firm's trust account. In addition, many state disciplinary authorities conduct random audits of attorney trust accounts in an effort to prevent these problems from occurring. Commingling of client funds is a common problem that nearly always results in harsh discipline being levied against the attorney.

BONDING FOR PEOPLE HANDLING FUNDS Law offices should routinely buy a dishonesty bond from an insurance company to cover all employees handling client or law office funds. If

***Anthony Cavuto (In re Cavuto,* 160 N.J. 185, 733 A. 2d 1174 (N.J., 1999).**

Attorney had practiced law for 33 years. The attorney settled a personal injury claim for a client for $36,000. The settlement proceeds were deposited in the attorney's trust account. The attorney was to pay himself a fee of $12,000, the client's health-care providers a fee of $12,727, and the rest to the client. Within a month of depositing the funds in this trust account, the attorney paid himself 22 checks from the trust account, for a total of $26,259. The attorney never paid the medical expenses. The client did not discover that the medical expenses had not been paid until more than five years later when the doctor refused to treat the client because the client's bill had not been paid. The client complained to the disciplinary authorities and an audit was done. The audit showed that the attorney had very few trust account matters and that the attorney did not keep a trust account receipts journal, a disbursement journal, or client record cards. The attorney did not reconcile his trust account. The attorney tracked his trust account through the running balance on the check stubs. The attorney said that he kept fees in his trust account to keep them from the attorney's spouse, since the spouse had authority to sign checks on the attorney's business account. The attorney said that he had tried to review the file after the client complained, but that the file had been mistakenly purged by his spouse. The attorney then asked the client to bring in the client's records. Still, the attorney could not remember whether the medical providers had been paid. The attorney told the client that he did not have the money to pay the bills at that time, but that he would pay them from another settlement that he was handling for the client. The attorney never paid the medical providers. The attorney suffered from diabetes, depression, fatigue, forgetfulness, and memory loss. The New Jersey Supreme Court found that the attorney knowingly misappropriated client funds and disbarred the attorney. At the time of the disbarment, the actions of the attorney were 13 years old.

***Committee on Professional Ethics and Conduct of the Iowa State Bar Association v. Minette,* 499 N.W. 2d 303 (Iowa, 1993)**

Attorney was client's financial advisor. Client was the recipient of a $40 million trust funded through 842,120 shares of stock. Attorney was authorized to write checks on client's bank account and to approve the sale of stock from the trust when greater funds were needed to pay client's expenses. Attorney paid himself $9000 from client's account to settle a professional negligence claim against him and paid himself a $2500-per-month retainer. When the complaint was received, attorney had misappropriated about $88,000 in client funds. Attorney had no written fee agreement to establish any of these payments. Attorney was disbarred.

In Re-Petition for Disciplinary Action Against Erickson, 506 N.W.2d 628 (Minn., 1993).

A bank notified the state bar that an attorney's trust account was overdrawn. The state bar found that the attorney's trust account records were incomplete; that client subsidiary ledgers for several clients had not been timely established; and that, on occasion, the trust account had contained both client and personal funds, because the attorney had not promptly withdrawn earned fees. In three instances where there were no client funds in the trust account, only earned fees, respondent wrote checks on the account for filing fees, thus using the trust account as a personal business account. Attorney was suspended for 60 days.

Exhibit 6-3 Commingling and Misappropriation of Client Trust Funds

an employee, covered by an employee dishonesty bond, steals client or law office funds, the insurance company would cover the loss up to the amount of the bond. Bonding is a prudent way to protect funds.

TRUST ACCOUNT MANAGEMENT Exhibit 6-4 shows a list of practices and strategies for proper trust account management. Careful and accurate record-keeping is crucial to properly maintaining a trust account. There are many computerized trust account programs available that allow even sole practitioners to inexpensively automate the tracking of a trust account. It is recommended that clients be notified in writing at least monthly regarding all activities in the trust account that affect their case. It is also recommended that the trust account be carefully reconciled every month and a document kept that verifies it. State disciplinary administrators routinely ask for attorney trust account reconciliation reports to prove that an attorney or office has such an account and that it is being properly used and maintained. Records should

Exhibit 6-4 Proper Trust Account Management

- Set up a trust account for all client monies and maintain written, detailed records (journals) of deposits and withdrawals from the trust account.
- On a monthly basis, review individual client balances and notify clients regarding all deposits and withdrawals.
- Unexpended costs and unearned fees should remain in the trust account until spent or earned.
- Promptly disburse funds owed to clients.
- Never commingle attorney/law firm monies in the trust account. Only a managing partner should sign on the account.
- Reconcile the trust account monthly and maintain a written record of the reconciliation.
- Follow the Interest on Lawyers Trust Account (IOLTA) Rules for your state and retain trust records according to state rules.

be kept regarding every deposit and withdrawal, including receipts, statements, and so forth, so that each transaction can be verified. *Rule 1.15(a)* regarding the rules of professional conduct requires that client trust account records be maintained for a minimum of five years after termination of the client matter, so it is important that records are carefully maintained even after a client's case is concluded.

Interest on Lawyers' Trust Account (IOLTA)

An interest-bearing account set up specifically to hold trust funds. The interest that accrues on an IOLTA account is given to a state bar foundation or other nonprofit legal organization for the good of the public.

INTEREST ON LAWYERS' TRUST ACCOUNT (IOLTA) An **Interest on Lawyers' Trust Account (IOLTA)** account is an interest-bearing account set up specifically to hold trust funds. The interest that accrues on an IOLTA account is given by the financial institution to a state bar foundation or other nonprofit legal organization for the good of the public, such as funding for legal services/aid offices. The exact way that IOLTA programs operate differs from state to state, but most states provide that IOLTA accounts can only be used for client funds that are a nominal amount or that are expected to be held for only a short time. If a large amount of client funds are involved, or if an amount is to be held for a long period, then the attorney should open a separate interest-bearing account for that specific client and the interest should be given to the client. In 2003, the United States Supreme Court upheld the use of IOLTA accounts in *Brown v. Legal Foundation of Washington*, 538 U.S. 216, 123 S. Ct. 1406 (2003).

Budgeting

Budgeting in any kind of law office is a good tool to control expenses and make a profit. Firms that develop and use budgets recognize that the budgeting process allows them to project and manipulate the profitability they want to achieve.

budget

A projected plan of income and expenses for a set period of time, usually a year.

A **budget** is a projected plan of income and expenses for a set period of time, usually a year. Budgets allow firms to plan for the future, to anticipate problems, needs, and goals for the firm, and to allocate and manage resources. A budget also is a management tool used to keep revenues and expenses moving toward the profit goal. Exhibit 6-5 shows an example of a typical law office budget. Notice that the budgeting process involves careful development of planned operating expenses, professional and administrative staff sizes, professional and administrative salaries, desired income, and planned capital expenditures for items such as computers, copiers, and furniture.

It is not uncommon for paralegals to prepare budgets for their department, their office, or, in small firms, for the whole practice.

STEP 1—Income Budget	Hours	Rate	Total
R. Adams, Partner	1750	$350	$612,500
C. Lee, Partner	1750	$350	$612,500
J. Brown, Partner	1750	$400	$700,000
J. T. Green, Associate	2100	$250	$525,000
H. Hammond, Associate	2100	$250	$525,000
L. Noland, Associate	2100	$250	$525,000
C. Miller, Paralegal	1700	$90	$153,000
B. Gonzales, Paralegal	1700	$80	$136,000
Other Income			$150,000
SUBTOTAL (Total Billing)			$3,939,000
Time-to-Billing Percentage (actually billed)			95%
TOTAL TO BE BILLED			$3,742,050
Realization Rate			90%
TOTAL GROSS INCOME			**$3,367,845**

STEP 2—Staffing Plan/Salaries	Expense
EXPENSE BUDGET—SALARY EXPENSES & BONUS	
J. T. Green, Associate	$140,000
H. Hammond, Associate	$120,000
L. Noland, Associate	$120,000
C. Miller, Paralegal	$62,500
B. Gonzales, Paralegal	$52,500
M. Harris, Legal Administrator	$85,000
J. Parks, Computer/Network Specialist	$70,000
J. Inez, Secretary	$47,500
J. Logan, Secretary	$42,000
C. Glazer, Secretary	$40,000
T. Monie, Secretary/File Clerk	$37,500
B. Dover, Bookkeeper/Clerk	$37,500
R. Hopper, Receptionist	$35,000
TOTAL SALARY EXPENSE	**$889,500**

STEP 3—Other Expenses *(continues on next page)*	Expense
Accounting Professional Services	$10,000
Amortization of Leasehold Improvements	$7,500
Association/Membership Dues	$7,500
Client Billings/Write-Offs	$75,000
Continuing Legal Education	$15,000
Copying Costs (not billed to clients)	$45,000
Depreciation	$50,000
Employee Benefits and Taxes	$225,000
Entertainment	$20,000
Equipment Purchase/Computers/Network	$85,000

Exhibit 6-5 Law Firm Budget—Master Budget

STEP 3—Other Expenses *(continued from previous page)*	Expense
Equipment Rental	$8,500
Forms, Stationary, Paper	$7,500
Insurance (P/C, Malpractice, etc.)	$125,000
Housekeeping/Cleaning Services	$7,500
Marketing	$30,000
Office Supplies	$25,000
Other Taxes	$10,000
Postage	$14,000
Reference Materials/Library/Westlaw	$40,000
Rent Expense	$200,000
Repairs/Maintenance	$35,000
Telephone/Internet/Communication/Mobile	$50,000
Travel (not billed)	$45,000
Utilities	$100,000
TOTAL OTHER EXPENSES	**$1,237,500**
TOTAL ALL EXPENSES	**$2,127,000**

STEP 4—Determine Acceptable Profit Goal
NET INCOME TO BE DISTRIBUTED TO PARTNERS $1,240,845

Exhibit 6-5 Law Firm Budget—Master Budget *(Continued)*

Budgeting and Planning

Budgeting and planning go hand in hand; a budget is just a specific type of plan. For example, if a firm's long-term strategic and marketing plans call for $30,000 of marketing expenditures, the budget needs to reflect that amount.

income budget

Estimate of how many partners, associates, legal assistants, and others will bill for their time, what the appropriate rates of hourly charge should be, and the number of billable hours each timekeeper will be responsible for billing.

Steps in the Budget Process

Step 1. Income budget—One of the first steps in developing a firm-wide budget is to draft an income budget (see Exhibit 6-5). An **income budget** estimates how many partners, associates, paralegals, and others will bill for their time, what the appropriate rates of hourly charge should be, and the number of billable hours each timekeeper will be responsible for billing.

time-to-billing percentage

System of adjusting downward the actual amount that will be billed to clients during the budget process, taking into account the fact that timekeepers are not always able to bill at their optimum levels.

When preparing an income budget, you should estimate as close to possible what the actual amount will be. However, if you are unsure of something, it is usually recommended that you be conservative in estimating the income budget; if you overestimate income and then rely on the overestimate in the expense budget and spend it, and income is actually lower than expected, you have a net loss. However, if you underestimate income and then the actual income is above the level (and expenses stay the same as budgeted), the firm makes a larger profit than was estimated and there is no harm done. One way to minimize this problem is to use a "time-to-billing" percentage. The **time-to-billing percentage** adjusts downward the actual amount that will be billed to clients, taking into account the fact that timekeepers are not always able to bill at their optimum levels due to vacations, sickness, and other unforeseeable events. Notice in Exhibit 6-5 that the firm used a time-to-billing of 95%, thus reducing its billing estimate by 5%. The time-to-billing percentage for most firms ranges from 85 to 100%. The purpose of the time-to-billing percentage is to build into the budget the fact that the firm may not bill all the hours it would like to.

Reasons that timekeepers may not bill their required number of hours include the following:

- Extended medical leave of timekeepers
- Too few clients
- Procrastination or other bad work habits
- Disorganization or inefficiencies in case management
- Failure to consistently report all billable hours
- Extensive use of the timekeeper on pro bono or other nonbillable tasks
- Marketing effects not as effective as planned

In some instances, paralegals' and attorneys' actual hours end up being greater than the budgeted hours. The firm makes an even larger profit than expected when this happens, as long as expenses remain as budgeted.

realization

Amount a firm actually receives in income as opposed to the amount it bills.

Realization is also an important concept in budgeting income. **Realization** is what a firm actually receives in income as opposed to the amount it bills. In Exhibit 6-5, the firm anticipates that it will actually receive or collect 90% of what it bills. Some firms strive for a 95% rate, while others are comfortable with a rate as low as 80%.

Notice in Exhibit 6-5 that the firm usually sets the hourly rates for the year at this point. Setting rates in the income budget can be difficult. If a firm sets the rate too high, clients may take their business to a competing firm, but if rates are too low, it could mean a loss of revenue. It also is quite difficult to try to project income if the firm has many contingency fee arrangements. One way to do it is to look at gross income figures for contingency fees for the past several years to help in estimating future contingencies.

staffing plan

Estimate of how many employees will be hired or funded by the firm, what positions or capacities they will serve in, what positions will need to be added, what old positions will be deleted, and how much compensation each employee will receive.

Step 2. Staffing plan—A staffing plan should also be established early in the budgeting process. A **staffing plan** estimates how many employees will be hired or funded by the firm, what positions or capacities they will serve, what positions will need to be added, what positions will be deleted, and how much compensation each employee will receive. One of the largest expenses of any professional service is salary costs. Thus, it is important that the firm determine whether positions will be added or cut, or whether existing staff members will receive cost-of-living adjustments or merit increases. A staffing plan also goes hand in hand with preparing the income budget.

Step 3. Estimating overhead expenses—Firms also must accurately estimate their general operating or overhead expenses. This can be fairly tricky because, in many cases, the estimates are covering a period that ends a minimum of a year in advance. For example, if a person is preparing a budget in November 2014, and the budget covers the period of January 2015 to December 2015, the person will not know until 14 months later whether the estimates were accurate. The time problem makes budgeting difficult; if insurance rates go up unexpectedly, if marketing costs rise significantly, or if large equipment breaks down unexpectedly, your budget will be greatly affected. When discussing the income budget, it should be noted that the preparer should be conservative in estimating income. However, when you get to the expense budget, the opposite is true. As always, you should try to be as accurate as possible in estimating expenses. However, if you question the validity of an item, you should be liberal in estimating the expense. This allows the firm to forecast unforeseeable events that might otherwise leave the budget short.

Step 4. Profit margin—The last step is to calculate income and expenses so that the firm budgets the targeted profit margin it needs. That is, if after the draft budget the firm is not happy with the profit margin, the preparer can manipulate and make changes in the budget—such as adding additional profit-making positions or cutting expenses further—to reach the desired goal. The following are some additional suggestions about budgets:

- **Communicate the budget to everyone involved.** For a budget to be effective, everyone in the firm should be aware of it, and there should be a consensus reached by the firm's management on major issues such as desired profits and equipment purchases. For instance, if even one timekeeper fails to charge the number of estimated hours, it can completely throw the budget off. Thus, it is very important that management stress the importance of the budget and communicate it effectively.
- **Track budgets year-round and consult them regularly.** For budgets to be useful, they must be taken out of the desk drawer. That is, if a firm wants to purchase a piece of computer equipment, it is important that the budget be consulted to see if the purchase was planned or if there is room in the budget to allow for it.
- **Track the progress of the budget on a monthly basis.** As suggested before, budgets are of little value if they are not updated and used throughout the year. One way to use the budget year-round is to compare "budget" versus "actual." This allows the firm to know whether it is staying in line with its budget or if it needs to make midyear adjustments.
- **Always document your budget.** Always document budgets well, making notes and narrative statements in the budget itself. It is common to make assumptions when formulating a budget, and unless the preparer notes why the assumption was made, he or she may forget its purpose. It also helps in preparing the budget for next year.
- **Use zero-based budgets.** Although it is common for organizations to start the budgeting process for a new year by using the actual figures from the previous year and adding 4 or 5%, this is not an effective way of controlling costs and managing the firm. By using a **zero-based budgeting system**, everyone in the organization must justify and explain his or her budget figures in depth without using last year's figures as justification. In short, each year's budget is taken on its own merit.

zero-based budgeting system

Procedure that forces everyone in the organization to justify and explain his or her budget figures in depth without using prior years' figures as justification.

Collection/Income

Collecting monies that have been billed to clients is an important financial aspect of any law office; this is particularly true in small-sized law offices but can cause problems in large ones as well. Collection and income are closely tied to each other. Most newcomers to the legal field quickly find out that it is easy to bill but much more difficult to actually get paid for legal services rendered. Billing large amounts of time and not getting paid is a direct path to bankruptcy for any law office. The first step in collecting a high percentage of billings is for the attorney to carefully select and weed out what clients' cases he or she will accept in the first place. Attorneys must do a good job of weeding out cases that will not be profitable; there is no substitute for this. Another strategy that many law offices take is to get monies up front using deposits in the form of earned and unearned retainers.

Other strategies law offices use for collecting fees billed include sending regular monthly billings and withdrawing from cases as soon as possible once it is determined the client will not pay. This is sometimes difficult to do since ethical rules put limits on when attorneys can withdraw from cases. *Rule 1.16* regarding the rules of professional conduct provides that an attorney may withdraw from representing a client when:

- the withdrawal can be done without negatively affecting the client's interests;
- the attorney believes that the client's conduct is criminal or fraudulent, or that the client has used the attorney's services to commit a crime or fraud;
- the client persists in a course of conduct with which the lawyer fundamentally disagrees;
- the client has not completed an obligation to the attorney regarding the attorney's services;
- the representation of the client is causing an unreasonable financial burden on the attorney;
- the client is unreasonably difficult to work with;
- there is some other good cause.

In most courts, an attorney must ask for permission to withdraw from the matter. If a court denies an attorney's request to withdraw, the attorney must ordinarily continue to represent the client. For example, if an attorney requests to withdraw from a complex criminal case right before trial, the interests of the client could be affected negatively and a court might reasonably deny the attorney's request to withdraw. If an attorney is permitted to withdraw from a case, the attorney must act prudently to protect the client's interests, such as giving the client reasonable notice, providing the client with his or her file, and refunding unused monies for fees or expenses.

Another strategy to collect on billings is for the attorney to actually sue the client for the fee. This is usually a method of last resort, as no attorney wants to be put in the situation of suing his or her own client; in some instances, however, this is the only option.

Internal Controls

internal control

Procedures that an organization establishes to set up checks and balances so that no individual in the organization has exclusive control over any part of the accounting system.

Law offices of every type—private, corporate, government, and legal aid—must establish good internal control procedures. **Internal control** refers to procedures that an organization establishes to set up checks and balances so that no individual in the organization has exclusive control over any part of the accounting system. Internal controls discussions are usually saved for accounting professionals. However, embezzlement by law practice personnel has become a major issue (see Exhibit 6-6) and is quite prevalent. If embezzlement occurs in an organization, it signals that its internal controls are weak and ineffective.

Internal controls must be established in both large- and small-sized firms. Interestingly enough, small-sized law offices need internal controls more than large-sized firms do. Why? Because fewer people handle the finances in a small-sized office, and there are typically fewer written and strict procedures. Thus, the opportunity to embezzle tends to be greater in a smaller office. Therefore, it is absolutely critical in a small-sized law office to have exceptionally good internal controls. The downside of internal controls is that it takes time to do them right and they can slow down the financial process (e.g., by requiring a partner to sign all checks instead of having a bookkeeper sign them). This is particularly true in small-sized firms, but it is the only way to ensure that embezzlement and fraud do not take place.

Legal Assistant Sentenced to Four Years in Prison

A legal assistant with five years of experience stole more than $102,000 by forging the names of attorneys he worked for on settlement checks that should have been deposited into the attorneys' trust account. The legal assistant passed himself off as a lawyer to the attorneys he was working for and kept the monies from 10 personal injury settlements. The legal assistant began the scheme by only taking the attorney's portion of the settlement check and quickly graduated to taking all of the monies in several settlements. The legal assistant was sentenced to four years in a state prison and restitution.

Legal Assistant Allegedly Launders Insurance Rebate Checks

A legal assistant allegedly stole approximately $724,000 from an insurance company over a two-month period. The legal assistant allegedly conspired with another person to issue 34 fraudulent rebate checks to policyholders. The legal assistant allegedly laundered the checks through a number of different accounts. The insurance company realized that something was wrong and started an investigation, but not before nearly three-quarters of a million dollars was gone. The legal assistant was charged with 5 counts of money laundering, 14 counts of embezzlement, and conspiracy and forgery charges.

Former Paralegal Sentenced in Embezzlement Case

A former paralegal was sentenced to two months of home detention and one year of probation for having embezzled $8,000 in funds belonging to a bankruptcy debtor while employed as a paralegal at an East Coast law firm. The paralegal faced a maximum penalty of five years' imprisonment and a $250,000 fine. The paralegal was custodian of the bankruptcy debtor's account and was responsible for preparing checks for the bankruptcy trustee. The embezzlement was discovered a few months after the paralegal left the firm while he was working at another firm. "We discovered certain irregularities during a routine inventory of accounts and turned the information over to the proper authorities," said one of the firm's directors. The case was investigated by the FBI. At the time of sentencing, the paralegal informed the U.S. attorney's office that he was no longer working at the new firm and that he voluntarily withdrew from law school entirely.

Exhibit 6-6 Embezzlement Is Common in Law Practices

Sources: N. J. paralegal jailed for theft. (2004, January/ February). Legal Assistant Today, 24; A "clean" getaway . . . almost. (1999, May/June). Legal Assistant Today, 19; Legal Assistant Today, (1992, July/August), 27.

What type of internal control procedures could limit the possibility of embezzlement? There are several.

- **Never allow a bookkeeper or person preparing checks to sign checks or to sign on the account.** Never let the individual who writes the checks sign on the account. In addition, never let any one person record the checks in the checkbook (or equivalent), prepare the checks, obtain signature(s) on the checks, and mail the checks. Embezzlement is more likely to happen in that case. A partner or ranking member of the firm should sign all checks, if possible. An alternative is to require two signatures on all checks.
- **Have careful, unannounced, routine examination of the books.** A partner or other ranking member of the law office with no direct accounting responsibilities should carefully look over the books on a weekly basis. A partner also should account for all monies on a regular basis (once every week or two weeks) by reviewing bank statements and canceled checks for the authenticity of the signatures, reviewing the reconciliation register, ensuring that check numbers out of sequence are not being cashed, and looking through cash disbursement records carefully. These procedures must be done for both the office business account and the trust account.

- **All documents must routinely be read and examined—no exceptions.** Never sign or let someone else sign checks, correspondence, or other important documents without carefully reading the material. It is very easy to hand documents to people and ask for their signature immediately. Do not do this, and do not let someone else do it. Everyone involved should always check all the supporting documentation of a check.
- **All checks should be stored in a locked cabinet.** All checks should be kept under lock and key at all times when not in use, and access for writing checks should be given to as few people as possible.
- **Never let the person signing the checks reconcile the account.** The person writing or signing the checks should not be allowed to reconcile the bank account or even open the monthly bank statement. If the person who is preparing and signing the checks is allowed to reconcile the account, that person will be able to write him- or herself a check, sign it, and destroy the check when it comes in the bank statement. This might tempt even a basically honest person. Oversight is the key. Never let anyone have the opportunity to embezzle; set up good procedures and follow them.
- **Use check request forms.** Check request forms are also used to bolster internal control procedures. If, for instance, an employee or attorney needed a check for a client expense or for an expense charged to the firm, the person would be required to complete a form similar to the one shown in Exhibit 6-7. Small-sized law offices should also use check requests whenever possible.
- **Establish guidelines for how the mail should be opened.** The mail should be opened by someone with no accounting duties, such as a receptionist, secretary, or mailing clerk. When a check is received, the person opening the mail should be instructed to immediately endorse the check on the back with "FOR DEPOSIT ONLY" in ink or with a stamp. If the bookkeeper or someone in accounting opens the mail, there is absolutely nothing to stop that person from taking the check and cashing it. This would be easy to do, because the firm would have no record of it.
- **Use nonaccounting personnel to help with internal controls.** An additional internal control would be for the receptionist, secretary, or another person to prepare the bank deposits, because he or she would be separated from the accounting department and would not have recorded the cash receipts in the accounts receivable system. In this way, all cash receipts and bank deposits are independently verified by someone completely outside the accounting department who has no access to accounting records.

  A very common way embezzlement occurs is through refund checks. For example, it is not uncommon for firms to receive large refund checks from insurance companies and other vendors. If a person in the accounting department opens the mail, he or she could endorse the check and deposit it into his or her own account with little possibility of someone finding out about it. Why? Because the original invoice would be shown as paid on the firm's books, and no one else would know that a refund had ever been received.
- **Require two signatures on checks over $10,000.** Checks over a certain dollar amount might also require a signature by a second individual (i.e., two signatures on the check). This is another example of an internal control; it would limit large checks from going out of the firm with the authority of only one individual.

ADAMS & LEE
ATTORNEYS AT LAW
11 Canal Street, Suite 2B
New Orleans, Louisiana 70115
(212) 585-2342

CHECK REQUEST FORM

Client Name and File Number: ______________________________

Date of Request: ______________

Request Made By: ______________________________

Bank Account: General Business Account   Trust Account   (Circle One)

Amount of Check: $ ______________

Check Should Be Made Payable To: ______________________________

Address of Payee: ______________________________

Detailed Description: ______________________________

____

____

____

Accounting Use Only

Account No./Code: ______________________________

Approved by: ______________________ Date: ______________

Exhibit 6-7 Check Request Form

- **Stamp invoices "CANCELED."** Once a check has been paid, the invoice should be stamped "CANCELED," so that no one could intentionally resubmit the same invoice for payment.
- **Have an audit done once a year or hire a Certified Public Accountant (CPA) to help you set up internal controls.** A yearly audit by an accounting firm can help find embezzlement, and strengthen and monitor internal control procedures. If your firm cannot justify the cost of an audit, hire a CPA to help you set up good internal controls and have him or her come in once a year to review them.

Lawyers and Nonlawyers Cannot Share Fees

Attorneys are generally barred from directly sharing their legal fees with a nonlawyer, such as a paralegal; in fact, *Rule 5.4* regarding the rules of professional conduct prevents a lawyer from sharing legal fees with a nonlawyer. The sharing of a fee between a lawyer and a nonlawyer could interfere with the lawyer's professional judgment and lead to the nonlawyer being concerned only with profits and not the best interests of his or her clients. Regarding paralegals, this typically arises when a paralegal refers a person to an attorney for representation. The attorney is prohibited from sharing the representation fee with the paralegal or paying the paralegal specifically for the referral. Exhibit 6-8 presents an example of lawyers sharing fees with nonlawyers.

Exhibit 6-8 Lawyers Cannot Share Fees with Nonlawyers

***In re Guirard*, 11 So.3d 1017 (La., 2009).** Respondents, E. Eric Guirard and Thomas R. Pittenger were partners in a law firm with locations in New Orleans and Baton Rouge. In 2000, the Office of Disciplinary Counsel (ODC) began its investigation into compensation arrangements for nonlawyers, including case managers, legal assistants, secretaries, and agents.

ODC found that five case managers received compensation as commissions on the firm's gross legal fees at a basic rate of 15% on cases directly assigned to the case manager and 7.5% on cases reassigned to them. The firm manager, a nonlawyer was paid 1% commission of the firm's total gross legal fees collected on all settled cases in addition to their salary. Legal assistants were paid either 6% or 6.5% of fees paid to the supervising attorney. Investigators were paid $50 for obtaining signed client forms for the law firm and additional compensation if additional clients were signed up while visiting the initial client.

ODC found that the nonlawyer case managers were paid a piece of the action if the case was settled and no commissions if the case was not settled and had to be litigated. Respondents had engaged in fee splitting with nonlawyers in clear violation of Rule 5.4(a) which prohibits lawyers and law firms from sharing fees with nonlawyers. Respondents were disbarred for among fee splitting violation, delegated the handling of their clients' cases to their nonlawyer staff, motivating them to settle claims quickly to receive commissions, in conflict with the clients' best interest and misconduct, noting their practices were egregious.

Summary

Ethical rules require that client funds not be commingled with law office operating funds, meaning that a law office must have a trust or escrow account. A trust accounting is a bank account, separate from a law office's or an attorney's operating checking account, where unearned client funds are deposited, such as unearned retainers or the proceeds of a settlement. Attorneys have an ethical responsibility to safeguard client property. Attorneys and law offices must carefully track all clients' funds in a client trust account. This includes having trust account ledgers for all transactions in the account, including ledgers for each individual client. In addition, the only time an attorney can have his or her own funds in the client trust fund is to pay for bank services charges. IOLTA is an acronym meaning Interest on Lawyers' Trust Account; an IOLTA account is an interest-bearing bank account set up specifically to hold client trust funds. The interest that accrues on an IOLTA account is given by the financial institution to a designated state bar foundation or other nonprofit legal organization (in accordance with state rules) for the good of the public.

A budget is a projected plan of income and expenses for a set period of time, usually a year. Most budgets consist of an income budget, staffing plan, general overhead expenses, and an estimated profit.

Collecting monies after they have been billed is an important issue for all law offices. Strategies for collecting monies that are due to an attorney or law office include carefully selecting and accepting cases; obtaining monies in the way of deposits/retainers up front, before legal work on a case has started; withdrawing from cases where a client will not pay (if allowed); and suing clients as a last resort if they do not pay.

Law offices must safeguard their assets by implementing internal control procedures, which establish checks and balances so that no individual in the firm has exclusive control over any accounting system. It is generally unethical for an attorney to share a fee with a nonlawyer.

Key Terms

budget
income budget
Interest on Lawyers' Trust Account (IOLTA)
internal control
realization
settlement
staffing plan
time-to-billing percentage
zero-based budgeting system

Test Your Knowledge

1. Another name for a trust account is ____________________.
2. True or false: it is okay to put an attorney's operating funds in the client trust account.
3. True or false: an attorney can put his or her own monies in the client trust account to cover bank service charges.

4. True or false: an attorney cannot commingle multiple client funds into one trust account.
5. True or false: it is alright for an attorney to borrow monies from the client trust account as long as it is paid back within one banking day.
6. What two things should an attorney do regarding a client trust account on at least a monthly basis?
7. According to the *Model Rules*, an attorney must maintain client trust fund records for at least ____________________ years after a client's case is concluded.
8. True or false: with an IOLTA, the interest monies are paid to the client.
9. There are usually two restrictions on the kinds of client funds that can go into an IOLTA account. Only ____________________ and ____________________ can go into an IOLTA account.
10. Name two strategies for collecting on client accounts.
11. ____________________ refers to procedures to set up checks and balances so no one individual has exclusive control of any part of an accounting system.

Practical applications

1. You are a paralegal in a five-attorney legal services/aid practice. The office manager, who writes all the checks for the organization, will not be back for several hours. Your supervising attorney asks you to get the checkbook out of the office manager's desk and issue a check that she needs right now. You fill in the manual check stub and type the check. Because the office manager is not there to sign the check, you hand the check to your supervising attorney to sign with several other papers. The attorney quickly signs her name while looking at the other documents. On your way to your office, the receptionist asks you to drop off the office manager's mail in his office. You notice that one of the envelopes appears to be a check from the local bar association that makes contributions to the practice as a community service. You also notice that another of the envelopes appears to be a bank statement and returned checks for the previous month. The office manager uses the returned checks and bank statement to reconcile the bank account. You place all the items on the office manager's desk as requested. Do you see any potential problems? Would it matter if the office manager had been there for 20 years, was extremely trustworthy, and refused to even take a vacation in that it might take him away from work? What recommendations would you make?

2. Your office represented a business client in litigation. During the litigation, the client made several cash advances. The matter has been concluded for approximately two months and the client has a balance in the trust account of about $20,000. The client has requested that the money be returned, but the supervising attorney has not gotten around to it yet. How would you analyze the situation and what would you do?

3. You have just been given the assignment to begin work on incorporating a new business. At the first meeting with the client, the client hands you a check for $5000 and states that although no work has been performed on the case, this was the agreement that the client and your supervising attorney worked out last week on the telephone. Later, you hand the check to the supervising attorney. The attorney says to just deposit it in the office's account. What problems would you face, what would you do, and why?

4. As a paralegal in a sole practitioner's office, you sometimes become "burned out" and tired. The attorney you work for is very appreciative of your hard work and would like to give you incentives when possible to keep you motivated. The attorney mentions that she will pay you a bonus equal to 10% of any new client retainers you are responsible for bringing in. How does this sound to you? Analyze this arrangement from an ethics perspective.

5. You are a paralegal in a relatively small office. One day, one of the partners in the office instructs you to transfer $5000 from the trust account into the office's general account. You ask him what case is involved. The partner says "There is no case name, but it doesn't concern you." What would you do? Explain your answer.

6. At 8:00 A.M. on a Monday morning, your supervising attorney rushes into your office. She states that at 10:00 A.M. she has a meeting with one of the firm's administrators to go over her draft version of the proposed budget

for her satellite office. Although the office is relatively small, she must submit a budget that will produce a reasonable profit for the firm. Unfortunately, she has a meeting with a client and a court appearance to go to before the 10:00 A.M. meeting. She hands you a list of her notes and asks you to please come through for her on this one. You reluctantly agree, but then remember that your bonus at the end of the year will depend on how profitable your office is. Suddenly, you feel better about the assignment.
Below are the attorney's notes.

- Rent is $5000 a month, but halfway through the year the lease calls for a 5% increase.
- The paralegals will bill at $80 an hour and must work a minimum of 1750 hours. You think that they will do this, since they will not be eligible to receive a bonus unless they work this amount.
- Utilities are included in the lease agreement, so do not worry about these.
- Associates will bill at $225 an hour. You figure that they will bill no less than 1900 hours because if they do not, they will not look good for a partnership position.
- From past history, the firm has determined that its time-to-billing percentage is 98% and the realization rate is 92%.
- Telephone cost is expected to be $4,000 a month.
- Staffing is as follows:

    Two paralegals
    Four secretaries
    Three associates

Last year, paralegals were paid, on average, $50,000; secretaries, $40,000; and associates, $90,000. Budget a 3.5% cost-of-living adjustment and a 2.5% merit increase.

- Fringe benefits and taxes are figured at 25% of the total of the salaries.
- Office supplies and stationery expenses will be about $20,000.
- The office must purchase four computers. Your best estimate is that they will cost about $3000 each when all costs are included (installation, cabling, software, printers, network hardware, training, maintenance contract, etc.).
- All other items, such as malpractice/general liability insurance and professional services, will be prorated to your office by the accounting office. You do not need to worry about this now.

What profit or loss is the office budgeted for?

7. You are a paralegal manager in a small- to medium-sized firm. The firm administrator asks you to prepare a proposed income budget for your department of six legal assistants. You are not required to do an expense budget, as this is handled by the administrators and the accounting department. From past years, you know that you must sit down with each of the paralegals and discuss billable hours, hourly rates, and so forth. You do not relish this much, because the firm has consistently pressed for more and more billable hours. Thus, this topic can be somewhat touchy for you as a manager. Below is the information you obtained to help you. Also, note that time-to-billing percentage is figured at 95%, and the realization rate is also 95%.

Paralegal #1 typically works for one of the firm's general litigators. Because of her extensive background in this area, her hourly charge is about $90. However, during trial and trial preparation, her hourly charge is usually about $100. She figures that about 40% of her time will be spent either in trial or preparing for trial. About 10% of her time is spent traveling to and from trials, finding witnesses, and so on. Her travel time is billed at $60 an hour. She is a very hard worker, and although she billed 1900 last year, she is requesting that her billable hours be lowered to 1800. You tentatively agree.

Paralegal #2 has recently been given a new assignment: to work almost exclusively on insurance defense cases. His typical hourly billing rate was $85. However, you know that the insurance company, he will primarily be working for, will only pay a maximum of $75 an hour for paralegal time. In addition, the insurance company is extremely picky about its invoices and absolutely refuses to pay for anything even remotely close to secretarial functions. The paralegal states he thinks that 1750 is a reasonable number of billable hours, considering his present salary. You figure that, based on your experience, the insurance company will either reasonably or unreasonably question about 40 hours that he bills. You reduce your estimate by this amount just to be safe.

Paralegal #3 handles workers' compensation cases. Unfortunately, these cases are almost all taken on a contingency basis. The firm typically recovers 25% of these types of cases. You estimate that the firm will receive about $600,000 in revenues from this gross part of its practice. You also note that about one-third of this is usually allocated to the work of the paralegal.

Paralegal #4 works mainly in the probate area. She typically receives about $70 per hour for her work. You note that although she billed more than 2000 hours last year, she did not take any vacation and took very little time off. Your conversation reveals that she is going to take three weeks off for an extensive vacation and that she may need to take an additional week off for medical reasons.

Paralegal #5 is new to the firm. From your past experience, you do not want to burn him out by putting too many billable hours on him at first. You also recognize that he will have many nonbillable hours during the first several months due to staff training and general unfamiliarity with the firm. You budget him for 1600 hours. He will be a rover, working for many different people, and thus his hourly billing rate is hard to estimate, but you budget $70.00 an hour.

Finally, Paralegal #6: yourself. You have many administrative responsibilities. You would like to set a good example, so you budget yourself at 1400 hours. You bill at $90 per hour. You are responsible for coordinating the efforts of the legal assistants under you, for handling personnel-related issues, and many other duties. You also remember that you are to take a greater role in marketing this year and that approximately 160 hours of your time will be nonbillable while you handle this function.

8. Your managing attorney has asked you to compute the current Balance in Trust for the Singer case for both fees and expenses. She asks you to track each of them separately. Here is what you find in the file:

- January 1, initial deposit/retainer against future fees (unearned) of $20,000 paid by client
- January 1, initial deposit/retainer against future expenses (unearned) of $10,000 paid by client
- February 1, client billed for $3500 in fees and the same amount paid out of the client trust fund to the attorney
- February 1, client billed for $2000 in expenses and the same amount paid out of the client trust fund to the attorney
- February 15, check from the client trust fund for filing fees of $100
- February 21, check from the client trust fund for $200 for service of process
- March 1, client billed for $5500 in fees and the same amount paid out of the client trust fund to the attorney
- April 1, client billed for $10,000 in fees and the same amount paid out of the client trust fund to the attorney
- April 17, check from the client trust fund for court reporting charges of $6000

9. A case settles in the amount of $120,000 for your client. The money has been deposited into the firm's client trust account. Your managing attorney has asked you to calculate the amount owed to all of parties. Below are the facts:

- Your firm is to pay medical expenses of your client out of the settlement of $10,000.
- Your firm has incurred $12,000 in legal expenses.
- Your firm billed hourly on the case in the amount of $40,000 but your managing attorney agreed to reduce the fee to $35,000.
- The client owes the firm $10,000 on another case and has agreed in writing to pay the firm that fee from this settlement.

On the Web Exercises

1. Go to the ABA Center for Professional Responsibility at http://www.americanbar.org. Find the *ABA Model Rules of Professional Conduct*; read and print out *Rule 1.15* Safekeeping Property and the Comment.

2. Visit five state bar association Web sites and find three articles on trust accounting, legal financial management, legal budgeting, law office profitability, or accounting for client funds. The following link will take you to a Web site that connects to all state bar sites: http://www.nationallist.com/resources/associations-state-bar-list.

3. Using a general search engine, such as http://www.google.com or http://www.yahoo.com, or state bar association Web sites, find a model chart of accounts for a law office.

4. Using a general search engine, such as http://www.google.com or http://www.yahoo.com, find a minimum of three sites (they do not need to be law related) that discuss what internal controls are and why they are important. Print out your results.

5. Using a general search engine, such as http://www.google.com or http://www.yahoo.com, find a minimum of three accounting or trust accounting programs (not listed in the Helpful Web Sites section of this chapter) that can be used in a law office.

Projects

1. Using a general search engine, such as http://www.google.com or http://www.yahoo.com, search for trust accounting procedures. Alternatively, go to a library or visit state bar association Web sites, such as the Alabama State Bar Association [http://www.alabar.org], and write a detailed paper on ethical trust account practices.

2. Research the issue of IOLTA accounts. Go to http://www.findlaw.com and print out and read the United States Supreme Court case of *Brown v. Legal Foundation of Washington*, 538 U.S. 216, 123 S. Ct. 1406 (2003). Try selecting "For Legal Professionals," scroll until you see "Cases and Codes," and then click on "Supreme Court" and "Supreme Court Opinions." You should then be able to enter the site of the case—538 U.S. 216. Why is the issue of IOLTA so controversial? What did the plaintiffs argue in the case? How did the Court decide? Why was there a descent in the case?

3. Research and write a paper on computerized financial management and trust accounting systems. Visit the American Bar Association Technology Resource Center http://www.americanbar.org/groups/departments_offices/legal_technology_resources.html and state bar association Web sites, as well as other legal technology Web sites, and review helpful articles and materials you find. Also go to the financial and trust accounting software Web sites listed in the Helpful Web Sites section of this chapter. Compare and contrast some of the different products that are available. Which one were you most impressed with, and why?

4. Using a general search engine, such as http://www.google.com or http://www.yahoo.com, search for law office profitability. Alternatively, go to a library or visit state bar association Web sites and write a detailed paper on how law offices can be profitable. Your paper should cover such topics as how to increase revenue, control expenses, increase collections, and related topics.

5. Using a law library, state bar journal magazine, Westlaw/LexisNexis, or the Internet, write a paper that summarizes a minimum of three attorney discipline cases regarding the misuse of client funds, client trust accounts, or related topics. Be sure to include an analysis of the case, what the court found, what ethical rules were at issue, what rules were violated, what discipline was imposed, and why.

Case Review

In the Matter of a Member of the Bar of the Supreme Court of the State of Delaware:

JOHN J. SULLIVAN, JR., Petitioner,
No. 698, 2013
SUPREME COURT OF DELAWARE

Board Case No 2011-0233-B

FILED: December 27, 2013

Submitted: January 16, 2014

Decided: March 7, 2014

Cite as: *In re Sullivan,* 86 A.3d 1119 (Del. 2014)

Before HOLLAND, JACOBS and RIDGELY, Justices.

ORDER

This 7th day of March, 2014, it appears to the Court that the Board on Professional Responsibility has filed a Report on this matter pursuant to Rule 9(d) of the Delaware

Lawyers' Rules of Disciplinary Procedure. The Office of Disciplinary Counsel filed no objections to the Board's Report. The Respondent did file objections to the Board's Report. The Court has reviewed the matter pursuant to Rule 9(e) of the Delaware Lawyers' Rules of Disciplinary Procedure and approves the Board's Report.

NOW, THEREFORE, IT IS ORDERED that the Report filed by the Board on Professional Responsibility on December 27, 2013 (copy attached) is hereby APPROVED and ADOPTED. The Respondent is hereby disbarred effective immediately.

BY THE COURT: Henry duPont Ridgely, Justice.

BOARD ON PROFESSIONAL RESPONSIBILITY OF THE SUPREME COURT OF THE STATE OF DELAWARE

In the Matter of a Member of the Bar of The Supreme Court of Delaware

JOHN J. SULLIVAN, JR. Respondent.

CONFIDENTIAL

Board Case No. 2011-0233-B

BOARD REPORT AND RECOMMENDATION

This is the report of the Board on Professional Responsibility of the Supreme Court of the State of Delaware (the "Board") setting forth its findings and recommendations in the above captioned matter.

The members of panel of the Board (the "Panel") are Wayne J. Carey, Esquire, Yvonne Anders Gordon, Ed.D. and Lisa A. Schmidt, Esquire (the "Chairperson"). The Office of Disciplinary Counsel (the "ODC") was represented by Patricia Bartley Schwartz, Esquire. The Respondent John J. Sullivan, Jr. (the "Respondent") appeared on his own behalf.

I. Procedural Background

On January 14, 2013 the ODC filed a Petition for Discipline. Respondent filed an answer on February 1, 2013. The ODC filed an Amended Petition on April 23, 2013 and a Second Amended Petition on May 9, 2013 (references to the "Petition" herein are to the Second Amended Petition). Respondent answered the Amended Petition on April 23, 2013 (references to the "Answer" will be to the Answer to the Amended Petition). [FN1]

FN1. The second Amended Petition was presented to the Panel at the May 9 Hearing to correct certain errors and changes intended to be addressed in the Amended Petition. The Respondent did not object and the changes did not require further answer by the Respondent. (Transcript of the May 9, 2013 Hearing ("May 9 Tr.") at 2-3, 143).

A telephonic pre-hearing conference was held on May 3, 2013. The Panel conducted a hearing on liability on May 9, 2013 (the "May 9 Hearing). [FN2] The parties provided the Panel with a Stipulation of Admitted Facts ("Admitted Facts"). At the May 9 Hearing, the Panel heard testimony from 4 witnesses; Ed Tarlov, Roseanne Goldberg, [FN3] Respondent and Sheila Pacheco. In addition, ODC Exhibits 6 through 27 were admitted into evidence. (May 9 Tr. 4) At the conclusion of the May 9 Hearing, the ODC presented an oral closing argument. On June 20, 2013, the Respondent submitted a written closing argument. On July 11, 2013 the ODC submitted a response the Respondent's closing argument.

FN2. A motion was made by the ODC to consolidate this matter with Board Case No. 2011-0234-B which shares common questions of law and fact. The respondents, in both this case and Case No. 2011-0234B did not object to consolidation. After consideration of the request, the Chair of the Board on Professional Responsibility denied the request noting: "based upon the lack of detailed information about the evidence and positions and defenses contemplated, I feel compelled to err on the side of caution and deny the motion." (Letter dated January 29, 2013). For the sake of economy, it was later determined, with the concurrence of the Chairperson of the Board, that the same Panel of the Board would hear both matters. Despite having several weeks of notice that the same panel would hear both matters, Respondent raised, for the first time at the May 9 Hearing, an objection to having the same Panel hear both matters. The Panel overruled the objection on the basis that the matters would be decided on two completely separate records and each would be decided on the record presented in the individual matter.

FN3. By agreement of the parties the testimony of Mr. Tarlov was presented by transcript from the hearing in Board Case No. 2011-0234-B and the testimony of Ms. Goldberg via deposition transcript (references to transcript testimony are to "Tarlov _" or "Goldberg_").

On August 7, 2013 the Panel notified the ODC and the Respondent that it planned to recommend to the Delaware Supreme Court that the Respondent violated Delaware Rules of Professional Conduct 4.l(a), 4.l(b), 5.3, 8.4(b), 8.4(c), 8.4(d) and l.15(a), as alleged in the Petition. On September 11, 2013 the Board reconvened to hear testimony and argument relating to sanctions (the "September II Hearing"). At the September 11 Hearing, the Panel heard testimony from: Kenya Smith, Gloria Henry, Montgomery Boyer, William Cheesman, Sherry Hoffman, John Williams, Christopher McBride, Stephen Dalecki, Mary Kathleen Glenn [FN4] and Respondent, followed by closing arguments. Exhibits 6-27(h) and (i), 29 and 30 were admitted into evidence.

FN4. The testimony of Mr. Dalecki and Ms. Glenn was presented by transcript from the criminal trial of Mr. Jamaar Manlove. The Panel considered only the non-hearsay aspects of this testimony. Respondent objected to other transcript testimony found at Exs. 28, 31 and 32 on the basis that he did not have an opportunity to cross-examine the witnesses. The Panel sustains the objection. Exhibits 28, 31 and 32 are not admitted into the record.

II. Allegations in the Petition for Discipline

The Petition alleges that Respondent violated Delaware Lawyers' Rules of Professional Conduct ("Rules") 4.l(a), 4.l(b), 5.3, 8.4(b), 8.4(c) and 8.4(d) in connection with residential real estate closings Respondent conducted between 2006 and 2008. Respondent is alleged to have certified that the representations contained in Department of Housing and Urban Development Settlement Statements ("HUD-1 Statement") were a true and accurate account of the transaction when in fact they were not. Specifically, the Petition charges that either the buyers did not bring the financial contribution set forth on the HUD-1 Statement and/or the proceeds from the transaction were disbursed in amounts that differed from those set forth on the HUD-1 Statement. The Petition alleges that the false certifications constitute violations of Rules 4.l(a), 4.l(b), 8.4(b), 8.4(c) and 8.4(d). The Petition further alleges that Respondent failed to ensure that the paralegals, who assisted him in connection with the closings, prepared checks for the disbursement of proceeds as set forth on the HUD-1 Statement in violation of Rule 5.3 relating to the supervision of non-lawyer staff. Finally, the Petition charges Respondent with violating Rule 1.15(a) for using his firm's client trust account to fund all or part of the buyer's contribution.

III. Factual Findings

A. Admitted Facts

Respondent is a member of the Bar of the Supreme Court of Delaware. He was admitted to the Bar in 1984. At all times relevant to this matter, Respondent was engaged in the private practice of law with the firm Sanclemente & Associates, LLC (the "Sanclemente Firm"). Respondent is still presently engaged in the private practice of law in Delaware but not with the Sanclemente Firm. (Petition and Answer 1 and 2, Admitted Facts1, May 9 Tr. 44-46). From 2006 through 2008, Respondent as the closing attorney for the following real estate closings, represented the borrower:

Phyllis Graham 405 Llangollen Blvd. New Castle, DE	405 Llangollen Blvd. Closing	Ex.6	10/30/08
Patricia Singleton 713 E. 7th Street Wilmington, DE	713 E. 7th Street Closing	Ex. 7	8/29/08
Lee Price & Tony Coleman 15 Cherry Road New Castle, DE	15 Cherry Road Closing	Ex. 8	8/20/08
Gloria Hemy 29 Dallas Road New Castle, DE	29 Dallas Road Closing	Ex.9	7/18/08
Evelyn Anders on Closing 123 Stroud Street Wilmington, DE	123 Stroud Street	Ex. 10	6/19/08
Charles & Jamie Holmes 411 Jefferson Street Wilmington, DE	411 Jefferson Street	Ex.11	4/28/08
Evelyn Anderson 1122 Elm Street Wilmington, DE	1122 Elm Street Closing	Ex.12	4/1/08
Craig Williams 1009 W. Seventh Street Wilmington, DE	1009 W. Seventh Street Closing	Ex.13	3/12/08
Dwayne & Sheree Manlove 104 Rita Road New Castle, DE	104 Rita Road Closing	Ex. 14	12/27/07

Anna Bennett 729 E. Tenth Street Wilmington, DE	729 E. Tenth Street Closing	Ex. 15	1/24/08
Dwayne & Sheree Manlove 230 Channing Drive Bear, DE	230 Channing Drive Closing	Ex. 16	12/10/07
Larry Manlove 54 University Avenue New Castle, DE	54 University Avenue Closing	Ex. 17	12/3/07
Gary and Lillian Wilson 314 W. 31" Street Wilmington, DE	314 W. 31" Street Closing	Ex. 18	10/23/07
Ramon Leak 2921 N. Broom Street Wilmington, DE	2921 N. Broom Street Closing	Ex. 19	9/12/07
Clifton Coleman 2511 Heald Street Wilmington, DE 2511	Heald Street Closing	Ex. 20	8/30/07
Clifton Coleman 2142 Culver Drive Wilmington, DE	2142 Culver Drive Closing	Ex.21	8/15/07
Derron Bowe 214 East 35th Street Wilmington, DE	214 East 35th Street Closing	Ex.22	6/22/07
Derron Bowe 107 West 30th Street Wilmington, DE	107 West 30th Street Closing	Ex.23	5/2/07
Kyle Steed 721 Wood Duck Court Middletown, DE	721 Wood Duck Court Closing	Ex.24	1/4/07
Reginald Johnson 417 E. 10th Street Wilmington, DE	417 E. 10th Street Closing	Ex.25	11/20/06
Kyle Steed 133 Sterling Avenue Claymont, DE	133 Sterling Avenue Closing	Ex.26	2/27/07
Theodore Jones 426 Eastlawn Avenue Wilmington, DE 426	Eastlawn Avenue Closing	Ex.27	2/4/08

Collectively these real estate closings are referred to as the ("Sullivan Closings"). (Admitted Facts 'il 2, Exs. 6-27, May 9, Tr. 49, 127) (Respondent confirmed at the May 9 Hearing that he conducted the 133 Sterling Avenue Closing), May 9, Tr. 151-154). Non-lawyer assistants would prepare the HUD-1 Statements and the checks for the Sullivan Closings. (Petition and Answer 'i[7, Admitted Facts 'i[3). The Sanclemente Firm's real estate escrow accounting records show that there were no deposits of funds from the buyers in eighteen of the Sullivan Closings and the buyers' costs were paid by others in nineteen of the twenty-one Sullivan Closings. (Admitted Facts 'il 4, 5). In the Sullivan Closings, funds were not disbursed according to the HUD-1 Statement but were disbursed as reflected in the disbursement statement. (Admitted Facts 'il 6, 7). As such, funds were disbursed to individuals not identified on the HUD-1 Statements. (Admitted Facts 'i[8).

B. Factual Findings from May 9 Hearing and Exhibits Admitted into Evidence.

Respondent has admitted facts sufficient to support a recommended finding that Rules 4.l(a), 4.l(b), 8.4(b), 8.4(c) and 8.4(d) were violated. Specifically, Respondent has admitted that (1) he was the closing attorney in the 22 transactions that form the basis for the allegations in the Petition; (2) that the Sanclemente Firm real estate escrow account records reflect that there were no deposits of funds from the buyers in 18 of the transactions and the buyers' costs were paid by others in 19 of the transactions; and (3) funds were not disbursed according to the HUD-1 Statement. The Panel believes that the factual findings described herein confirm that conclusion, support a recommended finding that Respondent also violated Rules 5.3 and 1.15(a), and assist in determining the appropriate sanction.

1. The Manlove Transactions.

While employed by the Sanclemente Firm, Respondent conducted settlements that involved Mr. Jarnaar Manlove, his relatives and associates. (May 9, Tr. 46-49). Respondent became acquainted with Jamaar Manlove when Manlove was a loan broker with Central Fidelity (May 9, Tr. 46). Jamaar Manlove had two organizations known as Master Builders for Christ ("MBFC") and Vision Builders Christian Center ("VBCC") (May 9, Tr. 46-47). Both organizations were used as fronts for an equity stripping scheme. Manlove, his relatives, friends, MBFC and VBCC received payments from the sale proceeds in many of the Sullivan Closings. [FN5]

FN5. In addition Mark Singleton and his entity MDS Enterprise arranged similar transactions and also received sales proceeds. (May 9 Tr. 114-115, Exs. 7, 10, 11, 12, 13 and 16).

Respondent explained that in the Sullivan Closings, the homeowners were in danger of losing their homes to foreclosure, and Jamaar Manlove would arrange for an investor to purchase the home to help them avoid foreclosure. The seller would remain in the home for a year and then repurchase the home from the buyer. (May 9, Tr. 62). Respondent never asked for any documentation of this purported agreement. (May 9, Tr. 76). Respondent testified that in order to compensate the buyer for the risk and to ensure that they had funds to make their mortgage payments, the seller would pay funds to the buyer at closing. (May 9, Tr. 62-63). Respondent also explained that funds were paid to MBFC and/or VBCC to be held for the one year period to enable the buyer to make their mortgage payments (May 9, Tr. 65). In short, the sellers were stripped of any equity they may have had in their homes in the guise of contributions to MBFC, and/or VBCC and/or some other entities.

The following chart shows the extent of the equity that was taken from some of the sellers in the Sullivan Closings:

Seller	Exhibit No.	Amount of Equity Stripped
Norlyn Ritter	6	$34,710.00
Ferris Properties	7	$30,189.00
Mary Glenn	8	$51,430.00
Michael Fisher	11	$41, 456.80
James Moss	13	$13,566.18
Donnell Fisher	16	$34,393.00
Stephen Dalecki	17	$24,906.36
Kenya Smith	18	$21,333.03
Adrienne Spencer	19	$66,727.34
Jamaar Manlove	20	$49,396.44
William Cheesman	21	$26,288.36
Jamaar Manlove	24	$23,073.56
Grace Cuff	25	$51,240.24
Gerald Hackett	27	$96,700.00

Respondent also testified that he initially believed people were contributing to Jamaar Manlove or his church to:

Thank him for saving their home, for–to express commitment to his church and things like that, and that they were paying in order–paying these funds to avoid losing their home at foreclosure.

(May 9, Tr. 74-75). Despite this belief, Respondent did not obtain any documentation indicating that the monies paid to MBFC and VBCC were gifts. (May 9, Tr. 75). Other than going over the entries on the HUD-1 Statement with the parties, Respondent did not question the monies going to the Manlove entities. (May 9, Tr. 81-82).

We find Respondent's position to be disingenuous at best. What was really happening was that the homeowners, who were at risk of losing their homes to a sheriff's sale because their current cash positions were insufficient to allow them to pay current obligations and to refinance their mortgages, were (without their knowledge) selling their homes and the equity that those homeowners had in their properties was diverted to MBFC and/or VBCC. The poor cash positions of the homeowners/sellers, along with the size of the purported donations to MBFC and VBCC should have alerted Respondent to the nefarious nature of the transactions from day one.

2. Buyers Did Not Make the Cash Contributions Reflected on the HUD-1 Statement.

The buyers in eighteen of the Sullivan Closings did not make any cash contribution (Admitted Facts4) despite the fact that checks were received by the Sanclemente Firm from many of the buyers for their HUD-1 Statement contribution amount. (See, e.g., Exs. 11, 12, 14, 16, 22, 25, 27). Those checks were copied and placed in the file to have a record of the buyer contribution but were never deposited. (May 9, Tr. 98, 101) (see, also, May 9 Tr. 113, 114, 124-25, 127, 132). Many of these personal checks were in excess of the $10,000 limit under Rule 1.15(k) and, despite a law firm policy that Respondent should not accept personal funds in excess of $2,000. (May 9, Tr. 113). Respondent admitted that in closings that did not involve Jamaar Manlove or related entities, he would not have accepted large personal checks. (May 9, Tr. 113).

Respondent claimed that he learned "probably sometime in 2007 that the borrowers" checks were no longer being deposited (May 9, Tr. 154), yet in the first of the closings at issue, in November of 2006 (Ex. 25) he collected a personal check from the borrower at closing for $15,000 in violation of Rule 1.15(k) and his firm's policy. [FN6] The acceptance of that check certainly suggests he knew it would never be deposited. Respondent never notified the lender that the buyers were not bringing their financial contribution as reported on the HUD-1 Statements and in some cases were receiving funds in the transaction because he knew that if the HUD-1 Statements were changed to reflect zero contribution from the borrower "it would have created red flags from the lender." (May 9, Tr. 99, 121).

FN6. Later Respondent testified he could not remember when he learned that the checks he was collecting were a fiction and were not funds from the buyer. (May 9, Tr. 162-63).

3. The Sanclemente Firm's Escrow Account Funds were Used to Cover the Buyer's Contribution.

Respondent admitted that in some instances funds due to the seller or a Manlove entity were disbursed instead to the Sanclemente Finn to meet the buyer's cash contribution. (May 9, Tr. 59-60). This was necessary because funds were being used from the Sanclemente Finn's escrow account to balance or zero out the transaction. The funds to reimburse the Sanclemente Finn's escrow account were taken from proceeds due to another party, either the seller or a Manlove entity. (See Exs. 6, 8 and 27; May 9, Tr. 137-141; 193-196). Respondent viewed this as a "zero balance transaction". He testified, "we took the money out of the escrow account and put it right back into the escrow account. (May 9, Tr. 194-195).

4. Funds were Disbursed to Persons or Entities not Listed on the HUD-1 Statement

Respondent claimed he was unaware of how the proceeds from the sales were being disbursed because the checks were prepared by a paralegal and given to him in sealed envelopes to disburse. (May 9, Tr. 163). Ms. Pacheco, the former paralegal at the Sanclemente Firm who prepared the documents for closings and "cut the checks for closings" (May 9, Tr. 198) indicated that Jarnaar Manlove would contact Ms. Pacheco directly and have her break down the checks in different ways. (May 9, Tr. 201-202). She indicated there would be no reason for her to tell Respondent about these changes post-closing. (May 9, Tr. 206). Ms. Pacheco testified, however, that when checks were distributed at the closing, the checks would not be placed in envelopes to be handed out by Respondent. (May 9, Tr. 207). Thus, Respondent could see the amounts being disbursed were inconsistent with the HUD-1 Statement.

5. Respondent Becomes Concerned.

Respondent testified that sometime during the period covered by the Sullivan Closings, he became concerned with the transactions involving Mr. Manlove:

Over time, it became clear that there were substantial amounts of money that were being received by Mr. Manlove, by MBFC, by VBCC, by his relatives, his friends, whomever, and that money that was supposed to be going to the seller wasn't going to the seller, but the seller's funds were being used to meet the buyer's obligation or they were being paid to Mr. Manlove or to his associates.

May 9, Tr. 166). Respondent indicated that he discussed the issue with Mr. Sanclemente and it was decided that they would no longer do transactions for Mr. Manlove. (May 9, Tr. 167). Yet, Respondent admittedly continued for some period of time to conduct Manlove closings. (May 9, Tr. 167). He claimed to be relying on Mr. Sanclemente's representations that they had no obligation to the seller. (May 9, Tr. 167).

As long as the seller was an adult and we were going over the settlement statements, that they were voluntarily signing them, and that they knew that they weren't getting the funds, or they were getting zero funds, and they were signing voluntarily, weren't questioning it, that satisfied our obligation. (May 9, Tr. 167).

While Respondent claims it became clear "over time" that large sums were going to Manlove entities, each of the Sullivan Closings followed a similar pattern throughout the two-year period. By way of example in the first closing at issue in November 2006, (Ex. 25) the HUD-1 Statement indicates that Reginald Johnson purchased a property from Grace Cuff for a contract price of $88,000.00. (Ex. 25A). According to the HUD-1 Statement, the buyer was to make a cash contribution of$15,200.71. (Ex. 25A). The seller was to receive cash at closing in the amount of$19,700.00. (Ex. 25A). The seller's proceeds were reduced by settlement charges that included a payment of $66,440.95 to MBFC. (Ex. 25A). According to the HUD-1 Statement, there was no mortgage lien on the property and the remaining settlement charges to the buyer were less than $2,000.00.

(Ex. 25A). The buyer wrote a personal check for $15,200.71 (Ex. 25C) which was never deposited. (May 9, Tr. 127). Respondent certified the HUD-1 Statement.

The last closing at issue was conducted by Respondent on October 30, 2008. (Ex. 6). The HUD-1 Statement for this closing reflects a $6,900.50 buyer contribution. (Ex. 6A). The buyer wrote a personal check in that amount which was never deposited. (Ex. 6C). Instead, funds due to another party were disbursed to the Sanclemente Firm to meet the buyer's contribution and cover the shortfall in the escrow account. (May 9, Tr. 58-61). The HUD-1 Statement reflects payments to VBCC7 of $60,500.00 and MBFC of $43,610.68. (Ex. 6A). MBFC received $34,710.00 in part to cover the buyer's contribution. (Ex. 6B, D).

6. Respondent Contacts the Department of Justice.

The pattern was consistent throughout the period yet it took more than 2 years before Respondent took any steps to remedy the situation. Respondent testified that:

I carne to realize they were stripping equity from these properties.

And it was at that point when I became aware of the fact that there was equity stripping going on, that's when I contacted the Department of Justice and spoke to Sherry Hoffman there because I was concerned about these transactions.

I carne in. I met with Ms. Hoffman. I went over a number of the transactions with her. We talked about ways to try to remedy the situation, to try to see if there was a way we could set aside the purchases, to put the homes back in the names of the original sellers. The problem was that the mortgage companies, of course, would not want to release their mortgages unless they were paid. And since Mr. Manlove and his friends and the investors didn't have the money any longer, there wasn't a way to undo the transaction.

(May 9, Tr. 159-60). Respondent indicated that he contacted the Department of Justice after the last closing he conducted related to Jarnaar Manlove. (May 9, Tr. 160-61).

There is some question regarding how Respondent carne to discuss the Manlove closings with Ms. Hoffman. John Williams, Esquire, a Delaware lawyer with a real estate practice, testified that the Hackett brothers came to see him about a real estate transaction involving a home they inherited from their mother. (Sept. 11, Tr. 72-73). Mr. Williams indicated that there was a $79,000 payment that he could not explain and the Hackett brothers received very little in the transaction. (Sept. 11, Tr. 73-74, see also Ex. 27). Mr. Williams contacted Respondent who told him that "he felt it was an arm's length transaction and that it involved some kind of lease or something." (Sept. 11, Tr. 74-75). It was after that conversation that Mr. Williams contacted the Department of Justice and went in to meet with Ms. Hoffman. (Sept. 11, Tr. 75-76). Ms. Hoffman testified that she had two meetings with Mr. Sullivan but could not recall who initiated the contact. (Sept. 11, Tr. 66). This testimony raises the question of whether Respondent initiated the contact with Ms. Hoffman.

7. The Lender's Decision to Fund Would Have Been Impacted if the True Facts were Disclosed.

The Sullivan Closings were inconsistent with Respondent's representations to the lenders on the HUD-1 Statement. The funding decisions by the lenders would have been impacted had the HUD-1 Statements been revised to reflect the true nature of the transactions. The ODC presented testimony from Ms. Roseanne Goldberg, Vice President of customer service for Freedom Mortgage, with 25 years of experience in the mortgage industry. (Goldberg 2-3). Ms. Goldberg testified that Freedom Mortgage requires that the HUD-1 Statement be faxed prior to the closing and there should be no changes once it has been approved by Freedom Mortgage. (Goldberg 5-6). Ms. Goldberg indicated that Freedom would want to know if a borrower comes to a closing without funds and if the borrower's contribution is coming out of someone else's settlement disbursement. (Goldberg 8-9). By way of example, Ms. Goldberg reviewed the HUD-1 Statement in Exhibit 14, which reflected a borrower's contribution of $22,466.77. Ms. Goldberg testified that if the borrower did not "come to the table" with money, that would have affected Freedom Mortgage's decision to fund the loan. (Goldberg 20). Similarly, Ms. Goldberg indicated that the fact that the borrower received a $10,000 disbursement at the time of closing would also have affected the decision to fund. (Goldberg 20); see, also, Goldberg 22-25 (similar testimony with respect to Exs. 16, 17, 19, and 20). Finally Ms. Goldberg testified that Freedom Mortgage expects the Delaware attorney who is the closing agent for Freedom Mortgage to ensure that the borrower's contribution is collected as reflected on the HUD-1 Statement. (Goldberg 37).

8. Respondent's Conduct was Inconsistent with His Obligation to Lender.

Mr. Tarlov, a member of the Delaware Bar, was called by the ODC to give expert testimony regarding residential real estate matters and the standard of conducting residential real estate closings in Delaware. (Tarlov 24). Mr. Tarlov has been a member of the Delaware Bar for more than 25 years and has represented the buyer in thousands of residential real estate closings. (Tarlov 23-24). Mr. Tarlov testified that the certification language contained above the lawyer's signature line on the HUD-1 Statement means that the "HUD-1 is an accurate reflection of the transaction" and "every single penny on the HUD is accurate." (Tarlov 44-45). At closing, Mr. Tarlov indicated that he is representing the borrower, but following the lender's instructions. (Tarlov 49-50). If Mr. Tarlov became aware at closing that the buyer was receiving settlement assistance from the seller he would revise the HUD-1 Statement and notify the lender for approval because "the lender approved the HUD and the HUD is a representation that you're putting cash into the transaction" (Tarlov 34; see also Tarlov 39 ("I would call the lender"); Tarlov 40-41 ("I am going to obey the lender 100 percent"); Tarlov 43 ("the HUD is being approved by the lender ... so just want the lender to sign off on my HUD"); Tarlov 60 ("I still would go back to the lender"). [FN8]

FN8. Mr. Tarlov testified that if the buyer's contribution as listed on the HUD-1 Statement was coming from a third party and not the seller, he would verify that the funds were not a loan, and he would also notify the lender. (Tarlov 40-42).

IV. Standard of Proof

Allegations of professional misconduct set forth in the ODC's Petition must be established by clear and convincing evidence. (Rules of Disciplinary Procedure IS(c)). That burden falls on the ODC. (Rules of Disciplinary Procedure 15(d)).

V. Discussion and Analysis.

A. Violation of Rules 4.1(a), 4.1(b), 8.4(b), 8.4(c), 8.4(d).

Respondent had admitted and the extensive record confirms that Respondent certified HUD-1 Statements that were not a true and accurate account of the transactions where the HUD-1 Statements indicated: (i) the buyer(s) made a financial contribution to the transaction when in fact the buyer(s) made no contributions; (ii) the funds were disbursed in amounts different than the amounts certified on the HUD-1 Statement; and/or (iii) the funds were disbursed to persons or entities not identified in the HUD-1 Statement.

Rule 4.1(a) provides it is professional misconduct for a lawyer, during the course of representing a client, to knowingly make "a false statement of material fact or law to a third person." Rule 4.l(b) provides it is professional misconduct for a lawyer, during the course of representing a client, to unknowingly "fail to disclose a material fact when disclosure is necessary to avoid assisting a criminal or fraudulent act by a client." (Delaware Lawyers' Rules of Professional Conduct 4.1(a) and 4.1(b)). The HUD-1 Settlement Statement contains the following certification above the attorney signature line:

The HUD-1 Settlement Statement which I have prepared is a true and accurate account of this transaction have caused or will cause the funds to be disbursed in accordance with this statement.

(Tab A of Exhibits 6-27). In the Sullivan Closings funds were not disbursed according to the HUD-1 Statements. (Admitted Facts 6). In addition, Respondent's clients did not provide funds reflected as "cash from borrower" on the HUD-1 Statement. Both Respondent and his client, the borrower, made false statements on the HUD-1 Statement. Respondent's certification of HUD-1 Statements that were not a true and accurate account of the transaction violates Rules 4.1(a) and 4.1(b).

Rule 8.4 provides that it is professional misconduct for a lawyer to:

(b) commit a criminal act that reflects adversely on the lawyer's honesty, trustworthiness or fitness as a lawyer in other respects; (c) engage in conduct involving dishonesty, fraud, deceit or misrepresentation; (d) engage in conduct that is prejudicial to the administration of justice.

The HUD-1 Settlement Statement contains the following language:

WARNING: It is a crime to knowingly make false statements to the United States on this or any other similar form. Penalties upon conviction can include: a fine or imprisonment. For details see: Title 18 U.S. Code§ 1001 and§ 1010.

(Tab A of Exhibits 16-27) Respondent knowingly executed HUD-1 Statements that contained false statements in violation of 10 U.S.C. § 1010.

Respondent argues that the ODC did not present any evidence that the HUD-1 Settlement Statements were offered or accepted by the Department of Housing and Urban Development or offered to the department "for the purpose of obtaining any extension or renewal or credit, or mortgage insured by such department or for the acceptance, release or substitution of any security or for the purposes of influencing in any way the action of such department" relying on the language of 18 U.S.C § 1010. Respondent did not offer any support for his interpretation of this provision. Instead, Respondent offered HUD-1 statements for federally insured loans that he knew to be false.

Respondent knew that each HUD-1 Statement was approved by the lender and that lenders were relying on the accuracy of the HUD-1 Statements in funding the loans. Respondent conceded that he never notified the lenders that the buyers did not make the: financial contribution listed on the HUD-1 Statements and that the funds were not disbursed as outlined because it would have raised "red flags" and the loans may not have been funded. In fact, copies of the checks collected from the buyer were made for the file even though Respondent knew the check would never be deposited in the firm's escrow account. In the Panel's view, Respondent's false statement to lenders to ensure loan funding constituted a "criminal act that reflects adversely on the lawyer's honesty, trustworthiness or fitness as a lawyer in other respects" under Rule 8.

As a result of these actions, and the facts outlined above, the Panel recommends a: finding that Respondent's action violated Rules 4.1(a), 4.1(b), 8.4(b), 8.4(c) and 8.4(d).

B. Violation of Rule 5.3.

Rule 5.3 states in part that in employing non-lawyer assistants:

(b) A lawyer having direct supervisory authority over a non-lawyer shall make reasonable efforts to insure that the person's conduct is compatible with the professional obligations of the lawyer; (c) a lawyer shall be responsible for conduct of such person that would be a violation of the Rules of Professional Conduct if engaged in by the lawyer if: (i) the lawyer orders or, with knowledge of the specific conduct, ratifies the conduct involves; or. (ti) the lawyer ... has direct supervisory authority over the person, and knows of the conduct at time when its consequences can be avoided or mitigated but fails to take reasonable remedial action.

(Delaware Lawyers' Rules of Professional Conduct 5.3)

The ODC argues that Respondent violated Rule 5.3 (i) by failing to make reasonable efforts to insure that the non-lawyer staff's conduct was compatible with the professional obligations of a Delaware lawyer and/or (ii) by ratifying the non-lawyer staff's conduct with respect to the disbursement of the real estate funds contrary to the HUD-1 Statements and/or (iii) by failing to take reasonable remedial action once Respondent had knowledge of the non-lawyer staff's conduct.

While Respondent denied having any managerial authority at the Sanclemente Firm, he did concede that he had supervisory authority over non-lawyer staff and could direct their conduct. For example, Respondent testified that if he needed a document changed during the preparation for closing he could direct non-lawyer staff to make changes. (May 9 Tr. 51). Respondent also conceded that if he needed something to be changed on the HUD-1 Statement or change the amount of a check during a closing he could direct the non-lawyer staff to make the changes needed. (May 9 Tr. 52, 191). Ms. Pacheco confirmed that if Respondent needed to have documentation changed during closing she would make the changes for him. (May 9 Tr. 207-208). Ms. Pacheco conceded that Respondent could direct her conduct to a certain degree. (May 9, Tr. 208).

Respondent took no action to prevent Ms. Pacheco from issuing checks inconsistent with the disbursement amounts listed on the HUD-1 Statement. Respondent knew that the checks received from the buyers in most instances were never cashed but that the legal assistants made photocopies for the file. Respondent also knew that the lenders were not notified of any of these actions. The Panel recommends a finding that Respondent violated Rule 5.3.

C. Violation of Rule 1.15(a).

Rule 1.15(a) requires, in pertinent part, that a lawyer "shall hold property of clients or third persons that is in a lawyer's possession in connection with a representation separate from the lawyer's own property", and that property of clients or third persons must be appropriately safe guarded. The ODC argues that by using other clients' funds that were in the firm's trust account to fund part or all of the buyer's contribution in certain settlements, Respondent violated Rule I.l5(a).

In three of the Sullivan Closings (Exs. 6, 8, 27), checks were disbursed to the Sanclemente Firm from proceeds from the sale to reimburse the firm's escrow account for the buyer's contribution. (May 9, Tr. 137-41; 193-96). Respondent viewed this as a "zero balance" transaction because they took money out of the escrow account and put it right back into the account. (May 9, Tr. 194-95). The fact that the funds were replaced does not negate the violation of Rule 1.15(a). See In Re Figliola, 652 A.2d 10711, 1076 (Del. 1995) (the Court rioted the issue was not whether the funds could be adequately reimbursed, but rather whether the money should have been taken without authorization) (citing In Re Librizzi, 569 A.2d 257, 261 (N.J. 1990)). The Panel recommends a finding that Respondent violated Rule 1.15(a).

D. The Panel's Recommendation is Supported by Precedent from Other Jurisdictions.

The Panel's recommended findings that Respondent violated Rules 4.1(a), 4.1(b), 5.3, 8.4(b), 8.4(c), 8.4(d) and 1.15(a) of the Delaware Lawyers' Rules of Professional Conduct are supported by case law from other jurisdictions involving similar fact patterns. North Carolina State Bar v. Rose, 10 DHC 17 Feb. 23, 2011; Cincinnati Bar Association v. Powers, 895 N.E.2d 172 (Ohio 2008); and In Re Barbare, 602 N.E.2d 382 (S.C. 2004). In Rose, there was one real estate transaction at issue. In that transaction Rose prepared a HUD-1 Statement reflecting a buyer contribution of $59,652.31 and a seller disbursement of $50,930.29. The Disciplinary Hearing Commission found that the HUD-1 Statement prepared by Rose was false and that the buyer brought no money to the closing and Rose did not disburse funds to the seller. The Commission further found that Rose was responsible for ensuring the HUD-1 Statement accurately recited the receipt and disbursement of funds in the transaction and that the HUD-1 Statement certification was false. The Disciplinary Hearing Commission found that Rose had violated Rules 8.4(b) and 8.4(c) which are identical to the Delaware Rul es. Respondent argues that this case is distinguishable because Rose represented both the borrower and the lender. Respondent, however, does not address the fact that Rose was also charged with a violation of Rule 8.4(g) involving intentional prejudice to his client, the lender, during the course of the professional relationship.

The ODC also relies on Cincinnati Bar Association v. Powers, where the attorney was charged with fabricating closing documents on over 300 loans causing lenders to lose nearly $3.5 million and for filing false income tax returns that concealed his profits. While Respondent did not profit from his actions or file false tax returns, there are some similarities with Powers. Mr. Powers knew that the buyer did not bring the down payment but that it was provided by others and that some of the buyers received funds from the sale proceeds. The Court found that these facts were not disclosed to the lenders and that the HUD-1 Statements were falsely certified. The Court found that Powers violated sections of the Ohio Disciplinary Code of Professional Responsibility which are nearly identical to Delaware Rul es 8.4(b), (c) and (d).

The ODC also asks the Panel to rely on In Re Barbare. Respondent concedes that the Barbare case is most similar to this matter. (Respondent's Closing Argument at 1f 14). In Barbare the Respondent pled guilty to a violation of 18 U.S.C. § 1010 in connection with his false certification of HUD-1 Statements where he certified that borrowers brought funds to closing when in fact no borrower's contribution had been made. In addition, the Respondent in Barbare permitted the clients to instruct non-lawyer staff on disbursements which were contrary to the amounts reflected on the HUD-1 Statements. The Court found that the Respondent's conduct violated Rules 4.1, 5.1, 5.3 and 8.4 of the South Carolina Rul es of Professional Conduct, which are identical to the corresponding Delaware rules.

The Respondent here argues that in Barbare the Supreme Court of South Carolina found that there were "red flags" which should have alerted Barbare to the criminal activity of third parties in connection with these closings. Respondent argues that he was deceived by Jamaar Manlove in his scheme to defraud the sellers of their homes. The Panel finds that Barbare is not distinguishable on those grounds. Moreover, that Respondent was deceived by Manlove is not credible. Respondent never sought documentation of the alleged buy-back agreements between buyer and seller. Respondent took action to hide the fact that buyers were not making the financial contributions as disclosed on the HUD-1 Statements and also because Respondent admittedly continued conducting closings after he testified that he became concerned with the "equity stripping" being conducted. Red flags were everywhere for Respondent to see.

The ODC also relies on In re Foley, No. BD-2010-005 (March 24, 2010) and provided a copy of the Petition for

Discipline filed with the Commonwealth of Massachusetts Board of Bar Overseers and the Order of Tenn Suspension issued by the Supreme Court of the Connonwealth of Massachusetts. Respondent argues that since neither document includes the findings of either a Board of Professional Responsibility or of the Supreme Court for the Commonwealth of Massachusetts, these documents do not represent appropriate precedent to be considered by the Panel and the Panel agrees.

VI. Sanctions.

A. Standard for Imposing Sanctions.

"The objectives of the Lawyer Disciplinary system are to protect the public, to protect the administration of justice, to preserve confidence in the legal profession, and to deter other lawyers from similar misconduct." In Re McCann, 894 A.2d 1087, 1088 (Del. 2005); In Re Fountain, 878 A.2d 1167, 1173 (Del. 2005) (quoting In Re Bailey, 821 A.2d 851, 866 (Del. 2003)). The focus of the lawyer disciplinary system in Delaware is not on the lawyer but, rather, on the damage to the public that is ascertainable from the lawyers' record of professional misconduct. In Re Hall, 767 A.2d 197, 201 (Del. 2001). It is the duty of the Panel to recommend the sanction that will promote those objectives.

In reaching its recommendation of an appropriate sanction, the Panel considered the ABA Standards for imposing lawyer sanctions (the "ABA Standards"):

The ABA framework consists of four key factors to be considered by the Court: (a) the ethical duty violated; (b) the lawyer's mental state; (c) the actual potential injury caused by the lawyer's misconduct; and (d) aggravating and mitigating factors.

ABA Standards for Imposing Lawyer Sanctions, at 9 (1992) (the "ABA Standards"), available at http://www.abanet.org/cpr/regulationlstandards_sanctions.pdf.

B. Application of the Standard.

1. The Ethical Duties Violated by Respondent.

As set forth above, the Panel recommends a finding that Respondent violated Rules 4.1(a), 4.1(b), 5.3, 8.4(b), 8.4(c), 8.4(d) and l.lS(a) of the Delaware Lawyers' Rules of Professional Conduct.

2. Respondent's Mental State.

The Panel must determine the Respondent's mental state in order to determine the level of culpability. The ABA Standards define the most culpable mental state as that of "intent" when the lawyer acts with purpose to accomplish a particular result. A less culpable mental state is that of "knowledge" where the lawyer is consciously aware of the attendant circumstances of his or her conduct but without the objective or purpose to accomplish a particular result. The least culpable mental state is negligence where the lawyer deviates from the standard of care that a reasonable lawyer would exercise in a given situation. (ABA Standards at 6-7). Based on the factual findings described above, the Panel concludes that the Respondent's mental state was intentional. Respondent acted with the intent of facilitating 22 real estate closings that defrauded those who relied on the accuracy of the HUD-1 Statements.

C. Injury Caused by Respondent's Misconduct.

Pursuant to the ABA Standards, the Panel must consider the potential or actual injury caused by the Respondent's action. (ABA Standards at 6-7). At the September 11 Hearing the ODC presented testimony from several witnesses to address the injury caused by Respondent's actions. Ms. Kenya Smith, Mr. Montgomery Boyer and Mr. William Cheesman were all sellers of properties in the Sullivan Closings.

Ms. Smith testified that the closing for her property took five minutes and she was presented with papers to sign but with no accompanying explanation and was in and out in five minutes. (Sept. 11, Tr. 12-15). Ms. Smith did not receive any proceeds from the sale of her home and she did not understand that the buyer was receiving funds as a result of the sale. (Sept. 11, Tr. 10-11). Ms. Smith and her children remained in the home paying rent to the buyer for less than six months when they were evicted by the sheriff. (Sept. 11, Tr. 8-9).

The testimony of Mr. Boyer was similar. Mr. Boyer acknowledged that at the closing for his property the lawyer showed him documents which he could not see due to poor vision nor could he understand the substance of the documents. (Sept. 11, Tr. 43-44). Mr. Boyer did not receive any proceeds in the sale and was unaware that the buyers received \$10,000.00 and Janlaar Manlove received \$1,700.00. (Sept. 11, Tr. 41). Mr. Boyer further testified that he had no understanding of why MBFC received \$34,000 at closing. (Sept.

11, Tr. 48). Mr. Boyer left his home when he could no longer afford the rent the buyers were charging which was more than his prior mortgage. (Sept. 11, Tr. 38-40).

Mr. Cheesman also testified that he was only in Respondent's office for 10 or 15 minutes for his closing and did not recall Respondent going over the HUD-1 Statement. (Sept. 11, Tr. 51-52, 56). Mr. Cheesman received no funds at closing. (Sept. 11, Tr. 53). He also had no understanding that he was making donations to an entity called MMBK and VBCC of more than $57,000 combined. (Sept. 11, Tr. 53-54). No one explained that he was also contributing $4,800 for closing costs. (Sept. 11, Tr. 57). Mr. Cheesman rented his home back from the buyer until it was put up for sheriff's sale. (Sept. 11, Tr. 55-56).

The ODC also presented the testimony of Gloria Henry. Respondent represented Gloria Henry who was the borrower in the 29 Dallas Road Closing. (Ex. 9). The HUD-1 Statement for this closing indicates that the borrower was making a cash contribution of $7,636.35 toward the $90,000 purchase price which Respondent admitted was not received. (May 9, Tr. 111). The HUD-1 Statement also shows payments to VBCC and MBFC of $16,700 and $5,000 respectively. (Ex. 9A). Ms. Henry testified that she did not understand that she was purchasing a home but instead thought that she was co-signing a loan for her nephew. (Sept. 11, Tr. 25, 28). She testified that she remembered signing the papers but did not understand them because she could not read well and no one went over the papers she was asked to sign. (Sept. 11, Tr. 27, 32-33). Ms. Henry indicated that prior to the transaction she had excellent credit which was impacted negatively by the transaction and she can no longer make purchases on credit. (Sept. 11, Tr. 30).

The ODC also offered the testimony of Christopher McBride, the real estate coordinator for the New Castle County Sheriffs Office. (Sept. 11, Tr. 89). Mr. McBride explained the sheriffs sale process and testified regarding 13 properties that were sold in the transactions at issue which were sold at sheriffs sale. (Sept. 11, Tr. 101-119). Mr. McBride explained that when the loans were not repaid and the properties were sold, Fannie Mae and Freddie Mac who guaranteed the loans took a loss on the properties. (Sept. 11, Tr. 38).

D. The Existence of Any Aggravating and Mitigatillg Circumstances.

The Panel considered whether there were any aggregating or mitigating circumstances which would warrant an increase or a decrease in the sanction.

ABA Standard 9.22 sets forth the following aggravating factors:

(a) Prior disciplinary offenses;
(b) dishonest or selfish motive;
(c) a pattern of misconduct;
(d) multiple offenses;
(e) bad faith obstruction of the disciplinary proceeding by intentionally failing to comply with rules or orders of the disciplinary agency;
(f) submission of false evidence, false statement or other deceptive practices during the disciplinary process;
(g) refusal to acknowledge wrongful nature of conduct;
(h) vulnerability of the victims;
(i) substantial experience at the practice of law;
(j) indifference to making restitution;
(k) illegal conduct, including that involving the use of controlled substances.

Based on the evidence presented, the Panel finds the following aggravating factors:

Respondent has a prior disciplinary record. (ABA Standard § 9.22(a)). Respondent testified that he did have a prior disciplinary history. (Sept. 11 Tr. 144-45). In 1999 he was suspended from the practice of law for eighteen months for violations of Rule 8.4(c)9 In 1996 he received a private probation for violation of Rule 1.4 and in 1995 he received a private admonition for violation of Rules 1.3 and 1.7.

Respondent has engaged in a pattern of misconduct. (ABA Standard § 9.22(c)). The evidence demonstrates that Respondent's misconduct occurred over a period of approximately two years and involved twenty-two separate real estate transactions.

Respondent's misconduct consists of multiples offenses. (ABA Standard§ 9.22(d)). The Panel has recommended a finding that Respondent violated Rules 4.l(a), 4.1(b), 5.3, 8.4(b), 8.4(c), 8.4(d) and 1.15(a).

The evidence presented at the September 11 hearing demonstrated that the victims of Respondent's misconduct were vulnerable.

Respondent has been a member of the Delaware Bar since 1984 and has substantial experience in the practice of law.

Lastly, although Respondent was not charged criminally, he falsely certified HUD-1 Statements which is a crime under 18 U.S.C. 1010.

I. Mitigating Factors.

ABA Standard§ 9.32 sets forth the following mitigating factors:

(a) Absence of a prior disciplinary record;

(b) Absence of a dishonest or selfish motive;

(c) Personal or emotional problems;

(d) Timely good faith effort to make restitution or to rectify consequences of misconduct.

(e) Full and free disclosure to disciplinary board or cooperative attitude toward proceedings;

(f) inexperience in the practice of law;

(g) character or reputation;

(h) physical disability;

(i) mental disability or chemical dependency including alcoholism or drug abuse when:

  (1) there is medical evidence that Respondent is affected by a chemical dependency or mental disability;

  (2) the chemical dependency or mental disability caused the misconduct;

  (3) respondent's recovery from the chemical dependency or mental disability is demonstrated by a meaningful and sustained period of successful rehabilitation; and

  (4) the recovery arrested the misconduct and recurrence of that misconduct is unlikely;

(j) delay in disciplinary proceedings;

(k) interim rehabilitation;

(1) imposition of other penalties or sanctions;

(m) remorse; and

(n) remoteness of prior offenses.

Based on the evidence presented the Panel finds the following mitigating factors:

Respondent made full and free disclosure to the disciplinary board and had a cooperative attitude toward the proceedings.

Respondent did not have a selfish motive only to the extent that he did not personally profit from the transactions except from the legal fees earned for his employer in connection with the closings.

VII. The Panel's Recommended Discipline.

The ODC argues that disbarment is the appropriate sanction. Respondent asks the Panel to recommend a substantial suspension. The ODC relies on several cases in support of its request that Respondent be disbarred. First, the ODC relies on In re Freebery, 947 A.2d 1121, 2008 WL 1849916 (Del. 2008). There, Ms. Freebery failed to disclose a loan on a personal mortgage application and pled guilty to a violation of 18 U.S.C. § 1014, a felony criminal offense. Ms. Freebery stipulated to a violation of Rule 8.4(b). The Panel in Freebery analyzed whether the mental state that formed the basis for her conviction was "knowing" or "intentional" As the Panel explained:

This distinction is critical, since the recommendations suggested by the ABA Standards are based on the mental state that forms the basis of an attorney's misconduct- i.e., more culpable mental states generally receive more severe sanctions. Specifically, under the ABA Standards, "knowledge" is defined as "the conscious awareness of the nature or attendant circumstances of the conduct but without the conscious objective or purpose to accomplish a particular result." ABA Standards Definitions (emphasis added) Given the language of 18 U.S.C. § 1014, Respondent's contention that her conduct was merely "knowing," and not "intentional," is misplaced. The federal statute under which Respondent was convicted specifically requires that Respondent's false statement be made "for the purpose of influencing ... any institution the accounts of which are insured by the Federal Deposit Insurance Corporation." Her guilty plea establishes this wrongful conduct. Respondent purposely omitted her \$2.3 million liability to ensure Commerce Bank's expeditious approval of her loan application. While Respondent may not have sought to defraud Commerce Bank, she did intend to have Commerce Bank rely on the erroneous application in granting a mortgage on her new home with favorable terms. Accordingly, her mental state cannot fall within the ABA Standard's definition of "knowledge", which excludes "the conscious objective or purpose to accomplish a particular result." Rather, the statute, on its face, requires purposeful influencing of a financial institution, a mental state the Panel considers in the context of this disciplinary proceeding to be substantially equivalent to intentional.

In re Freebery, 2008 WL 1849916, *5 (Del. Supr.) In adopting the Panel's Report in Freebery, the Court agreed that disbarment was the appropriate sanction for the conduct that led to a felony conviction and a violation of Rule 8.4(b).

Here while Respondent was not convicted of a felony, his conduct violated Section 1010 and implicates the same "intentional" mental state as found in Freebery, suggesting a more severe sanction under the ABA Standards. Section 1010 provides:

Whoever, for the purpose of obtaining any loan or advance of credit from any person, partnership, association, or corporation with the intent that such loan or advance of credit shall be offered to or accepted by the Department of Housing and Urban Development for insurance, or for the purpose of obtaining any extension or renewal of any loan, advance of credit, or mortgage insured by such Department, or the acceptance, release, or substitution of any security on such a loan, advance of credit, or for the purpose of influencing in any way the action of such Department, makes, passes, utters, or publishes any statement, knowing the same to be false, or alters, forges, or counterfeits any instrument, paper, or document, or utters, publishes, or passes as true any instrument, paper, or document, knowing it to have been altered, forged, or counterfeited, or willfully overvalues any security, asset, or income, shall be fined under this title or imprisoned not more than two years, or both.

18 U.S.C. § 1010. Respondent here admittedly violated 18 U.S.C. § 1010 by certifying HUD-1 Statements that he knew to be false and by failing to cause the funds to be disbursed in accordance with the HUD-1 Statements. He did not change the HUD-1 Statements to reflect that borrowers were not making financial contributions because it would have raised "red flags" with the lenders. Respondent intended for the lenders to rely on the HUD-1 Statement he certified. Although Ms. Freebery made false statements on a loan application for her own benefit and pled guilty to a felony, the Panel does not believe a lesser sanction is warranted here even though Respondent did not obtain any personal benefit other than his closing fees. Respondent made misrepresentations on the HUD-1 Statements in 22 transactions over a 2-year period and caused injury to his client, other parties to the transaction and the lenders.

The ODC also presented other cases in support of its recommended sanction. In re Lassen, 672 A.2d 988 (Del. 1996) (lawyer suspended for three years for multiple rules violations including 4.l(a), 8.4(b), 8.4(c) and 8.4(d) for falsifying invoices to clients); In re Fabrizzio, 498 A.2d 1076 (Del. 1985) (lawyer suspended for two years for violating (now) Rule 8.4(c) for falsifying settlement sheets in connection with one real estate closing); In re Faraone, 772 A.2d 1 (1998) (lawyer suspended for six months for violations of Rules 4.(a), 4.l(b) and 8.4(c) for representations made in connection with two real estate transactions); Cincinnati Bar Assoc. v. Powers, 895 N.E.2d 172 (Ohio 1008) (lawyer disbarred for multiple rules violations in connection with falsifying closing documents on over 300 loans). [FN10]

Respondent did not offer any cases in support of his request that the Panel recommend a substantial suspension.

FN10. While Powers is distinguishable on the basis that the lawyer personally profited from his actions and also falsified federal tax returns to hide his profit, the Panel believes that the Delaware precedents support the recommended sanction and is not relying on Powers for that purpose.

The Panel has considered the extensive factual record summarized above, the ABA Standards, including aggravating and mitigating factors and precedents of the Delaware Supreme Court and recommends disbarment as the appropriate sanction.

____

Lisa A. Schmidt (Bar No. 3019)

____

Wayne J. Carey (Bar No. 2041)

____

Yvonne Anders Gordon

Questions

1. What internal controls were lacking regarding both the trust accounts and supervision of nonlawyer staff?
2. What mitigating circumstances did the court consider when determining Sullivan's sanctions and what was the result?
3. What did the court address in connection with Sullivan's deposits from the real estate closing and the firm's trust account?

Case Review

In the Matter of James A. Cleland, 2 P.3d 700 (Colo. 2000).

2 P.3d 700 (Colo. 2000)
2000 CJ C.A.R. 2672
(Cite as: *In re: Cleland* 2 P.3d 700)

Supreme Court of Colorado, En Banc.

In the Matter of James A. CLELAND, Attorney—Respondent.

No. 99SA89. May 22, 2000

***700** John S. Gleason, Attorney Regulation Counsel, James C. Coyle, Assistant Regulation Counsel, Denver, Colorado, Attorneys for Complainant.

No Appearance By or on Behalf of Attorney—Respondent.

PER CURIAM.

The respondent in this attorney regulation case, James A. Cleland, admitted that he knowingly misappropriated funds belonging to his clients. We have consistently held that disbarment is the appropriate sanction for this type of misconduct, unless significant extenuating circumstances are present. No such circumstances exist in this case. Nevertheless, a hearing panel of our former grievance committee [FN1] accepted the findings and recommendation of a hearing board that Cleland should be suspended for three years, rather than disbarred. The complainant filed exceptions to the findings and recommendation, contending that Cleland should be disbarred. On review, we determine that certain of the board's findings are clearly erroneous, and we disagree with some of its legal conclusions. On the other hand, we agree with the complainant that disbarment is the only appropriate sanction in this case. Accordingly, we reject the panel's and board's recommendations and we order that Cleland be disbarred, effective immediately.

FN1. By order of the Supreme Court dated June 30, 1998, effective January 1, 1999, the grievance committee was superseded by the reorganization of the attorney regulation system. The same order provided: "All attorney discipline cases in which trial has occurred prior to January 1, 1999 before a Hearing Board ... shall be reviewed by the applicable Hearing Panel at a final meeting to be held in 1999. ..." Order re Reorganization of the Attorney Regulation System (Colo. June 30, 1998), reprinted in 12 C.R.S. at 605 (1999). This case was tried on April 29, 1998, and was reviewed by the hearing panel on February 20, 1999.

I.

James A. Cleland was first licensed to practice law in Colorado in 1989. [FN2] The amended complaint contained six counts. Count I charged Cleland with commingling his personal funds with a client's funds, knowingly mishandling contested funds, and knowingly misappropriating funds belonging to the client. Count II alleged that Cleland ***701** knowingly misappropriated $5000 of his client's funds to reimburse a third party for an earnest money deposit that Cleland was supposed to have held in trust. Count III of the complaint charged that Cleland consistently mismanaged his trust account from September 1995 to February 1996. Count IV alleged that Cleland unilaterally charged his client interest on past-due attorney's fees, without the client's authorization. In Count V, the complainant asserted that Cleland had failed to file a collection matter for a client; that he failed to keep the client reasonably informed about the status of the matter; and that he misrepresented that he had settled the case when in fact he had not. Finally,

Count VI charged Cleland with making misrepresentations to one of the complainant's investigators and a paralegal during the investigation of Count V. [FN3]

FN2. In an unrelated attorney regulation matter heard after the hearing panel acted in this case, the presiding disciplinary judge and hearing board suspended Cleland for two years, effective October 18, 1999. See In re Cleland, No. GC98B118, slip op. at 14 (Colo. PDJ Sept. 17, 1999).

FN3. The hearing board found that the charges in Count VI had not been proven by clear and convincing evidence. The complainant did not except to this finding; we therefore dismiss Count VI and do not discuss it further.

The evidence before the hearing board consisted of the testimony of the complainant's and respondent's witnesses (including Cleland himself), documents, and a stipulation of facts contained in the trial management order the parties submitted. As the facts are sometimes complex, we address each count of the complaint separately, together with the hearing board's findings and conclusions pertaining to that count.

A. Count I—The Kasnoff Funds

Cleland represented George M. Kasnoff Jr. and his various business entities. In 1994, however, Cleland and Kasnoff had a disagreement over the attorney's fees Kasnoff owed Cleland. One of the business entities involved was Kas-Don Enterprises, Inc., which was owned by Kasnoff and Don Shank. Kasnoff and Shank decided to dissolve Kas-Don in the summer of 1995; Shank agreed to buy out Kasnoff s interest in the real estate the corporation owned. Cleland was to prepare the documents that were necessary to transfer the property and to terminate Kas-Don. This was completed in August 1995 and the corporation was dissolved.

Because he was on his honeymoon in Europe on the closing date, Kasnoff made arrangements for Cleland to deposit the net proceeds from the closing into Cleland's trust account. The parties agreed that once the funds were in the trust account, they would be disbursed for certain business expenses. In addition, Kasnoff authorized Cleland to pay himself $5,000 for past attorney's fees. Cleland was to deposit the balance of the funds in Kasnoff's bride's bank account.

On August 16, 1995, Cleland deposited proceeds from the closing in the amount of $16,576.56 into his trust account. With his client's permission, Cleland paid certain business expenses that Kasnoff owed with funds from the trust account. On August 17, 1995, Cleland asked Kasnoff to pay attorney's fees over and above the $5,000 that Kasnoff had agreed to pay. Kasnoff did not authorize any additional sums to be taken out. Nevertheless, Cleland paid himself an additional $4,581.94 for legal services, including $600 for fees that had not yet been earned. Cleland deposited these unauthorized funds into his operating account and used them for his own purposes. When Kasnoff called from Europe on August 16, Cleland told him that he had deposited the balance of the funds (including the $4,581.94 he had paid himself without permission) into Kasnoff's wife's bank account. This was untrue.

The hearing board found that Kasnoff frequently paid the attorney's fees he owed Cleland slowly. Cleland also reasonably believed that Kasnoff was in financial difficulties. The exact amount of attorney's fees that Kasnoff owed was in dispute even at the hearing (although after these disciplinary proceedings were underway, Cleland returned the clearly unearned $600 in fees through his lawyer). The hearing board also found that at the time he paid himself the unauthorized funds, Cleland was under considerable financial and personal pressure, and that he was clinically depressed.

The board concluded that Cleland's conduct violated Colo. RPC 1.15(a) (failing to keep the client's property—in this case, the $4,581.94—separate from the lawyer's own ***702** property), and 1.15(c) (failing to hold separate any property that the lawyer and another—in this case, the client—both claim an interest in). The board found, however, that the complainant did not prove by clear and convincing evidence that Cleland violated Colo. RPC 8.4(c) (engaging in conduct involving dishonesty, fraud, deceit, or misrepresentation). The complainant did not specifically complain about this finding in his opening brief, and we find it unnecessary to address it.

B. Count II—The Clearly Colorado Matter

On June 19, 1995, about two months before Kas-Don was dissolved, Clearly Colorado, L.L.C. entered into a contract with Kasnoff to purchase the latter's one-half interest in Kas-Don real estate. The contract provided that Clearly Colorado would pay a $5,000 earnest money deposit, and that this would be held in Cleland's trust account. After receiving the $5,000, Cleland used the trust funds for his own use. This was not authorized. [FN4] The real estate transaction fell through and Clearly Colorado demanded the return of its $5,000 deposit. Because he had already diverted the trust funds, however, the balance in Cleland's trust account on August 3, 1995 was only $66.40. Nevertheless, on August 15, 1995, Cleland wrote a $5,000 check drawn on his trust account as a refund to Clearly Colorado. This $5,000 was paid from the proceeds of the Kas-Don transaction referred to in Count I above.

FN4. It is unclear why Cleland was not charged with initially misappropriating this $5,000 from his trust account.

The board concluded that Cleland knowingly misappropriated client funds to reimburse Clearly Colorado in violation of Colo. RPC 8.4(c) (engaging in conduct involving dishonesty, fraud, deceit, or misrepresentation).

C. Count III—Commingling and Misappropriation

Count II details numerous transactions that Cleland engaged in with respect to client funds and his trust account. For our purposes here, it is sufficient to note that Cleland admitted to commingling his own funds with those belonging to his clients in his trust account and that he knowingly misappropriated client funds without the authorization or knowledge of the clients affected. [FN5]

FN5. The board did find that client funds belonging to Donna Nazario were transferred to Cleland's operating account by mistake, and thus did not constitute commingling or misappropriation.

In particular, the hearing board found that Cleland: (1) knowingly misappropriated $1376.95 of client funds from his trust account to repay another client; (2) commingled personal funds with client funds in his trust account on numerous occasions between November 1995 and August 1996; and (3) disbursed trust account funds belonging to various clients to other clients, without the authorization or knowledge of the clients affected. The board thus concluded that Cleland's conduct violated Colo. RPC 8.4(c).

D. Count IV—Kasnoff Interest

Without his client's consent or agreement, Cleland charged interest on Kasnoff's past-due accounts. The board found that this practice violated Colo. RPC 1.5(a) (charging an unreasonable fee), and 8.4(c) (conduct involving dishonesty).

E. Count V—Robin Caspari

Robin Caspari hired Cleland to prosecute a landlord-tenant dispute, and gave him $91 to file suit against two tenants for past-due rent. The hearing board concluded that Cleland failed to keep Caspari reasonably informed about the status of the matter, in violation of Colo. RPC 1.4(a). In addition, Cleland told the client, falsely, that he had filed an action against one of the tenants, when he had not; that hearings had been set and orders had been entered in the case, when in fact there was no case; and that he had settled the matter with one of the clients for $600, which he then paid to the client. The $600 was actually from Cleland's personal funds. This conduct violated Colo. RPC 1.3 (neglecting a legal matter), and 8.4(c) (engaging in dishonest conduct).

*703 II.

[1] The hearing panel approved the hearing board's recommendation that Cleland be suspended for three years, with conditions. The complainant filed exceptions, claiming that certain of the board's factual and legal conclusions were erroneous, and that the appropriate disciplinary sanction was disbarment. The key to the appropriate discipline is also the most serious misconduct here—the knowing misappropriation of client funds in Counts II and III.

[2] As we have said numerous times before, disbarment is the presumed sanction when a lawyer knowingly misappropriates funds belonging to a client or a third person. "When a lawyer knowingly converts client funds, disbarment is 'virtually automatic,' at least in the absence of significant factors in mitigation." People v. Young, 864 P.2d 563, 564 (Colo. 1993) (knowing misappropriation of clients' funds warrants disbarment even absent prior disciplinary history and despite cooperation and making restitution); see also In re Thompson, 991 P.2d 820, 823 (Colo. 1999) (disbarring lawyer who knowingly misappropriated law firm funds); People v. Varallo, 913 P.2d 1, 12 (Colo. 1996) (disbarring lawyer who knowingly misappropriated client funds); People v. Ogborn, 887 P.2d 21, 23 (Colo. 1994) (misappropriating client funds warrants disbarment even in absence of prior discipline and presence of personal and emotional problems); People v. Robbins, 869 P.2d 517, 518 (Colo. 1994) (converting client trust funds warrants disbarment even if funds are restored before clients learn they are missing but not before the conversion is discovered by the lawyer's law firm).

[3] Consistent with our approach, the ABA Standards for Imposing Lawyer Sanctions (1991 & Supp. 1992) provides that, in the absence of mitigating circumstances, "[d]isbarment is generally appropriate when a lawyer knowingly converts client property and causes injury or potential injury to a client." *Id.* at 4.11. Neither this standard nor our cases require serious injury before disbarment is appropriate. On the other hand, "[s]uspension is generally appropriate when a lawyer knows or should know that he is dealing improperly with client property and causes injury or potential injury to a client." *Id.* at 4.12.

The hearing board found that the following aggravating and mitigating factors were present. In aggravation, Cleland has prior discipline in the form of a letter of admonition for neglecting a legal matter, see *Id.* at 9.22(a); and multiple offenses are present, see *Id.* at 9.22(d). The board also determined that there was a pattern of misconduct, see *Id* at 9.22(c), but only with respect to Cleland's "continuing recklessness and gross negligence in management of his trust account from approximately mid-1995 to mid-August 1996."

According to the board, mitigating factors included the absence of a dishonest motive or intention on Cleland's part, see *Id* at 9.32(b); Cleland admitted that he committed some of the misconduct and otherwise cooperated in the proceedings, see *Id* at 9.32(e), Cleland was relatively inexperienced in the practice of law, see *Id* at 9.32(f); and he has expressed remorse, see *Id* at 9.32(1). Additional mitigating factors found were the presence of personal financial and emotional problems, see *Id* at 9.32(c); and a timely good faith effort to rectify the consequences of at least part of his misconduct, see id, at 9.32(d). The board noted that Cleland was diagnosed with a depressive disorder that impaired his judgment, concentration, and thinking. The conclusion that Cleland tried to rectify some of the consequences of his misconduct stems from the board's belief that he offered to arbitrate the fee dispute with Kasnoff before he was aware that he was under investigation.

While acknowledging our statement in Varallo, 913 P.2d at 12, that disbarment is the presumed sanction when knowing misappropriation is shown, the board declined to apply what it deemed such a "bright-line" rule to the facts in this case. In particular, the hearing board cited three cases that we decided after Varallo that it believed contradicted a literal reading of the case: People v. Zimmermann, 922 P.2d 325 (Colo. 1996); People v. Reynolds, 933 P.2d 1295 (Colo. 1997); and People v. Schaefer, 938 P.2d 147 ***704** (Colo. 1997). However, these cases did not modify Varallo's "bright-line" rule. [FN6]

> FN6. The virtue of a bright-line rule like this one is not that it is easy to apply, although it is. Rather, such a rule strives to eliminate the disparate treatment of lawyers who have committed serious misconduct, when the unequal treatment may otherwise be based on invidious and irrelevant factors.

We decided Zimmermann three months after Varallo. The respondent in Zimmermann, John Delos Zimmermann, seriously mismanaged the funds in his trust account. He commingled funds that should have been placed in his trust account with funds that should have been deposited in his operating account; he improperly used clients' funds to pay his personal or business expenses; and refunded unearned attorney's fees to clients from funds advanced by different clients. See 922 P.2d at 326–29. We suspended Zimmermann for one year and one day. See *Id* at 330. Zimmermann's misconduct is similar to that charged in Count III of the complaint in this case, with one important exception. That exception serves to distinguish Zimmermann from this case, however, in the same way that we distinguished Zimmermann from Varallo. We stated that:

> The single most important factor in determining the appropriate level of discipline in this case is whether [Zimmermann's] misappropriation of client funds was knowing, in which case disbarment is the presumed sanction, People v. Varallo, 913 P.2d 1, 12 (Colo. 1996), or whether it was reckless, or merely negligent, suggesting that a period of suspension is adequate. People v. Dickinson, 903 P.2d 1132, 1138 (Colo. 1995).

Zimmermann, 922 P.2d at 329 [emphasis added]. However, the hearing board specifically found that Zimmermann's mental state when he was mismanaging his trust account was one of recklessness. See *Id* We noted that although the evidence before the board would have supported a finding that Zimmermann's conduct was knowing, rather than reckless, the board's conclusion found support in the record and we would not overturn it. See *Id* at 329 n. 1. Zimmermann therefore stands for the same proposition as Varallo—the lawyer's actual mental state is the most significant factor for determining the proper discipline. Because the board found that Zimmermann's mental state when he mismanaged his trust and operating accounts was reckless, not knowing, Dickinson (suspension) governed the result, not Varallo (disbarment).

We suspended the respondent in People v. Reynolds, 933 P.2d 1295 (Colo. 1997), for three years. John Kerz Reynolds engaged in an extensive pattern of "neglect of client matters, misrepresentations to clients, dishonesty, misuse of client funds, and assisting a nonlawyer in the unauthorized practice of law." *Id* at 1305. He also failed to account for, or return, unearned advance fees he received from various clients. See *Id* at 1296–1301. The case did not involve the knowing misappropriation of client funds, however. Reynolds was not charged with misappropriation, nor did the hearing board in that case make any findings on the issue. Reynolds is therefore distinguishable.

Finally, in People v. Schaefer, 938 P.2d 147 (Colo. 1997), we suspended Richard A. Schaefer for two years. Citing Zimmermann and Varallo, we concluded that "[t]he hearing board's determination that [Schaefer's] mishandling of his client's funds was negligent rather than intentional is not clearly erroneous and we will not overturn it." *Id.* at 150. Schaefer is thus completely consistent with Varallo.

The present case cannot be distinguished from Varallo. In two separate counts, Cleland admitted, and the hearing board found, that he knowingly misappropriated client funds. The board erred when it did not just accept Cleland's admissions and its own initial findings, and then go on to determine whether the factors in mitigation were weighty enough to justify a sanction less than disbarment. Because there is no evidence in the record that supports the conclusion that Cleland's mental state was merely reckless or negligent, that finding is clearly erroneous, and we reject it.

Having determined that disbarment is the presumed sanction in this case, we must now independently review the record with an eye ***705** toward the factors in mitigation. The hearing board first found that Cleland did not have a dishonest motive or intention when he committed the misconduct. As the complainant points out, this is directly contrary to the stipulation and a large part of the evidence. The hearing board specifically concluded that Cleland engaged in conduct involving dishonesty, fraud, deceit, or misrepresentation in Counts II (knowing misappropriation of client funds), III (knowing misappropriation of client funds), IV (unilaterally charging unauthorized interest), and V (misrepresenting the status of a case and that it had settled), in violation of Colo. RPC 8.4(c). The fact that Cleland may not have had a dishonest motive in every single instance of misconduct does not demonstrate that the mitigating factor exists. We reject this as a mitigating factor.

Next, the board found that Cleland's admissions of misconduct and his cooperative attitude in the proceedings were mitigating factors. See ABA Standards, supra, at 9.32(e). We agree that these constitute bona fide mitigating circumstances, but we accord them little ultimate weight, given Cleland's failure to appear and participate in this court, and his noncooperation and default in the proceedings before the PDJ for the misconduct (similar to that in this case because it involved mismanagement of trust funds) that earned him a two-year suspension. The reason we consider mitigating factors at all is so we may gauge the level of danger that an attorney poses to the public and, ideally, to arrive at a disciplinary sanction that adequately balances the seriousness of the danger against the gravity of the misconduct.

Although Cleland's cooperation before the hearing board warrants some consideration, we are troubled by his later noncooperation, and feel that this does not bode well for Cleland's future as a lawyer.

The board also considered Cleland's relative inexperience in the practice of law as a mitigating factor. It is such a factor; but inexperience does not go far in our view to excuse or to mitigate dishonesty, misrepresentation, or misappropriation. Little experience in the practice of law is necessary to appreciate such actual wrongdoing. On the other hand, Cleland's expressions of remorse are mitigating, as the board found. See *Id* at 9.32(1).

The hearing board also considered that the personal, financial, and emotional problems that Cleland was experiencing were mitigating. See *Id.* at 9.32(c). Specifically, the board noted that Cleland had been diagnosed with a depressive disorder that impaired his judgment, concentration, and thinking. However, we deem it worthy of note that, despite the advice of the psychiatrist who testified for him, Cleland had not sought treatment for the disorder. Moreover, we reject the proposition that Cleland's financial difficulties mitigate his misappropriation of client funds in any way. Finally, the board found that by offering to arbitrate the fee dispute with Kasnoff, Cleland made some effort to rectify the consequences of at least part of his misconduct. See *Id.* at 9.32(d). Despite the fact that Cleland's clients may not have suffered significant actual damages, as the hearing board found (a point that is debatable given the record in this case), the potential for injury was nevertheless substantial.

Taking all of the above factors into consideration, we conclude that they are not significant enough to call for any result other than disbarment. However, two members of the court disagree and would approve the recommendation to suspend Cleland for three years. Accordingly, we reject the board's and panel's recommendation, and we order that Cleland be disbarred.

III.

We hereby order that James A. Cleland be disbarred, effective immediately. Should Cleland ever seek readmission to practice law pursuant to C.R.C.P. 251.29, he must first demonstrate that he has complied with the following conditions:

(1)Cleland must pay George M. Kasnoff Jr. any amount awarded in Kasnoff's favor in the fee arbitration proceedings between Cleland and Kasnoff;

(2)Cleland must pay the costs incurred in this proceeding in the amount of $2,188.73, to the Attorney Regulation ***706** Committee, 600 Seventeenth Street, Suite 200 South, Denver, Colorado 80202.

END OF DOCUMENT

Case Review Exercises

1. Why did the court disagree with the board's findings that the attorney should only be suspended for three years and instead find that the attorney should be disbarred?
2. How did the attorney "consistently mismanage" his trust account?
3. In the Kasnoff matter (Count I), why could the attorney not place the $600 of unearned fees in his operating account?
4. How did the attorney complicate matters by writing a check in *The Clearly Colorado Matter* (Count II) for $5000 when there was only $66.40 in the account at the time? Apparently, the check cashed because another deposit was made. Where did this money come from?
5. In the Robin Caspari matter (Count V), what was wrong with the attorney's taking the $600 from his own personal account, as a client actually received a benefit and no client was harmed?
6. When considering mitigation, was the court persuaded by the fact that the attorney had been diagnosed with a depressive disorder that impaired his judgment, concentration, and thinking? Why or why not?

Helpful Web Sites

Organization	Description	Internet Address
Alabama State Bar—Law Office Management Assistance Program	Articles on a variety of law office management topics, including finance-related articles and information. The Web site has a comprehensive manual on trust funds.	http://www.alabar.org/
American Bar Association (ABA)	Association for attorneys. The Web site has a large amount of information and publications relevant to individuals working in the legal profession.	http://www.americanbar.org
ABA Law Practice Management Section	ABA Web site devoted to law practice management issues and including financial issues.	http://www.americanbar.org/lpm
ABA Legal Technology Resource Center	ABA Web site devoted to technology. Includes resources and articles.	http://www.americanbar.org/groups/departments_offices/legal_technology_resources.html
ABA Center For Professional Responsibility	Rules for auditing lawyer trust accounts, maintaining and tracking client funds, and trust account overdraft notification	http://www.americanbar.org/groups/professional_responsibility.html
Association of Legal Administrators	National association for legal administrators. Contains resources and information related to law office management and legal administration.	http://www.alanet.org
Law Technology News	Excellent periodical for legal technology issues.	http://www.lawtechnews.com and http://www.legaltechnology.com/

Organization	Description	Internet Address
State Bar Associations—and The National List of Attorneys	Articles published on individual states' bar association Web site. There are a variety of law office management topics, including trust funds, fees, and finance-related articles and information. The National List of Attorneys maintains a complete list of state bar association Web sites.	http://www.nationallist.com/resources/associations-state-bar-list You may also use search engines such as yahoo.com or google.com to reach a particular state's bar association Web site.
National Association of Paralegals	National association for legal assistants. Contains many resources for legal assistants.	http://www.nala.org
National Federation of Paralegal Associations	National association for paralegals and legal assistants. Contains many resources for paralegals/legal assistants.	http://www.paralegals.org

Financial and Trust Accounting Software

Organization	Product/service	Internet address
Abacus Data Systems	AbacusLaw—Full-featured legal accounting software.	http://www.abacuslaw.com
Aderant	Time & Billing—Full-featured legal accounting software.	http://www.aderant.com
AppFolio™	MyCase—Full-featured legal accounting software.	http://www.mycase.com
Clio	Full-featured legal accounting software.	http://www.goclio.com
LexisNexis	PCLaw® (0-20 lawyers); Juris® (over 20 lawyers); Time Matters® (customized features)—Full-featured legal accounting software.	http://www.lexisnexis.com/law-firm-practice-management/pclaw
Software Technology, Inc.	Tabs3—Full-featured legal accounting software.	http://www.tabs3.com
Thomson Reuters—Elite	ProLaw—Full-featured legal accounting software.	http://www.elite.com/prolaw

Suggested Reading

1. American Bar Association. *ABA Model Rules for Client Protection: Model Rules for Lawyers' Funds for Client Protection.*
2. American Bar Association. *ABA Model Rules for Client Protection: Model Rule for Trust Account Records.*
3. American Bar Association. *ABA Model Rules for Client Protection: Model Rules for Trust Account Overdraft Notification.*
4. American Bar Association. *ABA Model Rules for Client Protection: Model Rule for Random Audit of Trust Accounts.*
5. American Bar Association. *ABA Model Rules for Client Protection: Model Rule on Financial Recordkeeping.*
6. Munneke, G., & Davis, A. (2003, 2007, 2010). *The essential form book—comprehensive management tools, volumes I-IV.* American Bar Association.
7. Greene, A. (2012). *The Lawyer's Guide To Increasing Revenue, Second Edition.* American Bar Association.

Hands-On Exercises
Clio—Client Trust Funds

Training Manual Outline

Number	Lesson Title	Concepts Covered
Lesson 1*	Part A: Introduction to Clio Part B: Set Up Law Firm Profile	Understanding the Clio platform Details for Firm descriptions
Lesson 2	Entering Trust Deposits	Details on generating trust deposits
Lesson 3	Enter Trust Withdrawals	Details on creating trust account deductions
Lesson 4	Printing Trust Reports	Printing a trust report including a balance of trust monies for each case

*Note: Lesson 1—Introduction to Clio is the same for every subject matter. If you completed Lesson 1 in an earlier tutorial, you do not need to repeat it.

Welcome to Adams & Lee

Welcome to Adams & Lee! We are an active and growing firm with six attorneys and three paralegals. As you know, you have been hired as a paralegal intern. We are very happy to have you on board; we can certainly use your help.

At Adams & Lee, keeping detailed and accurate records of client trust monies is a priority. In this tutorial, you will learn how easy it is to track client trust funds in Clio. Clio does all of the work for you. You should review the "Getting Started" guide to help you become familiar with Clio. If you have completed Part A and Part B of Lesson 1 in a prior tutorial, please go directly to Lesson 2.

Getting Started

Introduction

Throughout these exercises, information you need to type into the program will be designated in several different ways.

- Keys to be pressed on the keyboard will be designated in brackets, in all caps and bold type (e.g., press the [**ENTER**] key).
- Movements with the mouse/pointer will be designated in bold and italics (e.g., ***point to File on the menu bar and click the pointer***).
- Words or letters that should be typed will be designated in bold and enlarged (e.g., type **Training Program**).
- Information that is or should be displayed on your computer screen is shown in bold, with quotation marks (e.g., "**Press ENTER to continue**").

Clio Installation (Appendix A)

Clio is not a downloaded program; it is accessed from the Web site. You may be invited by your instructor to join as a nonlawyer (paralegal) in a hypothetical law firm through your e-mail. ***Click the hyperlink or copy and paste it into your Internet browser. Follow the on-screen instructions for providing your name and creating a password.*** You will now have access to Clio and the hypothetical law firm.

Your instructor may have you create a Clio account and work independently. In that case, see Appendix A for installation instructions.

LESSON 1: Part A (Appendix B)

You should become familiar with the Clio Platform and its essential functions before you begin any of the lessons. *Note*: If you are already logged in, you will skip Steps 1 and 2.

1. Start your Internet browser. Type **www.goclio.com** in the Internet browser and press the **[ENTER] key**.
2. On the Clio Home page, ***click Log In. On the next screen, enter the e-mail address and password you provided in Clio and click SIGN IN. If you check the box next to KEEP ME SIGNED IN, you will be able to skip this step in the future.***
3. Clio will open in the hypothetical law firm on the PRACTICE page. At this point you are ready to explore the Clio platform and its essential functions. There are 11 tabs available in Clio. We will start with the PRACTICE tab.
4. ***Click* PRACTICE**. Your screen should now look like Clio Exhibit 1A-1. This is the Clio dashboard which provides a quick look at the agenda, calendar, and billing information. You will now explore the other 10 tabs.

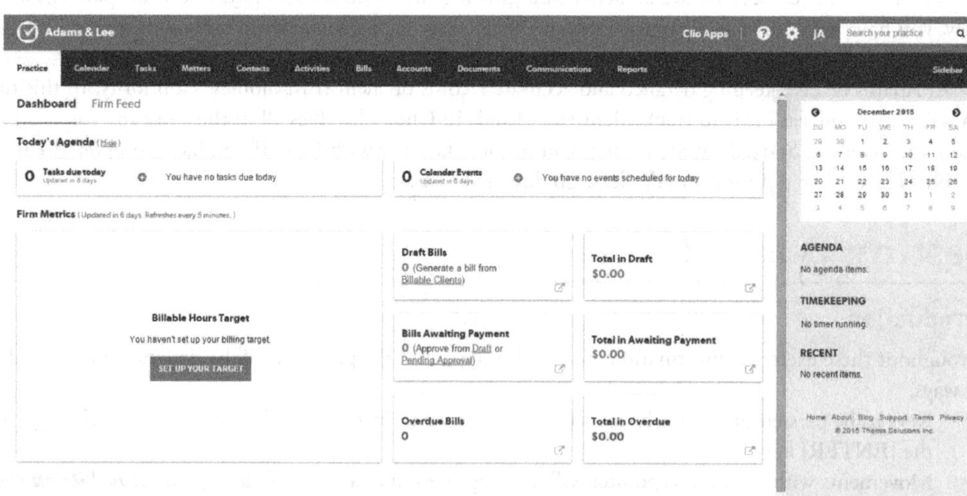

Clio Exhibit 1A-1 Practice Tab

Source: Themis Solutions, Inc.

5. ***Click*** **CALENDAR.** You may need to scroll down to see the entire page. You can change the view to see your Agenda, or Day, Week, Month, or Year views. You can view your personal calendar, the firm calendar or both.
6. To create a calendar entry, while in the Week view, ***select the Wednesday of that current week and double-click on the 10:00 am time slots.*** The Create Calendar Entry will open. See Clio Exhibit 1A-2. If you ***click Add Event***, the date will default to the current date.

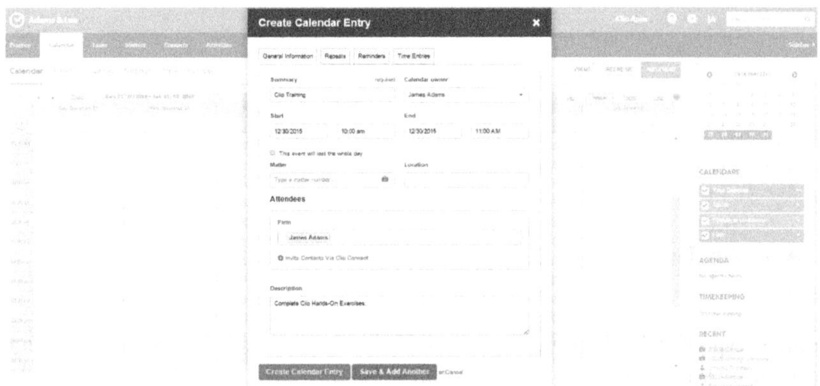

Clio Exhibit 1A-2 Create Calendar Entry

Source: Themis Solutions, Inc.

Under Summary, type **Clio Training**. Under **Start**, type **10:00 AM** and under **End** type **11:00 AM**. Leave Matter and Location "**blank**," and under Description, type **Complete Clio Hands-On Exercises.** ***Click Create Calendar Entry***. When adding multiple entries, ***click Save & Add Another***. After the entry is complete, it will appear in the calendar. ***Place your cursor over the new calendar entry*** to see the description. Your calendar should look like Clio Exhibit 1A-3. You can now move to the "Tasks" tab.

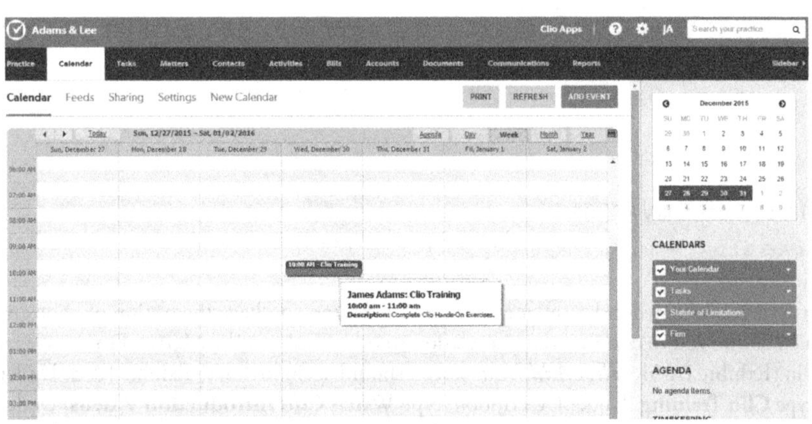

Clio Exhibit 1A-3 Calendar Entry - View

Source: Themis Solutions, Inc.

7. ***Click* TASKS.** This is where specific tasks can be assigned to specific individuals or groups. To create a new Task, ***click Add.*** See Clio Exhibit 1A-4. Under Task Name, type **Clio Training**.

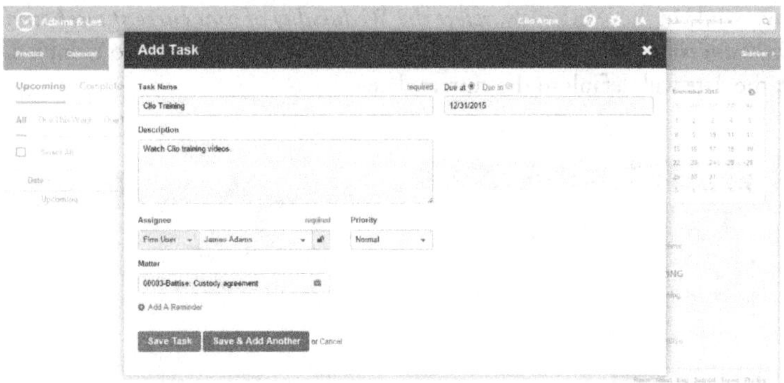

Clio Exhibit 1A-4 Add Task – "Due At"

Source: Themis Solutions, Inc.

Under Description, type **Watch Clio training videos.** Under Due: the radial button will default to **"Due at"** when there are no other tasks associated. ***Click the box under "Due At,"*** and a calendar will appear. ***Select Thursday of the current week.*** Under Assignee, ***select Firm User and then choose yourself.*** Under Priority, ***select Normal.*** Under Matter, ***type 00003-Battise: Custody Agreement*** (the case will appear in the list as you begin typing the number). Then ***click Save Task.*** When adding multiple tasks, ***select Save and Add Another.*** At this point you will be on the ***"tasks" under 00003-Battise.*** See Clio Exhibit 1A-5.

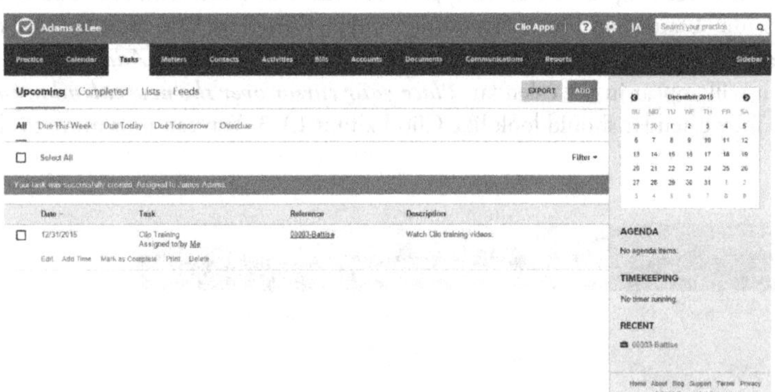

Clio Exhibit 1A-5 Task Entry – "Due At"

Source: Themis Solutions, Inc.

8. When you have several assigned tasks under a specific case matter, you have the option of choosing **"Due in"** which allows you to choose a date in relation to other Tasks in the Matter. From your current position in (Exhibit 1A-5), ***select Add.*** Your screen should again look like Exhibit 1A-3. Under Task Name, type **Clio Training**. Under Description, type **Watch Clio Introduction Videos**. Under Assignee, ***select Firm User and then choose yourself.*** Under Priority, ***select Normal.*** Under Matter, ***type 00003-Battise: Custody Agreement*** (the case will appear in the list as you begin typing the number).Then ***select 00003Battise: Custody Agreement.*** Under Due: the radial will default to

"Due at," however; you now have the option to choose **"Due in."** ***Select "Due in,"*** and a dialogue box will appear. See Clio Exhibit 1A-6.

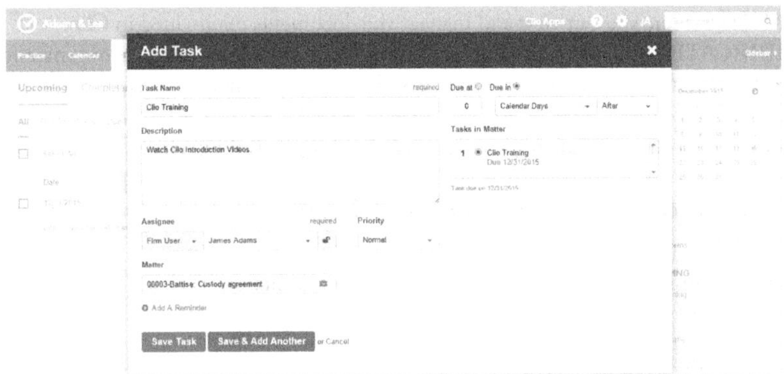

Clio Exhibit 1A-6 Add Task – "Due In"

Source: Themis Solutions, Inc.

ENTER **"1"** in the box marked with a 0. ***Select Calendar Weeks*** under the drop-down menu in the next box, ***Select before*** under the drop-down menu in the next box. Then ***select Clio Training*** under the radial button. ***Click Save Task***. The second task will now appear listed on the Tasks page. See Clio Exhibit 1A-7.

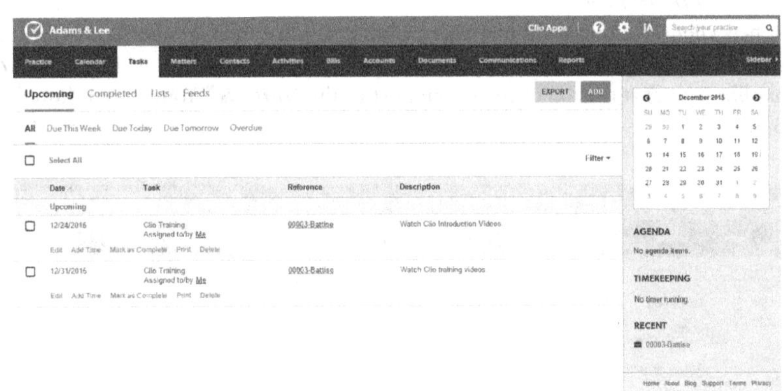

Clio Exhibit 1A-7 Upcoming Task Entries

Source: Themis Solutions, Inc.

9. ***Click*** **MATTERS**. Matters are what Clio calls for cases or files. Clio allows you to associate, or connect, matters with clients, tasks, bills, etc. In later exercises you will see how that works and you will create several new matters.
10. ***Click*** **CONTACTS**. Contacts are people and corporations that you do business with (clients, other attorneys, court reporters, etc.).
11. ***Click*** **ACTIVITIES**. "Activities" is what Clio uses for both time and billing entries as well as expense entries. Time entries can be billed as a flat rate or as an hourly rate. In later exercises you will create several new billing activities.

12. ***Click* BILLS.** Here, you can create a new bill, review a client's billing history, and create bill themes (designs) among other bill-related issues. In later exercises you will create several new bills.
13. ***Click* ACCOUNTS.** Here you can view and manage the various bank accounts of a law firm.
14. ***Click* DOCUMENTS.** Here you can view and manage the documents maintained in Clio.
15. ***Click* COMMUNICATIONS.** Here you can send and receive e-mails, maintain communication logs, interact with colleagues and Clio-connected users, as well as limit permissions between groups for file-related communications.
16. ***Click* REPORTS.** Here you can create reports on a variety of topics (billing client, mater, productivity, and revenue).
17. To end this Clio session, ***click your initials at the top of the screen. Click Sign Out and then close your Internet Browser.***

This concludes the introduction lesson on Clio's platform and essential functions review.

LESSON 1: Part B (Appendix C)

In this lesson, you will set up the firm profile in the hypothetical law firm, establish billing rate, create an activity description, set up bank accounts and establish the matter-numbering protocol.

Note: If you are already logged in, you will skip Steps 1 and 2.

1. Start your Internet browser. Type www.goclio.com in the Internet browser and press the **[ENTER] key**.
2. On the Clio Home page, ***click Log In. On the next screen, enter the e-mail address and password you provided in Clio and click SIGN IN. If you check the box next to KEEP ME SIGNED IN, you will be able to skip this step in the future.***
3. Before you enter new clients, contacts and matters in Clio, details for the hypothetical law firm should be entered. First, you will set up the account information for your hypothetical law firm. ***Click the "settings" icon*** (looks like a gear) at the top of the screen next to the "***initials***." Your screen should look like Clio Exhibit 1B-1.

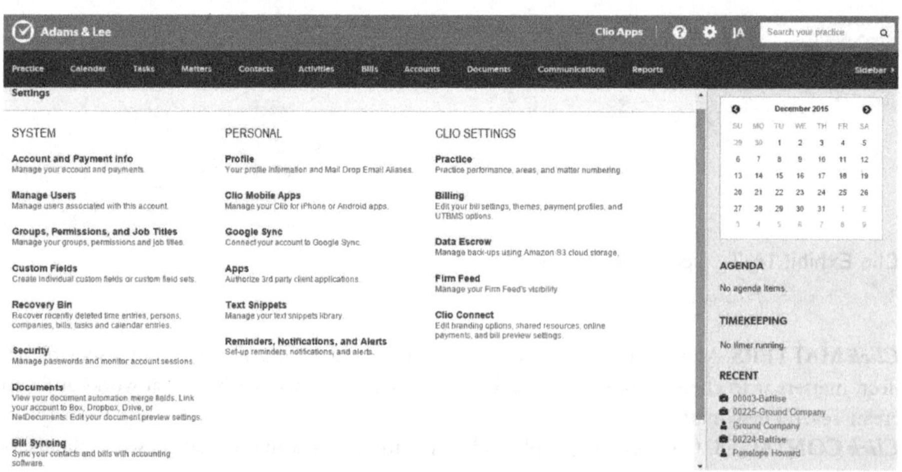

Clio Exhibit 1B-1 Clio Settings Screen

Source: Themis Solutions, Inc.

4. ***Click Account and Payment Info.*** The name of your hypothetical law firm will be established by your instructor (i.e., Adams & Lee) or your First and Last name if you create your own individual account (i.e., Law Office of "First name" "Last name" that you entered). Note: Free accounts do not have access to payment info.
5. ***Type the name, address, and contact information of your firm*** (i.e., sample check from Exhibit 6-1 (Chapter 6), instructor provided, or create your own).
6. Next, ***click the drop-down menu under Date format. Select*** the option that resembles ***12/31/2015.*** Then, ***click the drop-down menu under Time format. Select*** the option that resembles ***11:59 pm. Click Save New Information.***
7. You will now update profile and establish a billing rate. ***Click*** the "settings" icon (looks like a gear) at the top of the screen next to the "initials." Your screen should look like Clio Exhibit 1B-1. ***Click Profile*** and scroll down to **Billing Rate**. ***Type 175.00 next to $/Hr. Click Save New Information.*** See Clio Exhibit 1B-2.

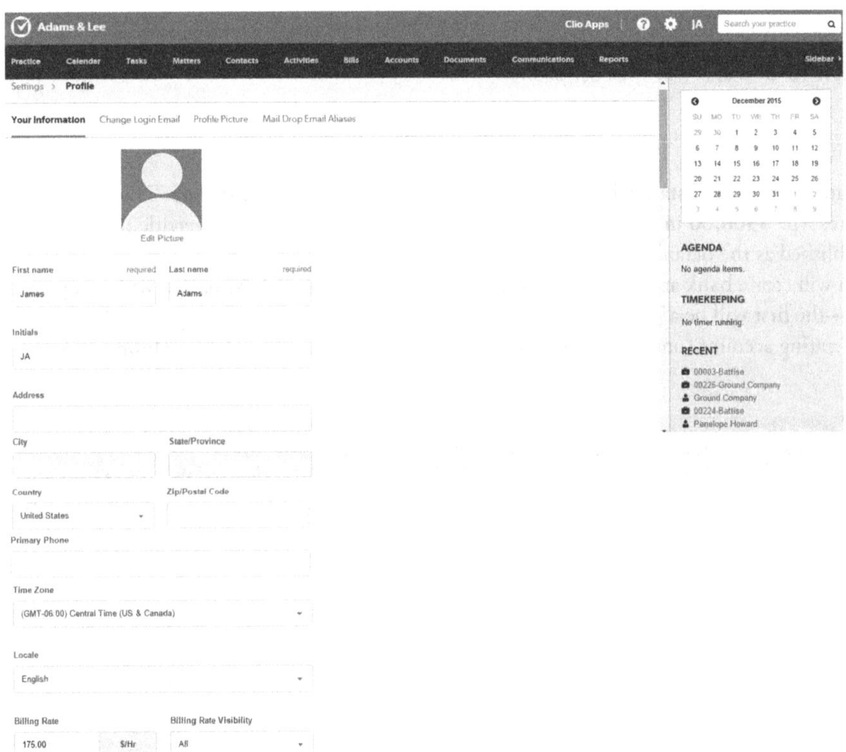

Clio Exhibit 1B-2 Update Profile – Billing Rate

Source: Themis Solutions, Inc.

8. Next, you will create an Activity Description. These are used to ensure a consistent description of commonly used time entries across a law firm. It can also be used as a shortcut—you can save text in the Activity Description and when you enter in a time entry, it will populate this text for you. Activity Descriptions can be shared across a law firm so that everyone in the firm can use them. ***Click the Activities tab, then click Activity Descriptions, then click Add.*** See Clio Exhibit 1B-3.

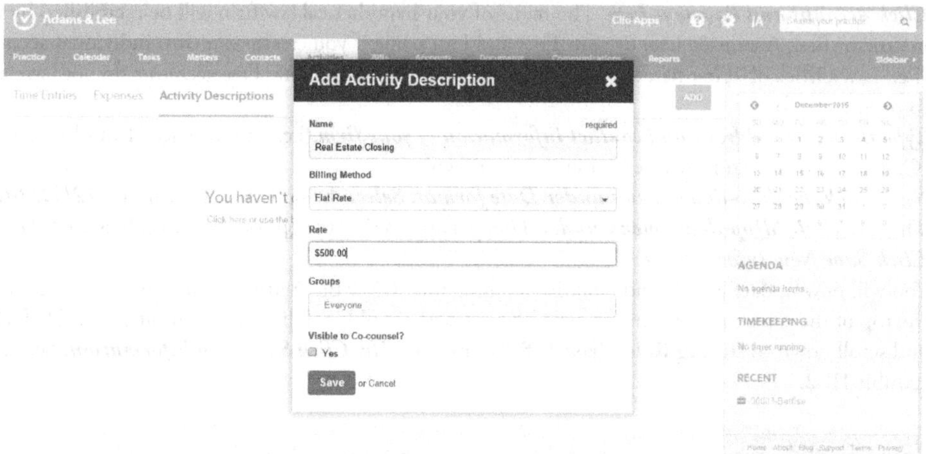

Clio Exhibit 1B-3 Add Activity Description

Source: Themis Solutions, Inc.

Under Name, type **Real Estate Closing**. Under Billing Method, ***select Flat Rate***. This opens a text box called Rate; type **$500.00** in the text box, ***Click Save***. This flat rate fee will override the $175.00 per hour established as the default rate.

9. Next, you will create bank accounts. ***Click the Accounts tab***, then ***click New***. You will set up two accounts—the first will be a Trust Account (one that contains only client money) and the second will be an Operating account (one that ***should not*** contain client money). See Clio Exhibit 1B-4.

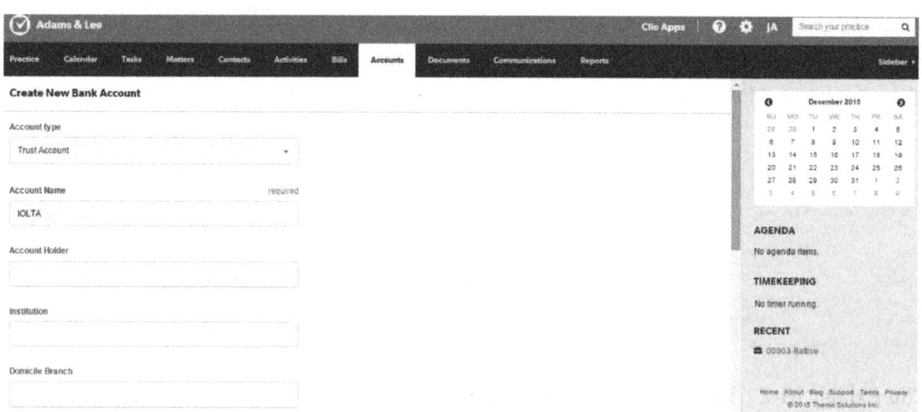

Clio Exhibit 1B-4 Create New Bank Account

Source: Themis Solutions, Inc.

10. Under Account type, ***select Trust Account.*** Under Account name, type **IOLTA** (this stands for Interest on Law Office Trust Account, commonly used for Trust accounts). It is not necessary, nor is it required, to complete the remainder of this form (although you are welcomed to do so). However, you should leave the Balance 0.0. ***Click Create New Bank Account.*** The screen will refresh (showing the new IOLTA account) so additional accounts may be created.
11. Now create the Operating Account. ***Click New,*** then under Account type, ***select Operating Account.*** Under Account name, type **Law Firm Account**. It is not necessary, nor is it required, to complete the remainder of this form (although you are welcomed to do so). However, you should leave the Balance 0.0. ***Click the box next to Default Account.*** (The default account will show up first on the Transactions tab found when a client file is opened under Matters.) ***Click Create New Bank Account.***
12. You will now create the matter-numbering protocol for the hypothetical law firm. ***Click the "settings" icon*** (looks like a gear) at the top of the screen next to the "***initials.***" Your screen should look like Clio Exhibit 1B-1. ***Click Practice,*** and then ***click Matter Numbering.*** See Clio Exhibit 1B-5. ***Under Select***

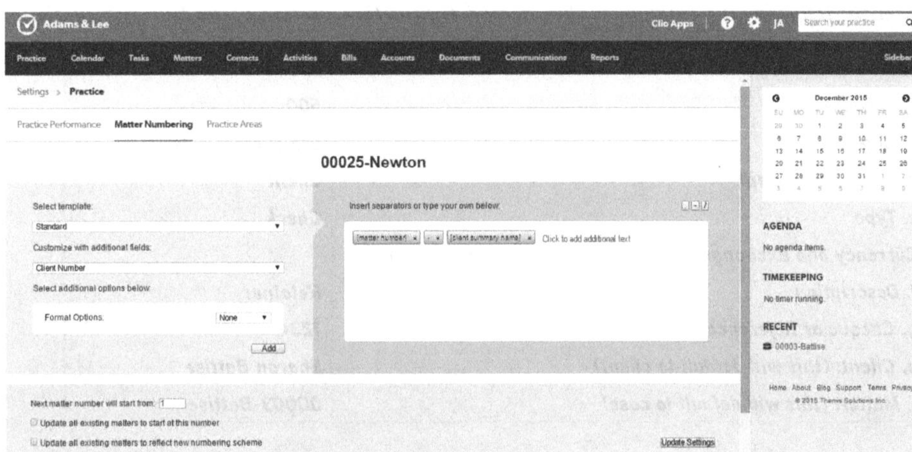

Clio Exhibit 1B-5 Matter Numbering

Source: Themis Solutions, Inc.

Template: click the drop-down menu arrow and click on each of the available options. As you do, notice how the sample matter number (00025-Newton) changes. Use the default (matter number—client summary name), then ***select Standard.*** Under ***Customize with additional fields, select Client Number. Click Update Settings.***

13. To end this Clio session, ***click on your initials*** at the top of the screen. ***Click Sign Out, and then close your Internet browser.***

This concludes the lesson on law firm profile and setup.

LESSON 2: Entering Trust Deposits

In this lesson, you will enter several trust deposits. You will use the current month and date for all transactions.
Note: If you are already logged in, you will skip Steps 1 and 2.

1. Start your Internet browser. Type www.goclio.com in the Internet browser and press the **[ENTER] key.**
2. On the Clio Home page, ***click Log In. On the next screen, enter the e-mail address and password you provided in Clio and click SIGN IN. If you check the box next to KEEP ME SIGNED IN, you will be able to skip this step in the future.***
3. Clio opens in the PRACTICE tab. ***Click the Matters tab.*** From the list of preloaded cases ***select*** "00003-Battise." (*Note:* If you have not preloaded files, see Appendix "A" for instructions or add a "new contact" (Chapter 4, Lesson 2). Next, ***click Transactions, click the drop-down box and select*** "IOLTA" account, then ***click Add.***
4. Now we will assume that the client has paid a $500 retainer for this matter. To record the retainer. ***Enter the following information in the "Record Transaction" section of the New Transaction form.***

a. Account	***IOLTA***
b. Amount	***500***
c. Date	***use current date***
d. Source/Recipient	***Client***
e. Type	***Check***
Currency and Exchange rate are set as default and left blank.	
f. Description	***Retainer***
g. Cheque or Reference	***1234***
h. Client: (this will default to client)	***Sharon Battise***
i. Matter: (this will default to case)	***00003-Battise***

5. ***Click Record Transaction.*** See Clio Exhibit 6-1.

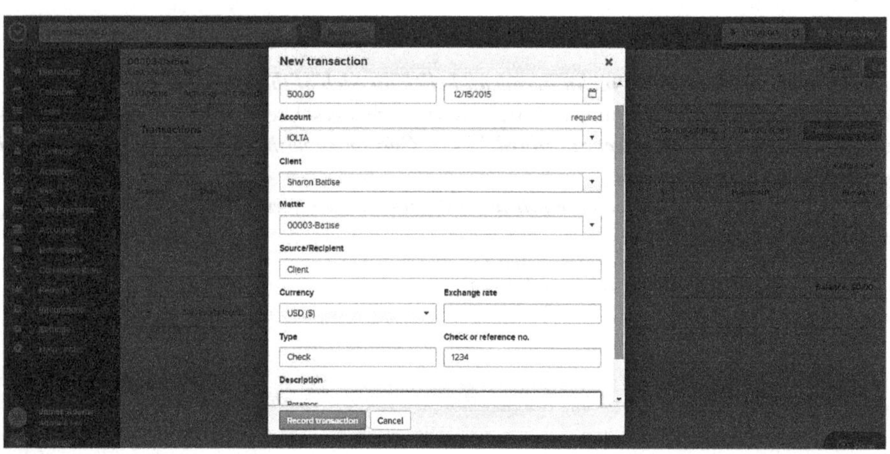

Clio Exhibit 6-1 Add New Transaction - Deposit
Source: Themis Solutions, Inc.

6. ***Enter Additional deposits for Matter 00003-Battise: For each deposit entry, repeat Step 5 with substituting the following information:***

Deposits	Description	Reference #
a. $2500	Witness fees	Check #2345
b. $5000	Travel expenses to take Depo of Expert	Check #3456
c. $1500	Prepay expenses	Check #5678
d. $2500	Transcript fees	Check #6789

7. The Matter 00003-Battise **Ledger** screen for the ***IOLTA balance now shows $12,000.00.***
8. To end this Clio session, ***click on your initials at the top of the screen, click Sign Out, and then close your Internet browser.***

This concludes Lesson 2 (Trust Accounts) of the Clio Hands-On Exercises.

LESSON 3: Entering Trust Withdrawals

In this lesson, you will enter several transactions to withdraw monies from the trust account. You will use the current month and date for all transactions.

Note: If you are already logged in, you will skip Steps 1 and 2.

1. Start your Internet browser. Type www.goclio.com in the Internet browser and press the [**ENTER**] **key**.
2. On the Clio Home page, ***click Log In. On the next screen, enter the e-mail address and password you provided in Clio and click SIGN IN. If you check the box next to KEEP ME SIGNED IN, you will be able to skip this step in the future.***
3. From the PRACTICE screen ***click the Matters tab.*** From the list of preloaded cases ***select*** "00003-Battise." (*Note:* If you have not preloaded files, see Appendix "A" for instructions or add a "new contact" (Chapter 4, Lesson 2). Next, ***click Transactions, click the drop-down box and select*** "IOLTA" account, then ***click Add.*** See Clio Exhibit 6-2.
   Here you will use the negative (–) symbol to create deductions from the account. Notice at the bottom of the Ledger screen you will see the client account balance.
4. Now we will assume that $500 has been paid to Advanced Court Reporting for a deposition. To record the deductions, ***enter the following information in the "Record Transaction" tab of the New Transaction form.***

a. Amount	-500
b. Date	Use current date
c. Source/Recipient	Advance Court Reporting
d. Type	Check
Currency and Exchange rate are set as default and left blank.	
Deposition	e. Description
1001	f. Cheque or Reference
Sharon Battise	g. Client: (this will default to client)
00003-Battise	h. Matter: (this will default to case)

5. ***Click Record Transactions.*** See Clio Exhibit 6-2.

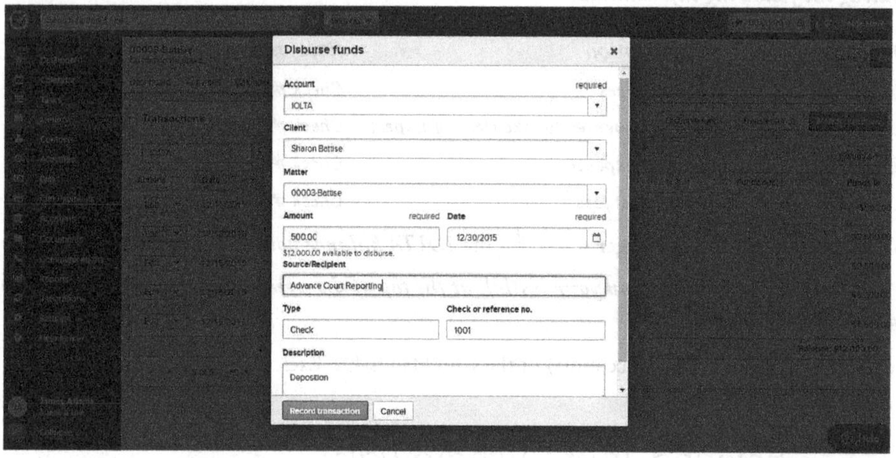

Clio Exhibit 6-2 Add New Transaction - Debit

Source: Themis Solutions, Inc.

6. ***Enter Additional deductions for Matter 00003-Battise: After each deposit entry, repeat Step 5.***

Amount	Check	Source/Recipient	Description
$150	1002	Clerk of Courts, State of New York	Court fee
$100	1003	U.S. Post Office	Shipping
$750	1004	American Reporting	Deposition of defendant
$2500	1005	Universal Investigation Services	Investigation re: damages

7. The Matter 00003-Battise **Ledger** screen for the ***IOLTA balance now shows $8000.00.***
8. ***To end this Clio session, click on your initials at the top of the screen, click Sign Out, and then close your Internet browser.***

This concludes Lesson 3 (Trust Accounts) of the Clio Hands-On Exercises.

LESSON 4: Printing Trust Reports

In this lesson, you will print a trust report that includes the trust balances for each matter. You will use the current month and date for all transactions.

Note: If you are already logged in, you will skip Steps 1 and 2.

1. Start your Internet browser. Type www.clio.com in the Internet browser and press the **[ENTER] key**.
2. On the Clio Home page, ***click Log In. On the next screen, enter the e-mail address and password you provided in Clio and click SIGN IN. If you check the box next to KEEP ME SIGNED IN, you will be able to skip this step in the future.***

3. From the PRACTICE screen ***click the Reports tab.*** From the list under Client Report ***select*** "Trust Ledger" (see Clio Exhibit 6-3).

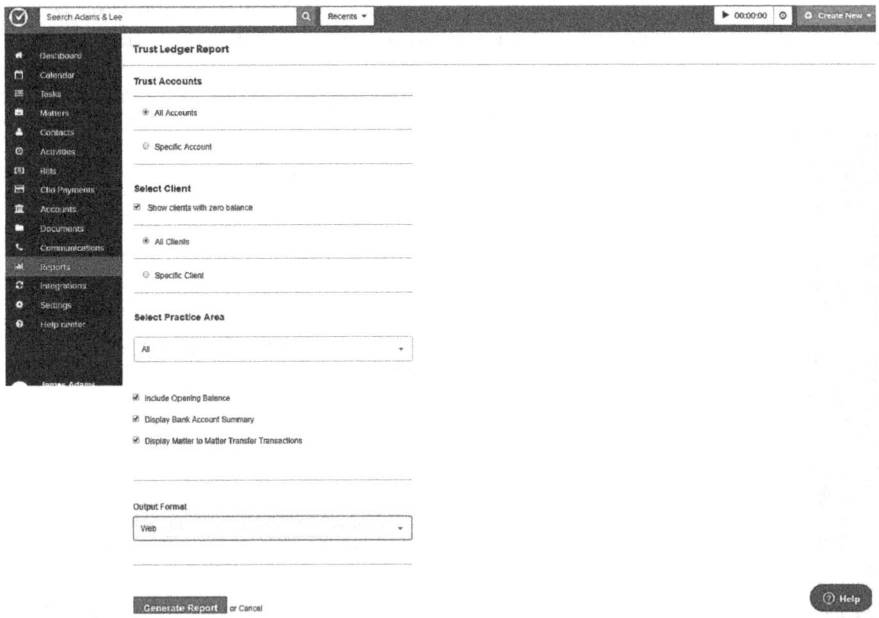

Clio Exhibit 6-3 Generate Trust Leger Report

Source: Themis Solutions, Inc.

Next, under Trust Accounts, ***select Specific Account, click the drop-down box and select*** "IOLTA" account. Next, under Clients, ***select Specific Client*** and begin ***typing the first few letters*** to locate the client file from the Lessons 2 and 3 (this would be Sharon Battise). Scroll down and ***select Generate Report***. All of the entries you made for this case should appear (see Clio Exhibit 6-4).

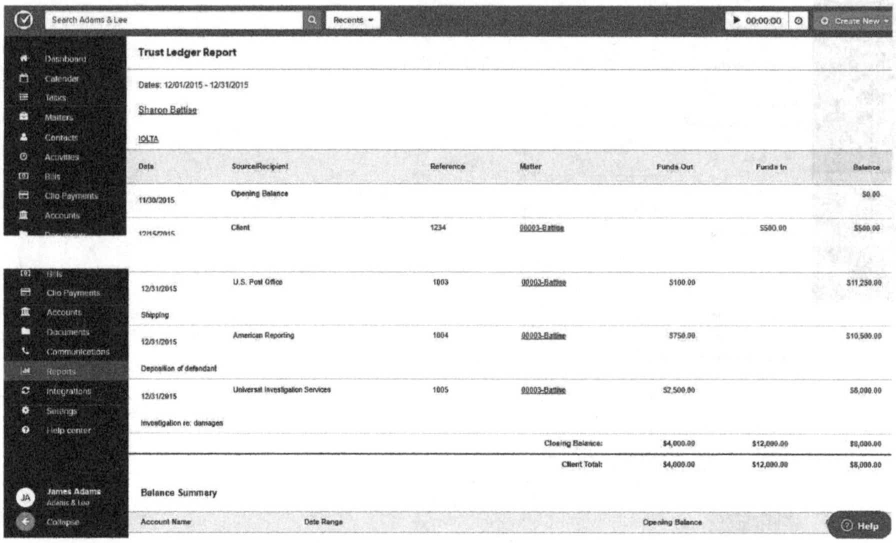

Clio Exhibit 6-4 Report – Trust Account

Source: Themis Solutions, Inc.

4. You can repeat Step 3 to run different report; under Clients, ***select All Clients.*** Now we will assume that a $500 has been paid to Advanced Court Reporting for a deposition. Scroll down and ***select Generate Report.*** All of the entries you made will be available for review.

This concludes the Client Trust Funds Hands-On Exercises.

Hands-On Exercises
Microsoft Excel

Basic Lessons

Number	Lesson Title
Lesson 1	Building a Simple Budget Spreadsheet—Part A
Lesson 2	Building a Simple Budget Spreadsheet—Part B
Lesson 3	Creating a Chart for a Simple Budget Spreadsheet—Part C
Lesson 4	Client Trust Account—Checkbook Register
Lesson 5	Client Trust Account—Client Registers
Lesson 6	Client Trust Account—Client Summary Ledger

Getting Started

Overview

Microsoft Excel is a powerful spreadsheet program that allows you to create formulas, "what-if" scenarios, graphs, and much more.

Introduction

Throughout these lessons and exercises, information you need to operate the program will be designated in several different ways:

- Keys to be pressed on the keyboard will be designated in brackets, in all caps and bold type (e.g., press the **[ENTER]** key).
- Movements with the mouse will be designated in bold and italics (e.g., ***point to File and click***).
- Words or letters that should be typed will be designated in bold (e.g., type **Training Program**).
- Information that is or should be displayed on your computer screen is shown in bold, with quotation marks (e.g., "**Press ENTER to continue**").

Overview of Excel

I. Worksheet

A. *Entering Commands: The Ribbon*—The primary way of entering commands in Excel 2013 is through the ribbon. The ribbon is a set of commands or tools that change depending on which ribbon is selected. There are seven ribbon tabs: Home, Insert, Page Layout, Formulas, Data, Review, and View (see Excel Exhibit 6-1). Each tab as a group of commands. For example, on the Home tab, the Font Group contains a group of commands that govern font choice, font size, bold, italics, underling, and other attributes (see Excel Exhibit 6-1).

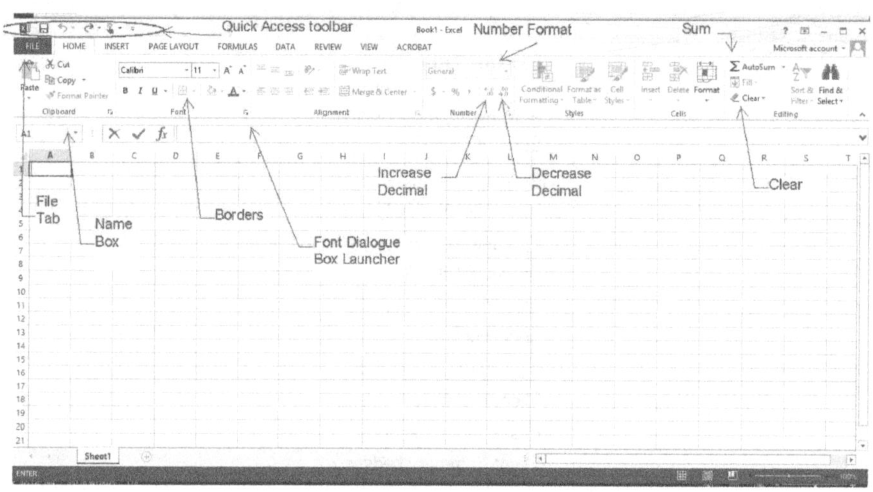

Excel Exhibit 6-1 Excel 2013 Interface

Used with permission from Microsoft.

B. *File tab*—The File tab is where a user accesses commands such as New, Open, Save, and Print. The File tab replaces the Office button used in Excel 2007.

C. *Entering Data*—To enter data, type the text or number in a cell, and press the **[ENTER]** key or one of the arrow (cursor) keys.

D. *Ranges*—A range is a group of contiguous cells. Cell ranges can be created by ***clicking and dragging the pointer*** or holding the **[SHIFT]** key on and using the arrow (cursor) keys.

E. *Format*—Cells can be formatted, including changing the font style, font size, shading, border, cell type (currency, percentage, etc.), alignment, and others by ***clicking the Home ribbon tab***, and then ***clicking "one of the dialog box launchers" in the Font group, Alignment group, or Number group.*** Each of these dialog box launchers brings up the same "Format Cells" window. You can also enter a number of formatting options directly from the Home tab.

F. *Editing a Cell*—You can edit a cell by ***clicking in the cell*** and then ***clicking in the formula bar.*** The formula bar is directly under the ribbon and just to the right of the "fx" sign. The formula bar shows the current contents of the selected cell, and it allows you to edit the cell contents. You can also edit the contents of a cell by ***clicking in the cell*** and then pressing the **[F2]** key.

G. *Column Width/Row Height*—You can change the width of a column by ***clicking the line to the right of the column heading.*** (This is the line that separates two columns. When you point to a line, the cursor changes to double-headed vertical arrows.) ***Next, drag the pointer to the right or to the left to increase or decrease the column width, respectively.*** Similarly, you can change the height of a row by ***clicking and dragging the horizontal line separating two rows.*** You can also change the width of a column or height of a row, by ***clicking the Home tab, and then clicking Format in the Cells group.***

H. *Insert*—You can insert one row or column by ***clicking the Home tab, then clicking the down arrow below the Insert icon in the Cells group, and clicking either Insert Sheet Rows or Insert Sheet Columns.*** You can also insert a number of rows or columns by ***dragging the pointer over the number of rows or columns you want to add, clicking the Home tab, clicking the down arrow below the Insert icon in the Cells group, and then clicking either Insert Sheet Rows or Insert Sheet Columns.*** Finally, you can ***right-click and select Insert from the menu.***

I. *Erase/Delete*—You can erase data by ***dragging the pointer over the area*** and then pressing the **[DEL]** key. You can also erase by ***dragging the pointer over the area, then clicking the Home ribbon tab, then clicking the down arrow next to the Clear icon in the Editing group, and then clicking Clear All.*** You can also delete whole columns or rows by ***pointing and clicking in a column or row, then clicking on the Home ribbon tab, then clicking on the down arrow next to Delete in the Cells group, and then clicking either Delete Sheet Rows or Delete Sheet Columns.*** You can also delete whole columns or rows by ***pointing in the column or row and then right-clicking and selecting Delete.***

J. *Quit*—To quit Excel, ***click on the File tab and then click Close.***

K. *Copy*—To copy data to adjacent columns or rows, ***click in the cell you wish to copy and then select the AutoFill command***, which is accessed from the small black box at the bottom right corner of the selected cell. Then ***drag the pointer to where the data should be placed.*** You can also copy data by ***clicking in the cell, right-clicking, and then clicking Copy, then clicking in the location where the information should be copied***, and pressing the **[ENTER]** key. Finally, data can also be copied by ***clicking and dragging to highlight the information to be copied, clicking the Home tab, and then clicking Copy in the clipboard group.*** Then go to the location where the information should be copied, ***click the Home tab, and click Paste in the Clipboard group.***

L. *Move*—Move data by ***clicking on the cell, right-clicking, selecting Cut, clicking in the location where the information should be inserted***, and pressing the **[ENTER]** key. Data can also be moved by ***highlighting the information to be moved, clicking the Home tab***, and then ***clicking Cut in the Clipboard group.*** Then go to the location where the information should be moved, ***click the Home tab***, and **click Paste in the Clipboard group.**

M. *Saving and Opening Files*—Save a file by ***clicking on the File tab***, then ***clicking Save or Save as***, and typing the file name. You can also save a file by ***clicking on the Save icon*** (it looks like a floppy disk) on the Quick Access toolbar (see Excel Exhibit 6-1). Open a file that was previously saved by ***clicking on the File tab***, then ***click Open***, and type (or click) the name of the file to be opened.

N. *Print*—To print a file, ***click on the File tab***, then ***click Print***, and then ***click Print.***

II. Numbers and Formulas

A. *Numbers*—To enter a number in a cell ***click in the cell***, type the number and press the **[ENTER]** key or an arrow (cursor) key.

B. *Adding Cells (Addition)*—You can add the contents of two or more cells by three different methods:

1. To add the contents of a range of two or more cells,
   a. ***Click in the cell where the total should be placed.***
   b. ***Click the Home tab***, then ***click the Sum icon ("Σ")*** in the Editing group (see Excel Exhibit 6-1). The Sum icon looks like the Greek letter "E." (*Note:* to see the name of an icon, point at the icon for a second and the name of the icon will be displayed.)
   c. Excel guesses which cells you want to add. Press **[ENTER]** if the correct range is automatically selected, or select the correct range by highlighting it (i.e., ***clicking and dragging until the range of cells to be added is selected).*** Then press **[ENTER]** key.
2. To add the contents of two cells, which need not compose a range:
   a. ***Click in the cell where the total should be placed.***
   b. ***Press*** = (the equal sign).
   c. Type the address of the first cell to be added (e.g., C4), or ***click in that cell.***
   d. ***Press*** + (the plus sign).
   e. Enter the address of the second cell to be added (e.g., C5) or ***click in that cell.***
   f. Press the **[ENTER]** key. (For example, to add the values of C4 and C5, the formula would read = ***C4 + C5***).
3. To add the contents of a range of two or more cells:
   a. ***Click in the cell where the total should be placed.***
   b. Type **=SUM(**
   c. Enter the address of the first cell to be added (e.g., C4), or ***click in that cell.***
   d. Press **:** (a colon).
   e. Enter the address of the second cell to be added (e.g., C5), or ***click in that cell.***
   f. Press **)** (a closing parenthesis).
   g. Press the **[ENTER]** key. (For example, to add the values of C4 and C5, the formula would read = ***SUM(C4:C5)*****)**.

C. *Subtracting Cells*—To subtract the contents of one or more cells from those of another:

1. ***Click in the cell where the total should be placed.***
2. Press = (the equal sign).
3. Enter the first cell address (e.g., C4), or ***click in that cell.***
4. Press - (the minus sign).
5. Enter the second cell address (e.g., C5), or ***click in that cell.***
6. Press the **[ENTER]** key. (For example, to subtract the value of C4 from the value of C5, the formula would read = ***C5 - C4***).

D. *Multiplying Cells*—To multiply the contents of two (or more) cells:

1. ***Click in the cell where the total should be placed.***
2. Press = (the equal sign).
3. Enter the first cell address (e.g., C4) or ***click in that cell.***
4. Press * (hold the [SHIFT] key and press the [8] key).
5. Enter the second cell address (e.g., C5), or ***click in that cell.***
6. Press the **[ENTER]** key. (For example, to multiply the value in C4 times the value in C5, the formula would read = ***C5 * C4***).

E. *Dividing Cells*—To divide two cells,
   1. ***Click in the cell where the total should be placed.***
   2. Press = (the equal sign).
   3. Enter the first cell address (e.g., C4) or ***click in that cell.***
   4. Press **/** (the forward slash).
   5. Enter the second cell address (e.g., C5), or ***click in that cell.***

Press the **[ENTER]** key. (For example, to divide the value in C4 by the value in C5, the formula would read = ***C4/C5***).

III. Basic Lessons

LESSON 1: Building a Budget Spreadsheet—Part A

This lesson shows you how to build the spreadsheet in Excel Exhibit 6-2—Excel Tutorial Budget Spreadsheet. It explains how to use the [CTRL] [HOME] command; move the cell pointer; enter text, values, and formulas; adjust the width of columns; change the format of cells to currency; use the bold feature; use the AutoFill and Copy features to copy formulas; and print and save a spreadsheet. Keep in mind that if at any time you make a mistake in this lesson, you may press **[CTRL] [Z]** to undo what you have done.

1. Open Windows. Then, ***double-click on the Microsoft Office Excel 2013 icon on the desktop*** to open the program. Alternatively, ***click on the "Start" button, point to "Programs" or "All Programs," point to Microsoft Office, and then click Microsoft Excel 2013.*** You should be in a clean, blank workbook. If you are not in a blank workbook, ***click on the File tab*** (see Excel Exhibit 6-1), ***click on New, and then click Blank Workbook.***
2. Notice that the cell pointer is at cell A1 and the current cell indicator (also called the name box by Excel) shows **A1**. The "name" box is just under the ribbon and all the way to the left (see Excel Exhibit 6-2). Also notice that you can move the pointer around the spreadsheet using the cursor keys. Go back to cell A1 by pressing **[CTRL] [HOME]**.

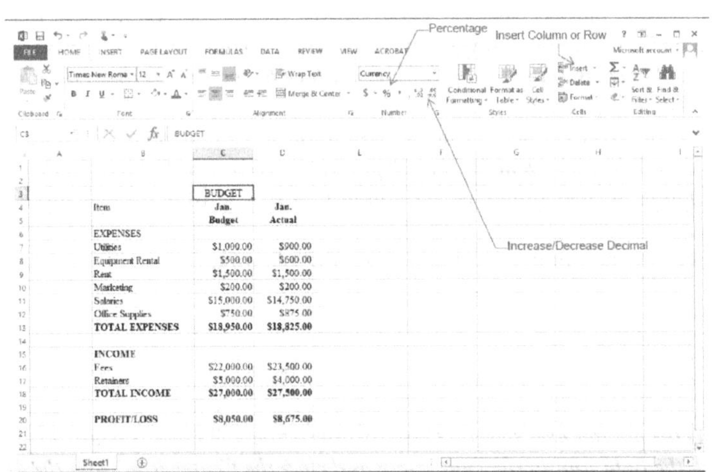

Excel Exhibit 6-2 Excel Tutorial Budget Spreadsheet

3. Go to cell C3 by ***clicking in cell C3*** or by pressing the **[RIGHT ARROW]** twice, and then pressing the **[DOWN ARROW]** twice.

   You will now enter the title of the spreadsheet in cell C3. Type **BUDGET** and then press the **[ENTER]** key.
4. Notice that the cell pointer is now at cell C4.
5. Press the **[UP ARROW]** to go back to cell C3. Notice that BUDGET is left aligned. To center **BUDGET** in the cell, ***from the Home tab, click the Center icon in the Alignment group.*** It is the icon with several lines on it that appear centered. *Note:* If you hover the mouse over an icon on the ribbon for a second, the name of the icon will be displayed. Alternatively, ***from the Home tab, click the Alignment Group Dialog Box Launcher. Next, on the Alignment tab, under the Horizontal field, click the down arrow and select Center. Click OK.***
6. You should now be ready to enter the budget information. First, move the cell pointer to where the data should go, then type the data, and finally, enter the data by pressing the **[ENTER]** key or one of the arrow (cursor) keys. ***Type*** the remaining row labels as follows:

   Item in B4
   EXPENSES in B6
   Utilities in B7
   Equipment Rental in B8
   Rent in B9
   Marketing in B10
   Salaries in B11
   Office Supplies in B12
   TOTAL EXPENSES in B13
   INCOME in B15
   Fees in B16
   Retainers in B17
   TOTAL INCOME in B18
   PROFIT/LOSS in B20
7. Notice that in Column B some of the data (such as "**TOTAL EXPENSES**" and "**Equipment Rental**") actually extend into Column C. To correct this, you must increase the column width of Column B. ***Put the mouse pointer in the cell letter B at the top of the screen. Move the pointer to the right edge of the column.*** The pointer should then change to a double-headed vertical arrow and the column width will be displayed in a small box. ***Drag the pointer to the right until the column width is 18.00.*** Alternatively, you can change the cell width by ***placing the cell pointer anywhere in Column B; then, from the Home tab, click Format in the Cell groups, click Column Width***, type **18** in the dialogue box, then ***click OK.***
8. Notice that all of the data entries now fit in the column. Enter the following:

   Jan. in C4
   Budget in C5
   Jan. in D4
   Actual in D5
9. ***Click in cell C4 and drag the pointer over to cell D5*** (so that the whole cell range is highlighted); ***then from the Home tab, click the Bold icon in the Font group and click the Center icon from the Alignment group.***

10. You are now ready to enter values into your spreadsheet.
11. ***Move the cell pointer to cell C7.*** Type **1000**. Do not type a dollar sign or comma; these will be added later. Press the **[ENTER]** key to enter the value.
12. Enter the following:

    500 in C8
    1500 in C9
    200 in C10
    15000 in C11
    750 in C12
    22000 in C16
    5000 in C17
    900 in D7
    600 in D8
    1500 in D9
    200 in D10
    14750 in D11
    875 in D12
    23500 in D16
    4000 in D17

13. The values you entered do not have dollar signs or the commas appropriate to a currency format. You will now learn how to format a range of cells for a particular format (such as the currency format).
14. ***Click in cell C7 and drag the pointer over to cell D20. From the Home tab, click the down arrow next to the "Number Format" box in the Number group, which should say General. Then, click Currency.*** Notice that dollar sign has been added to all of the values. ***Click in any cell to deselect the cell range.***
15. ***Click in cell B13, and drag the pointer over to cell D13; then, from the Home tab, click the Bold icon in the Font group.*** This will make the TOTAL EXPENSES row appear in bold.
16. ***Click in cell B18, and drag the pointer over to cell D18; then, from the Home tab, click the Bold icon in the Font group.*** This will make the TOTAL INCOME row appear in bold.
17. ***Click in cell B20, drag the mouse over to cell D20; and drag the pointer over to cell D18; then, from the Home tab, click the Bold icon in the Font group.*** This will make the PROFIT/LOSS row appear in bold.
18. Your spreadsheet is nearly complete; all you need to add are the six formulas.
19. ***Click in cell C13***
20. Type **=SUM(** and press **[UP ARROW]** until the cell pointer is at cell C7. Press **.** (the period) to anchor the range.
21. Press the **[DOWN ARROW]** five times, press the) (close parenthesis), and then press the **[ENTER]** key.
22. Go back to cell C13 and look at the formula in the formula bar. The formula should read **=SUM(C7:C12)**. The total should read $19,700. *Note:* you also could have typed the formula (=C7+C8+C9+C10+C11+12).
23. Enter the following formulas:

    =SUM(D7:D12) in D13
    =SUM(C16:C17) in C18
    =SUM(D16:D17) in D18

24. We now need to enter formulas for the **PROFIT/LOSS** columns. Enter the following formula:

    =C18–C13 in C20 (The total should read $8050.)

25. ***Go to cell C20 and click the AutoFill command*** (it is the small black square at the bottom right of the cell). ***Drag its one column to the right and release the mouse button.*** Notice that the formula has been copied. The total should be $8675. Alternatively, you could ***go to cell C20, right-click Copy, then move the pointer to cell D20***, and press the **[ENTER]** key.
26. The spreadsheet is now complete. To print the spreadsheet, ***click on the File tab, then click Print, and then click Print.***
27. You will need to save the spreadsheet, because you will use it in Lesson 2. To save the spreadsheet, ***click on the File tab and then click Save.*** You may save the file to your computer, to Microsoft SkyDrive or both. ***Under Save in: select the drive or folder*** in which you would like to save the document. Next to File Name, type **Budget1** and ***click Save.***
28. To quit Excel, ***click on the File tab, then click Close.***

This concludes Lesson 1.
To go to Lesson 2, stay at the current screen.

LESSON 2: Building a Budget Spreadsheet—Part B

This lesson assumes that you have completed Lesson 1, have saved the spreadsheet in the lesson, and are generally familiar with the concepts covered. Lesson 2 gives you more experience in copying formulas, formatting cells, and working with ranges of cells. It also shows you how to insert a row of data (see Excel Exhibit 6-3—Excel Tutorial Expanded Budget Spreadsheet). If you did not exit Excel after Lesson 1, skip Steps 1 and 2 below and go directly to Step 3.

1. Open Windows. Then, ***double-click on the Microsoft Office Excel 2013 icon on the desktop*** to open the program. Alternatively, ***click on the "Start" button, point to "Programs" or "All Programs," point to Microsoft Office, and then click Microsoft Excel 2013.*** You should be in a clean, blank workbook. If you are not in a blank workbook, ***click on the File tab*** (see Excel Exhibit 6-1), ***click on New, and then click Blank Workbook.***
2. To retrieve the spreadsheet from Lesson 1, ***click on the File tab and then click Open. Next, click the name of your file*** (e.g., **Budget** 1). ***If you do not see it, look under Recent Workbooks to*** find the file. When you have found it, ***click on Open.***
3. You will be entering the information shown in Excel Exhibit 6-3—Excel Tutorial Expanded Budget Spreadsheet. Notice in Excel Exhibit 6-3—Excel Tutorial Expanded Budget Spreadsheet that a line for insurance appears in row B9. You will insert this row first.
4. ***Click in cell B9. From the Home tab, click the down arrow below Insert in the Cells group. On the Insert menu, click Insert Sheet Rows.*** A new row has been added. You could also have ***right-clicked and selected Insert*** to open a dialog box with the option to insert another row.
5. Enter the following:

    Insurance in B9
    500 in C9
    450 in D9

6. Notice that when the new values for Insurance were entered, all of the formulas were updated. Since you inserted the additional rows in the middle of the column, the formulas recognized the new

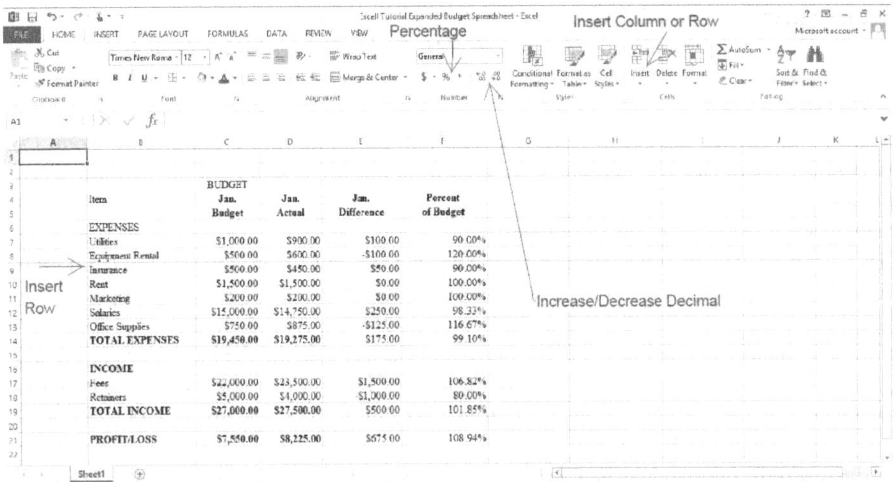

Excel Exhibit 6-3 Excel Tutorial Expanded Budget Spreadsheet

Used with permission from Microsoft.

numbers and automatically recalculated to reflect them. Be extremely careful when inserting new rows and columns into spreadsheets that have existing formulas. In some cases, the new number will not be reflected in the totals, such as when rows or columns are inserted at the beginning of the range that a formula calculates. It is always prudent to go back to each existing formula, examine the formula range, and make sure the new values are included in the formula range.

7. Change the column width in Column E to 12 by ***clicking the column heading (the letter E)*** at the top of the screen. ***Move your pointer to the right edge of the column.*** The pointer should then change to a double-headed vertical arrow. ***Drag the pointer to the right until the column width is 12.*** Alternatively, change the cell width by ***placing the cell pointer anywhere in Column E and, from the Home tab, click Format in the Cells Group, and select Column Width…***Then type **12** and ***click OK.***
8. Enter the following:

   Jan. in E4
   Difference in E5
   Percent in F4
   Of Budget in F5

9. ***Go to cell E4 and drag the pointer over to cell F5*** so that the additional column headings are highlighted, then ***Right-click***. Notice that in addition to a menu, the Mini toolbar appears. It has a number of formatting options on it including Font, Font size, Bold, and other. ***Click the Bold icon on the Mini toolbar. Point and click the Center icon on the Mini toolbar.***
10. ***Go to cell E14 and drag the pointer over to cell F14. Then right-click and click on the*** Bold ***icon on the Mini toolbar.***
11. ***Go to cell E19 and drag the pointer over to cell F19. Then right-click and click on the*** Bold ***icon on the Mini toolbar.***
12. ***Go to cell E21 and drag the pointer over to cell F21. Then right-click and click on the*** Bold ***icon on the Mini toolbar.***

13. You are now ready to change the cell formatting for Column E to Currency and Column F to Percent. ***Go to cell E7 and drag the pointer down to cell E21. Right-click and select Format Cells. From the*** Number ***tab in the "Format Cells" window, click*** Currency ***and then on*** OK. ***Click on any cell to get rid of the cell range.***
14. ***Go to cell F7 and drag the pointer down to cell F21. From the Home tab, click the Percent (%) icon in the Number group (see*** Excel Exhibit 6-3), ***then from the Home tab, click the Increase Decimal icon twice.***
15. ***Click on any cell to get rid of the cell range.***
16. All that is left to do is to enter the formulas for the two new columns. The entries in the **Jan. Difference** column subtract the budgeted amount from the actual amount for each expense item. A positive amount in this column means that the office was under budget on that item. A negative balance means that the office was over budget on that line item. The **Percent of Budget** column divides that actual amount by the budgeted amount. This shows the percentage of the budgeted money that was actually spent for each item.
17. You will first build one formula in the **Jan. Difference** column and then copy it. ***Click in cell E7***, enter **=C7–D7**, and press the **[ENTER]** key.
18. Using the **AutoFill** command or the **Copy** command, copy this formula down through cell E14. (To copy, ***right-click and then click Copy; highlight the area where the information should go; then right-click and select Paste.*** Alternatively, you can use the Copy and Paste icons in the Clipboard group on the Home tab.)
19. ***Click in cell E17***, type **=D17–C17**, and press the **[ENTER]** key.
20. Using the **AutoFill** command, copy this formula down through cell E21. Delete the formula in cell E20 ***by clicking on cell E20*** and by pressing the **[DEL]** key.
21. You will now build on the formula in the **Percent of Budget** column and copy it. ***Click in cell F7***, type **=D7/C7**, and press the **[ENTER]** key.
22. Using the **AutoFill** command, copy this formula down through cell F21. Delete the formula in cells F15, F16, and F20 by ***clicking on the cell*** and then by pressing the **[DEL]** key.
23. The spreadsheet has now been built. We will now build a bar chart that shows our budgeted expenses compared to our actual expenses.
24. Make sure you the save the changes to **Budget** 1 made in Lesson 2. To quit Excel, ***click on the File tab, then click Close.*** Make sure to save the changes ma

This concludes Lesson 2.
To go to Lesson 3, stay at the current screen.

LESSON 3: Creating a Chart for the Budget Spreadsheet—Part C

This lesson assumes that you have completed Lessons 1 and 2, saved the spreadsheet, and are generally familiar with the concepts covered in those lessons. Lesson 3 gives you more experience with creating charts to demonstrate the data entered in the previous lessons along with printing the material. If you did not exit Excel after Lesson 2, skip Steps 1 and 2 below and go directly to Step 3.

1. Open Windows. Then, ***double-click*** on the ***Microsoft Office Excel 2013 icon*** on the desktop to open the program. Alternatively, ***click*** the ***"Start" button, point to "Programs" or "All Programs," point to Microsoft Office, and then click Microsoft Excel 2013.*** You should be in a clean, blank workbook. If you are not in a blank workbook, ***click on the File tab*** (see Excel Exhibit 6-1), ***click on New, and then click Blank Workbook.***

2. To retrieve the spreadsheet used in Lessons 1 and 2, ***click on the File tab and then click Open.*** Next, ***click the name of your file*** (e.g., **Budget** 1). If you do not see it, look under ***Recent Workbooks*** to find the file. When you have found it, ***click Open.***
3. ***Click in cell B7 and then drag the pointer down and over to cell D14. The pointer changes shape depending on the action. To perform this action the pointer should look like a "thick white plus sign."***
4. At the lower right corner of the highlighted data, you should see the **Quick Analysis** icon. ***Click the Quick Analysis icon***, then ***click CHARTS***, then ***click More Charts*** (see Excel Exhibit 6-4). The Insert Chart box will open. ***Click All Charts*** in the Insert Chart box. ***Click Column*** (on the left side of the Insert Chart box), ***then click the fourth option from the left, 3-D Cluster Column. Click OK.***

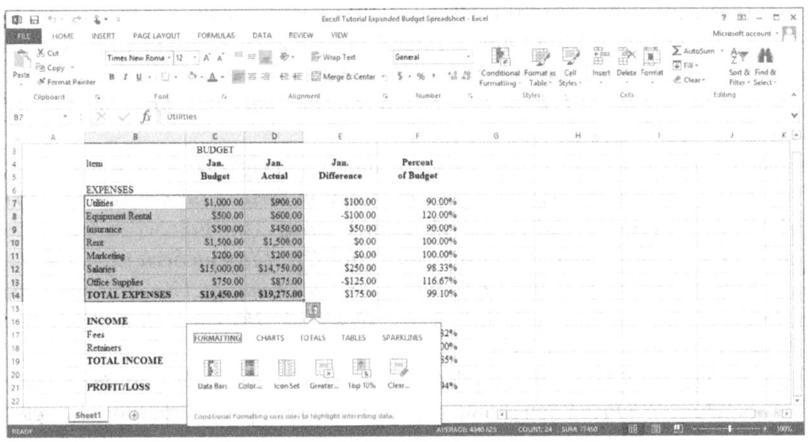

Excel Exhibit 6-4 Excel Tutorial Expanded Budget Spreadsheet with Quick Analysis

Used with permission from Microsoft.

5. Notice that a draft bar chart has been created. ***Move your mouse anywhere in the chart frame*** (see Excel Exhibit 6-5), ***and your pointer will turn to a four-headed arrow. Drag the chart across the spreadsheet so that the upper left corner of the chart is near cell G4.***

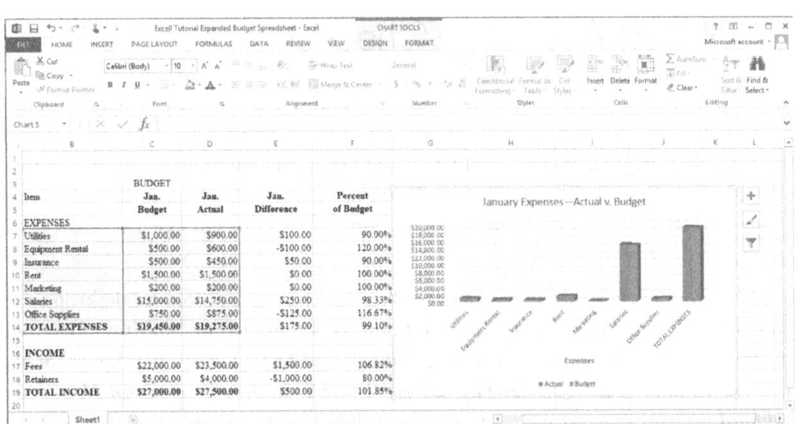

Excel Exhibit 6-5 Excel Tutorial Expanded Budget Spreadsheet with Bar Chart

Used with permission from Microsoft.

6. ***Using the horizontal scroll bar*** (see Excel Exhibit 6-5), ***scroll to the right*** so that the chart is completely in your screen (if necessary).
7. ***Move your cursor so it is on the bottom right corner of the chart frame.*** Your cursor should change to ***a two-headed arrow that is diagonal. Drag the chart so that the bottom right corner ends near cell K19*** (see Excel Exhibit 6-5).
8. Notice that new options have been added to the ribbon (Chart Tools Design and Format). ***Click the Design ribbon tab under Chart Tools.***
9. ***Click Chart Title in the chart and notice that a text box opens around the field "Chart Title."***
10. ***Click on the "Chart Title" text in the chart and press the [DEL] key and [Backspace] key until the text is gone.*** Type **January Expenses—Actual v. Budget.** If you would like to move the title—for example, if it is off centered—just click the title frame and drag it where you would like.
11. In the top left hand corner ***Click on "Add Chart Element" tab*** and ***click "Axis Titles"*** option. Then ***click "Primary (Horizontal)." Click the Axis Title at the bottom of the chart.*** Notice that a text box opens around the field ***"Axis Title." Click the Axis Title text in the chart***, then ***press the [DEL]*** and ***[Backspace] keys until the text is gone***. Type **Expenses.**
12. To change the legend from Series 1 and Series 2 to Actual and Budge, ***right-click on Series 1***, then ***click Select Data.*** The "Select Data Source" window will open. ***Click on Series 1 (under Legend Entries [Series]) to highlight it***, **then click on Edit** ***under the same heading.*** The "Edit Series" window will open. Type **Actual** in the text box under Series name; ***then click OK. Click on Series 2 (under Legend Entries [Series]) to highlight it, then click on Edit under the same heading.*** The "Edit Series" window will open. Type **Budget** in the text box under Series name; ***then click OK.*** Then, ***click OK in the Select Data Source Window.*** (See Excel Exhibit 6-5).
13. To print the chart, ***click on the File tab***, then ***click Print; under Settings, make sure Print Selected Chart is selected and then click Print.*** You should see a preview of the printed chart on the right side of the screen.
14. To quit Excel, ***click on the File tab, then click Close.***

This concludes Lesson 3.
To go to Lesson 4, you will need to create a new Excel spreadsheet.

IV. Advanced Lessons

LESSON 4: Client Trust Account—Checkbook Register

This lesson assumes that you have completed the previous three lessons and have a basic understanding of Excel. In this advanced lesson, you will learn how to build the spreadsheet in Excel Exhibit 6-6—Excel Tutorial Client Trust Account. After you have built the spreadsheet template, you will decide what information is entered into the spreadsheet based on facts that are given to you. Keep in mind that if at any time you make a mistake in this lesson, you can simply press [**CTRL**][**Z**] to undo what you have done. If you did not exit Excel after Lesson 1, skip Steps 1 and 2 below and go directly to Step 3.

1. Open Windows. Then, double-click on the Microsoft Office Excel 2013 icon on the desktop to open the program. Alternatively, click on the "Start" button, point to "Programs" or "All Programs," point to Microsoft Office, and then click Microsoft Excel 2013. You should be in a clean, blank workbook. If you are not in a blank workbook, ***click on the File tab*** (see Excel Exhibit 6-1), ***click on New, and then click Blank Workbook.***

2. Notice that the cell pointer is at cell A1 and the current cell indicator (also called the name box by Excel) shows A1. The "name" box is just under the ribbon and all the way to the left (see Excel Exhibit 6-1). Also notice that you can move the pointer around the spreadsheet using the cursor keys. Go back to cell A1 by pressing the [CTRL][HOME] keys.
3. To start building the spreadsheet in Excel Exhibit 6-6—Excel Tutorial Client Trust Account, you will need to increase the width of Column D. Put the mouse pointer in the cell with letter D at the top of the screen. Move the pointer to the right edge of the column. The pointer should then change to a double-headed vertical arrow and the column width will be displayed in a small box. Drag the pointer to the right until the column width is 38.00. Alternatively, you can change the cell width by placing the cell pointer anywhere in Column D; then, from the Home tab, ***click Format in the Cell groups, click Column Width***, type **38** in the dialogue box, then ***click OK.***

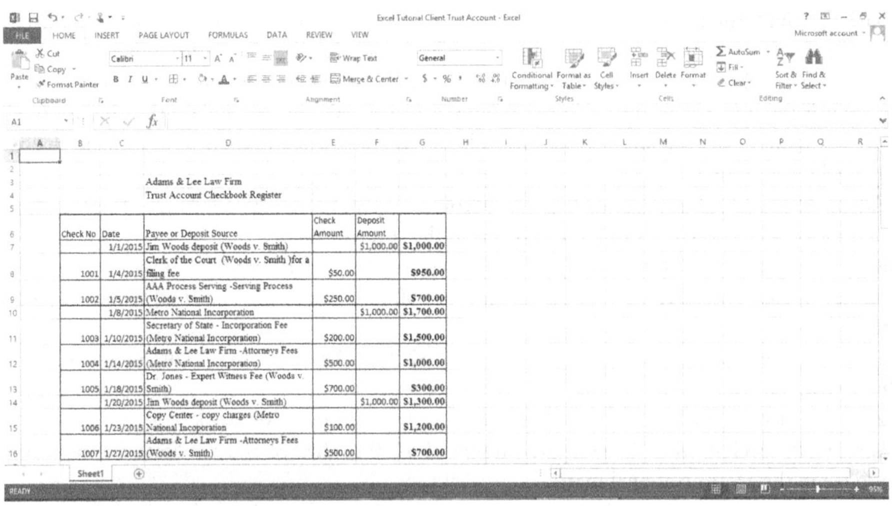

Excel Exhibit 6-6 Excel Tutorial Client Trust Checking Account

Used with permission from Microsoft.

4. You will need to add the "wrap text" feature to prevent the information you enter from going into the next column. ***Click at the top of*** Column D (the entire column should be highlighted). From the Home tab, ***click Wrap Text under Alignment.***
5. In cell D3, type **Adams & Lee Law Firm.**
6. In cell D4, type **Trust Account Checkbook Register.**
7. Change the format for cells C7 through C90 to a date column. ***Point and click on cell C7 and drag the pointer to cell C90.*** With cells C7 through C90 still highlighted, from the Home tab, ***click the drop-down menu under Numbers, and click "short date."***
8. Change the format for cells E7 to G90 to currency. ***Point and click on cell E7 and drag the pointer to cell G90.*** With cells E7 through G90 still highlighted, from the Home tab ***click the drop-down menu under Numbers, and click "currency."***
9. Looking at Excel Exhibit 6-6—Excel Tutorial Client Trust Account, enter the following data as column headings in cells B6, C6, and D6: in cell B6, type **Check No.**; in cell C6, type **Date**; in cell D6, type **Payee or Deposit Source.**

10. Enter the following data as column headings in cells E6, F6, and G6: in cell E6, type **Check Amount**; in cell F6, type **Deposit Amount**; in cell G6, type **Balance**. For cells E6 and F6, you will need to wrap the text down. ***Click cell E6***, then from the Home tab, ***click Wrap Text under Alignment. Click cell F6***, then from the Home tab, ***click Wrap Text under Alignment.***
11. Enter the value: **1000** in cell F7.
12. The following formula should be entered:

    In cell G7, type **=F7–E7**, then **ENTER.**
    In cell G8, type **=G7+F8–E8**, then **ENTER.**
    -***Use the*** AutoFill ***command to copy the formula series from cell G8 to cell G16. Click on cell G8***, then ***place the pointer in the bottom right corner of the cell (using the black plus sign) and drag it over the cells from G8 to G16.***

13. You have now built the template of the spreadsheet and you are ready to enter information into it. Using the spreadsheet, enter information into the Checkbook Register (see below). For each entry, you will need to input the check number (if it is a check), who is the payee or deposit source, the case name and what it is for (e.g., Clerk of the Court [Woods v. Smith] File Fee), and place the amount in either the check amount or deposit amount column. The spreadsheet will automatically calculate the balance in the checking account.
14. The Adams & Lee Law Firm opened the trust account on January 1 with a balance of zero in the account. Please record the following transactions in the spreadsheet:
    a. January 1, deposit for $1000 from Jim Woods regarding *Woods v. Smith.*
    b. January 4, check number 1001 in the amount of $50 to Clerk of the Court in Woods v. Smith for a filing fee.
    c. January 5, check number 1002 in the amount of $250 to AAA Process Serving in Woods v. Smith for serving process.
    d. January 8, deposit for $1000 from Metro National for incorporation work.
    e. January 10, check number 1003 in the amount of $200 to the Secretary of State for the incorporation fee in the Metro National matter.
    f. January 14, check number 1004 in the amount of $500 to Adams & Lee Law Firm for attorneys' fees incurred in Metro National incorporation matter.
    g. January 18, check number 1005 in the amount of $700 to Dr. Jones in Woods v. Smith for an expert witness fee.
    h. January 20, deposit from Jim Woods (Woods v. Smith) of $1000.
    i. January 23, check number 1006 in the amount of $100 to Copy Center, regarding copying charges for Metro National incorporation.
    j. January 27, check number 1007 in the amount of $500 to Adams & Lee Law Firm for attorneys' fees incurred in Woods v. Smith.
15. After entering all of the transactions, the balance in the trust account should be $700.
16. To add borders around the cells, ***click on cell B6, then drag the pointer***, (using white plus sign) ***to cell G16.*** From the Home tab, ***click the drop-down menu on the "Borders" icon under Font*** (looks like "four squares"), then ***click* "All Borders."**
17. You will next print out your spreadsheet on one page. ***Click File, then click Print.*** Under **Settings**, you will need to choose the last group of selections (scaling). ***Click on the drop-down menu and click "Fit Sheet on One Page,"*** then ***click Print.*** This will compress everything in the print area to one page.
18. To save the document, ***click on File, then click Save or Save As*** and ***type* Trust Account Spreadsheet** under File name, then ***click Save.***
19. To quit Excel, ***click on the File tab, then click Close.***

This concludes Lesson 4.
To go to Lesson 5, stay at the current screen.

LESSON 5: Client Trust Account—Client Registers

This lesson assumes that you have completed Lesson 4 and have a basic understanding of Excel. In this advanced lesson, you will learn how to build the spreadsheet in Excel Exhibit 6-7—Excel Tutorial Client Trust Account. You will be building subsidiary ledgers for each client (see Exhibit 6-2 earlier in the chapter). After you have built the spreadsheet template, you will copy information from Lesson 4 into them. Keep in mind that if at any time you make a mistake in this lesson, you can simply press **[CTRL][Z]** to undo what you have done.

1. Open Windows. Then, ***double-click on the Microsoft Office Excel 2013 icon on the desktop*** to open the program. Alternatively, ***click on the "Start" button, point to "Programs" or "All Programs," point to Microsoft Office, and then click Microsoft Excel 2013***. You should be in a clean, blank workbook. If you are not in a blank workbook, ***click on the File tab*** (see Excel Exhibit 6-1), ***click on New, and then click Blank Workbook.***
2. To retrieve the previously saved "Trust Account Spreadsheet" (from Lesson 4), ***click on the File tab, then click Open.*** Then ***click the name of your file* (e.g., Trust Account Spreadsheet)**. ***If you do not see it, look under Recent Worbooks*** to find the file. When you have found it, ***click Open.***
3. Look at Excel Exhibit 6-7—Excel Tutorial Client Trust Account and enter the following data: in cell D19, type **Jim Woods (Woods v. Smith) Subsidiary** Ledger; in cell D29, type **Metro National Incorporation Work, Subsidiary Ledger**; in D20 and D30, type **Description of Transactions.**

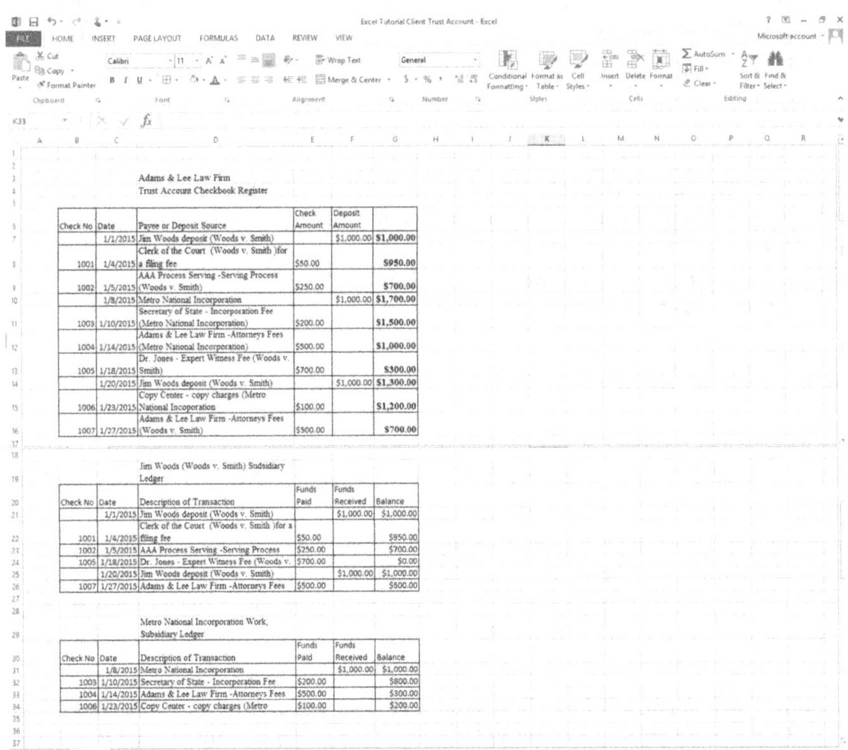

Excel Exhibit 6-7 Excel Tutorial Client Trust Accounts

Used with permission from Microsoft.

4. Use the "Wrap Text" and enter the following data: in cell E20 and F20, type **Funds** Paid; in cell E30 and F30, type **Funds Received.**
5. Draw separate borders for the subsidiary ledgers of Jim Woods (Woods v. Smith) and Metro National.
6. The following formulas should be entered:

   In cell G21, type **=F21-E21** and **ENTER.**
   In cell G22, type **=G21+F22-E22** and **ENTER.**
   -Use the AutoFill ***command to copy the formula series from cell G22 to cell G23 through G26. Click on cell G22,*** then ***place the pointer in the bottom right corner of the cell (using the black plus sign) and drag it over the cells from G22 to G26.***
   In cell G31, type **=F31-E31.**
   In cell G32, type **=G31+F32-E32.**
   -Use the AutoFill command to copy the formula series from cell G32 to cell G33 and G34. Click on cell G32, then ***place the pointer in the bottom right corner of the cell (using the black plus sign) and drag it over the cells from G32 to G34.***
7. With the subsidiary ledgers now built, you are ready to enter the data that applies to each client in his or her respective ledger. (You will not even have to retype the data.)
8. ***Click on cell C21, then type*** = (an equal sign), then ***click on cell C7, and press the*** **[ENTER]** ***key.*** Notice that the contents of C7 now appear in cell C21.
9. ***Click on cell D21. Then, type*** = (an equal sign), ***click on cell D7, and press the*** **[ENTER]** ***key.*** Notice that the contents of D7 now appear in cell D21.
10. ***Click on cell F21. Then, type*** = (an equal sign), ***point and click on cell F7, and press the*** **[ENTER]** ***key.*** Notice that the contents of F7 now appear in cell F21.
11. Using this method, copy all of the transitions from the Trust Account—Checkbook Register down to the appropriate subsidiary ledger for each client. When you are finished, the balance of the Jim Woods ledger should be $500 and the balance for Metro National should be $200.
12. Print out the Trust Account Checkbook Register and both subsidiary ledgers on one page using the method from Lesson 4.
13. To save the document, ***click on the File tab, then click Save.***
14. To quit Excel, ***click on the File tab, then click Close.***

This concludes Lesson 5.
To go to Lesson 6, stay at the current screen.

LESSON 6: Client Trust Account—Client Summary Ledger

This lesson assumes that you have completed Lessons 4 and 5 and have a basic understanding of Excel. In this advanced lesson, you will learn how to build the spreadsheet (Client Summary Ledger) in Excel Exhibit 6-8—Excel Tutorial. You will be putting the balance of the client subsidiary ledgers into a client summary ledger report (see Exhibit 6-2 example found earlier in the chapter). Keep in mind that if at any time you make a mistake in this lesson, you can simply press **[CTRL][Z]** to undo what you have done.

1. Open Windows. Then, ***double-click on the Microsoft Office Excel 2013 icon on the desktop*** to open the program. Alternatively, ***click on the "Start" button, point to "Programs" or "All Programs," point to Microsoft Office, and then click Microsoft Excel 2013.*** You should be in a clean, blank workbook. If you are not in a blank workbook, ***click on the File tab*** (see Excel Exhibit 6-1), ***click on New, and then click Blank Workbook.***

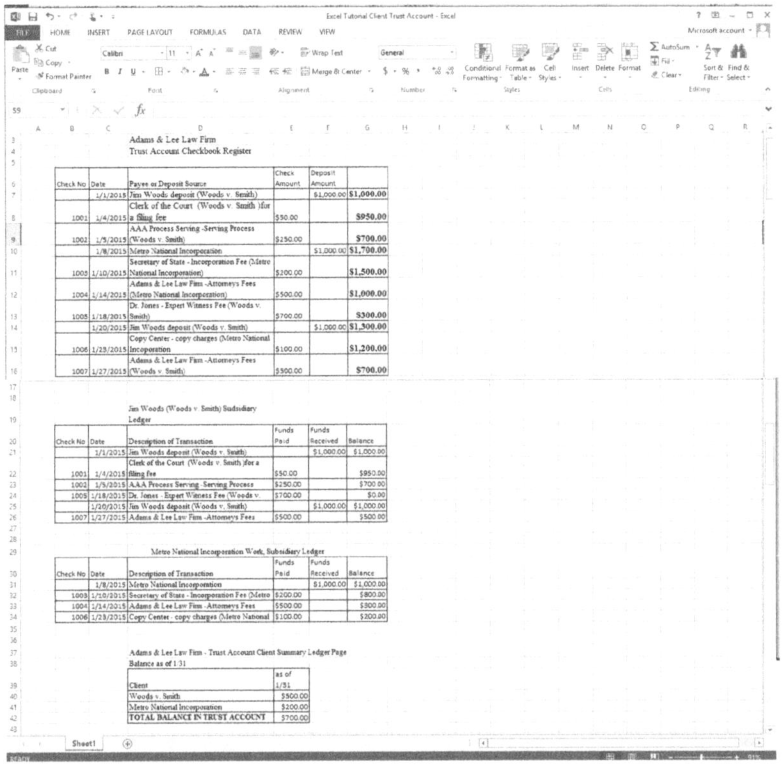

Excel Exhibit 6-8 Excel Tutorial Client Summary Ledger of Trust Accounts

Used with permission from Microsoft.

2. To retrieve the previously saved "Trust Account Spreadsheet" (from Lesson 4), ***click on the File tab, then click Open.*** Then ***click the name of your file* (e.g., Trust Account Spreadsheet).** ***If you do not see it, look under Recent Worbooks*** to find the file. When you have found it, ***click Open.***
3. In cell D37, ***type* Adams & Lee Law Firm—Trust Account Client Summary Ledger Page**. You may want the title to extend across cells. ***Click and drag the pointer*** (showing a white plus sign) ***across columns E and F.*** From the Home tab, ***click on Merge & Center under Alignment.***
4. In cell D38, ***type* Balance as of 1/31.**
5. In cell D39, ***type* Client.**
6. In cell E39, ***type* Balance as of 1/31.** ***Click Wrap Text*** from Home tab under ***Alignment.***
7. In cell D40, ***type* Woods v. Smith.** Go to E40 and ***type*** = (an equal sign), then ***click G26***, then press **[ENTER]**.
8. In cell D41, ***type* Metro National Incorporation.** Go to E41 and ***type*** = (an equal sign), then ***click G34***, then press **[ENTER]**.
9. In cell D42, ***type* TOTAL BALANCE IN TRUST ACCOUNT.**
10. In cell E42, use the AutoSum feature ∑. ***Click on cell E40 and drag the pointer*** (with white plus sign) ***to E42***, then ***click the AutoSum drop-down menu, then click sum.*** The total balance in the Trust Account should be $700.
11. To quit Excel, ***click on the File tab, then click Close.***

This concludes Lesson 6.

This concludes the Excel lessons for Chapter 6.

7

Calendaring, Docket Control, and Case Management

Chapter Objectives

After you read this chapter, you should be able to:

- Explain how to make docketing entries.
- Discuss how to calculate court deadlines.
- Explain why a poor docket system is harmful to a law office.
- Differentiate between manual and computerized docket systems.
- Explain how a poor docket control system leads to ethical and malpractice claims.

A client sued her former attorney for legal malpractice involving three different incidents: failure to timely file an appeal with the state appeal board, failure to file an administrative claim, and failure to determine the proper identities of persons to sue through inexpensive discovery methods. The discovery issue was noted by the court as grounds for denying her original action to recover from the auto accident resulting in the client's personal injuries.

The client sought the advice of another attorney and filed a legal malpractice claim against the first attorney. A jury awarded the client $473,000 in damages against the attorney and after appeals, the court reversed the district court's decision denying interest accrual, remanding it for a determination of additional sums owe.

Source: *Hook v. Trevino*, 839 N.W.2d 434 (Iowa, 2013).

Calendaring, Docket Control, and Case Management Definitions

The practice of law is filled with appointments, deadlines, hearings, and other commitments for every case that is handled; considering that a single legal professional can have a caseload between 20 and 100 cases at any one time, just staying organized and on top of what needs to get done is a big job. It is extremely important that these dates be carefully tracked for ethical, customer service, and general business reasons. Most, but not all, legal organizations track these deadlines by computer. This chapter introduces calendaring, docket control, and case management. These terms are somewhat confusing and are often used interchangeably.

calendaring

A generic term used to describe the function of recording appointments for any type of business.

Calendaring is typically a generic term used to describe the recording of appointments for any type of business. For example, an accounting or engineering firm might use a generic calendaring or scheduling form that comes with an office suite of software programs to track appointments.

docket control

A law-office-specific term that refers to entering, organizing, and controlling all the appointments, deadlines, and due dates for a legal organization.

Docket control is typically a law-office-specific term that refers to entering, organizing, and controlling all the appointments, deadlines, and due dates for a legal organization. There are many legal-specific software programs and manual systems that perform docket control functions for law offices, corporate law departments, and government law departments.

case management

A legal term that usually refers to functions such as docket control, things to do, contact information by case, case notes, document assembly, document tracking by case, integrated billing, and e-mail.

Case management is also a legal-specific term, but it always means more than just tracking appointments and schedules. The breadth of features in current case management programs seems to grow every day. Some of the features found in case management programs include docket control (scheduling/appointments), things to do, contact information database (name, address, e-mail, phone, fax, etc.) by case (parties, co-counsel, opposing counsel, judges, etc.), case notes, document assembly, document tracking/management, integrated billing, e-mail, and more. All information is centered around and tied to cases in case management programs. This is very helpful for legal organizations that view and organize most of their data according to the case to which it is tied. This is a different approach than general calendaring/personal information managers or docket control.

As the legal software market has matured, more and more manufacturers have entered the market. In addition, nearly all of the current legal products available in this market have gotten significantly more sophisticated at meeting the needs of attorneys, paralegals, and legal organizations.

A final term sometimes used to describe docket control is *tickler*, because it "tickles" the memory for upcoming events.

In many law offices, paralegals operate the docket control system for the whole office, while in others, paralegals only use the system to manage and track cases. Although the calendaring and docketing subject may seem trivial at first, the examples of dire consequences resulting from docketing system failures at the beginning of this chapter should indicate the grave nature and importance of this subject. Thus, it is critical for the legal assistant to know how to use docket control so that important deadlines are tracked and kept.

Appointments

A legal professional will have many appointments during the course of a case or legal matter: meetings with clients and co-counsel, witness interviews, interoffice meetings, and so forth. Keeping appointments is very important. Law offices that must constantly reschedule appointments with clients may find their clients going to other attorneys who provide better service. The concept of rescheduling appointments or legal deadlines is often called getting a **continuance** (e.g., the deposition was continued because the witness was sick).

continuance

Rescheduling an appointment or a court date.

Deadlines and Reminders

The practice of law is filled with deadlines at practically every stage of a legal matter. One of the most important types of deadlines is a statute of limitations. A **statute of limitations** is a statute or law that sets a limit on the length of time a party has to file a suit. For instance, some states impose a five-year statute of limitations on lawsuits alleging a breach of a written contract. That is, if a lawsuit is brought or filed more than five years after a contract is breached or broken, the lawsuit is barred by the statute, and a court dismisses the action. The purpose of a statute of limitations is to force parties to bring lawsuits in a timely fashion so that evidence is not destroyed, before witnesses leave the area, and so forth. If an attorney allows a statute of limitations to run or expire without filing a case, he or she may be liable for legal malpractice.

statute of limitations

A statute or law that sets a limit on the length of time a party has to file a suit. If a case is filed after the statute of limitations, the claim is barred and is dismissed as a matter of law.

There also are many deadlines that are set after a case has been filed. In some courts, the judge and the attorneys on both sides sit down and schedule a list of deadlines that the case must follow. The schedule may look something like the one shown in Exhibit 7-1. These deadlines must be adhered to and tracked; an attorney who does not adhere to the deadlines may be penalized or cause the case to be dismissed. Some courts are very reluctant to continue deadlines once they have been set.

Because attorneys and paralegals are busy, usually working on many cases, the law office must have a system of tracking upcoming deadlines. This is done not only by calendaring the deadline itself but also by creating reminder notices in the calendar so that a deadline does not catch a person by surprise. These reminders are called warnings. For example, regarding

Exhibit 7-1 A Typical Case Schedule

Deadline Item	Deadline Date
All Motions to Dismiss must be filed by:	January 31
Responses to Motions to Dismiss must be filed by:	March 1
Discovery (depositions, interrogatories, request for production) to be completed by:	December 20
Summary Judgment Motions to be filed by:	February 1
Responses to Summary Judgment Motions to be filed by:	March 1
Pretrial order to be filed by:	June 1
Settlement Conferences to be completed by:	June 30
Pretrial Motions to be completed and decided by:	July 15
Trial to start no later than:	September 1

the January 31 motion to dismiss in Exhibit 7-1, the attorney or paralegal may want to be reminded 30, 15, and 5 days before the deadline. Therefore, reminder notices would be made on January 1, January 16, and January 26, in addition to the deadline itself being recorded on January 31. It is common for an attorney or a paralegal to request from one to four reminders for each deadline. If reminders are not entered in the docket system, it may make it hard to meet the deadline. Thus, logging reminder notices of upcoming events is crucial to the effective practice of law.

Some deadlines are automatically set by the rules of procedure that are in effect in any given court. Rules of procedure are court rules that govern and tell parties what procedures they must follow when bringing and litigating cases. For instance, in some courts, the rules of procedure hold that after a final decision in a case has been rendered, all parties have 30 days to file an appeal.

For a law office that practices in the tax area, April 15, the date that federal income tax returns are due, is an example of an automatic or a procedural deadline that must be tracked. Thus, this automatic or procedural deadline must be tracked by the office's docket system, and appropriate reminders must be made so that returns are not filed late and penalties assessed.

Hearings and Court Dates

Hearings and court dates are formal proceedings before a court. It is extremely important that these dates be carefully tracked. Most courts have little tolerance for attorneys who fail to show up for court. In some instances, the attorney can be fined or disciplined for missing court dates.

In larger cases, especially when the case is being litigated in court, there may be hundreds of entries in the docket system. Exhibit 7-2 includes a list of common docket entries, including both substantive and law office management-related entries.

Exhibit 7-2 Common Docket Control Entries

- Expiration dates for statutes of limitations
- Judgment renewal dates
- Employee-benefit annual filings
- Renewal dates for copyrights, trademarks, and patents
- Renewal dates for leases and licenses
- Renewal dates for insurance coverage
- Trial court appearance dates
- Due dates for trial court briefs
- Due dates on various pleadings: answers, depositions, replies to interrogatories and requests for admissions, various motions and notices, etc.
- Due dates in probate proceedings, such as inventory and appraisal dates
- Appearances in bankruptcy proceedings
- Action dates in commercial law matters
- Due dates in corporate or security matters
- Closing dates for real estate transactions
- Due dates for appellate briefs and arguments
- Tax return due dates
- Due dates in estate matters, such as tax return dates, valuation dates, and hearing dates
- Dates of stockholder meetings
- Dates of board of directors meetings
- Review dates for wills
- Review dates for buy and sell valuations of business interests
- Review dates for trusts
- Renewal dates for leases on offices
- Renewal dates for attorney licenses
- Expiration dates on notary certificates
- Renewal dates for malpractice and other insurance
- Personal property tax return dates
- Dates for partner (and other recurring and nonrecurring) meetings
- Review dates for billings and accounts receivable
- Review dates for work-in-process
- Review dates for evaluation of associates and staff
- Review dates for raises and bonuses
- Due dates for quarterly payroll withholding reports

Receiving Documents, Following Court Rules, and Calculating Deadlines

Receiving documents that need to be calendared, calculating deadlines, and following the local court rules are important aspects of docket control.

Receiving Documents

When documents arrive in the mail, e-mail, or otherwise, response dates and other deadlines should be immediately and systematically entered into the law office's docket system. This includes pleadings, motions, discovery documents, and other documents that require responses within a certain time period.

Suppose that your office received interrogatories (written questions that your client must complete and send back) in the mail for one of your clients. Also, suppose that in the particular court where the suit is filed, interrogatory responses must be answered within 30 calendar days of the date they are received. When the interrogatories are received by the mail department (or whoever opens the mail), the documents with calendar entries should be routed immediately to someone who has the responsibility to record the deadlines in the docket control system. If there is confusion as to whose responsibility it is to enter the calendar item, or confusion as to when the documents should be calendared (i.e., there is no systematic system), there is an excellent chance that the calendar dates will not be entered into the docket system. If that happens, it is virtually guaranteed that deadlines, response dates, and so forth will be missed and ethical problems will follow.

Know the Local Court Rules

It is imperative to know the local court rules for each court in which your office has cases. Even courts in the same state can have vastly different rules, depending on the internal operating procedures of each court.

Calculating Deadlines

Calculating deadlines depends on the local rules. However, the following are some of the different ways that deadlines can be calculated, and some problems that may arise in making calculations.

CALENDAR DAYS V. WORKDAYS Some courts make a distinction between calendar days and workdays. For example, if a court rule says that a party responding to a motion has 15 days from the file date to file a response, you need to know if the 15 days refers to all days (i.e., calendar days) or only to workdays.

calendar days

System for calculating deadlines that counts all days including weekends and holidays.

When calculating deadlines, **calendar days** typically mean literal days, counting all days including weekends and holidays. For example, if a motion is filed on the 1st day and you have 15 calendar days to respond, the response must be filed by the 16th day. When you count days, you count from one day to the next; for example, the 1st to the 2nd day is one day, the 2nd to the 3rd day is two days, and so on. So, you actually start your count on the day *after* you receive the motion. When using the calendar-day method, a deadline may fall on a Saturday or Sunday; in many courts, the due date would simply be the Monday following the Saturday or Sunday. If the deadline falls on a holiday, the deadline is typically the next day the court is open for business.

workdays

System for calculating deadlines that refers to only days when the court is open.

When calculating deadlines, **workdays** typically refer to only those days when the court is open. Because courts usually are not open on holidays and weekends, these days are omitted from the calculation. For example, if a motion is filed on the 1st day and you have 15 workdays to respond, and assuming the 1st day is a Monday (with no holidays in between), the response would be due on the 22nd day (see Exhibit 7-3).

You need to know whether the court rules are figured on calendar days or workdays because there is a big difference between the two.

File Date v. Document Receipt Date

Court rules will typically state when and/or how deadlines are determined. Deadlines can be calculated either on the date the person actually receives the document or on the date when the document is stamped "FILED" at the clerk's office.

Monday	Tuesday	Wednesday	Thursday	Friday	Saturday	Sunday
1 Motion filed	**2**	**3**	**4**	**5**	**6**	**7**
8	**9**	**10**	**11**	**12**	**13**	**14**
15	**16** Response Due if 15 Calendar Days	**17**	**18**	**19**	**20**	**21**
22 Response Due if 15 Workdays						

Sample Event:	Number of days:	Due Date:
Motion filed on 1st	15 Calendar Days	Tuesday, 16th
Motion filed on 1st	15 Workdays	Monday, 22nd

Exhibit 7-3 Calendar for Calculating Calendar Days and Workdays Example

FILE DATE A typical court rule may state, for a civil action, that a party has 30 days from when the judgment is "FILED" to file an appeal. Assume the court files a judgment on the 1st day and that the party receives the judgment on the 3rd day; the deadline is calculated from the file date, and if there were 30 days in the month, the appeal would have to be filed by the 1st day of the next month.

DOCUMENT RECEIPT DATE Discovery document deadlines typically are calculated by receipt date. For example, a court rule may state that a party has 30 days to answer interrogatories. This is usually calculated from when the document is actually received by the law office needing to respond. So, if the document was mailed on the 1st day and actually received on the 3rd day, then the party will have until the 4th day of the next month to send responses to the opposing side. Thus, it can be very important for the law office to establish when a document was received. Law offices should routinely stamp all documents that come into the office with a received stamp that shows the date the document was received (e.g., "RECEIVED 10/1/2007").

Certificate of Service

A statement at the end of a court document that certifies or establishes when a document was placed in the mail.

Bates stamp

Stamps a document with a sequential number and then automatically advances to the next number.

In addition, when a party prepares a court document in a case there typically is a **"Certificate of Service"** at the very end of the document. The purpose of the "Certificate of Service" is to certify and establish when the document was placed in the mail. The "Certificate of Service" must also be signed. This way, the clerk of the court and the involved parties know when a document was placed in the mail.

A **"Bates stamp"** is sometimes used to number every page of a document. A "Bates stamp" stamps a document with a sequential number and then automatically advances to the next number. In this way, it is possible to establish the order of every page in a document, particularly large documents such as those that have been produced for evidence.

Due Date—File Date v. Mail Date

When reading court rules, it is important to know whether documents can be mailed in or if they must actually be "FILED" within the specified deadline. For example, assume you receive a document on the 1st day and the court rule says you have 20 days to respond; the response would be due on the 21st day. In some courts, it is acceptable to put the response in the mail on the 21st day. That is, you do not actually have to get the document stamped "FILED" on the 21st day. Some courts automatically give you three days' mail time before they say the document is late. Different courts have different rules; again, be sure you know if due dates are calculated on file dates or mail dates. This distinction becomes more important in rural areas.

Ethical and Malpractice Considerations

The ramifications of missing deadlines and otherwise failing to track the progress of cases can be severe. In fact, there are two types of negative outcomes that can result from case neglect: an ethical proceeding against the attorney and a legal malpractice claim filed against the attorney or firm. An attorney who neglects a case can be disciplined by a state ethics board. Such discipline in an ethics case may include reprimand, suspension, or even disbarment. In a legal malpractice case, the attorney involved is sued for damages by providing substandard legal work. These types of cases are not remote or obscure. There are thousands of legal ethics and malpractice proceedings filed throughout the country every year alleging case neglect.

Ethical Considerations

Studies of attorney disciplinary opinions have found that the number one and two reasons that clients file disciplinary proceedings and that courts discipline attorneys are (1) attorneys failing to communicate with their clients and (2) attorneys neglecting or not pursuing client cases diligently. Both of these problems are easily preventable when attorneys and legal assistants use good docket control systems and effective time management.

The ABA *Model Rules of Professional Conduct* gives direct guidance on these issues. The *Model Rules*, adopted and made a part of each states' rules of professional conduct, state that attorneys should be competent in the area in which they are practicing and that they are reasonably prepared to represent the client. The *Model Rules, as adopted by the states*, note that the attorney must act with reasonable diligence and promptness when representing a client, and finally, that an attorney must keep the client reasonably informed about what is going on in the representation of the client. While these ethical rules have been discussed in previous chapters, it is important to include them again in the context of docket control because it is through docket control and organization that a legal professional complies with these rules. Each of these areas is explored in detail.

COMPETENCE AND ADEQUATE PREPARATION The *Rules* regarding professional conduct holds that an attorney must be competent to represent the client; that is, he or she should reasonably know the area of law in which the client needs representation and, assuming the attorney does know the area of law, he or she should take the preparation time needed to become familiar with the case in order to represent the client adequately.

Rule 1.1 regarding rules of professional conduct states that an attorney must provide competent representation to a client, including reasonable preparation necessary to perform the legal work. The purpose of this rule is to ensure that an attorney does not undertake a matter in which he or she is not competent and to ensure that the attorney has had adequate preparation. The amount of "adequate preparation" depends on what type of legal matter the client has. Major litigation, for example, will require far more preparation time than the amount of time it takes to prepare a will. Attorneys should not undertake to represent a client if, for some reason, they cannot do it with the skill and preparation time necessary. Legal professionals use docket control systems to plan adequate preparation time for cases.

DILIGENCE *Rule* 1.3 regarding rules of professional conduct requires that an attorney act with a reasonable degree of diligence and promptness in pursuing a client's case. The rule specifically requires an attorney to act with commitment and dedication when representing a client and to avoid procrastination. Further insight concerning this rule comments that time passage may adversely affect a client's interest and/or destroy the client's legal rights. At the very least, time delays that are unjustified may create unnecessary anxiety for the client and raise questions as to the lawyer's integrity.

Furthermore, as noted by the rule's comment, an attorney should carry through to conclusion all legal matters undertaken for a client unless the relationship is properly and clearly terminated. If there is any doubt about the existence of an attorney–client relationship, the attorney should clarify the situation "in writing so that the client will not mistakenly suppose the attorney is looking after the client's affairs when the lawyer has ceased to do so." The purpose of this rule is to ensure that attorneys put forth reasonable effort and diligence to represent a client. Attorneys cannot adequately represent the interests of clients if they ignore the case, if they are lazy and do not work on the case, or if they do not have the systems in place to manage deadlines, appointments, and things to be done.

COMMUNICATION WITH CLIENTS An attorney also must communicate regularly with the client. *Rule* 1.4 regarding rules of profession conduct requires an attorney to promptly and reasonably consult with a client, to promptly comply to a client's reasonable request for information and to keep a client informed about the cases status and legal matters, as well as explain matter(s) to a client so that he or she might reasonable make informed decisions.

This rule specifically requires the attorney to maintain reasonable contact with a client, explain general strategies and keep the client reasonably informed regarding case status. "Reasonableness" is dependent upon the facts and circumstance for each case and is determined on a case-by-case basis. As noted in the rule's comment, a lawyer must meet reasonable expectations from the client, which is consistent with the lawyer's responsibility to provide quality representation, acting in the client's best interest.

Exhibit 7-4 Cases Regarding Lack of Diligence

Paralegal's Heavy Caseload Not an Excuse for Failing to Respond Timely to a Motion to Dismiss—Case Dismissed

An attorney filed an employment action for a client against the client's former employer one day after the statute of limitation. The defendant company moved to dismiss the complaint in August. No response was filed and in February of the following year the Court granted the motion and dismissed the client's case. In October of that year, more than a year after the Motion to Dismiss was originally filed, the plaintiff's attorney filed a Motion to Set Aside Judgment of Dismissal on the grounds that his paralegal had a heavy caseload and failed to respond to the motion to dismiss. The Court denied the motion and upheld the dismissal. The Court noted that the neglect of the legal assistant was not a reason to set aside the judgment and that even if a response had been filed, the case was filed outside of the statute of limitations and most likely would have been dismissed anyway. *Deo-Agbasi v. Parthenon Group*, 229 F.R.D. 348 (D. Mass. 2005).

Paralegal Scheduling Clerk Fails to Properly Docket Three Court Appearances for Attorney

An attorney's paralegal neglected to properly docket three court appearances for an attorney. As a result of this, the "answer" that was filed by the attorney for the client was stricken and the Court entered default judgment against the attorney's client. The attorney appealed the default judgment. The appellate court found that when the trial court granted the default judgment, it served to punish the innocent client for the paralegal's neglect. The appellate court reversed and allowed the attorney to file the answer. *Hu v. Fang*, 104 Cal.App 4th 61, 127 Cal.Rptr. 2d 756 (2002).

Attorney Files Suit for Special Education Student and Then Loses Interest

An attorney accepted $4000 to file a suit on behalf of a mother and her daughter, a special education student, so the daughter could be placed in a public school. The attorney then took no action in the case, never sent the client a detailed accounting, and refused to communicate with the client. Three and a half years later, the client received a letter from the attorney stating that in light of his "other business projects," he did not anticipate practicing law any longer. When the client requested the return of the $4000 in legal fees and her file, the attorney denied both requests. The attorney received a one-year suspension followed by a six-month period of supervised probation. *In Re Dunn*, 831 So.2d 889 2002

Exhibit 7-4 shows only a few examples of attorneys and paralegals failing to follow up on client cases. A basic element of due diligence to a client requires an attorney to meet deadlines and limitation periods and appear at requisite legal proceedings. Many of these failures could have been avoided by a good docket control system and attorneys' and legal professionals' willingness to plan, organize, and simply get the work done. There is little excuse for poor organization and poor docket control in the modern law office. Firms today have access to an unlimited supply of outstanding computerized docket control systems and case management programs made specifically for law firms, and an even greater supply of generic calendaring software that comes with most computers. With all these systems and technology, however, failure to properly perform work on time is a major reason that attorneys are disciplined in this country.

Conflict of Interest

Attorneys must take steps to prevent conflict of interest problems. A conflict of interest occurs when an attorney or a paralegal has competing personal or professional interest with a client's case that would preclude him or her from acting impartially toward the client. Before an attorney or a law firm accepts a case, he or she should perform a thorough conflict of interest search. Many attorneys and law firms use computerized software to perform such a conflict of interest search. Many case management programs allow attorneys to perform a conflict of interest search on current clients, past clients, law office contacts, adverse clients, counsel, and much more. A thorough conflict of interest search using computerized software is an effective way of avoiding conflict of interest problems.

Legal Malpractice Considerations

[A] client sued their former attorney(s) alleging that they were negligent with the fraud case that was dismissed by, among other things: failing to file a timely appearance, filing to attend certain depositions and advise of witnesses' testimonies in advance of other depositions, failing to properly prepare the case for trial, and failing to seek a voluntary nonsuit on date of trial, all leading to the client's case being dismissed. The jury returned a verdict for the client in the amount of $2,337,550, finding that but for the attorneys' negligence, the client would have been successful in their breach of contract and contract fraud lawsuit.

Source: *Tri-G, Inc. v. Burke, Bosselman and Weaver*, 817 N.E.2d 1230, 353 Ill. App.3d 197, 288 Ill. Dec. 580 (Ill. App., 2004).

legal malpractice

A claim that an attorney breached an ordinary standard of care that a reasonable attorney would have adhered to in that same circumstance.

In addition to the ethical considerations of neglecting a client's legal matter, the client may also have a legal malpractice claim against the attorney for negligence. The general theory in a **legal malpractice** claim is that the attorney breached an ordinary standard of care applicable to a reasonable attorney under those circumstances. In a legal malpractice case, both the plaintiff and defendant must rely on attorneys who are expert witnesses to testify whether the defendant did or did not act like a reasonable attorney would in the same situation.

Exhibit 7-5 shows some common deadlines that, when missed, may lead to malpractice claims. In fact, many malpractice insurers will refuse to write malpractice insurance for a law office that does not have an effective docket control system.

In recent years, the number of legal malpractice claims that have been filed has gone up dramatically. In some cases, the amount of damages can be substantial. Some insurance companies that offer legal malpractice coverage actually meet with staff members who are in charge of docket control to ensure that a docket control system is being used. Thus, attorneys and law offices have two powerful reasons to maintain a quality docket system.

Exhibit 7-5 Common Reasons for Malpractice Claims

1. Expiration of the statute of limitations
2. Failure to appear or plead, resulting in a default judgment
3. Dismissal of a lawsuit for lack of prosecution
4. Failure to file tax returns or other documents within the time required
5. Failure to file pleadings or to comply with an order within the time required
6. Failure to answer interrogatories within the time required
7. Failure to give timely notice when such notice is a precondition to a recovery of damages
8. Failure to communicate with clients
9. Not knowing what to do next (i.e., the attorney not being competent in an area)

Manual Docket Control Systems

There are many types of manual docketing systems, including a simple calendar, a card system, and others. Manual docketing systems work best for fairly small law offices. As a law office grows, manual systems become more difficult to manage.

CALENDAR Small law offices may use simple computer calendar programs or a page-a-day calendaring system. Many calendars provide a section to record "things to do" or reminders, in addition to providing a place to schedule appointments.

As cases or legal matters are opened, deadlines and reminders (i.e., "ticklers") are entered into the calendar. Notices from courts, attorneys, and so forth also are entered. In addition to the due dates or appointment date being entered, reminders also must be manually entered into the calendar. This process of manually entering due dates and reminders can be very time consuming; for instance, if a deadline with two reminders was entered, the whole entry would have to be manually entered a total of three times in three places.

In some offices, each attorney and paralegal maintains his or her own separate calendar. The issue with this approach is that often the attorneys and paralegals fail to coordinate their schedules and calendars. This can be a serious problem.

Finally, if attorneys wanted a short list of things to be done, appointments, or critical deadlines for a day, week, or month, it would have to be compiled and entered into a word processor by a staff member.

CARD SYSTEM A card system (sometimes called a "tickler card system") uses index cards or their equivalent to track deadlines and things to be done. A manual card or form is used for each deadline or task to be completed and includes client name, action to be performed, client number, reminder date, and due date. Cards can be color-coded to indicate different types of deadlines. In most cases, the card or slip of paper is kept in duplicate or triplicate; copies are used as reminders and filed before the actual due date. An index-card holder or expanding file folder with dividers for each month and each day must be maintained to file each card. When the date on a card tickler is reached, the card is pulled and given to the appropriate person to perform the task, or a list of the deadlines and things to do is made.

An individual must check the card system every day in order for it to work properly. However, if a slip is lost or misfiled, the system breaks down. Although computerized systems may occasionally break down as well, manual systems are far more likely to be error prone than them. In addition, like the manual calendar, any daily, weekly, or monthly card system report must be typed by hand.

Manual calendaring systems also lack the ability to track information by case. For example, if a client asked to see all the upcoming events for his or her case, a staff person would have to go through the calendar and manually put together a list. Depending on the case, there could be many entries. Again, this is a time-consuming process.

Another problem with a manual calendaring system is that successive calendars must be purchased every year (e.g., one for 2015, one for 2016, one for 2017, and so on). It is also difficult to schedule dates far in the future—five years down the road for a statute of limitations entry, for instance—because you will need the appropriate calendar.

Manual calendaring systems are prone to error and time consuming to administer. Because the process is slow and tedious, it encourages users to make as few docket entries as possible. Further, manual systems simply do not have the flexibility and reporting capabilities that computerized versions can deliver.

Types of Computerized Docket Control Systems

There are a variety of computer programs that can be used to schedule and track events for a legal organization. These include generic calendaring/personal information manager programs and case management programs. Most of these programs can be purchased for stand-alone computers or for local area networks. Networked systems, whether generic or legal specific, have the principal advantage of allowing individual users throughout an organization to see and have access to the calendars of other users in the office.

Generic Calendaring and Personal Information Manager Programs

Generic calendaring programs computerize the functions of a paper desk calendar. Since they are generic and can be used by any type of business, they lack many features that are helpful to a legal organization. These types of programs are usually very inexpensive and typically manage only the calendar, things to do, contacts, and e-mail functions.

personal information manager (PIM)

Consolidates a number of different tasks into one computer program. Most PIMs include calendaring, things to do, a contact database that tracks names and addresses of people, note taking, and other tasks as well.

A generic **personal information manager (PIM)** program consolidates a number of different tasks into one computer program. Most PIMs include calendaring, things to do, a contact database that tracks names and addresses of people, note taking, e-mail, and other tasks as well. Microsoft Outlook is a type of PIM that can come bundled with Microsoft's Office Suite of programs. Outlook is an extremely powerful program. As the generic calendaring and scheduling software market has matured, most new programs are PIMs. PIMs are very popular and convenient to use since they allow a user to organize a number of related tasks into one easy-to-use interface. Generic PIMs are not specifically suited to the needs of legal professionals but they still have many useful features, and some legal organizations use them. For example, for consistency purposes a corporate law department might use a product like Microsoft Outlook, which can be implemented throughout the corporation, instead of a legal-specific program that only its department can use.

Overview of Computerized Legal Case Management and Docket Control

Most case management programs offer a variety of features, including the following.

Monthly, Daily, and Weekly Calendar Views

Almost all case management programs have some type of monthly display, which allows the user to get an overview of his or her schedule. In addition to monthly and daily views, most programs allow users to see a weekly view of their schedules as well (see Exhibit 7-6).

Event Entry Screen

A typical event entry screen is shown in Exhibit 7-7; this is where new entries are entered into the case management program. These can include deadlines, things to be done, or appointments. The data entry process for most programs is easy and straightforward. Information that is entered into most entry screens includes the client, matter number, description, date, time, type of entry, place, who the event is for, notes, reminders, and other information.

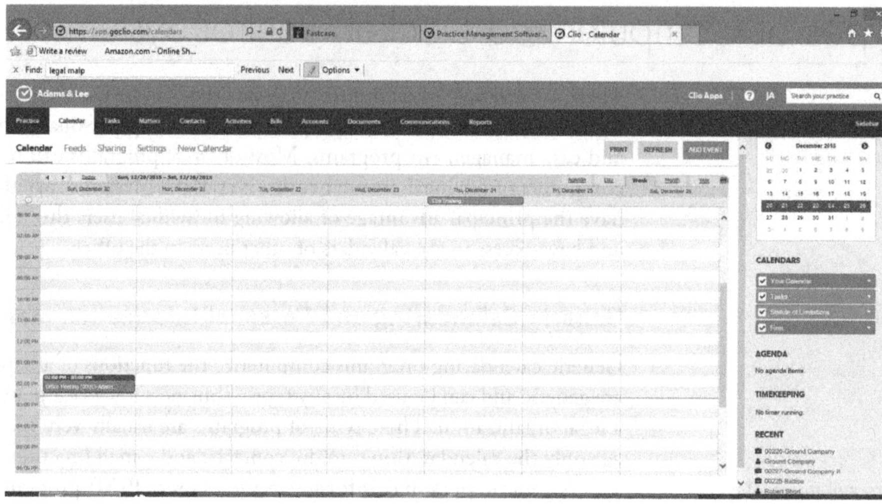

Exhibit 7-6 Case Management Program Weekly Calendar
Source: Themis Solutions, Inc.

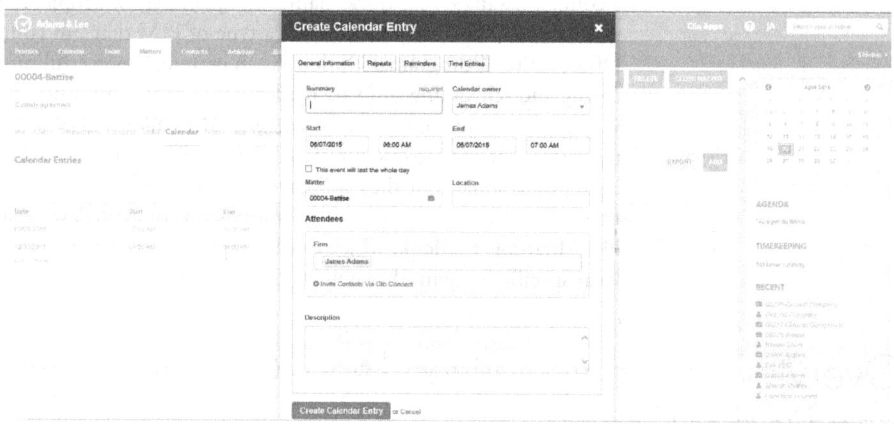

Exhibit 7-7 Event Entry Screen
Source: Themis Solutions, Inc.

Perpetual Calendars

Most computerized case management systems have built-in perpetual calendars that allow a person to see and enter data that will be used for many years in the future. Unlike manual calendars, a computerized system does not have to be updated annually (although purchasing updated versions of the software may be desirable). The perpetual calendar is an important feature of a computerized system, since it allows the user to make entries concerning dates that are far in the future, such as a statute of limitations.

Recurring Entries

recurring entry
A calendar entry that recurs.

One advantage of using computerized case management systems is that the user can automatically make recurring entries. A **recurring entry** is a calendar entry that typically recurs daily, weekly, monthly, or annually. For instance, if an office has a staff meeting every Monday morning, the entry could be entered once as a weekly recurring appointment, since most computerized case management systems can make recurring docket entries daily, weekly, monthly, quarterly, and annually. Thus, an entry that would have had to be entered 52 times in a year in a manual system would have to be entered only once in a computerized docket control program.

Date Calculator

Some case management systems have a date calculator that automatically calculates the number of days between dates. For instance, suppose you have 20 calendar days from a specific date to file a motion. The date calculator feature will automatically calculate the deadline. This is useful when you have deadlines that take into account only workdays (i.e., do not count Saturdays, Sundays, and holidays).

Scheduling Conflict Alert

Some case management systems automatically alert the user to possible conflicts. For instance, if a user mistakenly tries to schedule two appointments for the same date and time, nearly all computerized docket systems will automatically alert the user to the possible conflict. If the user has a conflict, most systems can be overridden and both appointments entered anyway. Some systems have a "lockout" feature that prevents users from scheduling more than one appointment for a given time period.

Some systems even allow the user to enter such information as the individual's regular office hours and days of the week that are usually taken off. If, for instance, an individual's office hours are from 7:00 A.M. to 4:00 P.M. and an entry is made for 4:30 P.M., some systems automatically recognize the problem and alert the user.

Scheduling Multiple Parties

Scheduling free time for an interoffice meeting can sometimes be difficult, since all parties must have an open block of time. Many case management systems that operate on a local area network can automatically bring up dates and times that a group of people have free, thus making scheduling meetings easy.

A computerized case management system also allows other individuals working on a case to see what docketing entries have been made and to find out what is going on in the case. This eases the process of multiple people working on the same case. It also allows for methods of communications between collaborative parties and features passwords and other encryptions to limit the personnel to the key people working on the case.

Centralized and Decentralized Systems

Most case management systems work well in either a centralized or decentralized system. In a centralized system, one person (like a secretary) can make time entries for many individuals; this is beneficial because only one individual is responsible for making the docketing entries. A decentralized system, where the attorney or paralegal enters his or her own deadlines into the docket program, also works well for some offices.

Automatic Reminders

Most computerized case management systems allow the user to make one entry into the system that also contains the reminder dates. For instance, when an appointment or a deadline is entered into the computer, the system automatically asks the user when he or she wants to be reminded of it. If a reminder date is entered, the computerized method automatically makes reminder entries. This is a great time-saving feature over manual systems where every reminder must be entered individually.

Calendaring a Series of Events from a Rule

Some case management programs allow a user to enter one event that, in turn, automatically triggers a list of subsequent calendaring events based on court rules. For instance, a complaint is filed. Sixty days after the complaint is filed, according to court rules the complaint must have been served. Therefore, the docketing program automatically enters a deadline to serve the complaint 60 days after the complaint is filed. This kind of feature is very powerful and can be a real time-saver. Many case management programs allow the user to program his or her own court rules into the program or to add on purchased court rule setups.

Reporting

Most computerized systems allow the user to generate a variety of reports that manual systems cannot produce, including daily, weekly, or monthly schedules and things-to-do entries for one person or a group of people. Most systems can also search and sort the entries in a variety of different formats.

DAILY CALENDAR REPORTS This is an in-depth listing of a timekeeper's or office's daily schedule. The daily report is sometimes called a "day-sheet." Many attorneys and legal assistants use this report every day for an accurate listing of the day's events.

DAILY CALENDAR REPORT FOR A WEEK This is similar to the daily calendar report except that the report shows docket entries for an entire week. Again, legal assistants and attorneys may want this report at the beginning of the week to get a "snapshot" of what their schedule looks like, so they can plan accordingly.

PER CASE DOCKET REPORT Most computerized case management systems allow the user to generate a docket report by case—that is, a report showing all the docketing dates for any one case (see Exhibit 7-8). This report can be very helpful in trying to determine how to proceed with certain cases. Exhibit 7-8 provides a listing of all entries for the case *00003-Battise Custody Agreement*. This is particularly helpful when scheduling other events for the same case and for providing details to the client. Keeping clients informed about their cases is very important when it comes to client satisfaction and when it is time for the client to pay the legal bill. A client who is consulted often and kept aware of the progress of the case is more likely to pay the bill and generally is more satisfied than a client who is not notified about his or her case's progress. Again, this report is very beneficial to clients who want to know what is going on in a case, and also to recently assigned attorneys or legal assistants who would like to see what has happened and where the case is headed.

James Adams
Schedule for Custody Agreement
Case Number: 00003

Date	Start	Last, First	Summary	Who	Note
12/28/15	8:30 A.M.	Battise, S.	DISCOVER	AMS	Discovery Deadline
01/02/16	9:00 A.M.	Battise, S.	HEARING	AMS	Hearing on Pending Motions
03/01/16	9:00 A.M.	Battise, S.	C-STATUS	AMS	Status Conference
03/15/16	1:00 P.M.	Battise, S.	PRETRIAL	AMS	Pretrial Conference
03/29/16	10:00 A.M.	Battise, S.	C-SETTLE	AMS	Settlement Conference
04/06/16	8:00 A.M.	Battise, S.	TR PR	AMS	Trial Preparation
04/07/16	8:00 A.M.	Battise, S.	TRIAL	AMS	TRIAL

Number of Events: 7

Exhibit 7-8 Docket Report for a Case

PAST DUE REPORT The past due report prints a listing of all docket entries that are past due (i.e., the deadline or due date has passed) or that have not been marked "Done." The past due report is a safeguard against forgetting or not completing items.

FREE TIME REPORT The free time report shows the times that one timekeeper or several timekeepers have unscheduled or open. This is useful when adding scheduling items or when setting up a conference of three or four individuals. Attorneys and legal assistants who have a lot of appointments and court dates also can use this report so they can see when free time is available for scheduling other matters.

Searching

Most computerized case management systems allow the user to search for entries. For instance, if a client calls and wants to know the date of his or her deposition, the user could enter the client's name into the computer and the system would retrieve the entry showing the deposition date.

Advanced Case Management Features

Up to this point, the case management program features, we have covered, have for the most part been confined to docket control. Now some advanced case management features will be covered as well.

Case Contacts

Case contacts allow the user to enter people into a contact database (which tracks phone, address, e-mail, etc.), just as in a PIM. The difference is that once they are entered in the database, the person(s) can be linked to a case or cases. So, if a user wanted to see or print a list of co-counsel or opposing counsel on a case, it could be easily done. Also, if the case management system is networked, the legal organization could have one master contact database (linked to cases) for the whole organization. Thus, there would be no duplication in multiple places throughout the legal organization.

Synchronizing with PIMs/PDAs

Most case management systems will synchronize calendars with PIMs (such as Outlook) and personal digital assistants (PDAs). Thus, if a corporate law department wanted to use a case management system, but the rest of the corporation was using Outlook, the two could be set up to share information or synchronize so that all of the entries in the case management program would not have to be entered by hand in Outlook.

Case Diary/Notes

Most case management systems provide a place to maintain a case diary or notes for the file. This allows legal professionals a central place to place their notes, record summaries of phone calls, and much more. A large benefit to case management programs is not only that the information can be stored electronically but that any users in a networked environment can immediately access and use the information at a touch of the button, without having to pull the hard copy of the file. Thus, a good case management system is also a communication enhancement tool (see Exhibit 7-9).

Document Assembly/Generation

As indicated previously, case management programs store a great deal of information about a case, parties, attorneys, case-related information, case numbers, and much more. Most case management programs can merge that information into a merge document (see Exhibit 7-10). So, a legal professional can automatically generate standard letters, forms, pleadings, and reports right from the case management system without having to reenter any additional data. Most case management systems also work with Word and Word Perfect, so they can merge documents into these programs as well. Also, when a case user creates a document in the case management system, in many instances it will automatically note this—including the date—in the case diary/notes. A user simply has to indicate what file the document needs to be merged with, and then the user is given a list of documents to choose from, including file reports, letters, memos, and others. Users are, of course, allowed to create their own forms as well.

Other Features

LEGAL RESEARCH LIBRARY Some case management programs give the user a place to store electronic legal research, or allow the user to access functions within Westlaw and/or other electronic research tools.

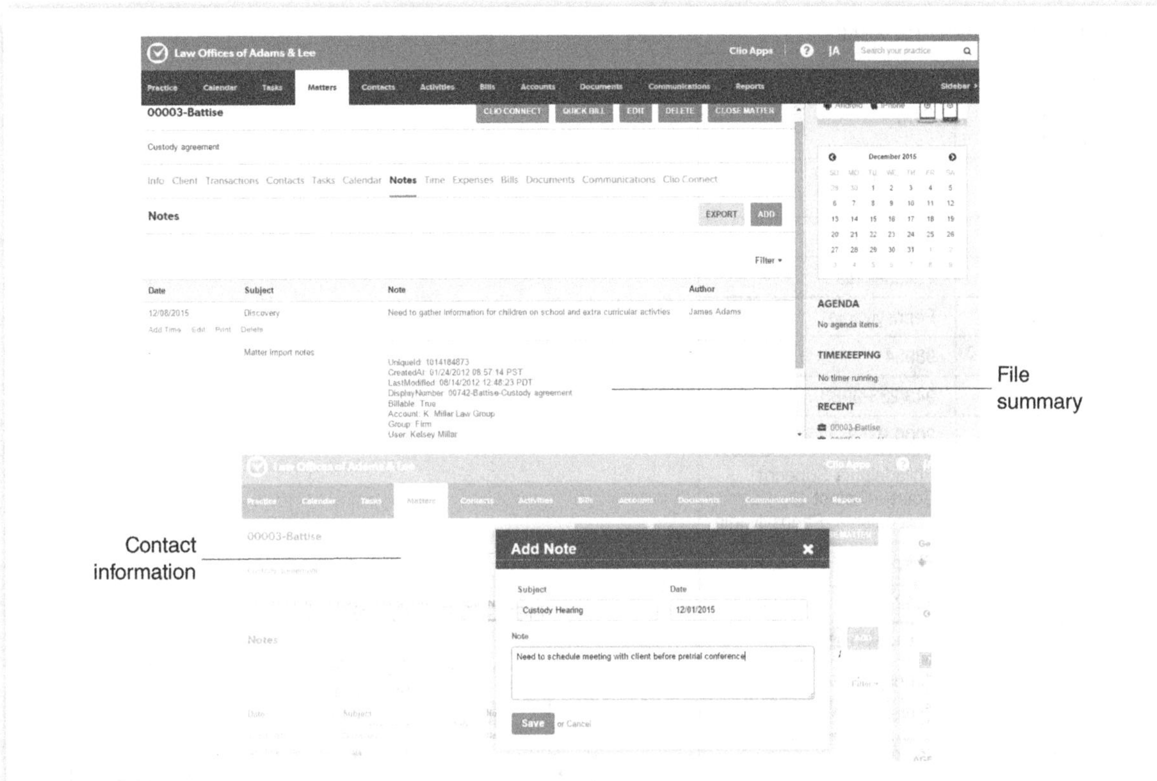

Exhibit 7-9 Case Diary Notes

Source: Themis Solutions, Inc.

CONFLICT OF INTEREST Most case management programs allow the user to do conflict of interest searches. Since the database tracks clients, parties, counsel, and much more case-related information, the conflict search can be very comprehensive.

E-MAIL INTERFACE Many programs now include an e-mail interface that allows users to link e-mails with cases. This is extremely important given the heavy use of e-mails in communicating with clients and handling client matters.

DOCUMENT MANAGEMENT Many case management programs can now associate documents with cases. A link can be made between a document/file and a case in a case management program. This allows legal professionals to index and manage case documents from the program.

TIME AND BILLING/ACCOUNTING INTERFACE Many programs share information with timekeeping and billing programs and, in some instances, accounting programs as well.

CASE MANAGEMENT DATABASE

Client Name:	First National Bank
Contact Person–First Name:	Sam
Contact Person–Last Name:	Johnson
Client Address:	P.O. Box 1000
Client City:	Philadelphia
Client State:	Pennsylvania
Client Zip:	98934
Client Phone:	943/233-9983
Case Number:	2006-9353
Court:	Philadelphia Superior Court—District 13, Philadelphia, Pennsylvania
Debtor Name:	Philip Jones
Debtor Address:	3242 Wilson Ave. SW
Debtor City:	Philadelphia
Debtor State:	Pennsylvania
Debtor Zip:	98984
Amount Owed to Client:	$25,234
Type of Debt:	Mortgage
Type of Asset:	House at 3242 Wilson Ave SW, Philadelphia, Pennsylvania

DOCUMENT TEMPLATE 1—"Complaint"

In the {Court}

{Client name}

Plaintiff

Case No. {Case Number}

{Debtor Name}
{Debtor Address}
{Debtor City}{Debtor State}{Debtor Zip}

Defendant.

COMPLAINT

Comes now the plaintiff, {Client Name}, and states that the defendant, {Debtor Name}, is indebted to the plaintiff in the amount of {Amount Owed to Client} on a {Type of Debt} regarding a {Type of Asset}. Attached to this complaint as Appendix "A" is a fully executed copy of the mortgage above referenced.

Merge function

MERGED DOCUMENT—"Complaint"

In the Philadelphia Superior Court – District 13,
Philadelphia, Pennsylvania

First National Bank

Plaintiff

Case No. 2006-9353

Philip Jones
3242 Wilson Ave. SW
Philadelphia, Pennsylvania 98984

Defendant.

COMPLAINT

Comes now the plaintiff, First National Bank, and states that the defendant, Philip Jones, is indebted to the plaintiff in the amount of $25,234 on a mortgage regarding a house at 3242 Wilson Ave SW, Philadelphia, Pennsylvania. Attached to this complaint as Appendix "A" is a fully executed copy of the mortgage above referenced.

Exhibit 7-10 Sample Document Assembly/Generation Sample

The Docket Cycle

The docket cycle refers to how information is entered into a case management program. There are three primary ways that information can flow into and out of such a program: a centralized method, decentralized method, and combined method.

Centralized Docket Control Cycle

In a centralized docket control cycle, one person typically is responsible for entering all docket entries into the docket program. This is usually a secretary or, in some cases, a legal assistant. In this type of system, first step would be for a user to manually complete a docket slip (see Exhibit 7-11). In the second step, the secretary enters the event into the docket control program. The third step is for reports to be generated, and the last step is for entries to be marked "Done."

Decentralized Docket Control Cycle

In a decentralized docket control cycle, the user enters docket information directly into the computer, controlling her or his own docket. In this type of system, the first step would be for the user to enter a docket entry into the case management program. Second, the user views or prints reports as necessary, and third, the user marks entries "Done." The advantage of this

ADAMS & LEE **DOCKET SLIP**

Client/Case Matter: Sharon Battise File No.: 00003

Event: Pre-Trial Hearing

Date of Event: 03/15/2016 Time of Event: 10:00 AM – 1:00 PM

Place of Event: U.S. Ct. House, Div. 8

To Be Handled By: JQA Reminder Dates: 03/01/2015

Priority: (1) 2 3 4 5 (Circle one, Top Priority is 1).

Slip Completed By: BRR Date Slip Completed: 02/01/2016

Notes: Meet Client at 9:45 at Ct. House

Docket Clerk Use Only

Date Entered in Docket: 02/03/2016

Entered By: JCC

Exhibit 7-11 Sample Docket Slip

system is that the user has ultimate control over his or her own docket; the disadvantage is that the user is doing the data entry instead of a clerk or secretary.

Combined Docket Control Cycle

In a combined docket control cycle, a user can decide whether to enter information into the program or have a clerk or secretary do it. Some docket control programs allow multiple people to enter data into a user's schedule. For example, some networked docket programs allow both an attorney and his or her secretary to enter information into the attorney's schedule. Both have full access to the attorney's calendar.

In this type of system, the first step would be for either the user or a third party to enter a docket entry into the case management program. Second, either the user or the third party views or prints reports as necessary, and third, either the user or third party marks entries "Done." In some ways, this is the best of both worlds, since the user still has control over his or her calendar but can delegate the data entry to someone else.

Summary

The practice of law is filled with appointments, deadlines, hearings, and other commitments for every case that is handled. It is extremely important that these dates be carefully tracked for ethical, customer service, and general business reasons. Calendaring is a generic term used to describe the function of recording appointments for any business. Docket control is a law-office-specific term that refers to entering, organizing, and controlling all of the appointments, deadlines, and due dates for a legal organization. Case management is a legal-specific term that usually refers to computer programs that not only have docket control but a number of other features, including contact management, document assembly, case notes, document management, and much more.

Ethical issues related to docket control include the duty to competently and adequately prepare for a client's matter, diligently and promptly serve clients, communicate with clients in a timely manner, and to avoid conflicts of interest.

Manual docket control systems include basic calendars and card systems. Computerized systems include generic calendaring and personal information management programs (such as Microsoft Outlook), and docket control/case management programs. Case management programs include a plethora of advanced and powerful features.

Key Terms

Bates stamp
calendar days
calendaring
case management
Certificate of Service
continuance
docket control
legal malpractice
personal information manager
recurring entry
statute of limitations
workdays

Test Your Knowledge

1. What is a legal-specific term for entering, organizing, and controlling appointments, deadlines, and due dates?
2. A legal term that usually refers to docket control and other functions, including things to do, contacting information, case notes, and document assembly is ________________.
3. When calculating deadlines, what two ways are there to count days?
4. A statement at the end of a court document that certifies or establishes when a document was sent is called a ________________.
5. Two major types of manual docket control systems are ________________ and ________________.
6. A generic computer program that consolidates a number of different functions including calendaring, things to do, contact, and e-mail is called ________________.
7. Name two features usually found in case management software.

Practical Applications

1. Your law office currently uses a manual docket system. It works fairly well because the office is small. However, several clients have requested a detailed listing of what is going on in their cases and what is coming up in the future. It takes a staff member quite a while to compile this information. Even though the office's manual system is working, should the office consider a change? What benefits would be realized? Please note that the office is driven by quality and productivity.

2. As a paralegal in a legal services/aid practice, you notice that one of the attorneys in the office filed a case on behalf of an indigent client. The defendant's attorney has attempted on three separate occasions to take the client's deposition. However, the attorney asked for and received continuances on each occasion. The client's health is deteriorating and the client has anxiety over the deposition. The client's deposition is set for tomorrow, but the attorney tells you that something has "come up" and to please call the defendant's counsel, the court reporter, and the client, and get it continued. Although you have covered for the attorney on multiple occasions, you know that the client really wants to talk to the attorney and not to you, and that the client would like to finish the deposition as soon as possible. Please respond to the attorney's request.

3. From time to time, you see new clients who come into the office. On this occasion, you interview a client who has a potential workers' compensation claim. After the client has left, you note that in a month the statute of limitations on the claim will expire. After discussing the case with your supervising attorney, the attorney says that he does not believe that the client has a viable case. The attorney tells you to not waste any more time on the matter and that you should simply call the client and tell her that the office will not be representing her. As you pick up the phone, you hesitate and then put the phone down. You go back into the attorney's office. What would you tell your supervising attorney?

4. You and your supervising attorney are overworked. You have two days to prepare for a trial that you really need 8–10 days to adequately prepare for. Your supervising attorney says, "It's okay, we'll just do the best we can." Discuss this situation from an ethical perspective.

5. One of the five attorneys you work for is taking on a new case. Unfortunately, the attorney has never handled a case like this before. This is particularly troubling you, because you doubt whether either the attorney or you have the time or inclination to do the necessary research to properly handle the case. Address any concerns you might have to the attorney. Try to be diplomatic. Give the attorney options that will address your concerns but will still allow the attorney to work on the case in some capacity.

6. Calculate the following due dates.

a. Motion for Summary Judgment filed 8/1/08; response due 17 days from file date. Court rules use calendar days in this case.

b. Motion to Compel filed Monday 3/5/08, response due 10 days from file date. Court rules use workdays only in this case. Assume there is one weekend.

c. Request for Admissions is received 6/1/08, response is due 25 days from receipt. Court rules use calendar days in this case. Response must be mailed by what date?

d. Request for Publication of Documents is received 12/10/08; response is due within seven days. Court rules use workdays only in this case. Assume there is one weekend and two holidays.

7. Set up and maintain a docket of class assignments for a semester. Use index cards to represent each assignment and file them in chronological order, or use a computerized calendaring program. For quizzes and assignments, give yourself a three-day reminder before the assignment or quiz is due, in addition to recording the quiz or assignment itself. For exams or lengthy papers, give yourself three reminders—a 10-day reminder, a 5-day reminder, and a 3-day reminder before it is due—in addition to docketing the deadline itself.

8. Read the disciplinary report section of your state bar association journal or magazine and prepare a short memorandum on several cases related to diligence and/or docket control.

On the Web Exercises

1. Go to the ABA Center for Professional Responsibility Web site at http://www.abanet.org/cpr/home.html, find the ABA *Model Rules of Professional Conduct*, and read and print out the Comments to *Rules 1.1, 1.3, 1.4, and 1.7.*

2. Visit several bar association Web sites (including the Georgia Bar Association) and find three articles on case management, docket control, or a related subject. The mentioned link will take you to a Web site that connects to all state bar sites: http://www.abanet.org/barserv/stlobar.html.

3. Visit the American Bar Association Technology Resource Center Web site at http://www.abanet.org/tech/ltrc/home.html and review any materials they have on case management software programs.

Projects

1. Research and write a paper on computerized case management and docket control systems. Go to the docket control and case management Web sites listed in the Web Links section of this chapter. Obtain demonstration copies of the programs, if you can. Compare and contrast at least two of the different products that are available. Which one were you most impressed with, and why?

2. Using a law library, state bar journal magazine, Westlaw/LexisNexis, or the Internet, write a paper that summarizes a minimum of three attorney discipline cases regarding the failure to complete work on time. Be sure to include an analysis of the case, the court's findings, the ethical rules that were at issue, the rules that were violated, and what discipline was imposed.

Case Review

74 P.3d 566 (2003).

The PEOPLE of The State of Colorado, Complainant,

v.

Matthew S. SMITH, Respondent.

Aug. 13, 2003.

Opinion and Order Imposing Sanctions

Sanction Imposed: Nine Month Suspension

A trial in this matter was held on February 27 and 28, 2003, before a Hearing Board consisting of the Presiding Disciplinary Judge, Roger L. Keithley and two Hearing Board Members, Robert A. Millman and Marilyn L. Robertson, both members of the bar. Kim E. Ikeler, Assistant Attorney Regulation Counsel, represented the People of the State of Colorado (the "People"). Gary D. Fielder represented respondent Matthew S. Smith ("Smith"), who was also present.

At the trial, the People's exhibits 1 through 4 and 6 through 37, and Smith's exhibit A, were admitted into evidence. Jennifer Reynolds, Roy Reynolds, Jr., Jeanette Ross, and Matthew Smith testified on behalf of the People. Smith testified on his own behalf. The Hearing Board considered the testimony of the witnesses and the exhibits admitted into evidence, the Joint Stipulation of Facts submitted by the parties, and made the following findings of fact which were established by clear and convincing evidence.

I. Findings of Fact

Matthew S. Smith has taken and subscribed the oath of admission, was admitted to the bar of the Supreme Court on May 13, 1993, and is registered upon the official records of the Court, attorney registration number 22681. He is subject to the jurisdiction of this court pursuant to C.R.C.P. 251.1(b).

During the relevant time period from 1999 to 2001, Smith was a sole practitioner. He handled a large-volume practice with approximately half of the practice devoted to domestic law. Jeanette Ross ("Ross") worked as Smith's legal assistant from 1996 to 2001. During the period of her employment, Smith put measures in place to assure that all communications, oral and written, were brought to his attention. Ross was required to receive, open, and sort mail and record telephone messages. Ross would review incoming mail and place matters requiring prompt attention on Smith's desk with the client file. Less critical communication was placed in sorted stacks for Smith's review. Smith would then review his mail or telephone messages and instruct Ross what action to take on a given case. It was Smith's practice to review all court orders. Smith did not utilize computer software to track deadlines in cases. Smith and Ross did, however, manually record dates on two calendars. In addition, Smith allowed Ross to prepare form pleadings, prepare and send correspondence, docket court appearances, communicate with clients by phone, and handle settings with the court. Smith periodically reviewed case files to determine if cases were properly advancing.

Smith did not give Ross permission to sign his name to pleadings. Ross was permitted to write checks on Smith's operating account and utilize his signature stamp on operating account checks without prior authorization from Smith. Ross testified that she signed Smith's name to routine pleadings. Ross's testimony that Smith permitted her to sign his name to pleadings was not credible.

Roy and Jennifer Reynolds were married in 1995. In late 1998, Roy Reynolds, Jr. ("Reynolds") retained Smith to represent him in an uncontested divorce and paid him $800. Reynolds's address and phone numbers were noted on the client intake sheet. [FN1]

> FN1. The Reynolds file disappeared when a new management company took over Smith's office. On January 27, 1999, Smith filed Reynolds's Petition for Dissolution of Marriage together with a Summons for Dissolution of Marriage or Legal Separation and Temporary Injunction in Arapahoe County District Court, Case No. 99DR0234. On the same day, the court issued a form order entitled "Domestic Case Management and Delay Reduction Order" requiring that Smith take specified actions by a date certain. The order

required Smith *569 to provide a copy to Mrs. Reynolds. Although Smith did not see the order, he was fully aware of the routine procedure in uncontested divorces and knew what deadlines were imposed by the court as a matter of course. Smith did not set a Temporary Orders Hearing or engage in the pre-hearing conference as required by the court's order. Smith knew that Mrs. Reynolds was pregnant and he felt it necessary to wait for the birth of the child before requesting that the court enter child support orders. Smith did not file a plan for alternative dispute resolution by the stated deadline due to his unconfirmed belief that Reynolds desired to forestall the divorce.

Thereafter, Mrs. Reynolds, who resided in Kansas, signed a Waiver and Acceptance of Service and Affidavit with Respect to Financial Affairs prepared by Smith, and returned both documents to Smith's office. Mrs. Reynolds did not obtain counsel at that time.

Between January and May, Smith and Reynolds were in communication. In May 1999, Smith drafted a Settlement Agreement and gave it to Reynolds to review. Reynolds took the Separation Agreement prepared by Smith to Kansas for Mrs. Reynolds to sign, and she signed it on June 16, 1999, had it notarized, and gave it back to Reynolds. Reynolds gave it back to Ross shortly thereafter. Reynolds failed to sign it. Smith was unaware that Reynolds had returned the Separation Agreement to his office.

On May 20, 1999, Ross filed a Notice to Set regarding a hearing on Permanent Orders. Ross affixed Smith's signature to the Notice to Set. Thereafter, she neglected to call the court at the appointed time to set the hearing.

On June 7, 1999, the court issued a form Status Order notifying the parties that the Reynolds case would be dismissed unless Smith took certain specific actions. Smith did not see the Status Order, did not take any of the actions the court directed him to take, and did not provide a copy of the Order to the parties. Smith believed that the case was proceeding on course and that he was waiting for a return of the signed Separation Agreement by the parties.

Ross, in an effort to cover her failure to follow through on the Notice to Set, filed another Notice to Set on June 10, 1999. Smith signed the notice but did not confirm with Ross that she set the hearing. A hearing was not set.

Ross attempted to contact Reynolds but was unable to do so. Smith told Ross to send a letter to Reynolds and advise him that the case may be dismissed if the Separation Agreement was not filed. Smith believed Ross did so, but did not check the file to confirm that she had. Ross did not send a letter to Reynolds.

During July and August 1999, Reynolds attempted to contact Smith several times but was able to only speak to Ross. The calls were not routed to Smith, and Smith was not advised that Reynolds was attempting to reach him.

On August 11, 1999, the court dismissed the case on the grounds that the parties had not complied with the court's June 7, 1999 Status Order and required Smith to provide a copy of the order to the parties. Smith did not see the order and therefore did not comply with it. Smith continued to believe that Reynolds had lost interest in pursuing the divorce.

In October, Ross contacted the court to set the matter for a Permanent Orders hearing. It was at this point that she discovered the case had been dismissed. She determined to conceal this fact from Smith. On October 25, 1999, without Smith's knowledge or approval, Ross filed a Notice to Set Uncontested Permanent Orders, an Affidavit With Respect to Financial Affairs and the Separation Agreement, both of which Mrs. Reynolds had signed on June 16, 1999. Ross hoped that the court would reopen the case. Nothing further occurred in Case No. 99DR0234.

In November 1999, Reynolds tried to reconcile with his wife, and she declined.

In early 2000, due to the lack of communication with Smith, Reynolds came to Smith's office to inquire about the status of his case. Reynolds never spoke directly with Smith; rather, he believed at the time that Ross was his lawyer. Reynolds confronted Ross with the court order dismissing the case in August *570 1999, which he first saw when he reviewed the court file at the courthouse. Ross told Reynolds the court had lost the paperwork and it would be necessary to file a new case. Ross did not tell Smith about Reynolds's visit to the office.

On March 6, 2000, without Smith's knowledge or approval, Ross commenced a new action on behalf of Reynolds by filing a Summons for Dissolution of Marriage and Temporary

Injunction in Arapahoe County District Court under Case No. 00DR0782. Ross affixed Smith's signature to the documents. Ross falsely notarized a Waiver and Acceptance of Service and affixed Mrs. Reynolds's signature without her knowledge or authority.

The next day, without informing Smith, Ross sent a letter to Reynolds enclosing financial affidavits, a Separation Agreement, and Child Support Worksheets. After receiving these documents, Reynolds came to the office and was angry with Ross. Ross did not inform Smith that Reynolds had visited the office. Smith believed the case was closed because Reynolds had not signed the Separation Agreement. Smith had no communication with Reynolds in 2000.

On March 20, 2000, Ross filed a Petition for Dissolution of Marriage and affixed Smith's name to the pleading.

In July 2000, Mrs. Reynolds believed the divorce had been finalized. She contacted Smith's office and spoke to Ross numerous times and to Smith once, asking for a copy of the decree. Ross informed her she would inquire into the status of the case and get back to her. Later Ross told Mrs. Reynolds she was not sure why there was no decree and that there was some confusion in Smith's office. After receiving a call from Mrs. Reynolds's father, Smith asked Ross about the status of the case. Ross said that Reynolds came in to sign the Separation Agreement and that they were waiting to receive a decree from the court. Smith then told Mrs. Reynolds that he was waiting for a decree from the court and that he would get back to her. Smith did not get back to Mrs. Reynolds.

On July 15, 2000, Ross drafted a second Separation Agreement. She affixed the signatures of Smith as counsel for Reynolds, Mrs. Reynolds, and the attorney's name who shared Smith's office as counsel for Mrs. Reynolds. Ross notarized the signatures stating that she witnessed the signatures in Adams County, even though Mrs. Reynolds continued to reside in Kansas. Ross filed it with the court. Neither Smith, Mrs. Reynolds, nor the attorney who was purportedly signing as counsel for Mrs. Reynolds knew that Ross had affixed their signatures to the document. Ross knew at the time that Smith would not condone her drafting the Separation Agreement and affixing signatures to it.

In August 2000, Ross filed an Affidavit for Decree Without Appearance of Parties with the court. She affixed the signatures of Smith and the attorney who shared Smith's office as counsel for Mrs. Reynolds without their knowledge or approval. Ross knew the court would rely on the document as containing valid signatures and knew at the time she filed the document that she was making a false statement to the court.

Finally, in the spring on 2001, Mrs. Reynolds hired an attorney in Kansas to commence a new divorce proceeding at a cost of $1,500. On April 3, 2001, Ross sent a letter to Mrs. Reynolds's attorney in Kansas stating that the dissolution of marriage action in Arapahoe County had not been dismissed. She wrote the letter on behalf of Smith and affixed his signature to the letter without his knowledge. On the same date, she notified the clerk of the district court in Shawnee County, Topeka, Kansas that the matter had not been dismissed, and again affixed Smith's name to the letter without his knowledge.

On April 12, 2001, a Decree of Dissolution of Marriage issued from Arapahoe District Court in Case No. 00DR0782. The Magistrate entered the Decree unaware that it had been presented by Ross with falsified signatures of the attorneys and parties.

Shortly thereafter, the divorce proceeding in Kansas was completed and Mrs. Reynolds obtained a decree.

Smith acknowledged that he was responsible for Ross's actions, but also believed that ***571** his actions were based on his belief that Reynolds had decided not to go forward with the divorce. Smith also believed that were it not for Ross's actions as an "intervening cause," he would have been aware of the court's orders and of Reynolds's communication with Ross.

Both parties suffered harm as a result of the delay in obtaining the divorce: Mrs. Reynolds applied for but could not obtain financial aid because she was required to include Mr. Reynolds's income on her application, and she paid additional attorneys' fees to resolve the divorce. Mr. Reynolds was required to resolve child support issues in another jurisdiction. Both parties suffered personal inconvenience and stress for over one and one-half years.

Smith refunded the $800 Reynolds paid to him. [FN2]

FN2. The second divorce action filed by Ross was eventually dismissed upon Smith's motion.

II. Conclusions of Law

The Complaint filed in this matter alleges that Smith's conduct violated Colo. RPC 1.3 (an attorney shall act with reasonable diligence and promptness in representing a client) in claim one; Colo. RPC 1.4(a) (an attorney shall keep a client reasonably informed about the status of a matter and promptly comply with reasonable requests for information) and Colo. RPC 1.4(b) (an attorney shall explain a matter to the extent reasonably necessary to permit the client to make informed decisions regarding the representation) in claim two; Colo. RPC 5.3(a) (a partner in a law firm shall make reasonable efforts to ensure that the firm has in effect measures giving reasonable assurance that the person's conduct is compatible with the professional obligations of the lawyer) and Colo. RPC 5.3(b) (a lawyer having direct supervisory authority over the nonlawyer shall make reasonable efforts to ensure that the person's conduct is compatible with the professional obligations of the lawyer) in claim three, and Colo. RPC 1.16(d) (upon termination an attorney take steps to the extent reasonably practicable to protect a client's interests) in claim four.

Colo. RPC 5.3 provides:

With respect to a nonlawyer employed or retained by or associated with a lawyer:

> (a) a partner in a law firm shall make reasonable efforts to ensure that the firm has in effect measures giving reasonable assurance that the person's conduct is compatible with the professional obligations of a lawyer;
>
> (b) a lawyer having direct supervisory authority over the nonlawyer shall make reasonable efforts to ensure that the person's conduct is compatible with the professional obligations of the lawyer....

[1] Smith entered into an attorney/client relationship with Reynolds, thereby forming an obligation to perform the agreed-upon professional services, including obtaining a divorce for Reynolds through the entry of permanent orders. By agreeing to perform the requested services, Smith inherently agreed that he would perform the services in accordance with the Colorado Rules of Professional Conduct. The Complaint alleges that Smith did not have measures in place which would give reasonable assurance that Ross's conduct was compatible with the obligations of a lawyer. [FN3] The evidence presented, however, revealed that Smith did have measures in place to reasonably assure that all communications with his office were promptly brought to his attention and that Ross would conduct herself in such a manner as was compatible with his professional responsibilities. Ross didn't follow those measures. Since such measures were in place, the charged violation of Colo. RPC 5.3(a) is dismissed.

> FN3. It is not clear that the provisions of Colo. RPC 5.3(a), referring only to partners in law firms, is applicable to a lawyer practicing as a solo practitioner. That issue, however, was not argued before the Hearing Board and is not decided here. For purposes of this decision we assume, without deciding, that Colo. RPC 5.3(a) applies to a solo practitioner.

[2] The charged violation of Colo. RPC 5.3(b) requires a different consideration. Colo. RPC 5.3(b) focuses upon whether the attorney having direct supervisory authority over a nonlawyer adequately supervises that ***572** individual. Smith had direct supervisory authority over Ross in this case. He delegated substantial responsibility to her and failed to review her work. Indeed, although the client file was in his office for the entire period of time the events were unfolding, he did not review that file to determine if Ross was, in fact, attending to the case as she described to him. Smith's failure to adequately supervise Ross allowed her to conceal the court's orders requiring that Smith take specific action on Reynolds's behalf, including setting a temporary orders hearing, engaging in alternative dispute resolution or informing the court that none was necessary, calendaring all deadlines set by the court, confirming that Smith's office was in contact with the client, and confirming the correct status of the case. A simple examination of the Reynolds file would have disclosed Ross's activities and alerted Smith of the problems developing in the case.

[3] Smith's failure to adequately supervise Ross resulted in her engaging in the unauthorized practice of law. Smith's acting as Ross's direct supervisor but failing to fulfill his professional obligations with regard to that supervision violated Colo. RPC 5.3(b). Allowing a nonlawyer assistant to engage in the unauthorized practice of law by failing to supervise the nonlawyer is grounds for discipline. *People v. Reynolds*, 933 P.2d 1295, 1298-99 (Colo. 1997); *People v. Stewart*, 892 P.2d 875, 877–78 (Colo. 1995).

Smith argues that but for Ross's failing to advise him of Reynolds's attempts to contact him, her failing to provide him with the court's orders, and her failing to advise him that the case had been dismissed, he would not have neglected the client's case. Smith's argument is without merit.

Other jurisdictions have examined this issue. The Restatement (Third) of Law Governing Law, § 11 (2003) concerning a lawyer's duty of supervision, provides:

Supervision is a general responsibility of a principal (see Restatement Second, Agency § 503, Comment *f*, & id. §§ 507 & 510). A ... lawyer with authority to direct the activities of another lawyer or nonlawyer employee of the firm is such a principal. Appropriate exercise of responsibility over those carrying out the tasks of law practice is particularly important given the duties of lawyers to protect the interests of clients and in view of the privileged powers conferred on lawyers by law. The supervisory duty, in effect, requires that such additional experience and skill be deployed in reasonably diligent fashion.

Lack of awareness of misconduct by another person, either lawyer or nonlawyer, under a lawyer's supervision does not excuse a violation of this Section. To ensure that supervised persons comply with professional standards, a supervisory lawyer is required to take reasonable measures, given the level and extent of responsibility that the lawyer possesses. Those measures, such as an informal program of instructing or monitoring another person, must often assume the likelihood that a particular lawyer or nonlawyer employee may not yet have received adequate preparation for carrying out that person's own responsibilities.

In *State ex rel. Oklahoma Bar Ass'n v. Braswell*, 663 P.2d 1228, 1231–32 (Okla. 1983) the attorney raised the same argument as Smith, intimating that losing track of the client's case may have been occasioned by the inaction or neglect of his law clerk. The Oklahoma Supreme Court stated "[w]hile delegation of a task entrusted to a lawyer is not improper, it is the lawyer who must maintain a direct relationship with his client, supervise the work that is delegated, and exercise complete, though indirect, professional control over the work product.... [t]he work of lay personnel is done by them as agents of the lawyer employing them. The lawyer must supervise that work and stand responsible for its product." *See, e.g.*, **In re Morin**, 319 Or. 547, 878 P.2d 393, 401 (1994) (lawyer responsible for unauthorized practice of law by paralegal where, following lawyer's initial warning to paralegal, lawyer took no further steps to enforce instruction or to test employee's ability to identify inappropriate activities); *In re Bonanno*, 208 A.D.2d 1117, 617 N.Y.S.2d 584 (N.Y.App.Div.1994) (attorney reprimanded respondent for his conduct in the supervision of a nonattorney employee and in the management ***573** of his law office in violation of the rules of professional conduct of New Jersey prohibiting gross neglect, aiding the unauthorized practice of law, and failure to supervise adequately a nonattorney employee); *Florida Bar v. Rogowski*, 399 So.2d 1390, 1391 (Fla. 1981) (noting that an attorney's nonlawyer personnel are agents of the attorney and attorney is responsible for seeing that the agents' actions do not violate the Code of Professional Responsibility); *State v. Barrett*, 207 Kan. 178, 483 P.2d 1106, 1110 (1971) (noting that the work done by secretaries and other laypersons is done as agents of the lawyer employing them and the lawyer must supervise their work and be responsible for their work product or the lack thereof).

[4] After initially pursuing the Reynolds matter and drafting a separation agreement, Smith lost contact with Reynolds and failed to inform himself of the status of the case. He failed to comply with the court's January 27, 1999 and June 7, 1999 orders. Even if, as Smith asserts, he did not see the court orders and therefore could not comply with them, he was fully aware of the procedures and deadlines set forth by the court in a divorce proceeding. Smith failed to make every effort to locate the client and acquire his signature on the Separation Agreement, and failed to take adequate measures to confirm the status of the case. Instead, he relied on Ross to oversee the file. Smith's failing to take the required steps to resolve the Reynolds matter constitutes neglect in violation of Colo. RPC 1.3.

[5] [6] Although Smith's conduct clearly constitutes neglect, it does not, however, rise to the level of abandonment. To find abandonment rather than mere neglect, the evidence must objectively indicate that counsel deserted, rejected, and/or relinquished his professional responsibilities. In the present case, although Smith should have taken measures to locate Reynolds, Ross did not inform Smith that Reynolds had come to the office inquiring about the status of the case. Smith continued to believe that Reynolds had lost

interest in pursuing the divorce. Ross fostered Smith's lack of awareness of Reynolds's numerous attempts to contact him. He did not, therefore, desert, reject, or relinquish his professional responsibilities. Smith's actions did not terminate the attorney-client relationship with Reynolds and the provisions set forth in Colo. RPC 1.16(d) were not triggered. Accordingly, claim four alleging a violation of Colo. RPC 1.16(d) is dismissed.

[7] Initially, for approximately the first four months of representation, Smith stayed in adequate contact with Reynolds and kept him informed of the case status. Thereafter, however, for a period of a year and a half, Smith violated Colo. RPC 1.4(a) by failing to keep Reynolds reasonably informed about the status of the divorce proceeding. Smith violated Colo. RPC 1.4(b) by failing to explain the procedural status of the case to Reynolds to the extent reasonably necessary to permit the client to make informed decisions. His failure to inform himself of the status of the case does not abrogate his responsibility to keep the client reasonably informed.

Smith's conduct regarding the Reynolds matter resulted in injury to Reynolds: his divorce matter was dismissed, both parties suffered considerable distress not knowing whether they were divorced over a considerable period of time, and Reynolds must suffer the inconvenience of pursuing his legal rights in another jurisdiction.

III. Imposition of Sanction

[8] The ABA *Standards for Imposing Lawyer Sanctions* (1991 & Supp.1992) ("ABA *Standards*") are the guiding authority for electing the appropriate sanction to impose for lawyer misconduct. ABA *Standard* 4.42(b) provides that suspension is generally appropriate when "a lawyer engages in a pattern of neglect and causes injury or potential injury to a client." Because Smith's continuing failure to properly supervise Ross in the Reynolds case covered a period of nearly 27 months, his conduct established a pattern of neglect. A six-month suspension is consistent with other disciplinary measures ordered by the Supreme Court. *See* *People v. Williams*, 824 P.2d 813, 815 (Colo. 1992) (attorney suspended for six months for continued and chronic neglect of three separate legal matters with requirement **574* of reinstatement); *People v. Barber*, 799 P.2d 936, 941 (Colo.1990) (attorney suspended for six months for handling legal matter without adequate preparation, neglect of legal matter, failure to seek lawful objectives of client and gross negligence); *People v. Larson*, 716 P.2d 1093 (Colo. 1986) (neglect of entrusted legal matter and failure to carry out contract of employment warrants six-month suspension); *People v. Bugg*, 200 Colo. 512, 616 P.2d 133 (1980) (failure to process estate, to file action, and to communicate with clients, when considered with the mitigating factor of personal problems, warrants six-month suspension).

Factors in aggravation and mitigation were considered pursuant to ABA *Standards* 9.22 and 9.32, respectively. In mitigation, Smith does not have a prior disciplinary record, *see id* at 9.32(a); he did not have a dishonest or selfish motive, *see id.* at 9.32(b); Smith made a timely, good-faith effort to make restitution by returning to Reynolds his retainer, and endeavored to assist in rectifying the filing of multiple divorce cases, *see id* at 9.32(d), and Smith has made a full and free disclosure and has demonstrated a cooperative attitude toward the disciplinary proceedings, *see id.* at 9.32(f). In aggravation, Smith declined to acknowledge the wrongful nature of his conduct. He testified that he did not believe he did anything wrong in the matter. *See id.* 9.22(g). Moreover, the length of time involved in his neglect of the Reynolds case and the supervision of Ross established a pattern of misconduct. *See id.* 9.22(c).

[9] In this case, Smith's lack of recognition of his wrongdoing in combination with the substantial damage imposed upon the administration of justice by the filing and processing of an unauthorized dissolution of marriage proceeding, as well as the injury suffered by his client arising from his neglect and failure to supervise a nonlawyer employee, suggests that a period of suspension greater than six months is required. The Hearing Board finds that a nine-month suspension is appropriate under both Colorado law and the ABA *Standards*.

IV. Order

It is therefore ORDERED:

- MATTHEW S. SMITH, attorney regulation number 22681, is suspended from the practice of law for a period of nine months, effective 31 days from the date of this Order.
- Pursuant to C.R.C.P. 251.32, Smith shall pay the costs in conjunction with this matter. Complainant shall file a Statement of Costs within fifteen (15) days of the date of this Order; Smith shall have ten (10) days thereafter to file a Response.

Questions

1. What parameters did the attorney (Smith) put on the legal assistant (Ross) to make sure she was properly supervised?
2. What did the attorney (Smith) do that was improper?
3. What did the legal assistant (Ross) do that was improper?
4. What did the court find?
5. Do you agree with the Court and the imposition of the nine-month suspension?

Case Review

In the Matter of Riva, 157 N.J. 34, 722 A.2d 933 (N.J. 1999).

722 A.2d 933

(Cite as: 157 N.J. 34, 722 A.2d 933)

Supreme Court of New Jersey.

In the Matter of Robert E. RIVA, an Attorney at Law.

Argued Sept. 28, 1998.

Decided Feb. 5, 1999.

****934 *35*** Lee A. Gronikowski, Deputy Ethics Counsel, argued the cause on behalf of the Office of Attorney Ethics.

Robert E. Riva, argued the cause pro se.

PER CURIAM.

This attorney discipline matter arises from a Report and Recommendation of the Disciplinary Review Board (DRB) that respondent be publicly reprimanded. Three members of the DRB concluded that a public reprimand would be insufficient discipline and recommended a three-month suspension. The majority recommendation is based on findings of the District VB Ethics **36* Committee (DEC), concurred in by the DRB, that respondent had been guilty of gross neglect, a violation of RPC 1.1(a), and a lack of diligence, a violation of RPC 1.3. The misconduct involved the failure to file a timely answer to a complaint against his clients and his subsequent failure to act with necessary diligence to vacate a default entered on the complaint. Respondent also failed to communicate with his clients in a timely manner and misrepresented the status of the matter.

Respondent does not deny the essential facts but asserts that the conduct resulted from a misunderstanding that his adversary had withdrawn the complaint and his failure to have received notice of the proposed default judgment. Respondent contends that the Court should not follow the DRB's recommendation that he be publicly reprimanded.

Based on our independent review of the record, we find clear and convincing evidence that respondent engaged in conduct proscribed by RPC 1.1(a) and RPC 1.3, and that a public reprimand is warranted.

*****9351***

The matter involves respondent's representation of Robert Palceski and his wife, Janet, who owned a company against which a former employee threatened to file an employment-practices claim. The disgruntled employee had hired an attorney in 1992. Respondent told that attorney that if the employee sued, the employer would file a counterclaim based on alleged financial improprieties engaged in by the employee. That attorney did not file an action. The employee hired a new attorney.

In January 1993, the new attorney served a summons and complaint on the employer. The employer retained respondent again. After some modification of the documents, respondent obtained a stipulation to extend the time for filing an answer to the complaint.

**37* Respondent never filed the stipulation or the answer and counterclaim. Although he testified that his conversation with the employee's attorney led him to believe that she would voluntarily dismiss the matter, the adversary testified that she had never made such a statement because her client was "adamant" about pursuing the claim. Meanwhile, respondent had told the Palceskis that he had filed the answering papers and that, because he had heard nothing further from opposing counsel, the case would just "go away."

The employee's attorney said that she called respondent several times and left a number of messages on his answering machine between March and May 1993 to determine whether respondent intended to file an answer to the complaint. She eventually learned by calling the court that respondent had never filed an answer on behalf of his client.

In May 1993, the employee's attorney obtained an order entering default. Her transmittal letter to the court and an affidavit of service prepared by her secretary indicated that the request for entry of default and a copy of the proposed default order had been sent to respondent by regular mail. Respondent denied receiving them.

The court entered a default judgment against the employer for $1.7 million in September 1993. A court officer seized the trucks, tools, and bank accounts of the employer. A constable sought to seize the personal cars and other assets of the Palceskis.

Robert Palceski telephoned respondent while the constable was at his home. Respondent assured him that he would go to court the next day to have their assets returned to them. He went to the Palceskis' home that evening to obtain copies of the papers served on them to prepare an emergent motion to vacate the default and assured them that he was working on the motion. The Palceskis asked for a copy of the motion, but respondent "put them off." It was only when Robert Palceski threatened to drive to respondent's office to pick up a copy of the motion that respondent agreed to fax him a copy. The faxed copy consisted of ***38** 14 blank pages. When later asked about the blank pages, respondent stated that he might have put the pages in the machine backwards or improperly transmitted the document.

When respondent went to court two days later, he was only able to obtain the release of the Palceskis' trucks and tools. (Respondent contends that the default judgment improperly included a business entity not named in the original complaint.) Although respondent filed a later motion to vacate the default in full, the trial court held that respondent's papers were deficient and that additional information was needed to set forth a meritorious defense to the claim.

From September through December 1993, respondent told the Palceskis on a number of occasions that he was consulting with other attorneys and conducting research on their defense. By the time that the court considered the motion again in December, the Palceskis had retained a new attorney. It was several weeks before respondent turned over the file. The only papers in the file were the motion to vacate the default with its accompanying inadequate certification, a cover letter to the employee's attorney with the draft stipulation extending the time to answer, and the draft answer and counterclaim. Only the motion to vacate had been filed with the ****936** court. The Palceskis later settled the lawsuit of the employee by a payment of $11,500.

In his testimony before the DEC, respondent acknowledged that although he knew that a stipulation of dismissal was necessary to have resolved the litigation once the complaint had been filed, he never obtained one. He believed that he had resolved the problem with the employee's attorneys.

The DRB agreed with the DEC that respondent's conduct displayed gross neglect and a lack of diligence from the time that he failed to file a timely answer to the complaint through his failure to act with necessary haste to vacate the default.

The dissenting members stressed respondent's continuous misrepresentations to his clients about the status of the matter both ***39** before and after the entry of the default, and the great financial and emotional injury suffered by the clients, who had relied on respondent's false assurances that their interests were being protected. The experience was a "nightmare" for respondent's clients, who were threatened with bankruptcy and the loss of their personal assets. In the dissenters' view,

> this is precisely the sort of attorney who contributes to the lamentable state of disrepute in which the attorney population has fallen, and who is responsible for the public's loss of trust in the legal profession. In order to assure the public that such conduct will never be tolerated, we believe that a period of suspension must be imposed. We would suspend this respondent for three months.

II

We have attempted to establish over a long period of years predictable standards for the imposition of discipline in cases of attorney misconduct. On one end of the spectrum are the cases in which disbarment of an attorney will be "almost invariable." In re Wilson, 81 N.J. 451, 453, 409 A.2d 1153 (1979) (misappropriating client funds).

Crimes of dishonesty touch upon a central trait of character that members of the bar must possess. In re Di Biasi, 102

N.J. 152, 506 A.2d 719 (1986). Such crimes are defined as a "serious crime" pursuant to Rule 1:20-13b(2). We have repeatedly held that "when a crime of dishonesty touches upon the administration of justice," id. at 155, 506 A.2d 719, the offense "is deserving of severe sanctions and would ordinarily require disbarment." In re Verdiramo, 96 N.J. 183, 186, 475 A.2d 45 (1984); In re Edson, 108 N.J. 464, 530 A.2d 1246 (1987) (counseling client to commit perjury and lying to prosecutor). Such conduct "poisons the well of justice." In re Pajerowski, 156 N.J. 509, 721 A.2d 992 (1998) (quoting In re Verdiramo, supra, 96 N.J. at 185, 475 A.2d 45). Serious crimes not touching on the administration of justice often warrant the same penalty of disbarment. In re Lunetta, 118 N.J. 443, 572 A.2d 586 (1989) (conspiring to receive and sell stolen securities); In re Mallon, 118 N.J. 663, 573 A.2d 921 (1990) (conspiring to commit tax fraud).

40 Nevertheless, "even in proceedings involving 'serious crimes,' mitigating factors may justify imposition of sanctions less severe than disbarment or extended suspension." Compare In re Imbriani, 149 N.J. 521, 533, 694 A.2d 1030 (1997) (disbarment for engaging in numerous acts of misconduct that involved substantial amounts of money) with In re Litwin, 104 N.J. 362, 517 A.2d 378 (1986) (five-year suspension for arson); In re Kushner, 101 N.J. 397, 502 A.2d 32 (1986) (three-year suspension for false certification); In re Labendz, 95 N.J. 273, 471 A.2d 21 (1984) (one-year suspension for instigating fraudulent representations to federally insured lender for purposes of obtaining a mortgage, despite excellent reputation, unblemished record, and lack of personal gain); and In re Silverman, 80 N.J. 489, 404 A.2d 301 (1979) (18-month suspension for filing false answer with the bankruptcy court to retain custody of certain assets).

Other crimes of dishonesty not touching upon the administration of justice nonetheless demonstrate an absence of character that ordinarily warrants extended periods of suspension.

[1] Crimes that subvert the public policy and good order of the State will ordinarily warrant a period of suspension. In re Kinnear, ****937*** 105 N.J. 391, 522 A.2d 414 (1987) (one-year suspension for criminal drug use); In re Herman, 108 N.J. 66, 527 A.2d 868 (1987) (three-year suspension for criminal sexual contact).

[2] Material misrepresentations of fact in sworn affidavits will warrant a long period of suspension. In re Lunn, 118 N.J. 163, 570 A.2d 940 (1990) (three years). Even misrepresenting a reason for an overlooked court appearance may result in a suspension. In re Johnson, 102 N.J. 504, 509 A.2d 171 (1986) (three months).

[3] Charges of client neglect "are serious and can have a detrimental impact on the confidence the public should have in the [b]ar of this state." In re O'Gorman, 99 N.J. 482, 492, 493 A.2d 1233 (1985) (citation omitted). When such ethical infractions demonstrate a pattern of neglect and of misrepresentation to clients, a period of suspension is warranted. In re Cullen, 112 ***41*** N.J. 13, 20, 547 A.2d 697 (1988); In re O'Gorman, supra, 99 N.J. at 492, 493 A.2d 1233; In re Getchius, 88 N.J. 269, 276, 440 A.2d 1341 (1982).

We have noted, however, in such cases that "the picture presented is not that of an isolated instance of aberrant behavior unlikely to be repeated. [The attorney's] conduct over a period of years has exhibited a 'pattern of negligence or neglect in the handling of matters.' "In re Getchius, supra, 88 N.J. at 276, 440 A.2d 1341 (quoting In re Fusciello, 81 N.J. 307, 310, 406 A.2d 1316 [1979]). The Cullen case involved two instances of neglect; O'Gorman involved four instances of neglect after being suspended for five prior similar complaints; and Getchius involved six instances of neglect. Other cases of suspension for client neglect and misrepresentation include In re Terner, 120 N.J. 706, 577 A.2d 511 (1990) (three-year suspension for pattern of neglect for failure to communicate with 13 clients despite potential mitigating factor of drug addiction, which respondent denied); In re Stein, 97 N.J. 550, 483 A.2d 109 (1984) (six-month suspension for "pattern of neglect" in handling three matters coupled with self-dealing in another matter); In re Goldstaub, 90 N.J. 1, 446 A.2d 1192 (1982) (one-year suspension for pattern of neglect involving three civil cases and one criminal case combined with long history of ethical complaints). In light of respondent's unblemished record for almost two decades, he does not fall within the end of the spectrum that warrants suspension.

III

[4] [5] [6] [7] "[T]he principal reason for discipline is to preserve the confidence of the public in the integrity and trustworthiness of lawyers in general," In re Kushner, supra, 101 N.J. at 400, 502 A.2d 32 (quoting In re Wilson, supra, 81 N.J. at 456, 409 A.2d 1153). In making disciplinary decisions, we must consider the interests of the public as well as of the bar and the individual involved. Ibid. "The severity of discipline to be imposed must comport with the seriousness of the ethical infractions in light of ***42*** all the relevant circumstances." In re Nigohosian, 88 N.J. 308, 315, 442 A.2d 1007 (1982). For that reason, we consider factors in mitigation of the seriousness of the offense. In re Hughes, 90 N.J. 32, 36, 446 A.2d 1208 (1982).

Although respondent's conduct was inexcusable in that he had compounded his initial neglect in not filing an answer with his later neglect and misrepresentation concerning his efforts to vacate the default judgment, the ethical misconduct is related to one client transaction. The closest analogous case, In re Kantor, 118 N.J. 434, 435, 572 A.2d 196 (1990), also involved a single failure to file an appellate brief and to represent truthfully the status of the appeal, but the one-year suspension reflected that it was conduct "viewed in combination with a prior ethics infraction and lack of mitigating factors." Generally, in the absence of conduct evidencing a disregard for the ethics system, cases involving a similar mixture of ethics infractions have resulted in a reprimand. See, e.g., In re Onorevole, 144 N.J. 477, 677 A.2d 210 (1996) (reprimand for gross neglect, lack of diligence, failure to communicate, failure to cooperate with disciplinary authorities and misrepresentation; attorney misrepresented to client that he had filed a complaint and that court was backlogged in filing complaints, when in fact attorney had not filed the complaint at all); In re ***938** Horton, 132 N.J. 266, 624 A.2d 1367 (1993) (reprimand for lack of diligence, failure to communicate, failure to provide sufficient information to allow client to make informed decisions and misrepresentation; attorney allowed an appeal to be procedurally dismissed, based on his belief that he could not win appeal, first allowing his client to believe that appeal was pending and then attempting to mislead client into believing that appeal was dismissed on merits).

[8] [9] "We ordinarily place great weight on the recommendation of the Disciplinary Review Board." In re Kushner, supra, 101 N.J. at 403, 502 A.2d 32; see also In re Vaughn, 123 N.J. 576, 589 A.2d 610 (1991) (adopting DRB's recommendation to reprimand publicly attorney who had failed to keep client informed, ***43** displayed pattern of neglect, and had failed to reply to DEC investigation). We greatly respect, as well, the views of the dissenting members of the DRB but believe that predictability and uniformity in the imposition of ethical decisions call for a public reprimand in these circumstances. We do not find that respondent's misconduct demonstrates dishonesty, deceit, or contempt for law, but rather an aberrational neglect of his responsibilities as an attorney. Respondent will suffer the reproach of his peers for the suffering inflicted on his client. Finally, we cannot overlook the fact that the default judgment of $1.7 million was entered (perhaps against the wrong parties) in a case that settled for $11,500.

For all of these reasons, we conclude that the appropriate discipline is a public reprimand.

Respondent shall reimburse the Disciplinary Oversight Committee for appropriate administrative costs, including the costs of transcripts.

For reprimand—Chief Justice PORITZ and Justices HANDLER, POLLOCK, O'HERN, GARIBALDI, STEIN, and COLEMAN—7.

Opposed—None

ORDER

It is ORDERED that ROBERT E. RIVA of SHORT HILLS, who was admitted to the bar of this State in 1979, is reprimanded; and it is further

ORDERED that the entire record of this matter be made a permanent part of respondent's file as an attorney at law of this State; and it is further

ORDERED that respondent reimburse the Disciplinary Oversight Committee for appropriate administrative costs incurred in the prosecution of this matter.

END OF DOCUMENT

Case Review Exercises

1. List each of the attorney's actions in this case that amounted to a lack of diligence, incompetence, or failure to communicate with his client.
2. Discuss how you might have felt if you had been the attorney's client in this matter.
3. Why did the New Jersey Supreme Court only reprimand the attorney?
4. After reading the case, did you tend to agree with the New Jersey Supreme Court that ordered the attorney be reprimanded or with the Disciplinary Review Board that recommended a three-month suspension of the attorney? Explain your answer.

Helpful Web Sites

Organization	Description	Internet Address
American Bar Association (ABA)	Association for attorneys. The Web site has a large amount of information and publications relevant to individuals working in the legal profession.	http://www.americanbar.org
ABA Law Practice Management Section	ABA Web site devoted to law practice management issues, including docket control and case management.	http://www.americanbar.org/groups/law_practice.html
ABA Legal Technology Resource Center	ABA Web site devoted to technology. Includes resources and articles.	http://www.abanet.org/tech/ltrc/home.html

Docket Control and Case Management Software

Organization	Product/Service	Internet Address
Abacus Data Systems	AbacusLaw (legal PIM/case management)	http://www.abacuslaw.com
Chesapeake Interlink, Ltd.	Needles (legal PIM/case management)	http://www.needleslaw.com
Clio	Full-featured legal accounting software.	http://www.goclio.com
LexisNexis	Time Matters (legal PIM/case management)	http://www.timematters.com
Thomson Elite	ProLaw and LawManager	http://www.elite.com/
Gavel & Gown Software	Amicus Attorney (legal PIM/case management)	http://amicusattorney.com/
Lawex Corp.	TrialWorks (legal case management)	http://www.trialworks.com
Legal Files Software	Legal Files (legal PIM/case management)	http://www.legalfiles.com
LegalEdge Software	Case management for criminal defense attorneys, prosecutors, and general law offices	http://www.legaledge.com
ADC Legal Systems, Inc.	Perfect Practice (case management)	http://www.perfectpractice.com
Aderant	Client Profiles (case management) and CompuLaw (case management)	http://www.aderant.com/products/aderant-total-office http://www.aderant.com/products/aderant-compulaw

Suggested Reading

1. *Law Practice* magazine, published by the American Bar Association Law Practice Management Section http://www.americanbar.org/groups/law_practice.html.
2. *Paralegal Today* magazine, published by James Publishing http://paralegaltoday.com/.
3. Munneke, G. A., & Davis, A. E. (2003, 2007, 2010). *The Essential Formbook: Comprehensive Management Tools for Lawyers, Volumes I-IV.* American Bar Association.
4. *Law Office Computing magazine*, published by James Publishing http://www.lawofficecomputing.com.

Hands-On Exercises
Clio—Docket Control

Training Manual Outline

Number	Lesson Title	Concepts Covered
Lesson 1*	Part A: Introduction to Clio Part B: Set Up Law Firm Profile	Understanding the Clio Platform Details for Firm descriptions
Lesson 2	Making Docket Entries	Entering docket entries in Clio
Lesson 3	Docketing by Rules and Searching and Retrieving Docket Entries	Making a docket entry with rules; searching and retrieving docket entries

*NOTE: Lesson 1—Introduction to Clio is the same for every subject matter. If you completed Lesson 1 in an earlier tutorial, you do not need to repeat it.

Welcome to Adams & Lee

Welcome to Adams & Lee! We are an active and growing firm with six attorneys and three paralegals. As you know, you have been hired as a paralegal intern. We are very happy to have you on board; we can certainly use your help.

At Adams & Lee, we take pride in carefully docketing and tracking all appointments and deadlines so that we meet and exceed our duty to our clients with respect to providing outstanding legal services. In this tutorial, you will learn how to use our computer system's docketing functions. We use Clio, a sophisticated legal-specific, Web-based program. Clio has many features related to docket control. It is important that you have a basic understanding of these features since most of our staff enter and track their own deadlines, appointments, and things to do. If you have completed Lesson 1 in a prior tutorial, please skip it and go directly to Lesson 2.

Getting Started

Introduction

Throughout these exercises, information you need to type into the program will be designated in several different ways.

- Keys to be pressed on the keyboard will be designated in brackets, in all caps and bold type (e.g., press the [**ENTER**] key).
- Movements with the mouse/pointer will be designated in bold and italics (e.g., ***point to File on the menu bar and click the pointer***).

- Words or letters that should be typed will be designated in bold and enlarged (e.g., type **Training Program**).
- Information that is or should be displayed on your computer screen is shown in bold, with quotation marks (e.g., "**Press ENTER to continue**").

Clio Installation (Appendix A)

Clio is not a downloaded program; it is accessed from the Web site. You may be invited by your instructor to join as a nonlawyer (paralegal) in a hypothetical law firm through your e-mail. ***Click the hyperlink or copy and paste it into your Internet browser. Follow the on-screen instructions for providing your name and creating a password.*** You will now have access to Clio and the hypothetical law firm.

Your instructor may have you create a Clio account and work independently. In that case, see Appendix A for installation instructions.

LESSON 1: Part A (Appendix B)

You should become familiar with the Clio Platform and its essential functions before you begin any of the lessons. *Note*: If you are already logged in, you will skip Steps 1 and 2.

1. Start your Internet browser. Type ***www.goclio.com*** in the Internet browser and press the **[ENTER] key**.
2. On the Clio Home page, ***click Log In. On the next screen, enter the e-mail address and password you provided in Clio and click SIGN IN. If you check the box next to KEEP ME SIGNED IN, you will be able to skip this step in the future.***
3. Clio will open in the hypothetical law firm on the PRACTICE page. At this point you are ready to explore the Clio platform and its essential functions. There are 11 tabs available in Clio. We will start with the PRACTICE tab.
4. ***Click*** **PRACTICE**. Your screen should now look like Clio Exhibit 1A-1. This is the Clio dashboard which provides a quick look at the agenda, calendar, and billing information. You will now explore the other 10 tabs.

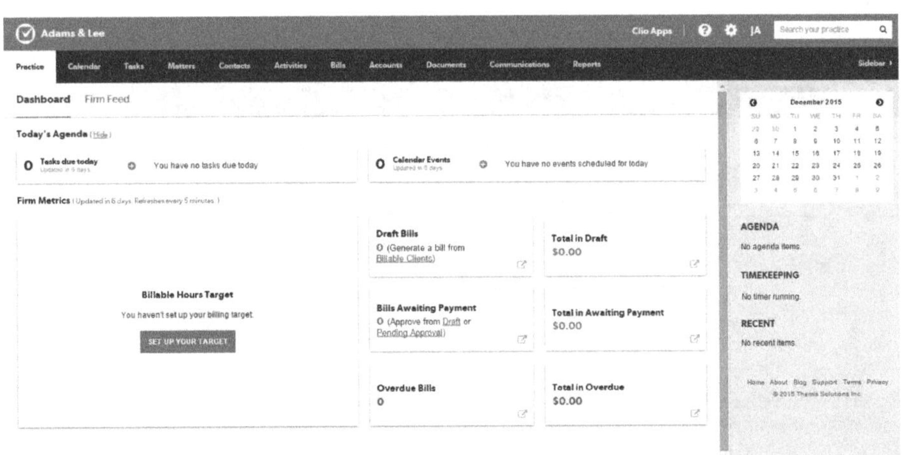

Clio Exhibit 1A-1 Practice Tab

Source: Themis Solutions, Inc.

5. ***Click* CALENDAR.** You may need to scroll down to see the entire page. You can change the view to see your Agenda, or Day, Week, Month, or Year views. You can view your personal calendar, the firm calendar or both.
6. To create a calendar entry, while in the Week view, ***select the Wednesday of that current week and double-click on the 10:00 am time slots.*** The Create Calendar Entry will open. See Clio Exhibit 1A-2. If you ***click Add Event,*** the date will default to the current date.

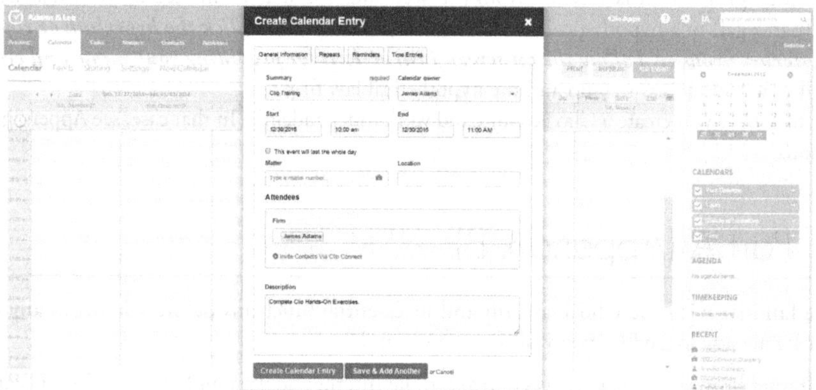

Clio Exhibit 1A-2 Create Calendar Entry

Source: Themis Solutions, Inc.

Under Summary, type **Clio Training**. Under **Start**, type **10:00 AM** and under **End** type **11:00 AM**. Leave Matter and Location "**blank**," and under Description, type **Complete Clio Hands-On Exercises.** ***Click Create Calendar Entry***. When adding multiple entries, ***click Save & Add Another***. After the entry is complete, it will appear in the calendar. ***Place your cursor over the new calendar entry*** to see the description. Your calendar should look like Clio Exhibit 1A-3. You can now move to the "Tasks" tab.

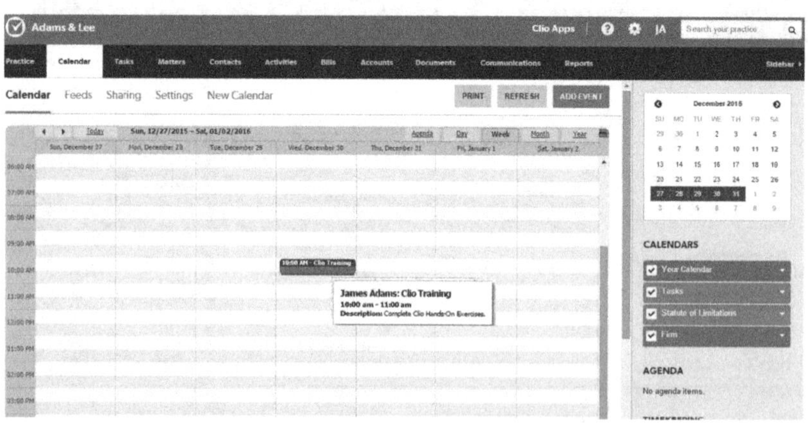

Clio Exhibit 1A-3 Calendar Entry - View

Source: Themis Solutions, Inc.

7. ***Click* TASKS**. This is where specific tasks can be assigned to specific individuals or groups. To create a new Task, ***click Add***. See Clio Exhibit 1A-4. Under Task Name, type **Clio Training**.

Clio Exhibit 1A-4 Add Task - "Due At"

Source: Themis Solutions, Inc.

Under Description, type **Watch Clio training videos.** Under Due: the radial button will default to **"Due at"** when there are no other tasks associated. ***Click the box under "Due At,"*** and a calendar will appear. ***Select Thursday of the current week***. Under Assignee, ***select Firm User and then choose yourself.*** Under Priority, ***select Normal.*** Under Matter, ***type 00003-Battise: Custody Agreement*** (the case will appear in the list as you begin typing the number). Then ***click Save Task.*** When adding multiple tasks, ***select Save and Add Another***. At this point you will be on the ***"tasks" under 00003-Battise***. See Clio Exhibit 1A-5.

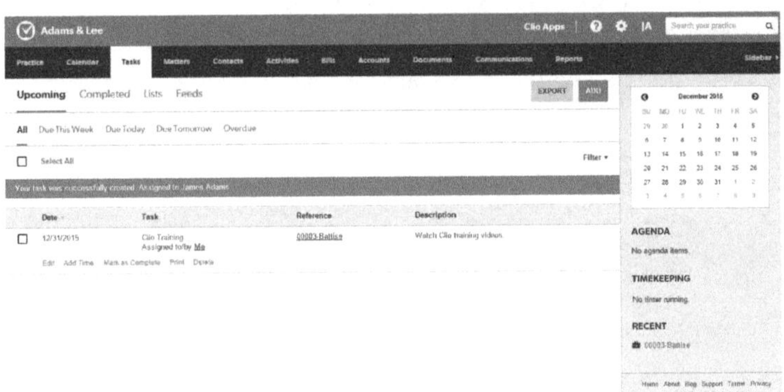

Clio Exhibit 1A-5 Task Entry - "Due At"

Source: Themis Solutions, Inc.

8. When you have several assigned tasks under a specific case matter, you have the option of choosing **"Due in"** which allows you to choose a date in relation to other Tasks in the Matter. From your current position in (Exhibit 1A-5), ***select Add***. Your screen should again look like Exhibit 1A-3. Under Task Name, type **Clio Training**. Under Description, type **Watch Clio Introduction Videos**. Under Assignee, ***select Firm User and then choose yourself.*** Under Priority, ***select Normal.*** Under Matter, ***type 00003-Battise: Custody Agreement*** (the case will appear in the list as you begin typing the number). Then ***select 00003Battise: Custody Agreement.*** Under Due: the radial will default to

"Due at," however; you now have the option to choose **"Due in."** ***Select "Due in,"*** and a dialogue box will appear. See Clio Exhibit 1A-6.

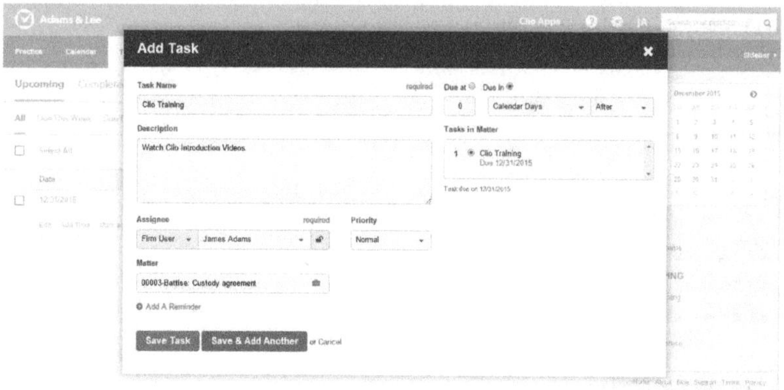

Clio Exhibit 1A-6 Add Task – "Due In"

Source: Themis Solutions, Inc.

ENTER **"1"** in the box marked with a 0. ***Select Calendar Weeks*** under the drop-down menu in the next box, ***Select before*** under the drop-down menu in the next box. Then ***select Clio Training*** under the radial button. ***Click Save Task.*** The second task will now appear listed on the Tasks page. See Clio Exhibit 1A-7.

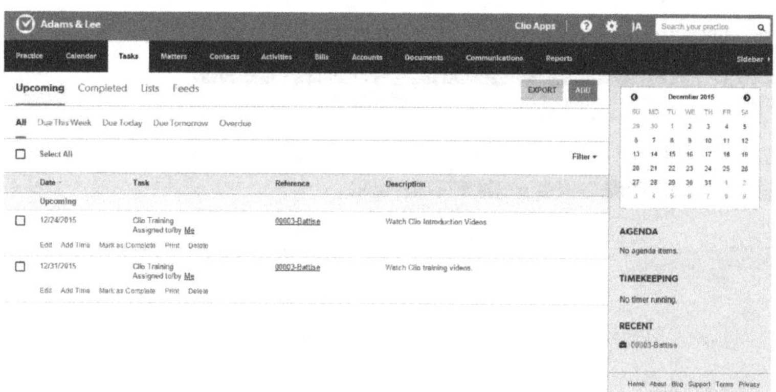

Clio Exhibit 1A-7 Upcoming Task Entries

Source: Themis Solutions, Inc.

9. ***Click*** **MATTERS**. Matters are what Clio calls for cases or files. Clio allows you to associate, or connect, matters with clients, tasks, bills, etc. In later exercises you will see how that works and you will create several new matters.
10. ***Click*** **CONTACTS**. Contacts are people and corporations that you do business with (clients, other attorneys, court reporters, etc.).
11. ***Click*** **ACTIVITIES**. "Activities" is what Clio uses for both time and billing entries as well as expense entries. Time entries can be billed as a flat rate or as an hourly rate. In later exercises you will create several new billing activities.

12. ***Click* BILLS**. Here, you can create a new bill, review a client's billing history, and create bill themes (designs) among other bill-related issues. In later exercises you will create several new bills.
13. ***Click* ACCOUNTS**. Here you can view and manage the various bank accounts of a law firm.
14. ***Click* DOCUMENTS**. Here you can view and manage the documents maintained in Clio.
15. ***Click* COMMUNICATIONS**. Here you can send and receive e-mails, maintain communication logs, interact with colleagues and Clio-connected users, as well as limit permissions between groups for file-related communications.
16. ***Click* REPORTS**. Here you can create reports on a variety of topics (billing client, mater, productivity, and revenue).
17. To end this Clio session, ***click your initials at the top of the screen. Click Sign Out and then close your Internet Browser.***

This concludes the introduction lesson on Clio's platform and essential functions review.

LESSON 1: Part B (Appendix C)

In this lesson, you will set up the firm profile in the hypothetical law firm, establish billing rate, create an activity description, set up bank accounts and establish the matter-numbering protocol.

Note: If you are already logged in, you will skip Steps 1 and 2.

1. Start your Internet browser. Type www.goclio.com in the Internet browser and press the **[ENTER] key**.
2. On the Clio Home page, ***click Log In. On the next screen, enter the e-mail address and password you provided in Clio and click SIGN IN. If you check the box next to KEEP ME SIGNED IN, you will be able to skip this step in the future.***
3. Before you enter new clients, contacts and matters in Clio, details for the hypothetical law firm should be entered. First, you will set up the account information for your hypothetical law firm. ***Click the "settings" icon*** (looks like a gear) at the top of the screen next to the "***initials***." Your screen should look like Clio Exhibit 1B-1.

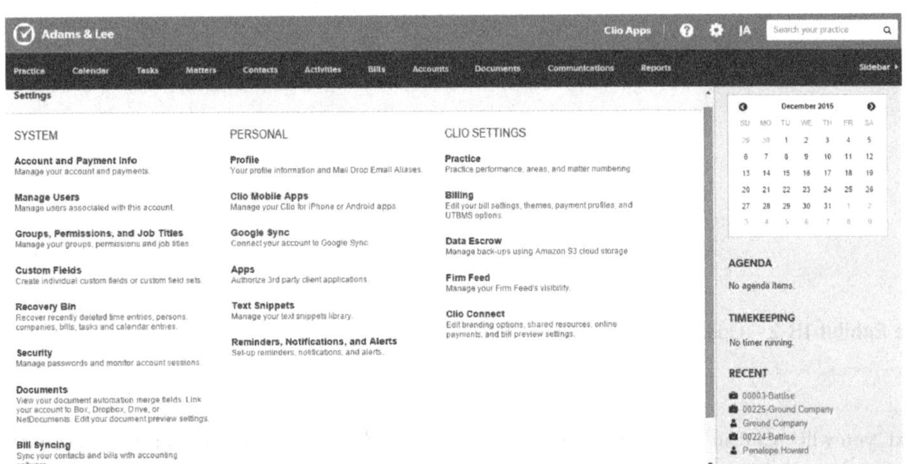

Clio Exhibit 1B-1 Clio Settings Screen

Source: Themis Solutions, Inc.

4. ***Click Account and Payment Info.*** The name of your hypothetical law firm will be established by your instructor (i.e., Adams & Lee) or your First and Last name if you create your own individual account (i.e., Law Office of "First name" "Last name" that you entered). Note: Free accounts do not have access to payment info.
5. ***Type the name, address, and contact information of your firm*** (i.e., sample check from Exhibit 6-1 (Chapter 6), instructor provided, or create your own).
6. Next, ***click the drop-down menu under Date format. Select*** the option that resembles ***12/31/2015.*** Then, ***click the drop-down menu under Time format. Select*** the option that resembles ***11:59 pm. Click Save New Information.***
7. You will now update profile and establish a billing rate. ***Click*** the "settings" icon (looks like a gear) at the top of the screen next to the "initials." Your screen should look like Clio Exhibit 1B-1. ***Click Profile*** and scroll down to **Billing Rate.** ***Type 175.00 next to $/Hr. Click Save New Information.*** See Clio Exhibit 1B-2.

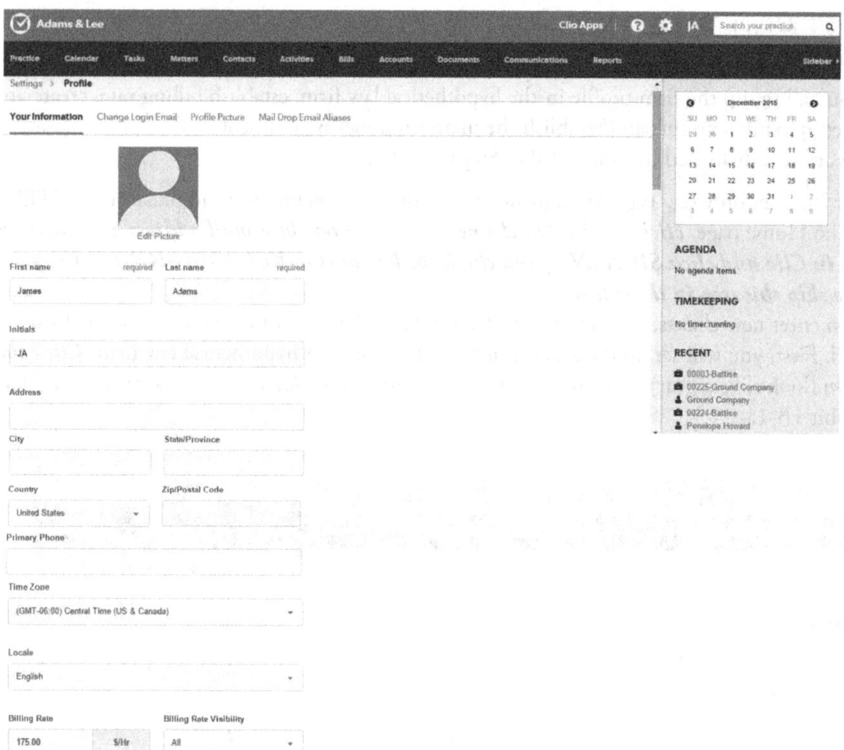

Clio Exhibit 1B-2 Update Profile – Billing Rate

Source: Themis Solutions, Inc.

8. Next, you will create an Activity Description. These are used to ensure a consistent description of commonly used time entries across a law firm. It can also be used as a shortcut—you can save text in the Activity Description and when you enter in a time entry, it will populate this text for you. Activity Descriptions can be shared across a law firm so that everyone in the firm can use them. ***Click the Activities tab, then click Activity Descriptions, then click Add.*** See Clio Exhibit 1B-3.

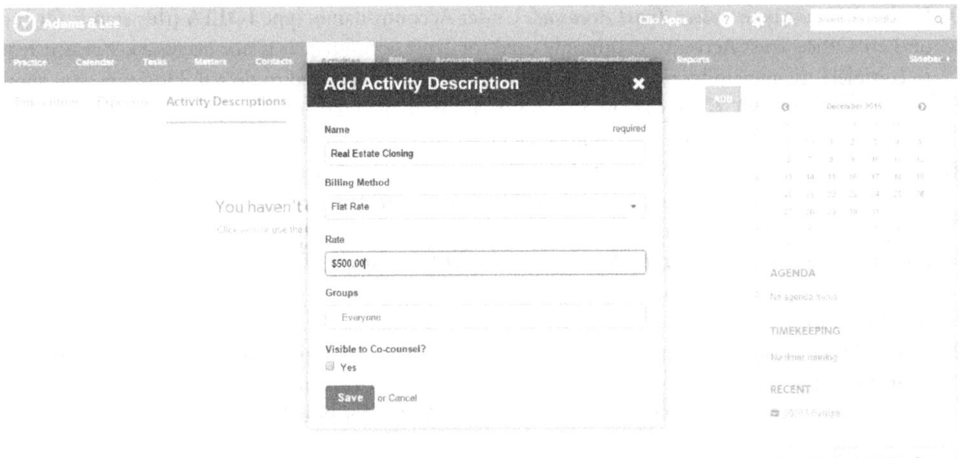

Clio Exhibit 1B-3 Add Activity Description

Source: Themis Solutions, Inc.

Under Name, type **Real Estate Closing**. Under Billing Method, ***select Flat Rate***. This opens a text box called Rate; type **$500.00** in the text box, ***Click Save***. This flat rate fee will override the $175.00 per hour established as the default rate.

9. Next, you will create bank accounts. ***Click the Accounts tab***, then ***click New***. You will set up two accounts—the first will be a Trust Account (one that contains only client money) and the second will be an Operating account (one that ***should not*** contain client money). See Clio Exhibit 1B-4.

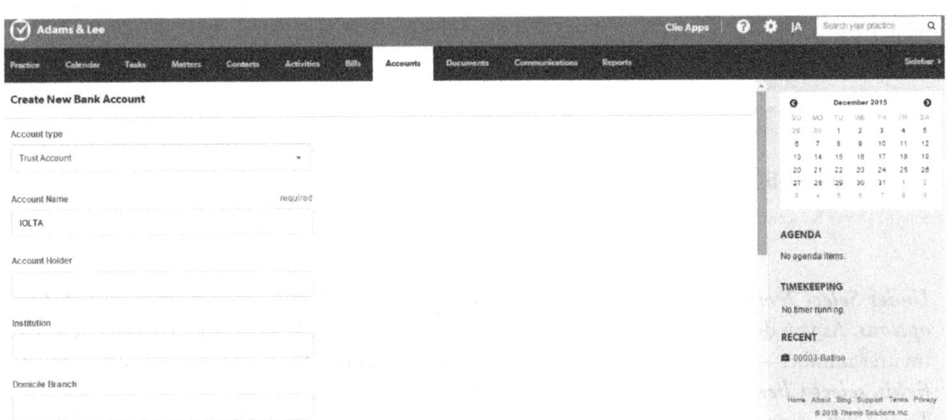

Clio Exhibit 1B-4 Create New Bank Account

Source: Themis Solutions, Inc.

10. Under Account type, ***select Trust Account.*** Under Account name, type **IOLTA** (this stands for Interest on Law Office Trust Account, commonly used for Trust accounts). It is not necessary, nor is it required, to complete the remainder of this form (although you are welcomed to do so). However, you should leave the Balance 0.0. ***Click Create New Bank Account.*** The screen will refresh (showing the new IOLTA account) so additional accounts may be created.
11. Now create the Operating Account. ***Click New,*** then under Account type, ***select Operating Account.*** Under Account name, type **Law Firm Account**. It is not necessary, nor is it required, to complete the remainder of this form (although you are welcomed to do so). However, you should leave the Balance 0.0. ***Click the box next to Default Account.*** (The default account will show up first on the Transactions tab found when a client file is opened under Matters.) ***Click Create New Bank Account.***
12. You will now create the matter-numbering protocol for the hypothetical law firm. ***Click the "settings" icon*** (looks like a gear) at the top of the screen next to the "***initials***." Your screen should look like Clio Exhibit 1B-1. ***Click Practice,*** and then ***click Matter Numbering.*** See Clio Exhibit 1B-5.

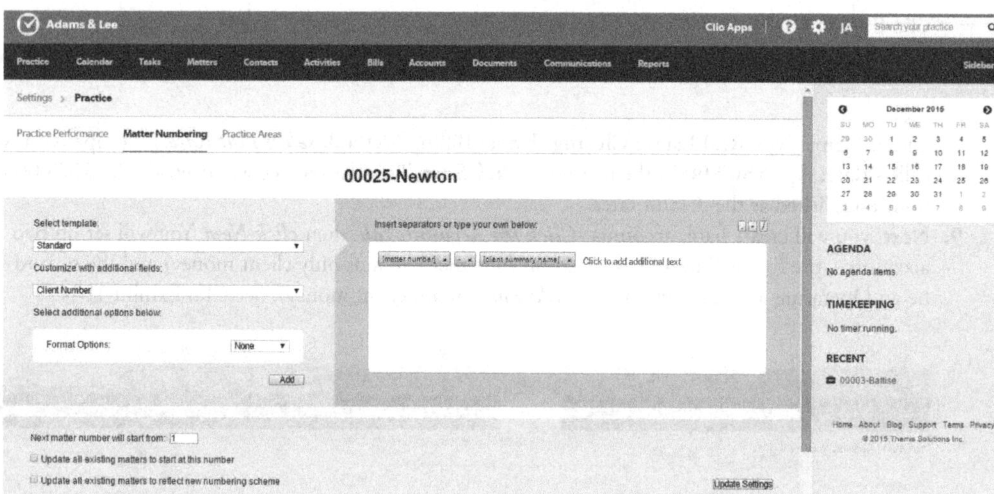

Clio Exhibit 1B-5 Matter Numbering

Source: Themis Solutions, Inc.

Under Select Template: click the drop-down menu arrow and click on each of the available options. As you do, notice how the sample matter number (00025-Newton) changes. Use the default (matter number—client summary name), then ***select Standard.*** Under ***Customize with additional fields, select Client Number. Click Update Settings.***

13. To end this Clio session, ***click on your initials*** at the top of the screen. ***Click Sign Out, and then close your Internet browser.***

This concludes the lesson on law firm profile and setup.

LESSON 2: Making Docket Entries

In this lesson, you will make a docket entry into Clio. You will use the current month and date for all transactions. *Note*: If you are already logged in, you will skip Steps 1 and 2.

1. Start your Internet browser. Type www.goclio.com in the Internet browser and press the **[ENTER] key**.
2. On the Clio Home page, ***click Log In. On the next screen, enter the email address and password you provided in Clio and click SIGN IN. If you check the box next to KEEP ME SIGNED IN, you will be able to skip this step in the future.***
3. Clio opens in the PRACTICE tab. ***Click the Matters tab.*** From the list of preloaded cases ***select*** "00003-Battise." (*Note*: If you have not preloaded files, see Appendix "A" for instructions or add a "new contact" (Chapter 4, Lesson 2).Your screen should look like Clio Exhibit 7-1. Your screen may show amounts under "Metrics," depending on which Clio exercises were previously done.

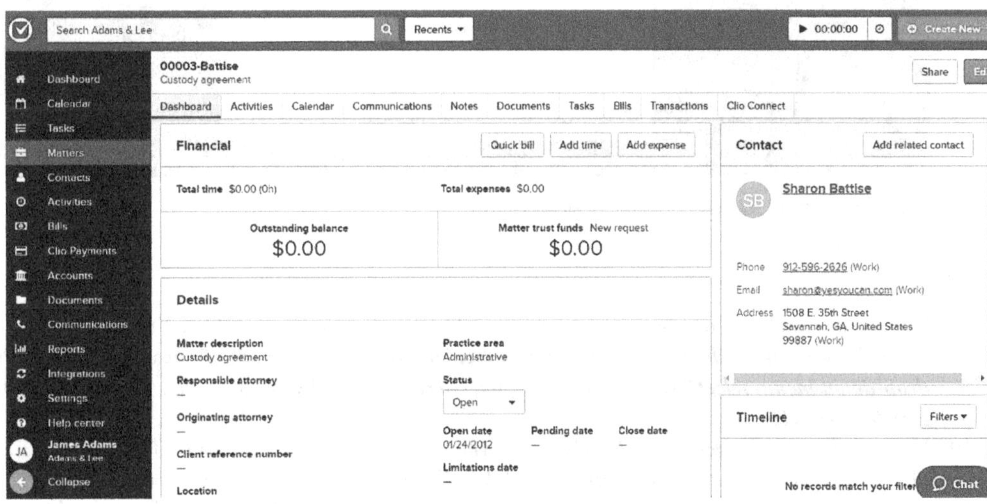

Clio Exhibit 7-1 Matters - Docket Details Screen

Source: Themis Solutions, Inc.

4. ***Click on the Calendar tab***, then ***select Add***. At this point you are ready to enter all the details about this docket entry.
5. Under Summary, type **Telephone Conference**. Under Start, use current date and calendar owner. Then ***select start*** type 3:00 P.M. Clio will automatically calculate the time as one hour for the end time, which will now show 4:00 P.M. We will leave the end time as the default.
6. In the location field, type **James' Office**.
7. The Attendees field will automatically show the default attorney. At this point you will add additional attendees. Clio will automatically suggest the client (in this case *Sharon Battise*). ***Click on Sharon Battise.*** It will now appear in the attendee Contacts box under attendees. (Please note: if the contact does not already exist, you will need to "invite" the contacts. You can add them as an Attendee).

8. Under Description, type ***Phone conference with client.*** At this point, your screen should look like Clio Exhibit 7-2.

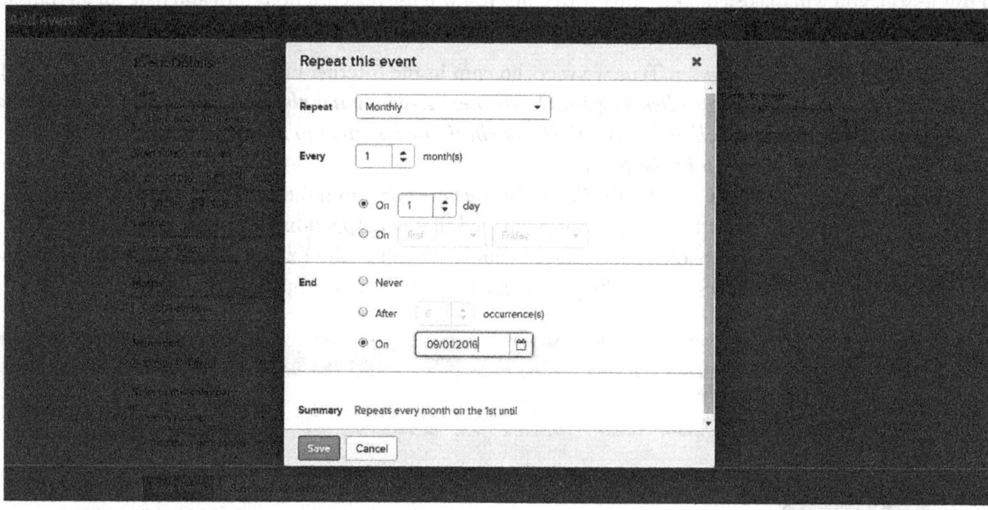

Clio Exhibit 7-2 Matters – Create Calendar Entry

Source: Themis Solutions, Inc.

You can now add information in the remaining tabs (Repeats, Reminders, Time Entries).

9. Under Repeats, ***from the drop-down menu, select "monthly."*** Then under **Repeat Every, *from the drop-down menu, select*** **"1."** Under **Repeat by, *select* "Day of the week."** Then, under "**Ends On,**" ***type 09/01/2016.***
10. Under Reminders, ***select Add A Reminder.*** It will default to the current e-mail. Then, type the number "1," and, ***from the drop-down menu, select "days."*** Do not change the default "before."
11. Under Time Entries **click Add A Time Entry**. Then under Activity Description, ***from the drop-down menu, select "Telephone Conference."*** Clio will automatically list the default rate. Then, ***click Create Time Entry.*** (Note: If no descriptions were added during the setup sessions, you can quickly create a description under the "Activities" menu and name it "**Telephone Conference**"). The default rate will appear based on the description selected. Under **Notes, type "Weekly phone conference with client.** Then, ***click Create Time Entry.***
12. When you have completed all the calendar options, ***click Create Calendar Entry.*** If you are have multiple calendar entries for the matter you are currently working with, you can ***click Save and Add Another.*** At this point, your screen should look like Clio Exhibit 7-3.

Note: It may take a few minutes for the entry to appear on your Calendar. Refresh on the Calendar will help the information appear quicker.

This concludes Lesson 2 (Making Docket Entries) of the Clio Hands-On Exercises.

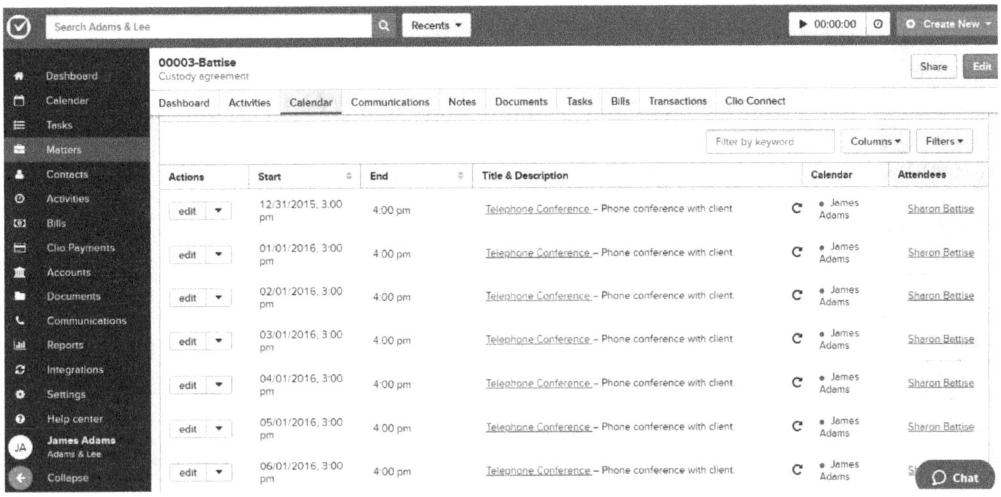

Clio Exhibit 7-3 Matters – Docket Calendar Entry

Source: Themis Solutions, Inc.

LESSON 3: Docketing by Rules; Searching and Retrieving Docket Entries

In this lesson, you will make a docket entry for an activity that must be performed by a certain date. You will use the current month and date for all transactions.

Clio has a feature included in the Elite subscription that allows users to keep track of important court rule dates. The information is configured to trigger appropriate dates that are for a specific court. When you specify a start date, your Calendar will automatically be populated with all the appropriate dates. Clio's Boutique plan, which you are currently using, does not have this feature, so we will manually calculate the number of days to trigger a date for review.

Note: If you are already logged in, you will skip Steps 1 and 2.

1. Start your Internet browser. Type www.goclio.com in the Internet browser and press the **[ENTER] key**.
2. On the Clio Home page, ***click Log In. On the next screen, enter the e-mail address and password you provided in Clio and click SIGN IN. If you check the box next to KEEP ME SIGNED IN, you will be able to skip this step in the future.***
3. Clio opens in the PRACTICE tab. ***Click the Matters tab, then select 00003-Battise and click to open.*** You screen should look like Clio Exhibit 7-1.
4. ***Click on the Task tab***, then ***select ADD***. At this point you are ready to enter all the details about this docket entry. A complaint was filed in federal court and served on the client (Sharon Battise). Under Federal Rules of Civil Procedures, an Answer must be filed within 21 days.
5. Under Task Name, type **Answer Complaint.** ***Select Due at*** and add 21 days from the current date and enter that date. Clio Exhibit 7-4 shows 12/31/2015 for the "Due At" date. This is based on a service date of 12/10/2015.

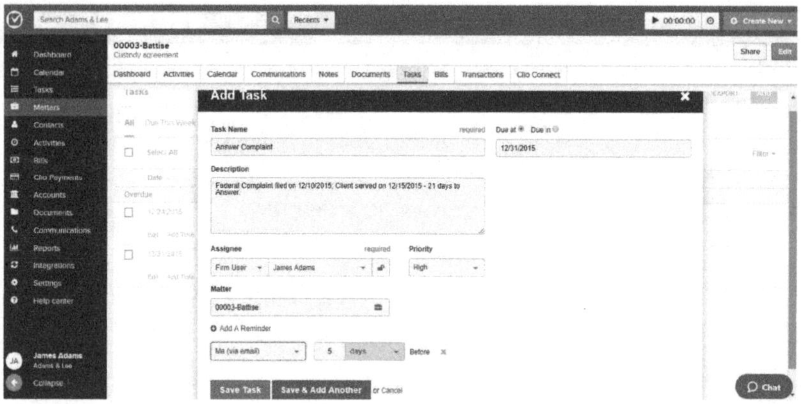

Clio Exhibit 7-4 Matters – Add Rules Based Task

Source: Themis Solutions, Inc.

6. Under the Description field type **Federal Complaint filed (use current date); Client served on (use 5 days after current date) - 21 days to Answer.**
7. Under Assignee, ***select*** **Firm User, your name**. Under **Priority,** ***from the drop-down menu, select "high."***
8. ***Click on*** **Add a Reminder**. Use the default e-mail and ***select*** **"5" days before**. Then ***Click*** **Save Task**. At this point your screen should look similar to Clio Exhibit 7-5.

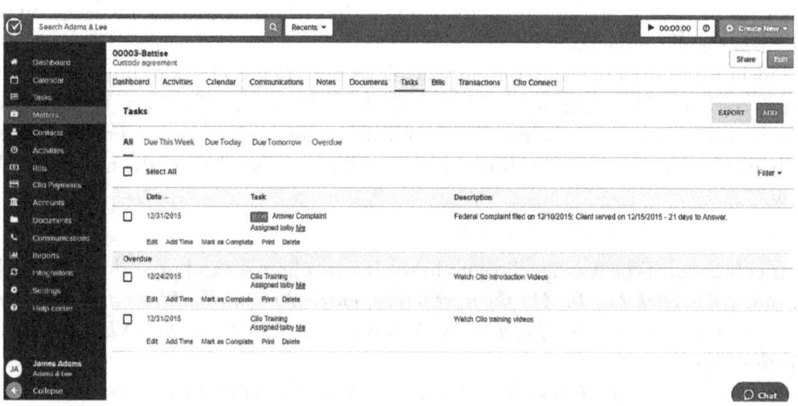

Clio Exhibit 7-5 Matters – Rules Based Task Entry

Source: Themis Solutions, Inc.

Note: Since the "task" was marked as "priority," the word **HIGH** appears in "red" to draw attention to that particular task.

9. Under the ***Search your practice*** bar, located in the right corner of the Clio screen, type **Answer** and this press the **[ENTER]** key. Notice that entries containing the word "Answer" appears on the screen. You should see "**Task**" listed, and "**Answer Complaint**" in "**00003 Battise.**"

This concludes Lesson 3 of the Clio Hands-On Exercises.

8

Legal Marketing

Chapter Objectives

After you read this chapter, you should be able to:

- Explain what marketing is.
- Differentiate between advertising and marketing.
- Discuss different marketing options that are available to most law offices.
- Identify ethical problems that may arise in carrying out a marketing plan.
- Explain what cross-selling is and why it is important in law offices.
- Discuss what the purpose of a marketing plan is.

Legal Marketing

legal marketing

The process of educating consumers on the legal and business activities a firm uses to deliver quality and ethical legal services.

Legal marketing is the process of educating consumers on the legal and business activities a firm uses to deliver quality and ethical legal services. Thirty years ago, law office marketing was virtually nonexistent. It was not until the landmark Supreme Court case of *Bates v. State Bar of Arizona*, 433 U.S. 350 (1977), that this began to change. In *Bates*, two young attorneys placed an ad in the *Arizona Republic* that stated: "Do you need a lawyer? Legal services at very reasonable fees." In response, the Arizona State Bar Association took disciplinary action against the attorneys. The U.S. Supreme Court held that a ban on attorney advertising was a violation of the First Amendment right to commercial free speech and that it was a restraint of trade. Today, attorney advertising is a given. With more than one million attorneys practicing law, the "Why should we market our practice?" question has long been forgotten. The increased competitiveness of the legal field has forced law practices to promote themselves or face the reality of getting left behind by losing business to more aggressive firms. In addition, law offices not only compete against other law offices, they also compete against accounting firms when it comes to handling some types of tax matters, real estate companies regarding real estate transactions, and other types of organizations as well. The only question truly left for a law office is *how* to market itself.

Why is Marketing Important to Paralegals?

Marketing is the job of everyone who works in a private law office. Your job depends on the firm's ability to find and serve additional clients. Therefore, the paralegal has a vested interest in the marketing function. Your friends, family members, acquaintances, social groups, and fellow paralegals are worthy of your marketing efforts. Make sure people know the name of the organization you work for, network with other professionals, and be prepared to talk to others about what your law office does. By marketing your firm, you will establish that you have an interest in and loyalty to the firm, and you also will be building some degree of job security. Law offices cannot do business without new clientele. In addition, many marketing-savvy law firms now require paralegals to participate in marketing efforts. After all, as an employee, a paralegal has a vested interest in the survival of the law firm.

Marketing Goals

There is a misconception that advertising and marketing are the same thing; they are not. Advertising is simply getting your name out to the public. Marketing, on the other hand, includes advertising, but is much more: marketing encompasses providing quality services to clients, gaining insight and feedback into client needs, having a good reputation in the community, and exercising good public relations. Law office marketing has focused objectives and goals:

- Educate clients and potential clients regarding the firm's array of services.
- Educate clients and potential clients as to the particular expertise of the firm in certain areas.
- Create goodwill and interest in the firm.
- Create positive name recognition for the firm.
- Create an image of honesty, ethics, and sincere interest in clients.
- Publicize the firm's accomplishments to the profession and community.
- Educate clients on changes in the law, thus creating client confidence in the firm.
- Improve the firm's competitive position in the marketplace.

- Obtain referrals from other attorneys.
- Maintain communication with existing clients.
- Increase client loyalty and retention.
- Increase staff morale and reinforce the firm's self-image.
- Obtain referrals from clients.
- Obtain repeat business from existing clients.

Basic Restrictions on Marketing

There are several restrictions on law office marketing. These restrictions involve ethical obligations and are discussed in depth at the end of this chapter, but the most fundamental restriction is that, no matter what the marketing entails, it must not be false or misleading.

The Legal Marketing Plan

marketing plan

It specifies a target audience the firm is trying to reach, the exact goals that the marketing program is to accomplish, and establishes a detailed strategy of how the goals will be achieved.

A law firm must have a marketing plan before it can begin marketing. A **marketing plan** specifies a target audience the firm is trying to reach, the exact goals that the marketing program is to accomplish, and establishes a detailed strategy of how the goals will be achieved. In specifying the target audience, it is important that law offices understand exactly who their clients are (see Exhibit 2-3 in Chapter 2 regarding practice management and strategic planning). Many law offices, even relatively small offices, hire marketing personnel or outsource for consulting, advertising, and other marketing efforts (see Exhibit 8-1). Exhibit 8-2 provides a sample job description for a legal marketing director. Due to the increased competition in the legal industry and the continual need for an influx of clients, marketing—as a part of a firm's overall management responsibility—simply cannot be ignored. Much of the research indicates that corporations typically spend from 10 to 13% of their revenues on marketing;

Exhibit 8-1 Legal Marketing Staff

Firm employment of legal marketing staff

Description	Percent of market staff employed
Solo Practitioner	0%
Between 2 and 10 lawyer firms	17%
Between 11 and 25 lawyer firms	41%
Between 25 and 50 lawyer firms	76%
Between 50 and 100 lawyer firms	93%
More than 100 lawyer firms	100%

Firm Outsourcing

Description	Percent
Graphic Design	11%
Public Relations	11%
Legal Marketing Consultant (on retainer)	26%
Advertising Agency	33%
Web Site Development	77%

Source: Larry Bodine, Esq. [n.d.], *Survey Report: How Law Firms Spend Their Marketing Dollars*, Law Firm Marketing, Law Marketing.com, http://lawmarketing.com.

MARKETING DIRECTOR

Job Description

Position Reports to: Executive Director/Marketing Committee/Managing Partner(s)

RESPONSIBILITIES

Overall Responsibility: Position is responsible for developing all aspects of the firm's marketing plan, coordinating all activities related to the plan and achieving the overall marketing objective.

PRIMARY RESPONSIBILITIES

Interoffice Relations

Collect, prepare, and maintain firm data.

Design or supervise the preparation of mailing lists and client and referral-source databases. Design, set up, and supervise maintenance of marketing databases that includes development, retrieval, and follow-up activities for members of the legal team.

Media relations

Work with news media, draft press releases, and coordinate for approval and distribution. Prepare placement of lawyer articles for target market publications such as editorial boards and social media Web sites. When applicable, serve as liaison between the firm and public relations counsel. Maintain file for all circulations or publications including previous copies of modified Web site pages on the firms' professionals both internally and externally.

Public relations

Plan and coordinate all of the firm's social- and community-related activities such as seminars and alumni programs. These activities should be designed to give visibility and name recognition to the firm.

Internal communications

Create and facilitate communications between professionals in various practice areas and offices with written and oral vehicles to promote awareness of the firm's marketing activities.

Publications and promotional materials

Responsible for development of newsletters, brochures, Web site materials, and other promotional publications. Prepare directory listings and announcement cards. Place professional advertisements.

Client relations

Develop or supervise client surveys.

Training

Provide or arrange for marketing training for partners and staff.

Proposals and presentations

Assist in preparing written proposals and in-person presentations for new business. Help with the technological aspects of presentation materials and maintain reference files of proposals. Help lawyers rehearse sales presentations.

Budget

Supervise and track a marketing budget and expenditures.

QUALIFICATIONS

Knowledge of

- Law office environment
- Marketing techniques and principles

Ability to

- Coordinate multiple functions
- Communicate with and motivate professionals

EXPERIENCE

Marketing manager in a law or other professional services firm.

EDUCATION

College or course work in marketing, writing, commercial art, or related fields.

Exhibit 8-2 Marketing Director Job Description

law offices spend on average about 2.0–3% of revenues on marketing. However, the trend shows an increase in spending for legal marketing. For example, a small firm with nine attorneys may be spending as much as $60,000 on marketing efforts.

Marketing must be done in an effective manner, and it is important that money not be wasted on efforts that are ineffective for a firm. A well-thought-out marketing plan will help ensure that money, time, and efforts are not wasted. A law firm's marketing plan should include the following:

- Overall goals of the marketing program
- Strategies and activities that will be necessary to achieve the goals (including who, what, when, how, and in what order the activities will be implemented)
- Estimated cost of the marketing program
- Estimated profit the successful marketing program would bring in

The marketing plan and the strategic business plan are related documents. To develop an effective marketing plan, consider the steps presented in Exhibit 8-3. A key component of the marketing plan is to conduct research. The drafter needs relevant information in order to write a good marketing plan, such as what the target group actually wants in the way of legal services; this is a departure from the usual method, which is to provide a target group with what you have to offer. Research in the way of studying competitors, interviewing clients, surveying clients, talking to experts, and really finding out what makes the target group "tick" forms the foundation of a good marketing plan. Another important part of the marketing plan is to develop specific strategies for reaching the target audience in the most effective way. There are innumerable ways to reach a target audience, but finding the most effective way that actually brings clients to the law firm takes thought, skill, and experience. Developing a marketing budget and funding an adequate marketing campaign are also integral parts of the plan.

Typical Law Practice Marketing Options and Strategies

The strategies and options that a law firm can use to market their services are many and varied. Exhibit 8-4 shows a number of strategies and marketing alternatives that are available, some of which are described in more detail in this section. One of the most important things an office can do is to actually *track* what marketing techniques are the most successful and then concentrate resources and funds on these methods. When a new client comes into the office, the New Client Questionnaire form should include a question regarding specifically how the client heard about the law firm, and statistics/reports should be maintained to show what sources are the most effective. Future marketing efforts should be based on the results of these reports.

- **Quality legal services**—There's that word again ... *quality.* Before a firm can market its services, it must have something of quality to market! Keep in mind that it is always easier to sell a quality product that people want to buy than to sell a product you want to sell. Earlier in this book, it was explained how important existing clients are for bringing repeat business back to the firm and for making referrals to others. This is why quality is so important. Everything a firm does affects quality and, therefore its marketing effort. Remember, it's easier to satisfy and keep a client for life by continually meeting and exceeding his or her expectations than it is to have to continually find new clients who stay for a while and then go to a competitor.

I. **Firm Approach**
The firm should develop an idea for the type of law it practices, the clients it will serve and the service to provide them, the competition and profitability, all of which will determine the market plan.

II. **Target Market and Marketing Plan Objectives**
The firm should determine the marketing plan's purpose for reaching a target market which could be a range of classifications from age, gender, occupation to marital and financial status. Is the firm trying to expand in a new area, increase its size, and maybe even focus on an expertise area of law? In selecting a target market, the firm's marketing plan should include the method for reaching these people.

a. **Client Types:**
   i. Individuals (impoverished, middle class, wealthy)
   ii. Business Organizations (small or large, private, public or nonprofit)
   iii. Labor Organizations
   iv. Government (local, state, federal, international)

b. **Legal Specialty Areas**
   i. This can range from Administrative Law to Workers' Compensation Law. Some examples below are areas commonly found; there are many others available.
      - Banking Law
      - Bankruptcy Law
      - Collections Law
      - Estates, Trusts, and Probate
      - Family Law
      - Insurance Law
      - Litigation
      - Mergers and Acquisitions
      - Oil and Gas Law
      - Real Estate Law
      - Social Security Law
      - Tort Law

III. **Market Research**
Become familiar with the groups' interest and background. The law firms must consider their target groups to determine how they can serve them—what do they want, need, or expect.
   a. Study marketing successes and failures.
   b. Generate surveys both inside the firm and outside for feedback.

IV. **Market Problems and Solutions**
The firm should try to anticipate marketing problems and have a plan in place to resolve them—this often includes alternate marketing plans.

V. **Marketing Action Plan and Strategy**
The firm must have a method in place—a game plan for accomplishing its marketing ideas. How will you deliver the information (mailings, seminars, trade shows)? Who will be responsible for implementing the plan? What is the time-frame to reach the target market and when will the firm adjust time frames consider market response?

VI. **Marketing Budget and Resources**
The firm must determine if the resources and finances are available to accomplish the marketing plan. At this point, the firm can proceed as designed or adjust to fit within their budget and resources.

Exhibit 8-3 Developing the Marketing Plan

- Internet site
- E-mail newsletter
- Online Yellow Pages
- Keyword searching advertising on search engine sites
- Firm brochures and resume
- Hard copy newsletter
- Promotional materials (folders, pencils, etc., with law office logo)
- Business cards/letterhead/announcement cards
- Subject area information brochures (e.g., tax, auto accidents, etc.)
- Public relations
    - Belonging to boards, associations, and community groups
    - Speaking at public functions
    - Writing articles on legal subjects for the local newspaper
    - Issuing press releases
    - Handling publicized pro bono cases
    - Volunteering in "law day" activities
    - Volunteering staff time to help with fundraisers for community groups
    - Running for public office
- Firm open house
- Public advertising
    - Yellow Page ads
    - Newspaper ads
    - Newspaper inserts
    - Television ads
    - Radio ads
- Client seminars
- Direct mail (not allowable in some states)
- Mining other legal professionals
    - Obtaining referrals
    - Joining legal associations
    - Networking with other legal professionals
- Mining friends, associates, and social contacts regarding the legal services offered
    - Making a call or contact list, including a mailing list
    - Contacting them monthly or quarterly
    - Breakfast, lunch, or dinner engagements regarding their needs and your services
- Mining existing clients
    - Contacting current and past clients monthly
    - Cross-selling
    - Breakfast, lunch, or dinner engagements regarding their needs and your services
    - Personal notes of congratulations for accomplishments
    - Holiday cards
    - Thank-you notes for referrals
    - Reading trade journals regarding a client's business

Exhibit 8-4 Marketing Strategies and Options

An employee who treats clients rudely, a docket control system that does not work, or billing practices that make clients upset in the end are all quality problems. Law office management must ensure quality; marketing and quality are parts of the same equation.

- **Firm Web site**—Operating a firm Web site is a standard marketing practice for most law firms. Solo practitioners have generally been the slowest to move to the Internet. However, in recent years, solo practitioners' presence on the Internet has dramatically increased, most likely due to technology advances, such as Web site builders that are easier and more affordable to maintain. A definite advantage of a firm Web site is that, unlike the office itself, it stays open 24 hours a day, 7 days a week, to local, national, and international customers and clients. A Web site is a particularly good idea for a legal organization with a specialized practice; a firm with a unique niche or specialized practice can reach potential clients anywhere in the world. Many organizations have found the marketing potential of a Web site to be enormous. In addition, because it operates all the time, it is cost effective when compared to other types of marketing alternatives.

  Depending on the information on the Web site, the organization can also provide timely information to current and potential clients. Many legal organizations offer information in their specialty area that would be useful to their clients. Thus, a Web site can provide a service to an organization's clients that hopefully will create goodwill toward the firm. Most experts say that "content is king." It is extremely important that the content of the law firm Web site be strong, fresh, and changed often. A Web site can also be used for recruiting employees, such as paralegals and other staff. Exhibit 8-5 presents a list of features that can help establish a top-notch law firm Web site.

While firms' Web sites are allowed, there is at least one case where an attorney violated a state's ethical rules by misusing e-mail. In *In re Canter*, Term. Sup. Ct., Nos. 95-831-O-H, etc. (6/5/97), the Tennessee Supreme Court found that an attorney who sent an e-mail

Tip	Explanation
List success stories	If the firm has been successful in a matter, tell the story on the Web site. Change the stories on a regular basis. You should not promise the same results, but you can tell the story.
Focus on the client	The whole Web site should be geared to the client. It should be user friendly and meet the needs of the client. It should clearly spell out in layperson's terms what services are available, including resources regarding the subject matters of the areas practiced. It's really about the client, not about the law firm.
List existing clients	Clients like to know that the firm has represented others "like them"; references help.
Demonstrate the firm's experience	Experience counts. Most clients want to know that the firm is an expert in the subject matter of the case they are bringing to the firm.
Keep content up to date	Out-of-date content gives the client no reason to come back to the Web site. Keep it updated and current at all times.
Include a search function	Clients want to be able to quickly find what they need; a search function on the Web site greatly helps in this process.
Make it printer friendly	The Web site should be printer friendly so that clients can print out information as needed.

Exhibit 8-5 Tips for a Strong Law Firm Internet Web Site

advertisement message to thousands of Internet groups and lists (called "spamming") had violated the state's ethical rules. The message did not comply with state rules that required noting that the message was an advertisement, and a copy was not filed with the Board of Professional Responsibility as required.

- **Firm brochure/resume/Web sites**—A firm brochure is typically a pamphlet that informs the general public about the nature of the firm. If the firm maintains a Web site, this information is often integrated on the Web pages in lieu of an actual brochure. In many ways, it is like a resume—some even call it a firm's resume. Firm brochures/resumes often contain the following types of information:
  (a) History of the firm
  (b) Ideology or philosophy of the firm
  (c) Services offered by the firm (e.g., the types of law it practices, specific departments, etc.)
  (d) The firm's fee or billing policies
  (e) Description of the firm's attorneys (background, items of interest, awards, degrees, etc.)
  (f) Description of the firm's support staff
  (g) Address, phone number, Web site address
  (h) Whether the firm has a newsletter or other types of client services
  (i) Notable firm accomplishments
  (j) Important clients the firm has represented (must have client's permission)

Exhibit 8-6 is a firm brochure/Web site page for a law office that has a law practice in several different areas of the law. Firms that practice a wide range of law or large firms typically take a different marketing approach; instead of having one piece of marketing material for the whole firm, they may have separate brochures or Web pages contained on the Web site for each department with material that targets specific industries. Some law firms maintain their law practice within a specific area of law such as health care, bankruptcy, immigration or social security law. Exhibit 8-7 is an example of a firm's brochure/Web site page for a law office that has a specialty area law practice.

- **Firm newsletters and e-mail newsletters**—Firm newsletters and e-mail newsletters are a popular way of maintaining contact with clients and generating goodwill. Firm newsletters can be on a single topic, such as real estate, or on a potpourri of topics. Some firms focus on a different legal issue in each issue: family law, real estate, tax, and so on. It is important that the firm knows and understands who its clients are and what type of information would be beneficial to them. Newsletters are also used to inform clients of legislative changes, whether local, state, or national. Newsletters can be produced in-house, by ad agencies, or by purchasing ready-made legal newsletters. With a ready-made newsletter, all the law office has to do is add its logo, firm name, and address. E-mail newsletters are popular because they are relatively low cost and can be distributed immediately.
- **Informational brochures**—These are brochures aimed at informing clients about a specific topic, such as "Why You Need a Will," "What to Do in Case of an Auto Accident," "How is 'disability' defined for adults by the Social Security Administration," "How to Set Up Your Own Business," or "How to Protect Your Ideas through Copyrights, Trademarks, and Patents." They are informational pieces that are used to inform clients about legal problems, and many firms publish them on their firm Web site.

Exhibit 8-6 Law Firm Brochure—Specialty Area Materials

Printed with permission of Bruno & Bruno, L.L.P.

Exhibit 8-7 Law Firm—Webpages for Law Firm Services and Lawyers

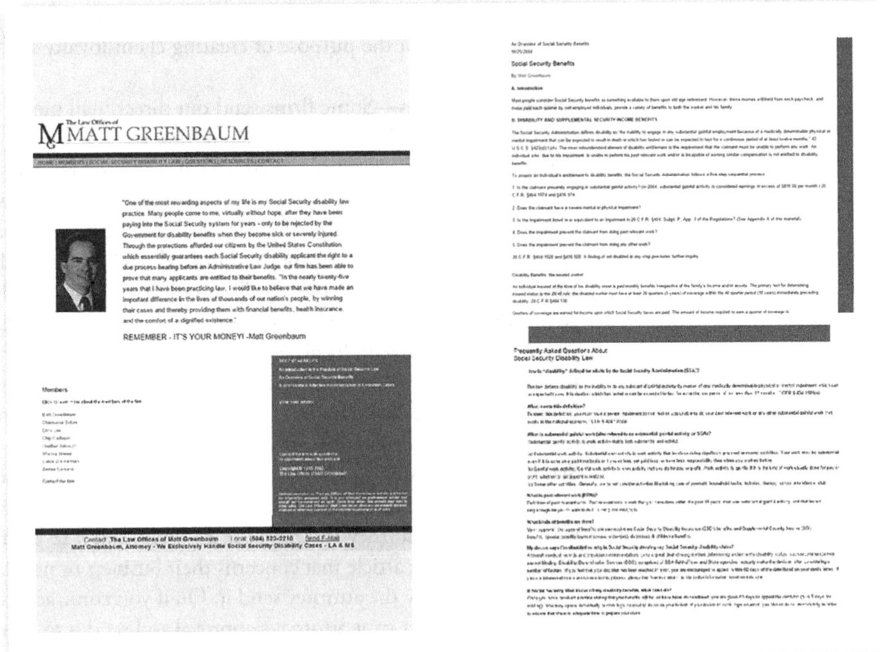

Printed with permission of Law Offices of Matt Greenbaum.

- **Public relations**—Generating goodwill and a positive public image is a long-standing, successful way that firms have marketed themselves. Paralegals and attorneys can promote themselves and their firms as members of social groups, churches, committees, nonprofit boards, and associations. Speaking at public and association meetings is another way to attract interest and goodwill; other methods of generating and maintaining good public relations include handling pro bono cases and issuing press releases when a firm wins a case or achieves other notable accomplishments.
- **Firm open house**—Some firms hold annual open houses, where clients and visitors can come to the firm and socialize with attorneys and staff members outside the normal pressures of coming to the office with legal problems.
- **Business cards, letterhead, and announcement cards**—Announcement cards are used quite frequently by law offices. An announcement card is usually a postcard that a firm sends to other firms to publicize a change, such as when new attorneys have been added or firms have merged. Business cards and letterhead are also a frequent way for firms to promote themselves and their staff.
- **Public advertising—yellow pages, newspaper, television, and radio ads**—Public advertisements are another popular form of marketing. They come in all sizes, shapes, and price ranges, and may appear in local yellow pages, newspapers, and television and radio stations.
- **Firm seminars**—Some firms hold seminars aimed at educating their clients or the general public (prospective clients) on legal issues. These seminars may be held on any legal topic that is of interest to clients. Businesses might be interested in the legal issues of hiring, firing, and evaluating employees and employee benefits, and individual clients

might be interested in tax planning, trusts and estates, and other issues. Client seminars are usually held for the purpose of creating client loyalty and should be conducted by an attorney.

- **Direct mail pieces**—Some firms send out direct mail pieces aimed at a specific audience. Usually, the pieces are unsolicited; that is, they are sent out to people without being requested. For example, if your firm primarily handles real estate matters, you might send out a letter to all real estate businesses. Note, however, that direct mail is very controversial, especially when the mailing is targeted to a specific group. Ethical rules in some states strictly prohibit targeted mailing under the theory that it is direct solicitation. Attorneys are specifically prohibited from directly soliciting clients.
- **Involvement in legal associations**—Attorneys and paralegals can also market themselves by being active in local, state, and national bar and paralegal associations. Many firms that involve themselves in these types of organizations gain the respect and goodwill of others and may gain referrals from another firm that may not have the expertise to handle a particular type of case.
- **Sending information to clients that you know will be of interest to them**—Whenever you come across information that you think will interest clients, bring it to the attention of your supervising attorney and have the attorney send it to them. For example, if you come across a newspaper article that concerns their business or new laws that might affect them, clip it out and have the attorney send it. Or, if you come across a case in which they might be interested in, get your attorney's approval and send it to them with a note (but do not bill them for it!). Clients appreciate a law office that takes a personal interest in them.
- **Marketing your services to existing clients**—A firm's current clients are among its biggest assets. Firms not only want to market to new clients but also need to keep the business of their current clients. Thus, firms will typically spend a great deal of time cultivating their existing clients using techniques described earlier, such as newsletters and client seminars. Firms also have other techniques for marketing to existing clients.

cross-selling

Selling additional services to existing clients.

(a) **Cross-selling—Cross-selling** refers to selling additional services to existing clients. For instance, suppose a law office represented XYZ business in a tax matter, but XYZ used another firm to handle its personnel disputes. If possible, the law office would like to cross-sell XYZ to use its firm for both the tax matter and the personnel matters.

(b) **Client questionnaires**—Many firms send out client questionnaires at the end of a legal matter to see how the client felt about the services that were provided. In addition to being a quality-control device, this is also a marketing technique because it is aimed at correcting problems that the client might have had.

(c) **Keeping the firm's name in front of the client**—What happens if a client's case is completely finished and the client has no other business for the firm at the time? Should the firm forget about the client? No, most firms continue to keep in contact with the client with newsletters, seminars, letters, and holiday cards. Firms want clients to feel wanted and to be reminded that the firm is there to serve them.

(d) **Developing client relationships**—With whom would you rather do business: friends or strangers? Friends are the unquestionable answer, because you trust and feel comfortable with them. This is the kind of relationship that firms want to promote.

(e) **Thanking clients for referring others to you**—Always send a thank-you letter to clients (or other attorneys) for making referrals to the office.

The Role of the Rainmaker

rainmaking

Bringing in new clients to a law office.

Rainmaking refers to the ability to bring in new clients to a law office. Sometimes law offices bring attorneys into the firm for the sole purpose of being "rainmakers." Some rainmakers are well connected politically or have inroads into certain industries. Rainmakers use their influence and skills to bring new clients into the firm. Helping clients achieve their business goals and dreams is often a factor in what makes a good rainmaker. It is important to pay close attention to any issues that affect the clients, which requires a special relationship with them. That relationship gives the clients a sense of security in knowing the attorney is watching out for their best interest. Many private law offices use rainmakers in their marketing schemes.

Marketing—An Ethics Perspective

Although ethical limitations on marketing have eased up over the past 20 years, there are still many pitfalls that can occur from an ethical perspective, including making false or misleading statements in an advertisement, failing to comply with general requirements about advertisements, directly soliciting a client, or putting forth an attorney as a specialist.

FALSE OR MISLEADING STATEMENTS *Rule* 7.1 regarding the rules of professional conduct states that attorneys are not allowed to make false or misleading statements in any kind of marketing or advertising piece. They may only promote themselves with advertisements that are completely true.

Thus, when an advertisement discusses a past victory it must be careful to not create an expectation that the attorney can always achieve the same result, since cases depend on the specifics of each circumstance. Exhibit 8-8 provides several examples of false or misleading advertisements.

ADVERTISING IN GENERAL *Rule 7.2* regarding the rules of professional conduct states some general guidelines that apply to all types of advertising, including that an attorney may advertise his or her legal services in the public media or through written, recorded, or electronic

Advertisement	Ethical Analysis
A statement of factual results (i.e., "Our firm recently won a $10,000,000 award)—coupled with a promise (i.e., "we can do the same for you.")	This would create an unjustified expectation and would imply that the next case would have a similar result, even though every case is different.[1]
"The Duke Law Firm: Better Than the Rest"; "The Premier Lawyers"; "After you've tried the rest, come to the best!"	Generally, the use of unsupportable, absolute terms are prohibited. It is also false or misleading for lawyers to compare their services to those of other lawyers unless that comparison can be factually substantiated.[2]
"One of the best firms specialized in the immigration and corporate law practice in the Washington, DC area."	Violates *Rule 7.4(a)* which states subject to the requirement of *Rule 7.1* "a lawyer shall not hold himself or herself out publicly as a specialist."[3]

[1] *Public Citizen, Inc. v. La. Attorney Disciplinary Bd.*, 642 F. Supp. 2d 539 (E.D. La. 2009).

[2] *Id.*

[3] *Attorney Grievance Commission of Maryland v. Runan Zhang*, Misc. Docket AG No. 11, September Term, 2013 (July 21, 2014).

Exhibit 8-8 Examples of False or Misleading Advertisements

communication. The rule generally prohibits an attorney from paying a person who recommends a client to him or her. The rule also provides that any communication shall include the name and address of at least one lawyer or law firm responsible for its content, so that the authorities will know who to contact if there is an ethical violation. This rule broadly allows lawyers to advertise using virtually any method.

NO DIRECT SOLICITATION OR "AMBULANCE CHASING" *Rule 7.3* regarding the rules of professional conduct restricts attorneys from directly soliciting persons they do not know either in person, by live telephone, or by real-time electronic means. The rule does not apply if the attorney is soliciting another lawyer, if the person is a family member or close personal friend, or if the person has had a prior professional relationship with the lawyer. In addition, the rule provides that an advertisement must include the words "advertising material" so that the public clearly understands the nature of the communication.

Direct, in-person telephone contact with individuals that the lawyer does not know is prohibited because of the possibility of undue influence, intimidation, or overreaching when a skilled attorney contacts a layperson. However, prerecorded communications may be acceptable, as the attorney is not "live." This rule also squarely prohibits attorneys from making harassing communication or bothering persons who do not want to be solicited.

A distinction is made in the rule between directly soliciting persons that are known by the attorney, such as family members or past clients, and soliciting unknown individuals. Attorneys and staff may solicit individuals they know. This is quite common, and there is nothing unethical about mentioning to friends and relatives that your law office handles certain types of cases and could help them if the need ever arose. What is prohibited is directly soliciting absolute strangers in person. Written solicitation, such as newsletters, brochures, and—in many jurisdictions—targeted mail, is allowed.

ADVERTISING FIELDS OF PRACTICE AND SPECIALIZATION *Rule 7.4* regarding the rules of professional conduct generally prohibits attorneys from presenting themselves as specialists. Attorneys are allowed to communicate that they practice in a particular field of law, but a lawyer generally cannot state that he or she is certified as a specialist in a particular field unless the attorney has been certified as a specialist by an organization approved by a state authority or the American Bar Association. The word "specialist" has a secondary meaning, implying formal recognition (this rule would not apply in states that provide procedures for certification in particular areas). There are a few stated exceptions in the rule related to patent and admiralty law.

Each state has specific ethical rules about lawyer advertising, so whoever performs the marketing needs to be familiar with the rules of your state. One way to avoid ethical problems is to show the advertisement to the disciplinary administrator for the state before it is run and ask his or her opinion on the matter.

Summary

Legal marketing is the process of educating consumers on the legal and business activities a firm uses to deliver quality and ethical legal services. Advertising entails getting your name out to the public, while marketing encompasses much more. A marketing plan specifies a target audience, sets goals for the marketing program, and establishes detailed strategies for achieving the goals. Marketing strategies and options for law offices include a law firm Web site, brochure/resume, e-mail newsletters, public relation activities, public advertising, law firm seminars, and much more. "Rainmaking" refers to the ability to bring in new clients to the office. Ethical regulations related to marketing include not providing false or misleading information in advertising, not directly soliciting clients, and not allowing an attorney to present himself or herself to the public as a specialist without some kind of certification from an accredited organization.

Key Terms

cross-selling
legal marketing
marketing plan
rainmaking

Test Your Knowledge

1. Why is the case of *Bates v. State Bar of Arizona* important?
2. What is the difference between marketing and advertising?
3. True or false: it is easier to sell a quality product that people want to buy than to sell a product you want to sell.
4. Before a law firm begins to market, it is essential that it has a ______________________.
5. What should an effective marketing plan contain?
6. Name two ways to obtain research for a marketing plan.
7. Name five ways a law office can market its services.
8. ______________________ is the ability to bring in new clients to a law firm.
9. True or false: a law firm ad can guarantee future results based on a recent victory of the firm.
10. True or false: according to the *Rules* regarding professional conduct, a lawyer may advertise services via written, recorded, or electronic communication, including public media.
11. Any ad or marketing piece an attorney or a law firm publishes *must* have two things somewhere in the ad; what are they?
12. True or false: an attorney may personally solicit legal business from family and people with whom the attorney has had a close personal or prior professional relationship.

Practical Applications

1. You and your supervising attorney have just spent 16 weeks in a complicated products liability case regarding vaccine immunization shots for children. Your firm's client contracted the disease from the immunization shot. Your firm received the largest verdict in history for this type of case. Given the success of this case, the firm would like to handle more of these types of cases. When you get back to the office, you are shown a draft of an advertisement that is going to run in newspapers across the country, which reads:

"MILLER AND HASTINGS Law office SPECIALIZES IN PHARMACEUTICAL CASES! Recently, our firm won a $100 million judgment against the manufacturer of a drug company for producing an unsafe drug. We can win for you too—please call us if you would like us to represent your interests."

Your supervising attorney asks you for your comment. How do you respond?

2. Your client from number 1 above is absolutely ecstatic about the verdict in the immunization case. She learns of your intentions and volunteers to appear in a television ad to do a testimonial about the verdict and the great services the firm provided. What do you think about this?

3. You work in a solo practitioner's office and she is considering a number of different marketing strategies. One is a high client turnover strategy that includes a high profile, big television campaign that would presumably generate a lot of new clients. What are your concerns?

4. As a paralegal for a small but respected firm, you know that the firm wishes to expand and move into more lucrative legal areas. You believe that environmental issues, such as toxic waste, would be a very good area for the firm to expand into and would also be a good fit, based on work the firm has done in the past. However, you know that you need to review the matter a little closer regarding the feasibility of this. Specifically delineate what you would do to research this (be creative), and then develop a draft plan of how you might present this to your managing attorney.

5. Your law office is considering placing a yellow-pages ad. You are to research the issue by looking in the yellow pages under "attorneys." You are to pick out two yellow pages ads that you like. Consider what it is that you like about the ads and what their messages are. Do the same with television ads. Which attorney ads are the best, and why?

On the Web Exercises

1. Go to the ABA's Information on Professionalism and Ethics in Lawyer Advertising and Marketing home page at http://www.americanbar.org/groups/professional_responsibility.html and read two ethics opinions related to lawyer advertising/marketing.

2. Using a general search engine, such as http://www.google.com or http://www.yahoo.com, or the ABA's Web site on Information on Professionalism and Ethics in Lawyer Advertising and Marketing, find and print out a copy of *The Handbook on Lawyer Advertising and Solicitation*, published by the Florida Bar Association.

3. The state bar of Texas requires that some marketing material be reviewed by the bar before it is published. Find the advertising review rules and read any "Frequently Asked Questions" document they may have. Try starting at the ABA's Information on Professionalism and Ethics in Lawyer Advertising and Marketing home page found within the ABA's Web site at http://www.americanbar.org.

4. Go to the ABA Center for Professional Responsibility http://www.americanbar.org/, find the *ABA Model Rules of Professional Conduct*, then read and print out the comments to *Rules 7.1, 7.2, 7.3*, and *7.4*.

5. Visit several bar association Web sites and find a minimum of five articles on legal marketing. The following link will take you to a Web site that connects to all state bar sites: https://www.hg.org/bar-associations-usa.html.

6. Visit the American Bar Association Law Practice Management section http://www.americanbar.org/groups/law_practice.html and review any materials they have on legal marketing.

Projects

1. Go to the ABA's Information on Professionalism and Ethics in Lawyer Advertising and Marketing home page at http://www.americanbar.org/groups/professional_responsibility.html. Review the "Cases on Lawyer Advertising" section and summarize three cases. Include the facts and an analysis of each case, what the court found, what the ruling was, and whether or not you agree with it.

2. Research and write a paper on any subject related to legal marketing. There are many resources available online or in most law libraries. Select a specific topic on legal marketing that interests you or cover the topic from a broad perspective. Your paper should cite at least five different resources.

3. Preparation of a marketing plan—several attorneys you currently work with are considering starting their own practice in your area. The practice will have five attorneys and other staff as needed. They would like to have three practice groups. The attorneys trust your business judgment and would like you to develop a detailed marketing plan for the first year of their practice. The attorneys agree that you cannot spend more than $20,000 for this first year. Your plan should be well thought out and be specific to your area. You will need to do research, get actual prices for what your marketing plan will cost, and attach examples or give narrative explanations of what the marketing will entail (e.g., if you will decide to have a TV commercial, you will need to develop a script; if you decide to have an Web site, you will need to attach an example, etc.).

Your plan should cover the following topics:

A. Practice Groups

- What practice areas do you recommend in your area, and why?
- Consider whether why you think the new firm will be able to get into this market.
- What firms are currently in the market (i.e., who will your competitors be)?
- What services will the practice groups provide?
- How will the services differ from services currently provided by existing firms?
- Who will be the targeted clients (be very specific)?
- How profitable are these areas?
- How will existing firms react to your firm getting into the market?
- How will you compete with existing firms (on quality, price, better location, etc.)?

B. Marketing Options

- What marketing options will you use, and why (be specific)? List the timing of your marketing options (e.g., 1st month = mailing announcing firm, 2nd month = newspaper advertising, etc.).
- How long will each marketing option last?
- How will your marketing options reach your targeted clients?
- How many people will your marketing options reach (you can obtain some of this information from the vendors you would use—newspaper subscription numbers, TV and radio ratings figures, etc.)?
- Attach examples or explanations, including the content of your marketing options.

C. Budget

- Get bids and/or estimates of how much your marketing plan will cost, and include a detailed cost projection.

D. New Client Business Projections

- Based on your marketing plan, how many new clients do you project you can bring into the firm?

4. Using the Internet, find three law firm Web sites. Try to find one Web site that is truly outstanding, another that is representative of an average Web site, and another one that is very simple and basic. From a client's perspective, compare and contrast the Web sites in terms of graphics/visual appeal, content, ease of use, depth of information about the firm and legal areas it specializes in, information about the attorneys, and so on. What are the things that you liked about the outstanding Web site and the things you did not like about the simple and average Web site?

Case Review

—*Doe v. Condon*, 532 S.E.2d 879, 341 S.C. 22 (S.C., 2000)

(Cite as: 532 S.E.2d 879, 341 S.C. 22 (S.C., 2000)

Supreme Court of South Carolina.

John DOE, Alias, Petitioner,

v.

Charles M. CONDON, Attorney General for the State of South Carolina, Respondent.

No. 25138.

Submitted May 23, 2000.

Decided June 5, 2000.

Assistant Attorney General Jennifer A. Deitrick, of Columbia, for respondent.

Disciplinary Counsel Henry B. Richardson, Jr., of Columbia, for amicus curiae Office of Disciplinary Counsel.

IN THE ORIGINAL JURISDICTION PER CURIAM.

*1 Petitioner sought to have the Court accept this matter in its original jurisdiction to determine whether certain tasks performed by a non-attorney employee in a law firm constitute the unauthorized practice of law. Specifically, petitioner asks (1) whether it is the unauthorized practice of law for a paralegal employed by an attorney to conduct informational seminars for the general public on wills and trusts without the attorney being present; (2) whether it is the unauthorized practice of law for a paralegal employed by an attorney to meet with clients privately at the attorney's office, answer general questions about wills and trusts, and gather basic information from clients; and (3) whether a paralegal can receive compensation from the paralegal's law firm/employer through a profit-sharing arrangement based upon the volume and type of cases the paralegal handles. The Office of the Attorney General filed a return opposing the petition for original jurisdiction.

The Court invoked its original jurisdiction to determine whether the paralegal's activities constituted the unauthorized practice of law, and, pursuant to S.C.Code Ann. § 14-3-340 (1976), John W. Kittredge was appointed as referee to make findings of fact and conclusions of law concerning this matter. A hearing was held and the referee issued proposed findings and recommendations.

[1] [2] We adopt the referee's findings and recommendations attached to this opinion and hold that a non-lawyer employee conducting unsupervised legal presentations for the public and answering legal questions for the public or for clients of the attorney/employer engages in the unauthorized practice of law. See *State v. Despain*, 319 S.C. 317, 460 S.E.2d 576 (1995). We further hold that a proposed fee arrangement which compensates non-lawyer employees based upon the number and volume of cases the non-lawyer employee handles for an attorney violates the ethical rules against fee splitting with non-lawyer employees. *Rule 5.4* of the Rules of Professional Conduct, *Rule 407*, SCACR.

PROPOSED FINDINGS AND RECOMMENDATIONS OF THE REFEREE

This is a declaratory judgment action in the Supreme Court's original jurisdiction. The Court referred this matter to me as Referee. Petitioner, a paralegal, has submitted a generalized list of tasks he wishes to perform and has inquired whether performing them constitutes the unauthorized practice of law. Petitioner also seeks a determination of the propriety of his proposed fee-splitting arrangement with his attorney-employer. Despite my repeated offers for an evidentiary hearing, neither party requested a hearing. The record before me is sufficient to address and resolve whether the activities in question constitute the unauthorized practice of law.

I find that a paralegal conducting unsupervised legal presentations for the public and answering legal questions from the audience engages in the unauthorized practice of law. Further, I find that a paralegal meeting individually with clients to answer estate-planning questions engages in the unauthorized practice of law. Finally, I find the proposed fee arrangement is improper and violates the ethical prohibition against fee splitting.

BACKGROUND

*2 Petitioner submitted the following questions to the Court:

> (1) Is it the unauthorized practice of law for a paralegal employed by an attorney to conduct educational seminars for the general public, to disseminate general information about wills and trusts, including specifically a fair and balanced emphasis on living trusts, including answering general questions, without the attorney being present at the seminar as long as the seminar is sponsored by the attorney's law firm and the attorney has reviewed and approved the format, materials, and presentation to be made for content, truthfulness, and fairness?
>
> (2) Is it the unauthorized practice of law for a paralegal employed by an attorney to meet with clients privately in the law office for the purpose of answering general questions about wills, trusts, including specifically living trusts, and estate planning in general, and to gather basic information from said clients for such purposes as long as it is done under the attorney's direction, and the clients have a follow-up interview and meeting with the attorney who would have primary responsibility for legal decisions?

(3) Can a paralegal receive compensation from the law firm he is employed by, through a profit-sharing arrangement, which would be based upon the volume and type of cases the paralegal handled?

DISCUSSION

To protect the public from unsound legal advice and incompetent representation, South Carolina, like other jurisdictions, limits the practice of law to licensed attorneys. S.C.Code Ann. § 40-5-310 (1976). While case law provides general guidelines as to what constitutes the practice of law, courts are hesitant to define its exact boundaries. Thus, the analysis in 'practice of law' cases is necessarily fact-driven. The Supreme Court has specifically avoided addressing hypothetical situations, preferring instead to determine what constitutes the unauthorized practice of law on a case-by-case basis. *In Re Unauthorized Practice of Law Rules Proposed by the South Carolina Bar*, 309 S.C. 304, 422 S.E.2d 123 (S.C.1992). I find that Petitioner's proposed actions constitute the unauthorized practice of law and that the proposed fee agreement violates the ethical prohibition against fee splitting.

Our Supreme Court has set forth a succinct standard of the proper role of paralegals:

> The activities of a paralegal do not constitute the practice of law as long as they are limited to work of a preparatory nature, such as legal research, investigation, or the composition of legal documents, which enable the licensed attorney-employer to carry a given matter to a conclusion through his own examination, approval or additional effort. *Matter of Easler*, 275 S.C. 400, 272 S.E.2d 32, 33 (S.C. 1980).

While the important support function of paralegals has increased through the years, the Easler guidelines stand the test of time. As envisioned in *Easler*, the paralegal plays a supporting role to the supervising attorney. Here, the roles are reversed. The attorney would support the paralegal. Petitioner would play the lead role, with no meaningful attorney supervision and the attorney's presence and involvement only surfaces on the back end. Meaningful attorney supervision must be present throughout the process. The line between what is and what is not permissible conduct by a nonattorney is oftentimes "unclear" and is a potential trap for the unsuspecting client. *State v. Buyers Service Co., Inc.*, 292 S.C. 426, 357 S.E.2d 15, 17 (S.C.1987). The conduct of the paralegal contemplated here clearly crosses the line into the unauthorized practice of law. It is well settled that a paralegal may not give legal advice, consult, offer legal explanations, or make legal recommendations. *State v. Despain*, 319 S.C. 317, 460 S.E.2d 576 (S.C.1995).

A. Educational Seminars

*3 Petitioner intends to conduct unsupervised "wills and trusts" seminars for the public, "emphasizing" living trusts during the course of his presentation. Petitioner also plans to answer estate-planning questions from the audience. I find Petitioner's proposed conduct constitutes the unauthorized practice of law.

I find, as other courts have, that the very structure of such "educational" legal seminars suggests that the presenter will actually be giving legal advice on legal matters. See, *In Re Mid-America Living Trust Assoc. Inc.*, 927 S.W.2d 855 (Mo. banc 1996); *People v. Volk*, 805 P.2d 1116 (Colo. 1991); *Oregon State Bar v. John H. Miller & Co.* 235 Or. 341, 385 P.2d 181 (Or. 1963). At the very least. Petitioner will implicitly advise participants that they require estate-planning services. Whether a will or trust is appropriate in any given situation is a function of legal judgment. To be sure, advising a potential client on his or her need for a living trust (or other particular estate-planning instrument or device) fits squarely within the practice of law. These matters cry out for the exercise of professional judgment by a licensed attorney. Thus, in conducting these informational seminars, Petitioner would engage in the unauthorized practice of law as a non-attorney offering legal advice.

Petitioner plans to answer "general" questions during his presentation. I have reviewed the Estate-Planning Summary submitted by Petitioner and his attorney-employer. This summary sets forth the subject matter to be covered by the paralegal. Petitioner would present information on, among other things, revocable trusts, irrevocable living trusts, credit shelter trusts, qualified terminable interest property trusts, charitable remainder trusts, qualified personal residence trusts, grantor retained annuity trusts, grantor retained unitrusts, and charitable lead trusts. It is difficult to imagine such specific estate-planning devices eliciting "general" questions or a scenario in which the exercise of legal judgment would not be involved. It is, after all, a legal seminar, apparently for the purpose of soliciting business. [FN1] To suggest that some "plan" would anticipate all possible questions with predetermined nonlegal responses is specious. And so complex is this area of law that many states, including South Carolina, have established stringent standards for an attorney to receive the designation of "specialist" in Estate Planning and Probate Law. SCACR, Part IV, Appendices D and E. This is the practice of law.

FN1. While this marketing method may raise ethical implications for the attorney involved, the issue before me is whether the activities of the paralegal constitute the unauthorized practice of law. See *Rule* 7.3, Rules of Professional Conduct, 407 SCACR; Matter of Morris, 270 S.C. 308, 241 S.E.2d 911 (1978) (lawyer improperly solicited employment); *Matter of Craven*, 267 S.C. 33, 225 S.E.2d 861 (1976) (an attorney's knowledge that his employee is engaged in solicitation of professional employment for attorney constitutes professional misconduct); *Matter of Crosby*, 256 S.C. 325, 182 S.E.2d 289 (1971) (attorney improperly solicited business). Thus, not only does Petitioner's solicitation of legal clients raise possible ethical concerns for his sponsoring attorney, Petitioner's involvement clearly constitutes the unauthorized practice of law.

I fully recognize the prevailing popularity of 'financial planners' and others "jump[ing] on the estate planning bandwagon." (Estate-Planning Summary submitted by Petitioner's attorney-employer, p. 1). This trend in no way affects the decision before the Court. This paralegal would not be presenting the estate-planning seminar as a financial planner. This seminar would be conspicuously sponsored by the paralegal's attorney-employer. The attorney's law firm is prominently displayed in the brochure submitted, e.g., name, address, telephone number, and "Firm Profile." In promoting the law firm and representing to the public the 'legal' nature of the seminar, neither the paralegal nor his attorney-employer can escape the prohibition against the unauthorized practice of law.

B. Initial Client Interview

*4 Petitioner intends to gather client information and answer general estate-planning questions during his proposed "initial client interviews." While Petitioner may properly compile client information, Petitioner may not answer estate-planning questions. See *Matter of Easler*, supra. Petitioner's answering legal questions would constitute the unauthorized practice of law for the reasons stated above. While the law firm in which Petitioner is employed plans to direct clients to an attorney for "follow-up" consultations, a paralegal may not give legal advice in any event. Moreover, permissible preparatory tasks must be performed while under the attorney's supervision. The proposed after-the-fact attorney review comes too late.

C. Compensation

Petitioner's law firm intends to compensate him based upon the volume and types of cases he "handles." A paralegal, of course, may not "handle" any case. [FN2] This fee arrangement directly violates *Rule 5.4* of the Rules of Professional Conduct, SCACR 407. [FN3] This limitation serves to "discourage the unauthorized practice of law by laypersons and to prevent a non-lawyer from acquiring a vested pecuniary interest in an attorney's disposition of a case that could possibly take preeminence over a client's best interest." *Matter of Anonymous Member of the S.C. Bar*, 295 S.C. 25, 26, 367 S.E.2d 17, 18 (S.C. 1998). This compensation proposal arrangement coupled with Petitioner's desire to market the law firm's services via the educational seminars and meet individually with clients creates a situation ripe for abuse. Indeed, the proposal by Petitioner presents the very evil *Rule 5.4* was designed to avoid. Accordingly, I find Petitioner's proposed compensation plan violates both the letter and the spirit of *Rule 5.4* prohibiting fee splitting with non-attorneys.

FN2. The suggestion that Petitioner and the law firm intend for him to "handle" cases speaks volumes about the anticipated role of Petitioner, far beyond the permissible tasks performed by paralegals.

FN3. Nonlawyer employees may certainly participate "in a compensation or retirement plan, even though the plan is based in whole or in part on a profit sharing arrangement." *Rule 5.4(a)(3)*, Rules of Professional Conduct, SCACR 407.

RECOMMENDATIONS

1. Offering legal presentations for the general public constitutes the practice of law.
2. Answering estate-planning questions in the context of legal seminars or in private client interviews constitutes the practice of law.
3. Fee-sharing arrangements with non-attorneys based on volume and cases "handled" by a paralegal violates *Rule 5.4*, Rules of Professional Conduct, SCACR 407.

Respectfully Submitted

/s/ John W. Kittredge Referee April 7, 2000 Greenville, SC

Case Review Exercises

1. Why was the court not persuaded by the paralegal's argument that, because an attorney had reviewed and approved all of the information in the public seminar, there should not be a problem regarding the unauthorized practice of law?
2. The paralegal seemed to argue that, in reality, he or she would be performing a good deed by educating the public on topics such as wills, trusts, and living trusts. Why was the court not persuaded by this argument?
3. If an attorney had been at the seminar, and the paralegal and attorney had jointly conducted the seminar, would the court have arrived at the same conclusion? Why?
4. Did the content of the seminar play a part in the court's decision? Why or why not?
5. The paralegal seemed to make the argument that, because other professionals such as financial planners were giving such advice, the paralegal should be able to as well. Was the decision to create a different standard for paralegals versus other professionals fair and consistent?
6. Read Footnote 2. How does the content of that footnote impact the rest of the decision? Why were the court's conclusions in Footnote 2 important to the case as a whole?

Helpful Web Sites

Organization	Description	Internet Address
American Bar Association (ABA)	Association for attorneys. The Web site has a large amount of information and publications relevant to individuals working in the legal profession.	http://www.americanbar.org
ABA Information on Professionalism and Ethics in Lawyer Advertising and Marketing	ABA Web site devoted to ethics related to attorney marketing.	http://www.americanbar.org/groups/professional_responsibility/resources/professionalism/professionalism_ethics_in_lawyer_advertising.html
ABA Law Practice Today	ABA Web site devoted to law practice management issues, including coverage of legal marketing.	http://www.americanbar.org/groups/law_practice.html
Legal Marketing Association	Nonprofit association for legal marketing professionals.	http://www.legalmarketing.org
Lawmarketing.com	Legal marketing portal, including articles and information on legal marketing.	http://www.lawmarketing.com
Legalmarketingblog.com	Legal marketing blog, including articles and information related to legal marketing.	http://www.legalmarketingblog.com

Suggested Reading

1. Rose, J. (2005). *How to Capture and Keep Clients: Marketing Strategies for Lawyers.* American Bar Association.
2. *Law Practice* magazine, published by the American Bar Association Law Practice Management Section http://www.americanbar.org/groups/law_practice.html.
3. Hornsby, W. (2000). *Marketing and Legal Ethics: The Boundaries of Promoting Legal Services.* American Bar Association.
4. Munneke, G. A., & Davis, A. E. (2003, 2007, 2010). *The Essential Formbook: Comprehensive Management Tools for Lawyers, Vols. I–IV.* American Bar Association.
5. American Bar Association. (2007). *The Lawyer's Guide to Marketing on the Internet.* (3rd ed.). American Bar Association.
6. Durham, J., & McMurray, D. (2008). *The lawyer's Guide to Marketing Your Practice.* (3rd ed.). American Bar Association.
7. Snyder, T. C. (2011). *Women Rainmakers' Best Marketing Tips.* (3rd ed.) American Bar Association.

9

File and Law Library Management

Chapter Objectives

After you read this chapter, you should be able to:

- Discuss why file management is important.
- Explain centralized and decentralized filing systems.
- Discuss the importance of closing and purging files.
- Explain why library ordering should be centralized.
- Give examples of how law library costs can be reduced.

- It was 10 days before Bruce returned from his honeymoon so we could not ask him about the wrongful seizure memorandum prepared. Bruce informed us that Sabrina worked on the memo, but he did not recall where she saved the file or its name.
- After several hours, we located the research file on bankruptcy petition preparers (11 U.S.C. 110) under "11."
- We spent several days looking on each computer hard drive attempting to find the salvage trucks lease purchase agreements involved with the loan refinancing. Eventually the agreements were found under "templates" on the network drive labeled "salvage trucks." The file name was saved as the first two words listed on the documents.

Why Paralegals Need an Understanding of File and Law Library Management

Paralegals work with hard copy and electronic files every single day. It is crucial that they know how to organize, track, and store clients' files. If a file or parts of a file are lost, misplaced, or misfiled, the effects can be devastating, both to the office and to the client's case. Information must be stored so that it can be quickly found and retrieved. Paralegals are responsible for organizing case files in many instances. In addition, many legal organizations are using automated file management systems. Paralegals must have a good understanding of automated systems as law firms progress toward a paperless office.

Paralegals also must have a basic understanding of law library management. Paralegals use the law library to conduct legal research, so it is important that they know how libraries work and be familiar with electronic research resources. In addition, many paralegals, especially in smaller offices, may actually be in charge of maintaining the library. Law libraries have changed drastically in recent years. More and more information is being stored electronically, so paralegals must have a good understanding of how to access electronic information and research.

Introduction to File Management

Law offices of all types need a file system that allows them to store, track, and retrieve information about cases in a logical, efficient, and expeditious manner. The outcome of many legal matters depends on the case information gathered, including evidence, depositions, pleadings, discovery requests, and witness interviews. File information generally is worthless unless it is organized and available to the paralegals and attorneys who will use it. File management is a large task, no matter the size of the law practice.

A. **Easy to Learn**—Well designed file systems are user friendly, simple, and straightforward, anyone can understand it.
B. **Easy to Use**—Well designed file systems are easily located with quick access and integrate electronic files within the office files' structure.
C. **Easy to Adapt**—Well designed file systems are easily adjusted as the business environment grows or changes focus.
D. **Comprehensive**—Well designed file systems are all-inclusive; hard copies and electronic files should contain all relevant case information.
E. **File Integrity**—Well designed file systems are reliable, dependable, accurate, and sound.
F. **Security Policy**—Well designed file systems provide a safe environment for both hard copies and electronic files to prevent unauthorized access to specific files as well as the system access.
G. **Retention Policy**—Well designed file systems have procedures for maintaining and preserving both hard copies and electronic file document based on required time frames.

Exhibit 9-1 File System Vital Components

Exhibit 9-1 presents the characteristics of a good file system, whether the system is paperless or uses paper. Each of these areas is vital to a law office, and none can be compromised. A poor file system has some or all of the following problems:

1. Files (hard copy and electronic) are lost and cannot be found.
2. Files are messy and disorganized.
3. Office staff is unclear about how the filing system works.
4. Attorneys and paralegals do not trust the file system and keep their own files or keep the office's files in their possession.
5. Staff is constantly aggravated and frustrated over the file system.
6. Large amounts of time and money are wasted trying to find the file and information.
7. Poor-quality legal services are given to clients because of the poor filing system.
8. Electronic file systems are unreliable or do not work.

File management is an important topic because law office management is responsible for providing an effective system that adequately supports its attorneys and paralegals. Files and file systems represent a tool that the attorney and paralegal use to provide their services.

Filing Methods and Techniques

There are different variations or filing methods that accomplish the objectives in Exhibit 9-1. Which filing method is used depends on the particular needs of each law office. These needs may be based on such factors as the number of attorneys in the firm, the number of cases that will be tracked and stored, the type and power of computer hardware and software in use, the size and length of time typical cases are kept open or active, how much paper typical cases generate, the amount of space available for storage, whether the files will be kept in a central location, or whether departments or attorneys will keep their own files.

Each Legal Matter Is Maintained Separately

No matter which filing method is used in a law office, each case or legal matter must be maintained separately. Even if one client has several legal matters pending, each case/legal matter should have its own separate file and should be given its own file number. There is the danger that documents will be misplaced or lost if all documents are commingled.

When matters are commingled, it affects other law office systems, such as conflict-of-interest checking (which determines whether the law office has a conflict of interest), docket control, and billing. Each case should be checked for conflict-of-interest problems, should have its own distinct and separate deadlines entered into the docket control system, and should be billed to the client separately.

Alphabetic Systems

alphabetic filing system

Filing method in which cases are stored based on the last name of the client or organization.

In an **alphabetic filing system**, cases are stored based on the last name of the client or name of the organization. There is a natural tendency to alphabetize because it is a system that most people understand. In addition, staff members do not need to memorize case numbers or use numerical lists: a user knows exactly where the file should be in the drawer.

The larger the number of cases the law office is handling, the more problems it will experience with an alphabetical system. This is because names are not all that unique; many clients may have the same last name. It is not efficient to search through four or five file drawers or cabinets of "Smith" files looking for the right case. It is also not uncommon for clients to have the same first and last names. Other systems, such as a numerical or an electronic system, can track almost infinite number of cases with a unique number and also protect the confidentiality of the client, because the client's name is not the identifier for the file and is therefore not written on all the files. In offices with a large number of cases, an alphabetic system may not be the best kind of filing system; they are difficult to expand and can require constantly shifting files to make room for more.

Numerical Systems

In a numerical filing system, each case or legal matter is given a separate file number. This is similar to when a case is filed with a court; a clerk assigns each action or lawsuit a separate case number. Case identifiers can be, but do not necessarily have to be, composed of all numbers (e.g., 234552). Variations can be used, such as alphanumeric, in which letters and numbers are used. For instance, a letter might be used in the case number to reflect which branch office is handling the case, and two of the numbers might reflect the year the case was filed, such as NO15-990004. The "NO" might stand for the office's New Orleans location, and "15" stand for 2015, the year the case was initiated.

Letters also may stand for types of cases ("PB" for probate, "TX" for tax, etc.) or for a particular attorney—"Patricia Burns," and so forth. Even in a numerical system, however, legal matters for the same client can be kept together. For instance, in the example "NO15-990004," "99" could represent the client's personal number and "4" could mean that this is the fourth case that the office is handling for the client.

Another numerical filing method is to assign a range of numbers to a particular type of case, such as 000–999 for trusts, 1000–1999 for tax matters, and 2000–2999 for criminal matters.

A filing rule that sometimes bears out is that the longer the case number, the more misfiling and other types of errors occur; shorter numbers can also be remembered more easily. Numerical filing solves the shifting problems caused by alphabetical systems. When a new case is taken, the next sequential number is given to the file, and it is stored accordingly. This is different than the alphabetic system, where a new file is stored by the client's name. When the new file is added to the existing drawer in the alphabetical system, the drawer may be full, and then someone must shift or move files to make room for the new addition.

Bar Coding

bar coding

A file management technique in which each file is tracked according to the file's bar code.

Bar coding is a file management technique in which each file is tracked according to the file's bar code. Each time a user takes a file, the file's bar code and user's bar code are scanned into a computer. The computerized system then tracks which user checked out which file. When the file is returned, the file's bar code is scanned back into the computer. A report can be generated any time, listing what files are checked out and by whom. Using this system, it is possible to find the location of files quite easily. Bar codes are used in many libraries to track the library's collection. Bar coding of law office files works much the same way.

The "Paperless Office"—Electronic Document Management

document management software

Organizes, controls, distributes, and allows for extensive searching of electronic documents typically in a computer-networked environment.

imaging

Uses a scanner to capture an image of a document. The image is stored electronically.

Document management software organizes, controls, distributes, and allows for extensive searching of electronic documents, typically in a computer-networked environment. In a "paperless" office environment, all information is stored electronically. Document management software easily tracks and stores computer files that are already in an electronic format such as word processing, e-mail, and spreadsheet files. It allows a legal organization to file documents electronically so they can be found by anyone in the organization, even when there are hundreds of users spread across offices located throughout the world. Document management software can also accommodate hard copy documents through the use of imaging. **Imaging** uses a scanner to capture an image of a document. That image is stored electronically and can be retrieved later. Given the enormous storage capacities of computers, document management software is the electronic equivalent of a filing room with thousands of file cabinets.

Document management software provides for extensive searching capabilities and allows users to associate files with cases and create profiles of documents for easy retrieval. Document management software tracks files from the time they are opened until they are closed. It also allows many reports to be generated regarding the records that are being kept. Records can be printed regarding files assigned to specific attorneys, types of cases, and more. Many law offices have some kind of document management software; while many are not completely "paperless," most law offices use document management software to some extent. Document management software has many advantages, including the ability to share information across vast distances, excellent tracking and reporting capabilities, reduced instances of misfiling, ability to easily and quickly create a backup copy of information, reduced space and storage costs, and the ability to quickly search and sort information, among others.

Unfortunately, document management also has some down sides. The cost of technology can be substantial, and training of staff is essential. In addition, like any system, a document management system must be maintained and properly administered. Law offices must have procedures and rules for those documents that are saved for long term. Discussion drafts and unfinished documents may need to be stored in a different place. In addition, firms should have a document retention policy that includes both hard copy and electronic documents.

Corporate, Government, and Legal Aid Filing Methods

Corporate law and government departments may arrange their matters differently. They may file matters by subject, by department, or by other means that suit their particular industry or need. Legal services/aid offices typically file cases alphabetically or even geographically, by city or county.

Centralized v. Decentralized

centralized file system

Method in which a file department or file clerk stores and manages all active law office files in one or more file rooms.

decentralized file system

System in which files are kept in various locations throughout the law office.

A fundamental law office filing consideration is whether the filing system will be centralized or decentralized. A **centralized file system** is where a file department or file clerk stores and manages all active law office files in one or more file rooms. In a **decentralized file system**, files are kept in various locations throughout the law office, such as each department storing its own files or each attorney keeping his or her own files.

A centralized system is typically used when the office has a complex filing procedure best handled by one department or file clerk staff; when the office wants a highly controlled system; or when several attorneys or paralegals work on the same cases. Even though a law office may want a centralized system, the office must first have the physical space to accommodate it. Law offices in which a single attorney or paralegal works on each case, such as real estate matters, or needs the case files for long periods of time may use a decentralized file system where the files are located in an individual's office or in a secretarial area. Some offices use a "pod," or team filing system, where several people—perhaps two or three attorneys, a secretary, and a paralegal or two—have offices located close to one another and have their files stored next to them. Some offices may use a combination. Whether an office uses a centralized or decentralized system depends on the size of the office, type of cases handled, and the needs of the personnel involved. Closed files are almost always kept in a centralized location.

Opening Files

When a new or an existing client comes into the office with a new legal matter, a new file should immediately be opened. The opening of a file should be standardized and requires certain information about the legal matter. A file-opening form or an electronic version (sometimes called a new client/matter form or case sheet) is customarily completed when opening a new file (see Exhibit 9-2).

file-opening form

A standardized form that is filled out when a new case is started. The form contains important information about the client and the case.

The **file-opening form** is used for a variety of purposes, including to check potential conflicts of interest, to assign a new case number and attorney to the matter, to track the area or specialty of the case, to set forth the type of fee agreement and billing frequency in the case, to enter the case in the timekeeping and billing system, to make docketing entries (such as when the statute of limitations in the matter might run), and to find out how the client was referred to the law office. Although file-opening forms are commercially available, most law offices choose to customize the form to reflect their own needs.

Copies of the file-opening form may be sent to the managing partner, other attorneys, accounting department, docket-control department, and the responsible attorney.

File Format and Internal File Rules

File format (or how case files are set up) and organization depend on the needs of each office. The type of file format will depend on the filing system that is used; for example, vertical file drawers require tabs in different places, while an open-shelf filing system requires tabs on the side.

Many offices use separate manila files as subdivisions in the same case to differentiate information in the same file, such as having files for "Accounting," "Discovery," "Pleadings," "Client Correspondence," and others (see Exhibit 9-3). The individual manila files are stored in one or more expanding files, so that all the files for one case are kept together. Many offices

New File

Client (Check one)

__________ INDIVIDUAL ____

Last First Middle Initial

__________ ENTITY ____

(Use complete name & common abbreviations; place articles [e.g., The] at end.)

__________ CLASS ACTION ____

(File Name, ex.: Popcorn Antitrust Litigation)

Matter (Check One)

__________ NON-LITIGATION

__________ LITIGATION

__________ Approved for litigation by—MUST BE INITIALED by submitting attorney!!

Nature of the Case

Area of law code: __________ Summary of work or dispute: ____________________

Client Contact (N/A for Class Actions)

Name: ______________________________

Company: ______________________________

Street: ______________________________

City, State, Zip: ______________________________

Telephone: ______________________________

***New Adverse Parties:**

***New Related Parties** (for Class Actions, Named Plaintiffs Only):

*Will be entered into computer system by Bus. Dept. *AFTER* approval by Managing Partner.

Closed File

Date Closed: __________ **Atty. Or Sec. Initials:** __________

__________ Attach pleadings and/or file indexes. If indexes are not available, attach brief description of what is contained in the file(s). SEND FILES, THIS FORM, AND INDEX TO FILE ROOM.

Routing Lists **(Initial)**

		New File:	Date:	Closed File:	Date:
Submitted by		____	____	____	____
Sec. of Submitting Person		____	____	____	____
Managing Partner		____	____	____	____
Business Department		____	____	____	____
File Department		____	____	____	____
Firm Newsletter		____	____	____	____
Docket for Litigation		____	____	____	____
EnviroLaw (Computer Center)	Add?	____			
IdeaLaw (Computer Center)	Add?	____			
JobLaw (Computer Center)	Add?	____			

Exhibit 9-2 File-Opening Form

Exhibit 9-2 *(contineud)*

Billing Address (N/A for Class Actions)

Name: ______________________________

Company: ______________________________

Street: ______________________________

City, State, Zip: ______________________________

Telephone: ______________________________

Team Information (Use initials)

_____ _____ _____ Managing Attorney(s) (for nonlitigation cases only)

_____ _____ _____ Bill Review Attorney(s)

_____ _____ _____ Originating Attorney(s)

_____ Calendar Attorney (for litigation cases only)

_____ Legal Assistant (for litigation cases only)

_____ Secretary to Calendar Attorney (for litigation cases only)

Referral Source (Check one)

_____ Existing Client ______________________________
(Name)

_____ Non-Firm Attorney ______________________________
(Name)

_____ Firm Attorney or Employee ______________________________

_____ Martindale-Hubbell ______________________________

_____ Other ______________________________

Fee Agreement (Check those that apply)

_____ Hourly

_____ Contingent _____ %

_____ Fee Petition

_____ Fixed Fee $_____ or Fixed Range from $_____ to $_____

_____ Retainer $_____

_____ Letter of Retainer sent by _____ on _____
(Initials) (Date)

Statement Format (Check those that apply)

Do you want identical disbursements grouped? _____ Yes _____ No

Do you want attorney hours reflected on each time entry? _____ Yes _____ No

Do you want fees extended on each time entry? _____ Yes _____ No

Conflict Check

Conflict Check Completed By: __________ Date: __________
(Initials)

Conflict Check Not Needed: __________
(Initials of Submitting Person)

Check One:

_____ No conflicts

_____ Potential conflict with the following existing parties (from computer system):

____

____

(Or attach computer printout from Conflict Check System.)

Exhibit 9-3 Typical Subcategories of Files

Accounting
Correspondence with Attorneys
Correspondence with Client
Deposition Summaries
Discovery
Evidence
General Correspondence
Investigation
Legal Research
Memorandums
Notes and Miscellaneous
Witnesses

also use metal fasteners to hold the papers securely in place; original documents, however, should not be punched. Instead, they should be maintained separately and a copy put in the regular file. Finally, information is typically placed in each manila file in chronological order, with the oldest on the bottom and the newest on the top of the file. This gives the user a systematic way of finding information. It is routine to find duplicate and draft copies of documents in a file; however, this makes the organization process more difficult. If duplicates must be kept, they should be in a separate file folder labeled "Duplicates."

Color Coding

Color coding files is a simple but effective way to reduce the number of misfiled documents. Files can be color coded in a variety of ways; for example, red-labeled files may be used for probate and green files for criminal matters. Color coding can also be done according to the year the case was opened or according to the attorney handling the matter.

Color coding may be used for cases that are especially sensitive or that need to be kept secure. For example, if the law office is trying to create an "ethical wall" or "ethical screen" to keep a staff member from participating in a case, others can be alerted to the need for security by assigning a certain color of file label to the case. Finally, color coding can be used in an alphabetic filing system—for example, A–E equals blue, F–J equals green, and so forth.

Checking Files Out

In some law offices where many people have access to files, users are required to check out files electronically (in a process similar to one used in a public library) or to simply leave a large card where the file is stored, showing who checked out the file. It can be quite frustrating to search for a client's file, only to discover that someone else took the file home to work on, or that the file is lost. Tracking the location of files is crucial to an effective file/record management system.

Closing, Storing, and Purging Files

After a legal matter has come to a conclusion and the final bill has been paid, the file is closed and taken out of the storage area of active files. It is boxed up and kept in the office's basement or an off-site storage facility for a certain number of years, until it is destroyed or put on microfilm, microfiche, or stored electronically on CDs or other storage devices.

A closed file is sometimes called a "dead file" or a "retired file." Some offices give the closed case a new number, to differentiate it from active cases. The closing of cases represents a problem for many law offices. Attorneys like to have access to closed files in case they someday need the information contained in them. Storage space can be quite expensive, however. Most law offices are continually opening and closing cases, which means that the flow of files never stops and that the required storage area gets larger and larger. Duplicate copies of documents should be removed in order to reduce file storage requirements.

A client must be made completely aware before his or her file is closed. It is strongly recommended that the law firm send a disengagement letter to the client, letting him or her know in writing that the file is being closed and that the client can have documents, evidence, or even the whole file returned to him or her. Electronic records also need to be purged or backed up at the same time the hard copy of the file is closed.

One solution to storage problems is to purge or destroy files after a certain period of time (see Exhibit 9-4). Some state ethical rules also govern file retention. Some law offices purge all files after a certain number of years, such as seven or eight, while others purge only selected files. Destroying hard copy files usually means shredding, burning, or recycling them. Simply throwing them away does not protect the client's confidentiality and should not be done.

Organization of Files—A Major Paralegal Duty

File organization is a large part of what many paralegals do. They must use files on a daily basis; therefore, for most paralegals to become efficient at what they do, they must be able to organize and—in some cases—index case files in a logical and systematic fashion so that they can quickly find information. Case material also must be organized in such a way that others, such as attorneys, can find the information quickly. A file that is a disorganized mess is useless in a law office. For instance, if the legal assistant is assisting an attorney at a deposition and the attorney asks him or her to find a specific answer in the discovery request, he or she must be able to locate it quickly. If the paralegal is not familiar with the case, does not have the file organized, or misfiled the document, he or she will not have the ability to find the information quickly, and the client's case may suffer.

File Management and Ethics

There are several ethical questions that should be addressed when considering filing and filing systems. These issues include performing conflict-of-interest checks before a new case is taken, maintaining client-related property that is turned over to the law office during representation, maintaining trust- and client-related accounting records, returning a client's file to him or her if the client decides to change attorneys, and ensuring that the office's filing system and/or file destruction procedures maintain client confidentiality.

Client Property

Offices should be careful when closing files and especially when destroying files containing documents or other information that were given to the attorney by a client. *Rule 1.15* regarding the rules of professional conduct address a law office's duty at the end of a case to give the client the option to pick up information that was delivered to the attorney for representation in the matter. Generally, unless the client consents, a lawyer should not destroy or discard items that

Exhibit 9-4 Sample Record Retention Periods

Law Office Administration	Retention Period
Accounts payable and receivable ledgers	7 years
Audit reports	Permanently
Bank statement and reconciliations	7 years
Cash receipt books	Permanently
Canceled checks (except for payments of taxes, real estate, and other important payments—permanently)	10 years
Contracts, mortgages, notes, and leases (still in effect)	Permanently
Correspondence, general	5–7 years
Important (significant) correspondence	Permanently
Deeds, mortgages, etc.	Permanently
Employment applications	3 years
Financial statements (year end)	Permanently
Insurance policies (expired)	10 years
Invoices	7 years
Minutes of directors' and stockholders' meetings	Permanently
Payroll records (after termination)	10 years
Retirement and pension records	6 years
Tax returns	4 years from date issued or paid
Time cards/records	3 years

Clients' Files and Documents—Important Note:

- Retention of a client's file and client-related documents depends on the ethical rules in your state.
- Before destroying a client's file, contact the client to make sure he or she does not want the file or want something out of the file.
- When destroying a client's file, burn, shred, or recycle them to ensure client confidentiality.

Source: Code of Federal Regulations (CFR) and The Sarbanes—Oxley Act.

clearly or probably belong to the client. In addition, an attorney should be especially careful not to destroy client information till the applicable statutory limitations period has not expired.

Duty to Turn Over File When Client Fires Attorney

An attorney also has a duty to turn over to a client his or her file when the client decides to fire an attorney and hire another one. What must be turned over to the client depends on the ethical rules and case law in each state. For example, Rule 3-700(D) of the *California Revised Rules of Professional Conduct* states:

> (a) [An attorney] whose employment has terminated shall ... promptly release to the client, all the client papers and property. Client papers and property include correspondence, pleadings, deposition transcripts, exhibits, physical evidence, expert's reports, and other items reasonably necessary to the client's representation, whether the client has paid for them or not.

In most states, the attorney must turn over any documents the new counsel will need to reasonably handle the matter. In some states, such as California, a law office cannot refuse to release a client's file just because the client still owes fees and expenses.

Destruction of Records of Account

Rule 1.15 regarding the rules of professional conduct also address the attorney's duty to maintain financial records related to a legal matter for five years after termination of representation. Law offices should carefully maintain accurate and complete records of the lawyer's receipt and disbursement of trust funds in every case.

Confidentiality

An attorney's duty to maintain the confidentiality of client-related matters should be a factor when considering a law office file management system. Files must be maintained so that sensitive information about a case or client is kept private. The confidentiality rule also does not stop once the case is closed. Law offices should be careful to destroy or dispose of files in a manner consistent with the confidentiality requirements.

Introduction to Law Library Management

Professional librarians may coordinate and manage the law library in medium- to large-sized law offices. In smaller law offices, however, paralegals or associate attorneys may perform these duties. Exhibit 9-5 contains a list of librarian-related duties.

Law libraries are changing. The Internet, CD-ROM libraries, e-Books, and data services such as Westlaw and LexisNexis have forever changed how and where lawyers and paralegals access legal research. While hard copy books will probably never be completely replaced by their electronic counterparts, many libraries are going digital, and this has changed how libraries are managed. Library management used to be centered around purchasing, maintaining, and storing shelf after shelf of books that constantly grew in number. This is no longer the case; many legal professionals do not even need a physical library at all. They can now

Exhibit 9-5 Librarian-Related Duties

- Trains and supervises staff
- Explains research techniques to lawyers and paralegals, and answers questions
- Compiles legislative histories and bibliographies
- Selects and orders books, CD-ROM libraries, and other library resources
- Reviews and approves bills for payment
- Plans library growth
- Catalogs and tracks library resources using computerized methods
- Routes library-related materials to appropriate staff
- Files loose-leaf services and other library-related documents
- Manages check out of books and reshelves material
- Performs or assists legal professionals in legal research, particularly regarding computer-assisted legal research and legal and factual research on the Internet

access a host of electronic legal research at their desk. That said, law firms will always have to provide some type of "library" for their staff, but many firms have moved from the expense of hard copy books to electronic alternatives.

Depending on the structure of the law office, the library may be supervised by a library committee, a managing partner, or an office administrator, or all functions may be controlled by the librarian.

Law libraries generally are thought of as an overhead expense and, regardless of size, are costly to maintain. Proper library management can, however, reduce overhead expenses and increase the quality of services to clients at the same time.

Some paralegals may be put in charge of the law library. Managing a law library may not seem at first like a difficult job, but in many instances it is. Books, periodicals, CD-ROM libraries, and other materials must be ordered on a regular basis to ensure the library is kept current; supplements to books (sometimes called "pocket parts") must be ordered and replaced regularly; the collection must be tracked using some type of computer or card catalog system (this requires quite a bit of time); books must be shelved and maintained; a library budget must be kept and tracked; and from time to time, books must be tracked down and found. Many librarians perform legal research themselves, as well. Proper law library management can be a time-consuming task.

Developing a Library Collection

There are many different types of materials that can be found in a law office library. The office's collection should mirror the type of practice and its specialties. As a law office's practice changes, the library also will need to change to keep information that is current with the needs of the law office. Exhibit 9-6 lists typical types of publications that are found in many law office library collections.

The extent of an office's collection will depend on many factors. Larger offices that have been in existence for many years will have much larger collections than will newer or smaller law offices. Some offices think that most, if not all, research should be performed in their own library, while other law offices that have large collections nearby, such as a law school or state or county law library, may want to keep their costs low and use these resources to the fullest extent possible.

A way to keep overhead costs low in the library is by purchasing CD-ROM libraries or electronic books with Internet access, maintaining Westlaw or LexisNexis, and keeping hard copy books and periodicals only as needed. This strategy limits the space requirements needed for most libraries and maximizes the use of computers already on the desks of most staff.

Exhibit 9-6
Possible Holdings in a Law Library

- Case Law
- Citators
- Digests
- Encyclopedias
- Index to Periodicals
- Periodicals
- Reference Works
- Statutes
- Treatises
- CD-ROM Libraries
- Westlaw
- Internet Access
- LexisNexis

CD-ROM and Electronic Legal Databases

CD-ROM legal database

A database like one found on Westlaw or LexisNexis, but packaged on CD-ROMs.

A **CD-ROM legal database** is a database like one found on Westlaw or LexisNexis, but packaged on one or more CD-ROMs. For example, the complete set of the *Federal Reporter*, which contains federal appellate court decisions from 1880 to the present, takes up more than 150 linear feet of shelf space in a law library, and this does not count the indexes necessary to use the reporters. The same *Federal Reporter* comes on CD-ROM disks, taking up 1-2 feet of shelf space, and includes a search engine that allows the user to search for needed material. Many CD-ROM publishers also offer connections to the Internet or online services so that research can be updated. Many online services now include access to electronic resources. The same *Federal Reporter* mentioned earlier, is now available electronically and downloaded directly onto the office computer system, further reducing the physical library space needed. Updates are simple and removing or reinstalling CD-ROMs are no longer necessary. Many electronic databases and resources, such as "e-Books" are compatible with devices such as smartphones and tablets. With a simple download of the resource's application ("app"), you can have access from multiple sources or locations.

CD-ROM AND ELECTRONIC LEGAL LIBRARIES Hundreds and hundreds of CD-ROM and electronic legal libraries are currently available. Many books and periodicals published for the legal industry are available on CD-ROM or in electronic "e-Book" format. This includes everything from criminal and family law to European tax laws, and everything in between. Most of the major legal book publishers, including West, BNA, Matthew Bender, and many others, offer a wide variety of CD-ROM and electronic "e-Book" products.

electronic legal database

A database containing law-related material on the Internet such as Westlaw or LexisNexis. Electronic sources, such as e-Books may be downloaded or accessed through applications ("apps").

CD-ROM AND ELECTRONIC SEARCH ENGINES Searching CD-ROM legal databases or electronic databases are similar to searching on Westlaw and LexisNexis. Every CD-ROM or **electronic legal database** uses a search tool, typically either Premise or Folio Views, to perform the search. Users are able to utilize terms and connectors including proximity searches, wild card searches, and other searches similar to Westlaw and LexisNexis. Most search engines also have hypertext, which allows a user to go directly to another referenced document immediately (similar to the Internet). For example, if a user is reading a case and another case is referenced, the user can click the mouse on the reference to the second citation, and the computer will immediately take the user to the second case.

Advantages and Disadvantages of CD-ROM and Electronic Legal Libraries

There are many advantages to using CD-ROM and electronic legal libraries, including the following:

- *Reduced space and expense considerations*—CD-ROM and electronic legal libraries take up a fraction of the space that similar information in book form would. While most law libraries will want some information in book form, there is much information that can be stored on CD-ROM. Using electronic law library databases further reduces the physically space, since everything is contained within the computer or through the Internet access. This has a tremendous impact on the annual operating cost of a law library for any legal organization. If a law firm or corporate law department can cut the size of its law library in half, it can save a tremendous amount on lease space, shelving, and other items. Because many legal organizations are in the business of making money, this is a very important consideration.
- *Portability*—Unlike rows and rows of books, CD-ROM and electronic legal libraries are inherently portable. Users can take the entire body of a state's case law into a courtroom on

a laptop or computer and have the information at their fingertips. Additionally, with the Internet connection and e-Book sources, you have immediate access to the most current legal information. This can prove extremely beneficial to the attorney or legal assistant.

- *Convenience*—Users can access information on their own computers without going to a library or even leaving their office. In addition, information on CD-ROM or electronic sources can be copied into a user's word processor, just like Westlaw and LexisNexis.
- *Cost*—The total cost of a CD-ROM or electronic legal library is often less than for hard copy books or for performing the research online using Westlaw or LexisNexis. It is also more cost effective for anyone who does a significant amount of legal research, because it can usually be done at the person's desk and, in many circumstances, electronic research is substantially faster than using books and indexes.
- *Maintenance*—The cost of maintaining books, and adding and deleting supplements and loose-leaf pages, should not be underestimated, particularly in a large law library. It takes library personnel numerous hours to do this, as compared to installing a new CD-ROM to replace an old one. As library personnel maintenance time lessens, productivity should increase in other areas, such as the amount of time library staff can spend to assist customers with research projects.

Disadvantages to CD-ROM and Electronic legal libraries include the following:

- *Maintenance*—Maintenance of the computer software can be an issue: most CD-ROM and electronic databases have a monthly, quarterly, semiannual or annual subscription service that must be purchased to keep them up to date. New CD-ROMs and updates must be installed; electronic database services must be downloaded to the computer system. In addition, search engines must be upgraded to new versions from time to time. Depending on the environment, such as whether the computers are networked or standalone, maintenance can be quite time consuming. Hardware needs (including RAM and hard disk space) as well as networking issues require constant updating to stay current. In addition, the technology involved (including interfacing with a network) must be maintained, the systems may not work, or they may be incompatible. Technical experts must be called in to make modifications, which can be both expensive and time consuming.
- *CD-ROM versus the Internet*—There is some question regarding the long-term validity of CD-ROMs, particularly when compared to the Internet. CD-ROMs must be continually updated, whereas Internet products never need to be updated because the product is always updated.
- *Switching CD-ROMs*—While there are CD-ROM towers that can hold multiple CD-ROMs, many systems still require users or information system professionals to change CD-ROM disks. This can be inconvenient and time consuming. Some legal organizations copy all their CD-ROMs to large network servers so that CD-ROM towers are not necessary. This also makes accessing the information faster, as server access is much faster than CD-ROM access.
- *Training*—Training staff to use CD-ROMs and electronic legal databases can be a problem when different publishers, search engines, or applications are used.

Cataloging and Classifying the Collection

Proper classification and organization of a collection are imperative for the office to know what material it has and where it is located. If information is not arranged or organized in such a manner so that attorneys and legal assistants can easily find it without wasting time, the whole purpose of an in-house library is thwarted.

Exhibit 9-7 Modified Library of Congress Classification Numbers

Administrative Law	Constitutional Law
KF5401	KF4501
Agency	Consumer Law
KF1341	KF1601
Appellate	Advocacy Contracts
KF9050	KF801
Civil Procedure	Corporations
KF8810	KF1384
Commercial Transactions	Criminal Law
KF871	KF9201
Conflict of Laws	Criminal Procedure
KF8810	KF9601
Conservation of Natural Resources	Decedents' Estates and Trusts
KF5505	KF746

Cataloging is the process of listing and organizing the inventory of a library. This usually includes giving each book a separate call number and listing the book's author, title, publisher, subject, publication date, and so forth. Some offices classify and catalog their collections according to the Library of Congress classification system or the Dewey Decimal System. The Library of Congress system uses the alphabet for its general divisions. For instance, "K" is the letter that represents American Law. Exhibit 9-7 contains a list of selected Library of Congress legal classifications. Other offices may simply group materials together, such as a tax section, labor section, or real property section. This is sometimes called a "neighborhood" classification system.

Computerized catalog systems can be created using almost any database management program. They are very easy to set up and are very flexible. There are also some commercially available library cataloging systems for many types of microcomputers.

Technology and the Law Library

Computer-Assisted Legal Research (CALR)

Computer-assisted legal research (CALR) uses computers to search the words of cases, statutes, and documents themselves; two familiar legal-information services are Westlaw and LexisNexis.

online

The user is connected to an information system and is running up charges.

off-line

The user is not connected to an information service and no charges are accruing except possibly a printing or downloading charge.

Because CALR systems use the full text of the document, there is no need for indexes or digests. Instead, the user simply enters common words that describe the issue that might appear in the full text of the case or document, and the system retrieves all cases and documents that meet the request. Since the information is stored on large mainframes, the database can be searched and the documents quickly retrieved. The documents that are retrieved can be read online, can be sent off-line to a printer, or the full text can be downloaded to the user's computer. **Online** means that the user is connected to an information system and is running up charges. **Off-line** means that a user is no longer connected to an information service and that no charges are accruing except possibly a printing or downloading charge. Alternatively, a list of the appropriate cases or documents can be printed or downloaded so that, if the user likes, he or she can go to a library and examine the full texts.

CALR can be significantly quicker than manual researching techniques. Further, when CALR is used correctly, it can also retrieve cases that might not otherwise have been found using manual methods because of poor indexing or other errors. CALR is faster than manual methods because it is possible to search many databases at once (e.g., searching the case laws of all 50 states on a specific subject). Using manual methods, the user would have to search through several sets of digests, supplements, and indexes.

CALR—in addition to being quicker and sometimes more accurate than manual researching—can also be more convenient. Nearly, all legal-information services are available 24 hours a day, unlike many law libraries. Also, the research can be done from the legal professional's office. As mentioned before, when using a law library, it is possible that an important book might already be checked out or unavailable. Sources are always available online with CALR. Another important factor to consider is that new cases are entered into legal-information services usually within a few days of being handed down or decided. Therefore, the information that is available online is almost always more up-to-date than information available in books.

Although CALR is both fast and convenient, it is not free. Most legal-information services charge a yearly subscription fee, along with a fee based on the amount of time a user is connected to their system. Some services also charge a fee for every search that is done on their system. Some services have connect-time charges of more than $200 an hour. In addition, some services have a minimum monthly charge, even if the service is not used. Because CALR is so expensive, new users can run up large bills quickly. Therefore, it is particularly important that new users have a thorough understanding of the CALR system they will be using. This is usually not a problem, because most CALR systems have off-line training tutorials. On the average though, most legal issues take approximately 15 minutes to research. Most offices bill this expense back to their clients; some even do so at a higher rate than charged to help cover related expenses, such as long-distance charges. The office must be careful, however, to not bill the client for general overhead costs; general overhead costs should already be figured into the office's attorney and legal assistant billing rate, so it would be inappropriate for the client to be billed for them again.

Westlaw

Westlaw is a full-text legal-information service provided by West Group. According to West, it is one of the largest law libraries in the world, with more than 40,000 databases available to its users. It contains cases from all West reporters as well as slip opinions, unreported cases, interactive databases, and much more. This site gives Westlaw users access to an enormous body of legal and nonlegal resources. Many of Westlaw's features are covered here, including its databases, types of search queries, and special features.

Westlaw is most commonly accessed through the Internet and Westlaw-specific proprietary software called with searches through Westlaw Next and West Search.

LexisNexis

LexisNexis is a full-text legal-information service. It was the first online, full-text legal-information service and is one of the world's largest services. LexisNexis and Westlaw are similar in many respects, with a few differences. LexisNexis can be accessed by using a microcomputer and specific proprietary software, or by using a microcomputer and a standard Web browser to connect via the Internet.

The Internet

Many, if not most, legal professionals are connected to the Internet and are using it in a variety of ways. Some of the most common include performing legal research, performing factual or business research, using e-mail to communicate with clients and colleagues, accessing court records, and performing marketing functions.

PERFORMING LEGAL RESEARCH ON THE INTERNET Performing legal research on the Internet can be done, but it is not at all like researching on Westlaw or LexisNexis. A user can look up, choose, and go to thousands of databases instantly using these two services; there is a uniform search engine and uniform Boolean language; and information is formatted neatly, succinctly, and uniformly. Even with all that, it still takes time, training, and experience to be proficient in Westlaw and LexisNexis.

Very little is uniform when performing legal research on the Internet. You must search for and find information where you can, and you must learn the nuances of many different searching techniques and languages. There is no one central depository of information. As with any kind of legal research, the more experience you have, the better, but it takes time, training, and experience to be good at it.

The following are some strategies to consider when beginning an Internet legal research project:

1. **Consider proper sources to find legal information.** Over the past decade research information has dramatically increased. If the user is looking for historic documents, including articles and statutes, or a solid case law background that dates before 1990, the Internet will more than likely have reference to the material. Nearly all traditionally law libraries include electronic resources and many have entire sections that are no longer available in hard copy. A user still uses the law library to perform traditional research, but often the Internet is the first stop. The Internet can have rich treasures of information, but you have to look for them. Many resources are free, others require the user to join or subscribe to a service for a fee to get access such as Westlaw and LexisNexis.

   A cost-conscience legal researcher should start by researching any CD-ROM or electronic legal databases and hard copy books that he or she has, since they are cheap and convenient. The user could then explore the Internet to see what is available online. Again, this is cheap (actually free) and handy. In some cases, an attorney may have free access to Fastcase, an online legal research tool, available through their state bar association membership. Finally, the user could go to Westlaw or LexisNexis, double-check and confirm the research, fill in any holes, and check citations ("Shepardize").
2. **Clearly understand the legal project and develop a method for completion.** You must know what information is being sought and a method for locating it to avoid wasting time. Because Internet resources are so vast, a user that starts his or her legal research without any direction may lose several hours of productivity "surfing" various Web sites without locating the needed research.
3. **Determine the proper search resources and finding tools.** A user should select search engines and finding tools that match the specific research that will be conducted. It is often difficult to determine what tools are the best suited for researching specific information. There are several good and free legal search resources to use, such as Cornell's Legal Information Institute, FindLaw the Oyez Project, and LexisWeb.
4. **Consider using a guidebook to locate specific information.** When a user is trying to locate a particular type of material, it is highly recommended to use a legal guidebook.

A guidebook provides useful starting points, such as a list with specific legal Web sites by topic, which improves user's ability to find the information he or she needs. Most major legal publishers have guidebooks available for purchase.

5. **Utilize an online starting point.** When a user is conducting legal research on the Internet, he or she must have a starting point. The starting point is often determined by the user and his or her technique or experience. Exhibit 9-8 provides a list of search engines, Exhibit 9-9 lists legal research starting points, and Exhibit 9-10 lists factual research starting points.
6. **Get help.** The Internet, along with providing resources for both legal and nonlegal research, also has many helpful tools. Some search engines incorporate methods to inquire like Google's Let Me Google That for You ("LMGTFY") and Ask.com. Additionally, there are listservs and discussion groups, blogs, tweets, and professional Web sites such as the American Bar Association and LinkedIn that offer groups to join providing topic-specific resources. It is more than likely that others have experienced similar Internet research problems. Always remember to be discreet and use proper "netiquette" when asking for help.

Exhibit 9-8 List of Search Engines/Gateways/Databases

Name of Web Site	Web URL (Address)
General Individual/Subject Directory Search Engines	
Ask.com	<http://www.ask.com>
Bing	<http://www.bing.com>
DuckDuckGo	<https://duckduckgo.com>
Excite	<http://www.excite.com>
Google	<http://www.google.com>
Lycos	<http://www.lycos.com>
Yahoo	<http://www.yahoo.com>
Specialty Search Engines	
Search (Government)	<https://www.usa.gov>
Search (Education)	<http://www.ed.gov>
Pandia Newsfinder (News)	<http://www.pandia.com/news>
Meta-Search Engines	
Dogpile	<http://www.dogpile.com>
Ixquick	<http://www.ixquick.com>
Profusion	<http://www.profusion.com>
Zoo	<http://www.zoo.com>
Library Gateways	
Academic Information	<http://www.academicinfo.com>
Digital Librarian	<http://www.digital-librarian.com>
The Internet Public Library	<http://www.ipl.org>
WWW Virtual Library	<http://www.vlib.org>
Subject-Specific Databases	
Monster.Com (employment)	<http://www.monster.com>
Peterson's (college and university Web site)	<http://www.petersons.com/college-search.aspx>
WebMD (health/medical information)	<http://www.webmd.com>

Subject	Additional Information	Web URL (Address)
	Legal Search Engine/Portal	
Legal search engine/portal	All Law	<http://www.alllaw.com>
Legal search engine/portal	FindLaw	<http://www.findlaw.com>
Legal search engine/portal	LawGuru	<http://www.lawguru.com>
	General Starting Points (Including Federal and State Case Law and Statutes)	
General legal-related information	CataLaw	<http://www.catalaw.com>
Large collection of links to legal resources	HierosGamos	<http://www.hg.org>
Large collection of links to legal resources	Internet Legal Research Group	<http://www.ilrg.com>
Law and politics institutions guide	Large collection of links to legal resources	<http://www.lpig.org>
One of the best sources of legal information on the Web	Legal Information Institute at Cornell	<http://www.law.cornell.edu>
Large collection of links to legal resources	The Virtual Chase	<http://www.virtualchase.com>
Well-organized and comprehensive legal information	WashLaw Web at Washburn University	<http://www.washlaw.edu>
General and legal-related information	World Wide Web Virtual Library	<http://vlib.org/>
	Federal Government Information, Regulations, and Laws	
FedWorld	Federal information	<http://fedworld.ntis.gov>
USAGov	Government search engine	<http://www.usa.gov>
	Legal Forms	
Internet Legal Research Group Forms	Free legal-forms database (also includes forms for purchase)	<http://www.ilrg.com/forms/index.html>
	Legal Encyclopedia	
Law About ... (from Cornell Law School Legal Information Institute)	Legal encyclopedia	<https://www.law.cornell.edu/wex>
	Federal Regulations	
Code of Federal Regulations	Database for the code of federal regulations	<http://cfr.law.cornell.edu/cfr/>
	News and Directories	
Chicago Tribune		<http://www.chicagotribune.com/>
Los Angeles Times		<http://www.latimes.com>
New York Times		<http://www.nytimes.com>
USA Today		<http://www.usatoday.com>
Wall Street Journal		<http://www.wsj.com>
Ultimate Collection of News Links	Contains thousands of news links	<http://ww4.pppp.net/>
News Link ARL Directory	Exhaustive list of publications available electronically	<http://www.newslink.org/news.html> <http://www.arl.org>
Virtual Chase News Sites	Links to news sites on the Web	<http://virtualchase.justia.com/wiki/business-news>

Exhibit 9-9 Legal Research Starting Points

Subject	Additional Information	Web URL (Address)
	Researching Businesses	
Justia Virtual Chase	Links to Web sites with general business information	<http://virtualchase.justia.com/research-resources/business-research>
Business phone/address listings	Bigfoot	<http://www.bigfoot.com>
Yellow pages	SuperPages	<http://www.superpages.com/>
Business fax lookup	WhitePages	<http://www.whitepages.com/name/Fax-Number>
Annual reports for companies	Public Register's Annual Report Service	<http://www.prars.com>
Federal Securities and Exchange Commission	Electronic Data Gathering Analysis and Retrieval (EDGAR) Database Business Information	<http://www.sec.gov/edgar.shtml>
Hoovers	Information regarding specific companies	<http://www.hoovers.com>
	Public Records (Free)	
Justia Virtual Chase	Large list of links to finding public information on the Web	<http://virtualchase.justia.com/>
Vital Records Information	Births, marriages, deaths, divorces	<http://www.vitalrec.com/index.html>
State Public Records	An excellent source of public records information is available from individual state Web sites. Many (but not all) states have a standard Web address, <http://www.state.xx.us>, where "xx" is replaced by the state's two letter abbreviation. For example, Florida = <http://www.state.fl.us> New York = <http://www.state.ny.us>	
Public Records Resource	Large portal to many Web sites with public records	<http://www.publicrecordsources.com/>
BRB Public Information Records	Large portal to many Web sites with public records	<http://www.brbpub.com/free-public-records>
NETR online	Real estate public records	<http://publicrecords.netronline.com/>
	Vendors of Public Records (Fee Based)	
AutoTrackXP by LexisNexis		<http://www.lexisnexis.com/risk>
DeepData		<http://www.deepdata.com>
USDatalink Information Services by Insperity		<http://www.insperity.com>
Westlaw		<http://www.westlaw.com>
LexisNexis		<http://www.lexisnexis.com>

Exhibit 9-9 *(Continued)*

Subject	Additional Information	Web URL (Address)
	General Web Sites	
Maps	Google Maps	<https://www.google.com/maps>
Maps	MapQuest	<http://www.mapquest.com>
Case citation guide	The Bluebook	<https://www.legalbluebook.com/>
Dictionary/Thesaurus	Merriam-Webster	<http://www.merriam-webster.com/>
Zip codes	U.S. Postal Service	<https://www.usps.com/>
National lawyer directory	Martindale-Hubbell	<http://www.martindale.com>
National lawyer directory	FindLaw	<http://www.findlaw.com/>
	Finding Expert Witnesses	
Expert witnesses	National Directory of Expert Witnesses	<http://www.national-experts.com/>
Expert witnesses directory	Expert.com	<http://www.experts.com/>
Expert witnesses directory	JurisPro	<http://www.jurispro.com/>
Technical advisory service for attorneys	The TASA Group	<http://www.tasanet.com>
Expert witnesses directory	Almexperts	<http://www.almexperts.com>
Expert witnesses network	Expert Witness Network	<https://www.witness.net>
	Finding People, Addresses, Phone Numbers, and E-mail Addresses	
People, addresses, phone numbers, e-mail addresses, yellow pages	Yahoo	<people.yahoo.com>
People, addresses, phone numbers	411.com	<http://www.411.com>
People, addresses, phone numbers, e-mail addresses, yellow pages	PeopleSmart	<https://www.peoplesmart.com>
People, addresses, phone numbers, e-mail addresses, yellow pages	InfoSpace	<http://www.infospace.com>
People search	ZABA search	<http://www.zabasearch.com/>
People, address, phone number locator	The Virtual Chase White Pages and Phone Directories	<http://virtualchase.justia.com>
	Other Information About People	
Federal campaign donors	Political Money Line	<http://www.politicalmoneyline.com>
Family information from census, marriage, Social Security, and other sources	Family Tree Maker by Ancestry.com	<http://www.familytreemaker.com>
Genealogy-related Web site link	Cyndi's List	<http://www.cyndislist.com>
Listing of military personnel	National Archives	<http://www.archives.gov/stlouis/military-personnel/about-ompfs.html>
Federal prison inmates	Federal Bureau of Prisons	<http://www.bop.gov>
Physician list	American Medical Association	<http://www.ama-assn.org/ama>
Ancestry database	Ancestry.com	<http://www.ancestry.com>
Government records database for finding people	Global-Locate by Integrity	<https://www.global-locate.com>

Exhibit 9-10 Factual Research Starting Points

Subject	Additional Information	Web URL (Address)
	Public Records (Free)	
Large list of links to finding public information on the Web	Justia Virtual Chase	<http://virtualchase.justia.com>
Births, marriages, deaths, divorces	Vital Records Information	<http://www.vitalrec.com/index.html>
Public records information from individual state Web sites.	State Public Records.	Many (but not all) states have a standard Web address, "http://www.state.xx.us,", where "xx" is replaced by the state's two letter abbreviation. For example, Louisiana = http://www.state.la.us
Public Records Resource	Public Records Resource	<http://www.publicrecordsources.com>
Large portal to many Web sites with public records	BRB Public Information Records	<http://www.brbpub.com>
Real estate public records	NETR online	<http://publicrecords.netronline.com/>
	Vendors of Public Records (Fee Based)	
Electronic Court Records for cases in Federal Courts	PACER (Public Access To Court Electronic Records) free registration—per page charges.	<https://www.pacer.gov>
State Court Internet Access to Records	Many state courts have free or monthly fee-based Web site access to records online	Various Web sites in state court locations
Legal Research and Resource for records	WestlawNext (by Thomson Reuters	<http://legalsolutions.thomsonreuters.com/law-products/westlaw-legal-research>
Legal Research and Resource for records	LexisNexis	<http://www.lexisnexis.com>
	News and Directories	
Chicago Tribune		<http://www.chicagotribune.com>
Los Angeles Times		<http://www.latimes.com>
New York Times		<http://www.nytimes.com>
USA Today		<http://www.usatoday.com>
Wall Street Journal		<http://www.wsj.com>
ARL Directory	Exhaustive list of publications available electronically	<http://www.arl.org>
	Researching Businesses	
Business service references and information	Library of Congress	<http://www.loc.gov/rr/business>
Directory of businesses lookup	Superpages	<http://www.superpages.com>
Business fax lookup	White Pages	<http://www.whitepages.com/name/Fax-Number>
Business information and insights	*Dun & Bradstreet*	<http://www.dnb.com>
Annual reports for companies	Public Register's Annual Report Service	<http://www.prars.com>
Electronic Data Gathering of business information required by public companies for filing	Federal Securities and Exchange Commission EDGAR (Electronic Data Gathering Analysis and Retrieval)	<http://www.sec.gov/edgar.shtml>
Information regarding specific companies	Hoovers	<http://www.hoovers.com>

Exhibit 9-10 *(continued)*

PROBLEMS WITH RESEARCHING ON THE INTERNET There are inherent problems with researching on the Internet that legal professionals should consider before beginning.

- *Research on the Internet can take longer to perform.* This is especially true when looking for cases, statutes, and other primary information, because it is spread over so many different Web sites. Experience is required to know where certain kinds of information reside on the Internet and which Web sites are better than others, especially when looking for historical cases or data.
- *Research on the Internet must be checked for accuracy and given a citation.* Unlike Westlaw, LexisNexis, and other fee-based information services, you need to make sure that the data you have collected on the Internet is genuine. You must be able to cite the source of the information.
- *There are no added features to information.* The legal researcher needs to remember that cases and other material on the Internet are raw in nature. No additional features typically exist like the case synopsis and keynotes that Westlaw adds to the beginning of a case. For the most part, the information has not been managed, at least not to the extent than it is when using a fee-based service.

Summary

Law offices of all types need a file system that allows them to store, track, and retrieve information about cases in a logical, efficient, and expeditious manner. When considering filing management techniques, each legal matter should be maintained separately and have its own case number. How a law office sets up its case numbering system is up to the office and its own needs. Alphabetical and numerical systems are common.

Some law offices are moving toward a "paperless" office, where all information is stored electronically. Document management software is a central part of any paperless office. Document management software organizes, controls, distributes, and allows for extensive searching of electronic documents, typically in a computer-networked environment. It can also accommodate hard copy documents through the use of imaging. Imaging uses a scanner to capture an image of a document. That image is stored electronically and can be retrieved later.

Law offices must also decide whether files should be kept in a central location in the office or whether they should be kept throughout the office using a decentralized approach.

Most law offices use a file-opening form to help track new cases. Because most offices cannot keep all files indefinitely, an office should close inactive files and destroy the closed files from time to time to reduce file-storage requirements. The *Model Rules* requires that attorneys safeguard client property. Many state rules require that attorneys turn over to a client his or her entire file when the client wishes to fire an attorney and retain new counsel.

Technology has greatly changed law libraries. Now, many legal resources are available online or in computer format. Most law libraries today include CD-ROM and electronic libraries, Westlaw or LexisNexis (or both), and the Internet.

Key Terms

alphabetic filing system
bar coding
centralized file system
CD-ROM legal database
decentralized file system
document management software
electronic legal database
file-opening form
imaging
off-line
online

Test Your Knowledge

1. Name three attributes of an effective file management system.
2. Name two types of file systems.
3. What does document management software do?
4. What are three advantages of document management software/the "paperless office?"
5. Legal research comes in a number of formats; name any two.

Practical Applications

1. Law libraries represent a large overhead cost to nearly every type of law office. List ways to reduce overhead costs of the library.

2. Your supervising attorney hands you a case file on which she would like you to do some work. It appears from the file that the client saw the attorney on two different cases: the purchase of a piece of property and a medical malpractice matter. When you ask the attorney, she states that the client has recently raised the medical malpractice matter, but that the client's primary focus is on the purchase of a piece of real estate. The attorney also states that she does not think the medical malpractice matter is significant, and that is why a separate file is not being opened. The attorney tells you not to worry about it. To your knowledge, the attorney is not doing any research on the malpractice matter. How would you handle the situation?

3. The solo practitioner you worked for is moving across the country and wishes to close his law practice. The attorney is going to destroy all files related to the law practice because he does not want to have to rent storage space in a city in which he will no longer live. The attorney is getting ready to dispose of the records by hauling them out to the dumpster. What is your advice to the attorney?

4. Your office represents a client who is suing his former partner in a business venture that went sour. Your office has represented the client for two years and has put about 300 hours into the case. In addition, your office has taken five depositions and paid for the transcripts. Your office also has hired an expert witness. The expert witness prepared a report that supports your client's case. The office has about $30,000 worth of fees and expenses in the case. One afternoon, the client comes into the office and gives the receptionist a letter stating that he is terminating the relationship with the law office and that he wants his files returned to him within one week. The attorney in the case states that there is no way he is going to hand over anything until the client pays the office's expenses. The attorney states that because the client has not paid for any work, the files are not legally his, and because the law office fronted the expenses, the law office at least owns the deposition transcripts and expert witness report. How would you handle the matter?

5. You have known for several months that your office's filing system is terrible. Documents are routinely lost, files are misplaced, and information is never filed in a timely manner. From an ethics and malpractice perspective, discuss the problems that may arise if a client's file or a piece of evidence regarding a client's file is lost and cannot be found.

6. The office you work for has recently added six attorneys and three paralegals. The file system is no longer efficient. Finding files is time consuming. You have been asked to come up with a new filing system. The following are some details you should keep in mind when determining the new system:

- The three tax attorneys want to start their own department. The tax attorneys will shortly move their offices to the basement, and they want to keep their own files so they do not have to run up and down the stairs to get to them. None of the other attorneys use or need access to the tax files.
- Staff employees can be very reckless about the condition in which they leave files.
- When a case is opened, all the documents are kept in a large expanding file folder.
- Documents tend to fall out of the files, and there is little organization to the case files.
- Many of the attorneys work on cases together and need access to the cases.
- People are constantly looking through the office trying to find a file.
- Last week, the accounting department found out for the first time that the office has been handling a case for about four months. The client has never received a bill.
- The office wants a file system in which it can immediately tell when the case is filed, what type of case it is (the office mainly handles tax, probate, corporate, and general litigation matters), and which partner is responsible for the case (there are five partners).

Develop a strategy that will help eliminate these problems.

7. The partners in your office are displeased with the way the office's library is being maintained. They say that the library is hemorrhaging money with increased costs, which is crippling the office's profits. Your job is to draw up a plan to bring this situation under control. You have noticed the following:

- Several copies of books are purchased by different partners and placed on their bookshelves.
- The library is a mess most of the time. Books are kept in attorneys' and paralegals' offices (they rarely check out the books and then fail to get them back to the library), there is not enough room for the materials the library does have, and books are stacked up on the floor.
- Many of the materials the library does have are outdated and no longer of use.
- You asked for several books, and while you know they were ordered, you have not seen them yet.
- The library has no budget as such; purchases are made when the office thinks it needs them. In addition, when an attorney orders a book, the book is sometimes kept on the attorney's own bookshelf.
- All library costs, including Westlaw and LexisNexis, are absorbed by the office.
- The library has no Internet access, although it has been talked about.
- The library has one old desktop computer that has Westlaw and LexisNexis only.

On the Web Exercises

1. Go to the ABA Center for Professional Responsibility at http://www.americanbar.org, find the *ABA Model Rules of Professional Conduct,* and read and print out the comments to *Rule 1.15.*

2. Using a general search engine, such as http://www.google.com or http://www.yahoo.com, find three manufacturers of legal document management software.

3. Visit five state bar association Web sites and find three articles on either filing, records management, record retention, law libraries, or opening/closing clients' files. The following link will take you to a Web site that connects to all state bar sites: http://nationallist.com/industry_resources/associations-state-bar-list/.

Projects

1. Research and write a paper on any subject related to law libraries. Many resources are available online or in most law libraries. Select a specific topic and cover it from a broad perspective. Your paper should cite at least five different resources.

2. Research and write a paper on any subject related to filing, records management, document management software, closing a law practice, or record retention. Many resources are available online or in most law libraries. Select a specific topic and cover it from a broad perspective. Your paper should cite at least five different resources.

Case Review

In re Cameron, 270 Ga. 512, 511 S.E.2d 514 (Ga. 1999).
Supreme Court of Georgia.

In the Matter of Johnnie CAMERON (Two Cases).
Nos. S99y0257. S99y0258.

Feb. 8, 1999.

***512** PER CURIAM.

The State Bar filed two Notices of Discipline against Respondent Johnnie Cameron alleging violations of Standards 4 (professional conduct involving dishonesty, fraud, deceit, or willful misrepresentation); 22 (withdrawal from employment without taking reasonable steps to avoid foreseeable prejudice to the rights of the client, including giving due notice to the client, allowing time for employment of other counsel, delivering to the client all papers and property to which the client is entitled, and complying with applicable laws and rules); and 44 (willful abandonment or disregard of a legal matter to the client's detriment) of Bar Rule 4-102(d). Upon Cameron's failure to respond to either of the Notices of Discipline within the time set by Bar Rule 4-208.3(a), Cameron was in default pursuant to Bar ***513** Rule 4-208.1(b) and subject to discipline by this Court. The State Bar has recommended disbarment as an appropriate sanction for Cameron's violations of Standards 4, 22, and 44 of Bar Rule 4-102(d). We agree.

In one disciplinary matter, Cameron was hired by a client to represent him in a Social Security disability claim. The client gave Cameron documents pertaining to the claim and tried to reach Cameron by telephone numerous times. Cameron did not return the client's calls even when the client tried to reach Cameron regarding an appointment scheduled with a physician regarding the client's disability claim. On July 28, 1997, the client spoke with Cameron by telephone and Cameron promised to return the call on July 30, 1997 but failed to do so. After the Social Security Administration scheduled a disability hearing, the client again tried unsuccessfully to reach Cameron. Subsequently, the hearing was postponed when the hearing officer also could not reach Cameron. The client, in making additional attempts to reach Cameron, learned that Cameron's office had been vacated and his home telephone number disconnected. On September 5, 1997, the client wrote a letter to Cameron terminating Cameron's services and demanding the return of all documents. Cameron again failed to respond. Due to Cameron's failure to represent the client, the client was not able to present his disability case to the administrative law judge.

In a second matter, a client hired Cameron on or about November 14, 1997 to advise her on a will and property deeds and gave the original documents plus $50 to Cameron. Although Cameron stated that he would copy the documents and return the originals to the client, he failed to return the documents or to contact the client. The client made numerous attempts to call Cameron at his home and his office but was not able to reach him; she also learned that Cameron's fax number was disconnected. The client and the client's daughter contacted Cameron at his part-time job and requested the return of the original documents. Although in both instances Cameron promised to return the documents on the day of the telephone conversations, he did not keep the appointments or return the documents. In sum, Cameron did not do any work on the client's behalf, did not return any portion of the $50 fee, and failed to return the client's documents.

Although Cameron has no disciplinary history, the State Bar noted the pattern of dishonesty and abandonment evidenced by the two grievances filed and Cameron's failure to respond to the Notices of Investigation as aggravating factors in its recommendation for disbarment. Cameron has failed to respond to disciplinary authorities during the investigation of these matters and the Court finds no evidence of mitigating circumstances.

***514** We agree with the State Bar that disbarment is warranted as a result of Cameron's violation of Standards 4, 22, and 44 of Bar Rule 4-102(d). Accordingly, Cameron is disbarred from the practice of law in Georgia. He is reminded of his duties under Bar Rule 4-219(c).

Disbarred.

All the Justices concur.

END OF DOCUMENT

Case Review Exercises

1. List each act committed by the attorney that violated Standard 22 of the state bar rules regarding the "withdrawal from employment without taking reasonable steps to avoid foreseeable prejudice to the rights of the client...."
2. If the attorney had argued that he should not be disciplined because the client had not paid him for the time spent on the case(s) (assuming it was true), would this have changed the outcome of the case?
3. What duty did the attorney have to his client(s) when he moved his office and had his home telephone number and office fax number disconnected?
4. Once the attorney took a part-time job, and assuming he quit the practice of law, what should the attorney have done?
5. Given the fact that the attorney had no prior discipline, do you think disbarment was appropriate?

Helpful Web Sites

Organization	Description	Internet Address
American Bar Association (ABA)	Association for attorneys. The Web site has a large amount of information and publications relevant to individuals working in the legal profession.	http://www.americanbar.org
ABA Law Practice Management Section	ABA section devoted to law practice management issues, including file and records management.	http://www.americanbar.org/groups/law_practice.html
Association of Legal Administrators	National association for legal administrators. Contains resources and information related to law office management and legal administration.	http://www.alanet.org
Law Technology News and Law.com	Excellent periodical for legal technology issues. Good white papers on technology issues.	http://www.legaltechnews.com/ and http://www.law.com/whitepapers

Suggested Reading

1. ARMA International. (2005). *Establishing Alphabetic, Numeric, and Subject Filing Systems.*
2. Cunningham, G.C. (2014). *The Lawyer's Guide to Records Management and Retention,* 2e. American Bar Association.
3. Levitt, C. A., & Rosch, M. E. (2011). *Find Info Like a Pro: Mining the Internet's Publicly Available Resources for Investigative Research, Volume 1.* American Bar Association.
4. Levitt, C.A., & Rosch, M.E. (2011). *Find Info Like a Pro: Mining the Internet's Publicly Available Resources for Investigative Research, Volume 2.* American Bar Association.
5. Munneke, G. A., & Davis, A. E. (2003, 2007, 2010). *The Essential Formbook: Comprehensive Management Tools for Lawyers, Volumes I-IV.* American Bar Association.

Appendix A:
Creating a Clio Account

I. Introduction—Read This:

Clio is a Web-based legal practice management system. Clio helps users stay on top of tasks, important deadlines, contacts, and conflict checks. The Clio demonstration version is a full working version of the program available for students and instructors 365 days after you create your account. It is highly recommended that you do not activate your account until you are actually ready to go through the Hands-On Exercises and learn the program.

II. Installation Technical Support:

If you face any problems creating a Clio account, you will need to contact Clio directly at caap@clio.com.

III. Clio Installation:

Unlike desktop applications, Clio is not a program that you download and install onto your computer. Instead, it is a Web site where you will be asked to open a free account and where you should act as a nonlawyer (paralegal) in a hypothetical law firm. (Note: the default is to set up the account as the attorney—you should change it to nonlawyer after creating the account. Once you create the account, there are two files (one with "contacts" and one with "matters") that you will need to download and load into Clio—you can access these files through the "Premium Web Site" associated with this text.

1. ***Open your Internet browser and log in to your CengageBrain.com account.***
2. Under "My Courses & Materials," find the Premium Web site for *Practical Law Office Management, Fourth Edition.*
3. ***Click "Open"*** to go the Premium Web Site.
4. Locate "Book Level Resources" in the left navigation menu.

5. ***Click on the link for "Clio."***
6. ***Click the link next to "To access the demo:"***
7. From the Clio Web Site, ***click "Get Started;" then click the link for "I have a promo or referral code."*** The code EDU should be typed. Enter your name, e-mail address, password and "999-999-9999" for the phone number, then ***click Start Trial.***
8. You will receive an e-mail from Clio with a link to activate your account. ***Click the* "Activate Account"** button or the hyperlink within the e-mail to access the Clio sign in page. If this does not take you to the Clio sign in page, copy and paste the link provided into your Internet browser. ***Follow the on-screen instructions to complete the registration process.***
9. Once you have completed the registration process, you may access your Clio account by typing **app.goclio.com** and press the **[ENTER] key.** ***On the next screen, enter the e-mail address and password you provided in Clio and click SIGN IN. If you check the box next to KEEP ME SIGNED IN, you will be able to skip this step in the future.***
10. Right now, there is no data in your Clio account. There are two files on the Premium Web site that you will now import into Clio that will provide you with some data to work with. ***Navigate to your CengageBrain account and locate on the Premium Web site the data file with Contacts named "democontacts_(1).csv" and the data file with Matters named "demomatters_output.csv." To do so, right-click on the link for democontacts(1).csv and, select Save Link As and using the default settings, save it to your computer. Then, right-click on the link for demomatters_output.csv, select Save Link As and using the default settings, save the file to your computer.***
11. To input the Contacts file, type http://app.goclio.com/imports in your Internet browser and press the **[ENTER] key**. At this point your screen should now like Clio Exhibit A-1.

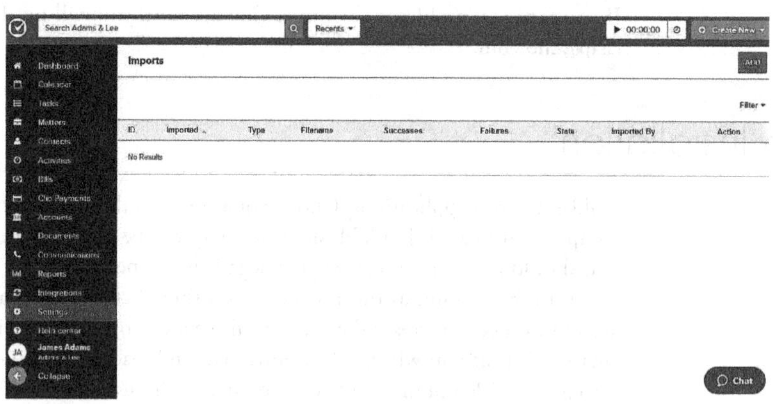

Clio Exhibit A-1 Clio Import Screen

Source: Themis Solutions, Inc.

Click Add and choose "Contacts from Outlook CSV" from the drop-down menu. Then, click "choose file" and browse to the location where you saved the .csv files and ***select and upload the file named democontacts_(1).csv from the save location. Click Upload File.***

12. To input the Matters file, type http://app.goclio.com/imports in your Internet browser and press the **[ENTER] key** (skip this step if you have already logged in Clio and remained on the Imports page). ***Click Add and choose "Matters from CSV" from the drop-down menu.*** You can leave Responsible Attorney **"unselected"** or choose the attorney names **(i.e., James Adams)** ***from the drop-down men.*** Then, ***click "choose file"*** and browse to the location where you saved the .csv files and ***select the file named demomatters_output.csv. Click Upload File.*** At this point you are ready to explore the Clio platform and its essential functions.
13. To end this Clio session, ***click on your initials at the top of the screen, click Sign Out, then close your Internet browser.***

This concludes the Clio Installation.

Appendix B:

Clio Introduction (Lesson 1, Part A)

Lesson 1, Part A: Introduction to Clio

You should become familiar with the Clio Platform and its essential functions before you begin any of the lessons. *Note*: If you are already logged in, you will skip Steps 1 and 2.

1. Start your Internet browser. Type www.goclio.com in the Internet browser and press the **[ENTER] key**.
2. On the Clio Home page, ***click Log In. On the next screen, enter the e-mail address and password you provided in Clio and click SIGN IN. If you check the box next to KEEP ME SIGNED IN, you will be able to skip this step in the future.***
3. Clio will open in the hypothetical law firm on the PRACTICE page. At this point you are ready to explore the Clio platform and its essential functions. There are 11 tabs available in Clio. We will start with the PRACTICE tab.
4. ***Click*** **PRACTICE**. Your screen should now look like Clio Exhibit 1A-1. This is the Clio dashboard which provides a quick look at the agenda, calendar, and billing information. You will now explore the other 10 tabs.

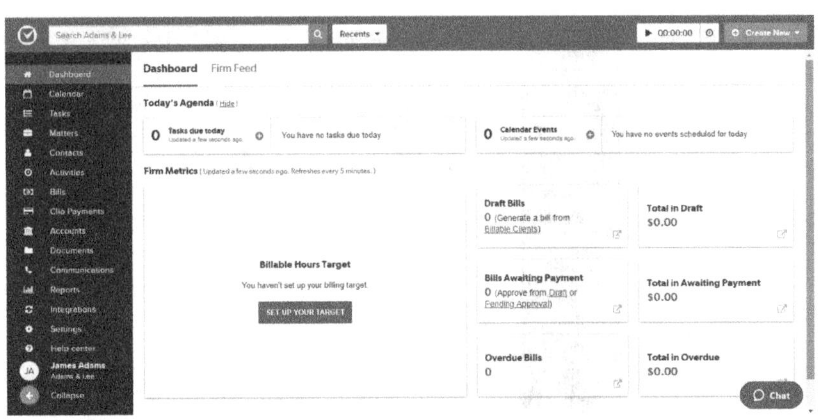

Clio Exhibit 1A-1 Practice Tab

Source: Themis Solutions, Inc.

5. ***Click*** **CALENDAR.** You may need to scroll down to see the entire page. You can change the view to see your Agenda, or Day, Week, Month, or Year views. You can view your personal calendar, the firm calendar or both.
6. To create a calendar entry, while in the Week view, ***select the Wednesday of that current week and double-click on the 10:00 am time slots.*** The Create Calendar Entry will open. See Clio Exhibit 1A-2. If you ***click Add Event,*** the date will default to the current date.

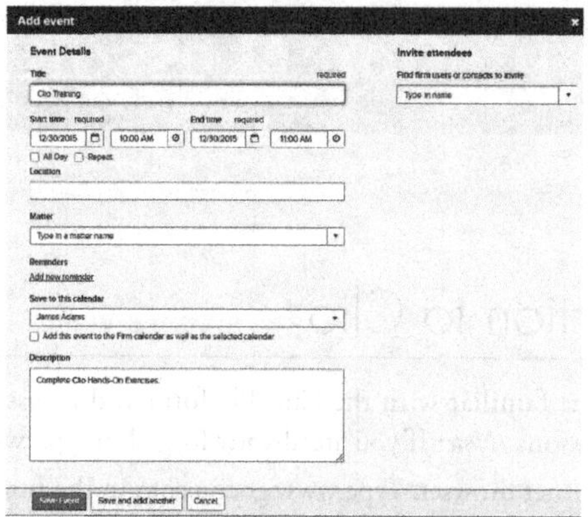

Clio Exhibit 1A-2 Create Calendar Entry

Source: Themis Solutions, Inc.

Under Summary, type **Clio Training.** Under **Start,** type **10:00 AM** and under **End** type **11:00 AM.** Leave Matter and Location "**blank,**" and under Description, type **Complete Clio Hands-On Exercises.** ***Click Create Calendar Entry.*** When adding multiple entries, ***click Save & Add Another.*** After the entry is complete, it will appear in the calendar. ***Place your cursor over the new calendar entry*** to see the description. Your calendar should look like Clio Exhibit 1A-3. You can now move to the "Tasks" tab.

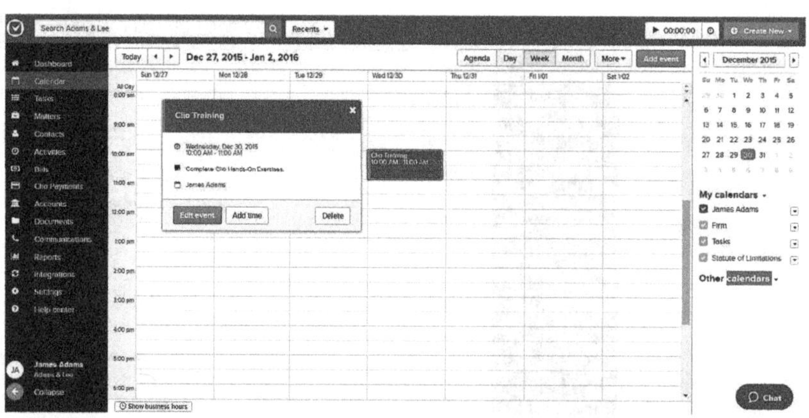

Clio Exhibit 1A-3 Calendar Entry - View

Source: Themis Solutions, Inc.

7. ***Click* TASKS**. This is where specific tasks can be assigned to specific individuals or groups. To create a new Task, ***click Add***. See Clio Exhibit 1A-4. Under Task Name, type **Clio Training**.

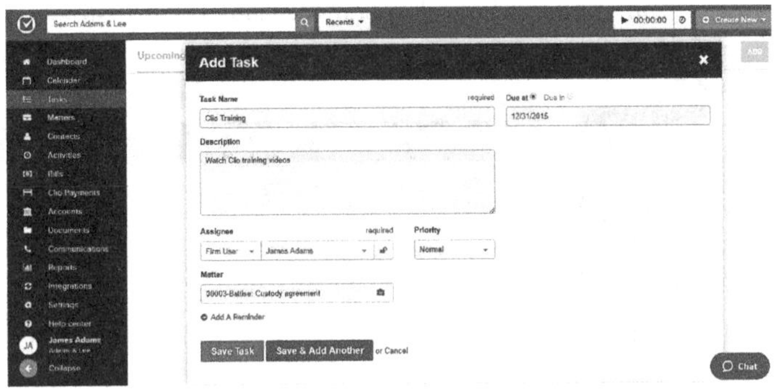

Clio Exhibit 1A-4 Add Task – "Due At"

Source: Themis Solutions, Inc.

Under Description, type **Watch Clio training videos**. Under Due: the radial button will default to **"Due at"** when there are no other tasks associated. ***Click the box under "Due At,"*** and a calendar will appear. ***Select Thursday of the current week.*** Under Assignee, ***select Firm User and then choose yourself.*** Under Priority, ***select Normal.*** Under Matter, ***type 00003-Battise: Custody Agreement*** (the case will appear in the list as you begin typing the number). Then ***click Save Task.*** When adding multiple tasks, ***select Save and Add Another.*** At this point you will be on the ***"tasks" under 00003-Battise.*** See Clio Exhibit 1A-5.

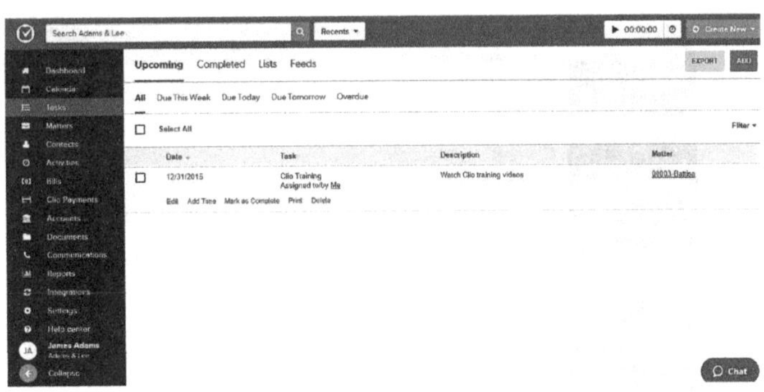

Clio Exhibit 1A-5 Task Entry – "Due At"

Source: Themis Solutions, Inc.

8. When you have several assigned tasks under a specific case matter, you have the option of choosing **"Due in"** which allows you to choose a date in relation to other Tasks in the Matter. From your current position in (Exhibit 1A-5), ***select Add.*** Your screen should again look like Exhibit 1A-3. Under Task Name, type **Clio Training**. Under Description, type **Watch Clio Introduction Videos**. Under Assignee, ***select Firm User and then choose yourself.*** Under Priority, ***select Normal.*** Under Matter, ***type 00003-Battise:***

Custody Agreement (the case will appear in the list as you begin typing the number). Then ***select 00003Battise: Custody Agreement.*** Under Due: the radial will default to **"Due at,"** however; you now have the option to choose **"Due in."** ***Select "Due in,"*** and a dialogue box will appear. See Clio Exhibit 1A-6.

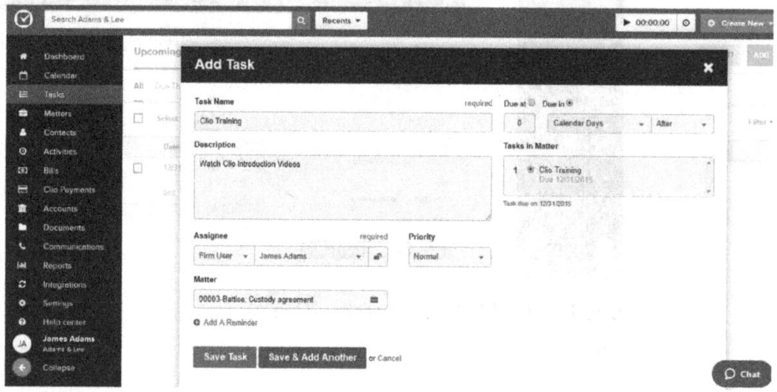

Clio Exhibit 1A-6 Add Task – "Due In"

Source: Themis Solutions, Inc.

ENTER **"1"** in the box marked with a 0. ***Select Calendar Weeks*** under the drop-down menu in the next box, ***Select before*** under the drop-down menu in the next box. Then ***select Clio Training*** under the radial button. ***Click Save Task.*** The second task will now appear listed on the Tasks page. See Clio Exhibit 1A-7.

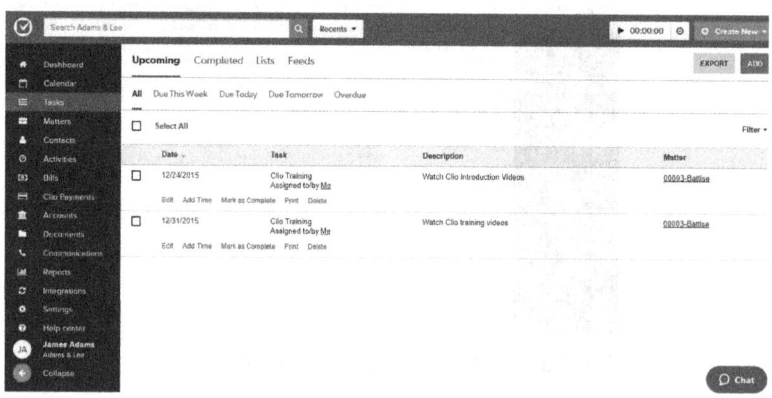

Clio Exhibit 1A-7 Upcoming Task Entries

Source: Themis Solutions, Inc.

9. ***Click*** **MATTERS.** Matters are what Clio calls for cases or files. Clio allows you to associate, or connect, matters with clients, tasks, bills, etc. In later exercises you will see how that works and you will create several new matters.

10. ***Click*** **CONTACTS**. Contacts are people and corporations that you do business with (clients, other attorneys, court reporters, etc.).
11. ***Click*** **ACTIVITIES**. "Activities" is what Clio uses for both time and billing entries as well as expense entries. Time entries can be billed as a flat rate or as an hourly rate. In later exercises you will create several new billing activities.
12. ***Click*** **BILLS**. Here, you can create a new bill, review a client's billing history, and create bill themes (designs) among other bill-related issues. In later exercises you will create several new bills.
13. ***Click*** **ACCOUNTS**. Here you can view and manage the various bank accounts of a law firm.
14. ***Click*** **DOCUMENTS**. Here you can view and manage the documents maintained in Clio.
15. ***Click*** **COMMUNICATIONS**. Here you can send and receive e-mails, maintain communication logs, interact with colleagues and Clio-connected users, as well as limit permissions between groups for file-related communications.
16. ***Click*** **REPORTS**. Here you can create reports on a variety of topics (billing client, mater, productivity, and revenue).
17. To end this Clio session, ***click your initials at the top of the screen. Click Sign Out and then close your Internet Browser.***

This concludes the introduction lesson on Clio's platform and essential functions review.

Appendix C:

Clio Law Firm Profile and Set up (Lesson 1, Part B)

Lesson 1, Part B: Set Up Law Firm Profile

In this lesson, you will set up the firm profile in the hypothetical law firm, establish billing rate, create an activity description, set up bank accounts and establish the matter-numbering protocol.

Note: If you are already logged in, you will skip Steps 1 and 2.

1. Start your Internet browser. Type www.goclio.com in the Internet browser and press the **[ENTER] key**.
2. On the Clio Home page, ***click Log In. On the next screen, enter the e-mail address and password you provided in Clio and click SIGN IN. If you check the box next to KEEP ME SIGNED IN, you will be able to skip this step in the future.***
3. Before you enter new clients, contacts and matters in Clio, details for the hypothetical law firm should be entered. First, you will set up the account information for your hypothetical law firm. ***Click the "settings" icon*** (looks like a gear) at the top of the screen next to the "***initials***." Your screen should look like Clio Exhibit 1B-1.

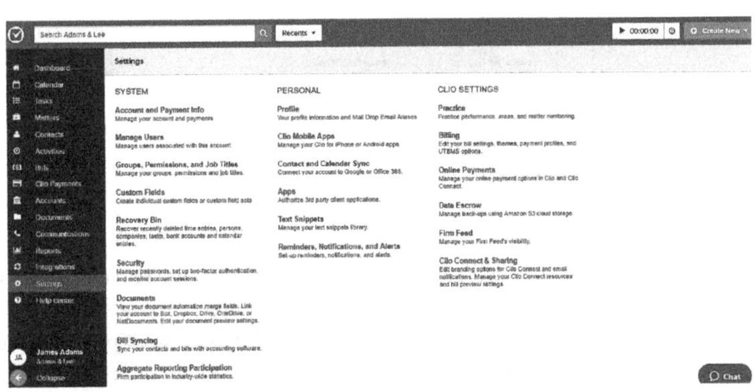

Clio Exhibit 1B-1 Clio Settings Screen

Source: Themis Solutions, Inc.

4. ***Click Account and Payment Info.*** The name of your hypothetical law firm will be established by your instructor (i.e., Adams & Lee) or your First and Last name if you create your own individual account (i.e., Law Office of "First name" "Last name" that you entered). *Note*: Free accounts do not have access to payment info.
5. ***Type the name, address, and contact information of your firm*** (i.e., sample check from Exhibit 6-1 (Chapter 6), instructor provided, or create your own).
6. Next, ***click the drop-down menu under Date format. Select*** the option that resembles ***12/31/2015.*** Then, ***click the drop-down menu under Time format. Select*** the option that resembles ***11:59 pm. Click Save New Information.***
7. You will now update profile and establish a billing rate. ***Click*** the "settings" icon (looks like a gear) at the top of the screen next to the "initials." Your screen should look like Clio Exhibit 1B-1. ***Click Profile*** and scroll down to **Billing Rate**. ***Type 175.00 next to $/Hr. Click Save New Information.*** See Clio Exhibit 1B-2.

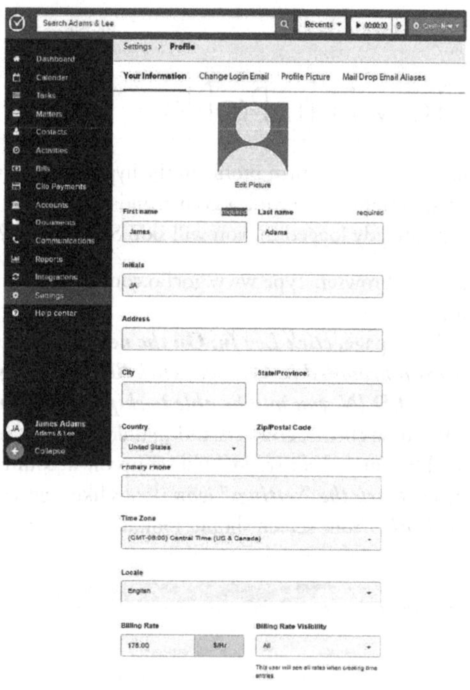

Clio Exhibit 1B-2 Update Profile – Billing Rate

Source: Themis Solutions, Inc.

8. Next, you will create an Activity Description. These are used to ensure a consistent description of commonly used time entries across a law firm. It can also be used as a shortcut—you can save text in the Activity Description and when you enter in a time entry, it will populate this text for you. Activity Descriptions can be shared across a law firm so that everyone in the firm can use them. ***Click the Activities tab, then click Activity Descriptions, then click Add.*** See Clio Exhibit 1B-3.

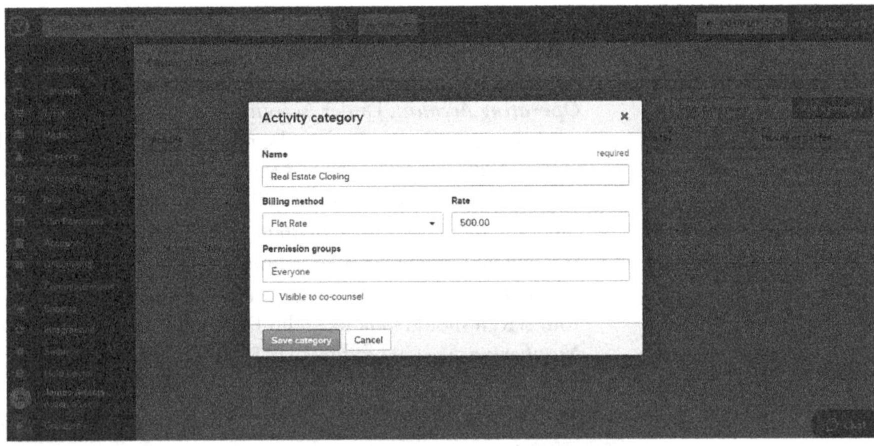

Clio Exhibit 1B-3 Add Activity Description

Source: Themis Solutions, Inc.

Under Name, type **Real Estate Closing**. Under Billing Method, ***select Flat Rate***. This opens a text box called Rate; type **$500.00** in the text box, ***Click Save***. This flat rate fee will override the $175.00 per hour established as the default rate.

9. Next, you will create bank accounts. ***Click the Accounts tab***, then ***click New***. You will set up two accounts—the first will be a Trust Account (one that contains only client money) and the second will be an Operating account (one that ***should not*** contain client money). See Clio Exhibit 1B-4.

Clio Exhibit 1B-4 Create New Bank Account

Source: Themis Solutions, Inc.

10. Under Account type, ***select Trust Account***. Under Account name, type **IOLTA** (this stands for Interest on Law Office Trust Account, commonly used for Trust accounts). It is not necessary, nor is it required, to complete the remainder of this form (although you are welcomed to do so). However, you should leave the Balance 0.0. ***Click Create***

New Bank Account. The screen will refresh (showing the new IOLTA account) so additional accounts may be created.

11. Now create the Operating Account. ***Click New,*** then under Account type, ***select Operating Account.*** Under Account name, type **Law Firm Account**. It is not necessary, nor is it required, to complete the remainder of this form (although you are welcomed to do so). However, you should leave the Balance 0.0. ***Click the box next to Default Account.*** (The default account will show up first on the Transactions tab found when a client file is opened under Matters.) ***Click Create New Bank Account.***
12. You will now create the matter-numbering protocol for the hypothetical law firm. ***Click the "settings" icon*** (looks like a gear) at the top of the screen next to the "***initials.***" Your screen should look like Clio Exhibit 1B-1. ***Click Practice,*** and then ***click Matter Numbering.*** See Clio Exhibit 1B-5. ***Under Select Template: click the drop-down menu***

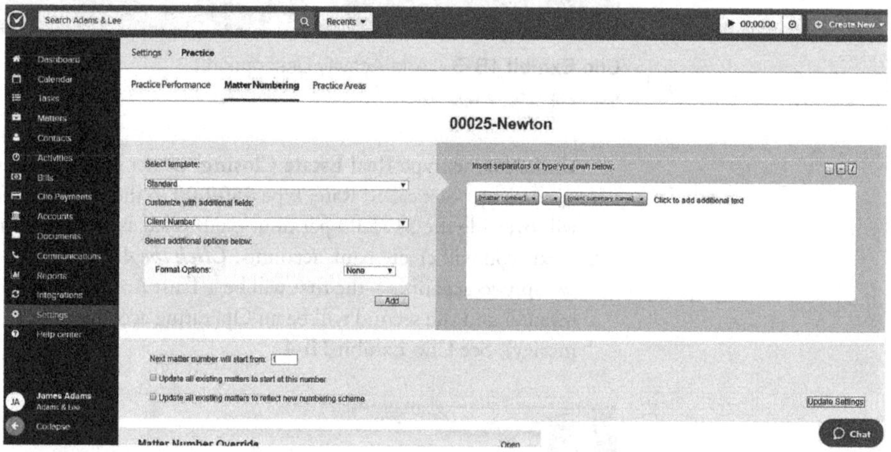

Clio Exhibit 1B-5 Matter Numbering

Source: Themis Solutions, Inc.

arrow and click on each of the available options. As you do, notice how the sample matter number (00025-Newton) changes. Use the default (matter number—client summary name), then ***select Standard.*** Under ***Customize with additional fields, select Client Number. Click Update Settings.***

13. To end this Clio session, ***click on your initials*** at the top of the screen. ***Click Sign Out, and then close your Internet browser.***

This concludes the lesson on law firm profile and setup.

Appendix D: Succeeding as a Paralegal

Paralegals must develop good management skills in order to succeed. They need to be accurate and thorough in everything they do. They must be routinely organized, prompt, and prepared. They must be team players and communicate effectively. These things do not come naturally; most are learned the hard, old-fashioned way: by trial and error over years. Read this section so that you can pick up some good ideas now that will save you from many headaches once on the job. Some of the suggestions may sound simplistic, but they really are not. The suggestions in this chapter come from many paralegals and legal assistants with varied experiences. These suggestions really work, and while some are fundamental, all of them are important.

Accuracy, Thoroughness, and Quality

"Accuracy" and "thoroughness" are easy to say but hard to accomplish. However, high-quality work is vital to the performance of a professional. A law office is a team, and everyone must be able to rely on everyone else; each client is paying for and deserves the absolute best work product the team can provide.

One element of quality work is careful documentation. It is important that, when you talk to witnesses, clients, opposing counsel, or others, you keep written notes of your conversation and send a confirming letter that documents your conversation. Some cases can drag on for years; if proper notes are not kept in the file, vital information can be lost. Keeping proper documentation about the work you have done on a case is very important.

Mistakes happen. If something does slip by, do not try to cover it up. Admit and/or report the mistake, correct the mistake to the best of your ability as quickly as possible, take precautions to make sure it does not happen again, apologize, and go on. Because mistakes are natural and almost inevitable, being accurate and putting out quality work is a daily battle.

Ideas on how to improve the quality of your work include the following:

- *Create forms and systems.* If you do a job more than once, create a system using forms and instructions for yourself. This will evoke memories from the last time you performed the job and speedup the work.

- ***Create checklists.*** Make a checklist for the jobs you regularly perform. Checklists will keep you from failing to perform specific details of a job that otherwise might be forgotten. In this way, the high quality of your work is maintained.
- ***Be careful and complete.*** Be prudent and careful in your work. Do not hurry your work to the degree that accuracy and thoroughness are compromised. Your work should always be neat and complete.
- ***Keep written documentation and notes.*** Keeping proper documentation about work you have done on a case is very important.
- ***Take pride in your work.*** Do not let work that you are not proud to call your own go out with your name on it.
- ***Work hard.*** Accuracy and thoroughness are seldom reached by slothfulness. Work hard at what you do, and the quality of the work will always be better for it.
- ***Ask for peer review.*** If you have a particularly important project due and you have a question about the accuracy of your work, have another paralegal or staff member look it over before it is turned in. While you do not want to become dependent on others or disrupt their productivity, sometimes a second opinion can really help, especially if you are new to the organization.
- ***Never assume.*** Do not assume anything. If you have the slightest doubt about something, check it out, conduct research, make sure that you pay attention to details, and double-check the accuracy of your work.
- ***Use firm resources.*** Use firm resources, like intranets, brief banks, and tools, to the fullest extent. You will learn from others and your work will be of higher quality if you use the collective knowledge of other experienced staff.

The Assignment

A paralegal was assigned a task by a senior partner to draft the necessary documents needed for an important filing with a deadline quickly approaching. The paralegal immediately drafts the documents and put them on the senior partner's desk for his review. The senior partner thought he told the paralegal to "take care" of the important filing. The deadline for the filing the matter was missed. Instead of admitting his error, he blames the paralegal for not properly handling the assignment.

When a task is being assigned to you, make sure you understand exactly what the assignment is and what the supervising attorney wants. Be absolutely certain that you understand the whole assignment; do not guess or extrapolate. One of the most common mistakes a new paralegal makes is to not ask questions. It takes a certain amount of maturity to say, "I do not understand," but it is absolutely critical. Your supervising attorney will not think any worse of you for it, and your chance of success on the task will be greatly enhanced. It is also a good idea to repeat the assignment back to the supervisor to make sure you understand all of the details. If a task is extremely complicated, ask the supervisor to help you break it down into smaller parts. You might say: "This appears to be a fairly good-sized job. Where do you recommend I start and how should I proceed; what steps should I take?"

It is also a good idea to write down your assignment. Have a pencil and a notebook or steno pad with you any time you talk to your supervisor about an assignment. A steno pad can serve as a journal, allowing you to keep all of your assignments in one place. If you record assignments, you will be able to refer back to them later if someone has a question or problem about work they gave you. Be sure to write down what the assignment is, who gave it to you, any comments the person made about the assignment, and when it is due. Always ask for the exact date an assignment is due, not "sometime next week" or "whenever you get to it." Also be sure to write down when you completed the assignment.

If an assignment gets a little fuzzy to you after you start it, ask the supervisor questions while you are still in the middle of it. Do not wait until the end of the assignment to realize you did something wrong; check in periodically and have the supervisor quickly review it. This is particularly important with large and complex tasks.

Do the following to communicate effectively when receiving assignments:

- ***Ask questions when the assignment is given.*** Ask questions about the assignment until you fully understand what you are being asked to perform. Be aware that miscommunication problems occur more frequently regarding assignments you have never done before.
- ***Repeat the assignment to your supervisor.*** Repeat the assignment back to the supervisor to make sure you understand all of the details.
- ***Break down complex assignments into small tasks.*** Ask the supervisor to help you break complex assignments down into smaller tasks and help you organize the priority of those tasks.
- ***Have a pen and paper ready.*** Always have a pen and paper (a legal pad works best) with you when you are being given an assignment. It allows you to remember when the assignment was given, by whom, any comments from the supervisor and when it is due.
- ***Always ask for a due date.*** Always ask for a specific due date. This prevents miscommunication regarding when an assignment should be completed.
- ***Continue to ask questions and check in periodically.*** As you work on the assignment, continue to ask clarifying questions and periodically check in with your supervisor to keep him or her updated on your progress.

Preparation and Organization

Successful paralegals are organized and prepared for everything they do. Being organized is not hard; it just takes planning and time. Always have an appointment calendar with you so that you can record important appointments and deadlines. In addition, use a "things-to-do" list each day and try to plan and prioritize tasks so that assignments and projects are never late. Begin with the most important assignment you have to do or with the task that has the most pressing deadline. When you are working on projects for two or more attorneys, ask someone to prioritize the tasks for you. If you have a computer program that has organizational features, use it.

The following ideas will improve your preparation and organization:

- ***Have an appointment calendar.*** Carry an appointment calendar with you at all times or be sure to constantly update your computerized versions and print out hard copies regularly. This way, if you are caught in the hallway and given an assignment or meeting date, you will know if you have a conflict.

- ***Make a "things-to-do" list.*** Plan your day in advance, every day. Make a "things-to-do" list and try to complete your list every day, marking off items once they are completed.
- ***Prioritize tasks.*** When you are preparing your "things-to-do" list, always prioritize the tasks so that you turn in assignments on time. Give priority to assignments that have the most pressing deadlines. If you have a question about what assignment needs to be done first, ask your managing attorney for direction.
- ***Be on time.*** Always be on time when completing assignments and attending meetings, and always take good notes so that you will remember important facts or information provided in meetings.

Manage Your Time

Are you using your time effectively, or are you wasting it? Time management and organization go hand in hand.

The following ideas can help you manage your time effectively:

- ***Set daily objectives.*** Always plan your day by setting daily objectives and prioritizing them accordingly. Try to stick to your plan and achieve your objectives every day. Do the most important things first.
- ***Do not waste your time on irrelevant tasks.*** Do not waste your time on unimportant or unnecessary tasks. When someone walks into your office to talk about an irrelevant subject and you have a job due, politely ask him or her to come back another time when you are free.
- ***Avoid procrastination.*** Do not put off what you can do today. Procrastination is unprofessional and leads to dissatisfied clients. Stick to your daily schedule and do not put things off unless you have a good reason.
- ***Avoid socializing in hallways.*** Socializing is not only a waste of your time, it is also a distraction to others around you. In addition, it looks very unprofessional to clients.
- ***Make a timeline or Gantt chart.*** When you have a large project, take the time to make a Gantt chart. A Gantt chart is a plan or timeline of projected begin and end dates for the various parts of a project. A Gantt chart will help you plan how you will complete the project and will also allow you to track the progress of the work.
- ***Have reference material close by.*** Lay out your desk and office so that important reference materials are located within arm's reach to minimize time spent looking for things.

Effective Communication with Attorneys

One of your most important tasks will be to establish mutual confidence between yourself and your supervisor. Because paralegals and attorneys must work together very closely, good communication is an absolute necessity.

The following practices will help you maintain effective communication with your supervisor:

- ***Always ask questions.*** If you do not understand something, ask questions.
- ***Listen.*** Do not forget to listen carefully when communicating with your supervising attorney. Listen and make notes so that you remember the details you will need to complete assignments.

- ***Be confident.*** Do not be so intimidated by attorneys that you act timid and fail to communicate. Carry yourself with confidence and authority. When you talk, always make eye contact.
- ***Check in.*** Check in with your supervising attorney on a daily basis so that he or she is informed of your progress on assignments.
- ***Do not make important decisions unilaterally.*** Include the supervising attorney in the decision-making process.
- ***Establish mutual confidence.*** Establishing mutual confidence with your supervising attorney is crucial. Your supervising attorney needs to have confidence in your work, and you need to have confidence in his or her work.
- ***Establish your limit of authority.*** Ask your supervising attorney what your limit of authority is when making decisions. You need to know as clearly as possible when he or she should be involved in decisions and what types of decisions they are.

The Client Comes First

When you are with a client, he or she should be given your undivided attention. Do not take phone calls, allow interruptions, play with your nails, or do anything else that would take your attention away from the client. Treat each client courteously and respectfully, and as if he or she is the only client you have.

The following measures will help ensure that the client comes first:

- ***Give clients your undivided attention.*** When you are with a client, be sure that you give the client all of your attention. Do not take phone calls, open mail, or do anything else that would take your attention away from the client.
- ***Give clients fast, courteous, respectful treatment.*** Treat the client courteously and respectfully at *all* times. Always return clients' phone calls and e-mails as quickly as possible, but never later than the same day, and always try to answer their questions as soon as you can.
- ***Treat each client as if he or she were your only client.*** A client's case is very important to him or her and should be important to you. Let your clients know that their welfare genuinely concerns you.
- ***Serve clients, but do not overstep your bounds.*** Do not let your zeal to serve clients cause you to overstep your bounds. Let the attorney answer complex client questions and give legal advice.
- ***Maintain client confidence.*** Always maintain the strictest standards regarding client confidentiality.

Keep Accurate, Contemporaneous Time Sheets

Attorneys and paralegals keep records of the amount of time spent on each case so that management will know how much to bill the client. Many firms require paralegals to bill a certain number of hours to clients each year or each month, so when you start with a firm always be sure to ask how many hours of billable time you are expected to have per month and annually.

Also ask when time sheets are due and when they are monitored for compliance (i.e., weekly, monthly, quarterly). Budget your time so that you know how many billable hours each month, week, or even day you will need to meet your goal, and then monitor yourself on your progress. Do not let yourself get behind, as you will not be able to make it up. If you are given a nonbillable task, delegate the task as much as possible to secretaries and clerks. There are simple techniques to keep accurate time sheets. Always record the necessary information on your time sheet *as the day progresses.* Do not try and go back at the end of the day or week and try to remember what you did; write it down as you perform the work.

Timekeepers, especially new timekeepers, have a tendency to subjectively discount their hours because they feel guilty for billing their time to clients. Record the time you *actually* spent working on a client's case: if it took 6 hours to research a legal issue, record the whole 6 hours. If your supervisor does not believe the finished product is worth that much, he or she can adjust the time billed. Simply put, it is not your call to reduce your hours. Record your actual time and go on.

To keep accurate time records, implement the following measures:

- ***Keep track of budgeted and actual billable hours.*** Your supervisor may tell you that you are responsible for billing 100 hours a month (i.e., 25 hours a week). You want to be sure every week that the time sheets you turn in to management show as close to the amount budgeted as possible. You need to track this.
- ***Keep a time sheet near your phone and computer.*** Always keep a time sheet next to your phone or computer so when you pick up the phone or prepare work on the computer, you can record the time for it.
- ***Fill out the time sheet throughout the day.*** Fill out your time sheet as you go throughout the day instead of trying to play the "memory game" to remember all the things you accomplished.
- ***Record the actual time you spent on a case.*** Always record the actual time it took you to perform the legal service. Let your supervisor make any decision to adjust or reduce time to be billed to the client.
- ***Be absolutely honest and ethical.*** Never bill a client for administrative tasks or for time you did not actually spend working on his or her case.

Work Hard and Efficiently

Everyone knows the difference between working hard and coasting. If you work hard, people will respect you and recognize you for it; if you do not, people will recognize this also and typically will resent you for it.

Do not be surprised if you have to work overtime. The question as to whether paralegals should be paid for overtime is a hot topic; some firms pay overtime compensation and some do not. In any event, if you have to work overtime, do it with a positive attitude. Be honest and sincere. Also try to work as efficiently as possible.

- ***Pull your weight.*** Do what is asked of you and produce quality work.
- ***Put in overtime when required.*** Be ready to put in overtime when it is required. Try to be pleasant and professional about it.
- ***Work efficiently.*** Work as efficiently as possible. If you have access to a computer, it makes sense to use it instead of doing something by hand.

Maintain a Positive Attitude and Team Spirit

A law office is a team that must rely on many different people to work together harmoniously in order to be successful. Approach your job with the goal of being a good team player and helping your team. Put the good of the firm above your own personal interest, and help the firm whenever you can, whether or not it is in your job description.

Good team players help other members of the team by passing along information and cooperating on tasks. They are able to give and receive help when it is needed. Another aspect of being a team player is knowing how to constructively criticize other players. First of all, be cordial and professional. Never criticize another staff member in front of a client, an attorney, or other staff members. Do not become emotional. Politely explain the problem and suggest a reasonable solution for solving it. Treat the other person as an equal. When you are the one being criticized, do not take the criticism personally; look beyond the finding of fault and try to make the adjustments suggested by the firm. Listen carefully and ask questions so that you understand the exact problem.

Your own effectiveness as a paralegal may depend on how well you work with others at your level within the team. You may strongly dislike some people. You will need patience and interpersonal skills to learn to work with them and develop mutual trust and confidence.

- ***Put the team first.*** Always put the needs of the team before your own personal interests. In the long run, what is good for the team is good for you.
- ***Delegate.*** Delegate tasks to other team members when possible. Use the team.
- ***Help other team members.*** Always remember to take time to help other team members. Otherwise, they will not be willing to help you when you need it.
- ***Share information.*** Never hoard information. Pass information along to other staff members, remembering to put the team first.
- ***Constructively and professionally criticize other team members.*** Just because you are a team player does not mean you cannot constructively criticize others. Try to be respectful, professional, and nonemotional. Explain the criticism, then suggest ways to fix the problem. Treat others as equals.
- ***Take criticism professionally.*** Try to avoid becoming defensive and listen to what is being said. Try to implement the suggestions of the other party as soon as possible.
- ***Get along with those you do not like.*** You will probably not like everyone you work with. But, for the good of the team, work at relationships and treat all coworkers with courtesy and respect.
- ***Know the employees of your firm.*** Get to know the employees of your firm and treat all employees as you would like to be treated.

Be a Self-Starter

Self-starters are valuable employees. Self-starters are people who do not need to be told what to do; they see a job that should be done or a need that should be fulfilled and they do the job or meet the need without having to be told. They seek out and volunteer for new work, assume responsibility willingly, and anticipate future needs.

Be flexible, open-minded, and creative; be a problem solver. Do not hesitate to courteously suggest new ways of doing things as long as the idea is well thought out (not off-the-cuff) and would provide the firm with a real benefit over the present way. However, before you try to implement a new idea or approach, be sure that you have researched, organized, and planned the project well in advance and have assessed the chances or risk of failure and the consequences of such a failure. Get others involved in the project, and ask for their help and input; this will help them accept the system later on.

Ideas on being a self-starter include the following:

- ***Anticipate.*** Anticipate what jobs need to be done or what need is unfilled, and then do the job or fulfill the need without being asked to do it.
- ***Seek out and volunteer for assignments.*** If a new assignment comes up (especially one with a lot of responsibility), volunteer for it.
- ***Be flexible and open-minded.*** Always be flexible and open-minded; have a positive attitude. All businesses must change with the times. Be adaptable.
- ***Be aware of risk.*** Before taking on a new assignment, research, organize, and plan. Assess your chances of success.
- ***Get others involved.*** Always include others in your development of new ideas. Get their thoughts and feedback. Not only is the information helpful, but people are far more willing to implement an idea to which they have contributed.

Stress Management

A law office is a very stressful place with a great deal of activities, deadlines, appointments, and problems. You must learn to manage your own stress, or it will manage you. Do not be so consumed with your work that you put it above your family or your own happiness. Learn to relax and participate in activities that allow you to do so. A healthy lifestyle and exercise can reduce your stress. You should also consider what causes your stress and how you can change your work environment to reduce it. Being a workaholic will only lead to burnout and frustration. Taking a vacation is also important; everyone needs an extended rest at least once a year.

To manage stress, follow these guidelines:

- ***Remember your family.*** Do not let your work rule your life. To be a complete person, you must work hard but you also have responsibilities to your family. Try not to go too far in either direction. You need a balance.
- ***Participate in relaxing activities.*** Learn to relax and participate in activities you enjoy.
- ***Exercise.*** A healthy lifestyle, with regular exercise, is another good way to reduce stress.
- ***Consider your environment.*** Consider where your stress comes from and how you can change your work environment to reduce the cause of your stress.
- ***Take a vacation.*** Take a vacation at least once a year. You need to rest and get away from the office from time to time.

Conclusion

A successful paralegal must have many attributes in addition to good technical skills. Being a team player, having a positive attitude, working hard, and keeping accurate records are just a few of the skills that paralegals must have.

Everything in this appendix must be considered in light of the corporate culture of the particular law practice in which you are working. **Corporate culture** refers to generally accepted behavior patterns within an organization; this will include the firm's values, personality, heroes, and mores. Most firms have written procedures or staff manuals that contain some of this information. Many policies, however, are never reduced to writing. Make it your business to understand your firm's position and how the firm views its clients, staff, and so on. Understanding how your particular firm looks at the world is very important.

Glossary

activity hourly rate Fee based on the different hourly rates, depending on what type of service or activity is actually performed.

administrative management Management decisions relating to operating or managing a law office, including financial and personnel matters.

administrative task A task relating to the internal practices and duties involved with operating or managing a law office.

Age Discrimination in Employment Act of 1967 Legislation that prohibits employers from discriminating against employees and applicants on the basis of age when the individual is 40 or older.

aged accounts receivable report A report showing all cases that have outstanding balances due and how long these balances are past due.

alphabetic filing system Filing method in which cases are stored based on the last name of the client or organization.

Americans with Disabilities Act of 1990 (ADA) Legislation that prohibits employers from discriminating against employees or applicants with disabilities.

associate attorney Attorney who is a salaried employee of the law firm, does not have an ownership interest in the firm, does not share in the profits, and has no vote regarding management decisions.

attorney-client privilege A standard that precludes the disclosure of confidential communications between a lawyer and a client by the lawyer.

attorney or paralegal hourly rate Fee based on the attorney's or paralegal's level of expertise and experience in a particular area.

attorneys Licensed professionals who counsel clients regarding their legal rights, represent clients in litigation, and negotiate agreements between clients and others.

bar coding A file management technique in which each file is tracked according to the file's bar code.

Bates stamp Stamps a document with a sequential number and then automatically advances to the next number.

billable time Actual time that a paralegal or attorney spends working on a case and that is directly billed to a client's account.

billing The process of issuing invoices for the purpose of collecting monies for legal services performed and being reimbursed for expenses.

blended hourly rate fee An hourly rate that is set taking into account the blend or mix of attorneys working on the matter.

bona fide occupational qualification An allowable exception to equal employment opportunity, for example, for an employee to perform a specific job, the employee must be of a certain age, sex, or religion.

boutique firm A small law office that specializes in only one or two areas of the law.

budget A projected plan of income and expenses for a set period of time, usually a year.

calendar days System for calculating deadlines that counts all days including weekends and holidays.

calendaring A generic term used to describe the function of recording appointments for any type of business.

case management A legal term that usually refers to functions such as docket control, things to do, contact information by case, case notes, document assembly, document tracking by case, integrated billing, and e-mail.

case retainer A fee that is billed at the beginning of a matter, is not refundable to the client, and is usually paid at the beginning of the case as an incentive for the office to take the case.

case type productivity report A report showing which types of cases (e.g., criminal, personal injury, bankruptcy, etc.) are the most profitable.

cash advance Unearned monies that are the advance against the attorney's future fees and expenses.

CD-ROM legal database A database like one found on Westlaw or LexisNexis, but packaged on CD-ROMs.

centralized file system Method in which a file department or file clerk stores and manages all active law office files in one or more file rooms.

Certificate of Service A statement at the end of a court document that certifies or establishes when a document was placed in the mail.

Civil Rights Act of 1964 Legislation that prohibits employers from discriminating against employees or applicants on the basis of race, color, national origin, religion, or gender.

clerks Employees who provide support to other staff positions in a variety of miscellaneous functions.

client confidentiality Keeping information exchanged between a client and law office staff confidential.

client hourly rate Fee based on one hourly charge for the client, regardless of which attorney works on the case and what he or she does on the case.

coaching technique Counseling that focuses on the positive aspects of the employee's performance and explores alternative ways to improve his or her performance.

communication The transfer of a message from a sender to a receiver.

communication barrier Something that inhibits or prevents the receiver from obtaining the correct message.

conflict of interest A competing personal or professional interest that would preclude an attorney or a paralegal from acting impartially toward the client.

contingency fee Fee collected if the attorney successfully represents the client.

continuance Rescheduling an appointment or court date.

contract attorney An attorney temporarily hired by the law office for a specific job or period. When the job or period is finished, the relationship with the firm is over.

controlling The process of determining whether the law practice is achieving its objectives, holding stakeholders accountable for their goals and making strategy adjustments as necessary so the firm achieves its objectives.

court-awarded fees Fees given to the prevailing parties pursuant to certain federal and state statutes.

criminal fraud A false representation of a present or past fact made by a defendant.

cross-selling Selling additional services to existing clients.

decentralized file system System in which files are kept in various locations throughout the law office.

disaster recovery plan A disaster recovery plan includes information on how the law office will rebuild and recover from a total disaster.

docket control A law-office-specific term that refers to entering, organizing, and controlling all the appointments, deadlines, and due dates for a legal organization.

document assembly software Creates powerful standardized templates and forms

document management software Organizes, controls, distributes, and allows for extensive searching of electronic documents typically in a computer-networked environment.

earned retainer Term for the money the law office or attorney has earned and is entitled to deposit in the office's or attorney's own bank account.

electronic billing When law firms bill clients using electronic means, such as the Internet.

electronic legal database A database containing law-related material on the Internet such as Westlaw or LexisNexis. Electronic sources, such as e-Books may be downloaded or accessed through applications ("apps").

employment-at-will doctrine Doctrine that states that an employer and employee freely enter into an employment relationship, and that either party has the right to sever the relationship at any time without reason.

equal employment opportunity Concept that requires employers to make employment-related decisions without arbitrarily discriminating against an individual.

Equal Pay Act of 1963 Legislation that prohibits employers from paying workers of one sex less than the rate paid an employee of the opposite sex for work on jobs that require equal skill, effort, and responsibility and that are performed under the same working conditions.

ethical rule A minimal standard of conduct.

Ethical Wall Term for a technique used to isolate the paralegal or attorney with a conflict of interest from having anything to do with a case.

exempt The employee is not required to be paid overtime wages over 40 hours/week.

expert witness A person who has technical expertise in a specific field and agrees to give testimony for a client at trial.

extranet A network designed to provide, disseminate, and share confidential information with clients.

facilities management encompasses planning, designing, controlling, and managing a law office's building or office space.

Fair Credit Reporting Act Federal legislation that governs the use of consumer reports in all employment decisions.

Fair Labor Standards Act Federal law that sets minimum wage and overtime pay requirements for employees.

Family and Medical Leave Act of 1993 (FMLA) Legislation that allows employees in certain circumstances to receive up to 12 workweeks of unpaid leave from their jobs for family- or health-related reasons.

feedback Information sent in response to a message.

file-opening form A standardized form that is filled out when a new case is started. The form contains important information about the client and the case.

financial management The oversight of a firm's financial assets and profitability to ensure overall financial health.

flat fee A fee for legal services that is billed as a flat or fixed amount.

freelance/contract paralegal Works as an independent contractor with supervision by and/or accountability to an attorney; is hired for a specific job or period.

Gantt chart A plan or timeline of the projected begin and end dates of a project.

general counsel The chief for a corporate legal department.

groupthink Term for when the desire for group cohesiveness and consensus becomes stronger than the desire for the best possible decision.

hourly rate fee A fee for legal services that is billed to the client by the hour at an agreed-upon rate.

human resources management Hiring, evaluating, compensating, training, and directing law office personnel.

imaging Uses a scanner to capture an image of a document. The image is stored electronically.

income budget Estimate of how many partners, associates, legal assistants, and others will bill for their time, what the appropriate rates of hourly charge should be, and the number of billable hours each timekeeper will be responsible for billing.

independent legal assistance services provided to clients in which the law is involved, but individuals providing the services are not accountable to a lawyer.

Interest on Lawyers' Trust Account (IOLTA) An interest-bearing account set up specifically to hold trust funds. The interest that accrues on an IOLTA account is given to a state bar foundation or other nonprofit legal organization for the good of the public.

internal control Procedures that an organization establishes to set up checks and balances so that no individual in the organization has exclusive control over any part of the accounting system.

intranet An internal information distribution system used only by a law firm staff.

law clerk A law student working for a law firm on a part-time basis while he or she is finishing their law degree. Law clerk duties revolve almost exclusively around legal research and writing.

law librarian A librarian is responsible for maintaining a law library, conducting legal research, and managing library resources.

leadership The act of motivating or causing others to perform and achieve objectives.

legal administrator Person responsible for some type of law office administrative system, such as general management, finance and accounting, human resources, marketing, or computer systems.

legal malpractice Possible consequence when an attorney's or law office's conduct falls below the standard skill, prudence, and diligence that an ordinary lawyer would possess or that is commonly available in the legal community.

legal marketing The process of educating consumers on the legal and business activities a firm uses to deliver quality and ethical legal services.

legal secretaries Employees who provide assistance and support to other law office staff by preparing documents, composing correspondence, scheduling appointments, and performing other tasks.

legal services office A not-for-profit law office that receives grants from the government and private donations to pay for representation of disadvantaged persons who otherwise could not afford legal services.

legal team A group made up of attorneys, administrators, law clerks, librarians, paralegals/legal assistants, secretaries, clerks, and other third parties. Each provides a distinct range of services to clients and has a place on the legal team.

legal technicians People who market their legal services directly to the public.

leveraging The process of earning a profit from legal services that are provided by law office personnel (usually partners, associates, and paralegals).

limited license legal technician in states where legislation has provided, a person qualified by education, training, and work to engage in the limited practice of law in the approved practice area as per the state's rules.

management The administration of people and other resources to accomplish objectives.

management by objectives A performance program in which the individual employee and the employer agree on goals for the employee.

management reports Reports used to help management analyze whether the office is operating in an efficient and effective manner.

managing partner An attorney in a law firm chosen by the partnership to run the firm, make administrative decisions, and set policies.

marketing The process of educating consumers on the quality legal services that a law office can provide.

marketing plan It specifies a target audience the firm is trying to reach, the exact goals that the marketing program is to accomplish, and establishes a detailed strategy of how the goals will be achieved.

mission statement A general, enduring statement of the purpose or intent of the law practice.

Model Code of Professional Responsibility/Model Rules of Professional Conduct Self-imposed ethical standards for ABA members, but they also serve as a prototype of legal ethics standards for state court systems.

negligent hiring Hiring an employee without sufficiently and reasonably checking the employee's background.

noise Any situation that interferes with or distorts the message being communicated.

nonbillable time Time that cannot be directly billed to a paying client.

non-equity partner One who does not share in the profits or losses of the firm but may be included in some aspects of management and may be entitled to certain benefits.

nonexempt The employee is required to be paid overtime wages (time and a half) over 40 hours/week.

of counsel An attorney affiliated with the firm in some way, such as a retired or semiretired partner.

office manager Manager who handles day-to-day operations of the law office, such as accounting, supervision of the clerical support staff, and assisting the managing partner.

office services management It refers to the administration of a number of internal systems and services in a law office. These include mail, copy, fax, and telecommunication services, among others.

off-line The user is not connected to an information service and no charges are accruing except possibly a printing or downloading charge.

online The user is connected to an information system and is running up charges.

organizing The process of arranging people and physical sources to carry out plans and accomplish objectives.

outside counsel Term referring to when corporate and government law practices contract with law offices (i.e., outside of the corporation or government practice) to help them with legal matters, such as litigation, specialized contracts, stock/bond offerings, and so forth.

overhead General administrative costs of doing business, including costs such as rent, utilities, phone, and salary costs for administrators.

paralegal manager Oversees a paralegal program in a legal organization, including preparing work plans, hiring, training, and evaluating paralegals.

paralegals A unique group of people who assist attorneys in the delivery of legal services. They have knowledge and expertise regarding the legal system in order to provide substantive and procedural law that qualifies them to do work of a legal nature under the supervision of an attorney.

partner or shareholder An owner in a private law practice who shares in its profits and losses.

personal information manager (PIM) Consolidates a number of different tasks into one computer program. Most PIMs include calendaring, things to do, a contact database that tracks names and addresses of people, note taking, and other tasks as well.

personnel handbook A manual that lists the formal personnel policies of an organization.

planning The process of setting objectives, assessing the future, and developing courses of action to achieve these objectives.

policy A specific statement that sets out what is or is not acceptable.

powerful managing partner A management structure in which a single partner is responsible for managing the firm.

practice management Management decisions about how a law office will practice law and handle its cases.

prebilling report A rough draft version of billings.

prepaid legal service A plan that a person can purchase that entitles the person to receive legal services either free or at a greatly reduced rate.

pro bono Legal services that are provided free of charge to a client who is not able to pay for the services.

procedure A series of steps that must be followed to accomplish a task.

pure retainer A fee that obligates the office to be available to represent the client throughout the time period agreed upon.

rainmaking Bringing in new clients to a law office.

realization Amount a firm actually receives in income as opposed to the amount it bills.

reasonable accommodation Accommodating a person with a disability, which may include making existing facilities readily accessible, restructuring the job, or modifying work schedules.

recurring entry A calendar entry that recurs.

rephrasing A technique used to improve communication by repeating back to a person your understanding of the conversation.

retainer for general representation Retainer typically used when a client such as a corporation or entity requires continuing legal services throughout the year.

rule by all partners/shareholders A management structure in which all partners/shareholders are included in decisions that affect the firm.

rule by management committee/board Management structure that uses a committee structure to make management decisions for the firm.

settlement A mutual agreement to resolve a dispute on specified terms.

sexual harassment Unwelcome sexual advances, requests for sexual favors, and other verbal or physical conduct of a sexual nature that create an intimidating, hostile, or offensive working environment. Exhibit 2-13 contains a sample anti-harassment policy.

staff attorney An attorney hired by a firm with the knowledge and understanding that he or she will never be considered for partnership.

staffing plan Estimate of how many employees will be hired or funded by the firm, what positions or capacities they will serve in, what positions will need to be added, what old positions will be deleted, and how much compensation each employee will receive.

statute of limitations A statute or law that sets a limit on the length of time a party has to file a suit. If a case is filed after the statute of limitations, the claim is barred and is dismissed as a matter of law.

strategic planning Determining the major goals of a firm and then adopting the courses of action necessary to achieve those goals.

substantive task A task that relates to the process of actually performing legal work for clients.

system A consistent or organized way of doing something.

time sheet or time slip A record of detailed information about the legal services professionals provide to each client.

timekeeper productivity report A report showing how much billable and nonbillable time is being spent by each timekeeper.

timekeeping The process of tracking time for the purpose of billing clients.

time-to-billing percentage System of adjusting downward the actual amount that will be billed to clients during the budget process, taking into account the fact that timekeepers are not always able to bill at their optimum levels.

total quality management Management philosophy of knowing the needs of each client and allowing those needs to drive the legal organization.

trust or escrow account A separate bank account, apart from a law office's or attorney's operating checking account, where unearned client funds are deposited.

unearned retainer Monies that are paid up front by the client as an advance against the attorney's future fees and expenses. Until the monies are actually earned by the attorney or law office, they belong to the client.

value billing A type of fee agreement that is based not on the time spent to perform the work but on the basis of the perceived value of the services to the client.

workdays System for calculating deadlines that refers to only days when the court is open.

zero-based budgeting system Procedure that forces everyone in the organization to justify and explain his or her budget figures in depth without using prior years' figures as justification.